Lord's Cricket Ground

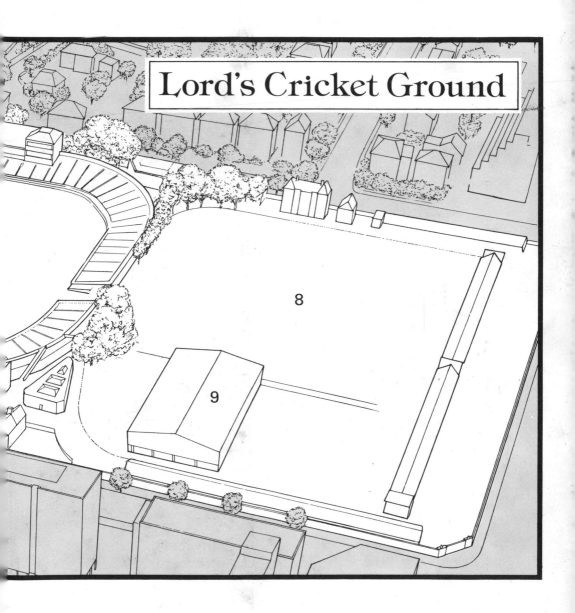

LORD'S

By the same author

The Other England
Against All Reason
Calcutta
The Missionaries
The Fearful Void
The Diplomats
The Boat and the Town
The Best Loved Game
India Britannica

LORD'S

Geoffrey Moorhouse

HODDER AND STOUGHTON
LONDON SYDNEY AUCKLAND TORONTO

British Library Cataloguing in Publication Data

Moorhouse, Geoffrey
    Lord's.
    1. Lord's Cricket Ground (London, England)
    I. Title
    796.35′8′0680942132   GV928.G7

    ISBN 0-340-28210-X

To JOHN ARLOTT

who has taught millions to appreciate cricket,
but has never made the mistake of thinking it
the most important thing in life, or of regarding
it chiefly as a vehicle for his own performance

Foreword

A few words on the genesis of this book, and the circumstances of its research and publication, might be useful to future historians of Lord's and to all who are fascinated by the workings of MCC. I am not a member of the Marylebone Cricket Club, nor have I ever sought to be, for reasons which are entirely to do with my view of the writer's profession and craft: I happen to think that he ought to be a steadfast non-joiner of any institution with a public function the better to maintain his detachment when he writes, which is probably the most valuable thing he has to offer. As a complete outsider, therefore, I had to request extraordinary facilities from MCC when I contemplated writing this book: not only a great deal of co-operation which would enable me to investigate all aspects of the club today, but permission to study archives more extensively, I imagine, than anyone but a senior member of the club has been allowed before.

I appeared as a supplicant before MCC's General Purposes Committee and I felt, as I was escorted into the Committee Room that day, as though I were taking part in a re-enactment of the court martial scene in *The Winslow Boy*. There were all my judges awaiting me, sitting in close order at long tables arranged into three sides of a square; only a sword in front of the President appeared to be missing from the tableau. I was questioned closely about my purpose in wishing to write the book, I was given to understand that no help would be forthcoming unless MCC were allowed to see the finished script before printing, and I was asked what right of reply I would allow MCC if it was thought that I had misrepresented the club. I agreed to submit the script – which is something I've done only once before in my professional life, when writing a book in similar circumstances about the Foreign Office – and I promised to incorporate in some way any views of MCC that differed from my own. I made it clear, however, that I would alter my own text only to correct matters of fact. On that basis, I was in due course given permission to go ahead.

As a result I spent a couple of years, on and off, enjoying the facilities and pleasures of Lord's to a degree that no complete outsider will have done before. I was not only given every assistance I sought, but I was also made to feel very welcome there. At an early stage in my research I had thought of asking if I might sit in on an MCC Committee meeting in order to absorb atmosphere; I was informed that this "might be difficult" and I let the matter drop, because it didn't seem important enough. Otherwise, there wasn't a single thing I asked for that I was denied. All manner of people who work at Lord's, and senior MCC men as well as ordinary members who simply belong, gave me hours of their time, patiently answered my questions, and dug up relevant facts. Similar co-operation was forthcoming from the Test and County Cricket Board, from the National Cricket Association, and from Middlesex County Cricket Club, as well as from MCC. If I mention only two people at Lord's by name, it is because the burden of my presence and my arrangements fell most heavily on them. One is Jack Bailey, Secretary of MCC; the other is that pivotal figure Stephanie Lawrence. I have a great deal to thank both of them for. I am no less grateful to their colleagues and everyone else who helped me on my way.

My search for information was not, of course, restricted to what was officially made available. There were some things I wanted to know that I couldn't reasonably have expected to glean from people whose loyalty to MCC, TCCB, NCA or Middlesex quite properly is stronger than any consideration they might have felt for me. I canvassed a number of sources outside the official circles of Lord's, and others on the fringes of cricket, for various things. Again I was offered help generously, and again I'm deeply in debt for this. No one in this category opened my eyes more than Dr W. A. Adams, of the Soil Science Unit in Aberystwyth, who furnished me with much data about the properties of wickets. I have also, obviously, drawn to some extent on what has been written before. I mention in the text E. W. Swanton's *Sort of a Cricket Person* and I might have added at several points that a nugget was excavated from the splendid *Barclays World of Cricket* that he and John Woodcock edited. Other books that I have referred to or quoted from, apart from innumerable editions of *Wisden*, are *Lord's 1787–1945* by Pelham Warner, *Lord's 1946–1970* by Ian Peebles and Diana Rait Kerr, *How to Watch Cricket* by John Arlott, *W. G. Grace* by Eric Midwinter, *Ashes in the Mouth* by Ronald Mason, *Illingworth* by Mike Stevenson and *The Summer Game* by Roger Angell.

When I had finished writing, I was well aware that some of the things I had set down might irritate or pain MCC in particular. I braced myself for "difficulties" when I despatched the script for the read-in at Lord's. What happened thereafter is something that ought to be carefully noted by all whose natural reflex is to mock MCC. A number of minor factual errors were courteously pointed out to me, and I corrected them. Some of my comments were questioned, but in a spirit of curiosity more than anything else, and no attempt was made to persuade me to alter them. One thing alone caused the perturbation that I had half expected on a larger scale. I had unearthed the full story of the happenings in the MCC members' enclosure during the Centenary Test of 1980, and its consequence (and I may say, in passing, that it came to me neither from within the Committee nor from the MCC Secretariat). It was not disputed that I had produced an accurate account; but I was asked if I would omit one part of it, for the following reason. The MCC Committee had persistently refused to indicate, even to members of the club, what form of disciplinary action had been taken after the fracas on the Pavilion steps. They were embarrassed at the prospect of these tidings being divulged, so to speak, behind their members' backs.

I'm afraid that I declined the request to drop the offending sentences, for reasons which should be obvious without description here, and I left everything as it had already been written. Maybe the Committee thought that an ungrateful response, after all the help they had afforded me. If so, they didn't show it. They accepted my decision with dignity, and I think that ought to be recognised by all who read this book.

Wensleydale 1983

9

Contents

Illustrations

Acknowledgments

1   MCC
2   Patrick Eagar
3   Patrick Eagar, reproduced by kind permission of MCC
4   *Wisden Cricket Monthly*
5   Bridgeman Art Library/MCC

CHAPTER ONE

Institution

By the time London has stretched itself to the postal zone of NW8, its commerce and its entertainment have almost all been left behind. The district of St John's Wood is loftier than a suburb but lowlier than those elegant estates situated centrally in Mayfair, Belgravia and elsewhere, whose rents and leases keep the wolf from many a dukedom's door. It is a residential district with a character, as Nikolaus Pevsner remarked, decidedly of its own – "a comfortable, verdant, early Victorian character, never showy and never mean". At the same time St John's Wood has become a thoroughfare for a good deal of the traffic leaving the capital for the northern provinces of England, an almost perpetual congestion of lorries, coaches and cars making for the motorway and the A1. Much of this swirls along two sides of the district's most notable landmark, a cricket ground: Lord's Ground to be precise, the word cricket being thought quite unnecessary to identify its function. Except on official stationery, on scorecards and on occasional notice boards, we know it simply and elliptically as Lord's, and are thus reminded of the Yorkshireman who established it on this spot in the winter of 1813–14, when Napoleon was licking his wounds after the Battle of Leipzig.

A little to the north-west of Madame Tussaud's, and just upwind of the London Zoo, Lord's is therefore the last significant feature on this segment of the city's inner circumference. It can be approached most pleasantly by pedestrians across Regent's Park, and the advent of a mosque with its burnished copper dome there has made navigation towards the cricket ground much easier for people coming from that direction. There was a brief period when the muezzin's amplified calls to prayer could be heard tantalisingly in the middle of the cricket pitch, but that all stopped after local inhabitants had secured an injunction against the romantic but distinctly alien sound. Other than the rumble of vehicles, or the hysterical hooting of police and ambulance sirens, the only intrusion since has been the tolling of a bell for Evensong, which must have caused many a batsman to supplicate as he has struggled to build an innings in an almost deserted stadium sometime between the tea interval and close of play. It issues from St John's Chapel which, with its white box pews and glazed galleries and one of London's prettier church-yards, stands to the east just across one of those main roads flanking Lord's. Petrol stations flourish nearby, and so do several blocks of high-rise flats, whose tenants are said to pay more stiffly for their accommodation the higher they are off the ground for the privilege of being able to overlook the cricket. There is also a modern hotel, where visiting players sometimes stay. Mostly, though, the sur-roundings of Lord's are, as Pevsner noticed, well-ordered sequences of early nineteenth-century villas, with jutting eaves and a faintly Italianate air, much dignified by an abundance of trees.

There are traffic lights between the chapel and the ground, and drivers obliged to halt there will often have spent the time from one set of changes to the next trying to absorb all the detail in the low-relief sculpture inset in the wall of Lord's. This is almost impossible for them, for it is a very busy composition, carved by the man who designed the Queen of Time who stands beside Selfridge's clock in Oxford Street. It includes two women and a man in tennis gear, a male golfer, a batsman holding the Ashes urn and a bowler facing him, a half-naked chap towelling himself, a Rugby player in a scrum cap, a Soccer player holding a football, an oarsman carrying his blade, a male and female swimmer, and another cricketer on his knees below the rest of the group, holding a bat. All of them appear under the exhortation "Play up, play up and play the game". This is not a sentiment one might look for on the exterior of, say, the Arsenal F.C. ground, where it probably wouldn't survive very long even if it had been thought of in the first place. But the thing has embellished the brick wall running round Lord's for half a century now and in that time it has remained unsullied. Decided respectability is the caste mark round here, and it is not at all surprising to discover that of all the nearby premises which might be expected to display photographs and souvenirs associated with the doings at Lord's – shops, garages and suchlike – none does so more enthusiastically than a bank half a mile away, where customers transact their affairs in a sort of picture gallery devoted to cricket at the ground (this is only a couple of blocks from the Abbey Road which illustrated the jacket of a Beatles record after the quartet had forsaken Merseyside for great substance and most serious recognition in *The Times*). There will not be many folk in the district who do not defer in some way to the existence of Lord's. Years ago there was a Mr McCarthy, cleansing superintendent of the local council and an ex-dustman himself, who made a point of urging his men to tidy the place properly on their regular visits. When he retired he left a notice above the switchboard at the municipal cleansing yard, which said "Take Care of Lord's"; as they have done ever since.

There is little in the way of decoration on the exterior, apart from the sculpture and the posters advertising matches to come. Yet the walls do not have that penitentiary air which generally makes the perimeter of a great sports stadium rather forbidding, even when people are shuffling along in a patient queue to get in. This is possibly because the buildings inside do not rear so high above the adjacent streets that they crushingly dominate everything else in sight. Only along St John's Wood Road, in fact, does the bulk of a stand heave up directly into the sky, and then not very far. That side of the ground is punctuated by a modest series of openings to admit the crowds (turnstiles generally are few and far between) and the outsider's impression is of a surprisingly unobtrusive place for its apparent size and known reputation. The only real hint of any splendour inside comes with the large and ornate cast-iron gates which have stood since 1923 to the almost sacred memory of W. G. Grace, who scored 12,690 of his runs and took 654 of his wickets at Lord's alone. Through those gates, open or shut, anyone passing can get an eyeful of the Pavilion's southern end, of the modern banqueting suite just inside the gates, of the Harris Garden between the two buildings, of herbaceous borders curving round a stand. There is a suspicion of a porte-cochère, the preliminary to a somewhat stately entrance by VIPs to that Pavilion. The structural surmise isn't quite accurate, but the manner of the approach very often holds good.

The secret of Lord's Ground's unobtrusiveness is plain to see the moment you step inside the Grace Gates and walk a hundred yards in any direction. Other than along the back of the Tavern and Mound Stands bordering St John's Wood Road, great distances separate the perimeter walls from the area where cricket is actually played and watched. Along half its entire outer limits the essence of Lord's is insulated from the world beyond by many of those private villas which give this part of London its character and charm; and, as a fair proportion of these are owned by the proprietors of the cricket ground, they ensure both its privacy and its own unaggressive effect on the locality.

One whole side contains very little but a wide open space between the wall running up Wellington Road and the back of the nearest stands. The space is occupied by a subsidiary cricket ground, where the nets are raised each season for practice, and where lesser matches sometimes occur. This is at the Nursery End of the ground, known thus because on its three and a half acres Henderson's Nursery grew celebrated pineapples and tulips until horticulture sold out to cricket

17

in 1887. Other than the expanse of grass, there is only a certain amount of car parking here, some dilapidated fragments of the arbours amidst whose rambler roses and trelliswork ladies and gentlemen once rested awhile from the fatigue of cricket-watching, and the quite recent shape of the indoor cricket school. There might have been a main railway line streaming across there on its way down to Marylebone, for that was what the Great Central Railway intended until cricket marshalled its considerable forces of influence and defeated the necessary Bill before Parliament in 1888. As it is, a tunnel carries the railway somewhere deep below Lord's, the strip of land above it, forty yards wide and now used to park cars on, being leased from the railway until 1996.

The casual observer may very well be charmed rather than impressed by what he has seen of the ground so far. Even after a thorough investigation he will probably still finish up with a feeling that everything about Lord's is understated, certainly if he compares it with Wembley Stadium or innumerable sports venues of one sort or another all over the world. An American accustomed to the baseball Yankee Stadium, or the places where his armoured footballers perform, would doubtless reckon to be doing Lord's a favour if he regarded it as simply cute. Even among cricket grounds, Lord's trails a long way behind some in physical stature. There is something almost rural about it compared with the massive amphitheatres of Melbourne and Calcutta, the one big enough to hold 130,000 people, the other regularly packing in 100,000 and more. The officially authorised capacity of St John's Wood is merely 27,000, though the biggest throng ever to cram itself in is logged as the 33,800 who came to see Wally Hammond complete an innings of 240 on the second day of the 1938 Test match against the Australians. "Merely", perhaps; but no other English ground comes anywhere near Lord's for accommodating crowds. Edgbaston and Old Trafford can officially manage 20,000, Headingley reckons on 17,500, Trent Bridge and the Oval no more than 16,000.

Size, though, was never any guide to anything worthwhile. Let the visitor stroll into the main arena of Lord's and he may catch his breath a bit. The Pavilion apart, there is scarcely a single feature that will account for this. The Mound Stand is frankly nothing more than a long and rudimentary shed. The relatively recent Warner and Tavern Stands are modishly curving and tricked out with some plate glass, but not enough to get worked up about. The first is not stylish enough to stifle regret at the passing of its humbler predecessor, where Lillie Langtry once sat (and judiciously averted her face from the approaching Prince and Princess of Wales). The second, for all

18

its up-to-date amenities, causes real heartache among those who recall the collection of idiosyncratic buildings that had to make way for it in 1966, especially the Clock Tower and the old Tavern, whose function has since been transferred affably to a new pub beside the Grace Gates, but unfortunately outside the ground. The Grandstand bordering the northern boundary of the cricket pitch has great character, with its old-fashioned boxes and scoreboard built in, not to mention its weather-vane of Old Father Time with his scythe: it is, however, a notoriously inconvenient structure, with too many stairs and alleys and not enough seats, a cast-off by Sir Herbert Baker (who also designed the Grace Gates) while he was collaborating with Lutyens in the building of New Delhi, which produced another sort of planning disaster. Then there is Q Stand, which is dapper and neat alongside the Pavilion, to which it is attached by an umbilical bridge, but tiny as these things go nowadays, almost apologetic for being there at all.

As well it might be so close to its illustrious neighbour, whose four storeys of mellowed red sandstone and brick do dominate everything else in Lord's Ground when seen from anywhere in the arena, but especially from the middle of the pitch itself. The scale of everything is such that a batsman taking guard at the Nursery End stumps is looking up at something that resembles a cliff in the background. This was not always the case at Lord's. The first pavilion, which was destroyed by fire in 1825, was a modest wooden structure. The second started off looking like a bungalow that a District Officer might inhabit in some far-flung part of the Empire, but evolved over the next sixty-odd years into a grander thing, though never boasting more than one balcony above ground level. By the penultimate decade of the nineteenth century this had become quite inadequate, and the architect F. T. Verity was given the commission (the most memorable of his entire career) to produce the third pavilion, which has now stood since 1890.

Pavilion is a word with its origins in medieval tent-pitching, usually with heraldic ornament, and it is maybe no coincidence that cricket's most celebrated adaptation depends for its effect on two great towers at either end of the whole structure, each rising to a peak, each adorned with a flagstaff, and each finally crowned with the monogram of the Marylebone Cricket Club, the owners of Lord's. Between these two extremities runs the famous Long Room at ground level, with further storeys of building above that, the two upper balconies even when full of spectators never quite obscuring the basic shape behind them. It is a building full of vantage points, with little balconies for players as well as long ones for MCC members, with large windows through which people solemnly watch or (for the broadcasting commentators are up there, too) intently describe. It works its way up from a solid-looking base, through ranges of cast-iron, teak-topped balustrading, to a flimsy-looking shelter which forms the roofline between those two peaked turrets with their filigrees of tracery wrought in iron. Some of the outside walls up there are decorated with terracotta figures and busts, one looking suspiciously like Lord Harris, who was a power in MCC when the Pavilion was planned. And although there are other distinguished cricket pavilions which have something of the same appearance (Old Trafford's for one, the Oval's for another) there is nothing at all as splendid in its setting as the Pavilion at Lord's.

Nor, as I say, is there another ground which quite seizes the attention and then holds it in the way that this one does. The impressiveness of Lord's is compounded of several things, quite apart from its history and associations. One secret is the scale of everything here; and whatever reservations one might have about the newer buildings, those responsible for them respected the existing scale of Lord's. Because buildings have made their first appearance here across the best part of 150 years, the view from the arena – or from the little roads that encircle the stands, within the outside walls – is of something as organic as most English High Streets were before mindless developers saw profit in making everything boringly and shoddily similar. You can stand anywhere on this ground and catch glimpses of funny old bits and pieces of brick and mortar that have not yet been demolished to make way for progress: the Lord's Shop, which once upon a time was part and parcel of a range of buildings which quartered the Clergy Female Orphans School; or the ground staff's depot, with its little clock tower and its private balcony, on which some of the staff spend sunny Test match afternoons; or the real tennis court behind the Pavilion, which is rare enough to be prized as a listed building; or the brace of telephone boxes abandoned now beside it, still painted green as these things used to be when public telephones first made their appearance in England. Another thing that is never missing from any view of Lord's is the loveliness of trees – chestnut and flowering cherry, lime and sycamore, poplar and copper beech and serviceable London plane – which have just taken their time and grown with the ground. The whole effect is very comforting, as well as of something that may be called a reticent grandeur; even, dammit, a graciousness.

It is difficult to visualise its Brideshead periods during two world wars. In the first it was used variously for the training of soldiers in the crafts of wireless, military cooking and artillery, while Lord's employees and some MCC members occupied themselves in the Pavilion making hay nets for horses quartered down at Woolwich. It was requisitioned by the RAF for less colourful purposes in the second, though cricket never stopped entirely at Lord's between 1939 and 1945. It was during a match between the Sussex Home Guard and the Surrey Home Guard in 1942 that Andrew Ducat collapsed and died at the wicket with his score on twenty-nine. It was during a game between the Army and RAF in 1944 that the descent of a flying bomb caused the players to fling themselves flat on the turf; and after they had picked themselves up, the next ball was hooked famously for six by Captain J. D. Robertson, lately of Dunkirk, always of Middlesex, and subsequently of England. Bombs, in fact, never actually landed on Lord's, though the roof of the tennis court was damaged by a near miss and Old Father Time was pulled from his perch by the cable of a stray barrage balloon.

This is, of course, something much more considerable than a place where cricket of the highest calibre is played and watched. It is nothing less than an international institution as well, because of its history and because of what it represents. The curious, or the sceptical, can pick and choose freely from an astonishing variety of sources who have left testimonials to what and how they feel about Lord's. Many are sentimental in the extreme, some are rather pompous, others are lyrical, but none has been set down without conviction and sincerity. One classic remark, embodying many of the elements in recurring genuflections, was that of an MCC President, General Sir Oliver Leese, who declared: "It is the Mecca of cricketers of all nations and the Headquarters of cricket from which come forth the Laws of Cricket, the spirit in which it should be played, and the encouragement to men of all ages and nations to play what we believe to be the finest game of all." People are always likening Lord's to Mecca, though Sir Robert Menzies spoke reverently of "the Cathedral of Cricket", and one of the institution's greatest luminaries, Sir Pelham Warner, produced a novel fancy by nominating it as the Caterham of Cricket; meaning that it was the place where the finest young cricketers, like the finest young Guardsmen, were reared.

For the lyricists we must naturally turn first to Sir Neville Cardus, a man who never seemed able to make up his mind whether he was stirred most by Old Trafford (which lay close to his own beginnings) or Lord's (which symbolised rather more what he eventually became). On the latter, the following may be considered his fullest benediction: "For your good cricketer the ends of the earth have come to a resting-point at Lord's, and wherever he may be at the fall

21

of a summer's day his face should turn religiously towards Lord's. Lord's is the Cosmopolis of cricket." The great jurist and after-dinner speaker, Sir Norman Birkett (later Lord Birkett), was pithier when he claimed: "To this historic ground cricketers all over the world turn in respect and homage." Another journalist, J. M. Kilburn, spelt things out a bit more than Cardus when he wrote that "Lord's is history modelled in turf and building . . . There idolator and iconoclast are touched by the magic of the game. They have visited a cricket ground and involved themselves in an institution." There are scores of quotations expressing that kind of view to be found in the writings on cricket. Just occasionally there is something subtler, like Edmund Blunden's reflection: "And truly he who sees present-day cricket at Lord's on many occasions is almost back to the country green and its felicity."

Umpteen poems have been turned on the inspiration of Lord's, many of them ham-fisted, some very moving, like Alan Ross's verse about the aged but still upright Sydney Barnes leading blind Wilfred Rhodes through the Long Room and down the Pavilion steps. Or like the best-known of all, *At Lord's*, which Francis Thompson wrote in 1907, though in his poverty he couldn't bear to visit the ground to see his native county play. There has been at least one waggish reference in verse, from Siegfried Sassoon (". . . One fact seems sure/That, while the Church approves, Lord's will endure."), and there has even been a poem devoted to the scoreboard at Lord's. There is also that exuberant celebration of West Indies' first Test win in England, achieved largely by "Those two little pals of mine/Ramadhin and Valentine" – *The Victory Calypso; Lord's 1950* by Egbert Moore, alias Lord Beginner.

It is not a local self-indulgence to suppose and claim that the rest of the cricketing world holds Lord's in special regard. Conceivably the fashion may decline before long, for attitudes in cricket are now changing faster than ever before. But that old and doughty Australian opener Jack Fingleton would have spoken for many overseas enthusiasts when he assured his readers that "No other ground, as I have seen them, can compare with Lord's in its calm and peaceful majesty . . . No player has walked on Lord's for the first time without his heart beating infinitely faster . . ." Lindsay Hassett, when saying farewell to an MCC official after the Melbourne Centenary Test, asked him to "give one of those bricks at the back of the Pavilion a kiss from me". The greatest of all Australian cricketers never waxed very eloquent about Lord's, being Sir Donald Bradman and there-fore inclined more than most men to express himself solely through his craft. But an unforgettable moment came after his last innings there. He had made 150 against the Gentlemen of England on his fortieth birthday and he was cheered all the way back to the Pavilion. Just before he reached it he turned to the crowd, his gloves hung round his bat handle. He raised them above his head, then bowed his good-bye. And while that was obviously an acknowledgment of the warmth flowing towards him, it was also Bradman's way of saying what he felt about Lord's. He batted on two other English grounds after that before the 1948 tour was over, but he did not repeat that gesture.

We may ask ourselves – ruefully, if we have any sense of proportion – when have so many people ever rhapsodised as extravagantly as in the case of Lord's about a theatre, a concert hall, a library, an art gallery, a museum or any other non-religious structure containing the mainsprings of civilisation? The answer can only be not often. The most extravagant tribute of all was that of an Australian Prime Minister, towards the end of the Second World War. He was John Curtin, and some thousands of his compatriots had been killed in the previous five years; more were still rotting in prison camps across Asia. What he said at a luncheon on the ground, indicating the wicket in the middle, was this. "Australians will always fight for those twenty-two yards. Lord's and its traditions belong to Australia just as much as to England."

Which brings us to the focal point of all that can be said and recollected of Lord's: the playing area. As a preliminary it would be tactful to notice its founder, because it was Thomas Lord who laid down the turf the cricketers still use – most of it, at any rate – and he had already carted this some distance around London before settling it here. The Catholic Lord family came from Thirsk in the North Riding of Yorkshire (more popular these days as the site of James Herriot's veterinary practice in real life) but had moved to farming in Norfolk before the adult Thomas shifted to the capital, where he performed as a bowler and acted as an attendant at the gentlemen's White Conduit Club towards the end of the eighteenth century. He found patrons there who were prepared to back him financially if he would start a new private cricket ground, and in May 1787 he opened one in Dorset Square, a few hundred yards from where Baker Street now crosses Marylebone Road. The first thing he did there was to fence it in, and soon followed that by charging spectators a sixpence admission fee. Lord had a nose for profit, which he would shortly exercise in the liquor trade as well as in property dealing, and it extended to welching on the £20 he had promised the first man to hit a ball clean out of Dorset Square. He abandoned that ground when the lease over-stretched his resources and was next found as a cricket impresario at North Bank, on the edge of St John's Wood. Within a couple of seasons he was obliged to move on again, this time because the new Regent's Canal was being navvied along a course that would take it straight across the middle of his pitch. He dropped anchor afresh half a mile or so to the north, on the present site of Lord's, which saw its first cricket on June 22, 1814, with a game in which MCC beat Hertfordshire by an innings and 27 runs. There Thomas Lord stayed put for eleven years until, in 1825, he sold out for £5,000 to William Ward, who was a leading member of MCC (a powerful hitter, too, who used a four-pound bat for fifty years), a director of the Bank of England, and MP for the City of London. His cricketing profit secured, Lord lived on in the district for several years before retiring to Hampshire, where he died in 1832 at the age of 76, having left a name that would resound across the world and be noticed even by people with little interest in the sport.

On each of his moves he carefully lifted the turf he had first established in Dorset Square and transported it to his new cricket ground. This is not to say that all the grass we see at Lord's today would have been recognised by Lord as his legacy. For some years after his retirement there were ponds in front of what is now the Mound Stand, sporadically filled in with broken bricks and other rubbish before the playing area was extended over them, which helped to account for the reputation of the Lord's field as a very rough one indeed. In 1859 Surrey refused to play there, as did Sussex a few years later, both because of the outfield and because the wicket itself was below standard. A customary citation of W. G. Grace's prodigious talent is the 134 runs he hit out of a 201 total in the Gentlemen v Players match of 1868, when he was only nineteen years old. He did so on a wicket described as follows by an onlooker: "The place where the ball pitched was covered with rough grass wetted and rolled down. It never had been, and never could be, good turf. I have no hesitation in saying that in nine cricket grounds out of ten within twenty miles of London, whether village green or county club ground, a local club could find a better wicket, in spite of drought and in spite of their poverty, than Marylebone Club supplied to the Players of England." Five years later the club took the hint and relevelled the area, and Lord's was never again regarded as the most dangerous pitch in the country.

This is not the largest playing area in the land, a title enjoyed across the Thames at the Oval, with its six acres, though commentators are apt to talk of it as though it were twice that size. Among the other English Test grounds, Trent Bridge runs to five and a quarter acres, Edgbaston to four and a quarter, Old Trafford and Heading-ley to an almost trifling four. All have distinguishing features of their own, quite apart from the wickets they produce, and the five and a half acres at Lord's are known above all for the gradient of the slope there. From the Grandstand boundary to the edge of the field in front of the Tavern, Lord's descends six feet six inches – or, as Pelham Warner quaintly put it, "About the height of a tall man in a top hat." It is most noticeable to spectators who let their eyes travel the full length of the Pavilion boundary, or to people on the Tavern side who have a distinct feeling that they are looking up at the opposite edge of the field. It is always noticeable to players, for it affects their batting, bowling and fielding techniques.

The other curiosity about the grassed surface at Lord's is what has become known as the ridge. This first became a topic of debate during the 1959 season, when players noticed that some balls pitching at the Nursery End behaved unpredictably, either shooting low or lifting abruptly. They attributed this to a fractional undula-tion in the surface, more or less on a length, which ran right down the table of wickets. It wasn't until a surveyor was summoned two seasons later that the existence of a second ridge, smaller than the first but potentially discomfiting nonetheless, was revealed in a corresponding position at the Pavilion End. One theory about the major ridge was that it had erupted along the course of an old drain; another about both was that they resulted from the final foot movements of bowlers, which, in effect, had tended to compact the earth into a faint ripple over two or three generations. The problem was first tackled by lifting the soil around the affected areas and dispersing it over the rest of the wicket, but in the past year or two the cricketers have been murmuring about the reappearance of the original ridge, whenever some balls have acted in ways that seem odd even to their bowler.

In the most intelligently helpful guide to cricket-watching that has appeared in modern times (out of print now, alas, for a generation, which is a publishing crime) John Arlott made the point: "The most important single factor governing any first-class cricket match is the wicket." The factor has become rather less important since that was written in 1948, because the habit of covering wickets has grown in the years between like a fungus, so that they no longer incorporate the wayward effects of climate as much as they did when cricket meant that players perpetually pitted their skills against each other and against nature as well. In spite of this, the wicket is still the crucial factor in any game, as anyone may guess from the number of times cricketers and cricket managers complain about the conditions teams have had to play in. The problem confronting any ground authority is to produce a regular schedule of wickets on which the players can feel that both batsmen and bowlers have had a chance to show themselves to best advantage, and on which spectators are liable to see an entertaining match. This is a doctrine of perfection. Even aspiring towards it, and surmounting the problems involved, stretches ingenuity a long way. Few first-class grounds anywhere in the world have as much cricket played on them as Lord's. None has to mount as many showpieces, when everything is expected to be at its best.

The central table or square – the area on which all the batting strips are prepared – has to accommodate no fewer than eighteen separate wickets here in the course of a season. It isn't possible to make do with a smaller number when Lord's is required to provide Test matches, county championship matches, Sunday league matches, cup matches and their finals, special matches (Oxford v Cambridge, Eton v Harrow), occasional MCC matches, and one or two matches below the first-class level of the game. In all, some forty fixtures are played at Lord's every season, varying in length from one to five days, which means that those eighteen strips must be rotated carefully so that each is in good trim when its turn comes up for use.

There are, of course, other considerations. The central strip is the one on which the annual Lord's Test is played, for obvious reasons, and it is therefore the one above all others which is expected to be in absolutely prime condition for the start of the match. To ensure this as nearly as possible, no cricket at all is allowed on that strip until the Test match begins; which means that one of the eighteen options is excluded from the rotation system until very nearly half-way through a cricket season; and the wear and tear on a wicket over the course of five days is such that the Test strip is good for only one other match before the season ends. Because all first-class cricket matches must be played with boundaries at a minimum of fifty yards from the wicket, the number of choices is further reduced for all but the minor games to a total of fourteen strips. Such fixtures as Eton v Harrow, MCC v MCC Young Cricketers, and the Village Cup Final, are played so close to either the Grandstand or Tavern sides of the ground as to be very distant indeed from spectators at the other side; and even some Sunday league games are played with one rather long midships boundary and one pretty short.

The full extent of the permutations is most apparent in the office belonging to MCC's Assistant Secretary (Cricket), where there is a coloured chart numbering off the Lord's wickets and earmarking them for various matches throughout the season. No. 1 strip is that nearest the Grandstand, No. 18 that closest to the Tavern, the Test strip being No. 9, all three-day matches being confined between Nos. 4 and 16. Occasional relief comes for the man who has to decide on which wicket any match is played if the weather more or less blots out a game, thus releasing that strip for further use earlier than originally scheduled. It also helps when Middlesex make an early exit from either of the two knock-out competitions, thus reducing a little more the pressure on wicket preparation. Such bonuses, however, can be offset by the unpremeditated damage that cricketers may do to parts of the table which are supposed to be lying fallow during their own match. When Colin Croft adopted a slanting run-up to the stumps, his approach and follow-through noticeably affected three different wickets at a time whenever he was bowling at Lord's.

The Assistant Secretary (Cricket) may be the official who supervises this aspect of Lord's, but another figure actually stakes his reputation on the playing area and nothing else. It was Cardus who said: "The history of cricket is one long battle between batsman and bowler, the groundsman holding the ring." If the Head Groundsman at Lord's since 1970 has been better known than any other man who had occupied the position, it is because the nation has become more accustomed to his appearance on its television screens than any predecessor. There, on each morning of every big match at Lord's, Jim Fairbrother has been standing by the stumps, waiting to hand over the bails to the umpires when they come out. At other times he might be seen looking anxiously at the sky, a cape rolled over one shoulder, like a matador before the arrival of the bull. Or, gumbooted and oil-skinned, leading his staff into action with their covers, their tractors, their thick hose-pipes and their squeegees, when a deluge has actually begun. There is something about that greyheaded stoop, that rather shambling walk across the middle of Lord's, those hands invariably behind his back, that suggests a yeoman reared and confident in relationship with his piece of earth. In fact, Jim Fairbrother started work as a wood machinist in his native Nottingham, coming to Lord's as assistant to Ted Swannell in 1968 after years on the ground staff at Trent Bridge. But the way he moves and speaks suggests that he was destined from birth to improve soil and nurture grass.

The time to appreciate fully the effect of playing cricket regularly on a first-class field is in September, when a season is done. If you look at any wicket the moment a three-day match is over you can see damage to the turf not apparent except by close inspection. Footholds, marks left by the bowler's run-up and the indentations caused by batsmen at the crease – all these are visible from afar, even without binoculars. It is the marks left by the ball that are inscrutable unless you stand over them, though they may be assumed from the batsman's habit of going up the pitch and prodding it – not always a nervous tic. There will be pink bruises on the earth, where the dye has been beaten in from the leather by repeated attack; even small concavities and rips on the surface, a rough that accurate length bowlers can produce without the assistance of footmarks. Multiply all the damage eighteen times over four months and more, and you have a cricket square resembling a barnyard by the autumn; which must be restored to a splendid sheen of turf by spring if you happen to be Head Groundsman at Lord's.

In September, Fairbrother and his staff – six men full-time – always tackle that table first, top-dressing it evenly with twelve cubic yards of soil obtained from the Surrey Loam Company, who have always been very secretive about where it comes from; after forty years at his craft, Jim Fairbrother still doesn't know the hideaway. Whatever the reason for such guardedness, this soil has one very striking property; after being thoroughly wetted and shaped into a ball or a cube, it dries out into something khaki-coloured as hard as a brick. Of such is the foundation of wickets made to last from start to finish of a long cricket match. The mowing machines are in action, too, during those last September days, for that is one of two periods in the year (late April and May the other) when grass grows at its fastest, and at that time you need to cut at least once a week in order to produce an outfield of quality, the blades no lower than one inch above the ground. The onset of autumn sees other forms of rehabilitation. To improve the aeration and drainage of the playing area, it is subjected to the attentions of a roller encrusted with hollow spikes, which stab the ground and remove tubular divots that are scattered across the surface as the machine rolls on, to be fragmented by subsequent frosts, and by raking, into a top dressing all over the field. Aeration by natural means can be less welcome because it may be less evenly spread. September nights have often seen Fairbrother coming from his house by the northern turnstiles to hunt for worm-casts and to sprinkle grains of poison wherever a concentrated patch of them appears.

Autumn, then, is a busy time; but spring is bustling with preparation for the coming season. During the winter the great expanse of grass has been resting, and the ground staff have been attending to the tools of their craft, mending, oiling and cleaning up. There comes the moment, though, in March, when they move into the middle once more and rake the surface over with scarifying tines, to remove dead growth and encourage new. On the threshold of the season the mowers are clattering away again, and fertiliser is spread wide (twenty per cent nitrogen, ten per cent phosphate, ten per cent potash) to help the spring bloom. Artfully, the same tonic is administered a little before each of the big matches Lord's puts on, because there is nothing like a dose of nitrogen to turn the central square vividly green, which is much admired by large gatherings of MCC members, and pleases the television producers as well. It is about this moment, after the middle of April these days, that the highest skills of groundsmanship are carefully mustered in preparing the first wickets of the year.

The basis of a Lord's wicket, apart from that quota of Surrey loam and the earth beneath, is grass. Someone once said that the secret of making a wicket was that you almost murdered the grass by slicing it off just above the root to create a mat. Well, sort of and up to a point. On all prepared wickets, wherever they are made, bare soil generally constitutes more than half the surface. Essentially, the grass is there to stop the impacted soil from breaking up under the pounding of the ball, though its degree of growth makes its own contribution to how the ball will behave after pitching. Fairbrother's practice is never to cut it closer than a quarter of an inch above roots that descend three to four inches into the heavy clay of the local subsoil. A fine old mixture of varieties with invigorating names they are, too, on the cricket table at Lord's. The predominant breed is Sprinter (forty-five per cent), a free-growing rye with a wide blade which stands wear and tear and is good at recovering from droughts. Then there is Majestic (forty per cent), another resilient crop which holds its colour better than Sprinter. Add to these Island Brown Top (fifteen per cent), and you have introduced what the experts call a bottom grower with a very fine blade, much used on golf courses, able to take violent temperature changes in its stride, continuing to grow even in the winter.

About a week before this concoction is to be played on, the meticulous cutting and rolling begins along the required strip. A machine with two rollers whose total weight can vary – by the addition of water in the hollow casings – between thirty-six cwt and two tons, trundles up and down those twenty-two yards at about 0.5 mph for hours on end; two in the morning and another session after lunch make a normal daily stint. At the outset the ground visibly sinks beneath the rollers, which will continue to trundle until there's no give left in the earth and until no faintly white lines are detectable on the surface where the roller's edge has pressed. Achieving that state is reckoned to be the evidence of a good and true wicket, which is what is demanded at Lord's. Tap such a strip of ground with your knuckles and it distinctly rings. It is ready to have all hell knocked out of it by twenty-two cricketers over the best part of a week. Afterwards, it will not be touched for two or three days, apart from some sweeping up of debris. Then the patches that have had most of the grass rubbed out of them will be re-seeded. Ideally, no wicket will be played on again for another month.

All that rolling is the groundsman's chief contribution to determining the pace of the wickets he is preparing; the roller affects the potential strength of the soil and that, together with the soil's clay content, is what makes for pace off the pitch – or lack of it. There is a recognised equation between the phrases cricketers use to describe the pitches they play on, and the amount of bounce when a cricket ball is bowled on them. A standard English ball dropped vertically on to a concrete surface from a height of 16 feet will bounce 52 inches into the air; on to soil there can be appreciable variation in the bounce, and the equation goes like this. A very fast pitch will produce a bounce of over 30 inches after that vertical drop, a fast one between 25 and 30 inches, a moderately fast one between 20 and 25 inches, an easy-paced pitch something between 15 and 20 inches, a slow pitch less than 15 inches. Any properly prepared pitch should have a bounce of at least 10 inches. This bounce is not always constant throughout the length of a wicket.

At the Oval some years ago, the average experimental bounce at the Pavilion End was 24.8 inches, while at the Vauxhall End it was only 19.6 inches. Constant or not, it is closely related to the clay content of the soil, which should be at least 33 per cent of the whole to produce a fast wicket. The higher the clay content, the faster the pitch.

Experts from the Soil Science Unit at the University of Wales in Aberystwyth, with the encouragement of MCC, conducted a series of tests around the English county cricket grounds during the seasons of 1966 and 1967 to determine local variations in bounce and clay. They found that the average bounce throughout the counties was 23 inches; the highest was at Worcester (30 inches), the lowest Old Trafford (11 inches) and at Lord's it was 19 inches. Worcester's high bounce was the result of two factors: a clay content of 42 per cent in the soil there and the consistent heavy rolling of the pitch from early spring onwards. At Lord's the clay content was 35 per cent, and the scientists surmised that the roller hadn't been applied as weightily or as often at the headquarters of the game in 1966 as it had up at New Road in the Midlands. Top dressing is a way of trying to regulate the consistency of the soil, whose natural clay content can vary from year to year as a result of leaching and other climatic factors. At Lord's, the 35 per cent of 1966 had become 38 per cent two years later, had dropped to 25 per cent by 1977, had climbed again to 30 per cent in 1981. That year, Jim Fairbrother's top coat of Surrey loam included 36 per cent of clay.*

These are the fundamentals of making it possible to play first-class cricket at Lord's. There are many incidentals which, in combination, add a further dimension to the groundsman's task and complicate his basic objective of providing proper conditions for the cricketers to use. Normal soil and grass pests he takes in his stride as much as the assiduously suburban gardener, reaching for his selective weed-killers whenever clover, buttercup or any other intruder comes in unwonted quantities. But there have been occasional invasions of a spectacular nature needing retaliation on a larger scale. In 1935 there was a plague of leather jackets (the larvae of the daddy longlegs) which bared Lord's of so much grass that it resembled a seaside beach. In the 1970s there were attacks of fusarium disease, a fungoid growth that arises when the covers are used for prolonged periods in humid weather, causing the turf to "sweat" underneath and acquire a mould which rapidly browns the grass and kills it. A perennial difficulty is providing enough good wickets at the nets on the practice ground, nets being in greater demand at Lord's than any other place in the country. MCC members have a right to use them, and do so quite a lot, especially at the beginning of a season. The young MCC professionals have a need to use them if they are to take fullest advantage of being drilled at the "Caterham of Cricket". So do the Middlesex players, if they are to sharpen themselves enough to leave a mark on the county championship and the one-day competitions. And while all these locals are being satisfied, the visiting tourists of the year must also be obliged. Lord's prides itself on its hospitality in many respects; it is never more generous than when offering good net facilities, more or less for the asking, to New Zealanders, West Indians, or whoever happens to have come over to do battle with England. Several days at the Lord's nets between the tourists getting off the plane and starting their first match is a regular feature of every spring now; as well as every other time they come through London.

But rain, obviously, is the biggest trial. It has fallen in such

* It is interesting to note how much faster some overseas wickets were at about the time of the English experiments. In Melbourne the clay content was 48 per cent and the bounce of an *English* ball was 31 inches. Other figures were: Adelaide and Sydney, both 52 per cent and 33 inches; Brisbane, 73 per cent and 41 inches; Sabina Park, Kingston, Jamaica, 49 per cent and 32 inches.

quantities over London at crucial cricketing moments in recent years that cynics have begun to agree that although Old Trafford has the reputation for producing bad weather for a Test, it is Lord's which actually delivers the goods. The Centenary Test with Australia in 1980 was ruined by it, ten hours being lost in the first three days alone. The year before, the Test against India had been visited by such a rainstorm – equal to anything Calcutta might produce at the height of the monsoon – that a lake formed in front of the Tavern Stand, long enough and deep enough for some spectators to dive into it. Out of eighteen Test matches played at Lord's between 1970 and 1982, only four were completed without any interruption from the weather (Old Trafford's tally was two out of eight). In that period, spectators became accustomed to the sight of Fairbrother and his men in the middle almost as much as the cricketers. At engrossing moments in a match the skies would darken, the white figures would charge – gratefully, it sometimes seemed – for the Pavilion, and in their place would come this platoon of workmen: hastening into the arena aboard accelerating tractors, stumbling into and fastening anoraks as they advanced, manhandling into place the mobile plastic-topped covers, and the lightweight plastic sheets, and the elephantine hoses to drain water off the middle. Some of this goes into sumps in the outfield, but even more gushes after heavy rainfall straight across the turf towards the Tavern boundary; and the Lord's slope, in a particularly mighty storm, produces a steady flow of water across the surface from the Grandstand side.*

The problem of waterlogging to some extent is insoluble, both because of the slope and because of the heavy clay underneath the subsoil of Lord's. It has defied the upheaval that followed the 1972 season, when drains laid across the ground in 1903 were dug up and a fresh set was substituted in a herring-bone pattern running from north to south down the slope, which leaves adequate covering and effective mopping up alone within the capabilities of the ground staff. Working as they do for an employer which, by its very nature, inclines towards the traditional and shrinks from the merely fashionable or the apparent gimmick (which also reaches decisions laboriously through committees and, at each stage, weighs up everything very carefully indeed), the ground staff have often seemed hampered by insufficient means. When covers were first used experimentally at

* A footnote to this depressing mention of bad weather at Lord's may be a less painful way of recalling that long ago, in 1876, the Eton v Harrow match was played in temperatures which varied between 142 degrees in the sun and ninety degrees in the shade.

Lord's in 1872, no one dreamt that they would ever be wheeled on as frequently or as extensively as is the custom now; and until the present generation, cricketers seemed content to play unless moisture was actually coming over the welts of their boots. Coverage of the area around the wickets at Lord's has therefore increased in a piecemeal way. The most recent introduction, in the 1975 season, was the series of large covers with corrugated tops, which provide perfect shelter and also allow air to circulate freely underneath; surrounded by plastic sheets which take the water running off the covers themselves, this combination pretty well takes care of the entire square. But a critical public is still apt to regard the solution as inadequate for the sort of weather London too often gets.

It may therefore be that one day Lord's will follow where Warwickshire alone has led so far, and instal the juggernaut that can cover the entire playing surface of Edgbaston in a few minutes (though if so, it is to be hoped that a cat and a fox are not found squashed into the ground in NW8, as happened during trial runs of the monster in Birmingham). What inhibits Lord's from taking such a revolutionary step as much as anything is the knowledge that installation of such a huge contraption would mean the loss of some seating capacity, and the worry that such blanket coverage of the playing area might be an open invitation to the spores of fusarium disease. Meanwhile, the ground staff do their best with the tedium of mopping up. In this they were reinforced the year after the Centenary fiasco by the arrival of their "Whale", the big double rolling machine, already proven at the Oval, which surges across the ground behind a small bow wave at times, soaking up the wet. This was a comforting sight to spectators in the open-air G Stand after Saturday's inundation during the 1982 Test with India. Contemplating it and all the other activities of Jim Fairbrother and his men as they laboured to make the waters recede, a rather damp fellow leaned appreciatively on the handle of his sopping umbrella. "You don't mind so much," he informed his equally long-suffering neighbour, "when they show a bit of willing."

Apart from the sheer thrill of performing here, as vouched for by Jack Fingleton and echoed by any cricketer you canvass on the subject, reaction to the playing conditions at Lord's is liable to vary as much as there are different skills in the game. The first thing any cricketer mentions, however, is the effect of that slope on almost any phase of a match. Its most pronounced influence is on bowling, and especially on which end a bowler will work from in order to gain the maximum

33

advantage in his craft. The wickets are unusual at Lord's in being pitched from east by north to west by south: unusual but not unique; they are the same at Headingley and Old Trafford, give or take a degree or two. This is an alignment which is sometimes criticised because a batsman at Lord's may have difficulty in picking up the ball when it comes out of the deep shadow cast by the Pavilion and Warner Stand as the sun goes glaring down the sky behind. More significantly, it means that the slope runs downhill across the wickets and can be harnessed by bowlers to added effect. Fast bowlers declare that it really doesn't do much for them either way, though some have seemed to pick and choose carefully the end they prefer to bowl at. Ray Lindwall was one who always opened with the Pavilion behind him, as did the Middlesex quickies Price and Moss a few years later; though lately most innings have appeared to start with attack from the Nursery End. Generally speaking, the spin bowlers are in no doubt at all which way they prefer the slope to be running for them. It is regarded as axiomatic that a slow left-armer shall not operate from the Pavilion End except in emergency, because he will have to turn the ball uphill. The off-spinner, on the other hand, is aided appreciably by performing with his back to MCC members, bowling as they say "through" the slope, the ball spinning down on to the Nursery End batsman. There have, of course, been notable cricketers to confound such rules of thumb. Hedley Verity, greatest of all English slow left-armers between the wars, operated entirely from the Pavilion End in 1934 when he destroyed Australia with fourteen wickets in a single day of the Second Test – though Australians would rightly argue that the effect of heavy rain on the wicket had much more to do with that haul than anything contributed by the slope. The more common spectacle has ever been according to the rule of thumb. The number of overs Titmus and Emburey between them have sent down from the Nursery End may not reach three figures. Blessed is the visiting cricket team which, like Yorkshire in the sixties, has someone with Illingworth's ability to send off-spin away from the members and a Wilson to turn the left-arm ball away from the bat in the next over.

The batsmen, of course, regard the slope as a factor mostly insofar as it aids certain kinds of bowling. But some of them claim to feel slightly off-balance when standing at the Lord's crease, as though they just might fall over if they don't look out; and left-handers taking guard at the Nursery End will sometimes say that they have especial care for the precise location of their leg-stump. Otherwise, the slope's chief effect on batsmen is to convey a greater sense of prosperity if they hit a ball towards the Tavern side than to the

Grandstand. But that can be a deception, as fieldsmen know best of all. Judging the flight of the hit ball through the air – safely if you're a batsman, hopefully if your job is to catch him out – is made much finer than normal when you have a six foot six inch incline to contend with. If Jackie Bond had been fielding at extra cover on the Tavern side rather than the Grandstand, it is conceivable that he would have heard the ball humming inches beyond his reach instead of taking it as he did, the most brilliant catch seen at Lord's for many a day, to dismiss Asif Iqbal and win the 1971 Gillette Cup for Lancashire against Kent. Boundary fielders in particular, standing before the Mound or the Tavern, find it difficult to judge high catches, for it is easy for them to move infield just a pace or so too far. In returning the ball from that side of the ground they must throw it higher if it is to reach the stumps on the full; they much prefer standing at long-off or long-leg in front of the Warner crowd, whence a flatter throw has a much better chance of skimming cleanly to the wicket.

Fieldsmen reckon Lord's to be one of the better grounds on which to sight the ball coming through the air, though some say they have much greater difficulty when the place is empty during a county championship game than when packed during a Test or Cup match; something to do with the pattern of split-level stands which makes for confusion in the background, with markedly different layers of colour one on top of another. Most complaints about sighting come from batsmen, though they are not nearly as frequent since the rolling sight-screens were installed along the top of the Pavilion steps in 1964. Before then the players had to be content with fixed canvas sheets hanging from the balcony above, and some even now mutter about the improvement that would follow if the screens could be rolled even further across the Pavilion front. There are, in fact, several holes drilled into the southern face of the Pavilion, to accommodate such an extension; but before the work could go further it was vetoed by the MCC Committee, which would have had its strictly private observation post covered by screen from time to time. As much of a nuisance, in the players' view, are the large expanses of window across the entire Pavilion front, shining or reflecting sometimes quite brightly on a sunny day. The sight-screen at the opposite end of the ground is regarded as one of the most effective in English cricket so long as bowlers of ordinary proportions are operating in front of it; which is to say that some batsmen – unusually short ones, perhaps – have sworn that as Joel Garner's hand comes over to deliver above his already extraordinary six feet eight inches, for a split second both it and the ball it contains are obscure above the uppermost edge of that screen. Normally, though, the only thing to distract a batsman facing the Nursery End is the movement of surrounding trees in a high wind.

The predominant wind at Lord's comes out of the west and tends to rush through the gap between the Pavilion and the Warner Stand, causing knowledgeable captains to put their fastest bowlers on with it at their backs. But wind is much less noticeable to players on the field at Lord's than on other first-class grounds, doubtless because it is more sheltered by its own buildings than the rest. Of much greater influence is the atmosphere that hangs over and upon the ground on many English summer days. It is usually believed that the high humidity of Lord's at such times is related to the proximity of the Thames, though no one ever remarks on the phenomenon at the Oval, which is considerably nearer the river. Yet an atmospheric curiosity most certainly exists at Lord's, and the only other major ground in this country with anything comparable is Headingley. In each case the ball of medium pace or more can behave quite differently through the air on the same day.

What makes the difference at Headingley is the appearance of cloud overhead, when the ball will swing more noticeably than under a clear sky. At Lord's there doesn't need to be any cloud at all; simply a morning when the sun shines warmly through a haze that it will later disperse. On such a morning a swing bowler opening the attack for his side can get the ball to move before pitching through an emphatic curve that he will try in vain to reproduce a few hours later, when the fully risen sun has burnt the heaviness out of the air. In June 1972 the heaviness persisted throughout most of three consecutive days and helped the Western Australian bowler Bob Massie, playing in his first Test, to devastate England with 8 wickets for 84 runs in the first innings, 8 for 53 in the second. That was the finest match analysis ever returned in a Test at Lord's, and one of the most impressive bowling feats of all time, almost every ball swinging prodigiously through the air. Massie never again returned figures like that, and by the end of that year his international career was over. In much less exotic circumstances, the bowler able to swing it a bit will hope for his opportunity during the first hour or ninety minutes of play at Lord's, knowing that if he doesn't pick up two or three wickets in that time, he'll have a long day ahead of him. By afternoon his captain will have resorted to working batsmen out by changing his bowlers a lot. By three o'clock on a good wicket, the sweating bowler will be finding it a job to get past the bat. A lot of captains, home or visiting, are apt to put opposing sides in first at Lord's if they win the toss, banking on the ability of their pacemen to enlist the atmosphere during the first session of play.

As for the wickets at Lord's, hard and true may be regarded as an exemplary recipe by the authorities, but some players beg to differ. Their anxieties about the reappearance of the ridge are a side issue, though *something* produces an uneven bounce at Lord's, so that a batsman is never wholly confident about whether he should be playing on the front or the back foot there. That apart, the reputation of the wicket has changed almost from generation to generation, sometimes as a result of policy decisions, sometimes by happenstance. When John Arlott was writing in 1948 he characterised the Lord's strips as "plumb to fair" (as distinct from Old Trafford – "Green"; Bath – "Sporting, *very* green"; Cheltenham – "Crumbling"; Bradford – "Fair; probably the best example in England of a fair wicket"). Some years later, cricketers knew Lord's for fast wickets with a lot of grass on them, a boon to bowlers like Moss and Bennett, who would pitch the ball up to get something off the seam; useful to their adversaries, too, who relished the ball coming on to the bat. In those days the pacemen monopolised the Lord's attacks – but not, as nowadays, because they had almost driven spinners out of the game – until the middle of July. By then the wickets were so worn that the spinners extensively replaced the fast men until September. It was a bit like having two separate seasons from a bowler's point of view.

The few men around who can recall those times, and still play at Lord's today, agree that the present wickets are better than they've ever been if the endurance of the strip is what you're after. Only, they say, that doesn't necessarily make for entertaining cricket. As a match proceeds these days, the wicket tends to get slower and the ball bounces lower. The batsman has to work for every run and the bowler has to exert himself more as his weariness grows, in order to produce the same effect. It is, say the critical performers, a terrible wicket to *win* matches on; an assertion which to some extent is supported by the experience of Middlesex teams which have won the county championship in recent years. In 1976 only five of the side's fourteen first-class victories were recorded at Lord's, in 1977 and 1980 six out of ten, in 1982 five out of thirteen. What the critics can't make up their minds about is what, fundamentally, makes for wickets at Lord's that are a bit less than the purist's dream. Surrey loam? Modern fertilisers? A change of tide in the policies of the game?

Some cricket matches have turned on the playing peculiarities of Lord's, and Massie's Test was one of them in modern times. So was the 1974 Test against Pakistan, who were 173 for three in their second innings at the close of play on the Saturday night, before a

Sunday deluge that prevented more cricket until late on the Monday afternoon. Within a couple of hours the Pakistanis were all out for 226 (had time not run out, they might easily have lost the match by ten wickets), cursing the slope at Lord's which had enabled water to seep downhill below the surface and produce a lasting damp patch on a length at the Pavilion End. It was this which Underwood exploited so effectively as to be virtually unplayable on that fourth evening, taking six wickets for nine runs in an hour at one stage, and finishing with eight for fifty-one. Cricketers can recall comparable dramas from almost every ground on earth, where local conditions have made for some phenomenal performance by a batsman or a bowler. Lord's is no more prone to the startling in this respect than any other cricket field, and it is much more predictably equable than some. It generally pays no outrageous dividends to the captain who wins the toss, and its biggest rewards are saved for consistent skill and perseverance.

Above all, it is permanently suffused in an atmosphere which is beyond measurement by the meteorologist or the analyst of soil. In part this is a matter of looks, the handsomeness of the setting. It also consists in the social and even the political history of cricket, which is in the fibres of this place more than elsewhere in the whole world. And when that has been said there is the playing tradition looming over all which, even in these self-centred and inflated times, cannot be overlooked by any cricketer taking the field at Lord's. This, he must surely know if he strides out with a bat in his hand, is where Jack Hobbs hit the ground record of 316 not out in 1926 against a Middlesex side which contained more amateurs than professionals. It is where Watson and Bailey managed one of the most famous of all rearguard actions in 1953, together defying everything that Lindwall, Miller and Co could hurl at them for over four hours, securing England a draw when defeat had earlier seemed inevitable. This was the scene of Fowler's Match in 1910, possibly the most sensational reverse of fortune in cricket history, even if it was Eton against Harrow. Bradman smashed the Middlesex bowlers for 160 out of 225 in just over two hours here, on a Saturday evening in 1934. Almost twenty years later, Dexter belted seventy off seventy-three balls he received from two extremely hostile West Indians, Wes Hall and Charlie Griffith – "the greatest onslaught on fast bowling I have ever seen", according to one old England player who watched it. That was a drawn Test which could have ended with any one of four results when the last over began. And its spectators still remembered Benaud's marvellous catch a few seasons before: taken with outstretched hands in the gully off a powerful slash by Cowdrey, the impact carrying the Australian several yards into a backwards somersault.

The mere cricket *watcher*, probably, is more susceptible to the intangible elements that make Lord's a unique institution in this international sport. But even players, obsessed as they always must be with their own performance, their private ambitions in the game, and as they now are with their finances as well, cannot be indifferent to those things apart from the state of the wicket and the effect of the slope, that amalgamate here and nourish this sovereign place. Don Wilson, sometime of Yorkshire and England, and for several years Head Coach at Lord's, says straight out: "If you can't play cricket here, you can't play it anywhere." He was thinking of things beyond the reliability of the turf and other facilities offered cricketers in NW8.

CHAPTER TWO

MCC

The calendar of the Marylebone Cricket Club, the owners of Lord's and chief defenders of tradition in the game, begins not in January but in October each year. That date sees the installation of a new MCC President at the first monthly meeting of a committee of senior members – *the* MCC Committee – which will itself have been slightly rearranged during the September holiday since its last gathering in August. The event takes place at the southern end of the Pavilion, in the Committee Room, which is much more exclusive than the adjacent Long Room. Not even a distinguished MCC member would dare to walk through those doors except at the Committee's invitation, and it beckons very rarely.

The room still feels spacious even with long tables ranged to form three sides for meetings such as the Presidential installation. By the great window overlooking the Pavilion steps and the playing area beyond, other furniture is deployed to help committee men watch their cricket in comfort and with all due assistance. There are several armchairs, with a little wooden stand to accommodate a scorecard beside each. Mounted on a tripod is a powerful (10 × 80) pair of naval glasses, worthy of an admiral with a beady eye for his fleet. A television set is parked near by, so that slow-motion replays can be mustered at will. A drinks cupboard, always well stocked, is within hailing distance. All this is surveyed from the walls by paintings of former Presidents, some looking faintly benign, the rest rather stern. A cabinet in the room contains pictures of every individual President since 1825. The only objects extraneous to cricket are the ormolu clock on the mantelpiece, with a Sphinx perched on top; and a highly polished jack arranged to commemorate the encounter on some antipodean green in 1947 between the St Kilda Bowling Club of Dunedin and MCC. If that overworked phrase the holy of holies may be used about Lord's at all any more, it properly belongs to the Committee Room.

In there since 1890, and in its equivalents for nearly a hundred years before that, all the major decisions affecting cricket have been taken. Nowadays they are mostly taken by officials of the Cricket

Council, the Test and County Cricket Board or the International Cricket Conference, because all these bodies muster for their most pregnant debates in that room. But even now, when MCC's power isn't all what it used to be, anything that matters about the game is spoken of in there by MCC's Committee at an early stage, discussed, weighed up, argued over, referred back, resurrected for more discussion, and finally pronounced upon with resonance. Great corporations with multi-national interests, and policies that may topple governments, do not consider such matters more exhaustively than do MCC's elders when applying themselves to the minutiae of cricket in their Committee Room. They are the self-conscious legatees of a tradition by which their club took upon itself ultimate authority in the sport the moment it was founded in 1787. The patrons who got Thomas Lord to make them a ground in Dorset Square simultaneously hoisted their new title, revised the existing Laws of Cricket, and reissued these under their own imprimatur, as MCC still does from time to time. From that moment the Hambledon Club, which had set the cricketing pace for a generation, went into decline as its lustre and its financial ability to attract the great players of the day to Hampshire were transferred to the arrivistes of Marylebone. The final gesture in this eighteenth-century takeover took place in 1793, when the Hambledon men played their last match, against MCC on Lord's Ground.

A succession of now hallowed figures, sometimes with national reputations in other spheres, have dominated the club from its beginning. An early one was the parson peer Lord Frederick Beauclerk, DD, descendant of Charles II's union with Nell Gwynne; he hit eight centuries on the first Lord's, spoke reverently of a game "unalloyed by love of lucre and mean jealousies", yet boasted of making £600 a year from playing cricket for stakes. William Ward, the banker MP who raised enough cash to stop Lord selling the present site for building development, hit 278 for the club against Norfolk in 1820, a ground record that lasted for over a hundred years. One who made little impression with bat or ball was the first secretary of the club, Benjamin Aislabie, a man rising twenty stone who pops up as a kindly character in *Tom Brown's Schooldays* and specialised in writing cricket songs and verses. Another was Sir Spencer Ponsonby-Fane, elected a member of MCC when he was sixteen, its treasurer for thirty-seven years and, above all, the man who began its superb collection of cricket art in 1864. Much nearer our own time there was H. S. Altham, the Winchester housemaster who had been a moderately successful first-class cricketer until he stopped playing in 1923 and became an administrator; a very fine

41

historian of the game, and the originator of many inspired ideas about encouraging young cricketers to play decently and deftly. The figures most venerated in MCC's pantheon tend to be those whose deeds on the field were complemented by their performances in the Committee Room. W. G. Grace does not qualify on those terms (though no name in all cricket is more hallowed than his) because although he was a devoted member of MCC for most of his life, he spared little time for anything but playing the game and making sure that he got as much money from it as possible.

If, for the moment, we dwell on only one more exalted ghost, it is because he personified many of the characteristics that hallmarked MCC during its most powerful period. He was the fourth Lord Harris (of Seringapatam and Mysore, and of Belmont), who is recognised much more – even by the *Dictionary of National Biography* – for what he did in cricket than for what he achieved as Governor of Bombay towards the end of the nineteenth century. Emerging from the cricket nurseries of Eton and Oxford, in time he became one of the most forceful batsmen of his period, quite worth his place in sides representing England. He played and was captain in four Tests, at the end of which his average was twenty-nine in six innings. Not even Grace lived more for cricket than Harris, who didn't play his last match until he was seventy-nine, only three years before his death. Within the game he moved in two neighbouring spheres. One was his native county club of Kent, which he first captained in 1875 and more or less ruled for the next sixty years. The other was MCC, of which he ultimately remarked that "my whole life has pivoted on Lord's". He was a trustee of the club for ten years, its treasurer for sixteen, its President in 1895, and for several decades no matter could be settled in the Committee Room without Lord Harris's assent, invariably given or withheld in unmistakable language. He was the very model of a Victorian and Edwardian autocrat.

He had a lot of guts, well publicised in 1879 when he was leading an English team in Australia and an angry crowd rushed on to the pitch at Sydney to protest against an umpiring decision in the match with New South Wales. Harris stepped forward to shield the umpire and was struck with a stick for his pains. There followed something of a crisis in Anglo-Australian cricketing relations which Harris himself ended, after some persuasion, the following year when he raised an England side to play Australia in the very first Test match held at home. But he was not on the whole a forbearing man. In his autobiography he told with some satisfaction of his response to the news that an old friend had been badly hurt at cricket: "The ball hit him in the mouth, driving his lips through his teeth, and in writing him a letter of sympathy I could not help adding that I should advise him in future not to put his head where his bat ought to be."

He was a stickler for well-defined principles, and no one in his hearing would get away with referring to cricket's written code as anything but the Laws of the game with a capital L. "Rules," declared Lord Harris, "are made to be broken. Laws are made to be kept." It was his rigorous adhesion to these Laws that made him such a fierce opponent of any bowler suspected of throwing. When he deemed two Lancastrians, Crossland and Nash, to be culpable, he ordered Kent to cancel all fixtures with the northerners until the pair were dropped from the Lancashire side. Wearing his MCC colours, he was just as adamant on the subject of a cricketer's qualification to play for any particular team. The most notable thing Harris did during his five years in Bombay was to foster cricket in India (because he reckoned that young men there needed "some healthy, active pastime as a counter-attraction to paise and politics") and in doing so launched Ranjitsinhji upon his career: but when the question arose of Ranji playing for England on the basis of his Cambridge and Sussex connections, Harris condemned the notion out of hand, losing that battle only because in those days the England teams were picked by the committee of the county organising the Test – and the Test in this case happened to be up at Old Trafford. Harris's hostility had nothing to do with race as such. An even more celebrated example of the same attitude was his discovery that young Walter Hammond had started playing for Gloucestershire, when he had been born in Kent. Promptly the edict went forth that this must stop until the lad had fulfilled certain requirements; which meant that his livelihood came to a standstill for a couple of years. Harris was in hot pursuit of yet another misplaced person when he was stopped one day in the Long Room by the President of Worcestershire: "May I congratulate you, my Lord," Lord Deerhurst is reputed to have said, "on having buggered the career of another young cricketer." No one but a fellow peer of the realm could ever have spoken to George Harris thus.

The hierarchy which he commanded remains a feature of MCC today, as well defined as it always was. It is topped by the President, but only for his year of office, which comes to him as the greatest favour the club can bestow on any man. Some resounding titles have sat in the Presidential chair since it was instituted in 1825, and until the Second World War only sixteen out of 111 occupants had answered to plain "Mr". It is some sign of our times that out of thirty-seven Presidents between 1946 and 1983, only twenty-one have had a more decorative handle to their names. The post-war

43

years have seen one Prime Minister (Sir Alec Douglas-Home), two supreme commanders (Earl Alexander and Viscount Portal), a Head of the Foreign Office (Lord Caccia) and the Earl Marshal and Chief Butler of England (the Duke of Norfolk); not to mention the monarch's husband, who has so far held the position twice. Other than the Duke of Edinburgh and the Duke of Norfolk, these gentlemen were at the time retired from their public duties, as they were almost bound to be, because MCC's President incurs rather a lot of time-consuming tasks one way and another.

It is expected that he will, for a start, attend each of the eleven monthly Committee meetings, together with as many sub-committees as he can manage, especially those specialising in finance and development. He is also in great demand as a speaker at various functions outside MCC's immediate bailiwick. He should turn up every day during the Test match at Lord's (often plural now) to act as host to the most distinguished guests, and more likely than not he will go abroad for a week or so during the winter to keep MCC's end up wherever the England side are on tour. On such occasions, he is also fulfilling part of his obligation to the International Cricket Conference, whose chairman he is and whose annual meeting he leads at Lord's. Likewise, he automatically became President of the Cricket Council (which since 1968 has assumed most of MCC's old role as the final arbiter on the game in England) until this body's constitution was changed at the end of 1982. If he wishes, an MCC President can quite easily fill his diary with official happenings from one end of his year to the other. Mr G. H. G. Doggart (at the time a headmaster in Somerset) had only reached the half-way mark in his 1981–2 Presidency when he calculated that he had already attended thirty-eight committee meetings, thirty-three dinners or lunches, and nineteen other occasions, one of which meant five days in Sri Lanka for the first Test ever played there.

A President may sometimes be little more than an eye-catching figurehead, as the Duke of Edinburgh was. But if he has earlier been an assiduous Committee – or at least sub-committee – member, as most of them have, he will have a clear idea of things more pressing than club tradition and the varied attractions of the game. He will know which round is about to come up in cricket's infighting (and there is much of it about) and just which corner MCC is punching from; or ought to be. He will be aware of the problems attending club solvency, which become more complex by the year. He will be all too familiar with the personalities he must sometimes grapple with if matters are to move forward at all: who is the Committee windbag who must be courteously deflated if everyone else is not to be driven daft; who tends to obstruct fresh ideas on a mysterious private principle of his own; and who can be relied upon to back the President through thick and thin. If a President-elect is strong-minded and has a clear strategy in his head when his October comes round, he can leave quite a mark on the club and some impression on the game in the twelve months before, as is the custom, his own nominee succeeds him.* One of the first things Hubert Doggart did in 1981 was to send a letter to all MCC match managers, asking them to make sure that the teams under their orders in the next season (well over 200 of them) behaved impeccably on and off the field and got in at least twenty overs of bowling every hour.

Because the President is but a temporary chief, the continuously most powerful leverage tends to be shared by two men, the Treasurer and the Secretary. The first is unpaid, a long-serving member of the Committee who is elected for five years at a stretch but may be appointed almost indefinitely if his colleagues wish it so. He deputises for the President on any club business the latter is unable to attend, but he sits on every committee in the club in his own right. He therefore has a distinctive voice of his own, and some very loud hailers have been Treasurers of MCC. Lord Harris, of course, was one. So was Lord Hawke, who held the position for six years before the Second World War. Another authoritarian figure, for whom Yorkshire played a comparable role to Harris's Kent, Hawke did a great deal during his long life to improve the working conditions of professional cricketers but is best remembered for his sometimes misquoted (though never misunderstood) exclamation, "Pray Heaven no professional may ever captain England!"; and for dismissing incontinent Bobby Peel from the Yorkshire side when the bowler's proverbial intake of ale got the better of him one day in the middle.

The Secretary is one of seventy people in the full-time employment of MCC and the tradition has been that, once appointed, he retains the job until he decides to retire. In the entire history of the club, from the moment Benjamin Aislabie appeared in 1822, only eleven men have been Secretary, and some of them have been very long servers indeed. Aislabie himself was there for twenty years, as was another nineteenth-century figure, Henry Perkins. Within living memory, Colonel R. S. Rait Kerr ruled the administration of Lord's for sixteen years as vigorously as he took charge of the Army's officer cadet training during the war. But for sheer staying power none has

* G. H. G. Doggart, for example, chose Sir Anthony Tuke, chairman of Rio Tinto Zinc Corporation, to follow him as President in October 1982.

matched Sir Francis Lacey, who became Secretary in 1898 and didn't
step down until 1926, whereupon he became the first man to be
knighted for his association with cricket. Lacey had been a barrister
before reaching Lord's, like Perkins his predecessor, but there their
similarities ended. "Don't take any notice of the damned Committee!" was the advice the one offered the other on handing over office,
for Perkins, like many of the masters he served, was an imperious
man. Lacey was cold, with a subtler mind that preferred to harness
other MCC energies rather than battle with them. Before long he
had devised the network of sub-committees that still keeps a large
number of senior members beavering away contentedly for many of
their afternoons: during the season of 1982, no fewer than ninety-
seven different people were engaged in these post-prandial pursuits,
some of them on as many as three or even four different committees.
Crucially, Lacey formed an alliance with Lord Harris. Between
them, they simply ran the place.

There has been nothing quite like that partnership since, though it
has remained a truth about MCC that if Treasurer and Secretary see
eye to eye – and they generally have – they can propel the affairs of
the club more or less in directions they have chosen. They can also
stretch their influence in other ways through the Secretary's connections elsewhere. In a more permanent version of the Presidential link
he acts as Secretary of the International Cricket Conference, and
until 1983 he was Deputy Secretary of the Cricket Council as well.
Whatever his role, he does much more than simply supervise
administration. He advises and persuades. In short, he has a hand in
making policy wherever he sits, which can generally be disregarded
by only a small handful of other men. In MCC, apart from the
President and Treasurer, only the Chairman of Finance and the
Trustees would have enough standing. The first of these is a modern
creation, since it was decided that the Treasurer had so many things
on his plate as the President's deputy that another officer of the club,
elected on the same terms as himself, should watch over money
matters alone. The Trustees have existed since 1864, *very* senior men
(three at the moment) pickled in the ways of club and game, elected
for three-year shifts which are quite often extended by popular
assent.

These seven figures, from the President down, constitute the top of
MCC's hierarchy. A little way beneath is the busy layer of sub-
committees that Lacey concocted, each pondering some aspect of
MCC and/or cricket in general. In alphabetical order there are ten of
them – arts and library, club facilities, cricket, development,
finance, general purposes, grounds and fixtures, indoor school man-

agement, property and works, tennis and squash. The smallest of them (property and works) has ten members, the biggest (cricket) nineteen. The Cricket Committee, with the Finance Committee, is regarded as the most important of all these invigilators. It concerns itself with standards of all kinds in the playing of the game at large, not just by MCC teams. It is loaded with men who have played for England, extending (in 1981–2) from old-timers such as Gubby Allen and Les Ames to someone as recent as Tony Lewis. Its members serve, like all other sub-committeemen, for as long as the full MCC Committee asks them. In due course, those obtaining the warmest approval from on high may expect to be elevated from whichever is the sub-committee on which they have made their mark to the senior body, if they aren't there already.

The full MCC Committee in 1981–2 consisted of thirty-one men, and only nine of them were without significant first-class cricketing experience. One was the Chairman of Finance, E. W. Phillips, a director of the merchant bank Lazards and nineteen other institutions which included Phoenix Assurance and the Woolwich Building Society. Another was Lord Caccia, retired from diplomacy but chairman of ITT (UK) Ltd and director of three other bodies including the Prudential. Another was J. T. Faber, Harold Macmillan's son-in-law and director of eleven companies, which included Cornhill Insurance and two firms operating in the Middle East. A fourth was Sir Oliver Popplewell, QC, the lawyer who, in a letter to *The Times* after the cricketing authorities had incurred High Court costs of £200,000 or so in litigation with World Series cricketers, urged that they should still stand firm against Kerry Packer until the Australian was prepared to make concessions.

Business experience was not confined to the non-cricketers. N. J. Cosh, who batted for Cambridge and Surrey in the sixties, was a director of thirteen companies, including the bankers Keyser Ullmann. His contemporary C. B. Howland, who kept wicket for Cambridge, Sussex and Kent, held fourteen directorships and had held another with the investment consultants Norton Warburg, who went into liquidation in 1981. Colin Cowdrey, who once strode to the wicket in a Lord's Test with his broken arm in plaster and is one of only four men alive to have scored 40,000 runs (also the youngest player ever to appear at Lord's; aged thirteen, Tonbridge v Clifton, 1946), was an executive director of Barclays International and on the boards of three other concerns. There was P. B. H. May, one of the most determined cricket captains England ever had, newly appointed chairman of England's selectors and a Lloyd's Underwriter for twenty years. There was D. J. Insole, May's vice-captain on the 1956–7 tour of South Africa, and marketing director of Trollope and Colls Holdings, the building contractors. There was C. H. Palmer, who personified the old amateur traditions when he batted for Worcester and then Leicester just after the war, with a commercial interest in steel. There were several others who could speak about playing top-class cricket with authority, and who also knew their way about the City and its dependencies. And there was E. W. Swanton, who had appeared once or twice for Middlesex before spending himself on journalism and becoming eventually the doyen (the word fitted him precisely) of cricket reporters.

In all, there were four former captains of England on the full Committee in 1981–2: G. O. Allen, F. R. Brown, May and Cowdrey. There were also four other men who had played for their country: A. V. Bedser, S. C. Griffith, G. H. G. Doggart and Insole. Each of those eight apart from Bedser had been a county captain in his time, as had the Treasurer D. G. Clark (Kent), C. G. A. Paris (Hampshire), A. C. D. Ingleby-Mackenzie (Hampshire) and Palmer. Out of the twenty-two former first-class cricketers, thirteen had appeared in their youth for one of the two major universities, and the old Cambridge players outnumbered the Oxford Blues by eleven to two. Added together, they had experience of playing cricket at home and abroad since shortly after the First World War. The oldest Committee man of all, Sir Cyril Hawker, a retired banker who played for Essex just once, only missed the nineteenth century by a few months. The majority were old or middle-aged men, but a couple weren't yet born when that flying bomb landed near Lord's in 1944. With the addition of J. A. Bailey, Secretary of MCC since 1974, captain of Oxford in 1958 and a useful Essex fast bowler for a time, they amounted to an impressive body of cricketing knowledge. And though some were undoubtedly creaking a bit, they couldn't reasonably be regarded as an unmitigated bunch of old fuddy-duddies, which has tended to be a popular image of those at the top of MCC.

One of them, like Lord Harris before him, has come to dominate the club in his lifetime; and if his effect on cricket in general has been marginally less pervasive – though that's a debatable point – it is because in recent years the tide of history has taken some things beyond his influence that Harris was able to order at will. He is George Oswald Browning Allen, widely known as Gubby – which is a familiarity, it is worth remarking, that George Harris wouldn't have tolerated for a minute. This may or may not have something to do with Allen's antecedents, which are largely Australian, though the "Browning" is a family gesture to the English poet, who belonged to the maternal ancestry. Allen's mother was half

Australian and half French; his father was a son of the man who founded the biggest firm of solicitors Down Under. Himself born in Sydney, Allen and his parents came to England when he was six; they never went back except, in his case, for cricket and business. He got into Eton and the first time he played at Lord's was in the game against Harrow in 1919, when he was run out without receiving a ball. As he says himself, he did rather better later. He returned to the ground as a Cambridge cricketer, easily his most conspicuous achievement at university where, he admits, he never did a hand's turn at history, which is what he'd been sent to study. With that background and in that part of the twentieth century, he naturally played all his cricket as an amateur during a very long career. This accounts for odd periods when he went missing from the game, to take care of his bread and butter. First there was a spasm with the Royal Exchange. Then there was a spell in France, working in the silk business under the patronage of Lord Bicester, who was a friend of his father. After that he was beckoned into the management of Debenham's, didn't enjoy it much, and was profoundly glad – when he returned from the Bodyline tour of Australia in 1932–3 – to join a firm of stockbrokers, on which his substance has been based ever since. The connection was severed only by the war, which Allen began with one pip in an anti-aircraft unit, and finished as a Lieutenant-Colonel responsible for all intelligence on the ground-to-air defence of Germany to both the RAF and the Americans (who gave him their Legion of Merit). Somewhere between the two postings, he had taken in a mysterious job with MI 14E.

As a cricketer he was often much more than a useful batsman and a very good fast bowler, possibly the fastest in the country after Harold Larwood at one period. He appeared for Middlesex between 1921 and 1950, and set Lord's aglow one day in 1929 when he swept through Lancashire's batting to take all ten wickets for forty runs. That is especially memorable on two counts. No one else, before or since, has taken all ten wickets in a county match at Lord's; and when Allen did so, Lancashire had been batting for twenty minutes without loss before he arrived at the ground, having had to go to work first to let them know that he would be playing cricket that day. His career average was not quite as impressive as that analysis, though 778 wickets at 21.22 apiece put him high in the lists almost every year he played; and though he never quite managed to hit 10,000 runs, his batting average in the end was 28.67, with a top score of 180. He (122) and Ames (137) still hold the world's record Test partnership for the eighth wicket, 246 against New Zealand at Lord's in 1931. He played twenty-five matches for England in the days when Tests were a rare treat and not a sometimes tiresome commonplace as nowadays. Eleven times he captained his country and twice led touring sides abroad. Once was to Australia, in 1936–7, for one of the most palpitating series of all times, which Allen's side lost 3–2. It is reckoned that they had some pretty sore luck with the tosses and the weather; but it is also generally held that they did an enormous amount to heal the wounds caused by the Bodyline tour. His other captaincy abroad was on that searing visit to West Indies in 1947–8, when the 45-year-old Gubby was invited to lead virtually an England Second XI into battle against what was expected to be easy meat. The selectors had not then heard of Worrell, Weekes and Walcott, whose batting so devastated the Englishmen that the tourists were glad in the end to have drawn two Tests out of four.

What he is always remembered for during his playing days, and deserves to be, was his refusal to bowl bodyline against Woodfull's Australians for Douglas Jardine. Some cynics who will allow no quarter to any Establishment figure (and Gubby Allen is most certainly that) have said that, as an amateur, he could afford to snub his captain, where none of the professionals on that team – Larwood, Voce and Bowes – would have dared to for fear of their livelihoods. That may be so, though Allen might easily have lost his place in the England side, which he was as keen as anyone to keep. But the main point surely is that Jardine, too, was an amateur and didn't share the principled stand that Allen took; or, for that matter, the Nawab of Pataudi, who refused to field in the leg trap. In his prime, Gubby was quite liable to bounce one at a batsman from time to time; but he didn't believe that systematic intimidation was a fair way to play cricket.

There had been talk on the boat going over of the need to hate the Australians, which Allen had openly scoffed at. But – he is quite clear about this – there had been no mention in his hearing of tactical bowling on the line of the batsman. It is his belief that this had been theoretically worked out before the team left England in discussions between Jardine, Larwood, Voce and Arthur Carr (county captain of the two Nottinghamshire players), which had been concentrated on the need to bring Bradman under control. Jardine had also been discussing leg theory that summer with Frank Foster of Warwickshire and Percy Fender, the Surrey captain. By the time the Second Test was due to start in Melbourne, Jardine's strategy for dealing with Bradman in particular was beginning to emerge, though matters were not to come to a head until the teams faced each other again in Adelaide a couple of weeks later. Half an hour before the Melbourne Test began, Jardine came to see Allen, whose account of the subsequent conversation goes like this:

> Jardine: "I was talking to the boys last night."
> Allen: "Which boys?"
> "Oh, Larwood and Voce and one or two others. They all say it's because you're worried about your popularity with the crowd that you won't bowl bouncers to a leg-side field . . ."
> "I've never bowled like that, and I don't think it's the way cricket should be played."
> "Well, you've got to, now."
> "I'm sorry, but I'm not going to."
> "But you must."
> "Douglas, you've got twenty minutes to make up your mind whether you want me to play or not. But I'm telling you that if you leave me out every word you've just said will be made public when I get back to England."
>
> And with that Allen, in his own words, "stormed out of the dressing-room".
>
> With less than ten minutes to go before start of play, he went back to Jardine and said, "Well, am I playing?"
> "Of course you're playing. Don't know what you're talking about."
> "But you do understand, don't you . . .?"
> "Don't know what you're talking about."

End of conversation. Allen did play, in that and each subsequent Test. He bowled as he'd always been accustomed to bowl, and he took twenty-one wickets during the series in the process. His self-exclusion from the bodyline attack was not mentioned again by Jardine – "to his credit," Allen now says. "We remained the best of friends throughout the tour."

Distinguished as his playing career was, in the scales of cricket history it is likely to be outweighed by his record as an administrator of the game; and it has puzzled many people who attach importance to such things that he has never been awarded more than the CBE (which he collected for his services to cricket in 1963) "despite", he believes, "several recommendations". Here is a man who has sat almost without interruption on the MCC Committee since 1935, who was the club's President in 1963–4, its Treasurer from 1964 to 1976, and since then has been one of its Trustees. He was chairman of the England selectors from 1955 to 1961 (shrewd enough to bring the long-absent Washbrook, Sheppard and Compton back into a weakling side, which then proceeded to beat the Australians by an innings twice) and has been a vice-chairman of the Cricket Council as well. For twenty years he represented England at the ICC.

The measure of Gubby Allen's involvement in the game since he stopped playing is perhaps most clearly made by the list of appointments he still held on his eightieth birthday in July 1982. That day he sat on MCC's Committee both as Trustee and as a member of the Special Advisory Committee (the innermost cabal, which does not appear on the printed list of sub-committees, and which acts as rudder to the full Committee on the most crucial issues like who is to be the next Secretary or Treasurer, or who are to chair the ten sub-committees). He was also a member of MCC's Cricket, Finance, and General Purposes Committees. He was an MCC representative on the Cricket Council, and a member of the council's Emergency Executive. For the Test and County Cricket Board he sat on Cricket, Overseas Tours and Adjudication Committees. He was a member of the Middlesex Committee (had been since 1931) and of the county's Cricket Committee. He was on the Coaching Committee of the National Cricket Association. To cap the lot, he was President of the Association of Cricket Umpires. There was, in short, no sphere of the game in the British Isles where Gubby Allen could not make his voice heard and his views known. There was nothing at Lord's, or remotely to do with Lord's, that wasn't marked by his presence. And ever since his election to the MCC Committee nearly half a century before, he had invariably been there or thereabouts.

Several things made this possible, quite apart from a passionate interest, force of character and proven expertise. One was the fact that, as a lifelong bachelor, Allen had more time to spare than most family men. Another was that, certainly after becoming a successful stockbroker, he had the means to afford a great deal of spare time beyond even a bachelor's average. It has also helped that he has lived on the doorstep of Lord's for fourteen years, in one of those MCC properties (he bought the lease) which border two sides of the ground; a gate leads from the rose garden at Lord's into his own, and he could probably still throw a cricket ball from there into the rear of Q Stand. On top of these advantages, he was always regarded as a coming man in MCC by those with the power to raise him high.

He confesses that although Lord Harris could be an awkward cuss, "a tyrant at times as well as a great administrator", he personally got on well with the old man, as one of Gubby's stories certainly bears out. He had been given out lbw when batting for the Gentlemen against the Players and thought it was a rotten decision, but walked without demur, which was the custom then. His bad temper, though, was obvious when he reached the dressing-room and encountered Lord Harris, who had watched the dismissal. "Satisfied, young feller?" enquired his Lordship. Allen made it plain that he was far from that. Whereupon Harris had the offending umpire struck off the first-class list. After Harris had died, the subtler influence of Sir Pelham Warner began to spread through Lord's and Allen admits that he was even more of a favourite with dear old "Plum", lucky to have been picked by him and the other selectors for the Bodyline tour; he hadn't had a very good season by his standards, and reckons it was his eight wickets in the Gents v Players match that put him on the boat.

Until he became a power in his own right, Gubby Allen made excellent use of such patronage, though he never failed to speak with the distinctive voice characterised by those exchanges with Jardine in Australia; blunt, self-confident and imperative. His own rise to eminence in the club began immediately the war was over, when he noted with despair that the Committee was still packed with "Lord Hawke's yesmen" (Hawke, "a dear old man but not very clever", had died in 1938) and decided that they must be replaced by people who thought for themselves. Gubby and five or six others with like minds used to meet at his home to work out voting strategies that would shortly see the old men through the Committee door. He has never had any time for anyone merely decorating the Committee, or any other post. Later on, quoting the instance of Lord Dartmouth, President of MCC in 1932 and a Trustee for many years, during the last twelve of which he didn't attend a single meeting, Gubby argued the Committee into a time limit to Trusteeships, which had hitherto been indefinite. He also put an end to electing the Treasurer for life. Just as radically, he later created the Chairman of Finance's position. At about the same time he divided what had been a single Finance and General Purposes Committee, on the grounds that current financial expertise was needed in the club and could only be obtained from men unavailable to MCC except at evening meetings, to which old buffers were generally averse. These undoubtedly are the most important marks that Gubby Allen has made on the structure of MCC. One other is unquestionably the most inspired. It was he who suggested, in 1949, that distinguished professional cricketers on retirement should be made Honorary Life Members of what had always been a determinedly amateur gentleman's club – which instantly admitted Hobbs and Larwood, Paynter and Leyland, Hirst and Rhodes and the great Sydney Barnes, and nineteen others like them, a tremendous band that has been added to in the years since.

In the game generally there is one instance of his following exactly in the footsteps of Lord Harris: in a campaign against throwing.

Allen was chairman of MCC's Cricket Committee towards the end of the 1950s when reports of suspect actions began to circulate, some of the worst cases involving Australian bowlers playing Peter May's touring side in 1958–9. The Australian Board's first reaction to complaints was to tell MCC to mind its own business, and Gubby decided to do that – but challengingly. He spent the next domestic season ranging the counties, looking for anything amiss, naming the players and ordering them to straighten their bowling actions or face the end of their careers. Among the bowlers he named were two England Test players, Loader and Lock.

That year also saw the visit of McGlew's South Africans and the miserable saga of their fast bowler Geoff Griffin, who was called for throwing in three matches before the Second Test started at Lord's in an atmosphere of some tension. Before the game began MCC's President, H. S. Altham, spoke to the two umpires, Lee and Buller, who were to stand in the match, reminding them: "It is for you and only you to interpret Law 26 without fear or favour on the simple basis of what you see. I'm glad that I can assure you on the best possible authority that the South African team and their manager have complete confidence in the ability and integrity of the umpires of this country, and whatever may be your judgment, they will accept it without question . . ." After that young Griffin proceeded to perform the hat-trick, the first ever seen in a Test at Lord's. But he was also called eleven times for throwing during England's solitary innings by Frank Lee; and in an exhibition match which followed the Test, Sid Buller no-balled him four times out of five deliveries in an over which extended sensationally to eleven balls, the last three sent down underarm. Poor Griffin bowled no more in England; his career, indeed, was finished. So, too, by the end of that season, were the most serious infringements of legitimate bowling actions seen since the nineteenth century. Gubby Allen's aggressive cleansing of his own stables did the trick with the Australian Board, which followed suit with a tough policy of its own.

His other great impact on the international game was in the duration and frequency of Test matches. When Allen started playing at an international level no Anglo-Australian Test in Australia had been drawn since 1882, because the Australians believed in playing matches to a conclusive finish on their own turf, however many days that took. It was Allen who persuaded Bradman after the war to consider and follow the English practice of a time limit to Tests of thirty hours, in the hope that this would make the cricket more eventful (a forlorn hope, it now seems, with seventeen games drawn in Australia between 1946–7 and 1983). And it was Allen with S. C.

Griffith, as Treasurer and Secretary of MCC, who went to India and persuaded the Cricket Board there to share a touring season of England with Pakistan in 1967, as the New Zealanders and South Africans had shared one two years before. The Indian Board had earlier rejected the notion almost unanimously and, had they remained obdurate, the custom of double tours – which Allen thinks has been tremendously successful since – would never have taken root.

Yet of all the things he has been responsible for in cricket, he remains proudest of something he did for the domestic game. It is now over thirty years since he sat down at an MCC Committee meeting and told his colleagues of the dreadful thing he had seen on Putney Common a day or two before: young men playing cricket with all the enthusiasm in the world, but without a clue about technique. Never having attended a public school, they had never been coached, and Gubby was aghast at this unsuspected state of affairs. "It is," he declared – and we may be sure that he didn't merely voice an opinion – "high time we did something about this." The result was the birth of the MCC Youth Cricket Association and its coaching award scheme in 1952, which was eventually incorporated into the highly organised workings of the later National Cricket Association. Another by-product of that unacceptable vision at Putney was the publication of the standard text-book on technique, the *MCC Cricket Coaching Book*, which has now gone into four editions and nine reprints with a circulation throughout the cricket-playing world. He and Harry Altham wrote that.

There are those who will say that Gubby Allen has never been averse to bullying his way through on what he has thought important, though it is usually added that his targets have invariably been pompous or weak men. Certainly he seems to divide the world clearly into "deadbeats" and those who are "awfully nice", anathemas and accolades both delivered in a cultivated rasping voice, with the faintest of squeaks lining it when he gets really worked up. It is an old-fashioned amateur's voice, and it pronounces golf (which he still plays) in the clubbable manner "goff". Very young Australian cricketers on their first visit to Lord's delight in a mild form of bear-baiting by hailing him matily with " 'Ow's it goin', Gubby?" which he takes equally in his stride; and for all his dogmatic reputation he can be a surprisingly sympathetic observer. He took a rather dim view of Boycott's behaviour on the English tour of India in 1981–2, but was at pains to make the point that the man had always been worried about the possibility of his health failing out there, having had his spleen removed many years ago.

55

And though it was well remembered by his co-selectors once that the choosing of an English team for Australia was somewhat lengthened because, between the picking of the batsmen and the bowlers, Gubby embarked on a dissertation about the state of Hoover shares, it is said by those who have had most dealings with him that here is a man who thinks more clearly and continually about cricket than anyone else alive. Some people arrive at a committee and apply themselves to the agenda only when they sit down, but G. O. Allen has worked out his own position on each item days before. He has always been a great one for picking the brains of younger cricketers than himself round his dinner table, and for choosing them single-mindedly. He once invited Tony Lewis to discuss some technical points of batsmanship, and both were wondering who else to include at supper. "I know," said Gubby, "we'll ask Parfitt. He's a left-hander."

Not naturally a penitent man, he deeply regrets having voted for the change in the lbw law when he first sat on the Committee in 1935. In his last report as Treasurer in 1976, he dwelt on this topic at some length, because it was central to his views about the game of cricket as a whole. "I am now more than ever convinced that this change in the Laws, to which in my infancy and to my everlasting shame I was in some small degree party, was the most disastrous piece of cricket legislation in my lifetime. The 1935 Law was designed to prevent batsmen padding up to balls pitching just outside the off-stump. Well, this it has done to some extent, but the administrators of the day clearly failed to examine in depth the possible by-products of their brainchild. It was argued that it would help all types of bowlers equally and increase off-side play. In the event it has done precisely the opposite, as, looking back, it was surely going to. As it has helped disproportionately the bowlers who bring the ball into the batsmen, it has in fact reduced off-side play, has contributed in no small way to the demise of the leg-spinner and orthodox left-armer and, perhaps worst of all, it has bred a race of front-foot batsmen for safety reasons.

"So what have we got now as a general pattern: seamers bowling endlessly at a funereal over-rate, off-spinners and an occasional left-armer pushing the ball through flat, to batsmen pushing endlessly forward. Containment is the theme. Efficient it is, backed by brilliant fielding, but variety and a sense of urgency, once among the charms of our game, are no longer there."

Not naturally tolerant, either, Gubby Allen makes no bones about the inadequacies of people who have appeared from time to time on the Committee. "Some years you can count on the fingers of one hand the number who come here except on Committee days, Test matches, and one-day finals. As a result, how can they know what the hell's going on round here?" For all that, the Committee gave him a birthday party in the Long Room when he became an octogenarian, something that had happened only once before, for his old patron Plum Warner. The tables were illuminated by the flicker from silver candlesticks, the paintings glowed beneath their soft strip-lights, while through the great glass windows could be seen the floodlit scoreboard reading "80 not out". All the pomp and circumstance that MCC could manage was laid on, with 143 guests to savour a bit of history being notched. Gubby sat on one side of the President, Sir Alec Douglas-Home on the other, and the tables were loaded with many lustrous names from half a century of English cricket, including eight captains of England, thirty-five old Test players, a dozen former Presidents of MCC. Les Ames, Bob Wyatt and Freddie Brown, companions from the Bodyline tour, were there. So were Edrich and Compton, the Bedser twins and Godfrey Evans, D'Oliveira and Dexter, Hutton, Graveney, Laker, May, Wooller and "Hopper" Levett, now almost as gnarled as his hands had become when he finally put aside his wicket-keeping gloves. So, too, was the legendary Dick Gaby, the Ground Superintendent many years ago at Lord's.

The chief guest of the evening was grateful for all this and he was gracious: but also, being Gubby Allen, he fulminated a bit about some things in the state of cricket today which, he advises, had better be corrected or the great game will go bust. The advice ought to be heeded. After all, that slight and gruff figure, which now rolls like a seadog after the hip operations of recent years, has seen and shrewdly assessed a vast amount of cricket in its time. When G. O. Allen has gone, an epoch at Lord's which stretches back to the First World War will also, reluctantly, have drawn its last breath.

Until 1968 there was very little in English cricket that the Marylebone Cricket Club, with the acquiescence of cricketers in general, didn't directly control. The Laws of the game were in its custody, and to that extent it controlled cricket throughout the world, too. At home it appointed the selectors who chose the teams representing England wherever they were to play. It picked the men who were to umpire all first-class matches in this country, and its recommendations about hiring and firing cricketers were accepted without question by the county clubs, who sent any unusually recalcitrant player up to Lord's to appear before the MCC sub-committee dealing with discipline. It organised the systematic coaching of young cricketers, as nobody else did, and in the remotest leagues and non-leagues of the British Isles any club with any sort of problem would sooner or later, if the problem became large enough, get in touch with Lord's; which in those days meant only MCC. The most famous example of this arose in 1947, when MCC supported the Cheetham Hill Cricket Club morally and financially all the way through the courts to the House of Lords, in a case which began when an unlucky lady called Bessie Stone, who had been standing in the street outside her house, was hit by the ball which one of the club cricketers had just knocked out of the ground for six. The combined forces of cricket ultimately triumphed, too.

MCC's breadth as a court of appeal may be judged by three items considered by the Committee between August 1962 and the following February. Just before E. R. Dexter's team left for Australia that winter, the Committee deliberated the matter of Mrs Dexter, who planned to be Down Under in time for Christmas and would be doing a certain amount of modelling while she was in the country, but would only be in contact with her husband and the rest of the English team in the major cities. The Committee solemnly came to the conclusion that it had no objection to this. Shortly afterwards it contemplated a letter from the Foreign Office, which sought financial assistance to sponsor cricket in Prague. That matter was deferred for more information on the subject. A few weeks later the Secretary reported correspondence with Messrs Stuart Surridge and Messrs Gunn & Moore "on the subject of Watermark Disease which attacked cricket-bat willows. Mr G. C. Newman suggested that county authorities should be asked to appoint an officer . . . to cut down the affected trees". The club's primacy was such, and had been since its formation, that if any public figure attempted to involve cricket in any other aspect of our national life, it was to MCC that he automatically turned. Thus, when the Archbishop of York, William Temple, in 1935 decided to enlist every British institution of influence in an approach to Adolf Hitler against persecution of Jews and others in Germany, he asked MCC to join the Olympic Games Committee in a letter to Berlin which appealed to "your Excellency to show yourselves no less generous than the Greeks and to issue a general act of amnesty for the benefit of all who are suffering imprisonment for religious or racial reasons". The MCC Committee decided that this was not a matter in which it could intervene.

The club embodied the virtues and the vices of the landed aristocracy and the substantial gentry from which it sprang. This meant above all that it flung itself wholeheartedly into the sustenance of a cricketing tradition which MCC itself had largely created or fostered by judicious patronage. In its disbursements of what can only be described as largesse, it often bore a striking resemblance to the English squire with some concern for those of his tenants who had served his purposes well and faithfully. In 1867 the club ceased to contribute to the Cricketers' Fund Friendly Society because it was decided that some of the northern professionals were too unbiddable for its taste; instead it established the Marylebone Professional Fund, "which shall have as its object the support of the professional players who during their career shall have conducted themselves to the entire satisfaction of the Committee of MCC". The club always has selected its good causes very carefully indeed. In 1963 it refused the Queensland Cricket Association's request for a donation to Ken Mackay's benefit, though the following year saw it subscribing to the funds of nine English cricketers (£40 apiece for Ken Barrington, Tommy Greenough and J. M. Parks; £25 each to Jack Bannister, Don Bennett, Henry Horton, Jim Presdee, Terry Spencer and R. C. Wilson). It can sometimes be caught rendering a spot of first aid when a genuine hard luck story comes its way. When news reached London that Wally Hammond's widow was having a rough time financially (he had lost all his money in the collapse of a motor business in South Africa, took work as a groundsman, and died not long after), the Committee recommended that Gloucestershire should launch on her behalf an appeal which MCC would support.

If the club appeared unbendingly severe in many respects, that was no more than the traditional posture of rulers in any sphere; and MCC did rule cricket. A penalty of this position was to be criticised from time to time by those jealous of its primacy or impatient of the pace at which it moved. The regular sniping by Michael Parkinson from a column of the *Sunday Times* throughout the 1960s and early 1970s was no more than a faint echo of the campaign run a hundred years earlier by many county contemporaries and newspapers, which agitated for the formation of a "cricket Parliament" that would depose the Marylebone club and its "deplorably lethargic and out of date" Committee. There always have been moments when such defects have been noticeable. Gubby Allen is the first to concede that the club ought to have done something for young cricketers years before he stumbled on those untutored lads in Putney. And in some extremely practical matters, MCC has now and again been almost unbelievably behind the times. Its priceless art collection was virtually unprotected until, in the wake of the 1970 anti-South African tour demonstrations, the insurers refused to do any more business unless the most sophisticated alarm systems were installed at Lord's. Until 1937 all details of MCC's membership – amounting to 7,000 names and addresses in those days – were noted in a large ledger and nowhere else; and the recently appointed Secretary, Colonel Rait Kerr, had a hard time convincing the Committee that it would be much more efficient if a filing system were adopted instead. There was not even a methodical and day-to-day accounting system for the club until 1968 – just single card entries, with a yearly visit by an auditor who totted up all transactions and committed them by hand to a heavily bound tome. Indeed, there was not to be an accounts department until 1972, all money matters previously having been logged by the club office, which handled half a dozen other daily tasks as well.

Things have changed in almost every way since then, down to the appearance of natty Sasco Year Planners on practically every office wall in the Pavilion, and the hiring of computer time for processing the payroll. With an organism whose finances are as complex as those of Lord's, such advances are no more than prudent. MCC, after all, is an institution with assets of approximately £2 millions, though that scarcely takes account of the money that would be distributed among the members if they collectively abandoned their interest in cricket one day and put their premises on the market. So fantastic is the sum that might be raised by selling such an expanse of property in that part of London, that for actuarial purposes speculation has been minimised by reckoning the value of the ground itself "within the curtilage of Lord's" at precisely £1. The £2 millions include such things as stock (£91,000 in 1981), and short-term deposits in the bank (£170,000), plant and buildings (though it's doubtful whether there is an alternative use for a cricket pavilion except in war). Among the buildings are those properties adjacent to Lord's – the six dwellings in Elm Tree Road, one of which is always inhabited by the Secretary, and the seven in Grove End Road. They were regarded as an asset worth over £760,000 in 1981.

That year the books were balanced at about £1 million each way. Quite the largest source of income was the £351,000 collected in members' subscriptions (36 per cent of the total sum), with £247,000 coming from cricket activities of all kinds, £138,000 from investments, £136,000 from ground advertising, and £64,000 from the hire of boxes at the big games. The rest of the incomings were from a variety of sources like property rents, catering concessions, the Lord's Shop, and indoor school fees. The match receipts are intricately arranged. For mounting a Test at Lord's, MCC gets seven and a half per cent of the advance ticket sales as a commission from TCCB, and this just about covers the cost of selling them. It also collects a lump sum for putting on the match, as do all Test grounds (£21,000 in 1981), and then receives a percentage of any surplus profit the match makes – fifteen per cent if there is a single Lord's Test in the season, twelve and a half per cent of the double takings if there are two. For a Cup Final, MCC simply receives five per cent of the gross receipts. For regular county matches the deal is again straightforward, MCC taking thirty-five per cent of the Middlesex gate money; this 35 per cent amounted to something under £20,000 in 1981.

The expenditure of the club is deployed in a number of fascinating directions. In 1981 it cost £150,000 to maintain the buildings at Lord's alone and £4,000 to take care of the laundry bills and the paper towels. The ground expenses were calculated at £89,000, which included the wages of ten men, repairs to covers and other equipment, fertilisers, seed, and the annual increment of Surrey loam. Some £14,000 was spent on official hospitality, on which Lord's has never stinted, and even more (£18,500) on Committee and sub-committee expenses – a figure which has been rising more steeply in recent years than ever before, as the people involved now tend to claim travelling money, which their predecessors used to disdain. The real tennis and squash facilities required £2,200 to keep going, the museum and library £17,000; and "sundries" amounted to £25,000, which included such things as the MCC's contribution to TCCB public relations, a staff canteen subsidy and medical cover, as well as the cost of the President and Secretary going to Sri Lanka for that inaugural Test. Two goodwill tours by MCC teams – one to Hong Kong and Singapore, the other round East Africa – set the club back another £20,000 or so.

By far the biggest item was the £650,000 needed to pay the wages and pension fund bill of MCC's full-time employees – not counting, that is, the army of stewards and doorkeepers and gatemen and cleaners who are mustered on a part-time basis in fluctuating numbers which depend on the importance of the occasion at Lord's. A large proportion of these are retired chaps, content to pick up an extra quid or two to supplement the old-age pension without crossing the income threshold established by the Inland Revenue. Their recruitment leaves MCC open to accusations of getting its man-power on the cheap; and it is true that until quite recently the club taxed the loyalty of its workforce at all levels to a degree that the TUC might think shameful. Twenty years ago, when the Pavilion staff were paid only £429 per annum, it was the habit to give a voucher worth £3 to those with over twenty years' service as a Christmas present, one worth £2 for those with less than two decades behind them.

In 1979 the salary of the Ground Superintendent – a sort of regimental sergeant major in the hierarchy of Lord's – was but £5,500. That year, however, saw a review of the whole wage structure, some eye-opening comparisons being made with what was being paid in the civil service, the banks, the GLC and by patrons of the Brook Street Bureau. As a result, everyone's pay packet was instantly inflated by sixteen and a half per cent, another twelve and a half per cent being added the following year, with a further increase of eight per cent at the start of 1982. This, it should be noted, was without any trade union activity. There isn't a single trade unionist at Lord's. Even the MCC's three printers, who might belong to the most aggressive of unions if they wished, choose to set their type under the Grandstand in St John's Wood without benefit of cards issued by Sogat 82 or the NGA. And whatever the world outside might think of this state of affairs, the plain fact is that the turnover of staff at Lord's is very low; except that it was the need to be constantly replacing young female secretaries that led to the 1979 review. Employees there seem to be as susceptible to the mystique of the place as any MCC member, or even a besotted cricket-watcher who can never enter the Long Room, but is content to sit on a cushion at the Nursery End. One man who has toiled there since before the war, and whose views on life in general suggest that politically he may lie somewhere between Mr Foot and Mr Benn, tells of his contentment in being "a servant of this club". It was he who offered me the opinion: "So long as we have an MCC Committee that tries to keep up standards, this will always be a bit better than other places."

CHAPTER THREE

The Members

The Marylebone Cricket Club happens to be two things at one and the same time, which produces a nice grammatical problem for anyone who writes about it. MCC is a voice of authority and it is also a considerable mass of members. Yet that commanding voice, a Committee of thirty-one men, is also all too plural in number; and there lies the problem. Shall one follow instinct and refer to authority as a singular presence in the atmosphere, or face up to reality and recognise the existence of Them? People who can spot a split infinitive at 500 yards even when one hasn't actually been split, will already have savoured a certain indecision in what has been written so far: they should take notice that the problem will not have been clearly resolved by the end of this book. No such difficulties are presented by the membership, however, which is most distinctly a collective of several thousand chaps who are neither more nor less amiably keen on watching cricket than anyone else.

It is quite likely that those who are employed by MCC have changed far less over the years than the members, for this is no longer the rarefied club it once was; certainly at its beginnings, when its small coterie of playing members habitually took the field dressed overall in sky blue, a colour that MCC shared with Eton College and Cambridge University. Even fifty years after its foundation, MCC had admitted no more than 300 men to its ranks, though by the end of the nineteenth century there were something just under 4,000. By the time the Second World War finished there were 7,174, and today there are 18,000 people entitled to flaunt that eye-crossing necktie with its thick red and yellow stripes; an article of clothing which some members thoughtfully leave at home, wearing instead the so-called City tie of MCC, as designed by Messrs Castell of Oxford, with its neat club monogram on a dark blue ground.* Less exclusive

---

* Precisely, there were 18,170 members of MCC on December 31, 1982, divided into the following categories: Town members 11,003; Country members 2,341; Over-65 members 2,990; Under-25 members 514; Schoolmaster members 228; Abroad list members 765; Life members 86; 60-year Life members 20; Honorary

MCC may be than it has been even in our own lifetime, yet there remains a cachet in belonging to this club, for social as much as cricketing reasons; though Sir Pelham Warner's remark that "In the Long Room . . . you may meet men who have seen and done things" – he meant Governors-General, Prime Ministers, Cabinet Ministers, members of Bench and Bar, "famous Bishops and Church dignitaries . . . and great Civil Servants" – now seems passé as well as fulsome. The most charming example of a social advantage following membership occurred in 1942, when a Mr Gordon Johnston was admitted to the club. He was, alas, unable to use its facilities at once, being at the time a prisoner-of-war in Italy. But his family were able to convey the glad tidings that he had been "elected to Lord's", and the new MCC member thereafter received much greater consideration from his captors, who assumed they had an English peer on their hands.

Election to MCC is as complicated a process as that required by any of the purely social clubs down in Mayfair, and takes much longer to achieve as a rule. No one may apply to become a member, though several hundred people try to every year, and are usually advised to join Middlesex for a start. You have to be proposed by two existing members. And then you wait. In 1939 a newly proposed fellow might expect to wait anything up to thirty years before achieving his membership, the initial step in this aspect of his life having been taken probably the day he was born by Father and some crony in the club. Even in the 1950s a man might face a couple of decades before he was finally "elected to Lord's", which made a nonsense of the minimum age for membership, which was fourteen years old, shortly afterwards raised to seventeen. For various reasons which we shall come to shortly, the size of membership has been progressively increased since then. But in 1983 there were still 8,408 people waiting hopefully to join MCC, some of them with no assurance of doing so until at least 1991.

Anyone wearing that famous and gaudy tie, therefore, may be instantly identified as a trier if nothing else. He will have persevered with his original intention, he will have found two further sponsors when his waiting time is almost up, he will have secured at least eight Committee votes in his favour, he will have avoided two black balls being cast against his name (two or three persons are blackballed

---

Cricket members 41; Honorary Life members 182. There were also 35 Out-match members and 8,408 candidates waiting to become members of the club. In 1982, some 587 vacancies had occurred, due to death (233), resignation (209) or lapsing (145).

every year) and he will have instructed his bank to pay his entrance fee and first year's subscription – a double subscription at one go. There is just one way in which he may have avoided at least the long years of wondering whether or not he will be allowed in. If he's still under forty and an active cricketer, he may seek playing membership of MCC. In which case he will be invited to play in at least five MCC matches over the next couple of seasons and, if thought good enough, will be put at the head of that great waiting list. About half those who seek entry in this way do, in fact, gain it. Their sartorial reward is not only to wear the MCC tie, but to be even more conspicuously dressed on a cricket field beneath the club's encircled red and yellow cap, which is guaranteed to produce a marked respect in all opponents – in the northern hemisphere at least. First-class cricketers of standing are usually invited to become playing members of MCC and quite often turn out for the club's sides when not otherwise engaged for their counties.

The rate of admission normally, of course, is regulated by the numbers departing from the club and (quite literally) making room for those patiently waiting to arrive. Something between 400 and 600 are crossed off the books every year, mostly because they have died, though maybe a hundred will have resigned. The majority of these are usually aged men who live so far away that they can no longer get to Lord's (many's the Highland laird whose tartan clashes with that tie) and reckon that the pleasure of belonging to MCC is at last outweighed by the cost: the numbers resigning on some matter of principle can usually be counted on the fingers of one hand. Not that the cost of MCC membership is exorbitant in these inflated times. Members of all first-class cricket clubs in England have long had this bit of their lives on the cheap, and to no one does this apply more than to members of MCC. The subscription had stood at £3 from 1858 until it went up to £4 in 1948. By 1979 the top subscription – for Town members living within a hundred miles of Hyde Park Corner – was £25. By 1982 it had risen to £35, which was no more than that paid by members of Sussex County Cricket Club at Hove. The following January it reached £50 at last, in exchange for which a member could enjoy not only a full season of top-class cricket at the game's most illustrious venue, but very considerable indulgences on the side.

He could drink fairly steadily if he had a mind to, for a start, with at least one of the Pavilion's several bars being open throughout any day of the year he cared to drop in: and he could do so confident that he would be most discreetly helped on his way if he ever had a drop too much (the formula is for one of the Ground Superintendent's men to come alongside and ask, very gently, "Shall I order you a taxi, sir?"). The member might also, if at a loose end on winter nights, attend the monthly dinners MCC holds during the off-season in the Committee dining-room on the top floor of the Pavilion, where some of those men who have seen and done things hold forth on their accomplishments for anything up to half an hour. If he is agile enough, an MCC member may play squash at his club, or practise real tennis with a lop-sided racquet to a baffling and ancient set of rules, smiting the ball off walls, galleries and high-pitched roof in one of the very few real tennis courts in the land. If he confines his agility to cricket he may, apart from playing for the club, use the nets beyond the Nursery End between 10 a.m. and 7 p.m., six days a week, whenever a major match is not in progress at Lord's; as many members do on spring and summer evenings, including a seventy-six-year-old physician who still likes to keep his eye in in this way.

The biggest indulgence of the lot will be, certainly in the view of less privileged cricket-watchers, the freedom of the Pavilion, the knowledge that you can roam around the Long Room whenever you like. All you have to do is produce the little booklet with red covers bound in cloth, which is your MCC pass, to satisfy the scrutineers just inside the Pavilion door, and you're in. Some steps descend to a row of wash-basins, each with its own soap and nailbrush by the taps, a shelf bearing mirrors and hairbrushes above. To the left are the gents, through swinging doors whose other sides are respectively signposted "Out" and "Not out". Above these basement facilities are the steps which lead up to the most famous and memorable viewing gallery known to cricket.

And it is quite a Long Room at Lord's – ninety-three feet long by twenty-seven feet wide, to be exact – as it needs to be to accommodate everything MCC has accumulated in there. There are several immense tables in the middle, on which members are wont to sit and swing their legs over the edge. Between these and the windows there are two or three rows of chairs, the ones at the back having extra-high seats so that their occupants can see over the heads of those who have nabbed the window places. Almost always a number of members are simply standing, watching carefully through the glass. A pause in the play; and one of them probably turns away to inspect some precious thing that helps to decorate the pale green walls and make the Long Room something much more than a place to see cricket from in the coolly handsome atmosphere of classical mouldings and furniture polish.

Here is the nucleus of the art collection that Ponsonby-Fane so splendidly began, the rest being dispersed throughout the building and across the roadway behind the Pavilion in the Memorial Gallery, whose contents may be inspected by anyone who visits Lord's. Worried by the threat to all these valuables after the London blitz began in the last war, the Committee first wondered whether it might be possible to deposit them in the vaults of Canterbury Cathedral for the duration. It evidently wasn't, because in August 1941 the paintings and a large proportion of the curios and historic photographs were packed off to Stoke Hammond Rectory, near Bletchley, and stayed there for the next four years. Restored to their proper place and added to from time to time (invariably by bequest; MCC's resources no longer stretch to the crazy prices now demanded in the sale rooms) they are best appreciated with an hour or two to spare and no distraction of cricket being played outside. Here are portraits, not all of them masterpieces, of names that have rung across two centuries and more. Thomas Lord himself, naturally, as well as Billy Beldham, Alfred Mynn, John Wisden and George Parr; and, of those within our own time, Bradman, Jardine, Warner and Allen. Then there are about twenty oils which either depict cricket being played or picture individuals with some piece of equipment from the game. The widely reproduced painting of four young Nottingham chimney sweeps "Tossing for Innings" is here; and so is Francis Hayman's description of cricket at St Mary-le-bone Fields in 1740. Once there was a miniature of Lord's by Landseer, but it vanished a few years ago and the culprit was never found.

Poised between these pieces of art are glass cases containing a mixture of historical possessions. There are rows of bats, some of them illustrating evolution from the middle of the eighteenth century – a curved bat of 1750, a bowed bat of 1770–90, Little Joey of 1792–3, an early straight bat of 1774 – all stained with the deep darkness of extreme old age. Then there are bats which belonged to great players: pieces of timber that Alfred Mynn, Fuller Pilch and Tom Hearne used, the one W. G. Grace had when making his highest score (334 for MCC v Kent, 1876), the last bat Victor Trumper used in England, the one Jack Hobbs made his last century with, and the one Wilfred Rhodes was carrying in his famous partnership with George Hirst ("We'll get 'em in singles, Wilfred") at the Oval in 1902. There is also the cricket ball with which Rhodes took fifteen Australian wickets at Melbourne two years later, though bowlers do not seem to have parted with their trophies as readily as batsmen, and so the Long Room collection is not nearly as impressive as that of the bats. Rhodes's gift is supplemented by a couple of curiosities and not much else; one is a five-ounce blue ball, specially devised for women's cricket in 1897, the other a string ball improvised by prisoners-of-war in the 1940s. They lie close by an assortment of plates and jugs and cut glass things, all of which bear inscriptions with some significance in the game; and a faded photograph of Ranjitsinhji, portlier than he used to be on the cricket field, fully rigged in his alternative role as the Maharajah Jam Sahib of Nawanagar state. The whole array is surmounted by a board bearing the names of every MCC President, and a dutiful colour photograph of the Duke of Edinburgh and his Queen who is, among many other things, the Patron of MCC.

The Queen is one of the very few women to have set foot in this masculine game reserve. The girl secretaries who work upstairs are quite liable to take short cuts through the Long Room during the winter, when few members are in the building, but they know the house rules and keep well out of the way when cricket is on. The daughter of one MCC secretary (Miss Rait Kerr) was actually present as a guest at an anniversary dinner one year, and the daughter of another (née Griffith) was allowed to hold her wedding reception here. And that is just about it, apart from a handful of female cricketers once or twice. The Women's Cricket Association held its annual general meeting in the Long Room in 1970, which was the startling preamble to an event even more extraordinary. As far back as 1951 the Australian women's cricket team had been allowed to practise at the nets during their tour of England that year, but no lass had ever been permitted to step on to the main playing area with a bat in her hand until 1976. That date brought the fiftieth birthday of the WCA, and with it the only time so far that women have played cricket at Lord's, a one-day fixture against the Australians which England won by eight wickets. The teams emerged from the Pavilion just like any other cricketers, having made use of the normal dressing-rooms, and they played their match before a fair-sized crowd which was most appreciative of this turn of events. But perhaps the women in the stands around the ground, who follow cricket there all season and don't discriminate much about its sex, did clap a little more vigorously than they usually do.

Once upon a time, not so very long ago, it was axiomatic that anyone becoming a member of this club should pass at least one of the extant definitions of a gentleman, even though it was well understood that these are numerous and not always congruous. What they had in common, however, was a background of education obtained at the very least in a grammar school; and a conversational habit which never fell below a recognised mark on the scale the English have evolved over the years to equate speech patterns with social worth (Colonials are excused this particular test). There was one other unwritten rule and it was this. One might behave like a blackguard in private, but there were certain things no man but a bounder did outside his own home, and the antique system of blackballing had been specifically devised to keep bounders out of institutions like MCC.

R. A. Butler's Education Act of 1944 marked the beginning of the end of one philosophy behind all this, by admitting to higher forms of schooling, and their consequent rewards, large proportions of the population that had never dared dream of them before. Post-war economic history has completed the adjustment in MCC's case, by obliging the club to accept more and more members in order to pay its way. The 7,174 MCC men who eagerly resumed their contact with Lord's as soon as the 1939–45 hostilities were over, cautiously voted to increase themselves to 8,000 in 1950, but costs proved that inadequate by the time the figure was reached. By 1958 another 3,000 members had been added; by 1962 there were 11,671 members of MCC, by 1967 there were 14,000, by 1971 there were 16,000. In 1975 the membership jumped up to 18,000, which is thought to be as many as the premises will physically hold without collapsing under the strain. Not that any of these increases have done much to relieve the annual battle against running into deficit. What they unquestionably have done is to alter the composition of MCC to a point that might seriously disturb Lord Harris were he to waft through the Pavilion half a century after his death.

Never before in its history can MCC have included such an assortment of people as it embraces now. Old gentlemen turn up in straw boaters with the club colours in a ribbon encircling the crown, to find themselves sitting cheek by jowl with young men in imitation leather jackets, and shoes that haven't seen boot polish for a month or more. It is an observable fact before play starts, or at any interruption in the game, that MCC readers of the *Daily Telegraph* outnumber those of any other newspaper by at least ten to one, but nowadays the also-rans include a surprising number who goggle at the nude on a certain tabloid's Page Three. Before the umpires came out on the first day of the 1981 Test with Australia there were scattered on those Pavilion steps people reading their various newspapers, a man with his nose deep in Summerson's study of John Nash, and many members simply chatting to pass the time. From these last, the following fragments drifted across this exclusive sector of Lord's:

"How's X getting on?" – "Oh, Lord. His son dropped a draw-bar on his foot and now the Admiral can't walk."

". . . magistrate or something, isn't she?" – "Oh, no, she's not a JP in London. To be a JP in London these days, I understand you've got to be a female black plumber."

". . . and we've been away three times this year. Morocco. West Indies. Majorca." – " 'Ow was Majorca?" – "Fuckin' awful, mate. Arsehole of the world."

The extent of change had been all too publicly revealed twelve months earlier during the Centenary Test, at the memory of which MCC officials still groan with the anguish caused by "that awful day". Here was an occasion which the Lord's authorities had intended to make one of the most memorable in the history of the game, something to equal the precedent of Melbourne in 1977, when a magnificent cricket match celebrated a hundred years of Anglo-Australian Tests Down Under, and when all things connected with the anniversary were in harmony with the match itself. MCC and TCCB had spared nothing to make the English Centenary something that would also be fondly recalled for decades by people counting themselves lucky to have been there. Some 200 ex-Test players had been invited, and the Australian contingent alone was something to make an Englishman blink. Here, in the flesh, were players of generations before one's own, men whose legends one knew without ever having seen. There actually was Bill Ponsford, a shy and gentle man with his burnished face set at benign; and "Stork" Hendry, who went so far back that you had to look him up in the reference books; and Bill O'Reilly, "Tiger" himself, whose views on cricket are as adamantly traditional as any to be found in MCC. And there, not always instantly recognisable after the passage of thickening and balding years, were one's own first Aussies – Neil Harvey, Ray Lindwall, Arthur Morris, Ernie Toshack, Sam Loxton, Keith Miller and the rest. They made you want, in middle age, to rush for your autograph book again. Five marvellous days were in prospect, and the old-timers were the part of the promise entirely fulfilled.

The weather turned the match into something approaching disaster. Rain wiped ten hours off the first three days and from that it never recovered as a contest, though there were centuries by Wood, Hughes and Boycott, and one incident of play will linger in the memory of those who saw it. On the Monday evening, before the Centenary started dawdling to a draw, Kim Hughes took two steps down the pitch to the sharpish bowling of Chris Old and hit him clean into the top deck of the Pavilion. Had he lofted his shot fractionally more, he might have put the ball where only one has ever been hit, over the top into gardens behind, Albert Trott's doing in

1899 when he faced Monty Noble, playing for MCC against the Australians. As it is, Gubby Allen reckoned that Hughes produced the best straight six he personally had ever seen. There was nothing much apart from the batting of Hughes to make the spirit soar in that game. And the occasion had already been astonishingly damaged two days earlier, on the Saturday.

It had rained for an hour and a half before the gates opened that morning, heavily enough to leave pools all over the ground, with no prospect of play starting on time. There was an especially messy area on two old pitches on the Tavern side – down the slope from the Test strip – but the ground staff thought that the game might easily restart after lunch. As did the crowd, who had sat through a morning of bright sun and strong breeze; perfect drying conditions, in fact. With the Australians in the stronger position at that stage of the match, Greg Chappell was interested in getting his men to grips with the Englishmen again as quickly as possible, Ian Botham being less enthusiastic about this idea. Meanwhile, the two men in whose hands the matter lay appeared at regular intervals, went through elaborate motions of inspecting the turf, discussing its dampness, canvassing Jim Fairbrother's opinion, surveying the skies, nodding to each other, apostrophising the crowd, and walking back to the Pavilion in a fashion that may have appealed to television watchers on at least two continents, but which the spectators at Lord's found increasingly tiresome. Umpires Harold Bird and David Constant were recognised as two of the finest to be found anywhere in the game, but on Centenary Test Match Saturday their local popularity was trickling away as quickly as the water going down the drains.

By mid-afternoon they were approaching the Pavilion after their fifth inspection, with the two captains in tow, when it was apparent from all parts of the ground that MCC members had gathered more thickly than is usual around the steps the umpires were about to ascend. Indeed, it wasn't possible to see any steps at all for the press of bodies on them, blocking the way. And then, heaven help us all, there was seen to be some swaying of bodies over there, some struggle by the umpires and captains to get to the sanctuary of the Long Room. It was 3.45 that afternoon before the umpires reappeared, this time preceding thirteen cricketers who were ready for or re-signed to a game. MCC's President, Mr S. C. Griffith, had uttered a word or two in the right ears. And, incredibly, an escort of policemen had been provided to see the umpires safely out of the Long Room and into broad daylight again.

This was no more than a fair precaution in view of what had already happened. Which was this. As Constant and Bird reached the Pavilion fence after their last virtuosi performance, they were met with a volley of questions which swiftly turned in some cases to abuse, from members who had had nothing to do but drink steadily for several frustrating hours. These were, as an official put it later, rather like railway passengers during a train-drivers' go-slow, who are left milling around the station for a long time and begin to vent their anger on any railwayman in sight. They were, moreover, physically preventing the umpires from going any further by simply massing in front of them; and David Constant gave one of them a push in order to make some headway. Whereupon the man grabbed Constant by the tie and almost pulled him down. At which there was something of a mêlée, with the captains of England and Australia striding to the assistance of the umpires in a repetition of Lord Harris's famous act in 1879. While it lasted, which was only a minute or so, it was quite a to-do. And it had happened at Lord's, in the MCC members' enclosure, with the long lenses of television cameras swivelling on to the scene like the barrels of six-inch guns.

Greg Chappell had picked out two members in particular as the chief culprits in this sorry affair and these were interrogated by Jack Bailey, Secretary of MCC, who then issued the following statement:

"Enquiries instituted today into the behaviour of certain MCC members towards the umpires and captains on Saturday leave no doubt that their conduct was inexcusable in any circumstance. Investigations are continuing and will be rigorously pursued with a view to identifying and disciplining the culprits. Meanwhile the club is sending to the umpires and captains of both sides their profound apologies that such an unhappy incident should have occurred at the headquarters of the game and on an occasion of such importance."

The investigation went on for rather a long time in the view of many people, who thought that identification of the culprits ought to be a fairly simple matter and that discipline should take a fairly obvious course: expulsion from the Marylebone Cricket Club. By the middle of September, a fortnight after the Centenary Test, nineteen members had been interviewed by the Secretary and the club had set up a sub-committee to decide what else to do. Two and a half months after the incident, the new President of MCC, Peter May, sent a letter to every one of the 18,000 members to say that the investigation was over. It had "shown conclusively that certain members did behave in a way wholly unbecoming to membership and this club, and appropriate disciplinary action has been taken".

There wasn't a word about who the culprits were (and not even those most incensed at their behaviour could reasonably have expected that) or what the disciplinary action had been. This second omission caused many with deeply cherished beliefs about the ethics of cricket to suspect MCC of whitewashing a club matter that would have been dealt with openly and heavily if the culprits had been rowdies on the Tavern side.

The disciplinary action, in fact, consisted of a very stiff letter from the Secretary to the member who had grabbed Umpire Constant by the tie; telling him that if ever his behaviour again was less than immaculate he would be expelled from MCC. The Committee had writhed over what to do after its special sub-committee had sat, some Committee members being keen to throw the fellow out without more ado. They decided to give him another chance because he clearly was only one of maybe fifty members who had behaved disgracefully that day, some of them half drunk, some quite soberly offensive. The scapegoat happened to be a non-drinker and claimed to have grabbed the umpire's tie to stop himself falling over when he was pushed. The Committee reckoned that it was impossible to decide who else in that noisy crowd on the steps was actually menacing the umpires and who was merely standing around in the manner of excited schoolboys when they see a couple of lads squaring up to each other. They were in no doubt at all that no MCC member should have been in either of these positions. But they felt that they couldn't make public what they had discovered and decided, because they would have had to mention Constant's gesture, which they were loath to do. By tying themselves into knots in order to be reasonable to everyone involved, they succeeded chiefly in giving the impression of a deliberate cover-up. It was the most painful exhibition of what MCC committees tend to do when considering many things on their agendas; dwelling on every question from every conceivable angle until everyone is so confused by alternatives that no clear decision seems possible or even desirable.

Within two more seasons, the hierarchy was faced with further unwelcome activity among the members, this time directed at the Committee itself in a couple of special conclaves in 1982. Mass gatherings of MCC are not uncommon, with an annual general meeting every May, and with special general meetings called from time to time whenever something of immediate importance to the club needs to be widely discussed. The AGM is usually a bland affair, and if 500 of the 18,000 eligible to attend do, in fact, turn up, MCC's officials feel that the muster has been rather good. Reports are presented about various aspects of Lord's and more often than not go through on the nod. Pats on the back are distributed among senior members, officials, players and servants of the club, each given its little round of applause and its "Hear, hear". Friction is restricted to question time from members, invariably handled with ease. In 1979 "A Member drew attention to derogatory remarks made by J. M. Brearley in a publication. The President said that a letter had been received from Middlesex CCC Committee regretting these remarks." In 1982 another member tabled no fewer than nine questions about catering and other facilities for himself and his kind, ranging from the sandwich fillings in the Long Room bar to his preference for screw tops on the mixers rather than ones that needed a bottle opener. (And it has to be said that although the catering for members in the Pavilion at Lord's would turn anyone obliged to queue at most of the ground's public eating and watering places bilious with envy, it is not in the same league as that normally provided by London clubs like the Garrick, the Travellers and elsewhere. In the Long Room bar MCC members have to eat their hot lunches off narrow ledges, mostly standing up. If it weren't for the red carpet and the display of touring team photographs going back to the year dot, which encrust three of the walls, the place would resemble something arranged by British Rail at one of its busier junctions.)

Annual General Meetings, however, are something the Committee takes in its stride. The Special General Meetings called in July and August were nothing of the sort. There was an insurrection at the bottom of them, most pointedly expressed by a Mr Prentice, a retired accountant who had been a member of MCC since 1958, what time he had not been vouchsafed so much as a glimpse of office in the club. He had remained a thorn in the Committee's side even after the President had taken lunch with him at Boodle's in an effort to win him round to the Committee's point of view. The excuse for the August meeting was the prospective increase in subscriptions to £50, and an impending development plan: it was called by the Committee itself in order to explain these matters to the membership. The July meeting, however, was instigated by the rebels. They were going bluntly for their target-in-chief by calling for a change in MCC's Rules, so that all members of the Committee would be elected by the general membership of MCC. Fifty members are required to lobby for a Special General Meeting before one can take place, and in this case sixty-one had slapped their petition on the Secretary's desk. Some of them had some trenchant points to make when combat was at last joined.

The existing rules for the construction of the MCC Committee –

and there are twelve of them on this topic alone among the fifty-one rules of the club – are not at all easy to grasp at one glance. For a start there are ex-officio members: the President, the Treasurer and the Trustees. To them is added the President-Designate, "such chairmen of sub-committees as the Committee may nominate annually, and fifteen elected members and such additional members as shall be nominated . . . who shall each serve for a period of three years." The Treasurer and the Chairman of Finance are nominated by the Committee and serve initially for five years, the Trustees like-wise, but only for three. There can be no more than two additional members, and five of the elected members must retire at the end of every September. Any MCC member may nominate another one for election to the Committee, but if a ballot is necessary the Committee circulates the list of candidates with a star against those names it wants to see voted in. It almost follows as a matter of course, because the majority of MCC members are loyal and dutiful, that the starred names are elected, as the Committee prefers. As a result, most Committee men always have been long servers: when their three-year term is over, they drop out for twelve months and are then hauled back on board for another run.*

The critics claimed that, out of thirty-one people on the existing Committee, twenty had been appointed by the Committee itself. Mr Prentice, in proposing the resolution for a change, asserted that about half the Committee were permanent fixtures, that all those over the age of seventy-five should now retire, and that the custom of the President nominating his successor was more in keeping with a dictatorship than a democratic institution like MCC. Someone else mentioned that the Electoral Reform Society had offered the opinion that it knew of no other body which ran a ticket of preferred candidates at its elections, and that such a system made it almost impossible to stop a hierarchy perpetuating itself indefinitely. A picture was drawn, by various rebels, of a Committee intransigently hostile to a change in the rules whereby everyone of its members would have to submit to regular election by the MCC membership at large.

Which, of course, Committee spokesmen at the meeting denied. They had just heard themselves accused of mismanaging some of the club's affairs in almost ungentlemanly terms, and they demons-trated a capacity to give in return quite as good as they were getting.

* The membership itself, in fact, requested the starred system twenty years ago; and on at least two occasions since, this method of balloting has been ratified anew by general vote in proportions of approximately 60–40 per cent.

Mr Prentice, for one, was referred to as the self-appointed scourge of the Committee, the members' SAS man. It was conceded that the Committee might have been too reluctant to let some of its more experienced members go, that perhaps there were one or two sub-committees too many. But the system of Committee appointments in some cases, rather than wholesale elections, was defended on the grounds of continuity, a word that was repeated every time someone spoke on the Committee's behalf. Not that this cut much ice with the critics, who were not much impressed either with the tremendous weight of cricketing experience on the Committee as it stood (one of them – pointing out that MCC had become a medium-sized business controlling valuable assets and with a turnover of a million pounds – said that "it is as irrelevant for the Committee to tell us that twenty-eight of their members have played first-class cricket as it would be, were the administration of cricket under criticism, to remark that twenty-eight members of the committee were directors of ICI"). What the critics wanted was greater access to the Committee, in every sense. What they were attacking was the notion of a separate club within the club.

There was no dramatic outcome of that meeting in July, though a fuse had been lit that might one day produce one. Of the 250 members bothering to turn up, a substantial majority voted for change, but when the postal votes had been counted the tide of opinion had swung strongly the other way, and the Committee representatives left after promising to think on these things. In fact, they did more than that. A Working Party was appointed to examine the whole structure of MCC. Led by the Treasurer, it included five other members of the existing Committee (Phillips, Cosh, Popplewell, the tennis player R. A. Sligh, and the old Middlesex cricketer E. A. Clark). Two of the rebels were given places on it, a Mr Sissons and a Mr Fry. So were two other people, who came betwixt and between: a Mr Leigh-Pemberton, who six months later would be appointed Governor of the Bank of England; and a Mr Bennett.

That August the Committee was even more heavily backed than in July in its proposals for increasing the subscription and for the development plan. Even the sternest of critics had accepted the inevitability of coughing up £50 in future to keep MCC's head above water. At the AGM in May they had, after all, defeated the Committee's attempt to raise more income by introducing 2,000 new associate members to the club, people who would have had few privileges apart from watching their cricket from the Pavilion. The existing members didn't want any more outsiders on the inside and they were prepared, for the time being, to pay the price in hard cash.

If this record of misbehaviours and insubordinations between 1980 and 1982 sounds sensationally unlike what the average outsider expects to happen in a supposedly decorous institution like MCC, it can only be because the outsider is forgetting two cardinal facts of life. One is that no group of people, from a domestic household to a community of nuns, is ever as tranquil behind its own doors as it may appear to be to those who do not belong. The other is that organisms which have been all-powerful, or nearly so, and find themselves having to adjust to a lesser role – whether nations or merely bodies with influence in some sphere – go through a period of disturbance, a kind of incoherence, until they become accustomed to their new bearings and settle down to a diminished way. Something of the sort is happening to MCC right now. The club still has influence on every aspect of cricket, but the only thing apart from Lord's itself that it actually controls today without let or hindrance from other quarters, are the forty-two Laws of the game, which cannot be changed by so much as a comma unless two thirds of MCC's members vote for alteration at a special meeting of the club. MCC's position in general is not so very different from that of Great Britain as a whole, which was once an imperial power, now rules nothing but itself and a clutch of tiny dependencies, yet hasn't quite adjusted completely to its reduction in the world: the biggest difference between the two is that whereas the British have now had a generation of trying to come to terms with their new selves, MCC's change of life began little more than a decade ago.

It is, therefore, a body which contains more glaring contrasts in attitude than ever before in its history, though these will become less conspicuous as time passes by. There are members today who get very cross if they aren't recognised with suitable deference by the gatekeepers at Lord's, and others who don't give a damn about genuflections of any kind. There are members who regard the Memorial Gallery and its museum as one of the inspirations of Lord's, and there are others who think it a white elephant, costing them insurance money and other upkeep for the benefit of the world and his wife. There are those who resent the dwindling exclusiveness of the club and the increasing likelihood that when they inform acquaintances that they are members of MCC, they will hear the reply "Well, who isn't?"; and there are those who would regard such a sensitive fellow as the quintessentially pompous ass. There are some who urge that MCC's mailing list should be offered to commercial houses, who might pay handsomely for access to such up-market customers, and there are those who disdain raising income for the club in such a blatantly mercantile way. (And MCC has always been very selective about outsiders bothering members in this fashion. In 1963 *The Cricketer* magazine, which Pelham Warner had founded forty-two years earlier, was given permission to circularise the club; a few months later Rowland Bowen's *Cricket Quarterly* had its application refused.)

Some members would have sailed into the club after waiting their turn at any period in its history, but others would undoubtedly have been blackballed on one pretext or another until a few years ago. They all, however, have one thing in common apart from a liking for cricket and belonging to MCC. They wonder just what the future holds for them and for Lord's. None of their predecessors across almost 200 years was ever in such an anxious state.

CHAPTER FOUR

Transfer of Power

When winter comes, Lord's can seem deserted, sometimes beautiful-ly so if snow has fallen and Jim Fairbrother's prized turf is concealed by a thick smoothness of white, crusted by the cold into the texture of meringue. Yet there are always keepers in their cubby-hole by the Grace Gates, ready to stump out and swing open those cast-iron portals so that a vehicle can enter through the slush. Traffic is steady throughout the off-season, bringing among others the tennis and squash players, of whom something between two and three hundred regularly use the courts at Lord's. And there are always officials coming in and out, as well as people with committees to attend. Lord's, after all, is not simply the seat of MCC and the home ground of Middlesex County Cricket Club. It is also the headquarters of three bodies which between them run all forms of cricket in the British Isles. The National Cricket Association supervises the re-creational game in this country. The Test and County Cricket Board, as its name implies, controls the professional game – and sends England teams on tour abroad. Both NCA and TCCB, together with MCC, supply the principal delegates to the Cricket Council, which for nearly twenty years has been the supreme arbiter of cricket here. One way and another, no fewer than 322 meetings were held at Lord's in 1981 by the bodies headquartered there: of these 83 were MCC meetings, 75 were held by TCCB, 68 by Middlesex CCC, 38 by NCA. The administration of cricket con-tinues almost every day of the year, and nothing exasperates those who labour in the multitude of offices beside, above and below the Long Room, than the public assumption that between September and April the place goes pretty well dead. If ever Lord's seems deserted, the illusion is strictly confined to those parts of it in the open air.

What's more, cricket itself continues on even the most appalling day that London in mid-January can produce. In the great buff shed of the Indoor School beyond H Stand at the Nursery End, batsmen and bowlers are liable to be working out at any time from shortly after breakfast until ten o'clock at night. The building looks rather like a small aircraft hangar from the outside, or some place where the Ministry of Defence might be conducting secret experiments that nobody in his right mind would want to know about. Inside, in a chamber 120 feet by 88 feet, the cavernous echo of ball on bat is not much reduced by the nets which hang in rows from ceiling to floor to separate one "pitch" from the next. At one end is a viewing gallery, with cricketing pictures on the wall between it and a bar; and spectators are almost always there, while their offspring, or their spouses, or their colleagues are jumping to it on the Uniturf below.

The idea of an indoor school at Lord's was first raised by Middlesex in 1955. But it would have needed a grant, as well as permission from MCC, which was then going through one of its financial crises, and the matter was dropped. The county eventually acquired a school in Finchley, and Lord's did not see its like until the end of 1977, when MCC opened this one of its very own. It cost £200,000 to put up, which would certainly have been more if both the architect and the builder hadn't been members of MCC; and the hole this knocked in club finances would have been bigger than it was if £75,000 hadn't been donated by "Union Jack" Hayward, the millionaire engineer who delights in spending his fortune patriotically, in ways other than those schemed by the British income tax system, from his base in the Bahamas. As a result of this generosity, the school's interior is known as the Hayward Hall, and it has been a total asset from the day Gubby Allen performed the opening ceremony, regretting only that he was unable to bowl the first ball ("I'm afraid," he said at seventy-five, "it's *just* beyond me now").

There are seven strips laid in plastic Uniturf on the board floor and they have been carefully designed for the two chief types of bowling. Four of the nets are regarded as fast; the other three, made from softer PVC containing more air cells, take more spin and produce less bounce. Orthodox cricket balls are mostly used, though sometimes they come in two colours for instructional purposes, so that novices can see the spin more clearly, or whether the seam is really being kept up as the young fast bowler intends. Hordes of novices now go through the school every year, ranging in age from seven to rising sixty, some with a natural talent that can be developed into something impressive, others with no hope from the outset of anything more than great pleasure at having been coached at Lord's. Apart from the novices, scores of good club cricketers, as well as first-class players in need of a net on a rainy midsummer's day at Lord's, have found the indoor school a boon. The Parliamentary cricketers who represent the teams fielded by the Lords and Commons practise there; so do those optimistic chaps from the *Guardian* newspaper, with their ambitions set on yet another tour of California or somewhere on the Indian sub-continent. The demand is such that people are clamouring to reserve evening nets in March for the following winter, at £9.60 an hour for a group of six, an arrangement which means that each one of them gets about ten minutes of batting. Continuous, though; no waiting for every bowler to take a constitutional between delivering each ball.

On top of the practice sessions, there are also the six-a-side competitive games, with the nets down and the entire chamber open to play, with batsmen hitting balls that rebound from the walls (often straight to a fielder, which accounts for the fact that sixty per cent of the dismissals are run-outs). The Laws of Cricket, obviously, are somewhat rearranged for this sort of thing. An innings lasts for twelve overs, bowling and batting are confined to one end apiece. It's said to be great fun by those who've become addicted to it, as many have, about 200 games a year taking place now, with competition sometimes disconcertingly fierce. It obliges a batsman to control his shots very finely, a bowler to be very accurate because the umpires are extremely strict about wides. It peps up a fielder's reflexes and it requires batsmen to run and call more nimbly than they sometimes do in the open air. But no one, certainly not at Lord's, pretends that indoor cricket has any major contribution to make to real cricket, apart from keeping cricketers in trim during the off-season. As it patently does.

While exuberant shouts reverberate round the school during the drab days of the year, while typewriters clack and filing cabinets slam in the Pavilion offices, while Fairbrother and his men dismantle their White and their Allet mowers for overhaul, another platoon in MCC's small army of workers is busily making what advances it can before the place gets really cluttered again in the spring, when the members return in droves and the public spectators start to trickle through the turnstiles. The Works Department at Lord's runs to twenty hands, who include one electrician, one plumber, one bricklayer, two carpenters, seven painters and six labourers. As may be guessed from these numbers, painting Lord's regularly is somewhere on the celebrated scale of the old Forth Bridge. Only a week or so before a season's start, the year's quota of repainted seats is still in the process of drying out, and if there's been an unusually rugged winter, the first outside visitors of the spring are likely to encounter the decorators slung beneath the Mound Stand, feverishly sloshing away with their brushes in order to make good lost time. Other forms of upkeep are attended to simultaneously, and the end of March is likely to see scaffolding still attached to some part of the Pavilion that has needed repair. Yet invariably, when the opening fixture between MCC and last season's champions begins, every paint pot and every length of tubular steel will have gone back into the stores, and Lord's will yet again be spruce and beguiling, the way many good people have been dreaming of it across six barely tolerable months.

The maintenance of Lord's has become quite a desperate thing. The Pavilion, after all, is approaching its century and some of the other buildings on the ground are 150 years old. They are not all in very good shape. There was a rainstorm of tropical proportions not so long ago which left some of the Pavilion offices taking in water through unsuspected holes like a submarine under depth charge. Much worse, and even earlier, two dressing-room walls and a viewing gallery in the squash court had collapsed through dry rot; and rain had been coming through the Listed tennis-court roof for several years. The MCC Committee had not been indifferent to all this, but its resources had been bespoke for other purposes and therefore no more than running repairs had been carried out for rather a long time. MCC was badly shaken when surveyors reported early in 1982 that something in the order of £1 million would *have* to be spent on the existing fabric of Lord's over the following five years. This was one of the recurring issues raised at those aggravated meetings of the club in the year of the surveyors' report. Some members wondered whether the best way out of this scrape, in view of the fact that they were guardians of an international institution, might not be to launch a building fund appeal to Save Lord's, as any other cathedral would.

The report could hardly have come at a worse moment, when MCC was already getting ready to commit itself to a new development plan likely to cost it anything up to £515,000 if it were completed by the end of 1983. Indeed, this combination of circumstances drew MCC on to ground it likes to occupy least of all, its experiences of maintenance and development in the past not having been wholly felicitous. Some years ago a property company offered to develop some of the club's deteriorating Elm Tree Road houses into something more profitable to both parties, with contracts and money having changed hands before it was discovered that planning permission would not be forthcoming from the local authority; and although MCC received compensation from the company, it was lumbered with squatters on the site for much longer than it would have wished. The first row ever known between the Committee and the membership took place in 1966 over the redevelopment of the Tavern side of Lord's, when a block of rebels demanded (by way of an advertisement in the personal column of *The Times*) that the Committee should appear before a special meeting and explain more comprehensively than it already had just what it was up to in that beloved corner of the ground. According to the last historian of Lord's, there was almost a late reprieve for the old and sociable buildings there "when the Committee, learning that there was, without satisfactory explanation, a substantial increase in the cost of the Tavern, paused to think again about the stand". But the new stand did go up, and the Clock Tower and venerable pub came down.

The 1982 development plan also produced commotion for reasons besides those of finance. The proposal was for a new building to be erected behind the Pavilion, adjacent to the Memorial Gallery and the tennis court. This would produce some improvement in the facilities for the squash and tennis players, but its basic purpose was to rehouse the officials of Middlesex, the TCCB and NCA. The Middlesex men have for years occupied a detached bungalow of sorts, but the others have been quartered in the Pavilion itself, taking up several offices in the southern end of the building high above the ground. Some of MCC's more possessive and claustrophobic members have complained bitterly about the limitation of their freedom to wander around the whole of their Pavilion, imposed by the presence of "bureaucrats" not directly connected with their club. Also, the pressure on office space in the Pavilion has become no joke for anyone working there, and MCC's secretariat alone could well use extra accommodation. So, for that matter, could the secretariat of TCCB and the staff who run the affairs of NCA. What the commotion attending the 1982 development plan boiled down to in essence, though, other than the tortured matter of money, was the politics of cricket and MCC's position nowadays.

The attitude of some MCC members is easier to understand if the transfer of cricket power away from the club is properly grasped; and especially if it is appreciated that in a very real sense the Test and County Cricket Board has become a kind of cuckoo in the nest at Lord's. The big turning point in this aspect of the game's fortunes in England came in the middle of the 1960s, when the Government began to offer grants for leisure activities through its newly formed National Sports Council. Cricket, however, did not qualify for such disbursements of public money because it was effectively controlled at all levels by a private club situated at Lord's. There existed a number of bodies which supervised the workings of British cricket, but their independence was more nominal than real. A Board of Control (dating back to 1898) was one, and it attended to Test matches alone. The Advisory County Cricket Committee (originating in 1904) was another, watching over the rest of the first-class game. A medley of organisations, ranging from the English Schools Cricket Association to the Women's Cricket Association, kept an eye on every form of the game below the first-class level. The Board of Control and the ACCC, in fact, were no more than extensions of MCC, which had founded them, funded them and performed all their administration, as well as influencing their policies when it chose to. The hotch-potch of bodies which ran the rest of British cricket also looked to Lord's for cash when they needed it, and received steering orders from the same source, often without asking for them.

The trouble was that MCC's affluence had declined markedly in the post-war years, and the club saw a partial solution to the financial problem by gaining access to the Government grants. So in 1965 the National Cricket Association was constructed as an umbrella under which all non first-class cricketers might shelter with some Government aid, its decisions taken by an autonomous constituent council, but its headquarters still at Lord's and its administration carried out by MCC's secretariat. Two years later MCC again found itself financially hard-pressed with the biggest annual deficit recorded in its history; £14,200. The club at last faced the fact that it could no longer support Test and county cricket either, with as much money as had been its habit for several generations. But the price of being relieved of this burden was relinquishing even more control of cricket in the British Isles. In 1968, therefore, the second and more crucial step was taken. The Test and County Cricket Board was established to supervise all manifestations of first-class cricket in England, as well as to select the English touring teams abroad.* Simultaneously, the MCC Cricket Council – soon shorn of the preliminary initials – was set up as the new ultimate authority for cricket as a whole in this country, on every matter except the Laws of the game. As if to emphasise that cricket had just adopted a new look, umpires the following season began to appear in short white coats, as the Australians had done for a long time, instead of the traditional garment which came well below the knees.

The reorganisation was peppered with anomaly from the outset. The NCA, consisting of fifty-two county cricket associations from all

*It is surprising how many people still believe that MCC selects and authorises every England team, so many years after this ceased to be the case. In January 1983 a correspondent in *The Times* referred to the current "MCC tour" of Australia, and he was by no means alone in his misunderstanding.

over Britain (each of which might represent dozens of bodies within its own area), was not alone in being administered by MCC staff. The TCCB likewise had all its paperwork done by the MCC secretariat, though MCC itself was but one among nineteen members of the new board; the others were the seventeen first-class counties and the Minor Counties Cricket Association. As for the Cricket Council, the game's new Parliament for which some people had been calling for generations, it only existed by kind permission of everybody in sight. Its Chairman and Vice-Chairman were automatically MCC's President and Treasurer, though later its Chairman was elected by the council's members, who sat in three quotas of five supplied by MCC, NCA and TCCB, with one representative of the minor counties making a grand total of eighteen voting members (the President was supernumerary). The balance of 5-5-5 between the main parties was MCC's own idea when it handed over its powers to the council, so as to prevent any one group's interests dominating the others. Once again, however, MCC provided the administration.

For a few years after the reorganisation, the new bodies were supervised by two of the Assistant Secretaries of MCC, D. B. Carr handling the affairs of TCCB and Cricket Council, J. G. Dunbar attending to the business of NCA, under the leadership of S. C. Griffith who was Secretary of TCCB as well as Secretary of MCC. These services were provided in grace and favour by the Marylebone club. In 1974 a certain amount of disentangling took place, when Carr and Dunbar ceased to have any MCC responsibilities and TCCB and NCA began to operate with separate staffs of their own. Simultaneously, J. A. Bailey, another Assistant Secretary at Lord's, charged with special responsibility for public relations and promotion, succeeded S. C. Griffith as Secretary of MCC, thus becoming the first man to occupy a position of traditionally widespread power, most of which had just been redistributed elsewhere. Yet even after this more pronounced division of cricket authority, MCC continued to house the other bodies at Lord's free of charge, though certain overhead costs have been worked out between them. As for finance in general, NCA qualified for some Government aid (£90,000 in 1982) but, like the Cricket Council, was otherwise kept afloat by MCC and TCCB. The latter paid the lion's share because it now controlled the major revenues of British cricket, which come from Test and county matches, from television fees and from sponsorships.

Since then NCA has paddled away industriously in its own realm, not over-impressed by the glimpses of cricket politics it has caught through its membership of the Cricket Council. It has quite enough on its hands covering a much larger area, in all senses, than either of its partners in the governing body. Most notably it runs the National Coaching Scheme, with six full-time regional officials doing that and nothing else between Edinburgh and Taunton under the general direction of Keith Andrew, the ex-Northamptonshire and England wicket-keeper. It organises high-class competitive cricket for young players of all ages up to and including international matches: the Tests between Young England and Young West Indies are part of NCA's handiwork, and a lad called David Gower was in the team that went on the first overseas tour arranged by NCA, to Holland in 1975.

It has run six-a-side indoor competitions sponsored by the manufacturers of chewing gum, and eleven-a-side outdoor tournaments subsidised by the distillers of whisky. And it has acted as father confessor to all those county associations which constitute NCA, with ramifications that are very considerable indeed. The association not so long ago found itself lending its weight to the South Staffordshire League when a dispute with one of the league's professional players finished up in court. By 1982 NCA was drafting model rules of discipline for distribution among the various cricket leagues of the land. It was already much involved in the insurance of local club cricketers against anything from public liability (someone's greenhouse being smashed by a splendid six) to dental or optical treatment for players who might themselves be damaged by a cricket ball. With such an extensive operation to run, the current secretary of NCA, Brian Aspital, was not really surprised to discover that in 1981 he had travelled some 27,000 miles around the British Isles.

The politics have been almost wholly restricted to MCC and TCCB, and an early sign of the vigour with which they were to be conducted in future came in 1972, when Raman Subba Row walked out of and then resigned from a Cricket Council Reorganisation sub-committee at Lord's. He had been a good enough batsman a decade and more earlier to play for England thirteen times, had gone into managerial public relations after leaving the game, and was destined within a few more years to become chairman of Surrey, where he started to revive an ailing county club with the application of business techniques that were quite foreign to the administration of first-class cricket in England until the 1970s. He had gone to that meeting at Lord's with a similar purpose, specifically to propose that management consultants should be called in to examine the workings of the Cricket Council and propose whatever they thought fit to bring its administration into line with modern practice in the world outside.

The MCC Committee Room, where the meeting took place, was not used to people just walking out in Subba Row's fashion, but he had just spent two and a half hours fruitlessly trying to get support for his idea from colleagues who preferred instead to concentrate on MCC's role in the future of cricket, and the desirability of the Cricket Council's chief executive being Secretary of MCC as well. It had seemed to him, he said subsequently, that it was "the policy of some MCC Committee members to ensure that MCC retains as many fingers in as many pies as possible. Their motives, I am sure, are honourable but in my view quite misguided ... MCC's apparent reluctance to allow the new organisations which they themselves created to develop in their own way at Lord's is, in my opinion, bad for the game and bad for MCC". Subba Row reckoned that such a policy would only encourage certain voices in TCCB which were already hinting at running their own show somewhere other than Lord's.

The voice he had most distinctly in mind was that of Cedric Rhoades, a textile manufacturer and former club cricketer from Manchester, who had led a palace revolution in Lancashire County Cricket Club eight years earlier. An unsettled team had been playing badly for many seasons, and when Yorkshire won the 1964 Roses Match at Headingley by ten wickets after bowling out Lancashire for fifty-seven, Rhoades decided that his county committee had outlived its time. He called for a special meeting of members, got a vote of no confidence passed by 656 to 48 and when the committee resigned en bloc he was one of those elected to take its place. By 1969 he was chairman of Lancashire (has been ever since) and within twelve months the team had begun its remarkable sequence of successes in one-day cricket, especially in the Gillette Cup. As chairman, Rhoades represented his county on the new TCCB, where he soon became a dominant figure with very strong views on the way cricket generally ought to be played; and these were not at all in accordance with the traditional precepts of MCC. Among other things, he believes that women should be allowed into county cricket club pavilions on the same terms as any man, a notion that he hasn't so far managed to get accepted even on his home ground.

Within a few weeks of Subba Row's walk-out at Lord's, Rhoades had written to Warwickshire's chairman, Edmund King, suggesting that there was no logical reason why TCCB should operate from Lord's, and that there would be no loss of prestige if the administration moved elsewhere. He reckoned that the average cricket follower, as things were, was unable to distinguish between the two; and he believed that although people inside cricket tended to think that

MCC was sacrosanct, its image outside was not a good one. He felt that for the good of the game's future, TCCB should be as remote as possible from any suggestion of MCC influence. And he added that the waste of manpower at Lord's was apparent to anyone who stopped to think what a small staff did on an average county ground. Rhoades estimated that a Test and County Cricket Board which was detached from Lord's would need nothing more than a Secretary, Assistant Secretary, a shorthand typist and a junior, whose salaries would total £8,600 and whose administrative costs would amount to £4,000 a year. This was an attractive supposition. As Rhoades well knew, and was aware that King knew, too, MCC's Secretary alone was drawing a salary of £6,300. Rhoades then added his personal preference for the ideal headquarters of TCCB. It ought to be in Nottingham, which was easy to get to with the motorway close by.

The management consultants were, in fact, called in to adjudicate on the Cricket Council, and some of their recommendations were adopted, though the rearrangement of 1974 was still brought about by the time-honoured and time-consuming method of discussion in committees. This was not a method Subba Row wished to dispense with entirely, merely one that had long since got out of hand in his view – as became even more apparent in 1978, when a dramatic document emerged from TCCB. Its immediate genesis was the turmoil cricket had been thrown into by the phenomenon of Kerry Packer, whose extravagant recruiting of international players for his imitation American World Series tournament, and whose buc-caneering attitude towards traditional authority had led to the High Court action which the international authorities expensively lost. The TCCB, one of the defeated bodies, was heavily under the influence of that blow and its imminent repercussions when it set up a working party to examine the long-term administrative structure of cricket in Britain. "The recent High Court action," according to the terms of reference, "would seem to have lent weight to the view that responsibilities are not very well defined and that the process of decision-making is too often protracted." The working party was to consist of three men: Raman Subba Row, Cedric Rhoades and Ossie Wheatley, sometime captain of Glamorgan and its recently ap-pointed chairman, a man whose business interests were in the wine trade.

The three spent six months meeting representatives of MCC, the minor counties and NCA before producing their report in July 1978. This first made the point that the Cricket Council was essentially a negative organisation because it contributed little to the actual running of the game at any level, because it raised no revenue of its own and could only influence the distribution of other people's money, and because it rarely initiated anything, acting as a watch-dog over the decisions of other bodies. The existing structure of TCCB was criticised on the grounds that it was too cumbersome; in theory no decision could be taken unless all members had been consulted after being given the chance to consult their individual county or club committees, and the working party estimated that this could involve over 500 people at a time. Another weakness built into TCCB was that the Players' Association, the cricketer's trade union, regarded the board as an employers' organisation because they had to negotiate wages and playing conditions with it alone; and yet Mr Justice Slade had ruled in the High Court that TCCB could not be regarded as any such thing, simply because it was not the controlling body of English cricket. "However correct from a legal point of view," the working party declared, "this judgment seems to make a nonsense of the fact that TCCB controls the first-class game in reality, by raising and distributing income, controlling the nature of employment of players, and deciding the type of cricket which is played." TCCB, moreover, shouldered much of the responsibility to act as trustee for the welfare of British cricket in general because it raised nearly all the revenue on which everything depended.

NCA got pretty good marks from the working party, but the Minor Counties Cricket Association was regarded with something between bewilderment and scorn. There appeared to be no common objective in the Association, each club deciding its own policy. There was sharp contrast between the semi-professional clubs of the north and the largely amateur clubs of the south and west. There was no apparent contact or co-operation between the minor counties and NCA, and very little between the first-class and minor county clubs. The working party had gathered that MCCA was perfectly happy with the present state of affairs, in which the association was part of TCCB, but Subba Row, Rhoades and Wheatley themselves were not. They pointed out that the minor counties had received £104,000 from the board the previous year and TCCB "does not question how – or even if – the money is spent. There is, therefore, no evalua-tion of the investment."

As for the Marylebone Cricket Club, the working party trod softly at first. The club was easily the biggest money-earner among the Test match ground authorities and it had retained considerable influence by having five representatives on the eighteen-man Cricket Council, and two votes in TCCB, where the first-class counties had only one apiece. MCC was naturally anxious to retain its historical link with the rest of cricket, and saw its role as one offering (i) an independent mind to cricket problems; (ii) a source of people of high calibre to provide administrative and technical skills; (iii) a head-quarters known world-wide; and (iv) a possible source of financial assistance or underpinning – particularly to NCA – in the event of sponsorship or other cricket income drying up.

Nevertheless, the working party concluded as it warmed to its task, "From a strictly practical point of view the contribution of MCC cannot be significant to either the professional or amateur games. In the case of the former, MCC does not participate as a club nor does it provide players for Test matches, etc. In the latter case, as a private members' club, it is part of the amateur game but it could not be considered democratic if it was seen to dominate this area. With regard to providing administrative skills, etc, it appears that nearly all the people who contribute to TCCB and the Cricket Council are connected with a first-class county and, in theory, their MCC association is not relevant. Should cricket run into financial problems in the future it is doubtful if any contribution by MCC could be expected to make much real difference even if MCC members agreed to granting such aid."

The Cricket Council also got it in the neck as a superfluous tier of administration, defective in planning for the future of the game, which was a vital role for a governing body when conditions were changing so much. The TCCB had failed to adjust its management system to meet the pressures of modern life and it had neglected to accept financial responsibility for developing the amateur game through NCA. NCA should receive its share of TCCB monies so that it could expand and plan for the future, and it should remain part of cricket's governing body in Britain. The minor counties should become part of NCA and receive no more money from TCCB as a separate entity. Finally, while acknowledging that TCCB and NCA were fortunate to have been accommodated at Lord's on beneficial terms, "the working party does not believe that the present condi-tions lend themselves to an efficient operation. A new purpose-built block is required for UK cricket, either at Lord's or elsewhere in the country, where modern businesslike facilities can be provided."

This wasn't the only thing the triumvirate were recommending. Their crucial suggestion was that the Cricket Council should be wound up and replaced by something called the United Kingdom Board of Control. This would consist of the seventeen first-class counties, eight representatives from NCA (including the voice of the minor counties), one man representing Scotland, one Ireland, and one the universities of Oxford and Cambridge. The last three wouldn't, however, have any voting powers on the board, which would meet twice a year to receive reports from an executive committee. That committee would meet every six to eight weeks and would consist of a chairman and thirteen members (five from the first-class counties, three from NCA, four sub-committee chairmen and "one representative of MCC for liaison purposes and to recognise MCC's independent position as custodians of the Laws of the game"). The sub-committees would be termed Cricket (with nine professional and three amateur members), Amateur (nine amateurs and three professionals), Finance (five professionals and three amateurs), and Marketing (five professionals and three amateurs). Lastly, the UK Cricket Board would be managed by a Chief Executive, with a Secretary responsible for administration. The working party urged that if this master plan was accepted by TCCB and then by the Cricket Council and its other constituents, no time should be lost in putting it into practice.

There was never any chance of the report going through all those hoops one after the other, just like that. The very things which the three critical county chairmen had seen as defects in the existing system would make sure, at the very least, of a long delay until any clear decision could be reached where it mattered most – in the Cricket Council. What's more, the Cricket Council had been very carefully constructed by MCC in the first place to ensure that no one could dominate it. If MCC and TCCB found themselves totally opposed on some topic, NCA would in effect hold five casting votes. This was a principle that would be fought over for several years still to come.

The TCCB at least tried to speed things up as much as it could by circulating the report not only among its own members but around every part of the Cricket Council, too. It soon found that the first-class cricketing counties were not by any means of one mind about the substantial changes proposed; and in some cases they seemed unable to make up their minds at all. Surrey, Lancashire and Glamorgan, naturally enough, supported the report without any reservations. Sussex, too, agreed with the conclusions and most recommendations. Kent accepted the basic thinking of the working party but were concerned lest the overall control of cricket should fall into too few hands; they wanted to see a more comprehensive study, perhaps by management consultants. Nottinghamshire agreed that the present system of administration was unwieldy, and thought that the balance of power on the Cricket Council should be tilted in favour of the first-class game. Northamptonshire were simply non-committal, Somerset said that there must be no impetuous rush at such an important subject, and Hampshire thought the document no more than a basis for discussion. Derbyshire didn't think the proposals would do anything to solve cricket's present problems, and Leicestershire were against any attempt "to bulldoze a rapid reorganisation", adding that MCC should certainly be represented on a new board, as on the Cricket Council. Essex were against any drastic changes to the present structure, and Gloucestershire certainly weren't going to support the proposals as a package, though they thought that there was merit in the idea of a chief executive.

Warwickshire reacted as though they had considered every item in the report, and a few that hadn't even been mentioned. They wouldn't accept it as a whole, though they welcomed some recommendations. They thought that MCC had too much influence in TCCB, as had the minor counties. But "we cannot believe that a Gillette Cup Final played at Edgbaston, much though we would welcome this, would have quite the same significance as the games played at HQ". Middlesex agreed with many of the comments and some criticisms, but not with the proposed solutions: there should be two governing bodies, one for the professional game and another for the recreational, with an overriding body to bring both sides together; and MCC should still be represented on a reconstituted Cricket Council, but in smaller numbers. Worcestershire's committee rejected the report unanimously, with the rider that MCC should continue to play a role in the administration of the game. Yorkshire, too, turned out to be one of MCC's strongest backers. The Club's "tremendous tradition and influence overseas cannot be wasted" and the working party "degraded its status by its not being a full member of the UK Board of Control. This is unacceptable." The view from Headingley was that reform and not revolution should be the aim.

NCA was well pleased with an analysis that had placed it in such a favourable light, with even greater prosperity dangled before it, though it confessed itself worried about the reduction of MCC. The Minor Counties Cricket Association was very angry indeed, as might be expected, and replied that the report revealed a lack of knowledge about cricket at that level; heavens, the three men didn't even know what they were talking about when referring to the balance between professionals and amateurs; there had been nineteen paid minor county players in 1976, twenty-two in 1977, twenty-one in 1978.

MCC's official response was cool, as though it were considering something quite detached from its own future. "Prompt decision-making is called for in many aspects of cricket administration," it said, "but there are others in which it can be dangerous. Longer-term policy and planning and far-reaching reforms merit careful scrutiny and consideration before decisions are taken. Cricket, like Government, benefits from the use of a 'second chamber' which is to some extent detached and which includes different minds from those promoting the measures under consideration." Wasn't there a risk, it asked, that the new Board of Control might be subject to just the same weaknesses attributed to the Cricket Council; the more it delegated to the executive committee, the likelier it was to become a rubber stamp itself? It then referred to "MCC's entitlement to a significant place in the government of the game". This was based on three things. In the first place Lord's was the Test ground which made the biggest contribution to the overall surplus on Test matches. Secondly, MCC provided the chairman and secretariat for the International Cricket Conference, and to do this it must be fully au fait with what was going on in the first-class game, where its status must also be such as to command the confidence of all ICC members. Thirdly, MCC was responsible for framing and updating the Laws of Cricket, "for which duty it must again be seen to occupy an adequate place in the counsels of the game". There were other factors, of course, and after a fashion they had already been noted by the working party.

The response behind the scenes in MCC was rather less measured than the club's official reply. One Committee member thought the attack on the Cricket Council was "insidious". Another referred to the working party as "the Three Blind Mice". Someone else declared: "This report must be fought with every weapon of defence the club has at its disposal, just as a takeover bid is fought by a company against an unwelcome bidder." They needn't, for the time being, have worried. The status quo was quite capable of taking care of itself. Not only had the individual first-class counties failed to produce any coherent response to the report; the TCCB chairman's advisory committee had also been divided.

In February 1979 there was a full meeting of TCCB, with cricket's future at the top of the agenda. The meeting was invited to consider both the working party report and a variant that had been put forward by some members of the advisory committee, led by Mike Turner, the secretary of Leicestershire. This plan suggested that the existing structure of the game should basically be retained, but that "significant changes" should be made to the composition of the overall governing body, among them an alteration of name from Cricket Council to Board of Control for Cricket in the UK. TCCB, "being charged with full responsibility for the professional game", should have far greater independence than in the past, without needing to refer decisions to the superior board for confirmation. The board of control should receive an agreed percentage of the proceeds from international cricket and with it would allocate funds to the recreational game and also cover its own administrative costs. This board would consist of TCCB, NCA, MCC, Scottish and Irish representatives, but TCCB would have an overall majority; and MCC's role in British cricket and its responsibilities within the board should be properly defined.

The two plans were put to the vote and the original working party's report went down by 16–4. The alternative scheme was backed by seventeen straight votes, and so some further details were hammered out on the spot. It was agreed that a new board of control should consist of eight TCCB members, five representing recreational cricket (at least three of them from NCA), and two MCC representatives. The secretary of TCCB should become secretary of the Board of Control. Having come to these conclusions, the Test and County Cricket Board people left their officials to work out the fine print of what had just been decided before submitting it to the full Cricket Council. They hoped that there wouldn't be too much obstruction up there; that their approach to change, more restrained than that threatened by the working party, might meet with a bit of give in other quarters. Eventually, it did. But the process took another four full years of lobbying, horse-trading and much overtime by the committee system of cricket.

When the great reorganisation was announced at the end of 1982, one thing stayed put. The supreme authority for cricket in the British Isles was still to be known as the Cricket Council. But its structure had been significantly changed. It was to contain one representative each of the minor counties, the Scots and the Irish, but none of them was to have a vote. The Test and County Cricket Board was given the weight it had been seeking for so long, with eight votes in council, compared with five from the National Cricket Association and only three from Marylebone Cricket Club. TCCB was invested with total authority to run all aspects of the professional game affecting English cricketers, and NCA similarly empowered to organise all forms of the recreational game. MCC's prerogative and copyright in the Laws of Cricket were acknowledged and it was also charged with organising cricket tours to associate member countries of ICC, the minor counties of the international scene. Otherwise it had to grin and bear the fact that, if ever push came to shove in the Cricket Council, and TCCB found itself opposed by a combined assault from MCC and NCA, the outcome would only be settled by the casting vote of the chairman – who might easily be Cedric Rhoades himself.

The immediate consequence of the change was that Gubby Allen withdrew from the Cricket Council, where he had been one of MCC's representatives for many years. It was a very pointed gesture from one of the two men who had been instrumental in establishing the council in the first place, when it was the MCC Cricket Council, in 1968. In a letter replying to one from the council's chairman, C. H. Palmer, he explained exactly why he had taken this step.

"Billy Griffith and I were responsible for the foundation of the Cricket Council because we felt that there should be a governing body for cricket representative of all levels of the game. At its inception we were in favour of MCC having the largest representation, as both the TCCB and NCA were in their infancy and we thought they might need guidance. Later, when both those bodies had found their feet, we suggested the 5-5-5 representation.

"In the discussion on the current reorganisation, I made it absolutely clear that I was not opposed to a reduction in MCC's representation if that was the consensus of opinion. But it is my firm conviction that a national body cannot be controlled by one faction, in this case the professional side of the game, regardless of how much money it may in its generosity provide for the recreational side of it.

"Further, at no time has anyone explained to my satisfaction either the reasons for or the advantages of TCCB having control of the council, bearing in mind that under the new constitution both it and the NCA have been delegated absolutely the control of their respective activities. It certainly cannot become a more effective body . . ."

This was the first time the Old Man had resigned from anything in his cricketing life.

By far the greatest curiosity in all these manoeuvres is the fact that complicated allegiances abound almost wherever you look. This isn't an example of unadulterated TCCB fellows from the provinces versus unalloyed MCC chaps in London, as distinctive as a team of West Indians playing a side from one of the white countries. It is hard to think of anyone who has taken a leading role in TCCB since it was invented, who isn't also a member of MCC; even Cedric Rhoades has belonged to the Marylebone club since 1972. Some people have frequently been senior members of both bodies at one and the same time. During the 1982 cricket season, the eight members of the TCCB's Executive Committee – the board's chief power group, formerly the chairman's Advisory Committee – included three men who were currently sitting on the MCC Committee as well. They were M. G. Crawford, for many years Yorkshire's treasurer and now its chairman; A. G. Waterman, a retired timber merchant from Essex, for whom he had played before the war; and D. J. Insole, ex-Test player and chairman of the Essex Cricket Committee.* Of the thirty-one MCC Committee men at the time, a further seven were then serving on various other committees belonging to TCCB. In other words, one third of the entire MCC Committee were also running the Test and County Cricket Board's operations in some way or other. Two of them, Peter May and Alec Bedser, were on TCCB's Selection Committee, its Cricket Committee and its Overseas Tours Committee (and Bedser additionally sat on the Adjudication and Umpires Committees). Gubby Allen belonged to the Cricket Committee, the Overseas Tours Committee and the Adjudication Committee. Colin Cowdrey was on Cricket and Overseas Tours (as was Insole, chairman of both). D. G. Clark, MCC's treasurer, was on TCCB's Finance and General Purposes Committee, under the chairmanship of A. G. Waterman, with M. G. Crawford also a member (and Waterman was on Overseas Tours as well). F. W. Millett, a minor counties stalwart from Cheshire who once scored a century against the West Indians, was on the Cricket Committee. So was Freddie Brown, the former England captain, who was also chairman of the TCCB County Pitches Committee that year (and, since 1977, either chairman or president of NCA).

These are but the most senior men of MCC accounted for. Of eighty-seven people serving on TCCB's dozen committees, the vast majority were at least ordinary members of MCC at the same time. The composition of the two cricket committees is especially illuminating. Until TCCB was founded, MCC's Cricket Committee was the all-powerful body on anything to do with the actual playing of the game, from infringements of the Laws, to the need for Laws to be changed; even to the spirit in which cricketers should approach the sport, which could involve anything from deliberate wasting of time to contrived declarations in order to produce a conclusive result. The Marylebone Club's Cricket Committee decided what was or should be what, and its rulings were ratified more or less on the nod by the full Committee of MCC. Since 1968, it has been the TCCB Cricket Committee which has fulfilled this arbitrary role so far as first-class cricket is concerned. The MCC Cricket Committee since then has

* The other members of the TCCB executive were: F. G. Mann (chairman) (Middlesex), B. Coleman (Surrey), A. C. Smith (Warwickshire), F. M. Turner (Leicestershire) and O. S. Wheatley (Glamorgan).

Four of the finest batsmen who have been associated with Lord's. Above: W. G.
Grace coming out to bat for the Gentlemen versus Players in 1895. Below left: Patsy
Hendren, of Middlesex and England, who scored over 25,000 of his runs and hit 74
centuries on the ground. Below right: One of the most exciting partnerships English
cricket has ever known — W. J. Edrich (left) and Denis Compton, both of
Middlesex and England.

The Eton v Harrow match, 1900. The fixture was notable, until some time after the Second World War, for the stage coaches drawn up along the Tavern boundary and for the lunchtime perambulation around the playing area of women dressed in high fashion and men clad in formal morning suits with top hats. Vestiges of this tradition still persist even today. The arches of the old arbours may be seen distantly beyond the Nursery End seating.

Opposite: England v Australia, photogravure after H. Barrable and R. Ponsonby Staples, 1887. This is an imaginative composition of no particular match. But W. G. Grace is batting, F. R. Spofforth is bowling, and T. W. Garrett is stooping to field the ball. Some well-known spectators in the old "A" enclosure (demolished twenty years ago to make room for the Warner Stand) are also depicted. The Prince and Princess of Wales (later King Edward VII and Queen Alexandra), she shaded by a parasol, are approaching the seats; while Lillie Langtry, the actress, her face turned towards the artist, sits just to the right of the slender iron pillar.

A memorable gathering at the Centenary Test with Australia in 1980. The players and umpires, together with some current officials, are grouped with a large proportion of all living former Test cricketers from the two countries. Meanwhile the Lord's Ground Staff stand beside the covers that were too often required in the

match. In the background (left to right) a corner of the Tavern Stand, "Q" Stand, the Pavilion, the MCC members' "cosy bar" — which used to be the professionals' dressing room — and the Warner Stand. A key to the individuals in the group may be found overleaf.

Above: A rare view of the interior of the Long Room with members intent on events outside.

Below: The unacceptable face of cricket, Lord's 1980. After a long and frustrating delay because of rain in the Centenary Test with Australia, the umpires and two captains were involved in a fracas with MCC members on the Pavilion steps. When the officials reappeared from the Long Room some time later, they were provided with a police escort down those steps to the edge of the field.

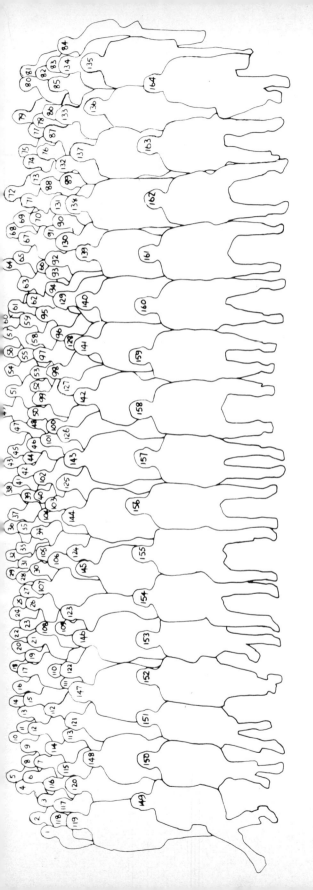

1. F. J. Bryant (Australian Cricket Board) 2. T. C. J. Caldwell (ACB) 3. L. V. Maddocks 4. A. N. Connolly 5. M. H. N. Walker 6. A. E. Moss 7. P. E. Richardson 8. C. R. Ingamells (ACB) 9. K. R. Stackpole 10. R. A. L. Massie 11. R. B. Simpson 12. R. T. Simpson 13. W. M. Lawry 14. A. Turner 15. R. Tattersall 16. R. A. Gaunt 17. M. J. McInnes (ACB) 18. A. W. Walsh (ACB) 19. J. W. Gleeson 20. A. C. Smith 21. G. B. Hole 22. D. L. Richards (ACB) 23. D. A. Allen 24. R. M. Prideaux 25. H. W. H. Rigg (ACB) 26. R. Subba Row 27. T. R. Veivers 28. F. J. Titmus 29. F. W. C. Bennett (ACB) 30. K. D. Mackay 31. T. W. Cartwright 32. R. Edwards 33. J. T. Murray 34. W. Watson 35. R. M. Cowper 36. C. S. Serjeant 37. J. S. E. Price 38. M. J. K. Smith 39. J. M. Parks 40. C. C. McDonald 41. B. L. D'Oliveira 42. A. S. M. Oakman 43. J. A. Flavell 44. J. A. Ledward (ACB) 45. L. J. Coldwell 46. R. Benaud 47. I. R. Redpath 48. G. R. A. Langley 49. P. H. Edmonds 50. G. A. R. Lock 51. F. E. Rumsey 52. J. H. de Courcy 53. K. V. Andrew 54. R. B. McCosker 55. H. B. Taber 56. J. H. Hampshire 57. F. M. Misson 58. T. W. Graveney 59. A. K. Davidson 60. K. D. Walters 61. G. D. McKenzie 62. P. J. Loader 63. E. W. Freeman 64. G. D. Watson 65. G. E. Corling 66. A. J. W. McIntyre 67. D. B. Close 68. G. J. Gilmour 69. I. M. Chappell 70. F. H. Tyson 71. R. Illingworth 72. D. J. Colley 73. J. B. Statham 74. K. Taylor 75. P. H. Parfitt 76. R. Appleyard 77. P. J. Sharpe 78. C. G. Howard (MCC) 79. I. J. Jones 80. E. R. Dexter 81. A. R. Barnes (ACB) 82. I. D. Craig 83. C. S. Elliott (TCCB) 84. V. J. W. M. Lawrence (MCC) 85. K. F. Barrington 86. J. H. Wardle 87. W. E. Bowes 88. J. G. Dewes 89. A. G. Chipperfield 90. C. J. Barnett 91. T. G. Evans 92. E. W. Clark 93. J. A. Young 94. W. Voce 95. J. C. Laker 96. Sir L. Hutton 97. E. R. H. Toshack 98. E. L. McCormick 99. W. A. Johnston 100. K. E. Rigg 101. A. R. Morris 102. D. T. Ring 103. F. R. Brown 104. S. J. E. Loxton 105. K. R. Miller 106. D. V. P. Wright 107. A. V. Bedser 108. K. Cranston 109. M. G. Waite 110. C. Washbrook 111. C. L. Badcock 112. N. W. D. Yardley 113. A. L. Hassett 114. H. E. Dollery 115. W. A. Brown 116. J. T. Ikin 117. L. G. James (MCC) 118. W. E. Hollies 119. J. A. Bailey (MCC secretary) 120. A. R. Border 121. J. Dyson 122. G. Dymock 123. R. J. Bright 124. B. M. Laird 125. G. M. Wood 126. G. N. Yallop 127. K. J. Hughes 128. R. W. Marsh 129. L. S. Pascoe 130. J. R. Thomson 131. A. A. Mallett 132. D. K. Lillee 133. P. M. Lush (TCCB) 134. J. R. Stephenson (MCC) 135. D. B. Carr (TCCB secretary) 136. D. J. Constant (umpire) 137. P. Willey 138. J. Emburey 139. C. W. J. Athey 140. R. D. Jackman 141. D. L. Bairstow 142. M. W. Gatting 143. C. M. Old 144. M. Hendrick 145. G. Boycott 146. G. A. Gooch 147. D. I. Gower 148. H. D. Bird (umpire) 149. W. J. O'Reilly 150. L. S. Darling 151. E. L. a'Beckett 152. W. H. Ponsford 153. A. Sandham 154. R. C. Steele (ACB) 155. P. B. H. May 156. G. S. Chappell 157. S. C. Griffith (MCC president) 158. I. T. Botham 159. R. J. Parish (ACB chairman) 160. F. G. Mann (TCCB chairman) 161. H. S. T. L. Hendry 162. G. O. B. Allen 163. R. E. S. Wyatt 164. P. G. H. Fender

LORD'S GROUND

CORNHILL INSURANCE TEST SERIES
ENGLAND v. PAKISTAN

THURS., FRI., SAT., SUN. & MON., AUGUST 12, 13, 14, 15 & 16, 1982   (5-day Match)

PAKISTAN	First Innings		Second Innings	
1 Mudassar Nazar ...United Bank	c Taylor b Jackman	... 20		
2 Mohsin Khan ....Habib Bank	c Tavare b Jackman	...200	not out	39
3 Mansoor Akhtar ...United Bank	c Lamb b Botham	 57		
4 Javed Miandad ......Habib Bank	run out	6	not out	26
5 Zaheer Abbas .................P.I.A.	b Jackman	75		
6 Haroon Rashid ......United Bank	l b w b Botham	1		
†7 Imran Khan ....Lahore	c Taylor b Botham	12		
8 Tahir Naqqash ..............M.C.B.	c Gatting b Jackman	... 2		
*9 Wasim Bari ....................P.I.A.	not out	24		
10 Abdul Qadir ....Habib Bank	not out	18		
11 Sarfraz Nawaz ....Lahore	Innings closed			
	B 3, l-b 8, w , n-b 2,	13	B 1, l-b 10, w 1, n-b ,	12
	Total	428	Total	77

FALL OF THE WICKETS

1—53   2—197   3—208   4—361   5—364   6—380   7—382   8—401   9—   10—
1—   2—   3—   4—   5—   6—   7—   8—   9—   10—

ANALYSIS OF BOWLING		1st Innings				2nd Innings				
Name	O.	M.	R.	W.	Wd. N-b	O.	M.	R.	W.	Wd. N-b
Botham	44	8	148	3	... 1	7	0	30	0	1 ...
Jackman	36	5	110	4	... 1	4	0	22	0	... ...
Pringle	26	9	62	0	... ...	...	...	...	...	... ...
Greig	13	2	42	0	... ...	...	...	...	...	... ...
Hemmings	20	3	53	0	... ...	2.1	0	13	0	... ...

ENGLAND	First Innings		Second Innings	
1 D. W. Randall..Nottinghamshire	b Sarfraz	29	b Mudassar	9
2 C. J. Tavare.......................Kent	b Sarfraz	8	c Miandad b Imran	82
3 A. J. Lamb ...Northamptonshire	c Haroon b Tahir	33	l b w b Mudassar	0
†4 D. I. Gower ....Leicestershire	c Mansoor b Imran	29	c W.-Bari b Mudassar...	0
5 I. T. Botham ....Somerset	c Mohsin b Qadir	31	c Sarfraz b Mudassar ...	69
6 M. W. Gatting ....Middlesex	not out	32	c W.-Bari b Mudassar	7
7 D. R. Pringle....................Essex	c Haroon b Qadir	5	c Miandad b Qadir	14
8 I. A. Greig.......................Sussex	l b w b Qadir	3	l b w b Mudassar	2
9 E. E. Hemmings...............Notts.	b Sarfraz	6	c Wasim Bari b Imran..	14
*10 R. W. Taylor ....Derbyshire	l b w b Qadir	5	not out	24
11 R. D. Jackman ....Surrey	l b w b Imran..............	0	c Haroon b Qadir	17
	B 11, l-b 12, w 13, n-b 10,	46	B 10, l-b 19, w 5, n-b 4,	38
	Total	227	Total	276

FALL OF THE WICKETS

1—16   2—69   3—89   4—157   5- 173   6—187   7- 197   8—217   9- 226   10—227
1—9   2—9   3—9   4—121   5—132   6—171   7—180   8—224   9— 235   10—276

ANALYSIS OF BOWLING		1st Innings				2nd Innings				
Name	O.	M.	R.	W.	Wd. N-b	O.	M.	R.	W.	Wd. N-b
Imran	23	4	55	2	10 ...	42	13	84	2	1 ...
Sarfraz	23	4	56	3	1 5	14	5	22	0	... ...
Tahir	12	4	25	1	... 3	7	5	6	0	... 4
Qadir	24	9	39	4	1 2	37.5	15	94	2	... ...
Mudassar	4	1	6	0	1 ...	19	7	32	6	4 ...

Umpires—H. D. Bird & D. J. Constant   Scorers—E. Solomon & R. M. Costan

† Captain   * Wicket-keeper

Play begins 1st, 2nd, 3rd & 5th days at 11.00, 4th day at 12.00

Luncheon Interval 1st, 2nd, 3rd & 5th days 1.00—1.40, 4th day 2.00—2.40

Tea Interval 1st, 2nd, 3rd & 5th days 3.40—4.00, 4th day 4.40—5.00; or when 35 overs remain to be bowled on any day, whichever is the later. (May be varied according to state of game). Stumps drawn 1st, 2nd, 3rd & 5th days at 6.00, 4th day at 7.00; or after 96 overs have been bowled on any day, whichever is the later. In the event of play being suspended, for any reason, for one hour or more on any of the first four days, play may continue on that day until 7.00 (1st, 2nd & 3rd days) or 8.00 (4th day).

Pakistan won the toss

A memorable victory, and a model scorecard. Once upon a time many English cricket grounds provided cards printed as neatly as this. Nowadays, Lord's alone maintains the high standard.

considered every single topic coming before the TCCB men, and a club attitude to each has consequently been formed; more to the point, this has been passed on to the MCC representatives on TCCB and especially to those who also serve on the TCCB Cricket Committee, for repetition there. What is particularly interesting about the two committees, as they were composed in the 1982 season, is not only a certain overlap in membership, but their scarcely distinguishable balances between retired and still active first-class cricketers. The full musters were:

MCC Cricket Committee: M. C. Cowdrey (chairman), G. O. Allen, L. E. G. Ames, T. E. Bailey, A. V. Bedser, F. R. Brown, E. A. Clark, E. R. Dexter, C. S. Elliott, N. Gifford, R. M. C. Gilliatt, S. C. Griffith, D. J. Insole, A. R. Lewis, F. G. Mann, P. B. H. May, F. W. Millett, J. G. Overy.

TCCB Cricket Committee: D. J. Insole (chairman), G. O. Allen, H. D. Bird, A. V. Bedser, A. S. Brown. D. J. Brown, F. R. Brown, T. W. Cartwright, M. C. Cowdrey, C. S. Elliott, N. Gifford, K. Higgs, R. Illingworth, P. B. H. May, F. W. Millett, R. V. C. Robins, B. C. Rose, A. C. Smith, T. E. Smith, C. Washbrook.

In view of all that interweaving in the fabric of cricket administration, it is scarcely surprising that drastic decisions involving a further reduction of MCC's influence in the game took so many years to arrive at. The men on TCCB who believe that the administration of cricket in this country might be improved if it was totally dominated by the board, have been very reluctant to put the boot into the club which created TCCB, because they have a loyalty to it, too. It was significant that, by 1982, two members of the notorious working party were no longer to be found on any of TCCB's committees. Ossie Wheatley was still there, chairman of the Discipline Committee and a member of the Executive. Subba Row had just managed the England tour of India the previous winter, but both he and Rhoades only retained their places in TCCB by virtue of their positions within their own county clubs. Rhoades, in fact, was the longest-serving county chairman in TCCB, which made him one of its representatives in the Cricket Council, both before and after the reorganisation.

He had, perhaps, been a bit too abrasive for some other county administrators, though he was widely admired for what he had achieved up at Old Trafford: not so much demonstrated in the performances of the Lancashire side, which had been going through the doldrums again, as in his vigorous encouragement of young cricketers within the county catchment area and in the sheer energy he had brought to the business side of the club. He had become a kind of Lord Harris on his own patch, an autocrat whose word was local law. Someone said at the time that he shuddered to think what would happen to Lancashire if Cedric fell under a bus the following day: Rhoades had personally supervised so many necessities of its life for a decade that no one else was equipped to carry on as deftly as he had been doing. He had trimmed the county committee back from the thirty or more members who sat at the time of his 1964 revolt to one of only twelve elected men (while Sussex still functioned with a committee of forty-four, Yorkshire with thirty-seven, Somerset with twenty-eight) and sometimes gave the impression that he thought the trimming might usefully go a bit further. He made no attempt to disguise his belief that too many county committees were not only overloaded, but overloaded in favour of former first-class cricketers "living in the past". He exempted only three old England Test cricketers from this charge – the late Ken Barrington, Subba Row and Freddie Brown. It was common knowledge that Rhoades and Cyril Washbrook (Lancashire's old Test opener, a member of his county committee and also, in 1982, of TCCB's Cricket Committee) did not see eye to eye on most things to do with the administration of the game.

Rhoades can be scathing about the way most county cricket clubs are run, claiming that only Lancashire, Surrey and Warwickshire are at all professional in their approach to things. He thinks it ridiculous that there are almost as many different pay structures for cricketers as there are first-class counties, a mixture of permutations on the basic wage plus appearances, bonuses, cars and other perks, living accommodation and outside sponsorship. Notoriously, he would abandon first-class competition in England between seventeen counties anyway, replacing it with a two-division system of teams representing the cities and larger towns (Manchester v Leeds, Bristol v Southampton and so forth). These would play mid-week championship games lasting three or four days, with twenty points for a win, five points for first-innings lead, and no points awarded for anything else: and all one-day cricket at the weekend would be played to fifty-five overs for each innings, instead of the three different durations that exist today.

So revolutionary are many things Cedric Rhoades proposes that he is regarded in some quarters as a bogyman who would defile cricket at every point and turn it into something as unsavoury as soccer has too frequently become. In fact, he would do no such thing; at least, he wouldn't intend to. He is dismayed by bad behaviour on a cricket pitch and will not countenance any form of indiscipline in the Lancashire side. He is genuinely horrified at the prospect of a transfer system in cricket like the one that has defaced the Football

League and brought many of its clubs close to ruin.* But he is perhaps even more aggressive towards MCC's influence on the game, quite surprisingly so for a man who has been an MCC member for more than a decade. He has viewed the Cricket Council as something which exists only to preserve vestiges of MCC's power. He scoffs at the tradition by which the President of MCC escorts the monarch on to the pitch during a Test match at headquarters: he thinks the Queen should be entertained and introduced to the players by the chairman of TCCB instead. He refers disdainfully to "the gentlemen at Lord's".

The fact that he was voted off the TCCB hierarchy in 1980 when its chairman's Advisory Committee was transformed into an Executive, was an indication that few of the men at the head of county cricket clubs share Rhoades's vision of the future in all its drastically new perspectives, though many would be willing to follow him part of the way. Yet, as Rhoades stepped down, there was already rising a figure who might have been thought to appeal even less to traditionalists in the cricketing shires. This was Bernie Coleman, chairman of TCCB's Public Relations and Marketing Committee at the time of the working party, and subsequently elected to the Executive from which Rhoades was excluded. Coleman is a publican by trade, mine host of the Dog and Fox at Wimbledon, owner of one or two more hotels, and some time director of Wimbledon Football Club until he moved up to the Second Division for a similar position with Crystal Palace. He had also been one of the new men in Surrey's cricket administration alongside Subba Row, and there he was soon speaking of plans for a transformation of the Oval with a reduced playing area to make room for a general sports centre, a business centre and flats at one end of the historic ground. Already he has helped to persuade the London Brick Company and the Brick Development Association between them to rebuild the crumbling perimeter wall round the Oval for almost nothing instead of a market price near to £1 million. His approach to cricket itself was made apparent in August 1980 when he got the *Daily Mirror* to sponsor a match between Essex and the West Indies under floodlights at Chelsea Football Club's ground, which most regular cricket-watchers thought something close to farce; especially when the electronic scoreboard, trying to keep tally of Graham Gooch's regular striking of the ball into the crowd on the narrow ground,

* Genuinely horrified he may be, but in 1982 the wicket-keeper Chris Maynard joined Lancashire from Warwickshire; the first example in cricket of a player being transferred from one county to another in mid-season.

flashed a message in lights, "Slow down, Mr Gooch. I can't keep up with you." This was Packerism at its most illuminating, and it didn't go down at all well in many places quite apart from Lord's.

If men of Gubby Allen's vintage, reared in MCC's ways and exerting great power from positions within MCC, may be described as the Old Buffers of English cricket, then Coleman may become one of the New Buffers of the game. But then, so may his associate Raman Subba Row. So may another Surrey man, Peter May, now in charge of selecting the England teams, a distinctly establishment figure who was President of MCC in 1980–1. So may Doug Insole, who has been somewhere close to the levers of power in either MCC or TCCB or both since before he stopped playing cricket in 1963. So may George Mann, Chairman of TCCB from 1978 to 1983,* and first Chairman of the reconstituted Cricket Council. Mann in many ways is the oddest figure who could possibly be found to head any organisation seeking to demote the Marylebone Cricket Club. A deceptively languid character with a taste for monogrammed shirts, once Group Director of Watney Mann & Truman Brewers and now Deputy Chairman of the Extel Group, he descends from an orthodox MCC line and was, in fact, a starred candidate for election to the MCC Committee in October 1983. His father, F. T. Mann, captained Middlesex and England as an amateur, one of the biggest hitters of his time (he all but equalled Albert Trott's feat in 1924, when he twice put Wilfred Rhodes on to the top deck of the Pavilion off consecutive balls). George Mann himself could be exciting with the bat for Middlesex and England, too; in seven Tests he averaged 37.60. He was the last Etonian to captain England, against New Zealand in 1949. Both then and when taking a team to South Africa the winter before, he showed qualities of leadership that make for happy and successful sides, later applied to the strange mixture of people who are liable to settle the destinies of English cricket for a generation to come, through the Test and County Cricket Board.

A remaining key figure is the Secretary of TCCB, Donald Carr. Although he has been a member of MCC for years and was an Assistant Secretary of the club at the inception of TCCB, Carr's roots at county level were perhaps deeper and sturdier than those of most men who gravitate to Lord's. He had been an assistant secretary of Derbyshire for a couple of years before he became captain of the county side in 1955, and he mixed county administration with

---

* Mann's successor in this position was C. H. Palmer of Leicestershire, a Past-President of MCC and long-serving member of MCC Committee. He defeated Subba Row in the election to decide who should head TCCB.

batsmanship for most of his playing career. His 2,165 runs in 1959 remain a record for the Derbyshire club, but he was never quite consistent enough to play Test cricket at home; though he captained England once, in the Madras Test of 1952, because the touring party's leader Nigel Howard was unwell. A quiet and subtle person, in spite of the Superman cartoon which someone has stuck on the outside of his door, Carr works in an office high up in the Pavilion at the end nearest the Grace Gates.

Almost the full length of the building away is the office where Jack Bailey, the essentially genial Secretary of MCC, supervises the affairs of the club and of Lord's itself: after captaining Oxford, he never gave himself long enough bowling for Essex to realise his potential as a player, before going into industry for a while and writing about Rugby for the *Telegraph* en route to administration in MCC. His secretariat looks as if everything is well under control, with all the paperwork battened down inside filing cabinets; only the picture postcards spread along the wall above two of the office girls suggest that not everything in there is also conducted according to the Laws of the game. By contrast, the focal point of TCCB still has an air of improvisation after almost a decade, with temporary-looking shelves and stacks of stationery surrounding the staff. It could very well be a political party's downtown office during a general election campaign.

Yet this is the effective headquarters of first-class cricket in England nowadays. More than that: insofar as all forms of cricket throughout the British Isles have any common administrative centre, this is it, too, because Carr is Secretary of the Cricket Council as well as of TCCB. If the council were a more active body than it has been, this would be an impossible task for one man to discharge. But it is a fact that the number of times the Cricket Council (before its reconstitution took effect at the end of January 1983, at least) has pronounced on anything of sufficient importance to catch the public eye, can be counted on the fingers of one hand. It was the council, not TCCB, that the Government persuaded to cancel the 1970 South African tour. It was the council which issued a statement condemning bad behaviour by cricketers after the tour of Australia by Illingworth's team the following winter. It was the council which put the English point of view when Guyana expelled Jackman in 1980–1, because of his South African connections, the council which decided that the whole of Botham's touring party should leave because of this. And it was the council which was cranked into motion when the Indian Government threatened to stop Fletcher's team touring the sub-continent the following winter because Boycott and Cook had also spent time in South Africa. Otherwise, the Cricket Council has rarely been heard of outside the game; even under the reconstitution it meets only four times a year. The fact that Jack Bailey, Deputy Secretary of this body for many years as well as Secretary of MCC, has been situated as far away from the council's Secretary as it is possible to be in the same building, is an indication of how nominal more than real his Cricket Council title was; but that alone says a great deal about the putative high command of our cricket for the past fifteen years. In that time there always has been a large grey area in first-class cricket between the responsibilities of the Cricket Council and those of TCCB. Officials have sometimes not been quite sure which hat they were wearing when they have been required to issue statements.

Figures are not always a good guide to anything, but a fair indication of TCCB's growth, and the consequent complexity of its operations, is the amount of money it has been handing over in the past few years. Its total disbursements around English cricket in 1975 totalled £450,000. By 1981 that sum had risen to £3,058,000 – and national inflation was not by any means responsible for all of the difference. There was a lot more money going out in Test match expenses, and especially in Test players' wages, which defied any norms laid down for the nation at large by Government. There was also a much greater swag coming into the game from sponsorship in various forms. The TCCB finances, however, are only a convenient yardstick and do not demonstrate the full nature of increasing complexity. The growth rate of international politics affecting English cricket in recent years has been such that if it were applied to the domestic economy, unemployment and bankruptcies would now be a thing of the past. TCCB has had more discussions with lawyers since the Packer case than any sane man would wish to endure in several lifetimes. It has had politicians jumping up and down like yo-yos – sometimes on its doorstep, sometimes at a healthier but nonetheless distracting distance; sometimes on a matter of principle and sometimes because they have decided that there is now an amount of mileage to be extracted from cricket.

Such is the welter of administration connected with issues which are tangential to the game itself, on top of those urgent commercial matters which must be handled as they crop up if the game is to survive in this country in its present form, that Donald Carr now thinks himself lucky if he manages to see some cricket being played. He isn't, as it happens, in a very good position to watch even when he can make time to. Of all the officials at Lord's, only Jack Bailey and his two Assistant Secretaries of MCC can look at the playing area while still sitting at their desks. Everyone else has to move off to some other room. Carr's chief difficulty, however, is one of opportunity rather than locality. He has been ashamed to discover that at a TCCB meeting of county captains not long ago, he was struggling to put a name to each face. It has occurred to him that if he drifted out to watch his old team playing Middlesex any time Derbyshire came to Lord's now, he probably wouldn't recognise half the players on the field. He doesn't believe this is good enough for a man with his job. He takes the view that he ought to spend more time pondering cricket and matters implicit in the game itself, instead of being bogged down in affairs which are peripheral to that. "I've felt," he says, "that one ought to have the flexibility to do a bit of thinking, positive work, instead of leaping, jumping, slipping from crisis to crisis."

Because he's at the sharp end of every negotiation that now takes place in the first-class game, Carr appreciates more than most just how much English county and Test cricket has changed since the end of the war, when he had just left Repton for Oxford before his time with Derbyshire. When those of us now in middle age – he is one, and I am another – began to watch cricket in those years we had our county allegiances strongly enough, we thought. We wanted to see our teams win, certainly in some fixtures more than in others: Lancashire v Yorkshire, Somerset v Gloucestershire, Middlesex v Sussex and all the other traditional pairings that took place over the two Bank Holiday weekends. But except on such occasions of ancient rivalry involving local peculiarities of social history, we attended cricket matches more than anything in the hope of seeing individuals play marvellously, even if this meant that our own teams suffered in the process. A Lancashire lad would go to Old Trafford for the Kent game, wishing to see the extraordinary Evans at his best behind the stumps, hoping that Leslie Ames might hit half a century (but not too many more, please). A boy from North London would turn up at Lord's when Yorkshire came down and go home disappointed if Jack Young or Laurie Gray bowled Hutton for a duck.

A paradox has since developed in the appreciation of cricket in England, and it is this. Never before have individual cricketers been thrust as individuals into the public gaze as much as now – on television and in various forms of advertising, not to mention the columns written about them in the public prints – yet their individual performances no longer count for as much as the achievements of their teams. There are one or two exceptions to this: appearances by Ian Botham and Viv Richards, transcending rivalries, immediately come to mind. But generally speaking, the majority of cricket enthusiasts now seem to be attracted much more by the possibility of their team's success than by the spectacle of the big names on both sides playing brilliantly. They cheer on their own sides much more aggressively and they deride opponents much more contemptuously. They are cricket supporters first, cricket-watchers second. Cricket crowds always did vary according to whether their team was having a good season or not; but they never varied as much as they have done over the past . . . what? . . . twenty years? When Lancashire were having their great run of one-day successes in the 1970s, the gates at Old Trafford were more often than not closed on a full house at those fixtures, unless the weather was bad. In the 1981 season, when the county finished eleventh in the Sunday League, and disappeared from the knock-out competitions after a couple of home matches in each, the biggest one-day attendance only just topped 4,000 on a ground that could hold 20,000 or more.

County committees have also changed, both in composition and attitude, over the same period. Once they consisted of nothing but local gentry and former players (usually ex-amateurs, who therefore qualified on two counts) all with much spare time on their hands. A great deal of hereditary wealth and power adorned the game at this level, to the extent that just before the Second World War, the Presidents of the seventeen first-class counties included two Dukes, two Earls, two Lords, three Baronets and three Knights among their number; by 1982, all but four county Presidents were untitled men. Social and economic history had together begun to alter the old formula when the gentry found it necessary to busy themselves with something more demanding than a leisurely watch over their investments; and when ex-professional cricketers, with a sports shop or a pub to attend to, were at last deemed suitable committee material. By 1962, when the last Gentlemen v Players match took place at Lord's because the distinction between amateurs and professionals was about to end (a decision urged by MCC in spite of opposition from all but two counties), the final rearrangement of county hierarchies had already begun.

Ten years later a new species of committeeman had settled thickly on the scene and was making himself at home in pavilions across the land. He was the local businessman whose trade had thrived, liked his cricket, had some spare cash, and fancied a position of note within his community unrelated to his status as employer: he wished to be seen as something between a benefactor and a cavalier. Had his sporting tastes been different, he would have become a director of his local football club. And because he had reached his eminence the hard way – nothing handed to him on a plate when his birth certificate was signed – he measured most things in life by quite ordinary exhibitions of success. From the moment he arrived, and was joined by others of his kind, the measurement was applied to the county cricket club, too, more than it had ever been before. From being the landed gentleman's pet creature, which was given house-room and cosseted so long as it didn't misbehave, the club became the tradesman's reflection of his own self-image, which meant that it had to do better all the time.

There was one other inducement to success, and that was the financial plight of the game at county level. Produce a winning team and you might just keep your head above water. Fail to do so, and you might well go under. That was the thinking until the big sponsors came along and began to buttress walls that had started to crumble all round the game. And even though for some time now it has been recognised that success alone cannot save any county club from the bailiffs, the thinking has taken root; and, after all, if the crowds don't turn up to watch their successful teams, the sponsors are very likely to look elsewhere for what they expect from their deals. Gone forever, therefore, are the days when county cricket was regarded as fun and games as much as a striving to win. Up to the 1950s, but not much later, all county cricketers had this ambivalent attitude to their sport. They could assume that if their team wasn't in the top five by the end of July, it had no hope of winning the championship, the only trophy going in those days. The dozen also-rans therefore began to relax when August came round, and aimed above all to enjoy the last few weeks of the season.

The great drive for success from the quarters already mentioned coincided roughly with the introduction of a new competition which kept many more cricketers keen up to the last day of the season: the first of the one-day tournaments, which the Gillette razor-blade company sponsored in 1963. Joined before long by the other knock-out competition sponsored by Benson & Hedges, and the Sunday League backed by John Player & Sons, there soon came the time when every one of the seventeen counties might well have something to play hard for from start to finish of the cricketing calendar. The day had dawned of the totally professional approach in every sense of the words, including some that had never been dreamt of before. The business manager had been introduced to county cricket. A little later, so had the team manager, who had hitherto been confined to touring teams abroad. Somerset had even paid someone £4,000 a year to be their player liaison officer.

A result of all these phenomena is a change in strategy on the field of play, and again it involves paradox. Because captains feel the urgent need to supply success, much more than their predecessors of a generation ago, they are tempted to play more defensively in order to deny their opponents victory and therefore secure the prize themselves: and the conditions under which one-day matches in particular are conducted make such a rum equation perfectly feasible. Stop the beggars scoring until the overs are fast trickling away and they'll do more than half your job for you by heaving at the bowlers in desperation just before time runs out. So runs the theory and, more often than not, the practice. It is, of course, easier to be precisely scientific in playing any sport negatively in this way than it is to adopt a positive approach, which depends so much on the individual's sudden inspiration, on his eye for the opening which appears in a split second and vanishes again without profit unless he reacts on the instant. You can wear anybody down with the dreary application of friction, but it takes something more exhilarating to vanquish him in such a fashion that an onlooker will be glad that he was there for the sake of the feat alone. One-day cricket, which at first-class level was introduced for a commercial reason and nothing but, has improved the game technically in one outstanding respect, and that is in its fielding, which is a lovely craft, but a defensive one most of the time: no longer can a batsman assume, as he once did, that he'll automatically get a single if he pushes the ball somewhere between cover and mid-off; a Randall or a Gower will be on it like a flash and he'll be run out by a yard or two. Fielding apart, though, one-day cricket has detracted from the techniques of the game and, for all the high excitement of the final slog, its emphasis on interminable fast bowling has made cricket a duller game to watch than it was when no side would take the field without a brace of spinners in the attack.

These are among the things Donald Carr has in mind when he says that he wishes there were more time just to think about *cricket*. And it would be as well if someone in TCCB did apply himself earnestly to such matters, as many an Old Buffer in MCC has done in the past, for there is no telling where cricket will end up if its future is settled by market forces alone. Shaping that future – which includes an aesthetic and an ethic as well as techniques – for the first-class game in England is TCCB's biggest responsibility, though its greatest energies so far have been spent on finance and politics. The thoroughly baffling thing about all the wrangles that took place up to the reconstitution of the Cricket Council in 1983, is that hardly any differences of opinion exist between the MCC Committee and the TCCB Executive on major issues affecting the conduct and playing of cricket. They share the same stance on a whole range of matters, from the discipline of players to policy towards South Africa, sometimes out of principle, sometimes from expediency. So close are they in so many ways, so impregnated are they with common traditions, so frequently are individuals to be found with one foot firmly planted in each camp, that it is rather difficult to avoid the suspicion that the long debate has not really been about the ideal structure of administration at all. It may have been about that primitive pastime of human beings when power is at stake; jostling each other to determine who shall enjoy the greater share. Something of the sort happened once before, nearly 200 years ago, when the arrivistes of Marylebone shouldered aside the old guard from Hambledon.

CHAPTER FIVE

The Middlesex Connection

Somewhere towards the end of March, or even in April if winter has lingered that year, Lord's begins to stir out of doors once again. In the middle of the playing area the ground staff move about purposefully with their first concentrated preparations for the new season, bearing wooden boards and long strings and other tackle in order to mark out the eighteen wickets. Soon they will be working to the rumble of tractors and the clatter of mowing machines. That sweet and penetrating herald of cricket, the fragrance of freshly cut grass, will begin to drift across the ground, and shortly it will be so commonplace that no one will remark on it anymore. But right now people do sniff and wrinkle their noses at the pleasure of it and what it means. As they walk round the backs of the stands towards the Nursery End, they also incline their heads unconsciously so as to catch the first sound of a bat upon a ball. The nets have gone up again on the practice ground. Men in track suits or flannels or combinations of both are doing painful-looking exercises that were never associated with cricket until a few seasons ago. But others are already in the nets, running in to bowl or taking guard. The Middlesex players have returned from wherever they've spent the last six months.

When Patsy Hendren and his less illustrious brother Dennis were on the Middlesex books at about the time of the First World War, the players were contracted to work for both the Middlesex County and the Marylebone Cricket Clubs. MCC's Secretary in those days, Francis Lacey, used to stand with his chief clerk by the main gates of Lord's, waiting for the arrival of the cricketers in spring. By their side was a pile of contracts on heavy blue legal paper, every one tied with a piece of pink ribbon. As each cricketer stepped forward he was greeted by the secretary. "Hello, Hendren. Here's your contract, and here's" – giving him 6s 8d (33p) – "your first day's wages, and I hope you've wintered well." A few, like Patsy, might have wintered pretty well if there had been a tour overseas. Brother Dennis, however, who never made anything like the same mark on the game, appreciated much less the Secretary's jovial approach. "There was me," he would recall in later years, "with me bleedin' ribs pokin' out of me skin, breakin' me neck to get at that six-and-eight." Stories like that are apt to set the Middlesex players of today rolling with laughter, or shaking their heads in disbelief.

Though a disturbing number of county cricketers in the last few years have spent their winters signing on the dole, the successful ones are now upholstered against the worst that any English winter can bring. They have a basic wage for the playing season which ensures at least dignity, *provided* that they can obtain its equal throughout the off-season at home. Many do very much better than that, and we shall come to them in due course. The bulk of players today, even if they never reach the level of Test cricket, rarely know the penny-pinching and the humiliation that the likes of Dennis Hendren used to endure. For the decade or so when they are in their prime they have their basic wage and often their well-paid winter of coaching and playing overseas; and they have a mass of perks, like free cars for the summer months, that their predecessors of even half a generation back never knew.

The life of Middlesex players has been emancipated in other small but not trivial ways. Until quite recently, no player would have been allowed into the Pavilion at Lord's unless he was, according to the custom of MCC, properly dressed; which meant wearing a collar and tie and jacket while he was running the gauntlet from the entrance to the dressing-room upstairs. Mike Brearley, a resolute battler for his own and his players' working conditions and rewards, as well as a rare captain on the field, put an end to that. He appeared in open-necked shirts and simply ignored complaints about the Middlesex team being a scruffy lot. After his team had won the county championship outright in 1976 for the first time in almost thirty years, the complaints duly subsided and were not heard again, while Middlesex cricketers walked in and out of the Pavilion often looking like a bunch of rather smart picnickers heading for the beach.

A pointed indication of how the condition of cricketers has changed over recent years was to be seen in the Middlesex dressing-room during the 1982 season. Part of the furniture is a small writing table, with a rack in the middle to hold notepaper and envelopes. Among this stationery was a pamphlet entitled "Partnership and Share Purchase Assurance", which looked as if it had been well thumbed. Other than that, and the television set nearby, there was little in the room to suggest what a transformation has occurred in cricketers' lives since Patsy Hendren was in his prime; and even before that, when Albert Trott himself, Bernard Bosanquet and "Old Jack" Hearne were playing for the county before the nineteenth century was out.

Not that Trott, Hearne or Hendren would ever have been allowed into that dressing-room as Middlesex players in their days. All three were professional cricketers, and that room was reserved for amateurs until after the Second World War, the pros being accommodated below stairs in what has since been converted into the most comfortable of the MCC members' bars. It wasn't until May Day 1946, an appropriate date, when Middlesex played MCC in a one-day match to celebrate the start of the first post-war season, that the revolutionary step of undressing together in one room was taken at Lord's and, at the same time, the professionals were allowed to emerge on to the field of play through the centre door of the Pavilion, instead of from a less obtrusive exit round the side. The reflex died hard in some quarters, though. It is well remembered that just before a Middlesex match began some time before the distinction between amateurs and professionals ended in 1962, a loud-speaker announcement advising team changes made one other correction to the printed scorecard. "For F. J. Titmus, read Titmus, F. J." it said. On such minutiae did a whole segment of English social history depend.

Where everybody changes now, all being thoroughly professional cricketers together, is known as No. 1 Dressing Room, its counterpart at the other end of the Pavilion nearest the Warner Stand being curiously termed No. 5 Dressing Room. The intermediate three, in fact, are nothing more than locker-lined alcoves off the connecting corridor, where young and usually unprofessional players of MCC change before going for a knock-up in the nets. No. 5 Dressing Room, a bit bleaker than No. 1, though also having the benefit of a balcony overlooking the Pavilion steps, is where teams visiting Lord's get changed. No. 1, the "home" dressing-room, is the province of the MCC, the Middlesex, the England, the Cambridge and the Eton sides when they appear at headquarters; competing teams of rank outsiders have to toss up to decide who takes which.

No. 1 is spacious, as it needs to be with a dozen lusty men and their gear quartered there for days on end, not to mention the hangers-on who drift in and out continually when a match is in progress (though not without the captain's permission, as a notice outside the door warns: and even MCC Presidents and chairmen of the England selectors defer to that). Another notice, for the benefit of the players alone, on the inside declares: "Track suits may only be worn at Lord's for match fielding and training on the Nursery Ground. At all other times proper cricket clothing should be worn." At the far end are four washbasins – the baths and showers are outside along the corridor – and apart from tables on which one can sit and swing legs, there are a couple of dressing-tables with mirrors and hairbrushes laid out. One of the pale green walls is almost obscured by the lockers belonging, as they are the most frequent inhabitants, to the Middlesex players. A milk-vending machine is parked elsewhere, and a fancy-looking portable telephone with an enormous base, painted red overall. Of decoration there is little other than a faded photograph in sepia of the 1907 Middlesex side, an unaccountable survivor when that team finished no higher in the championship than fifth. The thick waterpipes, antique central heating running round the room, pre-date it by a handful of years. But that other relic, Denis Compton's artificial kneecap, which lay discarded here for several years after he retired, is no longer to be seen, unless it has been lodged out of reach beneath the benches that run part of the way round the dressing-room. Where, of course, the players of each generation make certain places their own.

Of the current Middlesex side, Daniel, Emburey and Gatting have tended to range themselves along the bench running between the door and the front windows, with Edmonds stationed in the corner nearest the view. Brearley used to drop anchor near the door leading out to the balcony, where he too could keep an eye on what was going on in the middle. When England take the place over, Botham establishes himself firmly by the end windows where, looking down, he can see who is coming up the roadway from the Grace Gates. A bit institutionalised, is No. 1 Dressing Room, in more than the seating arrangements preferred by its occupants. Its atmosphere can be boisterously jolly, blankly downhearted, pleasantly argumentative, testy or relaxed, depending on the state of play, the nature of wicket and weather, the condition of the stock market, or simply the mood of the captain when he first walks through the door. It is both a nerve centre concentrating itself against whoever are the opponents, and a refuge from people who have come to Lord's to applaud or criticise, but who do not often, in the view of the players, really understand. It is something much more complex, and intriguingly so, than a place where men change from one set of clothes into another. The cricketers are watchfully guarded by a dressing-room attendant and his assistant in a little office next door. These two intercept the unwanted visitors and the highly personal telephone calls that all athletes often get, they make sure that the bathroom towels are changed five times every playing day, and that near-boiling water is constantly on tap. A period piece in many ways it may be, but players will tell you that there is nothing better, and hardly anything as good, at any cricket ground anywhere in the world.

Another pamphlet at that writing table gave away another tendency of our times. This one was called "Physical Fitness for Players", and some recent Middlesex cricketers haven't needed to look at it (the exuberant Barlow, for example, whose working day invariably begins with an hour of squash; or Selvey, who spends a lot of time road-running and, in winter, felling trees). A cock-stride away is the treatment room where MCC's resident physiotherapist, John Miller, acts as something between a doctor and a father confessor to the players. His appointment in 1975 is an indication of just when physical fitness began to preoccupy, sometimes to the point of obsession, cricketers more than ever in the past; it was only a year or two earlier that the dapper shape of Bernard Thomas, on hire to TCCB from his own practice in Birmingham, became as familiar to crowds as the England cricketers he sometimes seems intent on publicly pulling limb from limb before a Test. Before these two para-medics arrived on the scene, men with their certified skills were virtually unknown in county cricket, though Yorkshire long ago boasted an old chap who used to give the players a rub-down in the Headingley dressing-room. Now most counties have their physio, and every cricketer is very keen indeed to maintain his physical peak; some say because there's much more money at stake these days.

As an MCC employee, Miller's services are available to any of the teams playing at Lord's, but the Middlesex players have become his charges-in-chief. It's an uncommon morning when the county is playing at home and when one or two players don't request a spell on his couch and the application of ultra-sound from the battery of electronic appliances at his fingertips. Sometimes it's genuine muscle trouble, and sometimes the unimagined pain is the mental one of being out of form, with a lousy batting or bowling average, and with having just been dropped from the team. For the authentic pulled muscle, the first aid is ice to contract it and stop any bleeding, though it's much better to head the trouble off before it happens by keeping the blood circulating well, which is why cricketers now make such a fetish of warming up. For the essentially mental anguish which can produce psychosomatic pain, John Miller goes through the required motions of his craft, but is really doing nothing more for the player than offering tea and sympathy; which is what the man most needs. Hypochondria is not unknown in the Middlesex dressing-room, or any other if it comes to that; but cricketers, like the dancers of the Royal Ballet with whom Miller has also dealt, are far less prone to it than footballers, as he discovered when he spent two winters with

Tottenham Hotspur FC. There is also a quota of stoics in No. 1 Dressing Room, men who will damage themselves severely before they will utter a word of complaint. When Radley once asked the physiotherapist to examine his leg to see if he was fit for the nets, he was instantly told that there'd be no nets for him that day: there was no need for a preliminary look, because it was the first time in seven seasons that Radley had put his head round the treatment-room door, and Miller reasoned that something was bound to be structurally wrong.

And then there are the accidents which crop up from time to time during a game. Dislocated fingers happen about once a week, and maybe half a dozen fractured bones in a season. Twice since 1975 Miller has had a broken skull on his hands, once because a Dane hooked a ball into his face when playing MCC, again when the Combined Services were playing MCC's young professionals; and there was a near miss during a Middlesex match in 1978, when Croft floored Gould and put him into hospital for a few days with bad concussion. There was also the time when Brearley got the ball not only on the bridge of his nose, but between the bars of the grille on his helmet first, and the bleeding couldn't be stopped for the best part of three hours. It was ironic that this should happen to the player who, in 1977, was the cricketer who began the modern craze for helmets by appearing first of all in headgear with a polythene fringe round the nape and temples, a strange-looking compromise between armour and the traditional cap. It was a long-delayed response to that day in 1870 when Summers of Nottinghamshire died after being hit between the eyes by Platts of MCC at Lord's, the only fatality that has yet resulted in first-class cricket from a batsman being struck by a ball.

There are plenty of cricket-watchers who reckon that, since Brearley's innovation, the game has taken an aesthetic turn for the worse, and that the use of helmets by close fielders at least ought to be legislated against. There may no longer be an active cricketer left to agree with those who sit safely in their seats, and the authorities, petrified by the thought of further legal actions in the game, are unlikely to make any prohibitive move. Some older members of MCC let it be known that they think the players of today are mollycoddled with all this physiotherapy and suchlike. To which Miller replies that if the old gentlemen had been treated in the same way in their own playing days, they might not now be as arthritic as many of them are. As for the helmets, he's still trying to construct the ideal, which has so far eluded the designers. They offer protection well enough but suffer from an acoustic defect, so that batsmen wearing them at Lord's can often catch the sound of clinking glasses on the balcony of the members' bar, yet fail to hear their partner's call clearly enough from the other crease.

A quibble most Middlesex cricketers have about playing at Lord's is that the practice nets are apt to be arranged more for the benefit of MCC members than for them. An even bigger qualification to their liking for the place is that they do not sense the same enthusiasm in their supporters that they know other county sides enjoy when playing at home. Even during one-day matches, when the crowds turn up in some strength, there is an air of restraint in the stands that wouldn't be evident at Headingley, Old Trafford or Trent Bridge – or on the other side of London at the Oval, where Surrey have always drawn in large or small numbers of spectators loudly identifying with their team. Various theories are advanced on account for this state of affairs, and particularly for the comparison with Middlesex's metropolitan rivals. One is that because the Oval is located in a working-class area on the South Bank, cricket fans there are much more likely to behave without inhibition than the middle classes who abide in the hinterland of Lord's; which assumes that the average Middlesex supporter comes from St John's Wood and comparable parts of North London. Another possibility is related to the fact that English county loyalty has traditionally encompassed many sides of life, support for the county cricket team being one expression of this; and it can therefore be argued that, as Middlesex ceased to exist as a geographical and administrative reality after the Local Government Act of 1972, the cricket team thereafter was bound to operate in an emotional vacuum. Yet another school of thought believes that the tepid support is something that follows from Lord's being the place it is, with powerful infusions (including a decorous tone set by MCC) that have nothing to do with its almost accidental role as the home ground of Middlesex CCC. It is conceivable that the majority of people who occupy the public seating there are not Londoners by birth or instinct, but expatriates from other cricketing counties who patronise Middlesex simply because they inhabit the finest ground in the land and because they are a handy substitute for more distant teams who would engage deep loyalty. Whatever the reasons for this sad circumstance, it obviously is not a figment in the imagination of Middlesex cricketers. When the team met Surrey in the 1980 Gillette Cup Final, both clubs collected a special allotment of tickets for their supporters. Surrey's went within a day or two of becoming available. Middlesex struggled a bit to get rid of theirs. Since writing that, it has been pointed out to me that some Middlesex supporters would have collected Cup Final tickets from the office at Lord's in person some time before the allocation for the game, thus reducing the rush for them later on.

Lackadaisical support at Lord's was not what caused Middlesex to start playing odd games at Uxbridge, however. The first of these happened a couple of weeks before that Cup Final, when Derbyshire were beaten by nine wickets, largely due to some fine fast bowling by the giant South African Van der Bijl, who took 10 for 59 in the match. The decision had been taken after MCC had asked Middlesex to consider occasional home fixtures elsewhere in order to relieve the congestion at Lord's and leave more time for preparing wickets for the big matches there. The solution was new but the problem has existed for a long time: the county's fixture list always has been contrived so as to keep Middlesex away from Lord's, sometimes for long stretches of a season, while greater priorities have been attended to at headquarters. Middlesex supporters of that attractive team which played just after the war became accustomed to losing sight of Edrich and Compton from the beginning of July to the middle of August, when those two were probably hitting bowlers out of grounds all over England on extended northern and western tours.

Expedient the Uxbridge move may have been to the authorities at Lord's rather than to Middlesex, but after the first experience of it, most of the players and officials have found it to their taste, and it looks as if it will be a permanent arrangement, possibly an expanding one. The players have been stimulated by the bigger crowds who have turned up there than is the habit at Lord's for county championship games. They like the greater proximity of spectators, too, the tenting that goes up, the generally festival air. As for the officials, the appeal of Uxbridge to them is not so much one of financial benefit (though it is slightly that) as it is one of running what is entirely a Middlesex show. The truth is that at Lord's they often feel, sometimes keenly, second-class citizens. They see Middlesex as a team which has evolved chiefly to provide MCC members with some cricket to watch when nothing more impressive or more appreciated is on offer. There is some substance in this view.

When Middlesex were founded in 1864 they started playing in Islington, but by 1871 had moved to West Brompton. The pitch there was so awful that the team played only one match on it that year and the county side almost went out of existence. At an annual general meeting only thirteen members turned up to discuss whether London could support their team in addition to those of MCC and Surrey, the first well established for eighty-four years by then, the second twenty-six years old and going strong. It was decided by only one vote to carry on, and in 1872 Middlesex were to be found playing their home matches on the ground newly opened by Messrs G. and J. Prince between Knightsbridge and Chelsea. Before the move to Prince's, and again after, the county club turned down invitations from MCC to play regularly at Lord's, but after a rupture with George Prince an emergency general meeting of Middlesex members decided that their team should now go where it was obviously wanted. The move was made after the 1876 season, and the new association between MCC and Middlesex was soon hailed by the *Lillywhite* annual in the following terms:

"Cricket at Lord's benefited greatly by the appearance of the Middlesex Club, which had migrated from its former headquarters at Prince's, and the addition of a few county matches to the Marylebone programme will certainly strengthen it in a point where it has undeniably been weak of late years. For some time there it has been a complaint that there was not so much first-class cricket at Lord's as the revenue and position of the Club warranted, and beyond all doubt, with the exception of the two fashionable meetings of the season, there had been for some time to the outside world an air of monotony and apathy about the cricket at Lord's. The addition of the Middlesex fixtures fitted a decided blank in the Marylebone programme, and there was certainly more life in the appearance of matters at headquarters than in the previous year."

The two "fashionable meetings" referred to would be the Gentlemen v Players of England and Oxford v Cambridge fixtures, though there was no reason to exclude the Eton v Harrow game if numbers watching and elegant atmosphere were to be the criteria of the big occasion.* Test matches were still seven years away in the future for Lord's, both the Oval (several times) and Old Trafford (only just) seeing them first. The county championship had been formalised in 1873, and its nine competing teams of those early years – Derbyshire, Gloucestershire, Kent, Lancashire, Middlesex, Notts, Surrey, Sussex and Yorkshire – were almost wholly absorbed in each other, visiting Lord's in what amounted to their spare time if they continued to come at all. The majority of matches played in St John's Wood were between the Marylebone Club and sides which sometimes had an artificial appearance, as though someone had

* In 1870 some 30,000 people had watched the schoolboys in the course of two days, so many that for the first time no one was allowed into the ground on horseback. And though Eton v Harrow has lately been reduced from two days to one, it continues to be a notably – nay, exotically – well-dressed affair.

been scratching his head to think of a team that might give the metropolitan gentry a game. The opening fixture of 1874 had been "12 of MCC and Ground versus Professionals who had never played at Lord's". The reason why MCC had been lobbying Middlesex quite steadily for some years was very plain: this was England's senior club becoming stranded by events outside its control, and it badly wanted to secure part of whatever action was going.

It got plenty after Middlesex arrived. Though predominantly a team of amateurs, and remaining so until well into the 1930s, the county did pretty well for itself in the championship. It was not to take the title until 1903, but even after the championship expanded first to fourteen teams in 1895, and then gradually to the present seventeen by 1921, it was not often found in the lower half of the table. The amateurs may have provided headaches for the committee trying to pick a settled team, owing to their habit of frequently putting other interests before playing for Middlesex, but some of them performed tremendously well when they did turn out.

One was Andrew Stoddart, who conspicuously didn't play ducks and drakes with the committee. He personified the gifted amateur sportsman of his era, one of the few men to have played for his country at both cricket and Rugby (and one of only two – the other was A. N. Hornby – to have captained England at both) but wearing such honours lightly enough to turn down twice an invitation to bat for England because he preferred to play for Middlesex instead. Stoddart was one of the most punishing batsmen of cricket's Golden Age, though he seemed to save his major performances for matches away from Lord's, except for his last game for Middlesex in 1900, when he made 221 off the Somerset attack. He made 285 on one of his four Australian tours and for some years (until the prodigious Clifton schoolboy Collins overtook him) he was the world's highest scorer after hitting 485 for Hampstead CC in a by no means insignificant club match. He was also one of that tragically and unaccountably long line of cricketers who have taken their own lives, blowing his brains out at the age of fifty-two.

Then there was B. J. T. Bosanquet, who contrived a peculiar method of spinning a tennis ball in a table game which he and other Oxford undergraduates called "Twisti-Twosti". When he transferred this ability to the cricket field, the delivery became known as the googly (in Australia, the Bosie), first exhibited in a first-class match when he was playing for Middlesex against Leicestershire at Lord's in 1900. According to Bosanquet, "An unfortunate individual had made ninety-eight when he was clean bowled by a fine specimen which bounced four times." According to *Wisden*, the batsman Coe had indeed made ninety-eight, but he was stumped – and Bosanquet in that match made 136 in the first innings, 139 in the second, his googly having taken just that one wicket for forty-seven runs.

There was Pelham Warner, a consistently good batsman and an even more successful captain, who eventually led every team he played for apart from Oxford, and whose career ended like a fiction from an adolescent's magazine. When the 1920 season reached August, Middlesex hadn't a hope of the championship, but they then ran up such a sequence of victories that by the time they met Surrey in the final game at Lord's they were still in with a chance, though Lancashire were so confident of taking the title that they had broached the champagne; prematurely as it turned out. At Lord's the game swung like a pendulum from the start, in front of great crowds: 25,000 on the Saturday, another 20,000 coming through the gates on the Monday. Warner declared, leaving Surrey to get 244 in just over three hours, and they failed by fifty-six runs only forty minutes before the match would have ended in the draw that would have given Lancashire the championship. For that, in his last match for the county, Warner was carried from the field shoulder-high.

There was Ian Peebles, the Scot who played for England with his leg spin and his googlies, and the most literate of all first-class cricketers until another Middlesex player, Brearley, took to print. There was also G. O. Allen and there was F. T. Mann. And there was that relatively small band of professionals (only five of them in Warner's last match) which included two who shared the name of Hearne, though they were unrelated. J. T. Hearne's Middlesex career lasted from 1888 to 1923, and in that time his medium-pace bowling took over 3,000 wickets at an average of 17.75. J. W. Hearne, who played for the county from 1909 to 1936, was the all-rounder who did the double five times, yet another leg-spinner and purveyor of the googly as well as an elegant bat. Among the professionals, however, Patsy Hendren stood tallest until Denis Compton came along; metaphorically that is, because Elias Henry Hendren's was a sturdy figure, that of a butty little man whose backside stuck out sharply when he was crouching at the crease. A nervous starter going in at No. 4, he was almost always among the runs before long, and Jack Hobbs reckoned that, with "Young Jack" Hearne, he virtually carried the Middlesex batting for a decade between the wars. He ended up with a tally of centuries (170) which is still second only to that of Hobbs himself, and once returned from an MCC tour of West Indies with an average of 126.14. He hit 301 not out against Worcester at Dudley, but Lord's also often saw him at his best; as when he made 277 not out in 1922, "cutting, pulling and hooking the

Kent bowling in dazzling style". But Hendren is remembered warmly for reasons other than pure cricketing skill. He was a character, the Derek Randall of his day, who delighted spectators with his good nature and his knock-about turns. Like Randall, again, he was one of the few English cricketers that Australian crowds have actually relished and enjoyed, and one of Hendren's own stories suggests a reason why. On a tour Down Under he was driving through the bush and stopped to watch a country cricket match. Not knowing who he was, the locals asked him to fill a vacancy in one of the teams and this he did, spending several hours fielding in the deep, his boundary being so far down a slope that he couldn't actually see the wickets. Occasionally balls came his way and dutifully he threw them back. Then a catchable one arrived, he took it, and ran to the middle holding the ball up; only to discover that out of his sight one innings had long since closed and he'd just dismissed a batsman from his own team.*

Patsy's career just overlapped Compton's, though the latter's name is inseparable from that of the amateur W. J. Edrich. ("They go together in English cricket," wrote R. C. Robertson-Glasgow, "as Gilbert and Sullivan go together in English opera."). The euphoria of post-war cricket in England was never higher than when those two were batting together, either for Middlesex or for England, and the season of 1947 in particular still stands out like a beacon for those who were around then. It saw Compton scoring 3,816 runs, Edrich 3,539; and between them they scourged the visiting South Africans time after time, taking 2,000 runs off the tourists alone – 388 in the Middlesex match, the rest mostly in Tests. Robertson-Glasgow reckoned that the difference between the two was that Edrich had talents which he had nurtured into riches, while Compton had genius. He had something unique which has become legendary, at any rate. He was a national folk-hero of his time, as Ian Botham has become for a succeeding generation, and his face looked down from billboards all over the country in an advertisement for a hair cream which was supposed to be a by-word for neat grooming. Fielding at Old Trafford once on a windy day, he kept sweeping the hair out of his eyes before crouching afresh in the slips, until someone in the

---

*Patsy Hendren was, so far as we know, the very first cricketer to wear protective headgear. In 1931 he had been hit on the head by a short-pitched ball, and when the West Indians toured England two seasons later, quite a lot of bouncers began to fly. Hendren appeared against the tourists at Lord's wearing a special cap made by his wife. It had three peaks, two of them covering his ears and temples, lined with foam rubber; in appearance not at all unlike the thing Mike Brearley was to adopt forty-four years later.

crowd shouted, "Why don't yer use Brylcreem, Compton?" at which Compton, cricket's D'Artagnan, nearly fell over himself laughing.

He may have been the greatest improviser the game of cricket has seen, a batsman who might visibly change his mind four times between the ball being delivered and him hitting it, reviewing alternatives in a split second before selecting the one to use. Compton could be perfectly orthodox at times and he had all the classical strokes – but no one ever had the sweep shot more, and frequently he did not pick any stroke until the last possible moment, which meant that his body could be in the most ungainly contortions when he struck the ball, as he did much more often than not. He was certainly the most dreadful run-caller, whose reputation has not only survived but perversely been glorified by such a flaw; even the lamentable Boycott never ran so many people out. Denis Compton's celebrated crack was that "If Compton calls for a run, remember it is only a basis for discussion": someone else has remarked that innumerable batting partners were run out after hearing something like this from the other end – "Yes. . . No. . . Wait. . . Yes. . . Bugger it. . . Sorry!"*

That Middlesex side of 1947 was the last one to win the championship straight out – though it shared the title with Lancashire three seasons later – until Brearley led the first of his victorious teams. But even when not in the running for the major prize, Middlesex have always brought a wealth of cricket to Lord's, whose patrons cannot once have had any good reason to regret MCC's invitation in 1876. For all that it was deeply self-interested, it was a generous invitation, too. MCC for many years made no charge for Middlesex's use of Lord's, accepting any donation the county committee felt able to make from its fluctuating resources. Arrangements varied from time to time. Just after the Second World War, the county paid a rent of £1,100 a year and kept the gate money. Nowadays they pay no rent but tip up thirty-five per cent of the gate, and many of the overheads that all other county cricket clubs have to bear are removed from Middlesex's shoulders and carried by MCC. They have almost nothing to find but the wage bill for their players and an administrative staff of six.

There is, however, a price to be paid for such enormous advantages. A lot of it is unseen, and perhaps even more is unrecognised. What it amounts to in essence is that the relationship between MCC

---

* His record in this respect must have been the five men he managed to run out in one innings of his brother's benefit match, including Leslie Compton – while Denis himself was making a century.

and Middlesex is the very old-fashioned one of the squire and his tenant. This had a great deal to be said for it, especially when the squire was a civilised man, provided the tenant didn't prize above most things the freedom to look anyone straight in the eye, up to and including the squire, and tell him to go to hell if he felt like it. Few people associated with Middlesex, other than very senior committee men and old-style amateur captains (of whom Brearley was temperamentally one, notwithstanding history and his extremely professional approach in all things), have ever felt in a position to dare any such thing at Lord's.

It was, after all, not until 1949 that Middlesex in any way other than team selection ran their own affairs. MCC not only administered the county club until that year, but also paid the professional players on those double contracts that the Hendren brothers had known thirty-odd years before, though the hiring fair no longer took place at the main gates. The little wooden structure which has served Middlesex's administration, as well as providing a county shop of sorts, in its own dilapidated way exemplifies the relationship. Squatting insignificantly in the lee of the Pavilion, it was erected in 1933 as a refreshment hut, and practically every ground in the northern cricket leagues has one much like it, where tea and sandwiches and sausage rolls are served every Saturday afternoon. This one happens to be the centre of operations for the club which in the past few years has more than once won the English county championship, not to mention some one-day trophies. It is as though the management of Tottenham Hotspur were quartered in a garret somewhere down a side street off White Hart Lane.

The reason for Middlesex's contentment with this subordinate status at Lord's probably has much to do with the composition of its committees ever since the club moved up from South-west London. Within a generation or so, such men had become personally incorporated into the life of MCC, and presently the leading lights of Middlesex were also rising and then commanding figures in the Marylebone club. Sir Pelham Warner and Gubby Allen are the two most conspicuous examples of this trend, but others who didn't achieve their eminence also came to regard themselves as MCC luminaries first, Middlesex administrators second. The tradition has continued up to our own times. The county committee in 1981–2 contained two of MCC's trustees (G. O. Allen and G. C. Newman) and one other member of MCC's Committee in E. A. Clark. Middlesex's President was yet another MCC Committee member at the time, W. H. Webster. The county's chairman was that enigmatic figure George Mann, long-time MCC senior and chairman of

TCCB. Of the twenty-three men on the Middlesex committee, two or three others, apart from those already named, sat on various sub-committees of MCC, and only one or two were not MCC members, though it may be assumed that they were awaiting their turn to get in.

Admission to the Marylebone club, after all, produces certain privileges that the solely Middlesex member cannot enjoy at Lord's, quite apart from a vote in MCC elections. A Middlesex member may enter the Pavilion on those days when Middlesex are playing, but at no other time; so, for that matter, may any member of whichever county club is providing the opposition on those days. That is the rule of thumb. In practice, provided the Pavilion isn't packed with MCC members, Middlesex members are admitted at other times too. But even then, certain areas are out of bounds to anyone who is not a member of MCC – like the cosy bar which used to be the professionals' dressing-room, and the reading room, with its news-papers, its *Wisden*'s and its comfortably deep armchairs. It is quite likely that a large proportion of Middlesex's 9,000 members are people who have joined the county club in order to enjoy half a loaf until that day some years hence when they may be allowed to nourish themselves fully at Lord's. It is a fact that when kindly souls in MCC wonder whether one might like to be put up for membership, they suggest joining Middlesex meanwhile as an interim measure.

The deferences of Middlesex to MCC were all very well and could be managed without noticeable friction, until the moment came when county committees had to look to their finances more franti-cally even than in the early sixties. That moment coincided with the retirement in 1980 of Arthur Flower, after many years as Secretary of Middlesex, an old-timer whose notion of jazzing up cricket probably went no further than his suggestion once that on big match days at the Test grounds, the flags of all seventeen first-class counties should be flown from a series of poles, in a modest imitation of the Olympic Games. His first successor, Alan Burridge, was a minor counties cricketer; but, more to the point, he had not arrived through the traditional channel of cricket administration, starting as an office-boy or player with some county club. He had lately been managing the civic amenities and entertainments of Watford. He stayed for a year in the little wooden hut at Lord's, then left, to be followed by Alan Wright, who more clearly represents the rising caste of cricket administrators. He's never played more than club cricket in his life, and had spent the previous twenty-seven years working for British Airways, first in its accounting department, latterly in marketing management. His brief was to get more of Middlesex's head than the nostrils above water, at a time of escalating expectations if not demands by the players, falling attendances, and a nerve-racking dependence on sponsorship.

This was easier said than done, when the man is headquartered at Lord's of all places, and when the Middlesex committee is even more static than that of MCC. No one in the Middlesex hierarchy has to drop out for twelve months after a three-year stint in office; which means that Committee members are usually there without interruption for a very long time indeed, whether or not they are as attentive or as acute as Gubby Allen, who has now been there for over half a century. There is unavoidably a tension between what such men now recognise as necessary to maintain their club's commercial equilibrium, and what they would probably like to happen; which is to keep cricket and commerce as far apart as possible, as was the habit well within living memory. The tension is heightened by the relationship with MCC, where this schizophrenic attitude to tradition and contemporary needs exists in its most acute form.

Such profits as Middlesex have made in recent seasons – and they have usually been at the lower end of the county scale, in spite of MCC's underwriting of so many costs – have generally been managed by running lotteries, a method of raising money which has been the salvation of other clubs. This is no longer as profitable as it was a few seasons ago, when a club might have expected to make £100,000 in this way, Government legislation having since tightened the rules under which lotteries are held, so that a county will now be glad to collect £20–£30,000 in a year. It has, nonetheless, sometimes meant the difference between going into and staying out of the red. The trouble with a lottery, however, is that it must catch the eye in order to achieve any success at all; and MCC's tolerance of what shall be eye-catching at Lord's is much more limited than a born entrepreneur would wish. Middlesex wanted to set up five lottery stations around the ground but were told that they could have only two, and neither of these was permitted in the prime positions which had been sought, right opposite the Grace Gates and the gates at the Nursery End, where they would have confronted everyone coming into Lord's on all but big match days.

The county has also been hampered in some of its relations with commercial sponsors. Like every other club on the English first-class circuit, it has attempted to fix its own deals with local commerce, to supplement whatever it may gratefully receive from national operators through arrangements made with the Test and County Cricket Board. Among other examples there is the one by which the North London car sales firm of Lex Brooklands has offered potential customers free life membership of Middlesex CCC if they will only buy a Volvo. The inducement has been offered in leaflets circularised with Middlesex's mailing list, and what the county club gets out of it is the prospect of £350 every time a car is sold. Another arrangement was made with the clothing firm of Austin Reed, but this one ran into trouble at Lord's. The clothiers had offered several emoluments to Middlesex players for performances on the field and appearances off it, and at the same time contributed a straight £5,000 to the club's exchequer in 1981. In return for this they wanted publicity for their products at Lord's, and they had in mind an exhibition stand, as well as half a dozen girls perambulating round the ground on match days with promotional material. Someone in authority drew the line at this, arguing that people coming to watch a cricket match don't want to be canvassed on the internal roadways of Lord's as though it were Oxford Street. And so, in 1982, unable to deliver the expected goods, Middlesex were deprived of the rag trade's offering from its advertising budget.

A man whose instincts are chiefly commercial, whether inside or outside cricket administration, is bound to be perplexed by MCC's view of such things. He has been trained like Pavlov's dogs to react sharply to the slightest likelihood of making a sale, whatever the commodity might be, and at Lord's he finds the supreme authority deeply uninterested in such an unqualified philosophy, picking and choosing very carefully what it wishes to sell and the methods that may tastefully be used. Alan Wright confesses his bewilderment at times, particularly when MCC now needs to make money itself as never before, with that £1 million for maintenance to be found over the next few years. He cannot understand why MCC do not encourage him to sell Middlesex for all it's worth, in return for ten per cent or even twenty per cent of what this might bring in, which he'd happily offer. This is the reaction of someone not only with the marketing instinct, but without the divided loyalty that seems to exist in so many corners of Lord's. He is not a member of MCC, not even on that long waiting list, and sees his responsibilities as ones to the Middlesex club alone. His chief worry is that of paying the bills, of which the £120,000 for players' wages was by far the biggest in 1981. After that his anxiety is getting the maximum benefit for and out of the club's 9,000 members. He is encouraged by the fact that membership has almost doubled in the past ten years, and was well content that at his first annual general meeting some 400 turned up. He gives the impression of a man who wishes to milk them of everything that they can yield to the club, while at the same time leaving them as agreeably disposed to the experience as a well-tended cow. He has, he says, no wish at all to turn Lord's into Caesar's Palace, though he suspects that some people in MCC think he might.

But in October 1982 he made some headway in crossing the gap between his own view of cricket's strategy for survival, and the usual qualifications made by MCC. A wine and cheese party was thrown for the various Middlesex sponsors and their friends, and as many of the players as could be dragooned into the evening were also there as a bait. Additional attractions as guest speakers were Bill Edrich and Denis Compton; the first a Middlesex committee man for many years, the second rather oddly not. Yet the most magnetic draw for the outsiders was possibly the setting of the party, the Long Room at Lord's ("The Long Room", said the invitation, "will be available by kind permission of the MCC"). It may have been the first time, except at rare formal dinners of the Marylebone club, that food and drink had been permitted in that splendid and historic chamber: they certainly aren't under normal circumstances. It was a notable change in contact between Middlesex and MCC, in place of a sometimes curious distance separating the two.

While the Middlesex players are exercising themselves with spring training, and while the ground staff are fettling the first wickets of the season, there is particularly feverish activity elsewhere at Lord's. In a den beneath the Pavilion, especially prone to flash flooding in a London monsoon, the MCC club office is grappling with its busiest time in twelve months. The title of this place does less than justice to its varied activities. When the season has begun and the public have arrived, it serves as a collection point for lost property, though nothing very remarkable ever seems to have been mislaid at Lord's. The end of the year will have seen no more than the usual jumble of handbags, glasses, pipes, brollies and the like handed in (and once, insensitively, someone attending a Gillette Cup match left an electric razor behind).

The most protracted labours here are caused by the MCC members, actual and in-waiting. This is where all their records are kept up to date, and whence the club's circulars to them are despatched. Every December they are sent a form inviting them to apply for special tickets for the big games ahead. Every April they are sent a copy of the annual report before the upcoming general meeting, and with it that precious little red ticket-book which alone will get them into the ground and the Pavilion without more ado. Special general meetings, of which MCC has had more than it might wish in the past few years, mean a repeat performance each time with the mailing list. Spring would be busy enough if only MCC members were attended to. It becomes positively hectic for a few weeks because on March 1 the postal applications from members of the general public wanting to be at the Lord's Test and the Cup Finals are also put on to the office's production line. They may have been arriving for some considerable time beforehand, but after being filed on the basis of first come first served, they are not opened until the beginning of March; after, that is, the requirements of MCC members have been fully met.

The equation, as usual, is not a simple one. There are 18,000 members of MCC and every one of them is entitled to watch any cricket match taking place at Lord's, and to do so free of charge. Of course they aren't all going to turn up at any one time, but even 2,000 of them would be many more than the Pavilion can comfortably contain. They therefore have reserved enclosures elsewhere, in the Warner, Tavern and Q Stands; and in these places they can also bring their guests on special Rover passes (for which the member pays a small surcharge on top of the guest's ground admission fee). If, whimsically, they prefer to sit with the hoi polloi in the public stands on the Mound and at the Nursery End – and some of them do – they may obtain seats there, too, but only up to a limit of four for themselves and their guests.

The special boxes are almost – but very importantly, not quite – the exclusive preserve of individual MCC members, too. There are seventeen of them in the Grandstand, twenty in the Tavern Stand, and one reason for the Tavern redevelopment of the sixties ending up in the shape that it did was to include so many boxes and to raise revenue from them; they brought in £64,500 in 1981. It is reckoned that each box can hold a dozen people in comfort and three are earmarked for official entertainments at every big match at Lord's. The Secretary of MCC holds court in a box in the Grandstand, the President of MCC and the Chairman of TCCB playing host in their boxes on the Tavern side. Four more boxes are open to ballot within the MCC Committee; the remaining thirty are theoretically open to any MCC member, but the cost trims the field somewhat and usually there is a ballot for them among 600 or so applicants. Perhaps a quarter of the boxes are let for stretches of two or three days at a time; for the rest you take all five days or nothing. In 1982 this cost an individual £650 on top of ground admission tickets for his guests and whatever catering he wished to have laid on. If a company took a box that year, the basic charge for the five days was £1,300. Some companies, apart from the major sponsors of cricket, take boxes regularly, and the names of Esso and ICI are frequently among them. This will mystify those curious people who make a point of studying the lists of who is occupying which box, when these are tacked up, as they are on big match days, behind the relevant stands. Never does a company name appear on any of the lists. For some reason connected with the preservation of the Lord's mystique, it is preferred that the box be labelled with the name of an individual; and so the company hiring it has to track down an MCC member on its staff, both to act as the nominal intermediary and to turn up on the day, though fortunately for him not to foot the final bill.

When all these matters have been arranged, and when all the first-class counties have been invited to submit applications for seats for their members, at the same time as the MCC list is compiled, the club office can turn its attention to those postal applications from the general public. It starts from the assumption, generally proved each year to be close to the mark, that some 3,500 MCC members will have wanted seats for themselves beyond the Pavilion, and another 6,500 for their guests on all four bookable days of a Test match. This leaves approximately 17,000 places at Lord's for the public at large, five or six thousand of which are not bookable in advance, but obtained by simply turning up on the day and paying at the gate. There may also be anything up to another five thousand sitting on the turf between the fences and the boundary ropes, if the grass is dry, and Lord's is the only cricket ground in the world that habitually accommodates spectators like this: in doing so, MCC quite deliberately denies itself a useful revenue, because no advertiser is going to pay for hoardings along fences that might be obscured by crowds of squatting people. In the stands, a few hundred seats are consigned to the big match sponsors, as some return for what they have put into the game, not always with the happiest results for the unsponsored cricket watcher who pays his own way all the time and expects to see every ball bowled in exchange.

During the Second Test with West Indies in 1980 it became obvious to people sitting in L block in the Mound Stand that half a dozen full rows in front of them were occupied by what appeared to be every Cornhill insurance agent in the home counties, each accompanied by a brace or two of clients. It was also evident that most of them had either never been to a cricket match before, were indifferent to its unwritten codes of spectating, pathologically thirsty, in serious trouble with their bladders, or suffering from St Vitus' Dance. Scarcely an over passed without at least half a row arising and shuffling out cumbersomely to the aisles, where a corresponding file would be poised to re-insert itself in the same

manner, the total effect being that the people behind were catching
sight of about one and a half balls out of every six bowled. The usual
cries of "Siddown!" produced no effect whatsoever on these manoeuvres. Nor did lengthier exhortations and implicit threats. Yet by
mid-afternoon the traffic had almost come to a standstill and there
was a noticeable degree of absenteeism among those insurance men
and their acquaintances, because at last someone behind had hit
upon the antidote. From lunch-time onwards, the slightest impulse
to get up and block the view again had been greeted shrilly, in
well-practised imitation of the original, with falsetto cries of "Wal-
kies!"

The careful art of cricket-watching is nowhere more apparent than
in the MCC club office when those postal applications come in from
the general public. Many simply ask for something like three tickets
somewhere in the middle of the Mound Stand, as near the front as
possible, please, without leaving the shelter of the roof. Just as many
ask for precise seat numbers in any one of several areas around
Lord's. There are those who prefer to sit in the Grandstand or just in
front of it, where they'll have the sun on their faces until the last hour
at least. There are people who specify a position high up in H or G
Stand at the Nursery End, as close to the sight-screen as possible,
where they can watch the ball's movement through the air and off the
pitch as well as any MCC member sitting opposite them in the lower
of the two Pavilion balconies. There are those who like to be in N
block on the Mound, where they can have a reserved seat yet at the
same time be within earshot of whatever the roisterers standing in
front of the Tavern bar may be coming up with that day. Obligingly,
the club office attempts to give everyone what he wants, putting
those who are down the queue of applications as near as possible to
where they wish to be.

It is also apparent at this stage approximately how successful a
season is going to be in financial terms, a matter which now more
than ever before depends upon which overseas team is touring
England that year. The Australians have always drawn the biggest
crowds, for cricketing reasons as well as those of historical emotion.
And since the West Indies became such a powerful force, growing
perceptibly with almost every tour after the one led by John Goddard
in 1950, they have vied with the Aussies in terms of crowd appeal.
Either of those two sides in prospect can be sure of attracting twice
the numbers of advance Test match bookings that a season of
England against New Zealand, India or Pakistan will produce. This
pattern suggests all sorts of things about the response of cricket
crowds, not all of them clear, even fewer perhaps understandable. Is

it the sheer blood-and-thunder of almost unrelieved fast bowling of the most spectacular kind that attracts? Is it the greater likelihood of a tight game, with matters in the balance up to the last session of play? Is it something to do with the comportment of the players, some distinction between famous (and occasionally infamous) Superstars and those who have not been exalted so much by the apparatus of publicity? Or do people simply assume that they will see greater technical skills from the Australians and the West Indians than from players representing the other Test countries?

Whatever the reasons for the comparative lack of enthusiasm on the one hand, the abundance of it on the other, it does not suggest an altogether judicious approach. Pakistan, after all, has demonstrated its ability in recent years to field a side as thrilling as anyone's. New Zealand is no longer everybody else's chopping block (and one day, Sri Lanka won't be, either). For sheer pleasure at an international level, for matches full of skill, full of subtlety as well as fire and brimstone, full above all of a feeling which the players communicate to each other and thence to the crowds that this is, after all, only a game and not outright warfare, there is nothing at all these days to match the visit of an Indian team. Yet the figures speak for themselves. When Gavaskar's 1979 Indians were in the offing, and he himself was destined to play one of the most memorable innings of all time in that cliff-hanger at the Oval, some 25,800 seats had been booked in advance of the five-day Test at Lord's. When Kim Hughes's 1981 Australians were due, 52,300 bookings had been made for the same fixture.

There is a strangely similar difference in the public response to the two domestic knock-out competitions. Both invariably play their final matches to capacity crowds at Lord's, so there's nothing for either the authorities or the sponsors to fret about in this case. But the totally knock-out competition which Gillette sponsored, until the National Westminster Bank took over in 1981, produces such a sense of anticipation that the final is a sell-out long before the event, very often by the end of March, within a month of bookings opening. Tickets for the Benson & Hedges Cup Final, on the other hand, although offered for sale simultaneously, never begin to shift in quantity until after the semi-finals have been played early in June, less than three weeks before the final. Can this be because the first competition is based on the principle of "sudden death" from the start, like soccer's F.A. Cup Final, whereas the Benson & Hedges goes through a series of preliminary group matches before the quarter-finals are played? Or is it because one competition finishes half-way through the season, with many rival attractions still on the fixture list, whereas the other Cup Final doesn't happen until September, and can be seen as a climax to the season itself?

All such tickets increasingly command a market value somewhat higher than the nominal price, and both are rising fast in these inflationary times. St John's Wood Road on a Cup Final day, or on the Friday or Saturday of an Australian or West Indian Test in particular, sees as many ticket touts offering a means of access as there are newspaper sellers, or people purveying overpriced substitutes for the official scorecard. On such occasions a ticket for the Grandstand, the Mound or the Nursery End can change hands for two or three times its nominal value. But those who wish to shorten the time it takes to get into Lord's without a reserved seat, or who want to be sure of a place somewhere other than on the grass, ought to beware of those offering the quick solution.

Like Wembley, like Twickenham, like Wimbledon, Lord's has seen its forgeries in recent years. The last of the Gillette Finals in 1980 produced a particularly heavy batch, though they were so implausible that only a handful got past the gatekeepers before the alarm went up, and it is surprising that anybody was fooled enough to buy. Ticket forgery for all the big sporting events around London, however, has become a considerable business for someone with sophisticated printing techniques at his disposal, which is why the club office in 1982 resorted to counter-attack. Since then, all the authentic tickets officially issued for games at Lord's have been printed to a formula devised by the De la Rue company which makes the paper money for the Bank of England. What may look like inferior material, similar to paper manufactured during wartime from recycled rags, is nothing less than high-quality stuff sprinkled with tiny chips of plastic. Tear the ticket, as the gatekeepers always do, and the chips are clearly exposed. If they don't protrude along the ragged edge, then the thing's a dud. This ought to be a fool-proof method of stopping ticket forgery at last. Anyone who's clever enough to imitate the process might just as well aim for even bigger profit by printing fake £20 notes.

CHAPTER SIX

The New Patronage

The first-class cricket season usually begins in the second half of April, with undergraduate mortifications shared by those counties prepared to hazard their players in the bitter cold of Cambridge or the perishing damp of Oxford. The metropolis wisely delays taking the plunge a little longer, for London's weather in spring is no more likely to be spring-like than that of East Anglia or the upper reaches of the Thames. A few seasons ago a start was invariably made here, too, in April, but now it seems to have settled on May 1 or the nearest convenient day. And there is a feeling throughout the land that, whatever the students and their gallant opponents have been up to, cricket has not really got under way until that opening fixture at Lord's. The newspapers invariably send a deputation of photographers to picture a few score of spectators muffled like Eskimos, which is thought to be worth a laugh in the early editions.

Within living memory, the opening game has always consisted of a team representing the Marylebone club against one of the counties. For a little while after the Second World War the choice of opponents was haphazard, but for almost two decades Yorkshire supplied the opposition year after year, though sometimes only for a two-day match. Then Glamorgan appeared in 1970, after lifting the championship in 1969, and since that time opening day at Lord's has seen an MCC team taking the field against whoever won the title the previous season. This, however, is not one of the regular Marylebone club sides, such as play well over 200 matches a year. Though chosen by the club and wearing its colours, though the MCC flag flies above No. 1 dressing-room, the appropriate county flag over No. 5, the team is selected with a careful eye on England's requirements over the next few months. It invariably includes two or three established Test players, half a dozen men who are in the running, and a couple of young and promising county cricketers who may yet make the higher grade.

If the fixture didn't so consistently suffer from the weather, it would be an extremely useful occasion for the England selectors, as well as an entertaining one for everybody on the ground. It is, however, enough for the enthusiasts who turn up in small quantities, and generally spend as much time relishing the dear old place again as watching any play, that cricket has at last, if not in due season, returned once more to Lord's. They can be relieved that Conrad Ritblat's business has wintered well enough to maintain his advertisement on the Grandstand balcony. They can pick up their new *Wisden* at the Lord's shop and rummage for new lines in cricketing merchandise that have appeared since last season, an increasingly indiscriminate array of prints and posters, books and placements, neckties and headscarves, ashtrays and keyrings, pot towels and pencils, and all the other bric-a-brac of the souvenir trade. They can relish that tingling moment when the Pavilion bell is struck for the first time in months to announce the appearance of players in five minutes' time.

They can usually count on an hour or two's interruption for bad light or rain, which is best spent in the warmth and nourishment of the museum at Lord's. There may be only one comparable place in the whole world, the splendid museum attached to baseball's Hall of Fame at Cooperstown in New York state, though Lord's is much better served by not having something as monotonous and ridiculously obsequious as the Hall of Fame itself. At Lord's there is simply, but comprehensively, this marvellous collection of illustrations and bygones belonging to an international game (and nuts to the pretensions of a World Series restricted to teams between Los Angeles and Montreal). Here are photographs, masses of them, where you can find any hero you ever had since the day the camera was invented. Here are some of the paintings which are not hung in the Pavilion, including what may be artistically the most important in MCC's collection, Sablet's oil of Mr Hope of Amsterdam, taking guard in front of three diminutive stumps. Here also are paintings with no claims to artistic greatness, which nonetheless make a curiously moving record of cricket grounds all over the world – from Auckland to Lahore, from Cape Town to Kingston, and back. Here are more famous bats, and Don Bradman's size six boots, and the cricketing clothes worn by both sexes in the nineteenth century. Here is a collection of cricket club ties, again from all over the world, a display the like of which neither Savile Row nor Bond Street can imitate. And here, of course, are the two most famous curios known to the game. One is the ball slung down by Jehangir Khan in the MCC v Cambridge match of 1936, which killed a sparrow in transit to T. N. Pearce, the scuffed red leather ceremonially mounted with the poor bird itself perched on top. The other is the urn belonging to the Ashes, over which England and Australia have tussled for over a century. There has lately been a tarradiddle about whether the urn and its contents were presented to Ivo Bligh after the Sydney Test match in January 1883, or a few weeks earlier "about Christmas time" (and, oh dear, there has even been a claim that a housemaid subsequently knocked the blessed thing over on Bligh's mantelpiece, decided to clean it out, and thus lost forever the original ash inside). No matter; there the urn is for us to see. A surprisingly small thing it is, too, when seen for the first time; no bigger than a large brown egg-cup. But representing no small thing at all in the history of two countries and their most nostalgic of games.

The acolytes at Opening Day will also collect their first scorecards of the season, which Vince Miller and his two accomplices produce in the print shop under the Grandstand scoreboard. They also produce much else that MCC requires, up to annual reports that can run to twenty-odd pages or more. This wouldn't be worth remarking were it not for the fact that everything coming out of the print shop has been entirely hand set. Inside, the place resembles any small jobbing printer's shop, with its high tilted working benches, its metal formes, its mallets, its inky smell; and with its long trays of type – Times and Granby, Clearface and Marina Script, Winchester Condensed, Wide Latin and Great Primer Abbey. But there isn't even an old-fashioned linotype machine in there; just an even older-fashioned flatbed on which all is impressed after those men in long dun coats have selected every character of type with their fingers, lined it up and inserted each line into the forme. Caxton would recognise those three instantly, from their ways of working.

The scorecards provide most of this exercise in craftsmanship; neat and beautifully printed things deliberately shaped oblong ages ago so as to fit, with only one crease down the middle, into a jacket pocket. Other cricket grounds used to produce them in the same style, but now the Lord's cards stand out uniquely from what has become a mess of poor printing and overpowering advertisement, more often than not the outcome of a Roneo machine in careless hands. They are, justifiably, regarded as collector's items by many. The print shop prides itself on producing the completed scorecard of every match played at Lord's within twenty minutes of stumps being drawn on the final day. After a county game they will expect to sell a hundred or so of these; after a Test between four and five hundred. And never does a match begin without a blank scorecard available before the players appear (other grounds again please note). Three times in a normal day's play is the card updated and reprinted, the necessary information descending into the print shop from the scorebox down a pneumatic tube, as in a long-established department store. The printers will expect to have made at least 18,000 cards by the end of a Cup Final, 42,000 during an Australian Test, only a few score for some county games in bad weather. Every one is craftsman's work, not botched.

Spectators at Lord's do well to cherish the tradition involved in this supporting act, as well as that embodied in an opening fixture with an MCC team. There isn't, if they come to think of it, too much tradition left intact in the game they hold so dear partly because of its long and appealing past. What we have been sitting through in the last couple of decades is nothing less than the nearest thing to a revolution the game has known, one that is not by any means over and done with yet. This is not to say that great changes were not wrought periodically from the start of cricket: they were, and sometimes they were of greater magnitude than the deepest traditionalists, who may often be detected having fantasies about the past, often care to admit even when the evidence is put before them. But never have so many things changed almost simultaneously in such a relatively short time. It is difficult to think of anything, including the Laws of cricket themselves, which is exactly as it was when cricket started up again after the Second World War. The same thing could not have been said, looking back to World War One, in 1946. The Laws have probably moved less dramatically than anything, but even they have been altered or amended on no fewer than five occasions between 1947 and the complete revision of 1980, to take account of changes that had happened or were happening throughout the cricket-playing world.

By far the most drastic difference between pre-war cricket in England and that of today – and many other differences spring from or are linked with it – is in the business of finding the money to keep the first-class game going. At once we must beware of fantasy about what used to be. There probably never was a time when county cricket achieved solvency simply because enough people paid enough money to go and watch it. It was born in an age of great and wealthy gamblers, and of patronage by the rich which took various forms; the provision of grounds and the expenses incurred in maintaining them, as well as something for the kitty besides. That age duly passed, but first-class cricket retained one advantage until some time after the First World War. It had a high content of amateur players and proportionately smaller wage bills than those of today. Even so, the county clubs would never have paid their way unless the wealthy had regularly dipped into their pockets to supplement membership subscriptions and what was taken at the gate. It has been estimated that in 1937 (when the pound, as they tell us, was worth a pound) English county cricket was being run at a loss of almost £30,000 a year; it was bailed out of its difficulties by cash gifts from its patrons. The county secretaries became accustomed to a financial cycle which revolved around the visits of Australian touring teams. These were always certain to attract huge crowds to every county ground in turn, but unfortunately they took place only once every four years. Unless the weather had been atrocious for its match with the touring side, each county could expect to balance its books with a bit to spare in a year when the Aussies had been here. The three intervening seasons before the next tour by the men in the floppy green caps were a different matter. It was then that county secretaries thanked providence and the English caste system for endowing them with a Duke or an Earl as county president.

Derbyshire's secretary at that time, Will Taylor, knew that he could rely on a phone call from the Duke of Devonshire towards the end of October, by which time he would have done his annual sums.

"Now then, Taylor," the voice on the line from Chatsworth would say, "what's the damage this time?"

"Well, my Lord Duke, I think £185 4s 3d would do it this year."

Brisk response from the other end. "Cheque in post tomorrow. Good day to ye." Similar conversations took place all over England each Michaelmas in those days.

In short, county cricket has always needed, and generally enjoyed, its substantial patrons. But there was an interregnum for some years after the Second World War, when the old order was dispersing in the wake of the upheaval and its social aftermath, and when the new order had not yet turned up. At the same time the need for patronage was increasingly apparent in the starkest terms. Cricket had prospered briefly in the elation following 1945, and by 1950 almost two million people a season were paying to watch the first-class game. Then attendances began to slide. By 1963 they were down to 700,000; by 1965 they had dropped to half a million; in 1982 they totalled 782,809, having numbered 1,046,269 during the Australian tour of the previous summer. County memberships declined, too: 141,707 in 1964, 135,045 two years later, by 1974 they were under 100,000. In 1982 the figure was 112,524, but that included the MCC membership as this head-counting always has. The individual county membership figures for 1982 went like this: Derbyshire 2,900, Essex 7,102, Glamorgan 4,556, Gloucestershire 2,767, Hampshire 4,941, Kent 5,120, Lancashire 11,458, Leicestershire 4,000, Middlesex 9,312, Northamptonshire, 2,095, Nottinghamshire 3,554, Somerset 6,500, Surrey 6,264, Sussex 4,621, Warwickshire 5,084,

Worcestershire 2,747, Yorkshire 11,250, MCC 18,253. Various reasons were advanced for this state of affairs other than an end of post-war euphoria, which was never a good enough reason anyway, because the sixties in Britain were a boom period in almost every other walk of life, when a Prime Minister told us that we had never had it so good. An anxious MCC, still the supreme authority in cricket, appointed one committee after another to fathom the causes of decline, and though their recommendations differed in detail, their conclusions were much the same: that the structure of the game needed overhaul at playing and administrative levels, that the attitude of cricketers themselves towards providing entertainment was often to blame.

Most counties survived this interregnum by running football pools. Leicestershire began the habit in 1951, and within twelve months had been followed by Worcestershire and Glamorgan. Then Warwickshire took it up, and in doing so began an astonishing exercise in self-help which has continued to this day. The Warwickshire Supporters' Association was formed and within three years had 50,000 members, which by 1973 had grown to 300,000. At the beginning, each coughed up 1s (5p) a week, of which 10d was the pool stake, 2d a donation to whatever purpose the association had in mind. Twenty years after its inception in 1953, the association had raised the staggering sum of £2 millions from those 2d bits and their inflated and decimalised equivalent, and it was actually dishing out money to parts of cricket quite unconnected with the county club. It handed over £70,000 to Worcestershire, who had shown it how to organise its football pool. It lent Essex the cash necessary to buy that county's headquarters at Chelmsford outright from landlords. It placed monies at the disposal of MCC, the Cricket Council and TCCB. On its own doorstep it raised £750,000 for the redevelopment of Edgbaston, and an early reward was the restoration of Test cricket to Birmingham in 1957 after a gap of twenty-eight years. All the impressive amenities there – from the Executive Suite and catering facilities which are hired out by the club at a profit throughout the year, to the so far unique method of covering the pitch rapidly by means of a gigantic roller stretching across the playing area – have been the handiwork of the Warwickshire Supporters' Association. The great mystery is why so very few of these midlands subscribers ever turn up to see a county cricket match when they have offered the local club so much goodwill and practical help. And it is ironic that cricket had to accept salvation from football pools, in default of anything comparable associated with the summer game. Vernons and Littlewoods briefly used the John Player League Sunday games for a section of their summer pools, but then abandoned them. Zetters, too, have dabbled briefly in cricket, but punters generally seem more attracted by Australian football until the great British kick-off in August.

Football pools in time were displaced by other forms of lottery while cricket groped for a solution to its mounting problems from within its own resources. A special MCC committee set up in 1956 under the chairmanship of H. S. Altham to look into "The Future Welfare of First-Class Cricket", had recommended that a knock-out competition to "stimulate the public's general interest in cricket" should be held, but only as a two-day proposition, with four innings limited to fifty-four overs apiece. The idea of one-day cricket worried the counties also, as too much of a risk with what was beginning to look like a fickle public; and most counties remained strongly opposed to the idea of Sunday cricket for some time after MCC had decided to explore the uncertainties of the Lord's Day Observance Act. Yet by 1963 the first of cricket's substantial new patrons had appeared on the scene to launch a one-day county tournament. By offering £6,500 to underwrite any financial risks the counties might be taking with increased overheads, the Gillette company led English cricket into, if not exactly a new dawn, at least the prospect of extended daylight.

The very first match in the Gillette competition – Lancashire v Leicestershire at Old Trafford – took place before only a small crowd. But the competition thereafter so captured the public imagination that four months later, in the final at Lord's, 25,000 people turned up on a miserable day to watch Sussex beat Worcestershire thrillingly by fourteen runs. Not for a long time had cricket known such a gate except at a Test. Every year after that, the Cup Final took place before capacity crowds, and gates also swelled satisfyingly at the county grounds during earlier rounds. Gradually the domestic finances began to lose the pallor of approaching mortality, and were made even healthier six years after the Gillette enterprise had begun. Hampshire's suggestion of a Sunday league became reality when Jack Bailey – at the time the MCC Assistant Secretary responsible for the promotion of all cricket – persuaded John Player & Sons to sponsor this formula to the tune of £75,000. Again the crowds began to turn up in wholesome numbers, and it soon became clear that one-day cricket in both knock-out and league form had come to stay. So successful was the formula that by 1972 two more competitions had been founded. Benson & Hedges that year began their own variant of the knock-out system, putting up £65,000 to the TCCB and another £15,000 in team and individual incentives, and promis-

ing to do so for at least two years. In the same season, the Prudential
Assurance Company offered £4,000 in prize money and £26,000 to
the TCCB, together with a trophy for which England would compete
in three one-day matches with the visiting Australian tourists. A
total of 55,000 watched those international games, and £46,000 was
taken at the gates.

By this time, the Editor of *Wisden*, whose annual Notes had been
suffused in gloom for what was beginning to seem like donkey's
years, had become buoyant once more. He had introduced his 1972
Almanack confident that "given the right direction, cricket will
prosper at all levels. That is how I feel while looking back on 1971
and into the future". Twelve months later, he was able to assure his
readers: "From most points of view the English season of 1972 was
the best for some time. The presence of the Australians coupled with
generous endowment from sponsorship brought beaming smiles
from the county treasurers. In other words, county cricket is back on
its feet again financially." This seemed no less than the truth. Some
£600,000 had come into cricket one way and another that year, and
every county had collected £25,000 as its share of the TCCB kitty, in
addition to what it picked up at its own gate and what it might have
won in prize money. By 1979 TCCB's income from all sources had
risen to £1,400,000 and each county was receiving £55,000 at least,
the Test grounds something between £73,000 and £78,000. TCCB,
by then, had so adapted itself to the market place and the values
there, that it was bargaining toughly with sponsors. It was this
approach that caused the Gillette company to relinquish its hold on
the first of the one-day competitions. The moment came for negotiating the contract, and Gillette felt they couldn't increase their previous outlay by more than thirty per cent. TCCB wanted it doubled
to £250,000; and so Gillette stepped down after the 1980 Cup Final,
and saw the competition taken over by the National Westminster –
who happened to be Gillette's own bankers.

TCCB was able to adopt this approach and get away with it
because towards the end of the 1970s it was well aware that
commerce was looking hard for things to sponsor in sport. At various
levels of the game, cricket had already attracted, or would shortly
attract, a swathe of sponsors other than those already named. They
included Schweppes, Cornhill Insurance, United Friendly Assurance, Commercial Union Assurance, Gordon's Gin, John Haig
whisky, Whitbread's beer, Younger's beer, Wrigley's Spearmint,
British Reserve Insurance, Bonusplan Ltd, Holt Lloyd Ltd and
Waverite Ltd, all operating on a national basis, with dozens of other
firms allying themselves with individual counties in the first-class

competitions. The attraction of the sponsors was, of course, chiefly the advertising of their names on cricket grounds and, even more, the transmission of those names through the press, radio and, above all, television. The value to a major cricket sponsor of this last form of exposure was clearly demonstrated by a table published in 1982, logging the hours on TV enjoyed by twenty different forms of sponsorship throughout British sport in the previous year. Five of the top seven places were occupied by cricket sponsors (the other two both backed snooker). Benson & Hedges cricket had been screened for 20 hours 5 minutes, Prudential cricket for 24 hours 25 minutes, NatWest cricket for 26 hours 25 minutes, John Player cricket for 33 hours 47 minutes. Top of the entire table was Cornhill cricket, which had been shown for a total of 166 hours 28 minutes.

The introduction of Cornhill to cricket, and its consequences for the company, has become one of the great talking points of the insurance and advertising worlds since it happened in 1977. Here was a name relatively unknown outside its own trade, where it had concentrated on non-life insurance and had advertised itself only to brokers through the trade press. This was a firm of unimpeachable rectitude operating from a highly respectable address in the City of London, but it was only eleventh in size of business even in its own restricted field; and its advertising agents reckoned that only two per cent of the population had ever heard of it. In the winter of 1976–7 they advised Cornhill to project themselves and their respectability in some national way, partly because a lot of companies dealing in car insurance (which forms some of Cornhill's own business) had lately gone bust and the general public was becoming leery of names it didn't know well. The following summer, by a fluke, opportunity sat down heavily on Cornhill's lap.

It was the summer which began with the bombshell news of Kerry Packer's venture and ended with the cricket authorities preparing themselves for the High Court hearing which was a financial disaster to them. In the turmoil of those months a wealthy office cleaning contractor called David Evans announced a plan to "send Packer Packing", in which he would buy back the contracts of five English cricketers who had been signed by Packer, sponsor every English Test player for £1,000 per match, and pay a retainer of £1,000 a year to fifty players who would guarantee to be available for England alone. Well, no; it wasn't quite an offer of immense open-handedness. It was conditional on Evans's company obtaining at least £3 millions' worth of business over the next three years, the profits going to TCCB. Nothing, in the end, came of it.

Cornhill, who knew nothing about the mechanics of sports

sponsorship at this stage, approached Evans – whose offices are not far from Cornhill's in the City – simply to pick his brains about the sort of money they might have to provide if they decided to dabble in cricket in order to get their name more widely known. It had occurred to them that cricket, being an up-market sport, might be good for the image of a modest City institution like theirs. Evans mentioned £200,000 and said he could arrange a meeting with someone from TCCB if Cornhill were interested. They decided that they were, and Evans's contact was produced. He was Doug Insole, Chairman of TCCB at the time. In the negotiations which followed, he was joined by Bernie Coleman, the TCCB man from Surrey, and Peter Lush, the board's Public Relations and Marketing Manager. Evans's forecast proved to be precisely correct. Within a week or two, Cornhill had agreed in principle to sponsor English Test matches to the tune of £1 million spread across the next five years. It was the first seven-figure deal cricket had landed, and it put Cornhill into a new league in every sense. Their expenditure on advertising until then had never risen above £25,000 a year.

They quickly had a generous slice of luck which was very sharply exploited. On August 25 the Fifth Test with Greg Chappell's Australians started at the Oval, and two days later the Saturday was ruined by rain. Not long after viewers throughout the country had been introduced to the sight of a sodden ground, the television front man Peter West, in default of play that could be described, was able to announce the dazzling sum of money cricket had been promised, and where it was coming from. There were discussions with various personalities about the significance of this latest sponsorship, and each time the BBC returned to the Oval to find out whether there was any play, the topic was revived as the only bright news of the hour. The stoppage lasted for four and three-quarter hours all told, and this meant that by the evening there could scarcely have been anybody in the British Isles with an interest in cricket who hadn't at last been made aware of the fact that a Cornhill Insurance Company existed. The announcement had been carefully timed for that Saturday, but the climate had turned it into a publicity triumph exceeding the wildest optimism. And at that stage Cornhill hadn't spent a penny. They had just received the most sustained "commercial" the non-commercial BBC is ever likely to broadcast, and had done so merely on a verbal agreement to make a contract which had not then been signed. Within a month the advertising agents reported that the public awareness of Cornhill had risen from two to eight per cent.

In practical terms, what Cornhill were getting for their money from the 1978 season onwards consisted of several things. They were allowed to put up banner boards (30 feet × 3 feet to begin with, later reduced to 24 feet × 2 feet 6 inches in the interests of uniformity) on all Test match grounds, in two prime positions so that the Cornhill name was bound to come in shot several times in every over as the television cameras panned throughout the match. The definition of a prime site has become something of a sore point, because some of the Test grounds have made independent deals with other firms, which have pre-empted the ideal position for this form of advertising, which is on the boundary right behind the bowler who faces the camera. Sometimes there's a bit of push and shove the day before a Test match starts, when a posse of advertising representatives descends on the ground to check that camera and banner board positions will serve their own clients best. In addition, the deal meant that the word Cornhill would be spoken regularly by commentators on television and radio, and reported by cricket writers in the press. It would also appear on every scoreboard sold. There was an agreement with TCCB that the "name, fame and likeness" of every cricketer in the Test squad could be used in any form of advertising Cornhill chose to originate independently, and Test cricketers have made personal appearances on Cornhill's behalf.

Then there were the facilities for entertaining Cornhill's own people and clients at Test matches. They were to receive fifty free tickets for every day of every Test, and as many more as they wished to buy, reserved in advance of the general issue. At Edgbaston, the Oval and Trent Bridge, Cornhill discovered that their free seats were situated among the members. Some of them were at Old Trafford, none at all at Headingley or Lord's. But at Lord's they could take advantage of boxes if they wished to, and they do, as well as the transformation of the Indoor Cricket School into a Cornhill entertainment centre for the duration of the Test. Marquees sometimes serve the same purpose on other grounds, but not at the Oval, where they are required to take a couple of rooms in Archbishop Tenison's Grammar School across the road. The entertainment value of being so closely associated with Test cricket is important to Cornhill, as it is to other big match sponsors. They invite the people they most want to impress on the first four days of a match, on the assumption that it may not run to a fifth day. Entertainment is also responsible in part for costing them between sixty and seventy per cent more than they actually contribute to the game. That, and incidentals like the production of fixture booklets bearing their name, which have been circulated by all the county clubs to members each year, meant that in 1981 Cornhill spent close on £500,000, of which only £280,000 (including VAT) was the sponsorship fee.

By then they were talking to Messrs Coleman and Lush again about a renewal of the contract which would end after the 1982 season. This negotiation was a bit harder than the one of 1977. Then, TCCB had been after £750,000 over three years, but had yielded to Cornhill's preference for £1 million over five. Coleman and Lush now began by asking Cornhill what they thought a new deal might be worth, and Cornhill offered £600,000 a year for three years. The TCCB men, hinting that other people would be only too happy to take up the sponsorship if Cornhill decided the price was too high, said this wasn't enough; £800,000 was the figure they had in mind. Eventually, there was compromise – in Cornhill's favour – and the new contract was made for £2 millions spread out to the end of the 1985 season.

Cornhill say that it is "very difficult to quantify" the effect on their business of their attachment to Test match cricket, and no doubt it is; though perhaps not quite so difficult as they, and other sponsors, who say the same thing, would have us believe. An early effect they do concede is the increase in morale among their own employees, who suddenly found that they no longer had to explain just what business this hitherto obscure company was in. Insurance brokers began to appreciate them more as well, revising their collective opinion that Cornhill simply weren't big enough to handle certain commissions. One manifestly quantifiable asset has been the £200,000 worth of business that Cornhill have picked up since 1977 by obtaining the National Cricket Association's invitation to run its club insurance scheme. There have also been cases of cricket enthusiasts transferring their various insurances to Cornhill from other companies as an expression of gratitude for what has been done for the game. And the public awareness of Cornhill by the start of 1982 had risen – according to the calculations of National Opinion Polls – to seventeen per cent. Only two other companies in the entire insurance business were still better known than Cornhill by then.

Hard-headed business it may be, but so tickled are Cornhill by the esteem they have acquired through the cricket connection that the first thing you notice in the reception area of their City headquarters is a large glass case containing a selection of bats autographed by the Test teams they have sponsored in the past few years. Thirty-odd miles away in St Albans, something similar was brandished for a few years at the head office of Cadbury-Schweppes, the confectionery and soft drinks firm which attached itself to cricket some six months before Cornhill did so in 1977 – and detached itself again after the 1983 season.

The firm is very careful to keep its brand names, the result of a merger, well apart. Cadbury = chocolate = family and caring. Schweppes = drink = fun and style. Contrary to what might be a widely held belief among a species of athlete which has been notable, sometimes distinguished, for its consumption of ale and even stronger beverages, Schweppes took the view that cricket was an ideal area for their sponsorship. It had a certain style and a dash of humour, too. They wouldn't have dreamt of backing all-in wrestling; not quite their self-image at all. They describe this as "mildly aspirational, but not in a snobby way".

They had never sponsored anything before 1977, though they had a record of experimenting with new ways of advertising their soft drinks. They were looking for another fresh avenue, and they wanted to cover the whole year and the whole country. Nothing available or appealing promised as much by itself, so they divided themselves between English county cricket and Rugby Union in both Scotland and Wales. Moreover, they wanted to be the first into whichever form of sponsorship they picked up. They would not under any circumstances have taken over the Gillette Cup, as the National Westminster Bank did ("I'm afraid", said the man from Schweppes, "I still think of it as the Gillette Cup run by NatWest"). Test cricket either hadn't occurred to them or sounded too expensive, but they were well aware that the counties were in deep trouble with income from the basis of the English game. So they made their pitch for the championship, offering £360,000 over three years, distributed in a number of ways: the champions were to get £4,000, the runners-up £2,500, the third team £1,250. The offer was snapped up.

For this outlay, Schweppes obtained two returns in the gift of TCCB. Hoardings were to be situated permanently on every county cricket ground, and their name was also to be on every scorecard during a county championship match. The permanency of the hoardings was particularly important. County championship cricket is never televised, being thought far too dull for vicarious spectators at home; as it sometimes is. But every ground is visited by the camera crews occasionally during the season, when they are covering cup matches or Sunday games in the John Player League, and Schweppes were anxious to take advantage of this. On top of the contractual deal, there was the usual spin-off in publicity through broadcasting and the press. Schweppes could be sure that their name was mentioned on the sports news bulletins every day of the championship, at 7.25 am, 8.25 am, lunchtime and evening as well. They were referred to in every match report printed in the papers – and in the posh ones this could amount to half a dozen separate references on a single page. Let a cricket writer doggedly continue to type in his old-fashioned way "the county championship" alone, and he would soon be gently but pointedly encouraged by Schweppes's PR people to do otherwise from now on. After all, they insisted, without sponsors cricket would go down the drain – and, implicitly, so would the cricket writer's bread and butter.

The players, too, were eased into the way of absorbing Schweppes more than some might naturally be inclined to do. A certain amount of soft drink was carefully deposited in every county dressing-room, chiefly because the company didn't want any of the players to be seen wandering into public view drinking someone else's product. (But no one seemed sure whether Boycott's well-publicised taste for Malvern Water was another gratuitous PR exercise, or whether he actually paid for the stuff.) Not nearly as many of the trimmings that Cornhill, for one, take up were thought necessary by Schweppes. Access to a box at Lord's was never part of their deal, but they knew that they could have one any time they chose. They took one for the Australian Test in 1981, but declined the offer for the matches with India and Pakistan in 1982. Nor did they expect players to turn out on their behalf, though once, when they were opening a new depot in Birmingham, someone thought it would be a great idea if Bob Willis could be pictured bowling to the depot manager in front of some crates, and Willis seemed happy to oblige. Their own comparable gesture was to drop £150 into every cricketer's benefit fund. Theirs was much less of a spectacular sponsorship than some, and as they themselves were quick to point out, it was a very small part of their whole operation. Their total advertising budget on TV and in the press ran to £3 millions a year. The separate allotment for cricket sponsorship, under a renewed contract in 1980, cost them not more than three per cent of that sum.

Schweppes gave the impression that they had made a thoughtful investment from which they did not expect more than modest returns. It was something whose dividends, whatever they might have been, could not be expected to accrue except across many years. They had never had any intention of sponsorship occupying a large place in their overall strategy, and they didn't employ a single person to attend to it and nothing else. All that mattered to them, they said, was that through their association with cricket their name should be mentioned nationally and locally for six days a week during the season. They claimed no association between public awareness of them through their cricket link and the sales of their goods. And they were still taking the view early in 1982 that the response of the public seemed to be mildly favourable. That November, however, someone in Cadbury-Schweppes revised his opinion of the entire strategy, and the company announced that it would be pulling out of cricket within twelve months.

The man at Lord's whose entire life is spent in selling cricket as hard as he can, and riding blows of that kind, is Peter Lush. Senior citizens of MCC groan nowadays at the very mention of the word marketing, but Lush gives the impression that it is the staff of life to him. His whole career, before being recruited by TCCB, had been spent in advertising agencies, latterly as a joint managing director. He had played a bit of club cricket in Sussex and at one stage fancied the idea of being a cricket commentator, but when Lord's advertised for someone to fill the newly created post of Public Relations Officer and Marketing Manager of TCCB in 1974, he says he submitted his application "for a bit of a laugh". He had never even heard of NCA at that stage and one of his interviewers, Gubby Allen, quickly exposed other blanks in Lush's cricket knowledge under questioning. But he got the job because he had the skills that cricket needed badly at that stage, when it was frantically trying to adapt to the changing circumstances of its world. It says much about that world now that, although Peter Lush in cricketing terms is easily the outsider among all the officials at Lord's, he has become quite the most familiar one to the public at large because it is invariably he who stands before the television cameras when cricket crops up in the news. He appears as the spokesman for either the Cricket Council, TCCB or NCA. Sometimes he has difficulty in remembering, just before his television interview begins, on whose behalf he is supposed to be speaking that day.

"C'mon, it's a great new ball game" is the slogan on an Australian cricket poster tacked up beside Lush's office door – out of American sports jargon by way of Kerry Packer, which makes it thrice removed from the customary temperament of Lord's. Inside, the preoccupation is what can be done with cricket in the market place. Peter Lush tells, with an air of astonishment still, how the price of everything in the game was so unsound when he arrived on the scene that it wasn't even keeping up with inflation. He set about correcting that without delay, once he had worked out the intricate strategy needed for getting certain Lord's committees on his side without falling foul of others. He renegotiated the television fees with BBC, and then came the deals with Schweppes and Cornhill. The monies extracted from the BBC for its television coverage of Tests, one-day internationals, cup matches and the John Player League (not to mention its radio Test Match Special) are one of the most carefully guarded secrets in the game. TCCB and the commercial companies make no bones at all about how much cash is passing between them in sponsorship.

But the only clue about broadcasting money has been a revelation in *Wisden* that in 1975, BBC paid £120,000 to cover all four Tests with the Australians that year. It is in the interests of neither party to let on about what agreements have been made since then, simply because BBC holds a monopoly in this field.

Only once has independent television attempted to cover cricket nationally for more than a recorded few minutes during news bulletins, and that turned into a fiasco. The full-scale treatment by ITV was given to one of the early Gillette Cup Finals, and the match was approaching its exciting climax when the transmission ended abruptly in mid-over, with another half dozen or so to be bowled. The inflexibility of independent television's networking system was responsible: the Cup Final had to be shed to make way for a scheduled quiz programme or somesuch, otherwise havoc would have been wrought in several permutations throughout the United Kingdom for the rest of the night. The fiasco was such that the new Test and County Cricket Board were not prepared to risk a repetition and ITV took them to court on the issue, claiming an option on the following season. The independent television companies, however, lost the hearing. In consequence the BBC, untroubled by the stringencies of networking to anything like the same extent, has sailed blithely on – almost certainly getting its cricket very cheaply indeed. As 1982 arrived, however, and with it the imminence of ITV's Channel Four, Peter Lush was flexing his muscles at the possibility of a competitor to the BBC at last. Confident that every avenue open to exploitation by TCCB in the past few years had now been tapped, he was biding his time, awaiting the moment when cable television and the proper coverage of events between England and Australia through satellites might open up – in the language of that poster outside his door – a great new ball game indeed.

Given a free hand, Lush might well imitate some of the devices introduced by Packer during the brief ascent of World Series cricket, simply to attract new customers to the sport; or, at least, that is the impression he conveys. Retarded as he is by the braking system inherent in English cricket's devotion to committees, there are limits to what he can introduce in the cause of making money for the game at all costs. Some time ago he came up with the idea of umpires issuing yellow cards to refractory cricketers on the pitch, in the manner of Football League referees, arguing that this would have impact in the middle, in the stands and on the television screens at home. TCCB thought little of the plan and turned it down. The board constantly struggles with the need to accumulate as much money as possible for the game, and its own desire to alter the shape and appearance of cricket as little as possible. One of the demarcation lines it has set itself was pointed out by Doug Insole in that opening conversation he had with Cornhill's representatives back in 1977. "There is no way," he said, "we'd accept your sponsorship if you were selling Kentucky Fried Chicken."

Nor is the board very keen on sponsorship attached to individual performances, which risks affecting the team game, with a captain in the dilemma of having to choose whether to allow one of his men the opportunity to cash in, or whether to pursue a different tactic on the field for its own sake. Some board members recall a Hastings Festival years ago, when Brylcreem were offering £100 for the player who had taken the most catches in a season, a prize for which Tony Lock and Arthur Milton were running neck and neck as the season finished. Lock was bowling in the festival match when someone hit him high into the air above the covers. Bellowing "Mine!", he charged twenty-five yards towards the falling ball – and dropped it, though two or three players who had left it to him could have taken the catch with ease.

What TCCB is after, in its perpetual search for solvency, is the sponsor who will provide funds which can be ploughed into the game as a whole without discountenancing backers who have already made a niche in cricket. In 1981 the French mineral water firm of Perrier offered good money to encourage fast over rates in county championship cricket, a scheme which delighted TCCB on two counts; but when Schweppes began to make uncomfortable noises the offer was quickly refused. And the search for solvency has become anxious again, as the economic recession of the country deepens and causes commerce to look carefully at its disbursements of cash. There are other reasons why sponsors apart from Schweppes have been backing out of the game recently. Gillette felt unable to meet TCCB's new terms partly because they were beginning to suspect that their name had become more associated with cricket than with razor blades. Holt Products stopped sponsoring county matches with touring sides because the counties themselves, by idiotic team selections that produced something akin to second elevens, were reducing the value of such fixtures to the sponsors, or to anyone else for that matter. John Player & Sons became very nervous indeed when the BBC extended its Saturday Grandstand programme to Sunday, with a consequent reduction of cricket viewing that day, and it required some persuasive talking by Peter Lush before they decided to hang on to their sponsorship.

Prudential Assurance announced in 1982 that they were backing out of cricket altogether after the World Cup of the following year for the opaque reason that "our marketing and publicity objectives are not the same as they were when we began sponsoring cricket". The decision, in fact, caused less depression in TCCB than it may have done among the public. Some senior people in TCCB had already come to the conclusion that they didn't want to see another World Cup competition in England, splendid spectaculars though these had proved themselves to be. The conclusion was based on hard-headed business sense and nothing else. Though undoubtedly a money-spinner, into which Prudential put £500,000 for their last throw in 1983, the World Cup dividends had to be distributed among all the participating countries. It was reckoned that English cricket would be about £100,000 better off in any season which brought the Sri Lankans alone to this country, rather than an international cast of dozens including the Australians and West Indians.

That response of the English authorities to the most impressive of all quick-fire cricket tournaments, demonstrates more emphatically than anything else might the economic edge on which the game is still poised in this country, for all the comparative affluence of the past decade or so. A few weeks before the Prudential announcement was made, the point had been raised dramatically with the news that one of the biggest firms selling advertising space on British sports grounds, Sports Space Marketing, had gone into liquidation. It was through this firm's agency that many football and cricket clubs all over the country received precious income from individual deals with companies wishing to advertise on hoardings at the grounds. At the time of the collapse it was reported that ten county cricket clubs were owed money by Sports Space – Warwickshire £65,000, Surrey £60,000, Lancashire £60,000, Nottinghamshire more than £30,000 – perhaps £300,000 in all. Not one of them could afford anything like those losses, especially after a season which had seen income arriving via TCCB reduced from the £3,058,000 of 1981 to about £2,400,000 – partly because the Test Match receipts in a year of Indian and Pakistani tours had been, as usual, no better than fair to middling. The seventeen counties by then required a total of £5 millions to keep going – sometimes as much as £350,000 each – and they had become accustomed to relying on TCCB to provide between thirty and forty per cent of it.

As the county treasurers totted up their accounts that autumn they were, without exception, in a state of gloom. Somerset, who had made a profit of £183,000 in 1981, were scarcely breaking even in 1982. Even worse, Lancashire had seen a profit of £118,000 turned into a deficit of £150,000. Kent had lost £75,000, Gloucestershire

£57,000 and Worcestershire faced the fact that they would have to cut running costs by £40,000 in 1983 if they were to stay alive. Derbyshire's income of £235,000 had included a mere £21,000 from gate receipts, only £44,600 from members' subscriptions; and, finding themselves £30,000 below par, they at once took the decision to shed four cricketers from their playing staff the following year. And so on . . .

That back end, while England's cricketers were playing for the Ashes Down Under, morose people at home were beginning to speculate as they hadn't done for the best part of twenty years, wondering whether county cricket could survive much longer in its present form in the face of the financial problems that beset each club. And always, in each glum conversation, the same names were mentioned as those of counties most likely to go to the wall – Derbyshire, Glamorgan, Worcestershire, Hampshire, Northamptonshire, Somerset, Gloucestershire and Sussex.

Towering unavoidably in these calculations about how to make ends meet was the prospect of having to find something like £1,600,000 in 1983 to pay the wages of the men who play county cricket in England. There were 326 of them at the end of the previous season and there are very considerable differences in their earnings, mostly dependent upon whether they are international players as well. But even among those first-class cricketers who never reach the level of Test Matches, there is sometimes sharp inconsistency between what the men playing for one county may obtain compared with those of another. The Middlesex players are said to be easily the best rewarded, when all forms of income are taken into account; those of Glamorgan, Hampshire and Worcestershire the least well off.*

The variety is generally a result of the individual county committee's ability to arrange forms of sponsorship that will supplement what the club itself can afford to pay its staff. At Old Trafford every cricketer who has been awarded his county cap receives the same amount of money from Lancashire CCC; but the appreciable difference between what Clive Lloyd or any other overseas player on the team has got purely for playing for the county and what the most recently capped man has received has come from cash deals made on their behalf by the club with local entrepreneurs. Other counties have made different arrangements to boost the basic wages of their players. One of the devices Middlesex adopted when they contracted

---

* Another comparison: In 1982 players' wages at Worcester totalled £168,000; in more substantial Lancashire they amounted to over £215,000.

the sponsorship of Austin Reed was for a Player of the Month to receive a voucher enabling him and his family to buy goods worth £250 from the store; the nominated Player of the Season was rewarded in kind with £1,000 for his four and a half months' work. In 1982 Middlesex's capped players were paid between £6,500 and £8,500 plus expenses and perks like the one provided by the clothing firm; in effect, they were picking up between £10,000 and £12,000 apiece, whether or not they also played in a Test that year. Worcestershire's men may have enjoyed something under two thirds of those amounts.

There was a time, not so long ago, when county cricketers were even more exposed to pot luck than they are today. They took what the clubs could (or would) give them, and they could expect no supplementary income until, usually ten years after receiving their county caps, they were rewarded by a tax-free benefit, for which they were duly grateful. This is not to imply that professional cricketers have always been meanly treated. Between the two world wars, in fact, when any workman earning £2 10s a week thought he was doing rather well for himself, and when the salary of a teacher with a first-class degree began at £248 a year, the average pay for a professional county cricketer was £10 a match – and he could expect to play about thirty games a season. As for benefits, they are as old as the professional game itself.

In 1851 MCC began the habit of giving each paid cricketer on their staff a benefit just before he retired, and in due time this was an annual feature of the county game. Yorkshire were applauded but not often imitated for attending to the economic welfare of their players, largely the doing of that autocratic man Lord Hawke, who not only instituted a system of regular payments throughout the year, but also began a provident fund on which his players could draw when they retired. For a long time, too, the most notable benefits collected on the county circuits were for men wearing the white rose on their caps. In 1904 George Hirst – who for fourteen seasons did the double of 1,000 runs and 100 wickets, and once performed the still unequalled feat of scoring 2,385 runs and taking 208 wickets – outstripped another record by a long way with a benefit realising £3,703. In the same year, lackaday, Webb of Hampshire could only muster £150 from his benefit match with Surrey, in spite of hitting a celebratory 162 not out.

The first five-figure benefit did not happen until Lancashire allotted their 1948 fixture with Bradman's Australians to Cyril Washbrook, which inflated his benefit to what was then thought the breath-taking figure of £14,000, a sum generous enough not to be surpassed until Colin Milburn collected £19,473 from North-amptonshire supporters in 1971. What had really inflated Wash-brook's collection, though, was the unprecedented organisation of his well-wishers in Lancashire, who arranged a series of all-star matches, produced a souvenir tie, and persuaded people from show business to give beneficial concerts free of charge; all this on top of the customary benefit match. Much the same recipe was adopted (minus the tie, which the Inland Revenue had subsequently classi-fied as an item of trade, and therefore inadmissible) when Lan-cashire folk raised no less than £128,300 for Jack Simmons in 1980, a figure that is likely to remain a record for some time to come. This could be seen as a remarkable (and deserved) tribute to a loyal and liked player, an exemplary character in county cricket, whose skills were never quite appreciated enough to give him a Test cap. It was also a testimony to the diligence of friends by the score and of the cricketer himself over a period of perhaps two years, when arrange-ments were being made for the events of the benefit season.

In modern times, since Washbrook hit his jack-pot, the difference between a gratifying benefit and a disappointing one has generally depended on what has been put into the benefit effort before the final income has been counted up. The case of Norman Graham, the Kent medium-pace bowler, in 1977 is a celebrated illustration of what this can amount to. For eighteen months he worked flat out on his benefit fund – and was perversely assisted by the fact that for most of his benefit season he was unfit to play cricket – making personal appear-ances and attending to paperwork. The appearances included tour-ing some 700 pubs in the region, where lotteries had been arranged on his behalf. The paperwork meant postage and bills among other things, an *expenditure* of about £40,000 on prizes, hire of premises, and communications, a costly public relations exercise to persuade cricket enthusiasts to give even more money in return. As they did. The people of Kent tipped up something like £80,000 that year, leaving Graham with a record benefit for his county of £38,000. As a windfall exempted from income tax, that is a sum which a skilled craftsman in any field (including my own) would think himself fortunate to enjoy. Until quite recently, though, the benefit was the only prospect of affluence that the average county cricketer could hope to entertain.

Things first began to change in the cricketer's favour in 1967, when the bowler Fred Rumsey, formerly of Worcestershire, then of Somerset, later of Derbyshire, conceived the idea that cricketers ought to have a trade union. With tepid enthusiasm from his co-workers at first, and some suspicion from cricket committees everywhere between Lord's and Taunton and Manchester, he succeeded in launching the Cricketers' Association. Within two or three seasons this had become an accepted body in the sport, included every registered county player in its membership, and saw its representatives welcomed at Lord's into some crucial committees of TCCB. Such stability as the game in England has maintained since then has been due in no small measure to the amicable working relationship which has now become well established between the CA and the cricket authorities in this country. Even so, the CA didn't succeed in negotiating a uniform basic minimum wage for its members until the season of 1979. The previous year, the counties had shelled out a total of £650,000 in players' wages, but the discrepancies between cricketers of equal service and approximately equal merit could be glaring from place to place. In 1979, however, TCCB guaranteed every senior capped county cricketer a wage of £4,500, with smaller sums for younger and uncapped players. Ten years earlier, in his last contract as a senior player with Warwickshire, the CA's Secretary, Jack Bannister (as valuable in county cricket as Jack Simmons) had earned £1,100. That first guaranteed basic wage in 1979 was arranged to include whatever individual counties might acquire in the way of prize monies and sponsorships. Subsequently it was rearranged as a straight payment from the counties, underwritten by TCCB, irrespective of whatever income might arrive from other sources. In 1980 it rose to £4,850, in 1981 to £5,450, in 1982 to £5,850, in 1983 to £6,250. By then, players belonging to the most victorious clubs could expect to be richer by several thousand pounds, one way and another. Cricketers playing for persistently unsuccessful counties might expect to gain as little as £300 in supplementary cash.

A number of cricketers have had to make do with that sort of money for a full twelve months at a stretch, and some in recent years (Reidy and Scott of Lancashire are two who come to mind) have found themselves in the dole queues during the off-season. Luckier have been those who have managed to secure winter contracts with state or club sides in Australia and South Africa, where cash flows more freely than it has at home for some time. But the majority of those who do not go abroad between autumn and spring, either to play Test cricket or on their own account, soldier on with jobs that very often have come their way as a result of their cricketing careers. There are firms throughout the country ready and willing to make use of sportsmen in their spare time, in or out of season, to tout their business or in other ways to associate their names with a commodity. During 1982 Barlow Butcher and Merry of the Middlesex side all had such connections with Abbey Life Assurance; while Edmonds, reputedly the English cricketer with the sharpest nose for business, was reckoned to be involved with half a dozen firms. As in the case of the counties themselves, it is by enlisting commerce for what they can get out of it that more cricketers today than ever before have made themselves at least men of some means.

They are better off than their predecessors, for a start, by what comes to them from commerce in deals made by the counties for various perquisites. The days are now some distance behind when a county cricketer had to provide his own gear. The makers of bats and clothing are very happy to supply a team with all its needs free of charge, for the sake of the individual and county endorsement, and for the flourishing of its products in front of crowds and television cameras (sharp-eyed small boys, with heroes they wish to emulate, are quick to spot the make of this and that, be the insignia ever so indistinct to the adult gaze). So worried had TCCB become in 1981 by the flaunting of commercial symbols by cricketers in public, very often as a result of deals they had made individually with companies, that it ordained a restriction on such devices. Henceforth no clothing was to be worn in county matches bearing a maker's symbol larger than four centimetres square, and then only if every member of the team wore it. In Tests there was to be no such oblique advertising at all.

Beyond TCCB's reach, naturally, is that mobile advertisement the motor car, which has increasingly become a feature of the landscape in every county parking lot. It cost the firm of Lex Brooklands £40,000 in 1982 to supply Middlesex with eight Volvos for the season; one for the county secretary, Alan Wright, and seven for players, who received them in order of seniority; every car decked in the Middlesex colours of white and blue, and all bearing the firm's conspicuous slogan along the sides, together with "Support Middlesex CCC". Other counties had made similar arrangements with other firms in their own areas. The Surrey players had six sponsored Talbot Solaras, Sussex eight Morris Itals, Hampshire six Cortinas, Warwickshire nine Talbots and one Matra, Nottinghamshire a bountiful assortment of four Escorts, five Cortinas and ten Fiestas. Saab were being lobbied so persistently down in Somerset on behalf of all and sundry connected with the county club that they were becoming quite disillusioned by this form of sponsorship. But West Country cricketers had travelled philosophically a considerable distance since the day when Harold Gimblett walked a mile or two with his cricket bag before hitching a ride on a lorry to his first match for Somerset at Frome.

Somerset players are of a breed which now sells itself as dearly as possible in the market place, opportunist enough to set up their own commercial company, Wyvern Sports Marketing Ltd, in 1978. Initially, this produced the first county handbook Somerset had seen for many a year; then followed a succession of sunhats, T-shirts, calendars, button badges and other baubles for supporters to toy with – "such a huge range of Cricket Souvenirs and Mementoes", according to an advertisement four years later, "that space does not allow us to give full details". By then, after some disturbed noises at this private enterprise from the club, the buoyant Somerset cricketers had decided to allow the county itself a half-share in their company, in return for which the company became responsible for all marketing and advertising of whatever Somerset has to offer. They were the first cricketers to obtain TCCB's approval for the wearing of commercial symbols on clothing on the field, and promptly did a deal with the knitwear firm of Lyle & Scott, whose "Little Birdie" emblem thus achieved widespread exposure around the first-class cricket grounds of England, unfailingly so when Somerset were performing before the television lenses. They were also the first cricketers to sponsor one of their own matches, underwriting the second day of the championship fixture with Leicestershire at Taunton in 1980.

A generation ago it was almost unheard of for a cricketer to equip himself with a personal agent who for a percentage would sell his client's "name, fame and likeness" in the market place. By now it is common for even young and uncapped players, on first securing a place in a county side, to be heard enquiring of their seniors "Who's the best bloke to be my business manager?". It is no good guessing how many county cricketers are now possessed of such promoters; it is safe to say that there are a lot of them about, all playing various forms of the money game on behalf of their clients. Alan Knott revealed during the High Court action in 1977 that, on hearing of Kerry Packer's proposal, he put the matter in the hands of his agents, Arolac, in the Isle of Man, where income tax exactions are not at all what they are on the mainland. Boycott has been a client of Mark McCormack, the American wheeler-dealer who represents an international assortment of performers in all the big spectator sports. And it is here, at the level of the Test player, that the cricketing agents and their clients are sharing great prosperity by anybody's standards.

The rewards have risen dramatically in the past few years; so much so that in 1979 the Cricketers' Association asked the Test and County Cricket Board not to increase Test match emoluments any more because an intolerable gap was beginning to open up between the earnings of the English Test cricketer and the man who was anchored in the county game. The gap was there in basic wages, without it being widened even further by the sums the celebrity can attract from quarters other than TCCB. Twenty years ago, in 1963, a man selected for England at home was allowed a first-class rail ticket from whichever town his county was playing in to the Test match venue; and another one to restore him to his county side wherever it had moved to in the next few days. He was bedded free in an hotel for the duration of the Test, but the bill paid on his behalf covered only his lodging and food; he was given ten shillings a day for drink, tobacco or anything else he might want. He also had a match allowance of £7 10s, which was supposed to take care of his laundry, his taxi fares, his tips. His payment was £100 for the match, £60 if he stayed with the side as twelfth man for the full extent of the Test.

The match fee edged up slowly in fits and starts until, by 1976, it had been doubled to £200. After that it took off, and TCCB have never concealed the fact that Kerry Packer's counter-attraction of 1977, which seduced Amiss, Knott, Snow, Underwood, Woolmer and, above all, England's current captain Greig, was the spur that produced galloping inflation of English Test rewards. The board, quite blatantly, not knowing what course international cricket was liable to take in the near future, was buying the loyalty of every other English cricketer of Test calibre whom Packer might have had a speculative eye on.

The first jump was from £200 to £1,000 per match. In 1979 the fee was increased from £1,000 to £1,200, with the prospect of sharing £1,500 if England won the match in question. The following year the straight fee had risen again to £1,400; and there it has stayed at the behest of the Cricketers' Association. That, it should be noted, is a ceiling figure for the transaction between the England players and TCCB. Cornhill's sponsorship ensures that the England cricketers can obtain even more. In 1982 each man stood to share £1,750 every time he played on a winning team; he might pick up an additional £350 for being chosen man of the match, an extra £700 as man of the series. An England player that year, chosen for all six Tests against India and Pakistan, drawing also the basic minimum wage as a capped county player, would have banked not less than £14,250. In fact, most of them enjoyed sums in excess of that, with payments for one-day internationals as well as the plethora of private arrangements made with sponsors on the side, not to mention county earnings above the basic wage for their trade. And the ones who toured Australia and New Zealand the following winter picked up an additional £10,000, plus £200 for every previous tour they had made.

On top of that they stood to gain large amounts of Australian dollars in prize money put up by a variety of sponsors Down Under, which included a Japanese car firm and an American fast-food chain. Even though the English players lost the Ashes on that tour, and failed to qualify for the finals of the triangular one-day tournament, their "pool" was to be swollen with the equivalent of another £28,000 from these commercial sources.

The team which Mike Brearley led Down Under in 1978–9 had raised the question of cashing in on its "name, fame and likeness" by offering itself to any Australian or English concern which wished to associate the players with its advertising. TCCB conceded the point, and when business was done, the resultant profits were distributed in the following order: sixty per cent to the cricketers, twenty per cent to TCCB and twenty per cent to the agent acting for the team. Similar arrangements have existed ever since both at home and abroad, and what is known as the players' "pool" for such transactions, supervised in the first place by Bob Willis and Bob Taylor, has lately been organised by the team physiotherapist, Bernard Thomas.

The agency which does the actual marketing of this valuable collective commodity is Championship Sporting Specialist Promotions. Its Chief Executive is Barrie Gill, whose biggest interest is in motor-racing. Its most notable director with a cricketing connection is Chris Howland who, until his three-year term of office ended in October 1982, was a member of the MCC Committee. Not only does this outfit handle the extra-curricular acquisitions of the England Test team; it also represents a number of individual players in whatever separate deals can be made on their behalf. Brearley and Willis have both been among its clients. Gower and Botham are its two most glittering commodities at present. The sums involved can only be the subject of wild guesses, but one small clue is the fact that in 1982 CSSP paid TCCB £8,000 for the concession to canvass on behalf of the England team that year. The same figure was demanded by CSSP in 1982 when Radio Rentals enquired about the possibility of using Ian Botham's picture in their showrooms.

The most common forms of advertising to which players lend themselves are, of course, for cricketing equipment. This has a long history. In 1889 both W. G. Grace and Ranjitsinhji were to be found endorsing the bats made by L. J. Nicolls at Robertsbridge in Sussex. By the time the Second World War was approaching, cricket publications invariably contained advertisements for "Maurice Leyland" bats, the "Duckworth" gauntlet, the "J. B. Hobbs" leg guard. Any man in his fifties now will recall that first cricket bat of his, cherished all the more because its plain and oiled surface was unobtrusively indented with the autograph of some cricketing hero. Denis Compton's association with Brylcreem was probably one of the earliest examples of an English cricketer exploiting his reputation hand in hand with a form of commerce which had nothing whatever to do with the game; though Don Bradman's name a decade earlier was linked with a portable gramophone which had been astutely presented to him on one of his tours in this country. Not until this generation, however, have so many players flung themselves so avidly into the business of making money on the side by offering themselves to commerce. Not until television came along, and especially colour television, was there such a demand for their services as there is now. As a symbol of our times there is nothing to surpass the performance of the distinguished England cricketer (Botham) who actually altered his appearance (by abandoning his beard) in order to illustrate on the screen the virtues of an electric razor made in Germany. He would not, presumably, be getting less than the £25,000 supposedly made by Imran Khan at about the same time for lending himself to a TV commercial on behalf of Pepsi-Cola.

A cricketer more assiduous in such matters than most in this country was Tony Greig, who lent himself especially to St Peter Sporting Goods Ltd, of Wakefield. This was an old-established firm which at one time numbered among its directors Boycott's solicitor Duncan Mutch. Greig, too, became a director in 1978, by which time, partly because of his ubiquitous advocacy, objects produced by St Peter were flooding the cricket fields of England. For a couple of seasons it seemed as if every other batsman in the land was wearing the distinctive gloves (though white, they looked as if they had been made for boxers, not cricketers) manufactured in Wakefield. There was also a sun hat, which caused some trouble in 1976, when Greig's county colleague John Snow had flaunted it and its unmistakable blue trade mark in front of the television cameras during a John Player match between Sussex and Nottinghamshire. Sussex were severely censured by TCCB for allowing Snow to get away with that piece of strictly private enterprise, and the bowler was later suspended for three Sunday matches. Greig himself, making the most of his opportunities with St Peter as with Kerry Packer, remained on the board of the company until suddenly, in October 1980, the Receiver was appointed to take care of its affairs. When the following season began, it appeared as if almost every batsman in first-class cricket had reconsidered his equipment and reverted to more traditional forms of glove.

What with one thing and another, Test cricketers now have it within their capacity to become wealthy men; in some cases as preposterously rich as some footballers, golfers and tennis players have become. It was estimated in 1982 that Ian Botham was earning between £60,000 and £70,000 a year, and he owned two racehorses by then; within twelve months he had turned down an offer amounting to £250,000 if he would go and play in South Africa for a couple of seasons. The fourteen English cricketers who went to the Cape under the patronage of South African Breweries in 1982 collected £40,000 apiece (more, it is said, in the case of Boycott) for less than four weeks' work. Most of those who went had nothing much in the way of Test careers to look forward to. But so strong was the lure of the quick financial killing that Graham Gooch, in his prime, put at risk his already substantial earnings as a member of the England team. It was reckoned that he had just made £20,000 out of a year's Test cricket, plus £8,000 as an Essex player, plus £15,000 for endorsements and personal appearances.

Gooch was among those in the South African party who were represented by lawyers when they learned that TCCB had suspended them from England Test cricket for three years: and if one thing above all others marks the man of means from the majority of people, it is the swiftness with which he reaches for a lawyer when he isn't getting his own way. The habit is gaining ground among cricketers. Attached to practically everything Boycott has done for a decade, in his dealings with Yorkshire and others, has been the figure of his solicitor Duncan Mutch. The most spectacular example of the effect legal intervention can have on the game was the High Court action successfully fought by Greig and other Packer players in 1977. Not far behind it is the case of Barry Wood who, in the words of *Wisden*, "left Lancashire within forty-eight hours of banking a benefit cheque of £62,420" at the start of the 1980 season. There had been a squabble with the club over the terms he would continue to play on, and Wood had decided to move to Derbyshire, who were very glad to recruit him. But TCCB forbade the move at once because, as its Registration Committee declared, "it is anxious not to encourage the development of a transfer system". At the same time it offered Derbyshire the prospect of successfully reapplying for Wood's services later on. Wood instantly took his case to the Appeals Committee of the Cricket Council and was told, at the end of April, that he might start playing for Derbyshire three months later. Enter Wood's lawyer. And within a couple of weeks, faced with court action, TCCB had retreated. Wood was allowed to become a Derbyshire player on June 4.

The threat of litigation by cricketers is only a recent phenomenon.

All else has a considerable pedigree, and we need turn only to W. G. Grace to demonstrate that. As we have already noticed, he was perfectly willing to lend himself to commercial advertisement, and we may be sure that he did not do so without profit to himself. For if anything was as remarkable as his cricketing prowess, it was Grace's industry in making money from the game. He was quite breathtakingly grasping when his eye caught the glint of hard cash. On his first tour of Australia in 1873 he extracted from the organisers the equivalent of £18,000 in today's values. On his second, in 1891, one fifth of the entire cost of transporting thirteen cricketers across the world, supporting them while in Australia, and paying them for what they did there, went into Grace's pocket. At home, testimonials galore regularly tumbled the sovereigns into his bank account. MCC organised one, whose purpose was to buy him a medical practice. So great was the cost of W. G. Grace that cricket grounds often charged twice the normal price of admission if he was playing in order to cover their expenses. It has been calculated by his latest biographer that he must have taken, in today's currency, something like £1 million out of the game. Cricket's greatest unanswered question may be how on earth such a man could ever have been classified, and deified, as an amateur.

Nevertheless, TCCB is worried, as it ought to be, by the steadily advancing trends of today. It is especially anxious about the lengths to which commercial companies and players together are prepared to go to disturb the aesthetic of the game by advertising. Bat advertising since the advent of colour TV, which has encouraged more and more flamboyant stripes on the blade, all but concealing the fact that it is made of wood, is particularly getting out of hand. Were it not for the fact that TCCB and the Cricketers' Association have so far worked largely in sympathy on these and other matters, there might well have been some serious breach between cricketers and their employers by now; strikes, after all, have not been unknown in other sports. On top of this, there is now the certainty that England's first-class cricket authority can no longer be sure of any player's loyalty to the Test match game in the face of enticing emoluments offered from other quarters. Twice in the past few years the board has been taken completely by surprise at what a clutch of England's Test cricketers have done; once when Packer crept into the game; again when South African Breweries dangled their Krugerrands.

If Donald Carr or George Mann or Charles Palmer ever have nightmares, they are probably centred on what would follow if Arabs were to become seriously interested in cricket. There is already a businessman called Abdul Rehman Bukhatir, who abides in the emirate of Sharjah on the Persian Gulf, where opulence is now greater than anywhere else in the world. He happens to be keen on cricket, to the extent that he has created a stadium for the game, with green turf that any English first-class county might be proud of, and only a cliché will serve to describe it: it is an oasis of green in an otherwise totally desert landscape. On that ground, in April 1982, Ian Botham and Clive Lloyd among others took part in a double-wicket competition; and the full Indian and Pakistani Test teams played two one-day matches. In 1983, a dozen members of Willis's side stopped off there on the way home from Australia and New Zealand in order to pick up over £1,000 each in an exhibition match. Mr Bukhatir is by no means a Kerry Packer figure yet. But if he decided to become one – and people of his kind in that part of the world do behave regardless of expense – what then?

In Vince Miller's print shop at Lord's there is a framed letter in the handwriting of a Test cricketer who played half a century ago, thanking Sir Pelham Warner for £40, the money allotted for expenses on an MCC tour in 1933. It is signed "Yours respectfully, Maurice Tate". The valediction, even more than the sum of money, marks that letter as a period piece, almost as an antiquity. There cannot be a player today who would dream of signing himself thus, who would not regard it as a self-inflicted indignity. It is the relic of an age which, if not exactly feudal, was most certainly based on an accepted and rigid relationship between a master and his servant. No professional cricketer in 1983 would regard himself as anybody's servant, though there are maybe some people around who wish that he did.

And though we may be thankful that the condescensions and the supplications of such times have passed, the truth is that the old-fashioned patronage of cricket had something to commend it, quite apart from the fact that it sustained the sport. It was, quite simply, rather more reliable than the modern patronage. The landed gentry who kept the county game afloat with their annual disbursements to balance the books were not in the habit of withdrawing their support on a whim, or even because their own budgets might have to be reduced in certain years. They were too closely identified with their county cricket clubs, which were extensions of their squire-archy in whichever part of England they lived, to turn their backs on them unless real disaster had struck their own affairs, or unless they had received a very considerable affront. They would as lief had turned their backs on their tenants; and to do that would have caused them to suffer something more than loss of face. The accountancies of

The neckties associated with Lord's. Top row, left to right: the MCC City, Middlesex County Cricket Club, the customary vivid tie of the Marylebone Cricket Club, the National Cricket Association. Bottom row, left to right: the tie worn only by England Test cricketers, Cross Arrows, National Cricket Association, Cross Arrows centenary.

Four commanding figures in the history of the ground. Above left: Thomas Lord, the founder, whose portrait hangs in the Long Room. Above right: The fourth Lord Harris, who dominated MCC and Kent for decades. Below left: Sir Pelham Warner, player, administrator and newspaperman. Below right: Gubby Allen, the last of a line, taking the field in an MCC cap towards the end of a long career.

Above: Cricket at Lord's in 1821. This was Thomas Lord's third and last ground, the one played on today. The small building on the right is its first Pavilion, which was burned down four years later. Below: Members of MCC in front of the Pavilion, 1874. This was the second building to stand on that site. It gave way to the present Pavilion in 1890.

The Committee of the Marylebone Cricket Club, the owners of Lord's, County Cricket Board and the National Cricket Association, April 1983. A

loyees, as well as staff of the Middlesex County Cricket Club, the Test and
tifying the individuals may be found overleaf.

CRICKET.

A GRAND MATCH

WILL BE PLAYED IN

LORD'S GROUND,

MARYLEBONE,

On MONDAY, JULY **31, 1848,** *& following Day.*

The Gentlemen against the Players.

PLAYERS.

Gentlemen.	Players.
Sir F. BATHURST	BOX
E. ELMHURST, Esq.	CLARK
N. FELIX, Esq.	DEAN
H. FELLOWES, Esq.	GUY
R. T. KING, Esq.	HILLYER
J. M. LEE, Esq.	LILLYWHITE
A. MYNN, Esq.	MARTINGALE
W. NICHOLSON, Esq.	PILCH
O. C. PELL, Esq.	W. PILCH
C. RIDDING, Esq.	PARR
G. YONGE, Esq.	WISDEN

MATCHES TO COME.

Wednesday, August 2nd, at Lord's—Harrow against Winchester

Thursday, August 3rd, at Lord's—Eton against Harrow

Friday, August 4th, at Lord's—Winchester against Eton

DARK'S newly-invented LEG GUARDS, also his TUBULAR and other INDIA-RUBBER GLOVES, SPIKED SOLES for CRICKET SHOES, & CRICKET BALLS, to be had of R. Dark, at the Tennis Court.

Cricket Bats and Stumps to be had of M. Dark, at the Manufactory on the Ground.

Admittance 6d.........Stabling on the Ground.........Ordinary at 3 o'clock.

Morgan, Printer, 38, Church Street, adjoining the Marylebone Theatre.

Cricket matches for a long time in the nineteenth century advertised themselves like theatrical perfomances, with similar playbills. This one, for the Gentlemen versus Players fixture of 1848 at Lord's, is especially interesting for the commercial puff on behalf of the Darks, who sold cricket equipment at the ground.

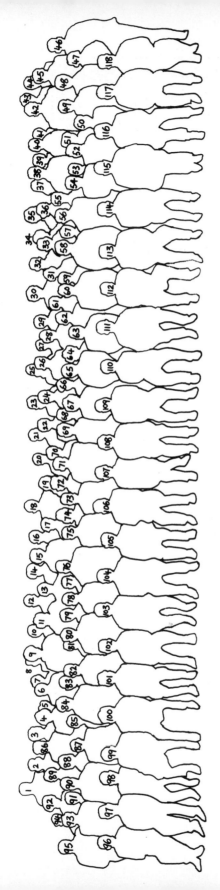

1. Mr. A. Q. W. Archdale 2. Miss B. Mitchell 3. Miss C. Tyler 4. Mr. A. M. Sheldon 5. Mrs. A. Young 6. Mr. A. C. Gull 7. Mrs. E. M. Hayes 8. Mr. M. Campkin 9. Mr. M. C. Lashley 10. Mr. P. G. M. August 11. Mr. N. Wilde 12. Mr. L. Wynne 13. Mr. A. J. Morgan 14. Miss T. J. Taylor 15. Mr. M. J. Hunt 16. Mr. J. O'Sullivan 17. Mr. C. Symmonds 18. Mr. M. J. Stammers 19. Miss A. Gibson 20. Mr. W. E. A. Higgins 21. Mr. C. Reason 22. Mr. C. Maynard 23. Miss L. Dobbie 24. Mr. M. W. Ryan 25. Miss D. H. Moore 26. Mr. J. F. Moody 27. Mrs. L. Kinsey 28. Mr. T. Hitchcock 29. Mrs. B. Forshaw 30. Mr. E. Symmonds 31. Mrs. A. E. Schrader 32. Mr. M. H. Lucy 33. Mr. R. G. P. Austin 34. Mrs. F. M. Ashmore 35. Ms. J. Warbrook 36. Mr. G. Jenkins 37. Miss S. Parsons 38. Mr. R. N. Berry 39. Miss R. Sarpson 40. Mr. D. A. Reeve 41. Miss J. Robinson 42. Mr. T. D. Topley 43. Mr. M. E. Gear 44. Mr. B. Langley 45. Mr. A. R. Wagner 46. Mr. P. M. Lush 47. Mrs. D. Taylor 48. Mr. A. J. Wright 49. Mr. K. V. Andrew 50. Mrs. N. Doyle 51. Miss A. M. Jones 52. Mr. H. D. Johns 53. Mr. M. E. Capitelli 54. Mr. D. W. Cull 55. Mr. C. D. Hitchcock 56. Mr. V. Miller 57. Mr. J. Thing 58. Mr. D. Norman 59. Mr. S. Weatherhead 60. Mr. E. W. Collins 61. Mrs. B. A. Hunter 62. Mr. R. J. Gamble 63. Mr. C. F. Farley 64. Miss A. E. Fletcher 65. Mr. A. W. P. Fleming 66. Miss S. A. Clack 67. Miss S. A. Lawrence 68. Miss J. Perry 69. Lt.-Col. L. G. James 70. Miss J. Reynolds 71. Lt.-Col. J. R. Stephenson 72. Miss L. M. Houston 73. Wg. Cdr. V. J. W. M. Lawrence 74. Miss W. Daniel 75. Mr. S. E. A. Green 76. Mr. D. Wilson 77. Mr. W. Leonard 78. Mr. T. G. Jones 79. Mr. G. Williams 80. Mr. R. G. Cook 81. Mr. G. Bantock 82. Mr. J. Miller 83. Mr. M. J. A. Cheney 84. Mr. S. R. Lynch 85. Mr. H. O. Powell 86. Mr. J. E. Fairbrother 87. Mr. R. Harrington 88. Mr. C. M. Sewrey 89. Mr. A. T. Bird 90. Mr. F. G. Mann 91. Mr. W. Cowie 92. Miss Y. Mason 93. Mr. D. B. Carr 94. Mr. G. Jenkins 95. Mr. T. Hawker 96. Mr. J. T. Faber 97. Mr. R. A. Sligh 98. Mr. M. E. L. Mellush 99. Mr. D. J. Insole 100. Mr. F. W. Millett 101. Mr. E. W. Swanton 102. Mr. M. C. Cowdrey 103. Mr. G. H. G. Doggart 104. Mr. F. R. Brown 105. Mr. R. Aird 106. Mr. E. W. Phillips 107. Mr. D. G. Clark 108. Sir Anthony F. Tuke 109. Mr. J. A. Bailey 110. Mr. G. O. Allen 111. Mr. C. G. A. Paris 112. Mr. P. B. H. May 113. Mr. J. G. W. Davies 114. Mr. J. S. O. Haslewood 115. Mr. D. R. W. Silk 116. Mr. A. V. Bedser 117. Mr. A. G. Waterman 118. Lt.-Cdr. A. N. S. Burnett

The very first cricket match on the present Lord's ground, in 1814, saw MCC beat Hertfordshire by an innings and 27 runs. One hundred years later the fixture was repeated, and this illuminated scorecard of the original match was printed as a souvenir.

today are quite otherwise, both as they affect the organisation of cricket, and the fortunes of cricketers themselves.

It is instructive to follow the course of advertisements placed by one manufacturer of cricket equipment – Sondico Sports, of Biggleswade in Bedfordshire – in cricketing publications between 1977 and 1980; and particularly to study the alliance reflected there between the firm and David Steele of Northamptonshire. Steele, to the public at large, was a highly competent county batsman unlikely to enjoy a Test career, which had eluded him to the age of thirty-three. Then England chose him, almost in desperation, to face Lillee and Thomson in 1975. In one of the most romantic episodes the game has known, Steele got the better of them with his skill and his even greater guts, scoring 50 and 45 in the Second Test at Lord's, 73 and 92 in the vandalised Test at Headingley, 39 and 66 in the final Test at the Oval. He became a national hero, showered with chops from a grateful butcher in his home town, received with acclaim wherever he appeared. The BBC dubbed him its Sporting Personality of 1975. *Wisden* picked him as one of its five Cricketers of the Year. He played in all five Tests against West Indies the following season, and finished third in England's batting array, with an average of 30.80. That, rather surprisingly, was the end of his short Test career, though he was to remain a heroic figure in the foreground of public consciousness for several seasons to come.

The Biggleswade firm began placing its full-page advertisements in *The Cricketer* magazine in March 1977. The Northamptonshire player was pictured hooking in a characteristic pose, beneath the slogan: "Steele yourself for action with Sondico!" The advert was repeated several times that season. In 1978 David Steele was again featured in a rearranged display, this time in colour; and again the advertisement ran prominently for months. By the end of that year two full seasons had passed since the batsman had appeared for England. In the second of them, however, a fresh star had appeared in the cricketing firmament, and he replaced Steele as the focal point of subsequent ads. "Sondico and David Gower face the ultimate test. . ." was the message in 1979, with picture lay-out adjusted accordingly. David Steele had not been utterly banished at this stage. Either because Sondico still had a lot of old stock on its hands, or because it was hedging its bets on which hero to suspend itself from, David Steele's face could be detected in the background of the advertisement otherwise dedicated to Gower: it decorated the packages of cricket balls lying about in the display. By 1980, however, when there could be no question of Steele being restored to his fame of five years before, his picture had disappeared from the ad. It was all about David Gower now, and the cricket balls were packaged accordingly.

The techniques and instincts of the market place had been at work. A cricketer had served its purpose.

CHAPTER SEVEN

Testing Time

On a Thursday in June, more often than not, Lord's reaches the most important occasion in its year, when its Test match begins. The introduction of double tours has sometimes meant that a second Test will be played at headquarters as well, for it is unthinkable that any team shall tour this country without facing England there. But in any year all activity round the ground has been bent for months on end towards that moment in June when the start of the Lord's Test swivels all attention on St John's Wood.

A day or two beforehand the tempo of preparation increases with the arrival of outsiders who have backstage parts to play in the dramas to come. Squads of people are drafted in by the BBC to erect bits and pieces of equipment around the playing area. Microphones for sound effects are carefully taped to the balcony railings of the Pavilion. The mobile gantry bearing one of the television cameras is manoeuvred behind the sight-screen at the Nursery End, where its yellow arm will be periodically flexed during five days, tracking some of the action and exposing a cameraman to vertigo. The broadcasters themselves begin to wander in, checking this and that, sniffing atmosphere, chatting everybody up: Brian Johnston, who will soon be giving the nation copious earfuls of rather Old Etonian (circa 1925) humour, makes a first leisurely circuit of the ground in his own Test match specials, his co-respondent shoes. The cricket writers, having detached themselves from the humdrum of the county game, drop by the Pavilion, where a notice has been pinned up to establish where they shall sit in the Press Box above the Warner Stand. There are 105 places for reporters up there and each is earmarked for a particular journalist: Woodcock of *The Times*, the thunderer himself and the dean of all he surveys since Jim Swanton and John Arlott retired, doesn't need to take a look; front row, corner nearest the Pavilion, is where he's been posted for many a year.

Outside contractors arrive in numbers. Gardeners come to tidy the herbaceous borders at the Pavilion end of Lord's, which they had planted with bulbs and annuals earlier in the year. Riggers come to put up marquees: for Ladbroke's and others down on the practice ground, for MCC alone behind the Pavilion. The big top there is where the club purveys its hospitality to its official guests. Months before a Test match begins treasured invitations have been despatched on behalf of the President and Committee of MCC, beckoning several score of acquaintances to take lunch and tea on appointed days of the match. Together with the families and hangers-on of the players, these watch the cricket from the exclusive Q Stand, where they are liberally plied with drinks from late morning onwards by the young ladies of the MCC Secretariat, who exchange their typewriters for waitressing during a Test and other big games. Then all are wined and dined most amply under canvas behind the stand at proper sit-down meals, a dozen or so to each table, with a menu to every place, the stiff card neatly bordered with the MCC colours of yellow and red.

The only folk served more handsomely than this are the exalted handful who receive an invitation to spend the whole of a Test match day in the President's box (in the Tavern Stand) or the Secretary's box (in the Grandstand). These invariably include the high officials accompanying England's opponents, personal friends of the host, distinguished old cricketers, and occasional performers in other fields (like Ronnie Corbett), hand-picked not so much for their entertainment value, but because in that particular year they have held office with the Lord's Taverners, the cricket charity – and sometimes the knockabout turn on the pitch – established in 1950 to raise funds for playing fields, underprivileged and handicapped children.

A man following a Test match from the President's box at Lord's may properly feel that he has attained the peak of his cricket-watching life. Within earshot of the Tavern crowd, yet safely distanced from its hurly-burly, elevated just above third man and with every corner of the field in full view, his is a comfortable as well as a lofty stance. He has leg room on his balcony seat. If rain stops play and the prevailing wind drives it inboard, he can take refuge behind plate glass and someone will almost certainly hand him compensatory refreshment as he goes through the door. Nor does he have to worry about scoffing his lunch in order not to miss a ball; he can dawdle through the trifle and the cheese absent-mindedly while he watches what's going on in the middle. He doesn't have to lament the absence of the slow-motion replay, for there's a television set perched high in one corner of the little dining-room (watch, next time you're at Lord's, how all necks on the President's balcony rotate every time a wicket falls). All this and the opportunity to question the likes of R. E. S. Wyatt about the cricket of a long time ago. And the chance to drop hints to the chairman of selectors about who should and should not be in the England team. A man who has spent a day at a Test in the President's box at Lord's can emerge quite pleased with himself, puffed up like a turkey cock.

Nothing requires more preparation before a Test than the victualling of 27,000 people through five six-hour days. The duration of all cricket matches means that more attention must be paid to the food and drink of spectators in this sport than any other, so that catering always has been a consideration of some moment at Lord's. There was a time (and it lasted for several years after the Second World War) when people would trek out to St John's Wood simply to buy the bread that was baked and sold there by the Mayfair Catering Company, whose barrows decked in MCC's colours were to be found inside and outside the ground, each hooded to keep the bread within warm. There was a bakery in those days under the Mound Stand, and fresh loaves were trundled for consumption at the Tavern and for loading into those barrows by the main gates along a miniature railway that ran under the stand, its rolling stock consisting of trolleys which were hauled along with ropes. Such simple arrangements, like many others, have long since gone. Small businesses operating as quaintly as that do not survive in the economic climate of our times. The catering at Lord's nowadays is done by the firm of Graison's, who lie at the end of a commercial chain linked through the Chef and Brewer, and Watney Mann, to Grand Metropolitan Hotels Ltd. Graison's pay MCC an annual fee for the concession at Lord's and then get on with the job themselves. They run the banqueting suite by the Grace Gates, with its restaurant open on cricketing days, its dinner-dances and wedding receptions as well at other times. They attend to the two dining suites in the Pavilion, one for the players, the other for MCC's Committee. They provide all that is consumed in the private boxes and the marquees. They handle the trade in the pub beside the ground. They organise the sixteen bars that are deployed around Lord's. The only things they don't control are the mobile bangers-and-chips shop at the Nursery End, the ice-cream vans, and the little seafood stall parked beside the Warner Stand.

Throughout the year Graison's have a permanent staff of sixteen to conduct their affairs at Lord's, augmented by another dozen for the whole of the cricket season. But for the Test and other major matches some 300 hands are shipped in to cope with the demand, semi-casuals who take what work the catering trade can offer them at a number of big sporting events which include Henley, Wimbledon and Ascot as well as Lord's. It is doubtful whether these earn their money more laboriously than they do when foddering a Test match cricket crowd. The important factor is not merely the quantities that are shifted; it extends to maintaining an acceptable relationship with the customers, which can be a tricky one when they come in two kinds. Backchat up to a certain level is acceptable enough in the public places at Lord's, much less so where MCC members congregate. The members, moreover, do not take kindly to waiting for what they want, which is why the Long Room bar is generally overstaffed a bit at peak periods, by the norms of these things. The general public don't much like queueing either, but they are more accustomed to having to. Everyone is distinctly rattier with the catering staff, it seems, when the weather is poor: there are twice as many complaints on a rainy day as when the sun shines on the ground.

We take yeoman appetites with us when we go to a Test at Lord's. The more delicate eaters will demolish 130 lb of strawberries and raspberries every day, not to mention the fresh salmon (originating in Scotland but killed on a fish farm outside Oxford at teatime and entering the Grace Gates before breakfast), of which Lord's takes in one and a half tons in the course of its season. The hoi polloi, meanwhile, is getting its teeth into 2,500 doughnuts every day, after bolting 3,000 sandwiches which a team of four has been making since four o'clock in the morning at a rate of seventy-five seconds per packet, including the time taken to wrap it in plastic. Meat pies and pasties are even more popular, with anything up to 4,000 going down the hatch every day of a Test. All this, of course, is supplementary to the vast amount of tucker people bring into the ground themselves in their shopping bags, their briefcases, their holdalls, their freezer boxes and their rucksacks. When the cricket season begins at Lord's, Graison's simply order 90,000 cardboard plates and 130,000 paper cups to contain part of what they expect to sell over the next few months.

They also stock up with 100,000 plastic pint holders and 40,000 plastic half-pint vessels to assist the drinkers. Only in the members' bars are glasses provided, on the assumption that no one belonging to MCC is going to be stupid enough to throw such an object on to the pitch, and in acknowledgement of the fact that at Lord's the tastes of MCC members must be obliged at all times. The assumption may no longer be as safe as it once was: the fact is that *no one* has yet thrown anything on to the pitch at Lord's during the course of a game. The cushions that have once or twice been showered on to the grass in the past few years have come in exasperation when play has been called off unreasonably early in the view of those who threw them. Doubtless drink had something to do with the reflex, for enough of it gets to those parts of Lord's that temperance cannot reach. Before a Test match starts, six lorry loads of beer, which means 500 ten-gallon kegs, roll into the ground and generally last for no more than half the game (the consumption is even more impressive at a Cup Final, when nearly 3,500 gallons may be expected to go through the system in one day). It is taken by the pint in the public bars more often than not, by the half-pint among the members, and no one has quite fathomed the reason for this discrepancy, unless it be that a high proportion of elderly bladders is accountable to MCC. The membership takes care of ninety-eight per cent of the spirits sold on the ground, though no bar at Lord's will expect to get through more than eight bottles of Scotch and a similar quantity of gin in a day. But the members, the sponsors and the restaurant between them cause up to 120 cases of wine to disappear every day of a big match.

The makings of a sociologist's thesis are there in the drinking patterns of Lord's. Much more draught ale than canned beer is sold during a Test match than during a Cup Final, for instance, and vice versa. The reason is the difference in rhythm between one form of cricket and the other: the action in a one-day game is always so liable to be hectic that nobody wishes to risk missing anything while he is away queueing for a pint, so he stocks up with a large number of cans before play starts and during the intervals. Canned beer is viewed with a certain amount of suspicion at Lord's. It's what spectators bring into the ground with them, often in staggering amounts, and therefore the form of drinking, with side effects, which cannot be controlled. The controls on what is sold on the ground are rather greater than occasional tipplers might suppose. High gravity beers are quite deliberately shunned by the caterers. There comes the rollicking point in some big match days when people queueing at the Tavern or any other public bar are informed that stocks have run out; which is a judicious way of handling matters when everyone has just about had enough. For the same reason, bar staff are sometimes told to take more breaks than usual, in order to slow the service down. But only once in the past few years has the Tavern bar been irrevocably shut before its normal closing time because too many drunks were already awash – Northamptonshire v Derbyshire, in the first NatWest Final in 1981. The crowds at Lord's, in fact, hold their booze pretty well; certainly better than the average hard drinker on an Australian Test ground. And though the quantities drained by spectators in NW8 will dismay the wowsers, Sydney Cricket Ground almost certainly outstrips everywhere else in this respect. It has been calculated that after the Fourth Test there against Denness's team in 1975, some 864,000 beer cans had to be removed by the garbage men.

The only place on the ground where little alcohol is consumed during a day's play is up in the players' dining-room. The odd beer, the occasional shandy, may slake a bowler's thirst during the lunch interval (what he puts back after close of play is another matter), but most of the cricketers stick to milk or soft drinks when they take their breaks. That dining-room is run by one of the great characters of Lord's: Nancy Doyle as ever was, as Irish still as when she came out of County Meath these many years ago, and her knowing naught of cricket (which she confused with rounders) at the time, which Colin Cowdrey painstakingly put right on the Pavilion balcony one day, since when her heart has been given to Kent, although she also has a soft spot for the Middlesex boys, that being natural enough because she sees them day in and day out when they're playing at home. A grandmother in fact, though her presence is that of an indulgent aunt, Nancy is paid by Graison's, answers to MCC, but is at all times and in all places very much her own lady, her independence emphasised by certain successes on the football pools, one of which paid for a trip to New Zealand a little while back, in order to see her son. She has been introduced to the monarch's consort as part of the furniture at Lord's. She has received from a Prime Minister (Sir Alec Douglas-Home) a brooch by way of thanks for her care and attention during his Presidential year in MCC, together with a letter which her paymasters would have liked for publicity purposes until Nancy told them where to go. She also has a collection of forty-eight cricket bats, signed by county and Test sides, some indication of her standing with the players who have sat at her table.

The truth is that Nancy Doyle feeds them better than anyone else does in England, and she is probably unrivalled anywhere in the cricket-playing world. The eternal salad of the county circuit (rarely as ambitious as the lobster and shrimp variety which has been known to appear at the Bath Festival) is something she wouldn't dream of serving, unless specifically asked for. Generally speaking, cricketers enjoy something more substantial only when county clubs concede their own inability to cater properly and shunt teams down to adjacent pubs; this can mean, in Northampton, heavy dumplings, which go down less than a treat with fast bowlers facing a hot afternoon. It is said that Sheffield once rose to a three-course lunch, which included wine and spotted dick; if so, it will have been the nearest thing any other venue has managed to what is commonly provided at Lord's. Nancy Doyle's regime there is based on roast beef, or lamb, or pork, or chicken, or steak and kidney pie, with potatoes and two veg, followed by a pudding, a cheese board and coffee. She switches the meats and the puddings around daily to avoid the players getting bored. When the Indians or Pakistanis arrive she simply omits the beef or the pork and the steak and kidney pie from the rotation, perhaps slips in fish on their behalf, but otherwise carries on as usual. She's not yet been asked for a totally vegetarian meal by South Indian eaters. At the second interval of the day she provides sandwiches, cakes and tea.

She panders, just a little, to notorious individual tastes. Some players never take anything in the middle of the day but the sweet, the cheese and the coffee. Botham is not such a big eater as his physique might suggest, but he does go in for more than one helping of meat, sometimes much more, and at Lord's he gets it. Boycott, who frequently eats alone when the other players have finished, has a vast appetite for apple pie and beef sandwiches, and a fair one for boiling water, which he takes down to the dressing-room in order to mash up his ginseng tea. It is customary for not-out batsmen to eat their lunch down there, sometimes whichever bowlers are in harness at the time, too. But Nancy draws the line when half a dozen other players decide to be waited on two flights of stairs below her own domain.

Nor will she allow them to enter her dining-room unless they're properly dressed, which means that bare feet are out at all times, likewise track suits unless worn by Middlesex players sneaking in for a late breakfast before they start their day's work. Once, when the Surrey team trooped in wearing full dress (blazers over their flannels), according to a new regulation issued by their county superiors, she observed that one fellow very obviously was doing his own number that day. When challenged he pointed out that, as team manager, he preferred to wear a track suit at all times during a match. This cut no ice with Nancy; and Mickey Stewart was sent to conform to Surrey rules before he got his lunch. She will take what she calls no nonsense from anybody. Poor Phil Edmonds once got on the wrong side of Nancy during his early days with Middlesex, wasn't spoken to thereafter for a month or more, and must have come close to starvation before a truce was called. She responds to Authority in much the same way, and is unofficially licensed to say what she thinks before all and sundry at Lord's to a degree that no one else shares. She was once catering to a Presidential box which contained three Prime Ministers (Home, Wilson and Macmillan), the Duke of Norfolk and the Chief Commissioner of the Metropolitan Police, as well as several altitudes in MCC, when the news was delivered that the IRA had planted a bomb on the ground. "My

God," says Nancy Doyle to this distinguished audience, "if they
threw a bomb in here they'd hit the flamin' jack-pot!" And made her
exit, perfectly timed, with a cackle that might have been heard all the
way back to the Bridge of Athlone.

That was in 1973, when the West Indies led by Rohan Kanhai
(who himself scored 157) were on their way to defeating Illingworth's Englishmen by an innings and 226 runs. The bomb threat
turned out to be a hoax, but while it was being taken seriously the
stands were cleared of people so that likely hiding places could be
properly searched, and for over an hour a watching nation was
treated to the spectacle of thousands mustered in orderly fashion on
the playing area of Lord's, except for an oblong in the middle, where
Umpire Bird sat alone to make sure that the wicket, if nothing else on
the ground, remained undamaged. There were thirteen separate
warnings of IRA bombs during the course of that game, which
provided the Ground Superintendent and his men with one of the
most torrid times ever known at Lord's.

It is they who attend to the business of ensuring that everyone is
where he ought to be on the ground, and during any big match this
can be an exhausting affair. They also take care that no one is where
he ought not to be. A nightwatchman patrols Lord's throughout the
year. For some time before and during big games, he is reinforced by
a uniformed squad which goes by the name of MCC Police, as well as
by regular London bobbies and dog patrols. The lesson of that
vandalised Test up at Leeds in 1975 has been carefully noted in St
John's Wood, but before that Lord's had become well known for its
careful security. Floodlights and barbed wire entanglements fes-
tooned the square overnight to thwart potential demonstrators
against the planned tour by South Africa in 1970. It is, some say,
easier for interlopers to penetrate Buckingham Palace than it is for
anyone to enter Lord's without the proper ticket or pass. Even
well-known cricketers have found the Pavilion door closed to them
when they have forgotten to bring their wherewithal to get in.

"Gus" Farley, Ground Superintendent until his retirement in
1983, brought the business of crowd control at Lord's to a refined
study in strategy and tactics, most elaborately detailed in the sixteen-
page briefing which he would issue to his troops on the eve of a Test,
revised each year in the light of previous experience. It included the
following:

SPECIAL NOTE: "Men in charge of Entrances must be on the
alert for spectators trying to introduce into the Ground anything
which could prove to be a nuisance factor – i.e. Flags, Banners,

Musical Instruments, Large Amounts of Alcoholic Beverage, Deckchairs, Prams, Outsize Hats etc. . . . Large Amounts of Alcohol means Large, i.e. one or more gallon plastic containers, Barrels, more than one large Party Size Can, Crates of Bottles, 24-can packs. Especially if these are carried by groups of obvious hooligan potential . . . Tact and discretion must be fully employed on such an occasion."

Tact and discretion, in fact, are as notable at Lord's as the scrutiny of passes; which is why a modicum of banners and flags and (technically) musical instruments do make their appearance at Tests there. The articles considered over the odds are deposited by the North Gates, where they may be picked up after close of play; but not the excessively large amounts of alcohol. They must either be drunk on the spot outside, in which case you may be in no fit state to stumble in, or else they must be dropped right there on the pavement, in which case some grateful wayfarer will dispose of them for you.

None of the 5,000 or so who may queue each day for a Test for unreserved places is allowed into the ground unless and until there is some prospect of play; partly on the principle that it would be unfair to take their money for nothing (ticket-holders take that risk as part of their deal), partly because no cricketing authority in the world has yet come up with a method of returning money or otherwise compensating its customers for not getting what they've paid for. The queues are invariably good-natured even when they have been required to exercise a lot of patience. The biggest trouble at the turnstiles is usually caused by some old body who gets stuck going through, panics, and causes the machine to lose count, thus producing awkward questions later for the gatekeeper, when the money in his possession and the figures on the counter don't match. And there can be embarrassing moments at the barriers by the Grace Gates, where the members and other privileged make their entrances, and where rank outsiders have been known to try the same thing by offering a fiver instead of a pass.

The ground is policed by the Metropolitan force during the big matches, their comings and goings organised from a control room on the east side of the Mound Stand. Their presence, by and large, is much more seen than felt, and there were 400 of them at Lord's for that 1975 Test precisely because IRA violence was generally in the air. Normally, no more than 120 are rostered for St John's Wood on each morning of a Test, and only forty of them will be inside the ground, the rest disentangling traffic and people in the roads outside. Compared with duty at the average British football ground, a policeman's lot at cricket's headquarters is a piece of cake. From time to time the MCC stewards need a constabulary hand to eject some fool who's had too much to drink and become too aggressive in supporting his team; but even then, tact and discretion are often employed. It is not unknown for a thick-headed supporter to be escorted out through the Grace Gates and allowed back in an hour or so later, when he's had a chance to cool off and reflect on his sins. If he's stupid enough to make for the middle, either to bestow felicitations on a batsman or merely to streak, the tacit agreement is that the stewards if need be will pursue him rather than the coppers, lest the dignity of the Metropolitan force be lowered by someone more agile than its constables.

Invasions of the pitch – which began in this country when Asif Iqbal reached his century in the Oval Test of 1967 and had to be rescued from idiotic well-wishers who rushed to the middle – have occurred from time to time at Lord's, as they have on every other major cricket ground. That is why the direst penalty of ejection from the ground is threatened politely each day before the umpires come out and ("May we remind spectators . . .") at the end of the intervals, on the public address system. The threat comes with all the combined weight of MCC and the Metropolitan Police, though the voice is that of an actor, Alan Curtis, who is said to do a very good Captain Hook on other stages. He is a spokesman of idiosyncrasy, who refers to play "commencing", not "starting", and rain "ceasing", not "stopping". But it isn't his fault when he asks someone to check in at "the door at the rear of the Pavilion". That used to be referred to more sensibly as the back door until Field Marshal Montgomery, who rarely visited Lord's but liked to make his presence felt when he did, one day objected to the loudspeaker request for a doctor to go to the back door; on the grounds that it reduced a general practitioner to the dreadful status of a tradesman.

Anything up to 350 stewards may be recruited by MCC for a Test or Cup Final, and the ones who have their work cut out are those who are expected to keep spectators clear of the boundary ropes. The habit of letting hundreds sit on the grass inside the fence may bring to Lord's a whiff of the old village green, but it is regarded as a pain in the neck by officials who have to keep the crowd under control. The fact is that, although infinitely better behaved than football crowds, cricket-watchers are no longer as biddable as they once were. The boundary squatters edge forward, bit by bit; they do not instantly retreat at the word of command, they sometimes answer back. Some of the counties contesting finals at Lord's now bring their quota of rowdies, and not all of them are grouped thickly by their refuelling station at the Tavern bar, which once upon a time was the only part of Lord's that could be relied upon to produce the sort of racket that charms only up to a point. When Lancashire and Surrey appear in big matches at headquarters these days they bring with them young lusties whose instincts have been moulded by winter dedication to Manchester United and Chelsea. Luckily for everyone else, the mobs who have been giving Leeds United a bad name do not yet appear to have inflicted themselves upon Yorkshire County Cricket Club.

Among the supporters of Test teams playing England, the New Zealanders are either so thin upon the ground or so introspective as to be almost inconspicuous. Indians and Pakistanis can make a noise and wave banners, but mercifully do not work themselves up into the sort of frenzy that has brought Tests in Calcutta and Lahore to a standstill; though once, when the politics of their homeland were unusually inflamed, a group of Pakistanis occupied a relatively empty portion of the Mound Stand for the purpose of demonstrating support for Mr Bhutto (or maybe it was the other way around), a manifestation which did not exceed democratic limits once a brace of London bobbies had been despatched to sit among them. More aggressive policing than that is almost always confined to Australian Test matches, when young larrikins from Earl's Court find even the Tavern's low gravity beer too much for them; they are not in the same league as their fathers were when it comes to drink, according to Gus Farley, who enjoyed fighting alongside Australians in North Africa.

As for the West Indians, they may be the noisiest of all cricket supporters, but they are also among the best behaved when they come to Lord's. They entered the mythology of the ground on that historic day in June 1950 which produced Lord Beginner's calypso extolling Ramadhin and Valentine. No West Indian side had ever won a Test match in England before, but Goddard's men trounced England that day by 326 runs, in spite of a second innings century by Washbrook. No one else in Yardley's team hit 50 in the match, but Wardle made 33 not out and 21, batting at No. 9. A not out 168 by Walcott in the second innings was the backbone of the 425 for six with which West Indies declared. But the victory really was secured by those two spinners.

They were first put on when England were 62 for no wicket in the first innings, a score which became 86 for five within an hour and a half. They were not exactly unplayable (England, in fact, made 151 and 274; and Test matches have been won with scores like that), but they baffled all the batsmen who faced them. The like of Ramadhin especially had never been seen before, with his curious action in bringing his arm up above his head as though – someone said at the time – he was about to shower himself with confetti. Most significantly of all, those two bowlers almost monopolised the West Indian attack after that first breakthrough, as their figures tell:

Valentine 45–28–48–4 and 71–47–79–3
Ramadhin 43–27–66–5 and 72–43–86–6

The rest of the West Indian attack, four men, bowled fewer than sixty-seven overs between them in the match. If a pair of spinners were given such opportunity today, they might well believe in the possibility of time warps back into the Middle Ages and beyond.

Among the 112,000 who watched that match (the gates closed with 30,500 inside on the first day) was the first substantial contingent of West Indians ever seen at an English Test. There may have been no more than a few hundred of them, but their participation in that match startled the traditional tranquillity of the place, which hasn't been quite the same since. A West Indian batsman would strike a ball which might or might not reach the boundary before a fieldsman headed it off, and just over the ropes a figure would arise, beckoning it on with ecstatic cries. When an English wicket fell, black spectators (we nervously weren't sure of the polite description then) were to be seen flinging themselves into the air and around each other's necks with joy. The inhibited whites (and, my Lord, we never called ourselves that in those days), most of whom had never seen anything like this in their lives, responded at first with uncertain grins. But by the end of that Test they had come to the conclusion that here was something that made cricket-watching even more fun than in the past. As for the West Indians in the crowd, when Worrell had Wardle lbw and the match was won, they went potty with pleasure. A gang of them formed up with guitars and things to beat time on, and shimmied their way round Lord's, singing their calypsos as they went. That was when the MCC members in front of the Pavilion stood and clapped as warmly as they had done when the players were coming in.

The West Indians have become much more numerous and a lot noisier in the thirty-odd years since that day. Yet they give very little trouble to anyone but those who think the din of empty Coke tins being beaten together non-stop a bit excessive. One reason may very well be that they do not drink beer in the quantities consumed by whites. Another is that every one of them seems keener on watching cricket than on mucking about. For a people whose natural inclination is to be much more demonstrative than any Anglo-Saxon, they have a nice sense of control, too; it just happens to be shaped differently from the native one. A feature of the first World Cup Final, when West Indies faced Australia and beat them thrillingly in the end, was the self-appointed custodian of law and order in front of the Grandstand. That area was full of West Indians, many of whom in their excitement were running across the ropes when their players did something to celebrate. They were paying less attention than they might have done to the injunctions of the police. Whereupon one of their number, a large fellow with a commanding voice, took it upon himself to walk the ropes from time to time, ordering them to behave. "The poh-leesman says you gotta get back," he bellowed, pointing a dramatic finger at the demarcation line. "So you jes' better get back!"

Gus Farley, instructed to do something about noise abatement during one West Indian Test, spent some time trying to identify two particular nuisances; a bugler and a whistler, who were blowing in duet more or less without interruption throughout the day. Eventually he tracked them down, surrounded by a dozen or so of their friends. What followed was a paradigm of that tact and discretion he urged on his own men, and also of the response by West Indians when it is employed.

"Now look here," said Farley, "I've not come to make trouble, but you've got to stop making such a bloody racket all the time. Do you know that we've been having complaints from as far away as Nottingham about you two?"

"Nottingham?" said the incredulous bugler. "They can't hear me in Nottingham, man."

"Too right, they can. They can hear you on the radio and they've been ringing up asking us to do something about it."

"Nottingham?" repeated the bugler, flabbergasted now by the unsuspected range of his ear-splitting notes. "They can really hear me in Nottingham?"

"That's right. And you've got to stop it. Not altogether, because we want you to enjoy yourselves. Blow your bloody heads off if Viv Richards gets his century, or if you take one of our wickets. But otherwise, just knock it off."

The duettists considered this for a moment, wondering whether there was a catch somewhere. Then, "OK, man," said the whistler, "That's reasonable. That's what we'll do."

The marvel is that a crowd of rising 30,000 people which can produce such a volume of sound as that at Lord's on the big occasion –

whatever the mixture of the crowd, whatever the contest they are watching – can on the instant be utterly still and silent, and can sustain this eerie rhythm for six full hours of play. Among outdoor spectator sports, only tennis, golf and show-jumping know a comparably concentrated quietness at the crucial moments of performance, but none of them also knows the pandemonium which breaks out at other times during a Test match at Lord's, and which throws the regular silences into such dramatic relief. Alan Fairfax, the Australian medium-pacer of the thirties, used to say that the Lord's crowds were so remarkably still from the moment he or any other bowler began his run in, until the execution of the batsman's stroke, that it was like playing on an empty ground. This is, perhaps, the last of cricket's traditions to survive virtually intact; perfectly so, were it not for the metronome clatter of empty cans when West Indians are performing in force.

One is conscious of it most of the time when sitting in the public stands, where conversation babbles ceaselessly all day, then stops with sentences unfinished or trailing away in a whisper, to be succeeded by a thunderclap roar, or a vast intake of breath, or continued speech. Six times in every over this sequence occurs, and the spellbound effect is even more emphatic after a wicket has fallen and a new batsman comes down the Pavilion steps. The tumult attending the dismissal may scarcely have died by the time that lonely figure reaches the wicket; and while he is making his mark on the crease, while he is taking note of the field, there can still be loud noise all around Lord's. But his act of taking guard against the waiting bowler brings the dramatic hush without fail. No orchestral conductor, with one motion, ever produced a more sensational response.

The phenomenon does not extend so powerfully to the incumbents of the Long Room. Little noise is ever produced in there, even when the chamber is crowded, with ancient cronies hunched over the window ledges, with men sitting raptly on high-legged chairs, with other fellows dangling their legs from the tables or standing shoulder to shoulder and gazing steadfastly at the play. They talk to each other between deliveries, but only the deaf old men speak loudly; the rest murmur sotto voce to each other, as though it were one of the rules of the house. Isolated spatters of clapping applaud the handsome stroke, the superb delivery, the athletic interception of the ball. Gruff phrases of dissent may be heard when a player has got something too obviously wrong. But any feat of high class is generously acknowledged when a cricketer returns to the Pavilion. Inside and out the members stand and clap in unison, and every platitude of acclaim may be heard with the possible exception of "Hear, hear".

But it can be an ordeal for any cricketer to pass through the Long Room at Lord's by himself, as every batsman must at least twice, unless he has already played well enough to be sure of the applause. When David Steele left the dressing-room for what was to be his memorable introduction to Test cricket, he was so nervous that he descended one flight of stairs too many and had to be redirected from the vicinity of the basement lavatory before he ran the gauntlet and got out into the open air. That sense of running a gauntlet was at its heaviest, so palpable that you could almost touch it, when Ian Botham returned to the Pavilion after batting against the Australians in the Second Test of 1981. He had just made his second duck of the match, and his captaincy of England (which he was to relinquish later that day) had not only been inadequate, but had clearly burdened him so much that he had briefly become a caricature of the magnificent cricketer he really is.

He came up those steps, bat under his arm, gloves peeled off, looking worn-out and miserable, taking care to catch nobody's eye. He need not have bothered, for there was nobody's eye to meet his. The members of the Pavilion seats sat stonily, trying not to notice him. In the crowded Long Room the attendant opened the door and people shuffled back to allow him through. Otherwise you could have heard a pin drop in that room, which was stifling in its display of studied ostracism. As Botham approached the Long Room's further door, young Dilley came through to take his place at the crease. They paused together as they met. Dilley whispered something to his captain, obviously asking if there were instructions. Botham, with a shrug of the shoulders and a weary expression around the mouth, made a small gesture with his hand: just play it straight. Then he turned and made for the stairs, quickly, yearning for the refuge of the dressing-room. At that point someone in the Long Room cleared his throat. The tension was released. The smothering silence lifted. The members became their discreetly conversational selves again.

They have, over the years, shown their warmer side to many a player from every land, who will have remembered the wonderfully impartial applause of Lord's to the end of his days. In 1972, between Bob Massie's 8 for 84 in the first innings and 8 for 53 in the second (for it was his match above all), Greg Chappell spent three hours at the crease before hitting a boundary, but this seemed to release a safety catch, and he went on to a superb 131, his first Test century in England. Twelve months later that greatest of all-rounders, Gary Sobers, majestically plundered England's bowling for 150 not out, which was his twenty-sixth and last century in Test cricket. In 1978 the visiting hero was New Zealand's Geoff Howarth, whose 123 was fashioned from five hours and forty minutes of extended courage, for he was suffering from influenza all the time he was at the wicket. When the Indians came to Lord's the following year, Vengsarkar and Viswanath, centurions both, kept their side in the game with a stand of 210 which some compared to the match-saving performance of Watson and Bailey against the Australians in 1953, and to the one with which Sobers and his young cousin Holford kept the Englishmen at bay in 1966. In 1980 the genius of Viv Richards was exhibited with a century in 125 minutes in what, quite surprisingly, was his first Test at Lord's, though he had shown his brilliance on the ground many times before in other games.

A couple of years later, Mohsin Khan scored precisely 200 runs for Pakistan, the first batsman to reach that figure in a Test there since the New Zealander Martin Donnelly did so in 1949. Across those decades there have been other individual performances that have thrilled, gripped the imagination, and occasionally astounded, by tourists and Englishmen alike. Not one of them has ended without the entire ground rising to its feet in homage (as well as to restore circulation around the fundament, for spectating takes its toll of a body, too) and applauding the cricketer, whether he be friend or foe. At such moments the members in the Pavilion stand beaming when the returning player strides past them, as though he were a son who'd just done well in a house match at school. Only a sense of propriety prevents some of them touching him to show him how fatherly they feel. Even Dennis Lillee has had his meed of praise at Lord's, where they make meticulous distinctions between a man's achievements with bat or ball, and his failure to reach acceptable norms in other respects.

The only thing at headquarters that its crowds usually fail to appreciate, is what happens when they have poured through the gates at the end of the day in a headlong rush for the nearest bus stops, or a steadier surge towards the St John's Wood and Baker Street Underground stations. The answer is mostly provided by that queue of fellows waiting to come in at the North Gates. They will have been patiently waiting there for hours, both to secure their position as keenly as any cricket-watcher and because most of them, in any case, have not much else to do. A majority are regulars who turn up to render Lord's tidy again, year in and year out. Officially they are referred to as casual cleaners, but Gus Farley, who recruited them, knew them for men of character. There is The O'Brien and his nephew Ginger (from County Monahan), who perform prodigies of shifting garbage in bulk. There is Pierre, the French-Canadian, who sings snatches of opera while he works. There are the Ryan Brothers, who let it be known that they'll take on anyone from Belfast. There are Cash and Carry, either brothers or accomplices, who switch a green and red tam o' shanter between them while one attends to the rubbish and the other scouts around for half-empty bottles of booze. There is Benito-the-Pope, who spends what he earns not on drink but on bets. There was once Bell, the Scotsman who would entertain the rest with his Highland dances, and died doing so when he reeled into the road and was hit by a lorry. They should be remembered in any roll-call of this ground. They sweep up and stockpile for the cleansing department's removal truck, about thirteen tons of garbage every evening after a Test or a Cup Final. They are as responsible as anyone for the model reputation of Lord's on the morning of a big match.

Nothing more precisely illustrates the diminished domestic role of MCC in this generation than the club's relationship with international cricket. Almost a full circle has now been turned since the days when cricketers first crossed the seas to play each other, with MCC in one sense very nearly back where it started in this sphere. It had nothing at all to do with the earliest tours abroad – by Englishmen to Canada and the United States in 1859, to Australia two years later – and little enough when the first tourists to England, the Australian Aborigines, came over in 1868. MCC acted as host and picked its own team when those visitors played at Lord's, but otherwise took no part in the venture; and that was part of a general pattern which continued to the end of the nineteenth century. Until then, teams representing England, in what had become known as Test matches against Australian touring sides, were chosen in turn by the committee of whichever club (county or otherwise) was allowing its ground to be used for the match. And English touring sides abroad were picked and organised by interested individuals, not by clubs or any central authority.

The first departure from this formula came in 1899, when MCC established a Board of Control at the request of the cricketing counties. It consisted of MCC's President, five members of the MCC Committee, and a representative of every county which had finished in the top ten the previous season, together with a delegate from any other county which was to mount a forthcoming Test. In time, this Board automatically included someone from every first-class county, as well as its quota from MCC, which always supplied the dominating influence if not numerical superiority. Until it was supplanted by the TCCB in 1968, the Board of Control appointed

179

the selectors of England's teams playing at home. The first panel in 1899 consisted of Lord Hawke, W. G. Grace and H. W. Bainbridge (plus England's co-opted captain, who was Archie MacLaren that year); and although the selecting trio nominally represented Yorkshire, Gloucestershire and Warwickshire, each was first and foremost a dedicated member of MCC. This tradition remained more or less intact until the Board of Control's demise, except that from 1949 until the end the number of selectors (other than the current captain) was increased to four. Significantly, no professional cricketer became an England selector until Leslie Ames reached the panel in 1950, though 1926 had seen the curiosity of both Hobbs and Rhodes being co-opted to assist P. F. Warner, P. A. Perrin and A. E. R. Gilligan.

Touring sides of Englishmen abroad remained matters of individual enterprise until the winter of 1903–4, when a party captained by Warner played in Australia wholly under the auspices of MCC. Those four years since the Board of Control's creation had firmly established the Marylebone club as the ruling authority in English cricket. Whereas earlier it had merely dominated by virtue of seniority, social power and its custody of the Laws, it had now become the great organiser as well. Henceforth MCC alone chose the touring teams and raised the necessary funds to despatch each party; it negotiated conditions with host countries and watched the cricketers sail and play their way around the world under its own house flag.* The parties which left England set off as MCC teams and every game they played was as an MCC side, until Test matches took place; at which point these nominally club cricketers were suddenly translated into *England* versus Australia, or whoever provided the opposition.

Not all these habits changed with the invention of TCCB in 1968. Thereafter the new board alone made all arrangements and appointed the selectors for international cricket played by Englishmen both at home and abroad, but touring sides were still known waywardly as MCC teams until after Mike Brearley and his men returned from New Zealand and Pakistan in 1978. Since then they have been officially called England sides from start to finish of every

* MCC raised the funds for these tours by selling some of its assets if need be, though host countries have always guaranteed a certain amount of money for visiting parties. But the Marylebone club met the cost of the journey to Australia of, for example, Jardine's tourists in 1932–3 by disposing of £3,000 worth of 5 per cent War Loan stock. When all the accounting had been done at the end of the tour, however, MCC had made a profit of £6,537. From this sum it offered £300 apiece to each of the first-class counties, the Minor Counties Association, the National Playing Fields Association, the London Playing Fields Association and the Cricketers' Fund Friendly Society. The balance it deposited in its own Foreign Tours fund.

tour. Yet even now one sentimental link with the Marylebone club remains. When Bob Willis took his side Down Under in 1982–3, it had been chosen by TCCB's latest selection committee – Peter May, Alec Bedser, Norman Gifford and Alan Smith – with the co-opted assistance of Willis himself, Donald Carr (as Secretary of TCCB) and Doug Insole (as chairman of the board's Cricket Committee, rather than as the team manager on tour). The board organised all its movements around the Southern hemisphere and paid those cricketers for their labours there. But every time one of those England players chose to wear an old-fashioned cap instead of a helmet or sunhat, he displayed the St George and Dragon badge which was first designed for MCC touring teams, and every time he pulled on his sweater, he was wearing the MCC colours of yellow and red.

If the arrangement of overseas tours and the picking of teams were all that there was to international cricket, then MCC's position in the world spectrum of the sport nowadays might indeed be thought rather a forlorn one when contrasted with its stature of not so long ago. Actually, it still holds a prime and increasingly vital position, because cricket administration always has meant more than team selection. At an international level it has also meant adjudication on the way the game should be played, according to both its codified and unwritten laws. MCC's prime position consists in its relationship with the International Cricket Conference, whose chairman is MCC's President each year, whose administration is entirely carried out by the Marylebone club under the direction of Jack Bailey, the Secretary of MCC, and whose meetings are held each summer in the MCC Committee Room at Lord's.

No international cricketing body existed until, in 1909, at the suggestion of the South African Abe Bailey, an Imperial Cricket Conference sat down in London. It was composed of half a dozen men representing England (which effectively meant MCC), Australia and South Africa, and it discussed the possibility of a triangular tournament between the three countries (which took place in 1912), as well as matters related to international umpiring, hours of play and the qualification of players. Three years passed before another meeting was held, and the conference gathered irregularly until 1929, after which it became an annual event. By then it also incorporated representatives from West Indies, India and New Zealand, but the three founder members retained supremacy by supplying twice as many delegates as the others were allowed. Not until 1958 was the principle of one man one vote (suggested by South Africa) extended to the member countries of ICC, which, with the addition of Pakistan, had grown to seven. Two years earlier, taking note of certain historical events which had been occurring for the best part of a decade, someone proposed that the word "Imperial" be dropped from the conference's style and title; but quite remarkably, nothing was done about this until 1965, when "International" was brought in as a substitute. In the very broadest sense, cricket had become an international sport by then, not just the amusement of nations which had belonged to the British Empire. It was played, at varying standards and frequencies, in more than fifty countries all over the earth – and they included the likes of Denmark and Israel as well as the United States.

It was to encourage the fortunes of the game in such lesser cricketing lands that 1965 also brought the inspiration of associate membership of ICC, offered in the first place to the Americans, to Ceylon (as Sri Lanka was still known) and to Fiji; later much more widely spread. By 1979 there were seventeen associates and that year saw the first competition between them for a new ICC trophy, another idea to stimulate their domestic cricket and give them a sense of community in the cricket-playing world. It was held on a number of club grounds in the English midlands that May, each match consisted of 120 overs, and despite bad weather throughout, it was judged a great success. As was the second competition in 1982, though that was blighted by even greater interruptions of English rain. Sri Lanka's victory over Canada in the first tournament helped her promotion to full Test-playing membership of ICC, causing many to suspect that Zimbabwe, who beat Bermuda in the 1982 Final, might be the next country eventually elevated to the company of the senior hands.

The associates can have no say on Test cricket, and their voting is therefore virtually restricted – beyond the Laws and the principles of cricket – to their own participation in the game. Indeed, the constitution of ICC ordains a hierarchy of three distinct levels, each embodying a different degree of power. There are the foundation members, of whom only the United Kingdom and Australia remain. There are the full members – West Indies, India, New Zealand, Pakistan and Sri Lanka now. And there are the associates, eighteen of them at the last count. All continue to debate the traditional and purist matters which were the reason for the conference setting itself up in 1909. But as international politics increasingly reach into all forms of sporting life, so the political attitudes adopted by the seven major ICC countries have become more crucial to the future of cricket than their views on the Laws of the game and the spirit in which it should be played. So, also, does the central role of MCC in this body become more important every year. The United Kingdom's two delegates to conference are nominated by the Cricket Council, and are invariably the chairman of the Cricket Council and the Chairman of the TCCB. But by permanently providing the chairman and, even more significantly, the administrative chief and his staff, the Marylebone club has a commanding voice in composing ICC's agenda and steering its discussions every time.

More and more, ICC meetings have been spent on deliberating the repercussions of apartheid in South Africa, the founder member which was obliged to leave the conference when its Government decided to withdraw from the British Commonwealth in 1961: ICC was still "Imperial" in those days, and its constitution would have no truck with such extreme forms of republicanism. A lasting result of that banishment has been that a generation of South African officials has been required to watch from beyond the boundary while others have settled South Africa's cricketing fate. And though it has become customary to speak of South Africa's progressive isolation from the rest of the cricketing world, as if this were some lamentably recent phenomenon, the reality is that South Africa always was isolated to a considerable extent. Even before the great ruptures which began in 1968, its teams had never played Test cricket against anyone but English, Australian and New Zealand sides; the rest had been excluded by the South Africans themselves on racial grounds.

But it was in 1968 that South African cricket was transformed, as far as ICC was concerned, from an embarrassing subject into something approaching an obsession. Outside forces such as the 1960 Sharpeville massacre and consequent international indignation against the policies of Pretoria, together with the rising power of ex-colonial countries (all with old grievances to work off in a number of directions), made some sort of political show-down with South Africa inevitable. At this distance the wonder of it is that cricket managed to keep out of the thick of things for as long as it did. The game was dragged in willy-nilly by the events which attended the selection of England's team which was to tour South Africa in the winter of 1968–9. MCC itself, therefore, was the catalyst. That team, coincidentally, happened to be the last England touring side chosen by the selectors of the Marylebone club before this responsibility was handed over to the new Test and County Cricket Board. Their names should be marked by history for that reason if for no other. They were D. J. Insole (chairman), P. B. H. May, A. V. Bedser and Don Kenyon, the former Worcestershire opening bat and captain with the co-opted assistance of the touring team captain and manager (M. C. Cowdrey and L. E. G. Ames), the President of MCC (A. E. R. Gilligan) and the club's Treasurer (Gubby Allen).

There had been question marks against the likelihood of that team ever getting to South Africa months before the selection was made, largely because it had been possible for more than a season that Basil D'Oliveira, the South African-born cricketer of mixed blood who played for Worcestershire, would be included in the side. Before the 1968 season began he had already represented England as an all-rounder in fourteen Tests, and he played in another two against Australia before the selectors sat down. By then the South African Prime Minister, Johannes Vorster, well aware that D'Oliveira might be included in the touring side, had made an opaque statement to the effect that racially mixed teams would be allowed into his country provided they came from lands which had "traditional sporting ties" with South Africa and provided that "no political capital is made out of this situation". There spoke the politician, craftily keeping his options open to the last moment. D'Oliveira, meanwhile, was having a mixed time with his cricket. The previous winter he had not done too well on England's tour of West Indies, finishing with Test averages of 22.83 with the bat and 98.66 with the ball. He had then been England's top scorer (87 not out) in the First Test at home against Lawry's Australians, had been dropped from the side because he had lost form, but was restored to it for the Fifth Test, when he hit a splendid 158. The night that match ended, the MCC selectors met at eight o'clock to choose the touring side. It was almost two in the morning when they finished, and D'Oliveira had not been picked.

Insole, as chairman of selectors, and MCC's Secretary S. C. Griffith, on behalf of the club, explained to the world next day that the omission had been made purely on cricketing grounds and no other: they had considered D'Oliveira only as a batsman this time and, like other batting possibilities of that season (including Colin Milburn), they had passed him over. This joint explanation did nothing at all to mollify the critics of the team selection, who now rose up in great numbers and much wrath all over the country, assuming that D'Oliveira had been omitted simply to ensure that the tour of South Africa would go ahead. Among them, nineteen members of MCC resigned by the next post (four of whom later had second thoughts and asked to be reinstated), as some indication of the passions raised within the club alone. These had clearly been there for some time before the selection was made. County cricketers playing at Lord's one day that summer had found their concentration a little disturbed by the sounds of what appeared to be a slanging match in the Pavilion behind them. One voice identified in the bout was that of D. R. W. Silk, a member of the MCC Committee, otherwise known and in due course widely televised as the Warden of Radley College. The other was that of the Rev David Sheppard, the former England batsman and a current member of MCC's Cricket Committee, a plain parson in the East End of London at the time but destined one day to become Bishop of Liverpool at least. Before the year was out they would be more openly at loggerheads before an audience of over 1,000 in Church House, Westminster. Sheppard, exercising his right as an MCC member, had called for a special meeting to be held within days of the touring party being announced, and so great were the numbers expected to attend that no room at Lord's was big enough to contain them all.

But before this meeting occurred, the selection of MCC's touring party took another turn. Tom Cartwright, the Warwickshire medium-pace bowler, failed to pass a fitness test three weeks after being chosen for the South African tour. At the time of choosing the team the selectors had stated that in the event of anyone dropping out, D'Oliveira or Yorkshire's Don Wilson might be asked to replace him. In plugging the gap left by Cartwright, however, they now chose D'Oliveira and the Glamorgan pace bowler Jeff Jones. From where Mr Vorster was sitting 6,000 miles away this was proof positive that MCC had bowed to political pressures directed against his country; at least, it was the excuse he needed to prevent the risk of demonstrations in his own land when the despised D'Oliveira came home a hero in an otherwise immaculately white man's team. The MCC side, he announced to an audience of fellow Boers, would not be welcome in South Africa that winter. Quickly, the MCC Committee in London made its formal proclamation that the tour was cancelled.

Two months later the Special General Meeting of the club took place in Church House, and David Sheppard tabled a motion which regretted "the Committee's mishandling of affairs leading up to the selection of the team for the intended tour". He was seconded by Mike Brearley, a 26-year-old at the time who had occasionally batted (moderately) for Middlesex that year when he wasn't teaching philosophy in Newcastle. The chief contestant in the opposite corner on the Committee's behalf was D. R. W. Silk, with Aidan Crawley, the chairman of London Weekend Television and an MCC President of the future, in close support. Between them all and their other assistants, they made for an evening of rip-roaring asperity. "Instead of following a firm policy," Sheppard declared, "the Committee chose to stumble from one selection of a player or not to another and hoped it would be all right on the night . . . I feel that, instead of resenting this debate, they should welcome it as a chance to air thoroughly the most important issue that cricket has ever had to tackle . . . Our protest is against racialism in cricket." He wondered at "the scorn which the Committee pour on us". He questioned some manoeuvres that had evidently taken place between MCC and the South African Cricket Association long before the MCC selectors had first met, even before the 1968 season in England had started. "A small group of us met the Committee this autumn, when Sir Alec Douglas-Home tried to persuade us of the good sense of this policy. He never told us that MCC had already written in January to the SACA. That was only told us by Mr Allen after half an hour of questioning."

The voice of Silk was on this occasion even more abrasive. "We do not stand as the social conscience of Great Britain any more than our Government stands as the social conscience of the world. South Africa is Britain's third largest export customer – £257 million's worth last year . . . We have never seen it as our role to act as Inquisitor-General – I cannot agree that Mr Sheppard has managed to rid himself of that tag . . . What a sorry look-out it will be for international cricket if the avowedly sincere fanatics are allowed to dominate the scene by asking the government of every country we play against to alter their policy before we arrive." He pointed out that Mr Sheppard hadn't attended any of the six cricket committee meetings between October 1967 and June 1968, and "We realise that David Sheppard in the work that he does is an extremely busy man. Some of us may think that his frequent appearances on television recently should have also allowed him to appear on this Committee." Oh dear, oh dear, oh dear.

There wasn't much to be said after that, temperately or otherwise. The civilities were restored in the taking of votes, some of which were cast in the hall, others sent by post. Sheppard's resolution was defeated by 4,357 to 1,570. A motion that "no further tours to or from South Africa be undertaken until evidence can be given of actual progress by South Africa towards non-racial cricket" went down by 4,664 to 1,214. A third proposal "that a special committee be set up to examine such proposals as are submitted by the SACA towards non-racial cricket" was sunk by 4,508 to 1,352.

Thus began the total isolation of South Africa as far as Test cricket was concerned. Within twelve months of that Church House meeting, all sporting links with the Republic had become one of the hottest topics in British political and social life, and a young South African engineering student in London called Peter Hain had started to organise spectacular and not always wholesome demonstrations against them. These disrupted several matches played in Britain by the Springbok Rugby tourists of 1969, and they threatened the cricket tour by South Africans which was scheduled for 1970. TCCB planned to insure the lives of every England cricketer who played in the forthcoming Tests for £15,000 apiece, so potentially dangerous had the situation become by that spring. In May 1970 the House of Commons debated the issue; almost at once South Africa was expelled from the Olympic Games movement, and the West Indies Cricket Board added its ha'porth by declaring its opposition to the prospect of South African cricketers touring England that year. Undaunted by – or heedless of – such portents, the Cricket Council made one of the first public utterances of its existence: by "a substantial majority", it had decided to proceed with the tour. By this time, with only a few days left before the South African cricketers set off for London, the subject had become one of controversy all over the world; in Britain it promised total upheaval in the following weeks. That was the point at which the Home Secretary, James Callaghan, summoned the chairman and secretary of the Cricket Council (M. J. C. Allom and S. C. Griffith) to his office and asked them to withdraw their invitation to the South African touring team. They had no alternative; that was that. The South Africans were to play no more Test cricket at all. At home, they had whipped Lawry's Australians 4–0 in the first three months of 1970, but that was their swansong in the international game.

Somewhere near the heart of the anti-apartheid movement's philosophy was the argument that on being cut off from international sport the obsessively sporting whites in South Africa would prefer to mend their racial ways rather than endure an indefinite ostracism; more, that they would feel so injured by isolation as to force their government to revise its racial laws. That there was some validity in the first of these propositions was amply demonstrated by what happened in South African cricket circles in the next decade. A tour of Australia, which never took place, was scheduled for 1971. During the final trial match before team selection every player walked off the field in front of an astonished crowd, to draw attention to their belief that racially mixed cricket should be taking place in the Republic. Within a few years it was taking place, as cricket officials began to follow where the top white players had led. In 1977 a momentous fusion of interested parties occurred. The all-white South African Cricket Association joined forces with the two bodies which represented Coloured and black cricketers, to form the new multi-racial South African Cricket Union, whose constitution forbade any form of racial discrimination within its membership. In the face of South African laws, which remained as repressive as ever, this was a triumph of determination against considerable odds; but it was a sadly brief one. Two months later, a rump of the old South African Cricket Board of Control for non-whites, one of the parties to the merger, reformed itself into the South African Cricket Board and hoisted a new slogan: "No normal cricket in an abnormal society." The asking price had not thereby been suddenly increased. Its total had been overlooked, but now it was being demanded in full. It became clear, from this point, that the opponents of apartheid both inside and outside South Africa were not going to relax their paralysing grip on cricket until the South African government had abandoned every one of its racial laws.

In their dealings with the International Cricket Conference since then, the officials of the multi-racial SACU have had some reason to feel bitter. At its 1978 meeting ICC decided to send a fact-finding mission to South Africa to verify the claims made there about integration in cricket. It took this step by thirteen votes to seven (West Indies, India, Pakistan, East Africa, Bangladesh, Sri Lanka and Malaysia being opposed to the idea). The mission returned and made a report so favourable that, at its 1980 meeting, ICC actually invited the South Africans to submit an application for readmission to the conference they had left nineteen years earlier; and of the major members, West Indies joined England, Australia and New Zealand in outvoting India and Pakistan this time. Yet twelve months later, when the application had been received, ICC didn't even put the matter to the vote, for the simple reason that South Africa's readmission could only be proposed by the remaining founder members of the conference; and neither England nor Australia was moved to propose. "What more can we do?" said the despairing SACU President, Rachid Varachia. He might well have asked, especially as at approximately the same time the Test and County Cricket Board had issued a warning to English cricketers that they would risk making themselves ineligible for Test selection if they took part in any unofficial tours of South Africa.

Cricket by now was completely pinioned by the harsh forces of world politics, and everyone but the optimistic South Africans and their lobbyists elsewhere knew it for an inescapable fact. The England tour of West Indies had almost foundered when the party left Guyana abruptly after the Surrey bowler Jackman was ordered to leave the country at once because he had played and owned property in South Africa. Had a Jamaican journalist not drawn the Guyanese Government's attention to Jackman's South African connections, the uproar over his presence might never have occurred. He became conspicuous because he was flown in as a replacement for the injured Willis; but the party already contained cricketers who had often wintered in South Africa, Boycott and Bairstow most notably among them. Boycott, in fact, together with Geoff Cook of Northamptonshire, moved to the centre of this particular stage a year later when there was some question of whether England's tour in India would go ahead, on similar grounds. The Yorkshireman's predilection for the Cape and its hinterland would very soon also bring him to the attention of the United Nations, where a special committee had begun to issue periodic blacklists of sportsmen who had performed in South Africa. One promulgated in November 1982 contained, among an assortment of golfers, horse riders, Rugby footballers, racing drivers and bridge players, some forty county cricketers in England. The sanctions against such deviants are not all clear; very obvious is the fundamental inconsistency of the blacklists when pallid Englishmen, burnished South Africans, and even darker men from Trinidad or Asia play together day in and day out for months on end in England each year.

It is scarcely possible to dispute the fact that South Africa has become a political football to be kicked about quite cynically by politicians in ex-colonial countries whose own domestic positions very often do not bear close examination; and if anyone doubts that he should pay some attention to the regular reports issued by Amnesty International for a start. At the same time, those who would be damned to the lot of them and resume full relations with South Africa are not in a more persuasive position. It is either ignorant or dishonest to equate the monstrosities of Soviet imperialism, as such plaintiffs usually do, with the monstrosities of South African apartheid (for a man may pretend to change political views he does not really hold in order to serve whatever purpose he has in mind, including self-preservation, at no cost except in hypocrisy; but he cannot change the colour of his skin even to save his life). Nor is it relevant to mock India for the excesses of caste there because, although caste is responsible for monstrosities too, it is not deliberately encouraged by the Indian Government, whose constitution refuses to recognise it and specifically forbids the practice of untouchability.

The relationship between the Indian government and Indian cricketers, however, does illustrate the grip that politicians can have, and have taken, on the sportsmen of ex-colonial countries who do not accept the prevailing political view. Twenty years before South Africa became the dominant issue of today, cables were being exchanged between the Secretary of MCC and the secretary of the Indian Cricket Board of Control, about a delay in preparations for the visit of M. J. K. Smith's touring side to the sub-continent. The delay was in New Delhi where, according to the Indian official, "I urged Government to expedite approval of the tour." At that stage the Indian Ministry of Education had recommended that the Englishmen's tour should take place, but the Finance Ministry had not yet made up its mind. In the event, this was no more than a matter of bureaucratic bumbling, a failure to get through the necessary paperwork as quickly as anxious cricket officials in two countries would have liked. The point is, though, that no cricket tour to or from India can take place without New Delhi's permission. Government can block any international enterprise it chooses to by, as a last resort, simply imposing financial exchange rate controls, which are most strictly regulated there.

India is not alone in holding such a handy ploy in readiness. The same goes for Pakistan, West Indies and Sri Lanka, too. Not one of the cricket authorities in those countries is in a position to defy the wishes of its politicians, either inside or outside the meetings of ICC. Were this not so, it is likely that by now South Africa would have been readmitted to the conference; it is even conceivable that official tours to and from the Republic involving all the major cricketing countries would be afoot. Some cricketers from the Third World, Viv Richards for one, have let it be known that they will not visit South Africa unless its racial laws are repealed; and that is an honourable view. But it is a matter of guesswork how many cricketers, of whatever colour, maintain the same attitude. Like most sportsmen they tend, on the whole, to be a notoriously apolitical breed. The three gangs of players, from England, Sri Lanka and West Indies, who toured South Africa unofficially in 1982 and 1983 in defiance not only of politicians but of their local cricket authorities, demonstrated very well the proposition that anything is possible provided the price is right. Cynicism may now be found in counterpoise on both ends of the scale weighing South African cricket up.

The proscription of the English authorities against any official contact with the Republic is based solely on their acceptance of the realities of the moment. The Test and County Cricket Board know very well that if they were even to hint at a resumption of the old playing relationship, a split in the world of Test cricket would immediately follow on racial lines. They simply and quite literally cannot afford to let this happen, whatever other considerations might influence them. Too much of the domestic budget depends upon the existing frequency of Test cricket between the seven competing countries. That includes the wages of all county cricketers in England; which is doubtless why, above any moral convictions, the Cricketers' Association endorsed the TCCB's three-year Test ban – on Gooch, Boycott and the twelve other Englishmen who toured South Africa unofficially – by 190 votes to 35.

The official English position was spelt out concisely by G. H. G. Doggart in his Presidential address to the 1982 Annual General Meeting of MCC. He pointed out that the Cricket Council adhered to the Gleneagles Agreement which was drawn up after the Commonwealth Prime Ministers' Conference of 1977: this meant that although the cricket authorities would not try to dissuade an individual from exercising his right in law to play and coach in South Africa, they would not support an English team playing a representative South African team anywhere except without ICC approval. He suggested that MCC members would feel sympathy for South African cricketers and their Cricket Union in their present plight, after what they had done over the previous twelve years. As for the decision to ban fourteen Englishmen from Test cricket, it "had been taken with a heavy heart. Nevertheless it had been unanimously decided that action had to be taken to preserve multiracial cricket on an international basis, and to safeguard the livelihoods of all English cricketers, including those who either had not been invited (by South African Breweries) or who had refused the invitation."

A number of weighty figures on the fringes of cricket at about the same time were loudly proclaiming their hostility to the ban. The cricket correspondent of *The Times*, John Woodcock, who is also Editor of *Wisden* these days, was the most persistently vocal of these. Normally a most sensible man, it became apparent in the course of 1982 that he had quite lost his balance on the issue. For months on end he inveighed furiously against the Test ban every time he appeared in print, often doing so at right angles to the purported subject of his articles. He repeatedly suggested that men such as Larkins of Northants and the Leicestershire bowler Taylor would have walked into the England party to tour Australia in 1982–3 had they not been deliberately excluded from consideration, although the first player had often failed in his previous Test opportunities (he had an average of sixteen in eleven innings) and the second had never even come near one. He chose to overlook the deceitful way in which Boycott, Gooch, Emburey, Underwood and Lever had prepared to tour South Africa while they were enjoying a tour of India as England players, though the deceit of Tony Greig and others when they had been readying themselves for a defection to Kerry Packer's organisation in 1977 in precisely comparable circumstances had raised Woodcock's blood pressure to bursting point. But in 1982 everything was to be excused except the action of those bounders in TCCB. It occurred to one of his readers that some English cricket correspondents might not be wholly averse to a realignment of Test cricket, if only to spare themselves the discomforts they complain about when they are obliged to follow England's cricketers into some of the less indulged corners of India, Pakistan and West Indies.

There was also Lord Chalfont, the newspaper reporter who was ennobled by Harold Wilson so that he might serve in a Labour Government. He later became disenchanted with Labour Party policies and assumed his new role as a perpetual member of committees and boards, so many of them that they occupy twelve lines of his entry in *Who's Who*. One of them is Freedom in Sport, of which Lord Chalfont is President. He is also a member of MCC, and it was during the club's 1982 AGM that, after the Presidential speech, he tried to get the Test ban discussed under any other business, but was overruled. He had already said his piece on the subject by writing an article for *The Cricketer*. TCCB, in his view, had "given in, without even a protest, to a straightforward and impudent piece of political blackmail". There had been "a deplorable capitulation to demands which carry with them the implication that our representative cricket teams are in future to be selected, in part at least, by their opponents". Chalfont thought it reasonable to suggest that "Boycott and his colleagues handled their arrangements with less skill than one is accustomed to expect from them on the field. This is not, however, an offence so outrageous that they should now be made the victims of arrogant and intimidating pressure groups who have decided to make cricket an instrument of their political prejudices." What the çi-devant Labour Minister was proposing was that if visiting touring sides – and he obviously had the 1982 Indians and Pakistanis in mind – were not prepared to play England sides of our choosing, "then it would be better for the long-term health, not only of international sport, but of the freedom of individual choice which we cherish in this country, if they stayed away". D. R. W. Silk couldn't have put it better.

And then there was Mr John Carlisle, a Conservative MP who has not so far featured in anybody's government and is only in Parliament by virtue of a 276 majority, also trying to use his MCC membership in order to succour the South Africans. In August 1982 a newspaper in Johannesburg reported that Mr Carlisle was the man behind moves to summon a special general meeting of the Marylebone club, the purpose of which was to demand that MCC should itself sponsor a tour of South Africa by English cricketers in defiance of the TCCB ruling on contacts with the Republic. The newspaper was quite right; Mr Carlisle was doing just that. The well-practised ways and means of his club were at once drummed up to block his ambitions in this venture, which made it at least likely that he would not succeed. If a Lord Chalfont could be stifled when he merely wished to pop a question under any other business, what hope had a precarious back-bencher from Luton of reversing history some twenty years, and despatching a fully-fledged MCC touring side, dripping with nostalgia and laden with meaning, to bring new hope to the laagered cricketers at the Cape? Mr Carlisle, however, was a determined man, who enlisted such resounding names as those of Compton and Edrich in his cause, and succeeded in summoning yet another special general meeting of the Marylebone club. The question was; would the majority of 18,000 members do the traditional thing and follow their Committee's advice, or would two thirds of them follow another instinct and thumb their noses at the Third World? Before that meeting was held, MCC's Secretary made it plain that if the membership instructed the Committee to send a team to South Africa – as they were quite entitled to – then MCC could not honourably continue to operate as a member of either TCCB or Cricket Council.

At the time of writing, the outcome of the meeting was still in the balance. Perfectly clear, however, was South Africa's position in international cricket as a whole. The lamps are likely to flicker fitfully down there for some considerable time to come. Only the South African politicians can tell us how long. They have 317 laws relating to apartheid to consider first.

CHAPTER EIGHT

A Standard for all Seasons

The Marylebone Cricket Club, in fact, has never stopped sending teams on tour overseas. These no longer play Test matches, and they no longer include the very best cricketers England has to offer at a given time. Instead they contain a variety of men, almost all of whom still play or recently have played at first-class level, some of them in Test matches, their only common denominator being that they have been selected to appear in MCC's colours. An MCC side which played eleven games in the United States in the autumn of 1982, for example, contained the former Test players Tony Lewis, Fred Titmus, John Jameson and Mushtaq Mohammed, as well as current English county cricketers such as Nick Cook, Nick Pocock, Simon Dennis and Bill Merry. The year before, two MCC sides had been sent overseas, one round East Africa, the other to Hong Kong and Singapore. It is a policy of the club to launch at least one tour every year, mostly to those countries which are associate members of ICC. The purpose, in the words of Jack Bailey, the Secretary of MCC, is "to spread the gospel of how cricket should be played – a matter of spirit as well as technique – and to give those countries a bit of a fillip from Lord's, the headquarters of the game". It was quite superfluous for the reconstituted Cricket Council at the start of 1983 to charge MCC with the responsibility of organising tours to lesser cricketing countries. MCC had been quietly getting on with the task for years.

So also does the club play a vast amount of cricket in this country every season without many people but those involved paying attention to it. Between the end of April and the start of September 1982, MCC teams played no fewer than 240 matches all over the British Isles, some of them taking place concurrently at several venues. Seven sides were fielded on just one day in May, spread out between Brentwood, Dover, Edinburgh, Ipswich, Cambridge, Repton and Dulwich. Most fixtures are one-day events, though a hardy annual lasting three days is MCC v Ireland, usually in Dublin or somewhere else over the water. A lot of public schools and a handful of grammar schools provide the opposition, as do university sides (the likes of Reading and Aberystwyth as well as Oxford and Cambridge), local cricket clubs (Ponteland CC, Luton Town CC), and old peculiars like the Honourable Artillery Company and Hampshire Hogs. Collectively, the games are known as the out-matches of MCC, which is precisely what they are: almost without exception they are played away from home, because the Lord's fixture list is crammed with Test and county cricket. That opening game with the champion county and perhaps a match against the season's touring side are just about the only MCC fixtures played in front of the members in the Long Room; but they are a different sort of cricket altogether, as professional as anything we know, with money changing hands. The out-matches are intended to be sheer sport all the way.

They exist to provide the playing members of MCC with pleasure because this is, after all – as the Marylebone officials repeatedly emphasise – a private cricket club above all other things. But it has always seen itself as something more than just that. It has believed itself to be, in Sir Pelham Warner's phrase, "a private club with a public function". Even in these chapfallen days the ambition still holds, though it is no longer as grand or as celebrated as it once was. To some extent the ambition is attained through the club's incorporation into administrative mechanisms of the game which have replaced the once overriding apparatus provided by MCC alone. In fulfilling the rest of it, those out-matches have a significant role. As in the case of the overseas tours, they are an area where MCC can spread its gospel of how cricket ought to be played.

The club devotes a fair amount of thought, as well as time and energy, to shaping all aspects of this missionary enterprise. The teams are selected very carefully so that none is likely to outclass any opposition it meets. The side meeting the Club Cricket Conference at Ilford will be theoretically more powerful than the one put out against Bradford Grammar School. Every MCC side has a match manager attached to it, and his responsibility extends well beyond the logistics of getting his players to the appointed location on time. If they're turning out against Eton or Harrow he may decide that spit and polish shall be in his order of the day, with every MCC cricketer immaculately equipped and dressed according to the old conventions, to set an example to those lads who have come to believe that the macho image of headbands, track-suit trousers and custom-built diaphanous shirts is the thing to pursue if you're to leave your mark on the game. He is unlikely to make a fetish of this if his side is appearing against an impecunious club side in the wastelands of Ell, where the stumper actually needs to save pennies by swathing his pads in bandages, in the fashion of Alan Knott. The axiom at all times, according to Jack Bailey, is "infinite courtesy to the people

who are your hosts on the day". And that, most distinctly, means on
and off the field. The MCC playing member who demurs at an
umpiring decision is unlikely to be selected for another out-match.
He is advised to watch his language, too, however often some young
lusty from the provinces sprays bouncers around his head.

And it is to spread the gospel at the heart of first-class cricket itself
that MCC spends some £30,000 a year in maintaining its own
professional Cricket Staff. On big match days we notice these young
men, clad in black blazers with the plain white letters MCC on the
breast pocket, selling scorecards and moving about with messages.
Others are up in the scorebox, manipulating the numbers on the
board. At less frantic moments of the cricket season they may be
observed in their playing gear down on the practice ground, going
through team drills of one sort or another, or bowling to MCC
members in the nets.

They are the heirs to a tradition which started with Thomas Lord
himself, whose cricket career began as a practice bowler to the
gentlemen of the White Conduit Club. When the Marylebone club
became a going concern, one of its first acts was to accumulate a
number of paid cricketers, known as the Ground Staff, to fetch and
carry for the gentlemen, to provide them with a work-out whenever
they felt like one, and also to stiffen their ranks when MCC teams
took the field in match play against powerfully professional opposition. At one stage in the nineteenth century, Lord's had sixty of these
players-cum-menials on its books. Some of them were among the
most illustrious players of their time. Nottinghamshire became an
especially fertile source of supply, providing among others the great
Alfred Shaw, that model medium-pace bowler of unvarying length,
who took 2,027 wickets in first-class cricket at 12.12 and, even more
significantly, yielded on average less than one run per over bowled;
just under two thirds of them were maidens.

In time, the MCC Ground Staff and the Middlesex professional
staff were interchangeable, as we have already seen. Hendren and
Compton both passed this way. But gradually in the post-war years,
as English cricket moved ineluctably towards total professionalism,
the position of the MCC Ground Staff became degraded into one
in which the fetching and carrying (and ground cleaning) predomi-
nated over any opportunity to exercise and sharpen professional
expertise. What Sir Pelham Warner had been pleased to regard as a
squad of trainees at the Caterham of Cricket had deteriorated,
during his administrative lifetime, into an unacclaimed unit of the
Pioneer Corps. Twenty-odd years ago, however, the thing was
pulled together again, and the Ground Staff was turned into the

Cricket Staff, a translation which pointed up a deliberate restoration of emphasis.

There were forty of these young professional cricketers in the mid-70s until, in a fit of cost-cutting, their number was approximately halved. Today there are twenty who have been recruited from all parts of the country, augmented in any year by a couple of lads from overseas who have been sent on scholarships to enjoy a Lord's apprenticeship. They are engaged as early as sixteen years old, for three consecutive seasons, and a young pro in his last term may have reached the age of twenty-two or twenty-three. Because a prime object of the exercise is to help young men with potential to make a career in the first-class game, they generally come to MCC's attention on the county grapevine, from clubs whose own facilities are not ample enough to give a good start to promising youths in their catchment area. Ian Botham is the prize exhibit so far, brought up from Somerset to be schooled at Lord's (where, it is said, he relished the opportunity to bowl bouncers during his weekly stint of servicing the MCC members in the nets) and restored to the county when he had been set on course for a glittering success. Not all who graduate from the Cricket Staff manage to secure a place with a county side but, in the 1982 season, twenty-nine of them were deployed around the circuit in the following dispositions:

Derbyshire: K. G. Brooks, R. J. Finney, S. J. Farrell. *Essex:* A. W. Lilley, K. R. Pont. *Glamorgan:* T. Davies, D. A. Francis, G. C. Holmes, J. A. Hopkins, M. J. Llewellyn, B. J. Lloyd, R. C. Ontong, N. J. Perry. *Gloucestershire:* R. J. Doughty. *Middlesex:* R. O. Butcher, N. G. Cowans, N. F. Williams. *Somerset:* I. T. Botham, J. W. Lloyds, K. F. Jennings. *Surrey:* A. Needham. *Sussex:* I. J. Gould. *Warwickshire:* Asif Din, C. Lethbridge, S. H. Wootton, P. A. Smith. *Worcestershire:* M. S. Scott, D. B. D'Oliveira.

The days are gone when the young professionals at Lord's could look to MCC members to provide them with employment during the winter months (a number could always rely on that old cavalier Percy Fender to recruit them for corking bottles in his wine business) and the creation of a Works Department has meant that they can no longer earn their off-season keep painting their way round the ground. They now have to make what winter shifts they can, of their own devising. But from the moment they turn up for their annual engagement at the end of April, they are paid a weekly wage until the beginning of September, which in 1982 varied from £52 to £68, depending on the lad's seniority. In addition, that year, they received a kit allowance of £68 which they could spend at discount rates in the Lord's cricket-school shop, luncheon vouchers for the canteen in the school, plus travelling and laundry allowances. They are quartered, unless they live locally, in a young men's hostel up in Hampstead. But from ten o'clock every morning until seven that night, Sunday excepted, their headquarters are in the Bowlers' Room above the groundsman's shed behind the clock tower at the Nursery End. That's where Alfred Shaw and his mates got changed before going out to do their duty by the gentlemen in the nets.

The boys are mustered in No. 5 Dressing Room in the Pavilion when they arrive for the start of a new term. There they are given a preliminary pep talk by John Stephenson, known as "The Colonel" (which is what he once was) to all and sundry at Lord's, where he may be observed publicly during inclement weather on big match days pacing the square anxiously with Jim Fairbrother, wondering how the hell to get play started again with all those puddles oozing over the welts of his shoes. He is the Assistant Secretary of MCC whose especial province is all that goes on in the middle, a job which also carries with it the position of OC the Cricket Staff. His pep talk to the young recruits is briskly engaging ("I don't wish to sound pompous, but . . .") as he rattles through a number of minor misdemeanours perpetrated the year before and on to a list of intimations about the months ahead. It is a friendly performance but it brooks no nonsense, and lately it has emphasised the standards MCC expects its employed cricketers to maintain, whether they're playing in a match, watching the superstars perform, or selling scorecards to the customers. The homily over, the young pros are stood down for the moment, to be sergeant-majored through the rest of the season by Don Wilson, the Head Coach.

They could scarcely be in the hands of someone who more typifies the standards of the old cricket professional, a species now all but vanished from the English game: and such characters never existed anywhere else, because no other form of cricket ever required men to play day in and day out for six days a week through five months to earn their bread and butter. "Required", in fact, is not the word Don Wilson would use there; "allowed" or even "privileged" would express more accurately his own feelings about the work he enjoyed during those eighteen seasons with Yorkshire which ended in 1974. His slow left-arm bowling (best performance eight for thirty-six) brought him 1,189 wickets at exactly twenty-one runs each and, though he only ever scored one century, he was a useful hitter even when batting down at number ten, who once slogged thirty in one over off Robin Hobbs during a Scarborough Festival match. He was also a brilliant field at mid-wicket, balancing Ken Taylor's swiftness in the covers in the last of those teams which made Yorkshire's reputation what it used to be.

And he wouldn't have swapped any minute of it, even though it wasn't all a bed of white roses. It pains him that so very few of the county and Test players he talks to now seem to get much enjoyment from the game; or – and he doesn't hesitate to use such an old-fashioned sentiment – a sense of honour at having been chosen to play for their county or for England. He remembers well the day he picked up the first of his half dozen Test caps, at Madras in 1964. Just before the team took the field, Barry Knight and Peter Parfitt both clapped him on the back, and one of them said: "Now Don, it's Don Wilson of Yorkshire *and* England. They can never take that away from you now!" This will doubtless fall on some contemporary ears as some archaic form of adolescent dialogue, but it happened less than twenty years ago and the feeling wasn't a spurious one.

Wilson is not, therefore, wholly in sympathy with the cricketers of today, who seem to him to be in the game for the money more than anything else. He's not dead nuts, either, on some of the techniques now employed, with cricketers warming up beforehand as though they're training for the Olympic Games rather than for the job they have to do. Men like Trueman, Statham and Bedser, he would remind us, bowled themselves fit by a lot of hard work in the nets and the middle at the start of a season. Batsmen are much more limited in their range than when he was around, mostly because they have to face much more fast bowling than a generation ago. You can, he points out, talk to some spinners now and find that by the end of June they've scarcely bowled fifty overs in all forms of the game.

Wilson's particular charges, then, are the young professionals, whom he nurtures in the crafts of the game that he himself first learned on the edge of the Yorkshire dales. On the practice ground in fine weather, on the floor of the indoor school in wet, he gets them going at their own speciality, bats and bowls himself in order to illustrate points, illuminates glaring defects with the aid of a video machine. But he doesn't believe in over-coaching anyone. If a bowler's got a funny run up he doesn't meddle with it, provided the ball is pitching where it should do and keeps the batsman guessing. If a batsman has a peculiar stance, Wilson may try to correct it to a certain extent, but if a lad is scoring runs that way the coach believes in leaving well alone. With the newcomers to Lord's, he effects the persona of martinet for a little while, just to make the point that there's to be no messing about; but nature seeps through before long and the customary atmosphere is one of mateyness, provided no one is silly enough to take advantage. When a dozen of them are sent off to play a team of Jazz Hats (as public school cricketers are known up in the Bowlers' Room) it is an avuncular figure who gives them last instructions before they depart. He himself leads them in the high-spot of their year, when they play a one-day match in the middle of Lord's (not on the Test strip itself, but near enough for any young cricketer with dreams) against an MCC side which may well contain half a dozen current county players.

The young pros are not Don Wilson's only charges. Quite a lot of old hands in the game turn to him for help when they are playing at Lord's, but worried about their form. None more than Boycott, of course, than whom no cricketer has ever been more dedicated to perfecting his technique. "Just watch my feet," or "Watch my head, will you?" he will say when he has persuaded Wilson to scrutinise him in the nets. Phil Edmonds will come down and ask that his arm, which he suspects is beginning to drop, should be checked; or his run up, which he thinks is going too wide. Wilson is quite clear about what he can and cannot do for a man of such standing in the game. "I can't," he says, "tell Edmonds how to bowl left arm. I can try to make him better than I am or was, though." His reputation as coach is such that overseas players come to him, too, when they're in town. Dilip Doshi spent a couple of days under inspection, just before returning to India in the winter of 1981, having his action videoed and analysed. Thus armed with Wilson's advice, he went home to become a thorn in the side of Fletcher's Englishmen. Something of the sort had happened earlier in the same year, when the Australian Ray Bright turned up, concerned by the fact that he couldn't get his line right. Wilson switched on the video again, with film of the spinner performing in the Tests at Lord's and Headingley, then had him out in the nets. After which he suggested that the problem might be eased if the Victorian bowled over the wicket all the time, instead of switching from side to side. Bright went on to Edgbaston and did just that, taking five good English wickets for sixty-eight in the second innings, after collecting a couple of cheap ones in the first.

It would be misleading to imply that anyone at all can be coached at Lord's, though this was very nearly the case in 1933, when MCC laid on special classes for the benefit of London's unemployed. But when Easter comes round the Grace Gates are flung more widely open than usual in the off-season, for a month of classes directed specifically at the young. These are basically an offering to the sons of MCC members, who can take advantage of them at reduced rates and have priority in booking places up to a month before the first of sixteen courses starts towards the end of March: after that any boy is welcome, provided Dad can come up with the £34.50 (in 1982) needed to pay for three days of tuition. They are under Wilson's direction, though he has the permanent assistance of a former young pro at Lord's, Andy Wagner, and reinforcements are generally provided by a clutch of county cricketers in the twilight or just past the end of their careers.

The pupils are graded carefully according to age, from eleven years old upwards, and the first thing Wilson does is to arrange them into teams and get them running about, to relax them and make them feel that they've come to enjoy themselves more than to be nervously put through a variety of hoops; also to encourage the competitive spirit, as patented in the county of York. The youngest start with tennis balls, so that their confidence shall be built, not damaged. Wilson remembers too well his own childhood, when some idiot of a schoolmaster would delight in hurling a cricket ball in catching practice at small boys who would be left wringing almost broken hands. He introduces the pull shot early, so that young batsmen shall know the sensation of hitting the ball with a satisfying thump. His eyes light up when he comes across a child who declares an interest in spin; but that is a rarity; the coaching classes are overwhelmingly full of twelve year olds eager to fling down balls in imitation of Willis and Botham. Occasionally he spots a prodigy with either bat or ball, whose rhythms are instinctively right, whose eye is sharp, whose mind is clearly working out the problems of technique. That boy, carefully handled, may have a future in the professional game if he wants one. But discovering such potential talent, in Don Wilson's view, is not really the point of the Easter coaching classes at Lord's.

The point of them is consistent with the attitude of the club to the game at large, at whatever level it is played. It is to encourage people to play cricket as well as they can, for the sake of doing that and nothing more. It is to persuade them that although a cricket match is of its nature a competitive event, and at a professional level a highly competitive one for preference, this is a worthless pursuit if it is exalted above the enjoyment of all who participate – which includes two umpires as well as twenty-two players. The philosophy has been most forcefully expressed of late by the enthusiastic Benny Green, in a reflection on the Bodyline series of half a century ago. The truth is, he wrote, that "winning Test matches can be child's play. You simply bash the opposition into insensibility. The essence of cricket is that you are supposed to win the game without bashing anybody into anything." He made one other point in the same article, a corollary to that. "The game you are frightened of losing is not worth winning." As disconsolate Fred Tate was reminded long ago, in

1902, after dropping that vital catch and getting himself bowled only four short of victory in the Old Trafford Test, cricket *is* only a game. No; perhaps not "only". Too fine a one to be burdened with some of the accretions that are beginning to weigh it down and distort a nature which – so far as law-makers can contrive – is essentially a fair one.

There was a time, MCC being at the height of its powers, when the club conceived part of its public function to put down most sternly all infractions against the spirit as well as the Laws of the game. Well, nearly all, and we shall look at the qualification more closely in a moment. Long after the autocratic figure of Lord Harris had departed from the Committee Room at Lord's, the deliberations of MCC's hierarchy were quite often spent on matters of discipline and how to punish some player who had offended against the codes. The most aggressive example of this in the post-war years concerned Yorkshire's slow left-arm bowler Johnny Wardle, who had been selected by MCC to tour Australia and New Zealand with Peter May's side in 1958–9. Three days after that team had been picked, the Yorkshire Committee announced that Wardle would not be re-engaged by the county the following season, for reasons undisclosed. He then wrote (or lent his name to) some articles in the *Daily Mail* which were highly critical of the Committee and his captain Ronnie Burnet. He was forthwith summoned to Lord's to explain himself, but his case did not impress his judges there. Next day he was dropped from the touring side, and MCC said that it had taken this draconian step for the welfare of cricket as a whole, to uphold the notion of loyalty and good behaviour. The same principle was applied to Jim Laker in 1963, after he had written a book of memoirs towards the end of a distinguished career. His old county, Surrey, were so incensed by some descriptions of life at the Oval that they withdrew his pass to the ground. MCC followed this up by removing his name from the list of Honorary Cricket Members of the Marylebone club, to which he had been added only three months before. As further penance, Laker was deliberately excluded from selection for the Old England XI v Lord's Taverners game at headquarters that year. Sitting in March 1964, and satisfied with its punishments, the MCC Committee solemnly "agreed that Laker should be invited to play in the next Old England/Taverners match". He was also to have his honorary membership restored.

Fred Trueman was another cricketer in the sixties disciplined for excursions into print, this time for articles in *The People* deemed offensive to Sussex and the Duke of Norfolk. The cast of mind which was applied to disciplinary matters at about this time is illustrated by a letter which Gubby Allen (absent ill) wrote to the MCC Committee for consideration at its meeting in August 1963, when it was formalising its plans for the winter tour of India by M. J. K. Smith's team. Allen was particularly worked up about the inclusion of two players in the party, "both of whom, on their previous tours, received thoroughly bad reports. As the MCC Committee accepted their names without comment when considering their letters of availability, I do not think they can now veto their selection. On the other hand, I feel very strongly indeed that both these players should be spoken to very firmly by the President in the presence of the Secretary of MCC and either the Manager or the Captain of the Team before leaving for India."

Four months later the Committee was considering a report from the Secretary that nine members of the side which Ted Dexter had led in Australia the previous winter had failed to acknowledge receipt of a memento of the tour which had been sent to them by the President and Committee of MCC. It was agreed that the Secretary should write to the respective chairmen of the clubs to which the negligent nine belonged. So obsessed by codes of conduct were MCC, that this arm of the unwritten law was extended even beyond the cricketers whose registrations the club controlled through its Advisory County Cricket Committee. During the tour of India by Smith's team, the cricket reporter E. M. Wellings blotted his copybook in MCC eyes. The Committee sat down to consider something Wellings had said in the press box at New Delhi, which "has given offence to India and, therefore, an apology to the Indian Board is essential". There was a long-running correspondence on this matter throughout 1964, but it eventually exhausted itself. Wellings evidently knew how to stonewall as well as any batsman.

Behaviour on the field which came below the desired standard could be drastically dealt with. Brian Close was relieved of the England captaincy because he was unrepentant about time-wasting tactics used by his Yorkshire side in a game against Warwickshire, when Close's men were in hot pursuit of the 1967 championship; a punishment presumably thought suitable by Norman Preston, Editor of *Wisden*, who had written of the Edgbaston incident that "the image of cricket was besmirched". Four years later the old morality still retained a firm grip on things in England even though MCC's sovereignty had by then been nominally transferred to the TCCB. MCC's Secretary, S. C. Griffith, was at that stage also Secretary of the board, for the demarcation lines between the two organisations had not yet been conclusively settled; and it was in his capacity as TCCB Secretary that he figured in an incident at Lord's during the

First Test of 1971 against Wadekar's Indians, which made the international headlines.

Just after the Indians started their second innings, their opening batsman Gavaskar was dashing for a sharp single when, in *Wisden*'s description, he "was barged to the ground by Snow as the pair ran up the pitch together". Appalled by this action of the England bowler, Griffith in the Pavilion went to MCC's President, Sir Cyril Hawker, and asked him to call for Snow's apology to the Indian side during the lunch interval. Hawker's response was, "You'll do it so much better, Billy." So, during lunch, Griffith went upstairs to have a word with England's captain outside the team's dressing-room. "I must tell you," he informed Ray Illingworth, "that that was the most disgraceful thing that I've ever seen on a cricket field, and for the sake of English cricket he's got to go and apologise. Has he done so?" No, he had not. Griffith therefore observed the local proprieties by asking the England captain's permission to enter the dressing-room, strode up to Snow and demanded the apology. The bowler made it plain that he was disinclined to oblige. Griffith's retort was a classic of its kind. "It's not a question of what you want to do," he told the Sussex player. "You will do this and you will do it at once." And he did; not quite at once, but before the match was over. Snow returned an analysis for the match of three for eighty-seven, moderate figures for him at the time. But they weren't the reason why he was dropped from the England side for the Second Test in Manchester. Then, having thus been publicly reproved by authority, he was selected again for the last Test of the series at the Oval.

The trouble with this old morality, sad to say, is that it was sometimes applied with a double standard; and the further one goes back in the history of cricket, the more obvious was this defect, intrinsically a moral one itself. Since that day in 1963 when the distinction between the amateur and professional cricketer in England was abolished there has been no cause for complaint. But before then there occurred instances of amateur cricketers being tolerated for actions which earned the professional player at least a good ticking off. The double standard was most vividly exemplified in the career of W. G. Grace, who was not only one of the outstanding mercenaries of all time, but one of the most conspicuous offenders against that spirit of cricket which became glorified during his era and which he was supposed to represent. Even so fair-minded a commentator on the game as E. W. Swanton has never been able to acknowledge in public anything worse than "a genial rascality" in the great Doctor, which is the blandest of euphemisms for practices he regularly resorted to. *Wisden* in 1897 took much the same view when it remarked that "the work he has done in perpetuating cricket outweighs a hundredfold every other consideration".

It is difficult to think of many actions by cricketers today, condemned when they occur, which were not in Grace's repertoire. On his first tour of Australia in 1873–4 he loudly criticised the pitches, was vehement about the incompetence of umpires, and had several public rows with a local administrator of the game, John Conway; and an Australian observer remarked that "for so big a man he is surprisingly tenacious on very small points". On his second tour Down Under eighteen years later, there were more wrangles over umpiring, there were disputed catches, and Grace led his team from the field in one match, in a blistering rage about the state of the pitch. At home his sharp practices were as notorious as his athletic skills were marvellous. He was quite capable of shouting "Miss it!" when a fielder was waiting for the ball to drop into his hands from Grace's bat. During the 1882 Test match at the Oval (the one that produced the mock obituary of English cricket), Grace put down the wicket and successfully appealed for a run-out against young Jones of New South Wales, when the poor lad was simply doing some gardening down the pitch. On the same Australian tour of England, Grace had made seventy-seven for Gloucestershire against Murdoch's men when he was given out lbw – "a decision at which he was highly indignant", according to Charles Pardon, who was reporting the match for *Bell's Life*. Twenty years later the *Sportsman* magazine was commenting on "the weakness of WG for dwelling at the wicket after the umpire's decision", which had continued unabated. As a bowler Grace appealed a great deal and often showed his disgust when the verdict went against him. He was also a terrible gasbag, especially when fielding with his brother E. M. Grace, with whom he would maintain loud cross-talk in order to disturb the batsman's concentration; so much so that even he was once reprimanded for it by Lord Hawke. And if any striker dared to stand his ground in Grace's own fashion after being given out, the Great Cricketer would point the way to the dressing-room, with the command, "Pavilion, you!"

W. G. Grace's place in the pantheon of Lord's is materially recognised by the main gates which were dedicated to him. Only two other men have been similarly memorialised by MCC for the esteem in which they have been held by cricketers in general and the club in particular. One is Lord Harris, whose name is given to the little garden behind the Pavilion where the Committee's marquee goes up during Test matches. The other is Sir Pelham Warner, patron saint of the stand which accommodates MCC members and their friends between the Pavilion and the Grandstand. If we now dwell on him it is both because he was one of the most influential figures in the history of the Marylebone club, and because he also exhibited a morality of his own where cricket is concerned.

Born the eighteenth child of Trinidad's attorney-general, Warner came to England as a delicate youth who failed to get into Winchester but was accepted for Rugby. In spite of ill-health which recurred through a very long life, he was a promising cricketer from the outset and in time a very good one at the highest levels of the game. He first stepped inside Lord's in 1887, shortly after arriving from the West Indies, to see MCC v Sussex, with Grace himself playing for the home club – "and I gazed with undisguised admiration, not to say awe, on the greatest personality the cricket world has ever known, or ever will know". Two years later young Warner – "Plum" now to his form-mates – played there himself in the Rugby v Marlborough match, and though he scored only three and sixteen he often recalled afterwards, in the sentimental fashion to which he was prone, that his second innings contained the first of many boundaries he was to hit on the ground.

He became a batsman of neatness and efficiency, a fine cutter of the ball, good against spin bowling, and for a frail-looking man he was surprisingly capable against the fast stuff. His captaincy was shrewd: he was a brilliant tactician and a very good judge of a player's capacities. His serious playing career lasted until that heady day in 1920 when he was carried shoulder-high from the field at Lord's after leading Middlesex to the victory which secured the county championship.* By then, he had scored 29,028 runs in first-class cricket, at an average of 36.33, with 60 centuries to his name and a top score of 244, which he made in 1911 for an England team against the champion county, Warwickshire. He had played for Oxford and therefore, as an Old Blue of that University, was qualified to wear the eye-catching cap of the Harlequins (segments of dark blue, maroon and buff) and did so frequently, whatever team he was playing for. His international career began when he returned to the West Indies as a member of Lord Hawke's team in 1897, and in the next two or three years he played cricket with English touring sides in America, Canada, Portugal and South Africa. These, remember, were still the days when such tours were private arrangements, and Warner's first visit to Australia in 1902 was as captain of an English side again under the patronage of Lord Hawke. It was

---

* He subsequently took a team round South America and one of its players was the young Lord Dunglass, later Sir Alec Douglas-Home.

there that he was himself invited to try and arrange the next tour Down Under. He told his hosts to "ask the MCC – they are the proper body". That was how the Marylebone club became the authority responsible for picking and despatching all English touring sides for the next sixty-six years.

Inevitably, Warner captained the first MCC touring side, which went to Australia in 1903–4 and won the Test rubber 3–2 against all the predictions, largely because of B. J. T. Bosanquet's googlies, the like of which had never been seen before out there. The victorious leader was rewarded, on his return home, with a place on the MCC Committee. He was thirty-one years old, and he was to retain that or some superior office in the club until only a couple of years before he died at the age of eighty-nine. He took another side Down Under, in 1911–12, and some still believe that it was the strongest touring party ever to leave England. It won the series four to one, though Warner played little part in the triumphs on the field, being laid low most of the time with one of his mysterious illnesses. They almost caused him to give up the captaincy of Middlesex, which he had taken in 1908, but was persuaded to hang on to with success until he had finished playing the first-class game. They also saw him invalided out of the Army during the First World War, after spending time with the General Staff and the Department of Information in London. It is remarkable that a man as sickly as Pelham Warner could recover the stamina to play cricket as conspicuously well and over as long a period as he did.

He had been called to the Bar in 1900, but he never practised law. Instead he made a profession of cricket journalism from 1903, when he began writing a weekly piece for the *Westminster Gazette*; more assiduously from 1921, when he became daily cricket correspondent for the *Morning Post* and founded his own magazine, *The Cricketer*. By then he was deep in the counsels of MCC and was shortly to become a selector of England teams, but neither Warner nor the club saw any incompatibility between these roles and that of newspaperman, though his juxtaposition remains one that is unique in the annals of the English game (*pace* E. W. Swanton, cricket writer and MCC Committee man). Warner could be relied upon in print to repeat doctrines dear to the collective heart of MCC, many of which he was responsible for. And so he rose steadily in the hierarchy of the club – Deputy Secretary during the years of the Second World War, Trustee from 1946 to 1961, President in 1950–1 – all the while writing his articles or editing his magazine, as well as turning out or having a hand in eighteen books. No one was better equipped to be a cricket writer. He had, after all, played the game at the highest level. One way and another, he almost certainly saw more first-class cricket than anyone else in his lifetime.

He venerated MCC, as it came to venerate him, and he cherished the concept of the amateur cricketer. For the rest, "we must not forget the professional", he once wrote. "Few, if any, men owed more to the professional cricketer than I do. I have travelled with him the world over and played with and against him in this country. I have always found him loyal to a degree and a splendid, happy companion both on and off the field." He wrote an account of the Gentlemen v Players games, and declared there that he was "fortunate to have lived to attempt to give some sort of history of an historic match which began long before Test matches were dreamed of, and which I pray, and believe, will never die out". That was a vain aspiration. Pelham Warner died in 1963 the very day before MCC took the decision to have done with the distinction between amateurs and professionals. In an extraordinary ceremony at Lord's they scattered his ashes on the boundary in front of the Warner Stand, as near as they could calculate to the spot where the ball crossed the edge of the field the day young Warner hit his first four on the ground. (Other cricket enthusiasts have sought a similar dispersal of their own remains, but they have always been turned down.)

Long before he died, Sir Pelham Warner had come to seem a very old-fashioned English gentleman of a certain kind. He never failed to wear a top hat when he attended the University match, which he did every year. If a player swore in his presence, the offender was made to apologise. He believed very deeply in a society based on hierarchy, in which every man knew his place and kept it. He once opened an exhibition of books about cricket and took the opportunity to let it be known that he thought little of the practice, by radio commentators, of referring to cricketers by their Christian names. Sir Pelham wasn't accustomed to being answered back and he was disconcerted when John Arlott was invited to address the audience and mentioned, en passant, "For my part, I shall continue to speak of Denis Compton as though he were my friend, and not as if he were my groom." Thereafter, whenever a new phenomenon appeared at Lord's to mark another step forward in Progress – advertisements propped up behind the bowler, bats with crimson blades, players with sweatbands round their wrists – Arlott could never resist the temptation to speculate within earshot of his radio listeners; "Oh dear. I wonder what Sir Pelham will make of this."

Few men have had so many testimonials to their character showered upon them, alive or dead. "He had innumerable friends of all ages and on a crowded day at Lord's would greet the humblest and most obscure with the same transparently sincere pleasure and interest as the most eminent" (H. S. Altham). ". . . Whilst Sir Pelham Warner, to whose courage and unquenchable enthusiasm cricket throughout the war years owed an incalculable debt. . ." (E. W. Swanton). "The most famous and recognisable figure at Lord's for half a century, he insisted on showing his membership card whenever he entered the ground or Pavilion, because he rightly thought that his example would greatly ease the task of the gatemen in carrying out their instructions" (Ian Peebles). "There have been many greater cricketers than Pelham Warner, but none more devoted to the game. Whether winning or losing he has always been the same" (*Wisden*, 1921). Invariably he was characterised as a very gentle prince among men. He was that period piece, the born leader who was approachable by all and beloved by his troops. He was kindness itself. He was dear old Plum.

But there was another side to him, not to be spoken of when he was alive, and a source of embarrassment even now, when he has been gone these twenty years. Gubby Allen has said that "it could be argued that he said or wrote a few half-truths to justify his actions or lack of them". Someone close to Warner has added that he was deft at blaming others for his own mistakes, that he made a rather vicious enemy if you fell out with him. It was perhaps this streak that accounted for his refusal to refer to the First or Second World Wars as such; to Warner they were the First German War and the Second German War, a peculiarity shared by the newspaper magnate Lord Beaverbrook, who was another good hater.* Certainly Warner could be quite grudging when he was on a losing side. He was President of MCC (an honour oddly delayed for a man so applauded by his peers) when Freddie Brown's side was defeated Down Under in 1950–1. At the end of the series, in his Presidential capacity, Warner sent the following message to the Australians: "I should like to congratulate Australia on retaining the Ashes. As they have so generously acknowledged, good fortune has not been with us. I think everyone would like to pay tribute to Brown's inspiring leadership and to his success on the field. Though beaten, he may well claim that he and his men surrendered with all the honours of war."

That was an unfortunate turn of phrase from the person who so carefully kept his head down when the shot was flying most furiously in the nearest thing to open warfare England and Australia have ever known. This is not the place to review the Bodyline tour extensively, but Warner's part in it is central to an understanding of the man. It

---

* Warner even entitled two chapters of his history of Lord's in this way.

also offers the oustanding example of that humbug which too often in the past coated the English cricketing establishment.

Warner was a powerful figure in MCC as the 1932–3 tour approached. Not only was he a Committee member of almost thirty years' standing; he was also chairman of the selectors who picked the team for Australia. On top of that, it was decided that he should manage the side in person, taking the Surrey secretary R. C. N. Palairet with him as assistant manager to attend to financial arrangements as the tour went along. Pelham Warner was in every way the senior Englishman in the party, though it is perfectly true, as his defenders argue, that the relationship between manager and captain of a touring side in 1932 was somewhat different from what has become the habit of today. Once appointed, the captain was allowed to get on with all strategical matters relating to the games themselves, including the team selection from match to match; and few captains took kindly to being corrected from beyond the boundary. Nevertheless, if any official ever carried the weight to influence an England captain, on or off the field, at home or abroad, that man should have been Pelham Warner.

Certainly, in Douglas Jardine he had an England captain as wilful as they come. A fine batsman and an astute tactical leader, he had many of the qualities most obviously needed to retrieve the Ashes lost at home to Bill Woodfull's side in 1930. Woodfull and several members of his team were to face the Englishmen again in the approaching series, and the visitors were in no doubt that the man they must somehow contain above all others if they were to have any chance of victory was Don Bradman, who had revealed himself at Headingley and Lord's in particular as the greatest batsman of the age, probably the greatest since W. G. Grace was in his prime. Warner himself had clearly thought hard about the threat from that quarter. After Bradman's superb 334 at Leeds, he had written: "We must, if possible, evolve a new type of bowler and develop fresh ideas on strategy and tactics to curb his almost uncanny skill."

Bradman was the main reason for all those tactical discussions which Jardine held in London during the weeks before the MCC team set sail. Although there is no record of Warner having been party to any of them, it is very difficult to believe that he didn't have some inkling of what was going on by way of preparation of what Jardine had in mind; not when he was at the centre of everything that happened at Lord's, where little in cricket escaped the attention of the influential, where words were always being whispered in receptive ears. Not when, in addition to being chairman of selectors, he was cricket correspondent of the *Morning Post*, and therefore able at least to overhear all the gossip of the press box as well. Pelham Warner wasn't a man living in an ivory tower, though he spent a lifetime doing his best to construct one round the realities of cricket.

He had been sitting in the press box at the Oval, and Jardine had been watching from the dressing-room, some weeks before the team was picked, when Bill Bowes of Yorkshire was admonished on the pitch by Jack Hobbs for bowling too many bumpers at him per over. Next day Warner's article in the newspaper deplored the Yorkshire-man's form of aggression. And in the next issue of his magazine *The Cricketer* he wrote: "Bowes should alter his tactics. He bowled with five men on the on side and sent down several very short-pitched balls which frequently bounced head-high and more. That is not bowling. Indeed, it is not cricket."

Douglas Jardine, who had faced his quota of this stuff shortly after Jack Hobbs, had neither ducked the bouncers nor protested against them. Presumably he was considering their value as a tactical weapon. He may properly stand condemned for what he unleashed in Australia, but at least he didn't take cover or whine when the same treatment was dished out to him. During the English season which followed the Bodyline tour, he found himself facing a prolonged assault from bouncers flung down by the West Indians Constantine and Martindale in the Test match at Old Trafford. He not only stood fast without uttering a word of complaint afterwards. In five hours at the crease he endured several blows about the body, managed to strike five boundaries, and grafted his way to a score of 127. This was the only century he ever made in Test cricket; and, as Ronald Mason, the latest historian of the Bodyline tour, has suggested, "he would have given his ears to have been able to make it against Australia". For he went there quite determined to even old scores. His conduct Down Under was not only designed to nullify the genius of Bradman in particular; it sprang from a dislike of crude colonials in general, which probably originated on his first tour there in 1928–9. He, too, was a Harlequin, whose cap was regarded by rough Diggers as clear evidence of the poncy Pom. Their barracking so nettled the lofty Jardine, another man who wasn't accustomed to being answered back, that – so Jack Hobbs told Gubby Allen years later – he actually spat in their direction when fielding on the boundary at Melbourne one day. After that, he couldn't really expect much less than open war between himself and the popular side of Australian grounds if ever he returned. But the hostilities on the field were entirely his own work, and more coolly organised.

It would be astonishing if Pelham Warner was without a clue of what might be forthcoming in the winter of 1932–3. Nevertheless, he picked Jardine to lead the team, and he also chose Bowes as a last-minute reinforcement, when Maurice Tate fell ill (although in fact, Tate subsequently joined the tour). And so the party sailed on a voyage across the globe which lasted for a month; what time, as Gubby Allen has recalled, there was at the very least talk of the need to hate the Australians. Again, Pelham Warner could scarcely have been unaware of this. The difficulty in reconstructing his part in what followed over the next four and a half months is that there is so very little documentary evidence one way or the other. It is remarkable that an epic (or whatever may be the more appropriate word) which excited so many passions, which achieved so much publicity, which has been analysed so often since almost to the point of tedium, is so devoid of first-hand observation about the behaviour and utterances of the man who had chosen the English team, who was actually managing it on the battlefield, who was to be knighted four years later for his services to cricket. This is so striking an omission that it really does seem as if that weary old cliché, the conspiracy of silence, is applicable here. We know that the England team met and decided to rally behind Jardine when he was being castigated for his brand of leadership. We also know that MCC went to extraordinary lengths to make sure that neither Larwood nor anyone else spoke to the Press about Bodyline until they reached St John's Wood again. Quite clearly, the protective coating was applied even more thickly to Pelham Warner than to England's captain on the field. Douglas Jardine has gone down in history as the villain or the hero of the piece, according to taste. Pelham Warner's public image has been consistently that of Mr Clean.

The most famous report of dear old Plum is of his encounter with Bill Woodfull, after the Australian captain had been staggered by a ball from Larwood which hit him over the heart in Adelaide. England's manager made his solicitous way to the dressing-room after Woodfull's innings was completed, to enquire about his health. There he was memorably told, "I don't want to see you, Mr Warner. There are two teams out there; one is trying to play cricket and the other is not." Thus rebuked, Warner retreated, apparently in some distress. Gubby Allen has said in print that "more than once I remember him in tears in his hotel room" in the course of the tour. He was apparently on the verge of tears after Allen, in Melbourne, went and told him of the ultimatum he had just given Jardine, concerning his own refusal to bowl Bodyline, before the bowler returned to the dressing-room to discover that he would be playing in the match after all.

"Oh, you can't have a row with Douglas," said Warner. "We really picked you because we thought you'd be the one person who'd get on with him. Please go down and be nice to him."

Allen replied, "When I go down there again, I shall simply repeat that I'm not prepared to bowl this stuff, and he can take it or leave it."

Warner's response to that was, "That's not very helpful."

We also know that during the Adelaide Test, the Australian Board of Control directly requested Warner and Palairet to put a stop to Jardine's tactics. The board was told that the managers had no control over the captain in anything to do with the conduct of that or any other cricket match. On receiving this limp reply, the board composed the first of the cables that shuttled back and forth between it and MCC over the next few weeks, which so heightened the international tension that eventually the two Governments were anxiously awaiting the outcome of events. The board's first message to Lord's about Bodyline ("Unless it is stopped at once it is likely to upset the friendly relations existing between Australia and England") was despatched on January 18, 1933, the fifth and penultimate day of the Adelaide Test. That same day in London, unaware of what was in transmission across the wires, the Secretary of MCC, W. Findlay, was writing a letter to his predecessor, Sir Francis Lacey. In it he quoted from a letter he had received from Jardine, which had remarked: "So far our bowling has in general been a shock and an unpleasant surprise to the old hands of Australia. The papers have put up a squeal rising to a whine about bowling at the man." To which Findlay added, in his own letter to Lacey, "Plum apparently has not told Jardine that he does not approve of this kind of bowling."

Nine days earlier he had written a brief letter to Warner himself which did little but pass the time of day in acknowledging some communication from England's manager. In it he had observed, "The paper reports are so unreliable and exaggerate." But on March 15, when the hostilities in Australia were over and the MCC side was playing in New Zealand before heading for home across the Pacific and the United States, he was more obviously comforting Warner after the recent tribulations he had endured. "You must not be bothered," Findlay declared, "by what some of the people say about the Press. In my humble opinion it is a blessing that there are still a few writers like yourself who understand cricket and all that cricket stands for."

Only a few more pieces of evidence can be adduced. When the

party returned to London, MCC summoned Warner, Palairet, Jardine, Larwood and Voce to give their versions of events in person; but neither Allen, R. E. S. Wyatt (vice-captain of the team) nor Herbert Sutcliffe (senior professional) were included in the interview. Back in the press box, though relieved of his position as Test match selector until he became chairman again in 1935 for four uninterrupted years, Warner once more preached sermons against intimidatory bowling. He also revised *The Book of Cricket* for a third edition in 1934 to include the following passages: "Practically every cricketer of every generation in Australia is convinced that the type of bowling employed by Larwood is contrary to the best interests and the spirit of cricket: they urge that it can only breed ill-feeling. It seems probable that time will probably confirm this verdict . . . To be pitch-forked into a tornado of trouble in the winter of one's cricketing life was something of a shock – and a bitter disappointment . . . I objected [in 1910] to a method of bowling which seemed to me to be utterly against the interest and spirit of cricket. From that view I have never wavered." In *Cricket Between the Wars*, which appeared in 1942, he wrote: "As for Bodyline, as the Australians called it, he [Jardine] thought this type of bowling was legitimate and within the rules. My own view was that it was wrong, both ethically and also tactically, and that Larwood often 'wasted his sweetness on the desert air' by sending down, for example, thirty-nine out of forty-two deliveries on the line of the batsman or just clear of him, as he did at Sydney in the first Test."

One of the few things quite clear about Pelham Warner is that he came to detest Douglas Jardine as a result of his experiences alongside him in Australia. In his book *A Sort of Cricketing Person*, E. W. Swanton reproduced a letter which Warner wrote in January 1934 to Sir Alexander Hore-Ruthven, subsequently the Lord Gowrie who became President of MCC in 1948. At the time he was Governor of South Australia, and as such during the Bodyline crisis he had made representations to the British Secretary of State for the Dominions, J. H. Thomas, in an effort to damp down the inflamed feelings between the two countries. When Warner wrote, the future of Jardine's leadership was in the balance. Was he to be reappointed captain for the 1934 domestic season, when the Australians would be visiting again, or not? "At present," wrote Warner, "I say 'No' unless he makes a most generous public gesture of friendliness, and then I am not sure I would trust him. He is a queer fellow. When he sees a cricket ground with an Australian on it he goes mad! He rose to his present position on my shoulders, and of his attitude to me I do not care to speak . . ."

All else about Pelham Warner's role in the Bodyline tour can be no more than inference, with many towering question marks. How, for example, does one square Billy Findlay's observation to Sir Francis Lacey that Warner had apparently not offered his views on Bodyline to Jardine, with Gubby Allen's assertion (in *The Cricketer*, May 1981) that "Plum made numerous efforts to get Douglas Jardine to change his tactics, or at least to modify Bodyline"? How did the lachrymose manager and chairman of selectors absolve himself from any of the stigmas which were attached to English cricket at this time, and especially to all who toured Australia in the winter of 1932–3? We do not know. For one of the most arresting features of the whole episode is the dearth of relevant material. As manager of that tour, Pelham Warner submitted to the MCC Committee a report on all that had happened from the moment the party left home until the day it returned. That document, quite simply, has vanished from the archives at Lord's. So has every letter he wrote from Australia to Findlay or anyone else in the hierarchy of MCC. The protective coating, it seems, has insulated him rather well from historical research.

It may be thought – it almost certainly will be thought in some quarters – that these matters are no longer of any moment; that they ought to be quietly forgotten, letting bygones be bygones, since they happened half a century ago. They are relevant today only because they concern the ethics of cricket, and that makes them very relevant indeed. For the spirit in which the game shall be played has become an issue in our time more pressing than at any other since that Bodyline tour. To point an accusing finger at Kerry Packer's intervention in the sport and blame all lapses since on the philosophy he introduced is facile and unfair, though it is difficult to rebut the argument that decline has accelerated since he dangled the prospect of considerable wealth in front of certain international players. The game *has* become more aggressively competitive, more orientated towards cash rewards and less towards the exhibition of sheer skill for its own sake since 1977. This has produced more gamesmanship (perhaps merely more overt gamesmanship), more deplorable badgering of umpires, more general hostility of an unpleasant kind in the cricketing air.

The symptoms and some of the examples were there before Packer had been heard of, however. It was at Adelaide in 1971 that Boycott flung down his bat in petulance when he was given run-out. It was during the captaincy of Ian Chappell, which began in 1972, that Australian Test teams acquired a reputation for the verbal bullying of batsmen, to which the anodyne "sledging" has been applied. It was after damaging several Englishmen with his fast bowling in the series of 1974–5 that Lillee put his name to the assurance that "I want it to hurt so much that the batsman does not want to face me any more". It was at Old Trafford in 1976, where Holding, Roberts and Daniel bowled so many bouncers that the first of them was warned for deliberate intimidation and their captain, Clive Lloyd, evidently thought he had excused and explained them by remarking that "our fellows got carried away".

Since 1977 the catalogue of offences against the unwritten codes has only lengthened each season. We have had an England captain (Fletcher) swiping at the stumps with his bat in his indignation at being given out. We have had a West Indian (Croft) shoulder-charging an umpire accidently-on-purpose because he, too, was upset about decisions against him. We have had another West Indian (Clarke) heaving a stone into the crowd. We have had an Australian (Lillee) holding up a Test match for ten minutes while he went through an elaborate pantomime, the chief purpose of which was to obtain the widest possible publicity for an aluminium bat he wished to sell in large quantities. We have had an Australian (Lillee again) and a Pakistani (Miandad) all but brawling in the middle of the pitch. We have had a New Zealander (Hadlee) inciting young spectators to chant mindless aggression at opposing batsmen. We have had two Australians (Lillee yet again, together with Marsh) actually placing bets against the Test team of which both were members, the bowler collecting £5,000 and the wicket-keeper £2,500. Could this really have been the same Marsh who, in the Melbourne Centenary Test of 1977, had warmed so many hearts by pointing out to the umpire that the catch with which he was reckoned to have dismissed Randall was not, in fact, a clean one? Perhaps the most dismaying thing of all about the bets placed at Headingley four years later is that the two players remained in the Australian Test side after the aberration was revealed. Onlookers could be forgiven for concluding at that point that values in the world of cricket had at last been turned completely upside down.

It is no use Englishmen making patronising noises when they notice that the most spectacular transgressions more often than not have been those of players from overseas; any more than it should comfort them that the abdication of responsibility by the Australian Cricket Board (which quite clearly has been demoralised one way or another by its bruising from Packer) is unlikely to be imitated by their own TCCB which, among other things, specifically forbids cricketers to bet on matches in which they play, on pain of losing their registrations, which means their livelihoods. The sounds of shock or snigger ought to be muted over here. All but the Australian offenders have been partly moulded by playing regularly for English county sides, whether or not they are qualified to appear in other Test teams. And the most lurid offences are no more than sharp illustrations of behaviour patterns which are doubtless as rife in this land as anywhere else. It sometimes seems as if the only major cricketing country where the game is still played by and large according to the old precepts is India: and even the Indians now practise deliberate time-wasting at home with a resourcefulness that almost defies condemnation. Behaviour in cricket is still a cut above that in many other field sports; but it most certainly isn't what it used to be within memory.

The question is, of course, just what were the old precepts? Anyone who contrasts Sir Pelham Warner's activities, or lack of them, during the Bodyline series with his lifelong pontifications about "the spirit of cricket" may well decide that the sentiment has been rendered everlastingly bogus by association. They may fairly come to a similar conclusion after studying the career of W. G. Grace and taking note of his observation once that he dreaded the prospect of totally professional cricket because "betting and all kindred evils will follow in its wake, and instead of the game being followed up for love, it will simply be a matter of £ s d". Prophetic words, perhaps, with much justification obvious now; but it ill became the mercenary Grace, of all men, to mouth them.

Cricket never has been the immaculate game that some of its windier eulogists have liked to pretend; its history from start to finish is studded with examples of imperfect behaviour, from the sly to the shoddy. Being the pastime of men who have also engaged in politics, warfare, commerce, marriage and religion, how could anyone expect it to be otherwise? There are few contemporary examples of bad behaviour which are not cases of history repeating itself. Games-manship? How about the University match played at Lord's in 1896, when the follow-on was compulsory? So as to prevent Oxford batting a second time straight off, the Cambridge captain ordered his bowlers to give away a dozen byes. Kicking the stumps out of the ground in a tantrum? Newman of Hampshire did that at Trent Bridge in 1929 after being barracked for slow play and having an argument with his captain. The bowler elated by having injured the batsman? John Jackson of Notts, well over a hundred years ago boasted: "I got nine wickets and lamed Johnny Wisden so that he couldn't bat. That was as good as ten, eh?"

If we must accept, and we must, that almost all forms of deviation from the model have been practised at least intermittently from the start, then we are left looking for a demarcation line between what is regarded as acceptable (in "the spirit of cricket") and what is not; and we have to ask ourselves just who decides where the line shall be drawn. At Melbourne, in 1981, Greg Chappell instructed his younger brother to bowl a final ball underarm along the ground, so as to prevent New Zealand tieing a match by the batsman hitting a six. In Sydney, twelve months earlier, Mike Brearley had ordered his wicket-keeper to take station on the boundary so as to reduce to an absolute minimum the chance of the necessary three runs being scored for a West Indian victory. Where stood the demarcation line in relation to those two incidents, which were both within the Laws of the game? Chappell's tactic was condemned by all detached commentators as an outrage against the spirit of cricket, Brearley's was merely frowned upon as a bit of one-upmanship. Was the line drawn between them simply because Chappell's ploy made it quite certain that his side would win the match, whereas Brearley's stratagem only made his victory highly probable: or was the arbitration based upon some subtler premise? Was so much made of both incidents because they took place in hectic one-day internationals with large amounts of instant cash awaiting the winners? Would either captain, indeed, have dreamed of offending the purists if he had been leading his team in a Test match rather than in the circus atmosphere of the knock-out stuff? The questions multiply and the answers are elusive.

At this distance the most interesting thing about Chappell's gaffe is the chorus of disapproval it provoked. The chairman of the Australian Cricket Board condemned it, speaking of Chappell's "responsibility as Australian captain to uphold the spirit of cricket at all times". The Prime Minister of New Zealand condemned it in the most offensive terms ("It was an act of cowardice and I consider it appropriate that Australia were wearing yellow") and the Prime Minister of Australia said that in his view "Greg Chappell has made a serious mistake". The cricket writers at both ends of the earth condemned it, a typical headline being "Greg Chappell outraged the spirit of cricket", and it received a dishonourable mention in the next edition of *Wisden*. Even Chappell's elder brother Ian – not a man of unswerving allegiance to the unwritten codes – went into print with the following solemnity; "Fair dinkum, Greg, how much pride do you have to sacrifice to win 35,000 dollars?" Only one prominent voice in cricket was raised in Chappell's defence. It was that of Mike Denness, the former captain of England, who said: "I don't think Greg Chappell can be criticised – he was playing to the Laws of the game. He notified the umpire, who notified the batsman. In a recent World Series match between Australia and the West Indies, Wayne Daniel hit a six off the last ball to beat Australia. Maybe that was going through Greg's mind. They were playing for high stakes." But by far the most fascinating reaction happened a few days after the incident in Melbourne. As Greg Chappell came out to bat at Sydney Cricket Ground, he was soundly booed on his way to the wicket, by what was presumably a mostly and patriotically Australian crowd (who gave him a standing ovation a little later, when he had scored 87).

Would that crowd, one wonders, have abused its national cricket captain if so much hostility had not already been flung at him from on high, and if the hostility had not been so vividly and widely publicised? Was it making up its own mind about Greg Chappell and the spirit of cricket, or was it the unwitting instrument of propaganda, a sort of Rentacrowd stimulated by the righteous? It is hard to be sure, though the history of cricket-watching (the history of the spectator in every sport) suggests that crowd reactions are much influenced by outside stimuli; and there never was a more potent stimulus of mass emotion than the selective processes of television, to which this generation alone has been fully exposed.

It is also difficult to escape the conclusion that television, together with the wilder forms of newspaper reporting, has had some part to play in the behaviour patterns of cricketers themselves. The man who is temperamentally an exhibitionist is liable to emphasise all mannerisms that single him out for attention, correspondingly as his audience increases. To perform quite literally before the eyes·of a whole nation – let alone on an international stage – is a mighty incentive to vanity. At the same time, the communication which broadcasts the individual's fame or notoriety so widely, whether it be television, radio or the press, also offers him images which may be suggestive, not necessarily from his own brand of sport. When the tennis player McEnroe can be seen to be making up his own rules as he goes along and pretty well getting away with it, who is to say that the cricketer of similar natural disposition is not encouraged to try the same thing in his own game?

Yet both crowds and players, stimulated as they may be by forces which are essentially dependants feeding off the behaviour of both, are also under the influence of limitations defined by authority, and they are inhibited to some extent by what has been the norm of behaviour accepted by their own predecessors until they themselves establish a new norm. The crucial factor would seem to be the role of authority, the clarity with which it settles limitations and the vigour with which it enforces them. In England the margins allowed between the acceptable and the impermissible were much narrower than they are today, when MCC was at the height of its autocratic powers. The fact that the club's powers might have been a great deal less effective if the mystique of infallibility had not been so carefully preserved by its exclusiveness is beside the point. It ruled professional cricketers in this country with its rod of iron, and cricket authorities elsewhere did likewise by taking their cue from Lord's. And though there was most certainly one set of unwritten rules for the gentleman cricketer and another for the professional (by no means all of the gents took advantage of them, however), there was also a high degree of the disinterested in MCC's attitudes, which had been shaped more than anything by that Victorian morality which genuinely strove for Augustinian notions of perfection – but at the same time was quite capable of sweeping what was domestically discreditable under the carpet, in the hope that no one else would notice. The disinterested response was evident after that Cambridge captain in 1896 had slyly stopped Oxford from following on, in order to secure advantage. MCC at once amended the Laws of Cricket so that the follow-on was no longer compulsory. The amendment was made solely to rid cricket of an opportunity for sharp practice.

Social and economic history alone ended MCC's old powers, and the same forces have meant that neither the Cricket Council nor the TCCB can ever enjoy them to the same extent, even though nominally they now occupy the ground MCC once held. It would have been perfectly feasible, for example, for the Marylebone club to have proscribed batsmen's helmets fifty years ago, when Patsy Hendren introduced a tentative version very briefly into the game. It would be quite impossible for TCCB to do so now, if only because of the legal implications which were undreamt of in the 1930's, when professional cricketers could not afford to consult lawyers. There are, however, areas of cricketing conduct which are rapidly approaching the disgraceful and which are still susceptible to old-fashioned forms of discipline.

By the start of 1983 the most urgent matter of all had become the attitude of players to umpires. So steeply had behaviour declined here that Bob Willis, captaining England in Australia, was being hailed in some quarters as a sort of hero for his studied refusal to criticise publicly those umpires whose decisions had sometimes been shown on television to have been incorrect (and there surely was something heroic about Willis standing doggedly by his principles when he was hectored for the comment that would inflame, and was intended in some quarters to inflame, the subject more). An abysmal development – a massive screen erected on the cricket ground to give slow-motion replays of any action the producers selected, in front of umpires, players, spectators and interested aircraft – had come to the game in Australia, to increase the tension inherent in the job of umpiring. For two or three seasons before that, however, it was becoming a thankless task owing to the wretched behaviour of a majority of cricketers, encouraged obliquely by commentators on the game, many of whom are ex-players themselves. The habit of fieldsmen appealing en masse when at least half of them can't have a clue whether the batsman is caught or lbw; the excrescence of the disappointed bowler dancing up and down in his fury like a demented three-year-old; the perpetual belly-aching of the touring party which lacks the human dignity to accept bad luck (real or imagined) with a shrug instead of a whimper: all these have become commonplaces of cricket now wherever it is played professionally. With a diminishing number of exceptions, it seems not to have dawned on any modern player that, were the same yardstick applied to his performances that he insists on measuring all umpires by – getting everything absolutely right every time he appears in the middle – the cricketer himself might be looking for another job before any season was half way through.*

In England a great deal depends upon the broad identity of purpose which has been established between TCCB and the Cricketers' Association, and which has been one of the healthiest features of the game here in recent years. There is no reason why, between them, they should not restore the fair-minded behaviour patterns of not so long ago where these have eroded, why they should not make sure that the erosion goes no further than it already has. It can be done with the mixture of authority and consensus that has so far preserved the English game from too intolerable a shift in some norms. But when authority decides to act, it will have to make more than a gesture in the right direction. Ian Botham may have been slightly more sinned against than sinning when remarks he thought he had made discreetly about Australian umpires found their way at once into 48-point type in a tabloid. It was a relief to hear that his manager, Doug Insole, promptly fined him £200 as punishment. But

---

* In *The Cricketer*, February 1983, one of Willis's team in Australia, Vic Marks of Somerset, was the author of a piece called "Despatch from the Dressing-Room", composed just after the Melbourne Test. In it he revealed that "the team was also urged to improve its appealing, an area in which the Australians are undoubtedly superior. When appealing the Australians make a statement: we ask a question". It seems pertinent to ask by whom was the England side "urged to improve its appealing"?

£200 to a man reputed to be earning between £60,000 and £70,000 a year will have as much impact as a parking ticket on a bank clerk.

The ultimate sanction, of course, lies in the hands of those who control the purse strings; as it always has. This is the Achilles heel of the professional game. And the purse strings are not really controlled by TCCB or even by the commercial companies who are propping up the game financially. They are held distantly, but nonetheless quite certainly, by all who appreciate and watch cricket. If spectators stopped attending matches, and especially if they stopped watching matches on television because they found them too offensive, the commercial support would very smartly be withdrawn. As it is, TCCB is very gloomy when the figures for home Test match attendances fall below a certain point. Now, the idea of a strike by cricket-watchers might seem like a pretty ludicrous proposition, but such a thing – undeclared and quite unofficial, of course – has happened lately in British sport: ask the Football League, which has suffered a catastrophic loss of revenue at the gate, related to the performances of footballers and the hooligans in football crowds, as well as to the national recession.

They evidently order things somewhat differently in Australia these days, but the bulk of cricket's followers in England have been reared according to precepts of the game which have only now started to seem old-fashioned. These people may have been naïve to swallow whole all that has been uttered about the spirit of cricket in the past, but the fact remains that they did swallow it and in their own way they represent it today (and even Greg Chappell used the phrase, and was very conscious of its implications, when he apologised for his action in Melbourne)* They are the . . . what? . . . tens

* Anyone who imagined that the Spirit of Cricket Past expired with Sir Pelham Warner would have been startled or relieved by a letter to *The Times* in January 1983 from a gentleman in South-west London:

"Sir: When a batsman sees his wicket thrown down long before he has reached the crease he knows that, whatever the umpire says, he is out and should return to the pavilion. If he does not, he is cheating. When a wicket-keeper catches a ball behind the stumps he can see far better than can the umpire whether the ball has touched the bat, or has been deflected by the player's body, or whether it has done neither of these things. If he can see that it has not touched the bat and still claims a wicket, he is cheating.

Cricket, and in particular Test cricket is, or has been for the aspiring player, one of the few remaining refuges of true sportsmanship. I think that Grantland Rice said all that was necessary when he wrote:

> For when the One Great Scorer comes
> To write against your name,
> He marks – not that you won or lost –
> But how you played the game.

Sincerely, etc."

of thousands? . . . who stay up into the small hours or rise well before a winter's dawn, so as to listen to commentaries from the other side of the world. They are the people who sit patiently under dripping umbrellas for hours on end, making wry jokes about their discomfort while they hope that those twenty-two players lolling about in the warmth of the Pavilion will perform again for them before the day is out.

If, one season (and the game's finances are so perilously balanced that it would take only one season), they decided that they had had enough of the prima donnas and the bully boys and the outright cheats, and turned to some other summer pursuit, then the purse strings of cricket would be drawn so tight that nothing could be extracted to pay all the bills. And what would the professional cricketers do then, poor things?

CHAPTER NINE

The Way Ahead

On the first Saturday in September, Lord's produces its last big occasion of the year, when the second of cricket's two Cup Finals is held. In blazing sunshine usually – and only once in twenty years has the weather really let this fixture down – the crowds come rollicking up to St John's Wood with a carnival air that is not repeated on the altogether more considered occasion of a Test, even when the West Indies are here. They pack the place to the seams with their banners and their bugles (Gus Farley's tact and discretion work overtime on Cup Final Day) and their other manifestations of loyalty. Men and women from Glamorgan have been seen with leeks tied to funny hats, antique farm labourers' smocks have been brought out of mothballs in many a Sussex bottom drawer, and stocks of corn purloined from the harvest fields of Somerset have made their appearance in front of the Tavern. The din is as tremendous when a wicket falls as the one made in that other seasonal climax at Wembley when a footballer scores a goal.

This relatively young Cup Final has already left its legendary marks on the history of the game. The catch that Bond made off Asif to turn the 1971 match Lancashire's way, above all perhaps, but there have been others not far behind in everybody's recollection. Boycott's 146 against Surrey in 1965 lingers on because it was made with uncharacteristic haste as well as with customary purpose. Illingworth's five for twenty-nine in the same match was the finest piece of bowling seen on Cup Final Day, a remarkable performance by a bowler limited to just a dozen overs, until Garner surpassed it in 1979 when he shattered Northamptonshire at critical moments with six for twenty-nine. In that game Richards had already scored one of his loveliest centuries, easing the ball to the boundaries time and again for 177 runs, turning the energy of the bowlers to his own account with unerring eye and perfectly angled bat. And there have been some close-run finishes on these September days at Lord's. When Sussex beat Worcestershire in the very first final, it was only by fourteen runs. Most rousing of all, Derbyshire and Northants actually managed cricket's least likely result by tieing their scores in

224

the final of 1981, in a last-ball dash, a desperate throw at the wicket and a flurry of tumbling pads, Derbyshire collecting the brand-new NatWest trophy for having lost only six wickets to Northamptonshire's nine.

Although it never happened before 1963, this sort of thing had been advocated seven years earlier by an agency which had nothing at all to do with cricket, and never would notice it again. The independent research organisation Political and Economic Planning, which was more familiar with bank rates and the gross national product, suddenly turned its attention to what it called The Cricket Industry in a report published in 1956. This took a fairly glum view of the game's prosperity, whose hollowness had not yet been publicly recognised by cricket's own authority. Among other things, it suggested that professional cricket in England should be reorganised completely and played only in short bursts during the weekend, a view which produced a memorable letter to the *Daily Telegraph*. "I have no idea," wrote a Mr Higgins from Nottingham, "who the members of this lugubriously named body are, but two questions arise. Why do not these people stick to their own depressing subject and leave cricket for those who understand it? And what has the practice in other countries to do with the matter?" The isolationist Mr Higgins hadn't much appreciated PEP's comparison between what happened in the English shires and what went on in the suburbs of Sydney and Melbourne, which occasionally resulted in the Australian part-timers tanning the hide off the more industrious English countryfolk.

At Lord's they were a bit more discerning, and the PEP report was the signal for MCC setting up the committee chaired by H. S. Altham to examine the future welfare of the first-class game, which put it on the road to the one-day match. When Gillette came along in the underwriter's role in 1963, the opportunity was seized with gratitude. Two years later Lord's was the scene of the very first Sunday cricket match with gate money taken in England, when twelve Middlesex players faced up to a side representing Lord's Taverners (and a regular Middlesex XI played Hampshire in 1967 in the first Sunday county match at Lord's).

A curiosity of the Sunday games, which are now an enduring part of the county cricket season, is that they still take place without anyone being quite sure whether they might not suddenly be disrupted by figures in black, rushing on to the pitch with hymn sheets and the Thirty-Nine Articles, denouncing all present as Godless and, what's more, criminal. The Lord's Day Observance Society (founded 1831) still broods upon Sabbath iniquity, fortified in the knowledge that the Act which gave it credibility in the first place has never been repealed. So aware of this far-fetched hazard to the game is MCC still that when, a couple of years ago, it was agonising over whether to introduce Sunday to the pleasures of Test cricket at Lord's, it sent all members some relevant extracts from the Sunday Observance Act, together with the club's own epistle on the subject: "Notwithstanding this [the dreadful penalties embodied in the Act], it has been common practice for a number of years for entrance to similar events to be effected by the purchase of a programme or by granting temporary membership upon payment. These methods provide no guarantee of immunity from prosecution, although it should be pointed out that they have not so far resulted in prosecutions being brought at Sunday afternoon cricket matches." Just so.

No such dark thoughts are in mind on Cup Final Day, however, when one of the sides is threading its way to victory, accompanied by yet another unsteady chorus from the Tavern crowd, a penance that others put up with because a long day in the sun has left everyone agreeably in the pink. Well, almost everyone. A few hundred stand stock still when the tumult attending the last over rises to crescendo at the last ball: they are the ones who have come all the way up from Taunton or down from Manchester, or wherever, and are still stone-cold sober enough to realise what a long way home it will be in the dejection of defeat. Everyone else seems to vault the rails, or at least negotiate them carefully on elderly legs, and streams, hurries or stumbles across what a minute or two earlier was the still sacrosanct turf. It is the only moment of the year when authority turns a blind eye to people doing this, and for some it is the only moment in a lifetime of cricket-watching, which they will remember as the occasion when they actually stood beside the batting strip at Lord's and pondered all the marks that a day's palpitating cricket had left behind.* They pause, these dedicated scrutineers, and look up towards the Pavilion balcony when loud cheers break out again. There are the victors, with their new trophy held high (and there, for sure, will be one of them shaking a bottle of bubbly to squirt over the man of the match or the great mob of supporters congregated on the turf below). There, too, are the vanquished, managing curt little nods and rather tight smiles as the runners-up medals are dished out. Every cricketer's hair is tangled into wet hanks after his day full of sweat.

* The only moment big crowds turn up, that is. It has always been a tradition for spectators to stroll upon the grass during the lunch intervals at the University Match and the Eton v Harrow fixtures.

When at last the players disappear, some of their travelling companions still linger a while in the middle, enjoying the licence to stroll there, before drifting off to join the crowds pouring away from the ground. The last of them cast a curious eye over The O'Brien and Ginger, Pierre and Benito, the Ryan Brothers, Cash and Carry and the rest of the boys who come hurrying in through the North Gates to begin the clearing up. By and by, the ground which has been noisy since not long after breakfast time has quietened enough for bird song to be heard again above the scrape of shovels, the clatter of empty beer cans and the tipsy laughter rippling from the members' bars. The place is still sticky in the heat of its Indian summer, though the sun now glows like a brazen gong quite low behind the Warner Stand. Lord's is almost ready to call it a day for another season.

Almost, but not quite. The place pauses for a day or two after its Cup Final, to get its breath back, and then it relaxes to the less demanding rivalries of the Cross Arrows games. The Cross Arrows Cricket Club is nothing less than the works team at Lord's. Everyone employed there is entitled to be a member and its players are a jumble of fellows who may labour during the year in any one of the departments at headquarters, augmented by the occasional MCC member and cricketer from the Middlesex staff (the 1982 fixtures saw Emburey, Cowans and Williams turning out for the side). The club was founded just over a hundred years ago with the express purpose of allowing MCC employees to have a spell of fun and games themselves after providing so much for others in the course of the season proper. At first it called itself the St John's Wood Ramblers Cricket Club, but then discovered that the name had already been pre-empted by another team in the same part of London. Therefore, in 1880, it designated itself the Cross Arrows; supposedly because an early fixture was away against the Northwood club and, on enquiring which direction that was, one of the team was told that "It's 'cross 'arrow way" – beyond Harrow.

Nowadays all the Cross Arrows games are played at Lord's, on the practice ground, where they put up a dapper little scoreboard of the kind familiar to all properly equipped village clubs, and rope the boundaries off, and set up a beer tent, and bring out the deck chairs for spectators who prefer not to sprawl on the grass. At 11 a.m. sharp each game begins, a different one every day with the exception of Sundays, right through to the end of September. A motley collection of visitors provide the opposition – Stage, Leprechauns, Tunbridge Wells, Mashonaland Country Districts, Ex-MCC Young Professionals, Frogs, Metropolitan Police D Divison, Barclays Bank and the like – and all the results go into fine print on the sports pages of

The Times, because the Cross Arrows have a special place in cricket's affections. Gary Sobers once turned out for this lot, and so would Frank Worrell if he hadn't had to cry off at the last minute; and a sixteen-year-old called Titmus in 1949 scored 660 runs for the club in eleven innings, at an average of 94.28. Cross Arrows matches are usually pretty high-scoring affairs, what with the short boundaries on the practice ground, and the fact that although the bowlers are trying hard enough, not one of them is taking himself quite as seriously as he might if he were performing in the big time on the other side of the Nursery End stands. Five hundred runs in the day are not uncommon, and in 1982 the home side hit 310 in 172 minutes against the Young Professionals. This is not a bad way to finish a season at Lord's. It's the way a lot of people there think cricket ought to be played more often than it is.

There is a Cross Arrows dinner every November, just like any other cricket function of its kind, with much tobacco smoke in the air, much booze going where it loosens tongues, much sentimentality, much mingling of the gentlemen and the players, much gossip making some sit up and others droop with boredom. There is a guest speaker, chosen for his knack of rolling people in the aisles above all, though occasionally his reputation has been misconstrued and he just about paralyses them instead. If he's really been hand-picked, though, ballpoints and the backs of menus are surreptitiously brought into action all over the Lord's banqueting suite, as the uninventive take careful note of the better jests, which are destined to resurface later in winter before impressed audiences all over the home counties of southern England. The President of Cross Arrows, who is always the Secretary of MCC, steers the evening adroitly from the top table. The captain of Cross Arrows, who is currently the Assistant Secretary (Cricket) of MCC, reports on the fortunes of September and distributes floral arrangements to one or two ladies without whom the evening, and some of the club's cricket, wouldn't at all be what it is. The immediate Past-President of MCC is very often there to reply to the toast of "Cricket", which will have been proposed by the chief guest. G. H. G. Doggart did so in 1982, and in a virtuoso performance told a story that ought to have a wider currency than the Cross Arrows dinner.

As an undergraduate he played in that historic game at Fenner's in 1950, when Cambridge University and the West Indies between them scored 1,324 runs in the course of three days, for the loss of only seven wickets all told. The pitch, according to *Wisden*, was "almost farcically unfavourable to bowlers" and four men hit centuries or double centuries. Topping them all, however, was Everton Weekes, who made 304 not out. He had reached, Doggart recalled, something like 293 when at the end of an over he ambled down the pitch to tidy it up, and was clearly heard muttering urgently to himself. He was saying, "Now steady on, Weekes, man, steady! Always go careful in the nineties!"

If that seems like a yarn from a fantasy past, on several counts, it will be a measurement of how much cricket has changed in three decades; just over one biblical generation, in fact. Another measurement is that English professional cricketers were picking up £75 per Test match then, with not much else to look forward to for being chosen to represent their country. Yet another is the remark made in 1982 by a cricketer who in 1950 was just beginning a spectacular career. He was Fred Trueman who, after taking more Test wickets than anyone in the history of the game before him, after revelling in a second reputation as a professional after-dinner speaker who habitually rolled them in the aisles (and didn't care much whether or not the ladies were present at the time), had finally found his level as the predictable old sweat on BBC Radio and Kerry Packer's Channel Nine. It was in this last capacity, on noticing the splendid attendance during the Melbourne Test match which began after Boxing Day 1982, that he declared: "That means money, and that's what cricket's all about."

The unnerving thought for those who believed that sport had nothing conceivably better to offer than the cricket played by men like Everton Weekes and Fred Trueman himself, is the possibility that the Yorkshireman thirty years later had very nearly put the state of the professional game in a nutshell. There are still many English county cricketers, and there will be any number of players overseas as well, who are so pleased to be doing what they are doing for work, who genuinely feel lucky to be playing for the sides that have picked them, that they would be prepared to pay for the opportunity if circumstances were different and they could afford to. But the impression that professional cricket as a whole now gives is that the majority of players have their eyes more on the money they can make than on the experience of cricket for its own sake. Well, why not? One has yet to hear of a lawyer, or a doctor or a writer who is indifferent to the cash he may receive for using his expertise. The answer lies in a sense of proportion. The man who is more concerned with his bank balance than with refining his skills and relishing his use of them even at the cost of tightening his belt, has lost something of his natural pride. What that costs him is for him to work out.

The manipulations of the money market over the past decade or so have already left a mark on the game which must now be indelible.

They seem likely to change its appearance and possibly its nature as well even more in the times immediately ahead. Kerry Packer has all but transformed the higher realms of cricket in Australia in half a dozen years, so that it barely resembles the sport that was played before 1977, except insofar as it still invites twenty-two players to compete in accordance with the Laws of the game: but cricket's character has always depended to a huge extent on what has never been laid down by authority; that has been one of its magnificent attractions. Packer may well be the biggest outside influence to disturb that character and that attraction. We may hope so. But we cannot be sure. Any number of entrepreneurs wait for the chance to make money out of the game if they can, and not all of them will be as careful with it as the sponsors in England have so far proved themselves to be. Not all the plans incubating come from expected directions either.

There is Mr Peter West's scheme, for example. For many years now, West has been familiar to all English cricket-watchers as the man who fronts the BBC's television coverage of the big games. He bids us welcome to the Test match ground, speculates on prospects for the day, hands over to the commentators for their descriptions of each session, but reappears at intervals to discuss matters with old players. He does all this knowledgeably and urbanely, the very image of an establishment figure; except when a Test match coincides with the Wimbledon fortnight. He then goes missing from the cricket coverage to report on the tennis, which is another interest of his. So is Rugby football. He was Rugby correspondent of *The Times* from 1971 until he resigned at the start of 1983 on what he called "a matter of principle". This turned out to be because the newspaper was refusing to send him to New Zealand later in the year – during the English cricket season, in fact – to cover the British Lions' tour. It never had sent its chief Rugby writer on such expeditions abroad; and West's contract with the paper never had extended beyond British winters.

Peter West also wears one other hat. He is the chairman of the West Nally Group, a public relations firm which specialises in promoting sport. "Nally" is Patrick Nally, whose particular interest is motor-racing, in which he has had a great deal to do with all the advertising seen on the grand prix circuits, some of which effectively camouflages the racing cars. West Nally have been involved in all sorts of events, from snooker to the London Marathon to the 1982 football World Cup in Spain. And cricket. Wearing one of his hats, Peter West was the man who in 1977 revealed from a rain-sodden Oval that Cornhill Insurance were to inject £1 million into English cricket over the next five years. Wearing another, he shortly afterwards saw his company undertake the cricket public relations job on behalf of Cornhill, a matter of West Nally representatives being around to arrange the smooth press conferences along; and having the old cricket reporter Crawford White hovering around the press box during Test matches to remind the lads not to omit the word "Cornhill" from their copy.

In June 1982 there emerged from the Berkeley Square offices of West Nally something called a concept paper entitled "Co-ordinated Marketing of English Cricket". This began by pointing out that West Nally had developed a new method of sports marketing which had brought more income to several sports in this country and abroad. The soccer World Cup had been the commercial culmination of a long programme in which a group of major companies had bought "exclusive Intersoccer 4 packages" giving each company exclusive use of all mascots and symbols associated with the events, the right to sell products inside the various football grounds, promotional rights, film, video and music rights and various other benefits. The companies included Coca-Cola, Seiko, R. J. Reynolds, Gillette, JVC, Fuji, Iveco, Canon and Metaxa, and they had been coached in the best ways of getting the maximum advantage from their purchased rights. Seminars had been held to this end, elaborate merchandising programmes had been devised, theme music and official videos had been orchestrated. None of these things, West Nally asserted, were to be regarded as refinements of commerce any more: they were the new standards that big sponsors now expected.

The company revealed that it was working closely with the English Rugby Union on a five-year programme of a similar kind which would be focused on Twickenham. It saw no reason at all why the same ideas shouldn't be applied to cricket; but if they were to be successful, certain criteria would have to be met. All the first-class counties and MCC would have to support the scheme wholeheartedly. Every county would have to guarantee that its prime advertising space on the ground would be made available. Entertainment facilities would have to be made available to all the sponsors everywhere, as would a number of free tickets. A new TCCB symbol would have to be agreed, and West Nally thought that old Jiminy Cricket might make an attractive mascot, to which, of course, the commercial companies would have exclusive rights, with every county cricket club making sure that the symbol received as much exposure as possible. Every county would also have to follow an established formula for the arrangement of advertising displays. A management committee would have to be formed, to take day-to-day decisions in liaison with West Nally.

A possible awkwardness had not been overlooked. The BBC's reaction to all this would have to be gauged (television, after all, is a vital component in the whole bag of tricks) but West Nally were able to point out that the Corporation had often screened big events where such arrangements had been made. The potential benefit to cricket would be enormous. There would be a consistent marketing policy for the game, less work for the individual counties, long-term relationships with big companies, potential spin-off benefits at the grass roots of the sport. West Nally were confident that they could raise sums of money for the TCCB and the counties far greater than anything any of them know at present. But, very clearly, it must be understood that West Nally were not prepared to act as any sort of guarantor to TCCB. The company's normal terms of business would apply – seventy per cent of income raised to TCCB, thirty per cent to West Nally – after general costs had been met.

Central to the prospect of plenty for all was not what is known in public relations jargon as venue dressing, or the consistent market-ing programme, or even the appearance of Jiminy Cricket around the land like something that has been superimposed upon Channel Nine's Test match coverage whenever a batsman is out for a duck. The central proposition offered as a means of securing this bonanza was nothing less than Diamond Vision, as manufactured by Mitsu-bishi Electric, the Japanese electronics firm. West Nally would supply one of these objects for all Test matches and any other fixture thought important enough. It would "provide a major refinement to English cricket and a considerable boost to potential gate".

Diamond Vision's specifications read like a robot's dream of orgasm. It has between 24,000 and 150,000 separate red, blue and green tubes, a screen that allows an image change of sixty frames per second just as on television, and it is a combination of giant television set and sophisticated electronic scoreboard. It will show commer-cials, live broadcasts, taped material, slow-motion replay, photos and art work, 35mm slides, superimpositions, character and graphic display, message crawl – every form of communication that the audio and video engineers between them can contrive. It gives the score. It entertains a crowd. It heightens their excitement. It pulls them in. There are twenty-seven of these things clamped per-manently in situ around the world now, and the one at the Singapore Turf Club is nineteen feet high and fifty-seven feet across (or the other way around). A couple are going to be installed at Twick-enham, at no cost to the Rugby Union. The marvel has already been seen in this country at the Grand National and the London Marathon. And here it is again, offered almost free, gratis and for nothing to Lord's and the Oval, to Old Trafford and Headingley, to Trent Bridge and Edgbaston. Let the cricket authorities of England but say the word, and any one of these grounds will enjoy the prestige of knowing that it is bang in the forefront of civilisation.

It so happens that one of the Diamond Visions, which West Nally are so eager to see embellishing English Test matches, was installed for the benefit of spectators, among others, at Melbourne Cricket Ground in time for the visit of Bob Willis's team in 1982. One of those who beheld the spectacle for the first time that December was Scyld Berry, cricket correspondent of *The Observer*. This is how he described it:

"Cricket yesterday went a stage further to Americanisation. The game's first video scoreboard went into operation in Melbourne, to record England's total of 275 against Victoria. The vast four million dollar structure provided replays in colour of all the dismissals, big hits and near misses for the 5,000 crowd, just as the television would have done at home, in addition to giving racing results, snatches of live tennis and the occasional bowling analysis . . . David Gower may have played a lovely innings of eighty-eight in two hours yesterday, but he was dwarfed by gigantic ads for The Great Australian Pie. As he returned to the pavilion, beautiful young people were to be seen pouring lashings of tomato sauce over what a few seconds earlier had been Ray Bright's bowling analysis, while we were assured that the great Australian pie is made of rich-filled pastry and the best of beef.

"The lunch and tea intervals were worse. Then the tannoys joined in as the drive-in screen went through its repertoire; 'You just can't get enough' the tannoys screeched about the great Australian pie. The board was built by Mitsubishi Electric, in return for holding the advertising franchise for it for the next ten years. Not surprisingly, therefore, their latest four-cylinder car is given the occasional plug – 'Australia's most powerful "four"'. Between dismissals we are more likely to be taken in it down some freeway at breakneck speed and fed with its slogan 'run like the wind' . . .

"Naturally, Australian umpires are concerned at what might happen in the Melbourne Test if replays of some controversial incident show them to be wrong. When it was done a few months ago at the Victorian Football League final on the same ground, fighting broke out in the crowd. However, the man in charge of authorising replays says the controversial umpiring incidents will not be replayed . . ."

The man authorising replays was either overruled or had second thoughts. Controversial decisions were exhibited on Melbourne's Diamond Vision. The Australian umpires were quite right to have been concerned, because what made some of their decisions controversial was the fact that they were replayed in front of everybody at MCG on this major refinement in cricket technology. There and then it was positively demonstrated that the umpire's eye had not always been infallibly keen. It never has been in the history of the game. But never before had an umpire been confronted with evidence more suitable to the Inquisition than to a cricket match. The perpetrators of this appliance had much to answer for in what was mildly referred to as "the debate" on standards of Australian umpiring which followed. Before the England tour was half over, Doug Insole, manager of the tourists and a senior member of TCCB, invited to speculate on how all umpiring might be augmented by technology at some time in the future, was cornered into the admission that "no doubt electronic aids will be looked at sooner or later, but it will be a sad day".

The cricket Down Under that winter had seen other drifts towards the Americanisation of the game, apart from the electronic cascade of tomato sauce down Ray Bright's bowling analysis. Earlier in England's tour, Matthew Engel of *The Guardian* had remarked on the appearance at the Test match in Perth of a hundred female gymnasts in leotards, who pranced around the pitch during the tea interval. And then there was the television advertising campaign designed to create interest in the Test series, which emphasised not cricket itself but antagonism towards that weary old cliché of an Englishman, the pin-striped imperialist. (The telly-ads did, however, produce one neat crack by that other caricature, the rugged Aussie: "I'm quite partial to Poms, so long as they're well done.") All this was the handiwork of Lynton Taylor, formerly an employee of Kerry Packer, now the man responsible for marketing all Australian cricket.

There are several avenues as yet unexploited if the Australians are really determined to follow the American philosophy of making all sport the tool of commerce. A combination of sex and violence is the most notable feature of American football, with the brutal collision of men's bodies on the field and the exhibition of nubile girls on the perimeter to stir other emotions throughout the game. Encourage your fast bowlers to sling down more bouncers and bring on more leotards from start to finish of play, and you'll have pretty well the same combination in the sport that Bradman and Woodfull, Hassett and Morris once graced. American football has another dodge geared to the circulation of dollars alone. Not all its tedious stoppages occur so that players can huddle in a tactical talk. A break in the action is ordained every few minutes so that a television commercial can be slotted in for the viewers sitting at home; and one referee has a radio headset so that he can hear the TV producer telling him just when to hold up play. How about that for an idea at the end of every over?

Or why not imitate a few things that baseball has made its own? The umpire there is now regarded as something between an adjudicating official and a serio-comic turn, the butt of the player or the team manager who comes chesting up to him, each threatening the other grotesquely and sometimes coming to blows, while the crowd howls its appreciation from the stands. Other pleasing spectacles have been introduced by inventive minds. At Kansas City twenty years ago the owner of the local team, name of Charlie Finley, brought in a flock of goats, dyed them in the team colours, and let them browse across a hillock some distance behind the pitcher's arm. Sometime later, in a brand-new stadium, the Kansas City Royals were performing in front of an aquatic equivalent of Diamond Vision, with the scoreboard built into a permanent water spectacular which embodied waterfalls ten feet high, fountains forty feet across, 638 nozzles which could fling 50,000 gallons into the sky at once, and 670 500-watt lamps which illuminated some 150 different light, colour and liquid effects. Wow! Down at Houston, the baseball teams had by then accustomed themselves to playing in The World's First Indoor Ballpark, the Astrodome, with its plastic seats, its plastic sky, its plastic turf, its plastic everything – except in the owner's suite, where the desk came in rosewood and marble, the wall panels in genuine onyx and the telephone in pure gold. The genius presiding over this apparition, name of Judge Roy Hofheinz, declared: "We have removed baseball from the rough-and-tumble era. We're in the business of sports entertainment." America's finest writer on the game, Roger Angell, went down into the arena to inspect the synthetic grass, the famous Astroturf. "I dug down with my fingers and found the spine of one of the hidden foul-line-to-foul-line zippers that hold the new infield together; I had a sudden feeling that if I unzipped it, I might uncover the world's first plastic worm."*

* One baseball invention that English cricket could do with following, however, is the rain-check. Spectators at major league games get a ticket, even when they pay at the gate. At the bottom is a tear-off stub – "the rain-check". If the game is rained off, even if it has to be abandoned only half way through, they can use the stub to gain

We can no longer doubt that any or all of these belongings to the world of "sports entertainment", where they have not already arrived, might be imitated before long in Australian cricket, if the marketing men there are allowed to follow their instincts. If such things came to pass in Sydney and Melbourne, then there would inevitably follow persuasion to introduce them elsewhere in the cricket-playing world; and there are people in England already receptive to some of the American tendencies which have either been adopted or are conceivable in Australia. We have lately had our experiments with floodlit cricket and coloured cricket clothes, and it is unlikely that we have heard the last of either. A man as influential in the English game as Raman Subba Row has suggested (under interview by Peter West the television front man) that it may be expedient one day to abandon turf-playing areas in first-class cricket and adopt "the sort of thing that Queen's Park Rangers play on", which is a variation of Astroturf. There is at least one county cricket captain, Brian Rose of Somerset, who takes the same view. In 1920 some English newspapers thought the appeal of cricket as it was then had fallen so low that baseball was likely to supersede it as our national game. It would be laughable (no, not really) if at some future date cricket were held to have maintained its appeal only by becoming a sort of transvestite version of America's most traditional sport. And shall the pitch one day not be twenty-two yards long, but 20.117 metres . . . ?

It is, of course, at Lord's that such matters will be settled. Traditionalists should perhaps take comfort from the fact that this ground has in the past seen some alien manifestations, admitted purely for entertainment, which have had no startling effect on cricket itself, the game having continued to potter on in its own evolutionary way, its patterns changing gradually so that nothing jarred too much. In 1837 someone made an ascent by balloon from this ground, and seven years later a company of Indians from Iowa encamped with their Great Mystery Medicine Man, while they gave exhibitions of archery and tribal dancing. In 1868 the Australian Aboriginal cricketers came to England and during the intervals of their matches at Lord's demonstrated the art of throwing boomerangs. Lord's actually did yield to baseball six years after that, when twenty-two Americans came over to give the English a taste of their

---

admission to a subsequent match. Adapting this principle to cricket ought not to be insuperable, when the American calendar is much more tightly packed than ours. A baseball team plays approximately 160 games in a season, almost every day between the middle of April and the beginning of October.

sport. At St John's Wood a team from Boston beat another from Philadelphia by twenty-seven runs to seven in a ballgame which was inserted into the middle of a cricket match. This was played between a XII of MCC gentlemen and an XVIII of the American baseball chaps – and, oh dear, the Americans won it by 107 runs to 105. *Wisden* said that it was "a result they were evidently proud of, and justly so, for this MCC twelve was undoubtedly the best English team the Americans met at cricket throughout their brief tour".

Of all the sports that have been played at Lord's, baseball never reappeared after that one exhibition in 1874. Lacrosse was played often in the winter until it vanished from the lists in 1954. Squash and real tennis are still firmly entrenched but confined to their own quarters, so that no one but a member ever catches sight of them. In its grace and favour, the Marylebone club still plays host to the hockey match between Oxford and Cambridge every March, with an anxious eye on possible damage to the grass only a few weeks before it must be in prime condition for the opening of the cricket season. Otherwise, the ground is used by cricketers alone.

And MCC long ago turned their backs on almost anything that smacked of the funfair at Lord's, except what might be provided by the crowds themselves in their enthusiasm for the game of cricket. Other examples are very few. A brewer's waggon drawn by Clydesdales, their gear polished and jangling, trundles through the Grace Gates on the occasion of the Village Cup Final to add a bit of atmosphere. For several years after the war a score or more of stage coaches would be drawn up by the boundaries during the Eton v Harrow game, vantage points for fond parents who would dress themselves up to match: but now only one coach makes its appearance as a token of nostalgia, parked down by the Nursery sightscreen, and attended by a lonely luncheon party sitting on tubular chairs. At the Centenary Test with Australia in 1980 the weather's interruptions of the game were occasionally relieved by a full-dress military band, which squelched and counter-squelched in front of Q Stand, where scores of the most honoured guests were ranged. Otherwise, Lord's nowadays makes few concessions to those who are not content with cricket and with contemplating cricket when it isn't actually being played.

It has usually kept pace with the times (ah, but the times are become disordered now) and often it has led the way in matters which demonstrably helped the cricket-watcher without disturbing the tradition of cricket itself. Television cameras first appeared here for the 1938 Test against Australia, and that was a notable lead by a good many years. A public address system was introduced in 1948;

lights on the scoreboard first twinkled beneath the relevant fieldsman's number in 1953; the restoration of betting to cricket was signalled with the arrival of Ladbroke's tent in 1973. In two conspicuous areas Lord's is still further behind the times than it ought to be. The scoreboard is a charming and familiar thing, and would be missed by many if it were replaced; but neither it nor any other in England is a patch on the one that Nottinghamshire have had for several years at Trent Bridge. And coverage of the playing area is still a sore point with many who were here at the Centenary Test and noticed the apparent effectiveness of the great roll-on appliance Warwickshire now use at Edgbaston.

What changes lie ahead depend ultimately on the relationship between MCC and TCCB, and the way their possibly conflicting interests can be resolved in the Cricket Council, where TCCB now has the distinctly upper hand. A proportion of members from top to bottom of the Marylebone club are so sickened by the commercialisation of cricket that they would wish Lord's to have nothing more to do with it. They would be glad to see TCCB and the whole apparatus of money-making in the professional game take itself elsewhere, so that MCC could revert to the role it enjoyed before the last two years of the nineteenth century, the very private club which acted as host to the best cricketers of the day on its own terms. The fact that this may no longer be a realistic proposition is something they are prepared to risk, rather than accept on their own doorstep any further encroachments by commerce. "It *does* belong to MCC, this ground," they say; a proprietary view that does not countenance any version of cricket which is not to their taste, but at the same time does not admit the possibility that the best cricketers in the world will not wish to play here, come what may, and in doing so bring the income necessary to maintain the fabric and running costs of Lord's.

There are others in MCC fearful lest such conservatives – most of whom tend to be the younger rather than the older men – should cause such a break between the club and the rest of the English cricketing establishment that Marylebone will be left high and dry, its already much reduced influence gone altogether, having no say at all in the shaping of cricket to come. They can see that in such circumstances Lord's itself might one day be catastrophically abandoned to its privacy, without sufficient resources to maintain itself. They are anxious that their old values and the gaudier ones purveyed by the new men of cricket – inside and outside the game – should achieve some sort of compromise, with what is old and tried and (above all) trusted, surrendering itself as slowly as possible, if surrender is indeed inevitable. They are the men who suspect that one of these days MCC will have to fight to prevent the custody of cricket's Laws being snatched from them by other hands.

There are many in the TCCB who think this way, too, men who belong to the hierarchy of MCC as well as to the first-class counties. But there are others who regard the old values, and those who would rather go to the wall than relinquish them, as a drag upon the march of progress in the game, by which they mean its economic prosperity, if not its survival. "The next five years will be crucial," says one of these. "Cricket in England will either become more profitable or it will go bust." The phrase is echoed in another quarter. "Something's got to be done about this game pretty quickly," says Gubby Allen, the old eminence of Lord's, "or it will go bust." The two men do not mean the same thing. The first is worried about a professional game in England that can no longer raise the money to pay the top players what they have come to expect, so that they will seek their high incomes elsewhere and be damned to a national tradition. The second fears that cricket will so abandon itself to the pursuit of money that it will have become a caricature of the game to which he has devoted his life.

Peter Lush, the TCCB marketing man, is not only impatient with what he sees as MCC's retarding influence upon the game as a whole. He is irritated by what he thinks is MCC's failure to make the most of the immense asset it has at Lord's. His catalogue of its failures runs from the need to queue for drinks at all times except when play is actually happening, to the seating at the Nursery End and in the Mound Stand, which he regards as deplorable and due for demolition in favour of more boxes and bucket seats. "This ground," he says, "should be the blue-chip stadium of all time." Ascot seems to be his model, where "you can go up to the stands in an elevator, and park your car without difficulty – it's wonderful". That's all very well, but open country in Berkshire affords certain facilities that are no longer possible among the crammed buildings of London NW8.

There is within MCC a recognition that, whatever part the club may or may not play from now on in moulding English first-class cricket as a whole, Lord's cannot very easily stay the way it is. Twenty years ago the club contemplated building a general sports centre at the ground, which would operate from September to March. The idea of a golf driving range on the practice ground had been rejected and the Club Facilities Committee was groping towards some alternative in the region of the Tennis Court when planning permission came through for the big redevelopment by the Tavern. There was no possibility of finding the cash for two schemes at once, and so the sports centre was quietly forgotten. But once again it is being talked about as something that perhaps ought to be built in the near future, to produce more income to keep cricket at Lord's the way MCC wants it. Like the owners of other major cricket grounds, they recognise that it is no longer realistic, in today's economic climate, to maintain a stadium where – the Indoor School and the Tennis Court notwithstanding – very little happens for almost two thirds of a year. Unfortunately, the passage of twenty years has not eased the financial problem at all. If anything, it's more pressing now than it was in 1966. The club has to find those huge sums for the pending maintenance work and the redevelopment behind the Pavilion; and, come 1996, it will have to renegotiate its Nursery End lease with British Rail – if that, too, has survived.

We who are detached from these writhings can but keep our fingers crossed and hope that the future deals more gently with cricket than has the immediate past. We may also fervently pray that at the headquarters of the game in this country, a lodestone still for cricketers everywhere, what changes may have come will be as carefully made as in the past. In all the places where the game has been enjoyed only Sydney Cricket Ground, perhaps, has ever seized the imagination, held affection and stirred recollection as much as Lord's. But SCG has lately been defiled by the totems of commerce, the pylons needed for flood-lighting, six of them, each 240 feet high, erected at the behest of men whose faculties do not include the ones which respond to the visually pleasing or to history. If ever the same thing, or anything comparable, were to happen to Lord's Ground, there would indeed be a vandalism. Interested parties should remember the ex-dustman's writing on the wall.

The lyrical Cardus, who was very fond of this place, often captured its qualities in sentences that were not always extravagantly overdone. He was here in 1930 when Australia all but annihilated England with 729 for six, when the upstart Bradman announced a new era in batsmanship with his innings of 254. "Bradman batted," wrote Cardus on the Saturday evening, "as though Duckworth did not exist, as though there were no wickets behind him . . . A bat is wider than a ball, when you come to think of it. Bradman brought the fact home once again to us today." On the Tuesday, with England well and truly licked, "The winning hit was made at five o'clock, and a memorable day was at an end. As the cricketers came from the field the sunshine fell on them, touching them with a lovely light. It might well have been a light cast by immortality, for this match will certainly never be forgotten."

Some eight years later, Bradman now the anointed and the

sceptred king but Lord's still the same, Cardus was waiting with the cricket correspondent of *The Times* for another match to begin. "Has it occurred to you that we are paid to do this?" he asked. "Yes, it has occurred to me," said the other. "And it's too good to be true, isn't it?"

Lord's has had that effect on many a man, whether he's an MCC member or not. Many a woman, too.

Some Lord's Statistics

Playing area: 5.5 acres.
Crowd capacity: 27,000 (authorised).
Record crowd: 33,800; England v Australia, June 25, 1938.
Record match attendance: 137,915; England v Australia, 1953.

Team Records

Highest Totals
Test: 729 for 6; Australia v England, 1930.
County: 612 for 8; Middlesex v Notts, 1921.
Lowest Totals
15; MCC v Surrey, 1839.
This century: 27; MCC v Yorkshire, 1902.
Highest match aggregate
1,601 for 29 wickets; England v Australia, 1930.

Individual Records

Batting
Highest Innings: 316 not out; J. B. Hobbs, Surrey v Middlesex, 1926.
Highest aggregate: 25,097; E. Hendren (Middlesex).
Most hundreds: 74; E. Hendren.
Fastest 50: F. T. Mann (53); Middlesex v Notts, 1921, 14 minutes.
Fastest 100: F. G. J. Ford (112); Middlesex v Philadelphians, 1897,
    55 minutes.
Fastest 200: G. L. Jessop (233); The Rest v Yorkshire, 1901, 135
    minutes.
Bowling
Best match analysis:
J. Southerton, 16 for 52; South v North, 1875 (all in one day).
All ten wickets in an innings:
E. Hinkley; Kent v England (no analysis recorded), 1848.
J. Wisden; North v South (no analysis recorded), 1850.
S. E. Butler; Oxford v Cambridge (10 for 38), 1871.

A. Shaw; MCC v North (10 for 73), 1874.

A. Fielder; Players v Gentlemen (10 for 90), 1906.

G. O. Allen; Middlesex v Lancashire (10 for 40), 1929.

Most wickets in career: J. T. Hearne; 1,719 (average 16.42).

Best all-round performance

B. J. T. Bosanquet; Middlesex v Surrey (103 and 100 not out; 3 for 75 and 8 for 53), 1905.

Wicket-keeping

Most dismissals in innings: W. F. Price 7 (all caught), Middlesex v Yorkshire, 1937.

Most dismissals in a match – 9:

A. E. Newton; Somerset v Middlesex (6 ct 3 st), 1901.

G. L. Langley; Australia v England (8 ct 1 st), 1956.'

J. T. Murray; Middlesex v Hampshire (8 ct 1 st), 1965.

Fielding

Most catches in an innings – 6

A. J. Webbe; Gentlemen v Players, 1877.

Most catches in a match – 7

A. F. J..Ford; Middlesex v Gloucestershire, 1882.

(All figures refer to first-class matches only, and individual performances are confined to Lord's alone).

Index

Compiled by Robert Urwin

Beauclerk, Lord Frederick, 41
Beaverbrook, Lord, 209
Bedser, Alec, 48, 57, 96 97, 181, 183, 199
Bedser, Eric, 57
behaviour in cricket (players and crowds), 215–23
  abuse of umpires, 220–1
  television effects on, 219–20
Beldham, Bllly, 67
Bell's Life magazine, 205
Benaud, Richie, 38
Bennett, Don, 37, 59
Bennett, Mr (MCC member), 76
Benson & Hedges Cup, 105, 129, 137, 139
Bermuda (in ICC cricket), 182
Berry, Scyld, 233
Bicester, Lord, 49
Bird, Harold ("Dickie"), 71, 97, 170
Birkett, 1st Lord, 22
Bligh, Hon. Ivo, 133
Blunden, Edmund, 22
Board of Control (founded 1898), 83, 84, 93, 94, 179, 180
Bond, J. D. (Jackie), 35, 224
Boodle's Club, 74
Bosanquet, B. J. T., 110
  inventor of googly, 117–18
Botham, Ian, 71, 103, 156, 157, 160, 169, 177, 221
  early years on Lord's Ground Staff, 197
  estimated earnings (1982), 158, 222
  leads West-Indian tour (1980–1), 101
Bowen, Rowland, 78
Bowes, W. E., 50, 211, 212
Boycott, Geoffrey, 55, 70, 101, 120, 144, 154, 157, 158, 169, 189, 191, 192, 200, 224
Bradman, Sir Donald, 38, 67, 132, 157, 234, 240
  agrees time-limit Tests, 54
  final appearance at and tribute to Lord's, 22–3
  leads 1948 Australians, 150
  target for Bodyline bowling, 50, 210, 211
Brearley, J. M. (Mike), 74, 109, 111, 118, 121, 218
  captain of England, 155, 180

innovates fashion for helmets, 113, 119n
  part in "D'Oliveira affair", 185
Brick Development Association, 99
Bright, Ray, 200, 233, 234
Brisbane Cricket Ground, 31n
British Broadcasting Corporation (BBC),
  TV and radio coverage of Tests and other cricket, 139, 140, 145–6, 220, 232, 237
  influence on crowds and players, 219–20
British Rail, *see* Great Central Railway entry
Brook Street Bureau, 62
Brooks, K. G., 197
Brown, A. S., 97
Brown, D. J., 97
Brown, F. R., 48, 57, 96, 97, 98
  leads 1950–1 Australian tour, 209
Bukhatir, Abdul Rehman, 160
Buller, Sid, 54
Burnet, Ronnie, 202
Burridge, Alan, 122
Butcher, Roland, 152, 197
Butler Education Act (1944), indirect effect on MCC membership, 69

Caccia, Lord, 44, 47
Cadbury–Schweppes company, 138
  sponsorship of county cricket (1977–83), 142–5, 147
  costs to company and benefits obtained, 143
Calcutta Cricket Ground, 32
  crowd capacity, 18
Callaghan, James, advises against 1968 S. Africa tour, 187
Canada, cricket in, 179, 182
Cardus, Sir Neville, 27
  on Lord's, 21–2, 240–1
Carlisle, John, attempt to change MCC policy on S. Africa, 192–3
Carr, A. W., 50
Carr, Donald, 159
  Secretary of TCCB, 85, 100–1, 102–3, 106, 181
Cartwright, T. W., 97, 185
Castell, Messrs (of Oxford), 63
Centenary Test (Lord's, 1980), 9, 32, 33, 70–3, 237, 238

Dexter, E. R., 38, 57, 97, 203
captains Australian tour (1962), 58
Diamond Vision, analysis of
capabilities of, 232–4, 235
Dilley, Graham, 177
Doggart, G. H. G., 44–5, 48, 191,
228–9
D'Oliveira, Basil, 57
the "D'Oliveira affair" and
aftermath, 184–93
D'Oliveira, D. B., 197
Donnelly, Martin, 178
Doshi, Dilip, 200
Doughty, R. J., 197
Douglas-Home, Sir Alec, 44, 57, 168,
169, 206
Doyle, Nancy, 168–70
Ducat, Andy, 21
Duckworth, George, 240
Dunbar, J. G., 85

Edgbaston cricket ground, 141 (see also
Warwickshire County Cricket
Club)
crowd capacity, 18
playing area, 25
Edinburgh, H. R. H. the Duke of, 44,
68
Edmonds, P. H. (Phil), 111, 153, 169,
200
Edrich, W. J., 57, 119, 125, 193
record 1947 season, 119
Electoral Reform Society, 75
Elliott, C. S., 97
Emburey, John, 34, 111, 191, 227
Engel, Matthew, 234
English Schools Cricket Association, 84
Essex County Cricket Club, 135, 136
Eton v Harrow matches, 32n, 116, 226n
Fowler's Match (1910), 38
Evans, David, abortive sponsorship
plan of, 139–40
Evans, Godfrey, 57, 103

Faber, J. T., 47
Fairbrother, Jim, Head Groundsman
at Lord's, 27, 28–9, 31, 32, 33, 71,
79, 81, 198
Fairfax, Alan, 176
Farley, Gus, 170, 173, 175, 178, 224
Farrell, S. J., 197
Fender, R. G. H., 50, 197

Fiji, cricket in, 182
Findlay, W., Secretary of MCC, 213,
215
Fingleton, Jack, 22, 33
Finley, Charlie, 235
Finney, R. J., 197
Fletcher, Keith, leads India tour
(1981–2), 101, 216
Flower, Arthur, 122
Ford cars sponsorship, 153
Foster, F. R., 50
Francis, D. A., 197
Freedom of Sport organisation, 192
Fry, Mr (MCC member), 76

Gaby, Dick, 57
Garner, Joel, 35, 224
Gatting, M. W. (Mike), 111
Gavaskar, Sunil, 129, 204
Gentlemen v Players matches, 116
last match (1962), 104
Gifford, Norman, 97, 181
Gill, Barrie, 156
Gillette Cup competition, 35, 105, 125,
129, 137, 146
1980 final (Surrey v Middlesex), 114
Gillette company relinquishes
sponsorship, 138, 147
Gilliatt, R. M. C., 97
Gilligan, A. E. R., 180, 184
Gimblett, Harold, 153
Glamorgan County Cricket Club, 91,
131, 135, 136, 149
Gleneagles Agreement (1977), 191
Gloucester, 116, 135, 148, 149
Goddard, John, 128, 173
Gooch, Graham, 99–100, 191
estimated earnings (1982), 158
Gould, I. J., 113, 197
Gower, David, 86, 156, 161–2, 233
Grace, E. M., 205
Grace, W. G., 156, 180, 206, 210
"genial rascality" on the field, 204–5
Grace Gates (Lord's), 17, 19, 205
mercenary image, 42, 159, 204, 217
record (runs and wickets) at Lord's,
17, 24, 67
W. G. Grace (Eric Midwinter), 8
Graham, Norman, 151
Graison's (caterers), 165–6, 168
Graveney, T. W., 57
Gray, Laurie, 103

Great Central Railway, Lord's lease
   from, 18, 240
Green, Benny, 201
Greenough, Tommy, 59
Greig, Tony, 155, 191
   association with St Peter Sporting
      Goods Ltd, 157
   captain of England, 155
   defection to Kerry Packer, 155, 191
Griffith, C. C. (Charlie), 38
Griffith, S. C.:
   Secretary of MCC, 48, 55, 71, 85, 95,
      97, 184, 187, 203-4
   daughter's wedding reception at
      Lord's, 68
Griffin, Geoff, throwing incidents, 54
Guardian, The, 81, 234
Gunn & Moore, Messrs, 58
Guyana, Jackman incident in, 101,
   188-9

Hadlee, Richard, 216
Haig, John, company, 138
Hain, Peter, 186
Hall, W. W. (Wes), 38
Hall of Fame, Cooperstown, New York,
   132
Hambledon Club, 41
Hammond, W. R., 18, 43, 59
Hampshire County Cricket Club, 91,
   135, 149, 153
Harris, Lord, 20, 46, 48, 69, 72, 97, 202
   career and character, 42-3, 45, 52, 53
   Governor of Bombay, 42, 43
   Harris Garden, Lord's, 17
Harvey, Neil, 70
Hassett, Lindsay, 22, 234
Hawke, Lord, 45, 150, 180, 205, 206
   captain of Yorkshire and cricket
      administrator, 45, 53
Hawkes, Sir Cyril, 48, 204
Hayman, Francis, 67
Hayward, "Union Jack", 80
Headingley cricket ground, 34, 36, 114
   crowd capacity of, 18
   playing area, 25
   vandalised Test wicket at (1975), 170
Hearne, J. T. ("Old Jack"), 110, 118
Hearne, J. W. ("Young Jack"), 118
Hearne, Tom, 67
Henderson's Nursery, see under Lord's
   Ground

Hendren, Dennis, 108-9, 121
Hendren, E. H. (Patsy), 108-9,
   109-10, 118-19, 121, 196
   first to wear protective headgear,
      119n, 220
   record tour in W. Indies, 118
Hendry, H. L. ("Stork"), 70
Higgins, Mr (of Nottingham), 225
Higgs, K., 97
Hirst, George, 53, 67
   career record and benefit, 150
Hitler, Adolf, 58
Hobbs, Sir Jack, 38, 53, 67, 118, 180,
   211
Hobbs, Robin, 198
Hofheinz, Judge Roy, 235
Holding, M. A., 216
Holford, D. A. J., 178
Holmes, G. C., 197
Holt Products sponsorship, 138, 147
Hong Kong, MCC tour to, 61
Hopkins, J. A., 197
Hore-Ruthven, Sir Alexander (later
      Lord Gowrie), 214
Hornby, A. N., 117
Horton, Henry, 59
Houston Astrodome, 235
How to Watch Cricket (John Arlott), 8
Howard, Nigel, 101
Howarth, Geoff, 178
Howland, C. B. (Chris), 47, 156
Hughes, Kim, 70-1
   leads Australian tour (1981), 129
Hutton, Sir Leonard, 57, 103

Illingworth, Ray, 34, 97, 204, 224
Illingworth (Mike Stevenson), 8
Independent Television, too inflexible
   for cricket coverage, 146
Indian Cricket Board of Control, 203
   relationship with Indian
      Government, 189-90
Ingleby-Mackenzie, A. C. D., 48
Insole, D. J., 47, 96, 97, 100, 140, 147,
   181, 183, 221, 234
International (Imperial up to 1965)
   Cricket Conference (ICC), 41, 44,
      46, 52, 181-3
   associate members, 182
   fact-finding mission to S. Africa, 188
   founder members (1909), 181;
      subsequent membership, 181-2

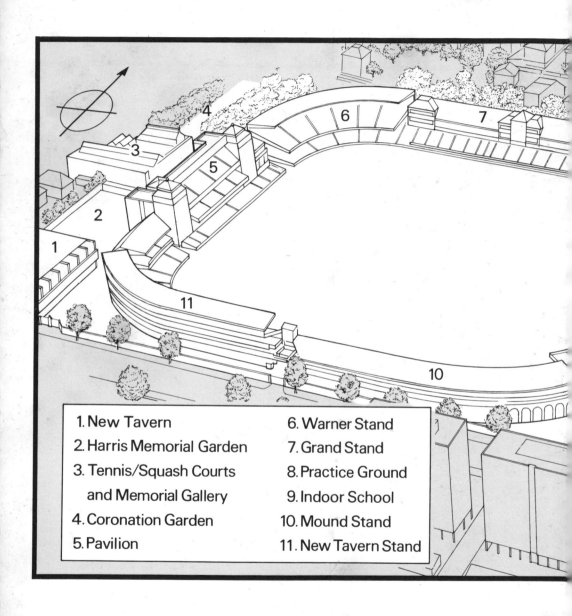

1. New Tavern
2. Harris Memorial Garden
3. Tennis/Squash Courts and Memorial Gallery
4. Coronation Garden
5. Pavilion
6. Warner Stand
7. Grand Stand
8. Practice Ground
9. Indoor School
10. Mound Stand
11. New Tavern Stand

The Genius of Jane Austen

ALSO BY PAULA BYRNE

Perdita: The Life of Mary Robinson
Mad World: Evelyn Waugh and the Secrets of Brideshead
The Real Jane Austen: A Life in Small Things
Belle: The True Story of Dido Belle
Kick: The True Story of Kick Kennedy, JFK's Forgotten Sister,
and the Heir to Chatsworth

AS CO-EDITOR
Stressed Unstressed: Classic Poems to Ease the Mind

The Genius of
Jane Austen

Her Love of Theatre and
Why She Is a Hit in Hollywood

Paula Byrne

WILLIAM
COLLINS

William Collins
An imprint of HarperCollins*Publishers*
1 London Bridge Street
London SE1 9GF
WilliamCollinsBooks.com

First published in Great Britain in 2002 by Hambledon and London
This updated edition published in 2017 by William Collins

1

A catalogue record for this book is
available from the British Library

ISBN 978-0-00-822565-0 (hardback)
ISBN 978-0-00-822566-7 (trade paperback)

Printed and bound in Great Britain by
Clays Ltd, St Ives plc

MIX
Paper from
responsible sources
FSC   FSC™ C007454
www.fsc.org

FSC™ is a non-profit international organisation established to promote
the responsible management of the world's forests. Products carrying the
FSC label are independently certified to assure consumers that they come
from forests that are managed to meet the social, economic and
ecological needs of present or future generations,
and other controlled sources.

Find out more about HarperCollins and the environment at
www.harpercollins.co.uk/green

For Jonathan

Contents

Illustrations

Unless otherwise stated, all pictures are from the author's private collection, © Paula Byrne.

Professional versus Private Theatricals: *Blowing up the Pic Nics* by James Gillray. Sheridan, manager of Drury Lane, leads a protest against the amateur aristocratic Pic Nic Society. The amateurs are performing *Tom Thumb*, while the professionals march under the banner of Shakespeare and Kotzebue (author of the German original of *Lovers' Vows*).

Dora Jordan as the Comic Muse. John Hoppner, *Mrs Jordan as the Comic Muse*: The Royal Collection © Her Majesty Queen Elizabeth II

The Comic Muse unveils herself and inspires the pen of Hannah Cowley: Jane Austen had particular admiration for comic plays written by women.

The Pantheon in Oxford Street where Austen's brother Henry owned a box.

Early nineteenth-century theatre-going: pit, boxes and stage, showing the experience that Jane Austen loved.

The 'illegitimate' Astley's, visited by Jane Austen and the location of the rekindling of the love affair between Harriet Smith and Robert Martin in *Emma*.

Jane Austen's favourite comic actor: her 'best Elliston'.

Eliza O'Neill as Juliet: Jane Austen called her 'an elegant creature' who 'hugs Mr Younge [her co-star] delightfully' – but did not live up to the example of the great Mrs Siddons. George Dawe, *Study for Miss O'Neill as Juliet*: Folger Shakespeare Library, Washington DC, licensed under a Creative Commons Attribution-ShareAlike 4.0 International License (CC BY-SA 4.0)

Sarah Siddons as Constance in Shakespeare's *King John*: 'I should particularly have liked seeing her in Constance, and could swear at her for disappointing me,' wrote Austen in 1811.

Frontispiece to the published text of *Lovers' Vows*, revealing its risqué content.

Mrs Inchbald's version of *Lovers' Vows* was immensely popular. Staged at the Theatre Royal, Bath, when Austen lived there, in 1799 it travelled as far as Philadelphia. Playbill for *Lovers' Vows*, New Theatre, Philadelphia. Pennsylvania, 25 May 1799: Library of Congress, Rare Book and Special Collections Division.

Emma Woodhouse, alias Alicia Silverstone as Cher, *Clueless* in Beverly Hills. Alicia Silverstone as Cher Horowitz in *Clueless*, directed by Amy Heckerling, © Paramount Pictures, 19 July 1995/Alamy Stock Photos

Fanny Price and Mary Crawford in Patricia Rozema's controversial *Mansfield Park*. Frances O'Connor and Embeth Davidtz in *Mansfield Park* (1999), directed by Patricia Rozema, © Moviestore Collection Ltd/Alamy Stock Photos

Mansfield Park made *Metropolitan* in upper-crust Manhattan. Isabel Gillies and Taylor Nichols as Cynthia Mclean and Charlie Black in *Metropolitan*, directed by Whit Stillman, © New Line Cinema, 23 March 1990/Alamy Stock Photos

Lady Susan: Whit Stillman's *Love & Friendship* takes Austen back to her comic origins. Chloë Sevigny and Kate Beckinsale in *Love and Friendship* (2016), directed by Whit Stillman, © Roadside Attractions/Amazon Studios/Atlaspix/Alamy Stock Photos

Foreword to the New Edition

Fifteen years ago, I published *Jane Austen and the Theatre*, a book whose central argument was that Austen's comic genius was shaped by her love of theatre. *Mansfield Park* was the first Austen novel I read, and, like many readers, I was intrigued by the spectacle of the amateur theatricals at the heart of the plot. Stuck in the country and bored to death, the young people decide to stage a play. But, as with Hamlet's 'play-within-the-play', the production is riddled with double meanings, intrigue and alarming consequences.

It seemed to me then, and does so now, that Austen's play-within-a-novel operates as a wonderful vehicle for exploring illicit flirtations between the young people, especially in the absence of a reliable chaperone. The play *Lovers' Vows* works as a meta-text for exploring important relationships between the characters. Edmund Bertram, the pious, shy clergyman, who is in love with a gorgeous, witty *femme fatale*, Mary Crawford, undertakes to play the part of a pious, shy clergyman who is seduced by a gorgeous, witty *femme fatale*, played by Mary Crawford. So many plot parallels, intrigues, allusions, moments of drama are contained in the amateur theatricals episode, which dominates the first quarter of the novel.

The play comes to a sticky end, and gives the reader one of the funniest moments in Austen's canon (and, incidentally, the only moment in Austen without a woman present), when the master of the household, Sir Thomas Bertram, returns from his slave plantations in Antigua to find himself on a stage next to a ranting young actor, who is a complete stranger to him. It's a beautifully orchestrated, highly comic scene, which humiliates Sir Thomas, giving him grave grounds for concern about the conduct of his children. His revenge is to burn all the unbound copies of the play. But the flirting doesn't stop.

Nevertheless, I was puzzled by the critical consensus, which, following the influential critic Lionel Trilling, took the view that the *Lovers' Vows* debacle meant that Jane Austen morally disapproved of theatre. Because Sir Thomas and the heroine, Fanny Price, disapprove of the play, then this must mean that Austen did too. This made no sense to me in the light of her letters and her other novels, which contain copious allusions to the theatre and to playwrights, from Shakespeare to Sheridan. Jane Austen wrote plays as a child and acted in amateur theatricals at home. She herself was said to be a fine actor, and played the part of Mrs Candour in Sheridan's *The School for Scandal* with great aplomb.

Furthermore, it seemed to me that a writer with such comic gifts (often overlooked in the pursuit of the romantic courtship and marriage plot) owed a debt to the plays she watched and read. This book is my attempt to redress that misconception and to examine the roots of Austen's comic genius. Her love for Shakespeare is well known (she pays tribute to him in *Mansfield Park*), but she also loved farce and comedies, especially those of now largely forgotten female dramatists, such as Hannah Cowley and Elizabeth Inchbald.

Some years ago, the book went out of print, partly the consequence of being with a small publishing house that no longer exists. Many of my readers have, over the years, expressed interest in the book, which was so generously reviewed. The bicentenary of the death of Jane Austen (2017) seemed to William Collins, the loyal publisher of my five subsequent books, a very good moment to reissue the book, with a new title and new material, as a companion to my full-scale biography *The Real Jane Austen: A Life in Small Things*.

The extra chapter takes a distinctive look at Austen in Hollywood, exploring a number of stage and film adaptations, from A. A. Milne (creator of *Winnie-the-Pooh*) to Whit Stillman, who recently adapted the juvenilia for the silver screen. The vogue for stage adaptations of the novels began in the early 1930s, but the explosion of interest in recent years has seen her novels refashioned, reworked and updated on stage, on screen and in the ever-expanding world of the Internet.

Fascination with Jane Austen does not wane. The bicentenary witnesses the appearance of her image on the ten-pound banknote. There are exhibitions about her life and work in Hampshire, where she was born and where she died. But the popular image of her is too often that of a novelist interested only in romance and marriage. Of course marriage is the traditional endpoint of comedy, but what really interested Austen were the misunderstandings and incongruous encounters along the way, not the happy ending. This book is an attempt to place Jane Austen where she properly belongs: alongside Shakespeare as one of the world's greatest comic writers. It was conceived as a love letter to the comic theatre of the late eighteenth and early nineteenth centuries, which I began to explore twenty years ago during a magical year in the incomparable setting of the Huntington Library in Los Angeles. While I was there, I regularly crossed town to Pasadena, Burbank, Hollywood and Westwood, in order to watch the latest movie releases. Among them were Emma Thompson's sparkling *Sense and Sensibility* and Roger Michell's tender, sombre *Persuasion*. Then there came a day when my partner said that he was going to take me to a teen movie called *Clueless* that was set in Beverly Hills. He was a Shakespeare scholar, also research-ing in the Huntington, so this seemed a very peculiar choice – until five minutes into the film, when I realised what was going on. I leant over and whispered, 'She's Emma, isn't she?' Since the film did not explicitly acknowledge at any point that it was a reworking of *Emma*, I think he was rather impressed that I worked it out so quickly. Perhaps that was why, soon after, he asked me to marry him.

As Jane Austen said herself, 'Let other pens dwell on guilt and misery. I quit such odious subjects as soon as I can.'

Acknowledgements

I am grateful to the Centre for Kentish Studies, Maidstone, for permission to quote from Fanny Knight's unpublished journals, and the Hampshire Record Office, Winchester, for permission to quote from Eliza de Feuillide's unpublished letters and James Austen's prologues and epilogues to the Austen family theatricals.

Abbreviations

Sense and Sensibility	(1811)	*SS*
Pride and Prejudice	(1813)	*PP*
Mansfield Park	(1814)	*MP*
Emma	(1816)*	*E*
Northanger Abbey	(1818)	*NA*
Persuasion	(1818)	*P*

All quotations of the above are from *The Novels of Jane Austen*, ed. R. W. Chapman, 5 vols (3rd edn, Oxford: Oxford University Press, 1932–34).

Minor Works   *MW*

Quotations are from *The Works of Jane Austen*, vi, *Minor Works*, ed. R. W. Chapman, rev. B. C. Southam (London: Oxford University Press, 1975).

Jane Austen's Letters, ed. Deirdre Le Faye (3rd edn, Oxford: Oxford University Press, 1995) is cited throughout as *Letters*.

Lovers' Vows   *LV*

Quotations are from *Lovers' Vows: A Play, in Five Acts. Performing at the Theatre Royal, Covent-Garden. From the German of Kotzebue. By Mrs Inchbald.* (fifth edn, London, 1798), reprinted in Chapman's edition of *MP*.

* Published December 1815.

Introduction

In 1821, four years after the death of Jane Austen, a critic in the *Quarterly Review* compared her art to Shakespeare's. 'Saying as little as possible in her own person and giving a dramatic air to the narrative by introducing frequent conversations', she created her fictional world 'with a regard to character hardly exceeded even by Shakespeare himself.'[1]

In the Victorian era, Austen was dubbed 'the Prose Shakespeare'.[2] George Eliot's common-law husband, George Henry Lewes, developed the comparison in an influential *Blackwood's Magazine* article on 'The Novels of Jane Austen':

> But instead of *description*, the common and easy resource of novelists, she has the rare and difficult art of *dramatic presentation*: instead of telling us what her characters are, and what they feel, she presents the people, and they reveal themselves. In this she has never perhaps been surpassed, not even by Shakespeare himself.[3]

Yet another nineteenth-century writer, the novelist Thomas Lister, ascribed her genius to revelation of character through dramatic dialogue: 'She possessed the rare and difficult art of making her readers intimately acquainted with the character of all whom she describes ... She scarcely does more than make them act and talk, and we know them directly.'[4]

Austen herself had a strong sense of the importance of dramatic dialogue in the novel. She and her family, like many others of their class, loved to read aloud together. The Austen women ranked novels according to how well they stood up to repeated group readings. Thus Charlotte Lennox's *The Female Quixote* remained a firm favourite (*Letters*, p. 116), whereas Sarah Burney's *Clarentine* failed the test: 'We are reading

1

Clarentine, & are surprised to find how foolish it is. I remember liking it much less on a 2nd reading than at the 1st & it does not bear a 3rd at all' (*Letters*, p. 120).

Jane Austen also had strict notions about how characters in her own novels should be rendered dramatically. To her chagrin, her mother botched the dialogue badly when *Pride and Prejudice* was read aloud to some friends: 'Our 2nd evening's reading to Miss Benn had not pleased me so well, but I beleive [*sic*] something must be attributed to my Mother's too rapid way of getting on – & tho' she perfectly understands the Characters herself, she cannot speak as they ought' (*Letters*, p. 203).

Perhaps Austen's frustration stemmed from her own aptitude for dramatic renditions. Her brother Henry noted her skill in the biographical notice written soon after her death: 'She read aloud with very great taste and effect. Her own works, probably, were never heard to so much advantage as from her own mouth; for she partook largely in all the best gifts of the comic muse.'[5] Her niece Caroline Austen recorded in her *Memoir*. 'She was considered to read aloud remarkably well. I did not often hear her but *once* I knew her take up a volume of *Evelina* and read a few pages of Mr Smith and the Brangtons and I thought it was like a play.'[6]

In *Mansfield Park*, it is typically tongue-in-cheek that Austen endows her villain Henry Crawford with her own gift for reading aloud. Edmund's commendation of Henry's reading of Shakespeare, 'To read him well aloud, is no every-day talent' (*MP*, p. 338), is seconded by Lady Bertram's approving comment, which curiously prefigures Caroline Austen's: 'It was really like being at a play' (*MP*, p. 338).

Austen's nineteenth-century critics defined her genius in terms of her dramatic powers. Her great achievement was in character study. As in Shakespeare, the fools are as distinctive and perfectly discriminated as are the heroines, and all the characters reveal themselves, unhampered by an obtrusive authorial presence, through dramatic presentation and conversations – by a kind of 'dramatic ventriloquism'.[7] Yet in the twentieth century there was a common perception that Jane Austen had a deep distrust of the dramatic arts. This was principally due to the notorious amateur theatricals in *Mansfield Park*: the disruption caused to the household by the performance of *Lovers' Vows* during Sir Thomas

Bertram's absence from home was taken as proof of the author's own distaste for theatre.[8]

There are, however, a range of judgements upon 'home representation' in *Mansfield Park*, not all of them hostile. It is an error to assume that Fanny Price's astringent judgement on the theatricals is Austen's own; after all, Fanny is by no means a disinterested commentator. Unlike her demure creation, who has never seen the inside of a theatre and is manifestly afraid of 'exposing herself' on stage, Austen herself was fascinated by professional theatre, visited it frequently, and, far from condemning private theatricals, participated in them herself, both when she was a child and when she was a woman in her thirties. Strikingly, only two years before writing *Mansfield Park*, she took part in a private performance of perhaps the most popular contemporary play of the Georgian period, Richard Brinsley Sheridan's *The School for Scandal*.

Jane Austen's letters reveal that she was steeped in theatre. As a young woman, she wrote short plays. She copied her brothers in the writing of burlesques in the style of Sheridan and Henry Fielding. She even turned her favourite novel, Samuel Richardson's *Sir Charles Grandison*, into a five-act comedy. Her interest in the theatre, both amateur and professional, and her lifelong preoccupation with the drama undoubtedly influenced her mature writing. She lived through a golden age of English stage comedy. Yet critics of Austen have barely touched upon this rich source, save in occasional nods to her extraordinary gift for theatrical dialogue and the creation of sustained comic characterisation.

This book offers the first comprehensive account of Jane Austen's interest in the theatre, but, more than this, it also suggests that her play-going and her reading of plays were a formative influence on her comic art. Part One of the book reveals her interest in the world of theatre and drama, while Part Two suggests that there is something intrinsically dramatic about her vision of the world in many of her major novels – not only *Mansfield Park*, but also *Sense and Sensibility*, *Pride and Prejudice* and *Emma*.

I make a number of passing references to *Northanger Abbey*, in which the heroine, Catherine Morland, resembles the naive 'country girl' of the comic tradition in the theatre, but of course the main thrust of this book's comedy is its parody of the Gothic novel. My argument about the importance of the theatre for Jane Austen is in no respect intended to diminish the importance of her engagement with the traditions of the novel. I draw attention to many neglected theatrical allusions in her work, but there are also many – frequently documented – allusions to eighteenth-century fiction. Indeed, it is an important part of my argument that from Fielding and Richardson through to Austen and her peers, especially Fanny Burney and Elizabeth Inchbald, there was vigorous two-way traffic between the new form of the novel and the ancient art of the drama. It must, however, be acknowledged that, unlike Inchbald and Burney, Austen never expressed the desire actually to write for the public stage.

Although Austen's final works are less obviously theatrical than her earliest ones – I do not offer a detailed account of *Persuasion*[9] – she participated in private theatricals well into her adult life, as may be seen from some fascinating and little-known passages in the unpublished journals of her niece Fanny Knight. She also took Fanny to the theatre whenever she got the chance. Her periods of residence in London, Bath and Southampton provided ample opportunities for theatre-going with her brood of nieces and nephews. In her letters she recorded her relish for the performances of the renowned tragedian Edmund Kean and the celebrated comic actress Dora Jordan, as well as her particular fondness for Robert Elliston, the star of the Bath Theatre Royal, whose fortunes she followed when he moved to the London stage. Even when in the country, when she was far away from the theatres, she maintained her interest by reading plays, both old and new. She also picked up theatre gossip from the newspapers and would have been able to keep up with reviews of new performances, for this was the age when professional theatre-reviewing grew to maturity.

Twentieth-century criticism was fixated on the assumption that Jane Austen was immovably attached to village life and deeply suspicious of urban pleasures – the theatre foremost among these.[10] This book presents quite another picture: an Austen who enjoyed urban life, who attended the theatre whenever she could, and who took enormous pleasure in the theatrical scene. A recovery of the theatrical Austen makes it difficult to persist in regarding her as a supremely parochial novelist, much less as an isolated, defensive, class-bound or reactionary one.

The first part of the book establishes Jane Austen's knowledge of the world of the theatre. The second part explores how that knowledge shaped her own art. It demonstrates how she makes allusions that assume considerable theatrical knowledge – of a kind now lost to us – on the part of her first readers. And it examines the ways in which the novels adapt a wide range of techniques from the stage tradition, including dramatic entrances and exits, comic misunderstandings, ironic reversals and tableaux.

A particularly important device is what I call the 'set-piece': chapters or episodes framed as set-pieces are often analogous in shape and length to a scene in a play. It is helpful here to cite a comment of Henry James, another nineteenth-century novelist much interested in scenic construction – and indeed in the writing of plays. His novel *The Awkward Age* was organised entirely on scenic principles. In his author's preface, James pictured each of his episodes as a lamp:

> Each of my 'lamps' would be the light of a single 'social occasion' in the history and intercourse of the characters concerned, and would bring out to the full the latent colour of the scene in question and cause it to illustrate, to the last drop, its bearing on my theme. I revelled in this notion of the occasion as a thing by itself, really and completely a scenic thing.[11]

The building bricks of Austen's novels were also dramatic scenes. This is one reason why they adapt so well to film representation.

We naturally think of Jane Austen as a pioneer of the nineteenth-century realist novel. But she also lived through a great age of English stage comedy. The aim of this book is to restore her to the company of such admired contemporaries as Richard Brinsley Sheridan and Hannah Cowley, while also setting her in the great tradition of English drama that stems from Shakespeare.

PART ONE

The Novelist and the Theatre

A love of the theatre is so general …

Mansfield Park

1

Private Theatricals

The fashion for private theatricals that obsessed genteel British society from the 1770s until the first part of the nineteenth century is immortalised in *Mansfield Park*. The itch to act was widespread, ranging from fashionable aristocratic circles to the professional middle classes and minor gentry, from children's and apprentices's theatricals to military and naval amateur dramatics.[1]

Makeshift theatres mushroomed all over England, from drawing rooms to domestic outbuildings. At the more extreme end of the theatrical craze, members of the gentrified classes and the aristocracy built their own scaled-down imitations of the London playhouses. The most famous was that erected in the late 1770s at Wargrave in Berkshire by the spendthrift Earl of Barrymore, at a reputed cost of £60,000. Barrymore's elaborate private theatre was modelled on Vanbrugh's King's Theatre in the Haymarket. It supposedly seated seven hundred.[2]

Private theatricals performed by the fashionable elite drew much public interest, and had profound implications for the public theatres.[3] On one occasion in 1787 a motion in the House of Commons was deferred because too many parliamentarians were in attendance at a private performance of Arthur Murphy's *The Way to Keep Him* at Richmond House.[4] Such private performances often drew more attention in the newspapers than the theatres licensed for public performance.

From an early age Jane Austen showed her own mocking awareness of what the newspapers dubbed 'the Theatrical Ton'. In a sketch called 'The Three Sisters', dating from around 1792, she portrayed a greedy, self-seeking young woman who demands a purpose-built private theatre as part of her marriage settlement (*MW*, p. 65). In *Mansfield Park*, the public interest in aristocratic private theatricals is regarded ironically: 'To be so near happiness, so near fame, so near the long paragraph in praise of the private theatricals at Ecclesford, the seat of the Right Hon. Lord Ravenshaw, in Cornwall, which would of course have immortalised the whole party for at least a twelve-month!' (*MP*, p. 121). Austen carefully distinguishes between the fashionable elitist theatricals of the aristocracy, of the kind that were mercilessly lampooned by the newspapers, and those of the squirearchy.[5] While Mr Yates boasts that Lord Ravenshaw's private theatre has been built on a grand and lavish scale, in keeping with aristocratic pretensions, Edmund Bertram shows his contempt for what he considers to be the latest fad of the nobility:

> 'Let us do nothing by halves. If we are to act, let it be in a theatre completely fitted up with pit, box and gallery, and let us have a play entire from beginning to end; so as it be a German play, no matter what, with a good tricking, shifting after-piece, and a figure dance, and a horn-pipe, and a song between the acts. If we do not out do Ecclesford, we do nothing.' (*MP*, p. 124)

Edmund's mocking comments are directed to his elder brother. But despite Tom Bertram's efforts to professionalise his theatre, the Mansfield theatricals eventually fall back on the measure of converting a large room of the family home into a temporary theatre for their production of *Lovers' Vows*. In reality, this was far more typical of the arrangements made by the professional classes and the minor gentry who had also adopted the craze for private theatricals. The private theatricals of Fanny Burney's uncle at Barbone Lodge near Worcester, for example, took place in a room seating about twenty people. At one end of the room was a curtained off stage for the actors, while the musicians played in an outside passage.[6]

In 1782, when the craze for private theatricals first reached Steventon rectory, Jane Austen was seven. The dining parlour was probably used as a makeshift theatre for the early productions.[7] The first play known to have been acted by the Austen family was *Matilda*, a tragedy in five acts by Dr Thomas Francklin, a friend of Dr Samuel Johnson and a fashionable London preacher. The part of the tragic heroine Matilda was later popularised by Mrs Siddons on the London stage. At Steventon the tragedy was acted some time during 1782, and James Austen wrote a prologue and an epilogue for the performance.[8] Edward Austen spoke the prologue and Tom Fowle, one of Mr Austen's Steventon pupils who later became engaged to Cassandra Austen, the epilogue.[9]

Francklin's dreary play, set at the time of the Norman Conquest, dramatises a feud between two brothers. Morcar, Earl of Mercia, and his brother Edwin are both in love with Matilda, the daughter of a Norman lord. Matilda has chosen Edwin. Morcar separates the lovers, sets up plans to murder his brother, and tries (unsuccessfully) to win over and marry Matilda. The tragedy takes an unexpected twist with Morcar's unlikely reformation: he is persuaded to repent of his crimes, reunite the lovers and become reconciled to his brother.

Matilda was a surprising choice for the satirically-minded Austen family. Its long, rambling speeches and dramatic clichés of language and situation made it precisely the kind of historical tragedy that Sheridan burlesqued in *The Critic*. The tragedy had only six speaking parts, however, and was perhaps manageable in the dining room.[10] Jane Austen was surely only a spectator at this very first Steventon performance, but it is probable that she disliked the play, given the disparaging comment she makes in her juvenilia about another historical drama, *The Tragedy of Jane Shore*, 'a tragedy and therefore not worth reading' (*MW*, p. 140). Perhaps the manager/actor James felt the same, for after *Matilda* no more tragedies were performed at Steventon.

Matilda was followed two years later by a far more ambitious project. In 1784, when Jane was nine, Sheridan's *The Rivals* was acted at Steventon. Once again James Austen wrote the prologue and an epilogue for the play performed in July 'by some young Ladies & Gentlemen at Steventon'.[11] Henry spoke the prologue and the actor playing Bob Acres (possibly James himself) the epilogue. James's prologue suggests that there was an audience for this production.[12] The play has a cast of twelve, and it seems that the Austens had no qualms about inviting neighbours and friends to take part in their theatricals. The Cooper cousins and the Digweed family probably made up the numbers.[13] Biographers speculate that Jane Austen may have taken the minor role of Lydia Languish's pert maid, Lucy, but perhaps it is more likely that she was a keen spectator.[14]

James's prologue is unequivocal in its praise of satirical comedy, rather than sentimental tragedy:

> The Loftier members of the tragic Lyre;
> Court the soft pleasures that from pity flow;
> Seek joy in tears and luxury in woe.
> 'Tis our's, less noble, but more pleasing task,
> To draw from Folly's features fashion's mask;
> To paint the scene where wit and sense unite
> To yield at once instruction and delight.[15]

Jane Austen was undoubtedly influenced by her Thespian brothers, and it is therefore unsurprising that one of their favourite comic writers was to have a major impact on her own writing. While Sheridan's influence is discernible in Austen's earliest works, his presence can be felt most strongly in her mature works, which, unlike the juvenilia, also set out to instruct and to delight, and sought to combine 'wit and sense'. In particular, the influence of *The Rivals* can be most keenly felt in Austen's own satire on sentimentalism: her first published novel, *Sense and Sensibility*. It is all the more bewildering that this aspect of her comic genius has been so sorely neglected.

It was shortly after the performance of *The Rivals* that Cassandra and Jane were sent off to boarding school in Reading. The eccentric headmistress of the school was a Mrs La Tournelle, née Sarah Hackitt, who (much to the amusement of her pupils) could not speak a word of French. She was notorious for having a cork leg, for dressing in exactly the same clothes every day, and for her obsession with every aspect of the theatre. She enthralled her young charges with lively accounts of plays and play-acting, greenroom anecdotes, and gossip about the private lives of leading actors. Plays were performed as an integral part of the girls' education. The Austen sisters' interest in the drama was fostered at this school. Jane later recalled their time here with memories of fun and laughter, reminding her sister of a schoolgirl expression: 'I could die of laughter … as they used to say at school' (*Letters*, p. 5).

When the girls returned home from school for good in 1786, they were delighted to be in the company of a real French-speaking person, their exotic cousin, Eliza de Feuillide, a French countess. Eliza had taken part in theatrical activities since she was a child and had also acted in private theatricals staged by her aristocratic French friends. In a letter to Philadelphia Walter (also a cousin of Jane Austen), Eliza regaled her cousin with tales of private theatricals: 'I have promised to spend the Carnival, which in France is the gayest Season of the year, in a very agreeable Society who have erected an elegant theatre for the purposes of acting Plays amongst ourselves, and who intend having Balls at least twice a week.'[16]

Family tradition records that the Steventon barn was used on occasions as a temporary theatre, but probably not until the Christmas theatricals of 1787 when Eliza was a guest at the rectory.[17] In a letter written in September of that year, Philadelphia Walter wrote: 'My uncle's barn is fitting up quite like a theatre and all the young folks are to take their part.'[18]

During September 1787 Eliza had asked her cousin to join her for the Tunbridge Wells summer season, and had requested that the comedies *Which is the Man?*, by Hannah Cowley, and *Bon Ton: or High Life Above Stairs*, by Garrick, be presented at the local theatre. Much to her delight, the house was full on both occasions.[19] These two modern comedies were clearly great favourites with Eliza. *Bon Ton* was an amusing satire on fashionable French manners, while *Which is the Man?* depicted a fascinating young widow, Lady Bell Bloomer, on the brink of remarriage. Eliza clearly longed for an opportunity to perform these plays at Steventon. Later, Philadelphia Walter informed her brother in a letter that these plays were to be given at Steventon that Christmas: 'They go at Xmas to Steventon and mean to act a play *Which is the Man?* and *Bon Ton*.'[20]

Eliza had already made plans with the Austen family for the Christmas festivities. James was home from his foreign travels and keen to begin organising theatricals on a grander scale than before, egged on by Eliza. Both she and the Austen family wished Philadelphia to be part of the theatrical ensemble, but, like Fanny Price, the meek and timid Phila resolutely declined the offer: 'I should like to be a spectator, but am sure

I should not have courage to act a part, nor do I wish to attain it.'[21] Eliza urged Phila, on behalf of the Austens, to take one of the 'two unengaged parts' that were waiting to be filled:

> You know we have long projected acting this Christmas at Hampshire and this scheme would go on a vast deal better would you lend your assistance ... and on finding there were two unengaged parts I immediately thought of you, and am particularly commissioned by My Aunt Austen and her whole family to make the earliest application possible, and assure you how very happy you will make them as well as myself if you could be prevailed on to undertake these parts and give us all your company.[22]

In the same letter, Eliza assured her cousin that the acting parts set aside for her were 'neither long nor difficult', and reminded her that the acting party were well-equipped: 'Do not let your dress neither disturb you, as I think I can manage it so that the *Green Room* should provide you with what is necessary for acting.' At the close of the letter she tried another means to persuade her shy cousin: 'You cannot possibly resist so many pleasures, especially when I tell you your old friend James is returned from France and is to be of the acting party.'[23]

Eliza was clearly used to getting her own way. But Philadelphia's firm resolve not to act surprised both Eliza and the Austen family:

> I received your letter yesterday my dear friend and need not tell you how much I am concerned at your not being able to comply with a request which in all probability I shall never have it in my power to make again ... I will only allow myself to take notice of the strong reluctance you express to what you call *appearing in Publick*. I assure you our performance is to be by no means a publick one, since only a selected party of friends will be present.[24]

According to Eliza, Philadelphia's visit to Steventon was dependent on her compliance with joining the acting party: 'You wish to know the exact time which we should be *satisfied with*, and therefore I proceed to acquaint you that a fortnight from New Years Day *would do*, provided however you could bring yourself to act, for my Aunt Austen declares "she has not room for any *idle young* people".[25]

Despite Eliza's repeated assurances that the parts were very short, Philadelphia resisted her cousin's efforts and stayed away. Eliza appears to have attributed this to Mrs Walter's interference: 'Shall I be candid and tell you the thought which has struck me on this occasion? – The insuperable objection to my proposal is, some scruples of your mother's about your acting. If this is the case I can only say it is [a] pity so groundless a prejudice should be harboured in so enlightened [and so] enlarged a mind.'[26] The Austens showed no such prejudice against private theatricals and *Bon Ton* was performed some time during this period. There is a surviving epilogue written by James.[27]

The first play that was presented at Steventon in 1787 was not, however, Garrick's farce, but Susanna Centlivre's lively comedy, *The Wonder: A Woman Keeps a Secret* (1714). As usual James wrote a prologue and an epilogue. *The Wonder* was an excellent choice for Eliza: she played the part of the spirited heroine, Donna Violante, who risks her own marriage and reputation by choosing to protect her friend, Donna Isabella, from an arranged marriage to a man she despises. The play engages in the battle-of-the-sexes debate that Eliza particularly enjoyed. Women are 'inslaved' to 'the Tyrant Man'; and whether they be fathers, husbands or brothers, they 'usurp authority, and expect a blind obedience from us, so that maids, wives, or widows, we are little better than slaves'.[28]

The play's most striking feature is a saucy proposal of marriage from Isabella, though made on her behalf by Violante in disguise, to a man she barely knows. Twenty-seven years later, Jane Austen would incorporate private theatricals into her new novel, and the play, *Lovers' Vows*, would contain a daring proposal of marriage from a vivacious young woman.[29]

The Austen family clearly had no objection whatsoever to the depiction in Centlivre's comedy of strong, powerful women who claim their rights to choose their own husbands, and show themselves capable of loyalty and firm friendship. James's epilogue 'spoken by a lady in the character of Violante' leaves us in no doubt of the Austens' awareness of the play's theme of female emancipation:

In Barbarous times, e'er learning's sacred light
Rose to disperse the shades of Gothic night
And bade fair science wide her beams display,
Creation's fairest part neglected lay.
In vain the form where grace and ease combined.
In vain the bright eye spoke th' enlightened mind,
Vain the sweet smiles which secret love reveal,
Vain every charm, for there were none to feel.
From tender childhood trained to rough alarms,
Choosing no music but the clang of arms;
Enthusiasts only in the listed field,
Our youth there knew to fight, but not to yield.
Nor higher deemed of beauty's utmost power,
Than the light play thing of their idle hour.
Such was poor woman's lot – whilst tyrant men
At once possessors of the sword and pen
All female claim with stern pedantic pride
To prudence, truth and secrecy denied,
Covered their tyranny with specious words
And called themselves creation's mighty lords –
But thank our happier Stars, those times are o'er;
And woman holds a second place no more.
Now forced to quit their long held usurpation,
Men all wise, these 'Lords of the Creation'!
To our superior sway themselves submit,
Slaves to our charms, and vassals to our wit;
We can with ease their ev'ry sense beguile,
And melt their Resolutions with a smile.[30]

Jane Austen's most expressive battle-of-the-sexes debate, that between Anne Elliot and Captain Harville in *Persuasion*, curiously echoes James Austen's epilogue. Denied the 'exertion' of the battlefield and a 'profession', women have been forced to live quietly. James's remonstrance that 'Tyrant men [are] at once possessors of the sword and pen' is more gently reiterated in Anne Elliot's claim that 'Men have had every advantage of us in telling their story ... the pen has been in their hands' (*P*, p. 234).

There were two performances of *The Wonder* after Christmas. The evident success of the play was followed up in the new year by a production of Garrick's adaptation of *The Chances* (1754), for which James, once again, wrote a prologue. This play was to be Eliza's final performance for some time.

Once again James and Henry chose a racy comedy: originally written by Beaumont and Fletcher, the play had been altered by the Duke of Buckingham and in 1754 'new-dressed' by Garrick. Although Garrick had made a concerted effort to tone it down, the play was still considered to contain strong dialogue. So thought Mrs Inchbald in her *Remarks*, which prefaced her edition of the play: 'That Garrick, to the delicacy of improved taste, was compelled to sacrifice much of their libertine dialogue, may well be suspected, by the remainder which he spared.'[31]

The Austen family did not share such compunction. Like *The Wonder*, Garrick's play depicts jealous lovers, secret marriages and confused identities. The two heroines, both confusingly called Constantia, are mistaken for one another. The first Constantia is mistaken for a prostitute, although she is in fact secretly married to the Duke of Naples. It is likely that the feisty Eliza played the role of the low-born 'second Constantia', a favourite of the great comic actress Mrs Jordan.

Eliza had played her last role, as the return of Mr Austen's pupils in the new year signified her imminent removal from Steventon. Both James and Henry Austen were 'fascinated' by the flirtatious Eliza, according to James's son, who wrote the first memoir of Jane Austen. Most critics and biographers accept that a flirtation between Henry and Eliza was begun around this time and resulted eventually in their marriage ten years later. Some critics have conjectured that the flirtation which the young Jane Austen witnessed between Henry and Eliza during rehearsals may have given her the idea for the flirtation between Henry Crawford and Maria Bertram in *Mansfield Park*.[32] That the young girl was acutely aware of the flirtation seems clear from one of her short tales, 'Henry and Eliza', where there are a series of elopements including one by Henry and Eliza, who run off together leaving only a curt note: 'Madam, we are married and gone' (*MW*, p. 36).

By all accounts, Jane Austen was an intelligent observer of the intrigues, emotions and excitement of private theatricals; of rehearsals, the reading over of scripts, and the casting of parts. James-Edward Austen's *Memoir* claims that his aunt Jane 'was an early observer, and it may be reasonably supposed that some of the incidents and feelings which are so vividly painted in the *Mansfield Park* theatricals are due to her recollection of these entertainments'.[33]

In *Mansfield Park*, Jane Austen devoted her creative energies to the rehearsal process rather than the performance. Furthermore the singular strength of the theatrical sequence lies in its depiction through the eyes of an envious observer. It has been suggested that in writing the *Lovers' Vows* sequence Austen distilled some of her own experience as an outsider, a partially excluded younger sister.[34] There is, however, no evidence to suggest that Jane was excluded from the family theatricals. Even if her youth prevented her from taking part in the actual performances, she began, at this time, to write her own short playlets. These were probably performed as afterpieces to the main play.

Henry Fielding's outrageous burlesque *The Tragedy of Tom Thumb* was 'acted to a small circle of select friends' on 22 March 1788 at Steventon, and this was followed some time later by 'a private Theatrical Exhibition'. Regrettably, James's prologue to the latter gives no indication of the play performed, though it imitates Jacques's 'seven ages of man' speech. The prologue also satirises the hypocrisy of the sentimental age where 'to talk affecting, when we do not feel' is described as a form of 'acting'.[35] The family perhaps wrote the entertainment themselves. It was probably at this time that Jane wrote and participated in her own burlesque playlet, 'The Mystery'.[36]

The last plays performed at Steventon in 1788–89 were *The Sultan: or A Peep into the Seraglio*, a farce by Isaac Bickerstaffe, and another farce by James Townley, *High Life Below Stairs*. Bickerstaffe's farce was first performed in London in 1775, but had only been recently published, in 1784. It was yet another comedy that depicted a bold, spirited heroine, posing a challenge to male prerogative and authority. Roxalana is an Englishwoman who has been captured for the Sultan's seraglio. She displaces the favourite concubine, Elmira, by winning the honourable affections of the Sultan. Moreover, she condemns his harem and demands the freedom of all his wives: 'You are the great Sultan; I am your slave, but I am also a free-born woman, prouder of that than all the pomp and splendour eastern monarchs can bestow.'[37] James's epilogue was yet another provocative declaration of female superiority over men, opening with the words,

> Lord help us! what strange foolish things are these men,
> One good clever woman is fairly worth ten.[38]

Two of the most popular contemporary choices for private representation were Fielding's *Tom Thumb* and Townley's *High Life Below Stairs*. The Burneys acted *Tom Thumb* in Worcestershire in 1777, ten years before the Austens chose it for performance. The part of the diminutive hero Tom Thumb was often played by a child, whose high-pitched voice would add to the comic incongruity.[39]

James Townley's satire on plebeian manners, *High Life Below Stairs* (1759), depicts a household of lazy servants who behave as badly as their masters. They ape their masters' manners, assume their titles, drink their expensive wine, gamble and visit the theatre. Like Gay's *Beggar's Opera* and Foote's *Mayor of Garett*, Townley's farce was a comedy that used low life to criticise high society. It was also an extremely popular choice for amateur theatricals. In part, this was because it was more prudent to poke fun at the lower orders in the safety of one's own home than in the professional theatre house. In 1793 a performance of *High Life Below Stairs* in an Edinburgh public theatre incited a row between a group of highly offended footmen and their masters.

George Colman the Younger's comedy about social transformations, *The Heir at Law*, was also a popular choice for the gentry to indulge themselves in stereotypical 'low' roles. Austen was to explore this contentious issue in *Mansfield Park* when the heir of Mansfield insists on staging *The Heir at Law* so that he can play the stage Irishman, Duberley.

Jane's playlet, 'The Visit', dedicated to James, contains a quotation from *High Life Below Stairs*, which suggests that she composed it around the same time as the family performance of Townley's farce, perhaps as a burlesque afterpiece. Austen repeats Townley's phrase, 'The more free, the more welcome', in her play. The allusion seems to be a nod to the main play performed that day at Steventon. Austen's habit of repeating phrases from the plays performed, or even merely contemplated for performance, at Steventon remained with her for a long time. Though Hannah Cowley's play *Which is the Man?* was considered for performance, it was finally rejected. Yet Austen quoted a phrase from it in a letter dated 1810, some twenty-nine years later.[40]

Which is the Man? is alluded to in Austen's 'The Three Sisters', written around 1788–90 (*MW*, p. 65). In this story, a spoilt young woman demands to play the part of Lady Bell Bloomer, just as Eliza had wished to in the 1787–88 Christmas theatricals. Again, a quotation from Cowley's popular comedy *The Belle's Stratagem* appears in a letter of 1801: 'Mr Doricourt has travelled; he knows best' (*Letters*, p. 73).

Though Eliza was now in Paris and unable to partake in the Steventon theatricals, the Cooper cousins came to Steventon for Christmas 1788–89 and Jane Cooper filled the gap left by Eliza. In a letter to Philadelphia, Eliza had hastily, though wistfully, scribbled a last message: 'I suppose you have had pressing accounts from Steventon, and that they have informed you of their theatrical performances, The Sultan & High Life below Stairs, Miss Cooper performed the part of Roxelana [*sic*] and Henry the Sultan, I hear that Henry is taller than ever.'[41] No prologue or epilogue by James has survived for *High Life Below Stairs*, but the prologue he provided for Bickerstaffe's comedy is (confusingly) dated 1790 and states it was 'spoken by Miss Cooper as Roxalana'.[42]

The Sultan and *High Life Below Stairs* ended the theatricals at Steventon, although there is a family tradition which claims that they were resumed in the late 1790s. The main reason why actor-manager James abandoned private theatricals seems to be that he was turning his mind to other literary interests, namely the production of a weekly magazine, *The Loiterer*. This periodical, like the theatricals at Steventon, was also to prove an important influence on Jane Austen's early writings.

Henry Austen tells us in his 'Biographical Notice', published in the first edition of *Northanger Abbey* and *Persuasion*, that his sister Jane was acquainted with all the best authors at a very early age (*NA*, p. 7). The literary tastes of Catherine Morland have often been read as a parody of the author's own literary preferences.[43] Catherine likes to read 'poetry and plays, and things of that sort', and while 'in training for a heroine', she reads 'all such works as heroines must read to supply their memories with those quotations which are so serviceable and so soothing in the vicissitudes of their eventful lives' (*NA*, p. 15): dramatic works, those of Shakespeare especially, are prominent among these. *Twelfth Night*, *Othello* and *Measure for Measure* are singled out. Catherine duly reads Shakespeare, alongside Pope, Gray and Thompson, not so much for pleasure and entertainment, as for gaining 'a great store of information' (*NA*, p. 16).

In *Sense and Sensibility*, Willoughby and the Dashwoods are to be found reading *Hamlet* aloud together. In *Mansfield Park*, the consummate actor Henry Crawford gives a rendering of *Henry VIII* that is described by Fanny Price, a lover of Shakespeare, as 'truly dramatic' (*MP*, p. 337). Henry memorably remarks that Shakespeare is 'part of an Englishman's constitution. His thoughts and beauties are so spread abroad that one touches them every where'. This sentiment is reiterated by Edmund when he notes that 'we all talk Shakespeare, use his similes, and describe with his descriptions' (*MP*, p. 338). Though Emma Woodhouse is not a great reader, she is found quoting passages on romantic love from *Romeo and Juliet* and *A Midsummer Night's Dream*.

Henry and Edmund agree on very little. It is therefore a fair assumption that, when they do concur, they are voicing the opinion of their author. Their consciousness of how Shakespeare is assimilated into our very fibre, so that 'one is intimate with him by instinct', reaches to the essence of Jane Austen's own relationship with him. She would have read the plays when a young woman, but she would also have absorbed famous lines and characters by osmosis, such was Shakespeare's pervasiveness in the culture of the age. She quotes Shakespeare from memory, as can be judged by the way that she often misquotes him. Her surviving letters refer far more frequently to contemporary plays than Shakespearean ones, but Shakespeare's influence on the drama of the late eighteenth and early nineteenth century was so thoroughgoing – for instance through the tradition of the 'witty couple', reaching back to *Love's Labour's Lost* and *Much Ado About Nothing* – that her indirect debt to his vision can be taken for granted.

In her earliest works, however, Jane Austen showed a certain irreverence for the national dramatist. Shakespeare's history plays are used to great satirical effect in *The History of England*, a lampoon of Oliver Goldsmith's abridged *History of England*. Austen mercilessly parodied Goldsmith's arbitrary and indiscriminate merging of fact and fiction, in particular his reliance on Shakespeare's history plays for supposedly authentic historical fact. Austen, by contrast, is being satirical when she makes a point of referring her readers to Shakespeare's English history plays for 'factual' information about the lives of its monarchs.[44] Just as solemnly, she refers her readers to other popular historical plays, such as Nicholas Rowe's *Jane Shore* and Sheridan's *The Critic* (*MW*, pp. 140, 147). The tongue-in-cheek reference to Sheridan compounds the irony, as *The Critic* is itself a burlesque of historical tragedy that firmly eschews any intention of authenticity.

From such allusions in the juvenilia it is clear that Jane Austen was familiar with a wide range of plays, although these are probably only a fraction of the numerous plays that would have been read over as possible choices for the private theatricals, read aloud for family entertainment, or read for private enjoyment. While it is impossible to calculate the number of plays that she read as a young girl, since there is no extant record of Mr Austen's ample library, the range of her explicit literary allusions gives us some idea of her extensive reading – references to over forty plays have been noted.[45]

Jane Austen owned a set of William Hayley's *Poems and Plays*. Volumes one to five are inscribed 'Jane Austen 1791'; volume six has a fuller inscription 'Jane Austen, Steventon Sunday April the 3*d*. 1791'.[46] Hayley was well known as the 'friend and biographer' of William Cowper, Austen's favourite poet, though he fancied himself as a successful playwright. The most well-thumbed volume in Austen's collection of Hayley was the one containing his plays. It contained five dramas in all: two tragedies, *Marcella* and *Lord Russel*, and three comedies in verse, *The Happy Prescription: or the Lady Relieved from her Lovers*; *The Two Connoisseurs*; and *The Mausoleum*.[47]

Like the Sheridan plays which the Austens adored, Hayley's comedies depict the folly of vanity and affectation in polite society. By far the best of them is *The Mausoleum*, which dramatises excessive sensibility and 'false refinement' in the characters of a beautiful young widow, Sophia Sentiment, and a pompous versifier, Mr Rumble, a caricature of Dr

Johnson. Lady Sophia Sentiment erects a mausoleum to house her husband's ashes and employs versifiers to compose tributes for the inscription on the monument. The comedy explores the self-destructive effects of sensibility on the mind of a lovely young widow, who refuses to overcome her grief because of a distorted conception of refined sentiment. The tell-tale sign of misplaced sensibility is Lady Sophia's obsession with black:

> If cards should be call'd for to-night,
> Place the new japann'd tables alone in my sight;
> For the pool of Quadrille set the black-bugle dish,
> And remember you bring us the ebony fish.[48]

But this sentiment is amusingly undercut by its correlation to hypocrisy and false delicacy:

> Her crisis is coming, without much delay;
> There might have been doubts had she fix'd upon grey:
> But a vow to wear black all the rest of her life
> Is a strong inclination she'll soon be a wife.[49]

This comedy is of particular interest as the main character has the name that was adopted in a satirical letter to James Austen in his capacity as editor of *The Loiterer*. The letter complains of the periodical's lack of feminine interest:

> Sir, I write this to inform you that you are very much out of my good graces, and that, if you do not mend your manners, I shall soon drop your acquaintance. You must know, Sir, that I am a great reader, and not to mention some hundred volumes of Novels and Plays, have in the two last summers, actually got through all the entertaining papers of our most celebrated periodical writers.[50]

The correspondent goes on to complain of the journal's lack of sentimental interest and offers recommendations to improve its style:

Let the lover be killed in a duel, or lost at sea, or you make him shoot himself, just as you please; and as for his mistress, she will of course go mad; or if you will, you may kill the lady, and let the lover run mad; only remember, whatever you do, that your hero and heroine must possess a great deal of feeling, and have very pretty names.[51]

The letter ends by stating that if the author's wishes are not complied with 'may your work be condemned to the pastry-cooke's shop, and may you always continue a bachelor, and be plagued with a maiden sister to keep house for you'. It is signed Sophia Sentiment.

It is highly probable that Jane Austen wrote this burlesque letter to her brother. It is very close in spirit to her juvenilia of the same period. *Love and Freindship* also has a sentimental heroine named Sophia. It seems plausible that *The Mausoleum* was among the comedies considered for performance by the Austens when they were looking at material for home theatricals in 1788. This may have been the time that Jane first became acquainted with the name Sophia Sentiment. If Austen was indeed Sophia Sentiment, by her own admission, she was a great reader of some hundred volumes of novels and plays.

Austen also owned a copy of Arnaud Berquin's *L'ami des enfans* (1782–83) and the companion series *L'ami de l'adolescence* (1784–85). Berquin's little stories, dialogues and dramas were much used in English schools for young ladies towards the end of the eighteenth century, being read in the original for the language or in translation for the moral. Berquin states in his preface to *L'ami des enfans* that his 'little dramas' are designed to bring children of the opposite sex together 'in order to produce that union and intimacy which we are so pleased to see subsist between brothers and sisters'.[52] The whole of the family is encouraged to partake in the plays to promote family values:

Each volume of this work will contain little dramas, in which children are the principal characters, in order that they may learn to acquire a free unembarrassed countenance, a gracefulness of attitude and deport- ment, and an easy manner of delivering themselves before company. Besides, the performance of these dramas will be a domestic recreation and amusement.

Berquin's short plays and dramatic dialogues were intended to instruct parents and children on manners and morals, on how to conduct themselves in domestic life, how to behave to one another, to the servants, and to the poor, and how to cope with everyday problems in the home. Some were directed towards young women, warning against finery and vanity. *Fashionable Education*, as its name suggests, depicts a young woman (Leonora) who has been given a fashionable town education, 'those charming sciences called drawing, music, dancing', but has also learned to be selfish, vain and affected.[53] The blind affection of Leonora's aunt has compounded her ruin. The moral of this play is that accomplishments should embellish a useful education and knowledge, not act as a substitute for them. A similar play, *Vanity Punished*, teaches the evils of coquetry, vanity, selfishness and spoilt behaviour.

Intriguingly, one of the playlets in the collection carries the same plot-line as Austen's *Emma*. In *Cecilia and Marian*, a young, wealthy girl befriends a poor labourer's daughter and 'tastes the happiness of doing good' when she feeds her new playmate plum cake and currant jelly:

> Cecilia had now tasted the happiness of doing good. She walked a little longer in the garden, thinking how happy she had made Marian, how grateful Marian had shewed herself, and how her little sister would be pleased to taste currant jelly. What will it be, said she, when I give her some ribbands and a necklace! Mama gave me some the other day that were pretty enough; but I am tired of them now. Then I'll look in my drawers for some old things to give her. We are just of a size, and my slips would fit her charmingly. Oh! how I long to see her well drest.[54]

Cecilia continues to enjoy her patronage until she is roundly scolded by her mother for her harmful and irresponsible conduct. By indulging and spoiling her favourite, Cecilia has made her friend dissatisfied with her previous life:

MOTHER: But how comes it, then, that you cannot eat dry bread, nor walk barefoot as she does?
CECILIA: The thing is, perhaps, that I am not used to it.

25

MOTHER: Why, then, if she uses herself, like you, to eat sweet things, and to wear shoes and stockings, and afterwards if the brown bread should go against her, and she should not be able to walk barefoot, do you think that you would have done her any service?[55]

Cecilia is an enemy to her own happiness and that of her 'low' friend Marian. She is only saved by the intervention and guidance of her judicious mother. In *L'ami des enfans*, mothers are often shown instructing, advising and educating their daughters: the plays were aimed at parents as well as children. In *Emma*, the variant on Berquin's plot-line is a similarly meddlesome, though well-meaning, young woman who painfully lacks a mother figure.

Like Berquin, Austen wrote her own short plays and stories for domestic entertainment.[56] But, rather than teaching morals and manners, Austen's playlets parody the moral didacticism of Berquin's thinly disguised conduct books. There are three attempts at playwriting in Austen's juvenilia. The first two, 'The Visit' and 'The Mystery' in *Volume the First*, were written between 1787 and 1790.[57] The third, 'The First Act of a Comedy', is one of the 'Scraps' in *Volume the Second* and dates from around 1793.

As mentioned earlier, 'The Visit' was probably written in 1789, the same time as the Steventon performance of Townley's *High Life Below Stairs*. The play depicts a dinner engagement at Lord Fitzgerald's house with a party of young people. Dining room etiquette is satirised in this piece, as the characters pompously make formal introductions to one another, then promptly discover that there are not sufficient chairs for them all to be seated:

MISS FITZGERALD: Bless me! there ought to be 8 Chairs & there are but 6. However, if your Ladyship will but take Sir Arthur in your Lap, & Sophy my Brother in hers, I beleive we shall do pretty well.
SOPHY: I beg you will make no apologies. Your Brother is very light.
(*MW*, p. 52)

The conversation between the guests is almost wholly preoccupied with the main fare of 'fried Cowheel and Onion', 'Tripe' and 'Liver and Crow'. The vulgarity of the food on offer is contrasted with the polite formality of the guests:

> CLOE: I shall trouble Mr Stanley for a Little of the fried Cowheel & Onion.
> STANLEY: Oh Madam, there is a secret pleasure in helping so amiable a Lady –.
> LADY HAMPTON: I assure you my Lord, Sir Arthur never touches wine; but Sophy will toss off a bumper I am sure to oblige your Lordship. (*MW*, p. 53)

Banal remarks about food and wine lead irrationally to unexpected marriage proposals for the three young women at the table, who eagerly accept without a second's hesitation.

On the surface, Austen's parody of a dull social visit derives its comic impact from the farcical touches and the juxtapositions of polite formalities with vulgar expressions. The young heroine, Sophy, like so many of Austen's early creations, is portrayed as a drunk who can 'toss off a bumper' at will. Above all, there is an irrepressible delight in the sheer absurdity of table manners. The Austens performing this play would, of course, be expected to maintain their composure when solemnly requesting 'fried Cowheel & Onion' and 'Liver & Crow' (*MW*, p. 53).

Austen's playlet, deriding the absurdity and pomposity of table etiquette, provides a mocking contrast to the morally earnest tone of Berquin's instructive playlets. His *Little Fiddler* also dramatises a social visit, where the exceptionally rude behaviour of a young man to his sister (Sophia) and to her visitors, the Misses Richmonds, leads to expulsion from the family circle. Charles, the ill-mannered brother and deceitful, greedy son, is eventually turned out of his father's house for his treachery and lies, and for his cruel treatment of a poor fiddler. In Berquin's play, the virtues of polite conduct are piously upheld:

> SOPHIA: Ah! how do you do, my dear friends! [*They salute each other, and curtsy to Godfrey, who bows to them.*]

CHARLOTTE: It seems an age since I saw you last.

AMELIA: Indeed it is a long time.

SOPHIA: I believe it is more than three weeks. [*Godfrey draws out the table, and gives them chairs.*]

CHARLOTTE: Do not give yourself so much trouble, Master Godfrey.

GODFREY: Indeed, I think it no trouble.

SOPHIA: Oh, I am very sure Godfrey does it with pleasure, [*gives him her hand.*] I wish my brother had a little of his complaisance.

The stilted artificiality of such social visits is precisely the target of Jane Austen's satire in 'The Visit'. She seemed to have little time for plays which dictated appropriate formal conduct, preferring comedies which satirised social behaviour. Jane Austen mocks Berquin and simultaneously begins to explore the incongruities and absurdities of restrictive social mores.[58]

As noted, a more direct source for 'The Visit' was Townley's *High Life Below Stairs*. Austen's quotation 'The more free, the more welcome' (*MW*, p. 50) nods to Townley's farce, where fashionably bad table manners are cultivated by the servants in an attempt to ape their masters. Berquin wrote didactic plays instructing the correct ways to treat servants, both honest and dishonest. Townley's hilarious farce of social disruption dramatises a lord who disguises himself as a servant to spy on his lazy servants, so that he can punish them appropriately for taking over his house.[59]

Austen dedicated 'The Visit' to her brother James. Intriguingly, in her dedication, she recalled two other Steventon plays. These 'celebrated comedies' were probably written by James, since Jane describes her own 'drama' as 'inferior' to his:

Sir, The Following Drama, which I humbly recommend to your Protection & Patronage, tho' inferior to those celebrated comedies called 'The School for Jealousy' & 'The travelled Man', will I hope afford some amusement to so respectable a *Curate* as yourself; which was the end in veiw [*sic*] when it was first composed by your Humble Servant the Author. (*MW*, p. 49)

28

James had recently returned from his travels abroad, so 'the travelled Man' may have been based on his adventures. The two play-titles echo the form of several favourites in the eighteenth-century dramatic repertoire: Goldsmith's *The Good-Natur'd Man* (1768), Arthur Murphy's *The School For Guardians* (1769), and Richard Cumberland's *The Choleric Man* (1774), Sheridan's *The School for Scandal* (1777), and Hannah Cowley's *School for Elegance* (1780).

'The Mystery' was probably performed as an afterpiece to the Steventon 1788 'Private Theatrical Exhibition'.[60] Austen dedicated it to her father, and it may well have been a mocking tribute to one of his favourite plays. It has been suggested that the whispering scenes in this playlet were based on a similar scene in Sheridan's *The Critic*.[61] Jane Austen's parody is, however, closer to Buckingham's burlesque, *The Rehearsal*, which Sheridan was self-consciously reworking in *The Critic*.[62] It is most likely that Austen was parodying the whispering scene in *The Rehearsal*, where Bayes insists that his play is entirely new: 'Now, Sir, because I'll do nothing here that ever was done before, instead of beginning with a Scene that discovers something of the Plot I begin this play with a whisper':

PHYSICIAN: But yet some rumours great are stirring; and if Lorenzo
    should prove false (which none but the great Gods can tell) you
    then perhaps would find that – [*Whispers.*]
BAYES: Now he whispers.
USHER: Alone, do you say?
PHYSICIAN: No; attended with the noble – [*Whispers.*]
BAYES: Again.
USHER: Who, he in gray?
PHYSICIAN: Yes; and at the head of – [*Whispers.*]
BAYES: Pray, mark.
USHER: Then, Sir, most certain, 'twill in time appear. These are the
    reasons that have mov'd him to't; First, he – [*Whispers.*]
BAYES: Now the other whispers.
USHER: Secondly, they – [*Whispers.*]
BAYES: At it still.
USHER: Thirdly, and lastly, both he, and they – [*Whispers.*]
BAYES: Now they both whisper. [*Exeunt Whispering.*][63]

'The Mystery' is closely modelled on this whispering scene. Austen's playlet is comprised of a series of interruptions and non-communications. It opens with a mock mysterious line, 'But hush! I am interrupted!', and continues in a similarly absurd and nonsensical manner:

> DAPHNE: My dear Mrs Humbug how dy'e do? Oh! Fanny, t'is all over.
> FANNY: Is it indeed!
> MRS HUMBUG: I'm very sorry to hear it.
> FANNY: Then t'was to no purpose that I …
> DAPHNE: None upon Earth.
> MRS HUMBUG: And what is to become of? …
> DAPHNE: Oh! thats all settled. [*whispers Mrs Humbug*]
> FANNY: And how is it determined?
> DAPHNE: I'll tell you. [*whispers Fanny*]
> MRS HUMBUG: And is he to? …
> DAPHNE: I'll tell you all I know of the matter. [*whispers Mrs Humbug and Fanny*]
> FANNY: Well! now I know everything about it, I'll go away.
> MRS HUMBUG & DAPHNE: And so will I. [*Exeunt*]
> (*MW*, p. 56)

The play ends with a further whispering scene, where the secret is finally whispered in the ear of the sleeping Sir Edward: 'Shall I tell him the secret? … No, he'll certainly blab it … But he is asleep and won't hear me … So I'll e'en venture' (*MW*, p. 57). In 'The Mystery', we are never told any information about the conversations between the characters, and it becomes as incongruous as Bayes's own 'new' play, which he proudly insists has no plot.

Austen's third playlet, 'The First Act of a Comedy', parodies musical comedy, an extremely popular mode of dramatic entertainment in the latter part of the eighteenth century.[64] A satirical passage from George Colman's *New Brooms* (1776) targets the vogue for comic opera:

> Operas are the only real entertainment. The plain unornamented drama is too flat, Sir. Common dialogue is a dry imitation of nature, as insipid as real conversation; but in an opera the dialogue is refreshed by an air

every instant. – Two gentlemen meet in the Park, for example, admire the place and the weather; and after a speech or two the orchestra take their cue, the musick strikes up, one of the characters takes a genteel turn or two on the stage, during the symphony, and then breaks out –

When the breezes
Fan the trees-es,
Fragrant gales
The breath inhales,
Warm the heart that sorrow freezes.[65]

Austen, like Colman, satirises the artificiality of the comic opera, its spontaneous outbursts of songs, and distinctive lack of plot.[66] Austen's playlet concerns the adventures of a family *en route* to London, and is set in a roadside inn, a familiar trope of the picaresque form popularised in Fielding's novels *Joseph Andrews* and *Tom Jones*.[67] Austen's play also nods towards Shakespeare's comic scenes set in 'The Boar's Head' in *Henry IV, Parts One and Two*. Three of the female characters are called 'Pistoletta', 'Maria' and 'Hostess'.

Chloe, who is to be married to the same man as Pistoletta, enters with a 'chorus of ploughboys', reads over a bill of fare and discovers that the only food available is '2 ducks, a leg of beef, a stinking partridge, & a tart'. Chloe's propensity for bursting into song at any given moment echoes Colman's burlesque of the inanities of comic opera: 'And now I will sing another song.'

SONG
I am going to have my dinner,
After which I shan't be thinner,
I wish I had here Strephon
For he would carve the partridge
If it should be a tough one.

CHORUS
Tough one, tough one, tough one,
For he would carve the partridge if it should be a tough one.
(*MW*, p. 174)[68]

As will be seen in the next two chapters, Austen clearly enjoyed musical comedy, even if, like Colman, she was conscious of its deficiencies as an 'imitation of nature'.

The three playlets in the juvenilia are parodic and satirical, and a strong sense prevails that Austen was writing to amuse her sophisticated, theatre-loving brothers. Whether she was composing a mocking counterpart to Berquin's instructive dramatic dialogues, or writing burlesques in the style of plays like *The Rehearsal* and *The Critic*, she endeavoured to impress her siblings with her knowledge of the drama. Two of her playlets, 'The Mystery' and 'The First Act of a Comedy', allude specifically to what was popular on the London stage, and mock it by drawing attention to its limitations and artificiality. 'The Visit' nods to the popular comedy *High Life Below Stairs*, so often dramatised for the private theatre, and begins to explore the incongruities and absurdities of genteel social behaviour.

In contrast with Berquin and William Hayley, who self-consciously used their plays to instruct, Austen entertains. Furthermore, even as she abandoned plays and turned to fiction, she began an apprenticeship in the art of dramatic dialogue and quasi-theatrical techniques that was to distinguish her mature writing. Austen's juvenilia reveals a deep familiarity with the most popular plays of the period: the works of Garrick, Fielding, Sheridan and Cowley.[69]

The Steventon theatricals took place between 1782 and 1790, coinciding with the period in which Jane Austen's juvenile literary works were written. Given the abundance of dramatic entertainment that she was exposed to at this time, it is not at all surprising that there were attempts at playwriting among her youthful literary efforts. Contrary to popular belief, however, it was not only in her childhood at Steventon that Austen developed her interest in the drama. In the period between the composition of the early versions of *Northanger Abbey*, *Pride and Prejudice* and *Sense and Sensibility* and the completion of the mature novels, Austen was taking part in private theatricals, writing dramatic dialogues and turning her favourite novel into a five-act comedy.

Jane Austen took part in private theatricals in 1805 when she was thirty. The death of her father early in the same year had a profound effect on the lives of the three dependent women whom he left behind, who were not to find a permanent home until they settled at Chawton in 1809. Some time after her father's death Austen may have redrafted and put the finishing touches to a short epistolary novel, *Lady Susan*. In June, the Austen sisters left Gay Street in Bath, collecting their niece Anna on the way, and set out for her brother Edward (Austen) Knight's Godmersham home. During her time at Kent, Jane spent many hours amusing her favourite nieces, Fanny and Anna, with play-acting. It was here that Anne Sharp, the children's governess, formed a friendship with Jane Austen that was to last for the rest of the latter's life. In the Godmersham private theatricals, Miss Sharp played the male roles and was clearly a great success.

The unpublished diaries of one of those nieces, Fanny Knight, reveal that aunt Jane had no scruples about play-acting. Fanny records a game of 'school' in which her aunts, grandmother and governess dressed up and took part:

> Wednesday 26 June. We had a whole holiday. Aunts and Grandmama played at school with us. Aunt C was Mrs Teachum the Governess Aunt Jane, Miss Popham the teacher Aunt Harriet, Sally the Housemaid, Miss Sharpe the Dancing Master the Apothecary and the Serjeant, Grandmama Betty Jones the pie woman and Mama the bathing woman. They dressed in Character and we had a most delightful day. – After dessert we acted a play called *Virtue Rewarded*. Anna was the Duchess St Albans, I was the Fairy Serena and Fanny Cage a shepherdess 'Mona'. We had a bowl of Syllabub in the evening.[70]

Although improvisational play was part of the fun, the small company of women also included their own plays in their repertoire. *Virtue Rewarded* may well have been composed by Anne Sharp, with roles written specifically for the children.[71]

The theatricals continued throughout June and July. Then on 30 July Fanny recorded two more amateur performances, including a play possibly written by Anne Sharp called *Pride Punished: or Innocence Rewarded*:[72] 'Aunt C and J, Anna, Edward, George, Henry, William and myself acted *The Spoilt Child* and *Innocence Rewarded*, afterwards we danced and had a most delightful evening.'[73] Bickerstaffe's *The Spoilt Child* was a great favourite on the London stage, popularised by Mrs Jordan who played the cross-dressed role of 'Little Pickle', the naughty child of the title. If Fanny played the part of Little Pickle and Anne Sharp his father, it is plausible that Jane Austen took the role of the spinster aunt, Miss Pickle. The most popular scene in the play is when the naughty child catches his aunt and her lover in the garden reciting love poetry and planning their elopement, and sews their clothes together.

It was during the 1805 Kent visit that Jane Austen read Thomas Gisborne's dour *Enquiry into the Duties of the Female Sex*. She would have been amused to discover Gisborne's assertion that play-acting was injurious to the female sex through encouraging vanity and destroying diffidence 'by the unrestrained familiarity with persons of the other sex, which inevitably results from being joined with them in the drama'.[74] Jane wrote to Cassandra, 'I am glad that you recommended Gisborne for having begun, I am pleased with it, and I had quite determined not to read it' (*Letters*, p. 112). This remark suggests a softening of her prior scepticism towards Gisborne, yet she clearly had no intention of putting his prescriptions into practice and giving up her involvement with private theatricals.[75] Jane Austen not only acted in plays at the same time that she was reading Gisborne, she also committed the grave offence of luring children into this dangerous activity, a practice that Gisborne particularly abhorred:

> Most of these remarks fully apply to the practice of causing children to act plays, or parts of plays; a practice of which parents, while labouring to vindicate it, sometimes pronounce an emphatical condemnation, by avowing a future purpose of abandoning it so soon as their children shall be far advanced in youth.[76]

Gisborne's prejudice directly opposes Arnaud Berquin's championing of the moral efficacy of family theatricals. Austen appears to have been more sympathetic to Berquin's view, judging by her enthusiasm for private theatricals among Edward Knight's young family at Kent. Perhaps she was rekindling memories of happier days at Steventon in her present uncertain state of home (she was to live at yet another brother's home in Southampton before eventually settling at Chawton).

In the meantime she continued not only to act with the children, but also returned to drama writing. It may well have been at this time that, with the help of her niece Anna, she put the finishing touches to her five-act play, *Sir Charles Grandison: or The Happy Man*, a burlesque dramatisation of her favourite novel, Richardson's *The History of Sir Charles Grandison*.[77]

There are two more notable occurrences that reflect Austen's interest in the drama. There still exists in the Austen-Leigh family collection a short unidentified document, untitled and consisting of two dramatic dialogues on the business of child-rearing in the early nineteenth century. From 1806 to 1809 Mrs Austen, her two daughters and Martha Lloyd were living in Southampton, for part of the time with Frank Austen and his newly pregnant wife Mary Gibson. As was the convention, the women read novels and plays aloud. This provided Jane Austen with another opportunity for the composition of amusing playlets on the subject of baby-care and motherhood.[78]

In these dramatic dialogues, a first-time mother, Mrs Denbigh, is seen neglecting her child, and spending almost all of her time in the garden looking at her auriculas. She pleads ignorance in child-rearing as 'I was just come from school when I was married, where you know we learnt nothing in the way of medicine or nursing'. The incompetence of Mrs Denbigh (and her Irish nanny) is contrasted with the sensible advice and practical skills of her friend Mrs Enfield:

MRS ENFIELD: [*Endeavours to look at the back*] Ah Nurse his shirt
    sticks! Do bring me some warm water & a rag.
MRS DENBIGH: [*rising*] I shall faint if I stay.
MRS ENFIELD: I beg you will stay till we can see what can be done.

MRS DENBIGH: [*takes out her smelling bottle*] I will try – how
   unfeeling [*aside*].
MRS ENFIELD: [*applies a mild plaister*] Now nurse you must change
   the plaister night & morning, spread it very thin, & keep a few folds
   of soft linen over it – Will you bring me a clean shirt.
NURSE: [*going out*] Yes Ma'am, if I can find one – I wish she and her
   plaister were far enough [*aside*].[79]

The dialogues are didactic, as they are meant to be, but the selfish Mrs
Denbigh is comically drawn. Her rattling conversations perhaps fore-
shadow the monologues of Miss Bates and Mrs Elton in *Emma*.[80]

The other significant event in these later years took place in 1809. It
was then, only two years before starting work on *Mansfield Park*, that
Austen acted the part of Mrs Candour in Sheridan's *School for Scandal*.
In writing of Sir William Heathcote of Hursley Park, Hampshire, in 1898,
the novelist Charlotte M. Yonge recalled: 'His mother was Elizabeth,
daughter of Lovelace Bigg-Wither of Manydown Park in the same country … She lived chiefly in Winchester, and it may be interesting that her
son remembered being at a Twelfth day party where Jane Austen drew
the character of Mrs Candour, and assumed the part with great spirit.'[81]

There is no reason to doubt this evidence. Jane Austen's friendship
with the Manydown family lasted all her life. Both she and Cassandra
often used to spend the night at Manydown when they attended the
Basingstoke balls as girls. Jane informed Cassandra of a twelfth day party
at Manydown in her letter to Cassandra of 27 December 1808:

> I was happy to hear, cheifly [*sic*] for Anna's sake, that a Ball at Manydown
> was once more in agitation; it is called a Child's Ball, & given by Mrs
> Heathcote to Wm – such was its' beginning at least – but it will probably
> swell into something more … it is to take place between this & twelfth-
> day. (*Letters*, p. 160)

The postscript to her next letter (10 January 1809) suggests that she
attended the festivities: 'The Manydown Ball was a smaller thing than I
expected, but it seems to have made Anna very happy. At *her* age it would
not have done for *me*' (*Letters*, p. 165). If this was the same party that Sir

William recollected, then Jane Austen was acting in a Sheridan play only two years before she began writing *Mansfield Park*. This would seem to be still stronger evidence against the notion that the novel offers an unequivocal condemnation of amateur theatricals.

Jane Austen's artistic development was clearly influenced by the vogue for private theatricals that swept Britain in the late eighteenth and early nineteenth century. Contrary to popular belief, it was not merely as a passive spectator that she was exposed to private theatricals as a young girl. Her plays show that she was actively engaged in the amateur dramatics at Steventon, and her involvement in private theatricals in Kent, Southampton and Winchester confirm an interest that was to be crystallised in the writing of *Mansfield Park*.

2

The Professional Theatre

In 1790 Jane Austen wrote *Love and Freindship*, a parody of the popular heroine-centred, sentimental novel. The cast of characters includes two strolling actors, Philander and Gustavus, who eventually become stars of the London stage. As a final joke, these two fictional characters are transformed into real figures: 'Philander and Gustavus, after having raised their reputation by their performance in the theatrical line in Edinburgh, removed to Covent Garden, where they still exhibit under the assumed names of *Lewis & Quick*' (*MW*, p. 109).

William Thomas ('Gentleman') Lewis (1748–1811) and John Quick (1748–1831) were well-known comic actors of the Covent Garden Company. The roles of Faulkland and Bob Acres in Sheridan's *The Rivals* were created for them, and Quick was also the original Tony Lumpkin in Goldsmith's *She Stoops to Conquer*. 'Gentleman' Lewis earned his appellation for his rendering of refined roles. A fellow actor, G. F. Cooke, called him 'the unrivalled favorite of the comic muse in all that was frolic, gay, humorous, whimsical, and at the same time elegant'.[1] Leigh Hunt considered that 'vulgarity seems impossible to an actor of his manners',[2] and Hazlitt's testimony ranked him high above the comedians of his day: 'gay, fluttering, hare-brained Lewis … all life and fashion, and volubility, and whim; the greatest comic *mannerist* that perhaps ever lived.'[3]

Quick, conversely, was a fine 'low' actor, 'the prince of low comedians'.[4] He was a diminutive man who breathed life into the roles of clowns, rustics and servants before he became famous with his performance of Tony Lumpkin. Unsurpassed in playing old men, he was George III's favourite actor.[5] Hazlitt records that he 'made an excellent self-important, busy, strutting, money-getting citizen; or a crusty old guardian, in a brown suit and a bob-wig'.[6]

By the 1790s Lewis and Quick were among the highest-paid actors in the Covent Garden Company.[7] Austen's reference to this comic duo reveals her knowledge of the contemporary stars of the London stage, and suggests the young girl's eagerness to be included in the theatre-loving clan of her brothers and her cousin Eliza de Feuillide, to whom *Love and Freindship* was dedicated (*MW*, p. 76). The joke is more than merely a glancing and amusing allusion to an immensely popular pair of eighteenth-century comedians: it also reveals a striking and specific interest in the nuanced world of high and low comedy in the late Georgian theatre. This interest was to have a strong influence on Austen's comic vision. As will be demonstrated, her sense of the interplay between genteel characters and low ones was an important part of her awareness of how comedy works.

The first reference to the professional theatre in Austen's letters is a mention of Astley's Theatre in London, in August 1796: 'We are to be at Astley's tonight, which I am glad of' (*Letters*, p. 5). The history of this theatre, and its importance in the growth of the illegitimate stage, has been overlooked by Austen scholars.

Astley's Amphitheatre was an equestrian theatre built on the south side of the river in Lambeth by Philip Astley in 1770.[8] When first opened it was merely an open-air circus ring with covered seats. By 1780 Astley had roofed over the whole of his ring, which was now called the Amphitheatre Riding House. It was renamed the Royal Grove in 1784, when Astley obtained a royal patent, and in 1787, he added 'burletta' to his amphitheatre licence.[9] It was popular not only for equestrian events, but for acrobatics, swordsmanship, musical interludes, songs and dancing. In 1794 the amphitheatre was burnt to the ground. It was rebuilt in the following year with the new name, the Amphitheatre of Arts.[10] In 1796, when the Austens visited Astley's, the entertainment was more elaborate than ever before. Thirty-five new acts were advertised, and, as a special attraction, two Catawba Indian chiefs performed dances and tomahawk exercises.[11] Astley's Amphitheatre survived two fires and lasted until 1841.

As with many of the minor, unpatented London theatres, Astley's circumvented the licensing laws by exploiting the ambiguity of the term 'burletta' and slipping in straight plays among the main entertainments.[12]

The Licensing Act of 1737 confined legitimate theatrical performances to two patent playhouses in London, Drury Lane and Covent Garden. The Act prohibited the performances of plays elsewhere for 'hire, gain or reward' and gave the Lord Chamberlain statutory powers to examine all plays.[13] The monopoly of the patents was broken in 1740, however, by Henry Giffard who re-established his theatre in Goodman's Fields and avoided the 'hire, gain or reward' clause by claiming to charge only for the music and giving the play free. The authorities tolerated Giffard's theatre until David Garrick joined the company in 1741. The unprecedented success of Giffard's new actor ensured that both he and Garrick were offered engagements at Drury Lane, and Goodman's Fields was closed once more.

Giffard had demonstrated that the law could be circumvented. Other theatre managers followed suit and found ways of evading the £50 fine and the threat of the loss of their licence. Samuel Foote sold tickets inviting the public to 'drink a dish of chocolate with him' at noon, and provided entertainments free of charge, thereby inventing the matinee. This led to his obtaining a summer patent for his Little Theatre in the Haymarket in 1766.[14]

Foote's patent was followed by a number of patents for provincial theatres. In London, by the early nineteenth century, the proliferation of illegitimate theatres posed a formidable challenge to the patents. By 1800 there were seven minor theatres offering regular entertainment: Sadler's Wells, Astley's, the Royal Circus, the Royalty in east London, Dibdin's Sans Souci, the King's, Pantheon and the first Lyceum.[15] In 1826 Edward Brayley included eleven minor theatres in his *Historic and Descriptive Accounts of the Theatres of London*, and F. G. Tomlins, in *A Brief View of the English Stage* (1832), listed thirteen minor theatres operating in London.[16]

Astley's was not only visited by Jane Austen. It was also chosen by her as the location for a major turning point in *Emma*.[17] It is Astley's Theatre where Robert Martin meets Harriet and rekindles the love affair between them, thus clearing the way for Emma and Mr Knightley to be united. Scholars have assumed that Austen was referring to the equestrian amphitheatre by Westminster Bridge in Lambeth. But following the success of his amphitheatre, which only operated on a summer licence, Astley opened a new theatre on Wych Street in the Strand in 1806.[18] He called his new theatre the Olympic Pavilion, but it was also known as Astley's Pavilion, the Pavilion Theatre, the Olympic Saloon, and sometimes simply Astley's.[19] The theatre specialised in equestrian events, but Astley also obtained a licence, through the influence of Queen Charlotte, for music and dancing.[20]

According to the testimony of one nineteenth-century theatre historian, though Astley conducted several other establishments, the new Olympic theatre was '*par excellence*, "Astley's" – a name which has become historic'.[21] It was an especially popular place to take children. Astley had built his new theatre from the remains of some old naval prizes that he had bought. The deck of the ship was used for the stage and the floors.[22] The new theatre was built like a playhouse, with a stage, orchestra, side-boxes, galleries and a pit surrounding the ring. It was the largest of London's minor theatres and accommodated three thousand people.[23] In writing about Astley's in his *A Brief View of the English Stage*, Tomlins notes that it was 'a name at which the youthful heart bounds, and the olden one revives. Jeremy Bentham pronounced it to be the genuine English theatre, where John Bull, whatever superior tastes he might ape, was most sincerely at home'.[24]

Jane Austen was not absolutely precise about dates in *Emma*: the theatre visit takes place some time in late summer and Harriet marries Martin shortly afterwards, in late September. This opens up the possibility of the Astley's reference being to either the summer amphitheatre in Lambeth or the winter Olympic house off Drury Lane. Strictly speaking, the summer season commenced on Easter Monday and closed about the end of September or the beginning of October.[25] Given that the Austens patronised the Lambeth Amphitheatre, Jane may well have intended the same theatre. On the other hand, the genteel John Knightleys visit Astley's as a treat for their young boys, and Harriet, on quitting their box, is made uneasy by the size of the crowds. This suggests the superior Olympic Pavilion.[26] The Lambeth Amphitheatre also had its own separate entrance for the boxes and the pit, with the gallery entrance fifty yards down the road, so it would be more likely that Harriet encountered large crowds at the Olympic.[27]

Nevertheless, whichever of Astley's playhouses Austen intended when she was writing *Emma* in 1813, the allusion is of considerable interest, as the long-standing battle between the minor theatres and the patents had once again flared up that year, with the name 'Astley's' at the centre of controversy. When Elliston opened up Astley's in 1813 with the provocative name 'Little Drury Lane Theatre', he was almost immediately forced to close. He was able to reopen the theatre by reverting to its old name. In 1812 Astley had sold his theatre and licence to Robert Elliston for £2800.[28] Almost as soon as the management passed into Elliston's hands, he remodelled the playhouse in the hope of attracting a superior type of audience. He introduced a mixed programme of farce, pantomime and melodrama, all of course concealed under the term 'burletta'. Though many of the minor theatres circumvented the law by similar methods, none had dared to do so in the direct vicinity of the patents. Perhaps Austen was sympathetic to Elliston's crusade to compete against the patents, for he was one of her favourite actors, and, as we will see, she followed his fortunes throughout his career.

Astley's was known for its socially diverse audience. It was 'a popular place of amusement for all classes'.[29] A friendly and unpretentious theatre, its tickets were priced well below those of the patents.[30] The spectacle that it offered clearly appealed to families, and to people of all classes, much as the West End musical attracts thousands of people today. Austen had no compunction about visiting the minor theatres when she stayed in London, and her reference to Astley's in *Emma* may indeed have been a gesture in support of them in their long battle to break the monopoly of the patents.

Given Jane Austen's scrupulous sense of class and realism, and the particular concern in *Emma* with fine discriminations within social hierarchies, it is by no means fanciful to attach considerable weight to her choice of Astley's for the reconciliation between Harriet and Robert Martin. Precisely because of its status as a minor, illegitimate theatre, it was a place where a yeoman farmer and a girl who is without rank (carrying the 'stain of illegitimacy', we are reminded in the same chapter) could mingle freely with the gentry.

Austen does mention the patented theatres in her other novels. In *Sense and Sensibility*, Willoughby 'ran against Sir John Middleton' in the lobby of Drury Lane Theatre, where he hears that Marianne Dashwood is seriously ill at Cleveland. In *Pride and Prejudice* Lydia Bennet, in complete disregard to the disgrace that she has brought on the family by her elopement, can only prattle: 'To be sure London was rather thin, but however the Little Theatre was open' (*PP*, p. 319). Lydia's elopement takes place in August, and, as Austen was aware, the 'Little Theatre' in the Haymarket was the only house licensed to produce regular drama during the summer season. This is a fine example of Austen's scrupulous sense of realism working in conjunction with her knowledge of the London theatre world. It is also worth noting that her favourite niece, Fanny Knight, with whom she often went to the theatre, was particularly fond of the 'little' theatre in the Haymarket, as opposed to the vast auditoriums at Covent Garden and Drury Lane. In her unpublished diaries Fanny complained that 'Drury Lane is too immense' and that she preferred 'the dear enchanting Haymarket.'[31]

There is only one other mention of playgoing in *Pride and Prejudice*, a vague reference to an 'evening at one of the theatres' in which Elizabeth Bennet and Mrs Gardiner talked over intimate family matters in what was presumably a theatre box, while the rest of the party watched the action on the stage (*PP*, pp. 152–54). In *Persuasion*, Austen includes only a few vague references to the Theatre Royal on Orchard Street in Bath.[32] However, she uses the same theatre in *Northanger Abbey* to structure an important plot link between John Thorpe and General Tilney. It is at the theatre that Thorpe, 'who was never in the same part of the house for ten minutes together' (*NA*, p. 95), falsely boasts to General Tilney that Catherine is the heiress to the Allen fortune, thus encouraging the General's plan to invite her to Northanger Abbey.

In *Sense and Sensibility*, *Northanger Abbey* and *Emma* Jane Austen uses the forum of the public theatre to implement crucial plot developments. In this, she was influenced by Fanny Burney, whose novels about the London *ton* used the playhouses as important meeting grounds for the advancement of plot lines. For example, in *Evelina* the heroine first attends Drury Lane to see Garrick in *The Suspicious Husband* and is later reunited with Lord Orville at a performance of Congreve's *Love for Love*. Here she is subjected to impertinent remarks by the fop Lovel, who compares her to the character of Miss Prue, an ignorant rustic young hoyden, a role made famous by the comic actress Frances Abington.[33] As

Burney and Austen demonstrate in their novels, the public theatres provided an arena for the exchange of news and gossip.

In *Northanger Abbey* there is a special irony at play, for Austen's novel about an ingenue's entrance into Bath society self-consciously mirrors Burney's *Evelina: or The History of a Young Lady's Entrance into the World*. In one of the more subtle allusions to *Evelina*, Catherine quotes from Congreve's *Love for Love* when she tells John Thorpe that she hates the idea of 'one great fortune looking out for another' (*NA*, p. 124). Like Evelina, Catherine delights in going to the play, though she has been told that the Theatre Royal Bath is 'quite horrid' compared to the London stage (*NA*, p. 92).

Northanger Abbey's status as a burlesque Gothic novel has unwittingly deflected attention away from Austen's parody of the heroine-centred sentimental novel popularised by female writers like Burney and Edgeworth. Instead of London's *beau monde*, unfamiliar terrain to Austen, the resort city of Bath becomes her microcosm of fashionable high society. *Northanger Abbey* was written in 1798–99. As Jane Austen and her mother were at Bath during the later part of 1797 visiting the Leigh-Perrots, her account could well have been based on actual experience.

In 1799 Jane Austen revisited Bath, staying at Queen Square with her brother Edward Knight. This visit included a trip to the Theatre Royal: 'The Play on Saturday is I *hope* to conclude our gaieties here, for nothing but a lengthened stay will make it otherwise' (*Letters*, p. 47). She does not name the play, but the account in the *Bath Herald and Reporter* for 29 June 1799 reveals that she saw Kotzebue's drama *The Birth-Day* and 'The pleasing spectacle of Blue-Beard' on that occasion. In the eyes of the Bath newspapers, the new Kotzebue comedy was considered to be a vast improvement on his previous works, which were notable for their immorality:

> If the German Author has justly drawn down censure for the immorality of his productions for the stage, this may be considered as expiatory – this may be accepted as his *amende honoyrable* [*sic*]; it is certainly throughout unexceptionable, calculated to promote the best interest of

virtue, and the purest principles of benevolence: and though written in the style of Sterne, it possesses humour without a single broad Shandyism.[34]

James Boaden, a professed admirer of Kotzebue, described the play as 'the *naval* pendant to the *military* Toby and Trim', and thought it contained 'one of the best delineations of human nature coloured by profession'.[35]

The Birth-Day, a comedy in three acts, was translated from Kotzebue's play *Reconciliation*, and adapted for the English stage by Thomas Dibdin (1771–1841).[36] The plot is centred on a feud in a Bertram family. Twin brothers, estranged over a law suit, are finally reconciled on their sixty-third birthday by the efforts of their children, cousins who are in love with each other. The heroine, Emma Bertram, is devoted to her father and has vowed never to marry until she is finally persuaded by her cousin: 'But if a man could be found, who would bestow on your father a quiet old age, free from every sorrow; who, far from robbing the father of a good daughter, would weave the garland of love round three hearts, who would live under his roof, and multiply your joys, by reconciling your father and your uncle.'[37]

Two of the best comic characters in *The Birth-Day* are a boatswain, Jack Junk, and a meddling housekeeper, Mrs Moral, who has taken over Captain Bertram's household and has contributed to the family estrangement for her own devious means.[38] *Mansfield Park*, in which a different Kotzebue adaptation is staged, shares with this other Kotzebue play not only the family name Bertram but also similar comic stereotypes in the persons of the bullying, interfering Mrs Norris and the rum-drinking, oath-swearing Mr Price.[39]

In May 1801 Jane Austen moved more permanently to Bath to live with her parents. She stayed until July 1806. Owing to the absence of letters during this time, very little is known of her theatrical activities there.[40] Her residence in Bath coincided, however, with one of the most prosperous and exciting times in the history of the local stage. The period from 1790 to the opening of the new theatre in Beaufort Square in 1805 marked an unprecedented time of 'prosperity, of brilliancy and of progress.'[41]

Bath was a fashionable resort town and was able to support a theatre of considerable standing for the society people who flocked there to take the waters. The theatre was run in tandem with the Bristol playhouse and was regarded as one of the best in the country. Provincial theatres in the Georgian era were not merely seasonal or summer playhouses, playing in the London off-season, but year-round operations. Their importance to the life and culture of their cities is suggested in the increasing numbers of royal patents granted by 1800.[42] The Bath theatre had been patented in 1768, becoming the first Theatre Royal of the English provinces.[43]

Outside London, Bath was one of the most important theatres, maintaining a regular company which was supplemented by London stars.[44] Many of the London stars had indeed cut their teeth in the Orchard Street playhouse. It was described variously as 'a dramatic nursery for the London stage' and a 'probationary school of the drama to the London stage'.[45] Mrs Siddons had begun her career there in 1778, and retained such an affection and loyalty to the theatre that she often returned during the summer seasons.[46]

One of the theatre's main assets was Robert William Elliston (1774–1831). Intended for the church, the young Elliston ran away to Bath and made his first appearance in Orchard Street in 1793.[47] Remarkably, he stayed until 1804, although 'by permission of the Bath manager' he was loaned to the London theatres, where he played once a fortnight, reinforcing the already strong links between the London and Bath playhouses. One of the reasons why Elliston refused to leave Bath, despite lucrative offers from both Drury Lane and Covent Garden, was his marriage. In 1796 he eloped with and married Elizabeth Rundall, a dance teacher, who, despite her husband's success, continued her occupation.[48]

Despite Sheridan's efforts to hire him, Elliston refused a permanent engagement at Drury Lane. His new wife had recently gone into partnership running a dance and deportment academy, and Elliston enjoyed his position as Bath's star attraction. Even when he was finally lured to Drury Lane in 1804, Mrs Elliston remained in Bath. Jane Austen was aware of the unusual arrangements of Elliston's private life. In February 1807, she shared with Cassandra some Bath gossip gleaned from her Aunt

Leigh-Perrot: 'Elliston, she tells us has just succeeded to a considerable fortune on the death of an Uncle. I would not have it enough to take *him* from the Stage; *she* should quit her business, & live with him in London' (*Letters*, p. 122). This remark, which has not hitherto drawn comment from Austen scholars, demonstrates her loyalty to Elliston, both in his professional and his private life. Even though Elliston was now based in London, Austen continued to take an interest in him, and she clearly disapproved of his wife's determination to remain with her academy in Bath.

Elliston's last engagement on the Bath stage, before leaving for London, was as Rolla in Sheridan's adaptation of Kotzebue's *Pizarro*.[49] Rolla was not a surprising choice for Elliston. His performance of the noble, virtuous warrior was one of his most acclaimed tragic roles. It was also the role that he played for his Drury Lane debut, later that year, when he took over from Kemble.[50]

Another Kotzebue adaptation, *Lovers' Vows*, was performed at least seventeen times in Bath from 1801 to 1806.[51] This suggests that Austen was familiar with the play long before she used it in *Mansfield Park*. Elliston played the part of Frederick. Kotzebue adaptations such as *The Birth-Day*, *Pizarro*, *The Stranger* and *Lovers' Vows* continued to flourish at Bath, despite objections by the *Anti-Jacobin Review* to 'the filthy effusions of this German dunce'.[52] In September 1801 Siddons played Elvira in *Pizarro* alongside Elliston at the Orchard Street Theatre.[53] Elvira, in particular, incited vicious attacks by the *Anti-Jacobin Review* which, with typically excessive rhetoric, described her as one of the most reprehensible characters that had ever been suffered to disgrace the stage. Such charges cut no ice with playgoers, who flocked to the Bath theatre to see Siddons as Pizarro's dignified paramour.

Another comment suggesting that the Austens were theatregoers while living in Bath is to be found in a letter written by Jane's mother to her daughter-in-law Mary Austen: 'Cooke, I dare say will have as full houses tonight and Saturday, as he had on Tuesday'.[54] George Frederick Cooke (1756–1811) was the name of the Covent Garden actor whose brilliance as a tragic actor was overshadowed by his notorious drinking problem. He was one of the great actors of the English stage, the hero of Edmund Kean. After Cooke's death brought on by hardened drinking,

Kean arranged for his remains to be removed to a better location, and kept the bone of the forefinger of his right hand as a sacred relic.[55] Cooke's reputation as a drunkard has obscured his acting abilities. His performances of Richard III and Iago were legendary, but he was considered to be an unreliable and erratic actor. One of his critics, to Cooke's great mortification, described him in the following terms: 'No two men, however different they may be, can be more at variance than George Cooke sober and George Cooke in a state of inebriety.'[56] At Covent Garden in 1803, while playing Sir Archy MacSarcasm in *Love à la Mode*, Cooke was so drunk that he was hissed off stage and the curtain dropped.

Like Kean and Siddons, Cooke started his career as a provincial actor before he became famous on the London stage.[57] In December 1801 Cooke returned to Bath where he played Richard III, Shylock and Sir Archy MacSarcasm. In that season, the same time that Mrs Austen was writing of him, he also played Iago to Elliston's Othello. Cooke wrote in his journal: 'I received the greatest applause and approbation from the audiences.'[58]

The last five seasons at the Orchard Street Theatre before the opening of the new playhouse in 1805 saw the introduction of several London actors onto the Bath stage. The appearance of such London stars gave prominence to the playhouse, and, coupled with the allure of Elliston, ensured its reputation as a theatre of the highest standing. Austen was fortunate in residing in Bath at a time when the theatre was in 'the zenith of its glory',[59] and where she could see her favourite actor performing all the major roles. Elliston's most famous roles in comedy were Charles Surface, Doricourt, Ranger, Benedick, Marlow, Lord Ogleby, Captain Absolute, Lord Townley and Dr Pangloss. In tragedy, Hamlet, Macbeth, Othello, Douglas, the Stranger, Orestes and Rolla were just a few of the characters that her 'best Elliston' made his own.[60]

Elliston was unusual in being a player of tragic and comic parts. Leigh Hunt declared Elliston 'the only genius that has approached that great actor [Garrick] in universality of imitation'. Though Hunt preferred him in comedy, he described him as 'the best lover on the stage both in tragedy and comedy'.[61] Others praised his diversity. Byron said that he could conceive nothing better than Elliston in gentlemanly comedy and in some parts of tragedy.[62] His obituary stated that 'Elliston was undoubtedly the most versatile actor of his day'.[63] Even William Oxberry's disparaging memoir conceded that 'Mr Elliston is the best versatile actor we have ever seen'.[64] Charles Lamb honoured him with high praise in his 'Ellistonia': 'wherever Elliston walked, sate, or stood still, there was the theatre'.[65]

Elliston finally moved on to the London stage, where Austen saw him perform. She complained, however, of the falling standards of Elliston's acting when she saw him in London. Austen's observations on his demise reveal her familiarity with his work from the Bath years. With the majority of Austen's letters from this time missing, destroyed after her death, much has been lost, for, as her London letters reveal, she was a discerning and perceptive critic of the drama.

When Austen left Bath in 1806 to live with Frank Austen and his wife, Mary, in Southampton, she was forced to make do with the French Street Theatre, a far cry from Bath's Theatre Royal. It was also during the first few months at Southampton that Austen wrote her two little playlets on baby-care. Frank Austen's young wife was pregnant with their first child, and writing the plays proved a welcome diversion during the winter evenings. Austen also attended the public theatre in Southampton. In her list of expenses for 1807 she noted that she had spent 17s. 9d. for water parties and plays during that year.[66]

The French Street Theatre in Southampton was served mainly by provincial companies, but stars from the London stage made occasional visits. Sarah Siddons and Dora Jordan made visits of a few days in 1802 and 1803.[67] The less talented Kemble brother, Charles Kemble, and his wife played there for a few nights in August 1808.[68] John Bannister (1760–1836), one of the most popular comedians of the London stage, was also well known to the provinces. His *Memoirs* record that he played the provinces during the summer months from 1797 to 1812. In the course of his career he took on the roles of some 425 characters.[69]

Although there is no record by Jane Austen of the plays that she saw at the French Street theatre, her niece recorded one of the performances that she attended with her two aunts. In September 1807 Edward Knight and his family visited his mother and sisters in Southampton. Austen's attachment to her niece Fanny Knight is revealed in her description of her as 'almost another sister' (*Letters*, p. 144). Austen had amused her niece with private theatricals in 1805, and when Fanny came to stay they visited the playhouse. Fanny recorded in her journal that on 14 September 1807 the party saw John Bannister in *The Way to Keep Him* and the musical adaptation of Kotzebue's *Of Age Tomorrow* for his benefit.[70]

Bannister's role in Arthur Murphy's comedy *The Way to Keep Him* was Sir Bashful Constant, a man of fashion in possession of the shameful secret that he is in love with his own wife, his '*Cara Sposa*'.[71] Jane Austen employed this fashionable Italianism to brilliant effect in *Emma*. For Emma, there is no clearer mark of Mrs Elton's vulgarity than her references to her husband as 'Mr E.' and 'my *caro sposo*': 'A little upstart, vulgar being, with her Mr E., and her *caro sposo*, and her resources, and all her airs of pert pretension and under-bred finery' (*E*, p. 279). Scholars have debated the source of Austen's use of the phrase, but no one has noticed its presence in Murphy's comedy, where, spoken by the coxcomb Sir Brilliant Fashion, it surely got a laugh in the theatre.

Bannister was best known for his low roles. Leigh Hunt claimed that 'no actor equals him in the character of a sailor'.[72] The sailor, Jack Junk, in Thomas Dibdin's adaptation of Kotzebue's *The Birth-Day* was one of his best-loved roles. Bannister was also praised for his ability to transform himself into many different roles: 'The greatest comedians have thought themselves happy in understanding one or two characters, but what shall we say of Bannister, who in one night personates six, and with such felicity that by the greatest part of the audience he is sometimes taken for some unknown actor?'[73] Leigh Hunt was thinking, in particular, of *A Bold Stroke for a Wife*, where Bannister transmigrated into five different characters. However the comic after-piece, *Of Age Tomorrow*, that Austen saw in Southampton was also used as a vehicle for Bannister's versatility.

Thomas Dibdin adapted *Of Age Tomorrow* from Kotzebue's *Der Wildfang*. Dibdin had already adapted Kotzebue's *The Birth-Day* and *The Horse and Widow*.[74] Michael Kelly, in his *Reminiscences*, records that Bannister persuaded Kelly and Dibdin to adapt *Der Wildfang* for Drury Lane.[75] Kelly describes *Of Age Tomorrow* as a great favourite. The ballad 'No, my love, no', according to Kelly, was 'the most popular song of the day … not only to be found on every piano-forte, but also to be heard in every street'.[76]

Dibdin's musical farce showed Bannister adopting three different disguises in his endeavours to woo his lover, Sophia, who is guarded by a dowager aunt, Lady Brumback, who stands to lose half her fortune if her niece marries. Bannister's disguise as Fritz the *frizeur* was extremely popular, especially for his comic rendering of a story of his master breaking his leg over a bannister, to which Lady Brumback remarks, 'Poor fellow! I wish there were no Bannisters in the world'.[77] Kelly wrote: 'Bannister's personification of the Hair Dresser, was excellent; had he served a seven years' apprenticeship to the trade, he could not have been more *au fait* in it, nor have handled the comb, curling irons and powder puff, more skillfully'.[78] Bannister's transformations into a Swiss soldier and a (cross-dressed) abandoned mother of a foundling child showed his powers of imitation at their very best.[79]

The appearance of London stars at the French Street theatre may be attributed to the rising popularity of Southampton as a spa town. Charles Dibdin, the Southampton-born dramatist,[80] partly ascribed this transformation to the increasing number of 'genteel families who have made it their residence', and also to the tourists who came to Southampton for the sea-bathing.[81] Though the theatre had acquired a poor reputation by the end of the eighteenth century, a new playhouse was opened in July 1803 by one John Collins.[82]

The French Street theatre also housed amateur theatricals from the local grammar school. The school's headmaster, George Whittaker, was passionate about the theatre and encouraged his pupils to stage amateur theatricals for charitable purposes. In 1807 Home's famous tragedy *Douglas* was acted for the benefit of British prisoners of war in France, to 'an uncommonly crowded house'.[83] In *Mansfield Park*, Tom Bertram's comic remarks about the efficacy of schoolboys reciting the part of young Norval in *Douglas* may have been an echo to such performances lingering in Jane Austen's memory of amateur theatricals.

Her comments a year later, in 1808, about the playhouse suggest that she had taken a dislike to its shabbiness: '*Our* Brother [James] we may perhaps see in the course of a few days – & we mean to take the opportunity of his help, to go one night to the play. Martha ought to see the inside of the Theatre once while she lives in Southampton, & I think she will hardly wish to take a second veiw [sic]' (*Letters*, p. 155).

Another family descendant, Richard Arthur Leigh, observed that while Jane Austen was living in Southampton she became friendly with a Mr Valentine Fitzhugh, whose sister-in-law was an ardent admirer of Mrs Siddons who would assist her in dressing and make-up for her shows.[84] There is, however, no record of any conversation that Austen might have had with Fitzhugh about the theatre, which is hardly surprising given that he was so deaf 'he could not hear a Canon, were it fired close to him' (*Letters*, p. 160).

During the Bath and Southampton years Austen's writing was put on hold. She had produced three full-length novels before leaving Steventon in 1801, and began working on them again in 1809. Biographers and critics have been puzzled by Austen's eight-year silence, attributing it to her evident unhappiness and displacement. But perhaps Bath and Southampton simply had more to offer in the way of public diversions and amusements than Hampshire and Kent. At Chawton Austen turned her mind once more to her novels and, with the help and encouragement of her brother Henry, began to think about publication. When Jane spent time in London with Henry, negotiating with publishers, she rarely missed a chance to visit the London theatres.

Had the majority of Jane Austen's letters not been destroyed after her death in 1817, we would have had a much more detailed sense of her passion for the theatre. But there is enough evidence in the few surviving letters to suggest that she was utterly familiar with contemporary actors and the range and repertoire of the theatres. Her taste was eclectic; she enjoyed farces, musical comedy and pantomime, considered to be 'low' drama, as much as she enjoyed Shakespeare, Colman and Garrick.

3

Plays and Actors

The year 1808 was a particularly busy one for Jane Austen. She spent most of the time travelling between her various brothers and family friends. After playing Mrs Candour in *The School for Scandal* at the Manydown Twelfth Night party, she visited the Fowles at Kintbury and in May she visited Henry and Eliza Austen at 16 Michael Place in Brompton. The latter two, whose love of the theatre went back to the home theatricals at Steventon, were delighted to live in close proximity to several famous London stars. The actress and singer Jane Pope lived next door to them at No. 17. She had been the original Mrs Candour in *The School for Scandal*, playing the part until she was in her sixties. By this time, she was the only member of the original cast left on the stage.[1] Having herself played the part of Mrs Candour earlier that year, Jane Austen must have been amused to be living next door to the actress who had inspired the original role.

At No. 15 Michael Place was Elizabeth Billington, the celebrated soprano singer. John Liston the comedian lived at No. 21.[2] Jane Austen stayed until July, enjoying the rounds of dinner-parties, theatre trips and concerts arranged by Henry and Eliza. Henry Austen owned his own box at one of the illegitimate theatres, the Pantheon in Oxford Street.[3] The Pantheon had originally opened in 1772 as a place of assembly for masquerades and concerts, which were all the rage in the 1770s.[4] Boswell and Dr Johnson visited and admired the magnificent building in 1772, and Fanny Burney distilled her own experience of the new Pantheon into *Evelina*; her heroine is 'extremely struck with the beauty of the building' when she is taken to a concert there.[5]

The Pantheon was converted into an opera house in 1791 but was destroyed by fire a year later, losing its hope of a royal patent to the King's

Theatre in the Haymarket. Thereafter the Pantheon was rebuilt and resumed its original function as a place of concerts and masquerades until 1812, when it reopened as the Pantheon Theatre, staging the usual mixed bill of burlettas and ballet to circumvent the licensing law.

Henry Austen's patronage of minor playhouses such as the Pantheon and the Lyceum, as well as the legitimate patent houses, suggests his unflagging interest in the theatre. Like his sister, he had no compunction about supporting the minor theatres. Unlike his brother James, who lost interest in the theatre after he was ordained, Henry's passion for the theatre carried on into maturity; and, whenever Jane and Cassandra were in town, he was to be found arranging seats at the various London theatres. Although there are few surviving letters to fill in the details of Jane's activities at this time (the letters stop altogether from 26 July 1809 until 18 April 1811), she surely took advantage of Henry's and Eliza's hospitality as she did in the following years. Starting at the latter date, there is a sufficient amount of information to provide a fair estimate of her theatrical activities up to 28 November 1814, the last time she is known to have attended a theatre.

In order to be available for the proof-reading of *Sense and Sensibility*, she went to London in April 1811, staying with Henry and Eliza at their new home in Sloane Street. Shortly after her arrival she expressed a desire to see Shakespeare's *King John* at Covent Garden. In the meantime, she sacrificed a trip to the Lyceum, nursing a cold at home, in the hope of recovering for the Saturday excursion to Covent Garden:

> To night I might have been at the Play, Henry had kindly planned our going together to the Lyceum, but I have a cold which I should not like to make worse before Saturday … [Later on Saturday] Our first object to day was Henrietta St to consult with Henry, in consequence of a very unlucky change of the Play for this very night – Hamlet instead of King John – & we are to go on Monday to Macbeth, instead, but it is a disappointment to us both. (*Letters*, pp. 180–81)

Her preference for *King John* over *Hamlet* may seem curious by modern standards, but can be explained by one of the intrinsic features of Georgian theatre: the orientation of the play towards the star actor in the lead role. Her disappointment in the 'unlucky change' of programme from 'Hamlet instead of King John' is accounted for in her next letter to Cassandra:

> I have no chance of seeing Mrs Siddons. – She *did* act on Monday, but as Henry was told by the Boxkeeper that he did not think she would, the places, & all thought of it, were given up. I should particularly have liked seeing her in Constance, & could swear at her with little effort for disappointing me. (*Letters*, p. 184)

It was not so much *King John* that Austen wanted to see as Siddons in one of her most celebrated roles: Queen Constance, the quintessential portrait of a tragic mother. In the words of her biographer and friend, Thomas Campbell, Siddons was 'the imbodied image of maternal love and intrepidity; of wronged and righteous feeling; of proud grief and majestic desolation'.[6] Siddons's own remarks on this 'life-exhausting' role, and the 'mental and physical' difficulties arising from the requirements of playing Constance provide a striking testimony to her all-consuming passion and commitment to the part. Siddons records:

> Whenever I was called upon to personate the character of *Constance*, I never, from the beginning of the play to the end of my part in it, once suffered my dressing-room door to be closed, in order that my attention might be constantly fixed on those distressing events which, by this means, I could plainly hear going on upon the stage, the terrible effects of which progress were to be represented by me.[7]

Though her part was brief – she appeared in just two acts – Siddons's impassioned interpretation was acclaimed. Constance's famously eloquent speeches and frenzied lamentations for her dead boy were newly rendered by Siddons, for she didn't 'rant' and produce the effects of noisy grief but was stunningly understated, showing grief 'tempered and broken', as Leigh Hunt put it.[8] While admitting that *King John* was 'not written with the utmost power of Shakespeare', Hunt nevertheless viewed the play as a brilliant vehicle for Siddons's consummate tragic powers.[9] Her biographer, Thomas Campbell, also claimed that Siddons's single-handedly resuscitated the play, winning over the public to 'feel the tragedy worth seeing for the sake of *Constance* alone'.[10]

Jane Austen certainly felt that 'Constance' was worth the price of a ticket. Though Henry Austen was misinformed by the box-keeper and Siddons had indeed appeared in *Macbeth* on Monday (22 April), Jane was less sorry to have missed her in Lady Macbeth than in Constance, which may imply that she had previously seen her in *Macbeth*. Sarah Siddons acted Lady Macbeth eight times and Constance five times that 1811–12 season, before retiring from the London stage, so perhaps Jane finally got her wish.[11]

On Saturday (20 April) the party went instead to the Lyceum Theatre in the Strand, where the Drury Lane company had taken their patent after the fire in 1809.[12] They saw a revival of Isaac Bickerstaffe's *The Hypocrite*.

> We *did* go to the play after all on Saturday, we went to the Lyceum, & saw the Hypocrite, an old play taken from Moliere's *Tartuffe*, & were well entertained. Dowton & Mathews were the good actors. Mrs Edwin was the Heroine – & her performance is just what it used to be. (*Letters*, p. 184)

In *The Hypocrite*, the roles of Maw-Worm, an ignorant zealot, and the religious and moral hypocrite Dr Cantwell were acted by the renowned comic actors Charles Mathews (1776–1835), and William Dowton (1764–1851), singled out by Jane Austen for praise. Dowton was famous for his roles as Dr Cantwell, Sir Oliver Premium and Sir Anthony Absolute.[13] Leigh Hunt described his performance in the *Hypocrite* as 'one of the few perfect pieces of acting on the stage'.[14]

The great comic actor Charles Mathews was also a favourite of Hunt's: 'an actor of whom it is difficult to say whether his characters belong most to him or he to his characters'.[15] Mathews was so tall and thin that he was nicknamed 'Stick'; when his manager Tate Wilkinson first saw him he called him a 'Maypole', told him he was too tall for low comedy and quipped that 'one hiss would blow him off the stage'.[16]

Mathews himself described the success of *The Hypocrite* at the Lyceum, and recorded his experiment in adding an extra fanatical speech for Maw-Worm, thus breaking the rule of his 'immortal instructor, who says "Let your clowns say no more than is set down for them". His experiment worked, and the reviews were favourable: 'It was an admirable representation of "Praise God Barebones", an exact portraiture of one of those ignorant enthusiasts who lose sight of all good while they are vainly hunting after an ideal perfectibility.'[17] Jane Austen dearly loved a fool – in *Pride and Prejudice* she portrayed her own obsequious hypocrite and ignorant enthusiast, in Mr Collins and Mary Bennet.

Elizabeth Edwin (1771–1854), the wife of the actor John Edwin, performed the part of Charlotte, the archetypal witty heroine, for which she was famous.[18] The Austen sisters were clearly familiar with Mrs Edwin's acting style. She had played at Bath for many years, including the time that the Austens lived there, and she was also a favourite of the Southampton theatre, where the sisters may have seen her perform.[19]

Elizabeth Edwin was one of many actors from the provinces who had begun her career as a child actor in a company of strolling players. She was the leading actress at Wargrave at the Earl of Barrymore's private theatricals.[20] She was often (unfairly) compared to the great Dora Jordan, whose equal she never was, though they played the same comic roles. Jane Austen's ambiguous comment about Edwin suggests that she did not rate her as highly as Dowton and Mathews, whom she regarded as the 'good actors' in *The Hypocrite*. Oxberry's 1826 memoir observed that although Edwin was 'an accomplished artist … she has little, if any, genius – and is a decided mannerist'.[21] She was an 'artificial' actress who betrayed the fact that she was performing:

> Though we admired what she did, she never carried us with her. We knew that we were at a display of art, and never felt for a moment the illusion of its being a natural scene.[22]

The preoccupation with the play as a vehicle for the star actor, popularly called 'the possession of parts', went hand-in-hand with the theatre's proclivity towards an established repertory.[23] It was common to see the same actor in a favourite role year in, year out. Dora Jordan's Rosalind and Little Pickle, both of them 'breeches' roles, were performed successfully throughout her long career. Siddons's Lady Macbeth and Constance were staples of her repertory throughout her career, and, even after her retirement, they were the subject of comparison with other performances. The tradition of an actor's interpretation of a classic role, which still survives today, was an integral part of an individual play's appeal. Critics and the public would revel in the particularities of individual performances, and they would eagerly anticipate a new performance of a favourite role, though innovations by actors were by no means a guarantee of audience approbation.

In the early autumn of 1813, Jane Austen set out for Godmersham, stopping on the way in London, where she stayed with her brother Henry in his quarters over his bank at Henrietta Street, Covent Garden. On the night of 14 September, the party went by coach to the Lyceum Theatre, where they had a private box on the stage. As soon as the rebuilt Drury Lane had opened its doors to the public, the Lyceum had no choice but to revert to musical drama. The Austens saw three musical pieces. The first was *The Boarding House: or Five Hours at Brighton*; the second, a musical farce called *The Beehive*; and the last *Don Juan: or The Libertine Destroyed*, a pantomime based on Thomas Shadwell's *The Libertine*. Once again, Jane Austen's reflections on the plays were shared with Cassandra:

> I talked to Henry at the Play last night. We were in a private Box – Mr Spencer's – Which made it much more pleasant. The Box is directly on the Stage. One is infinitely less fatigued than in the common way … Fanny & the two little girls are gone to take Places for tonight at Covent Garden; Clandestine Marriage & *Midas*. The latter will be a fine show for L. & M. – They revelled last night in 'Don Juan', whom we left in Hell at half-past eleven … We had Scaremouch & a Ghost – and were delighted; I speak of *them*; *my* delight was very tranquil, & the rest of us were sober-minded. Don Juan was the last of 3 musical things; – Five hours at Brighton, in 3 acts – of which one was over before we arrived, none the worse – & The Beehive, rather less flat & trumpery. (*Letters*, pp. 218–19)

The Beehive was an adaptation of Kotzebue's comedy *Das Posthaus in Treuenbrietzen*. Two lovers who have never met, but who are betrothed to one another, fall in love under assumed names. The young man discovers the ruse first and introduces his friend as himself; meanwhile the heroine, Miss Fairfax, in retaliation pretends to fall in love with the best friend. In the light of *Emma*, the conjunction of name and plot-twist is striking.

Austen clearly preferred the Kotzebue comedy to *Five Hours at Brighton*, a low comedy set in a seaside boarding house. Her 'delight' in *Don Juan* is properly amended to 'tranquil delight' for the sake of the upright Cassandra. Byron had also seen the pantomime, in which the famous Grimaldi played Scaramouch, to which he alludes in his first stanza of *Don Juan*:

> We all have seen him, in the pantomime,
> Sent to the devil somewhat ere his time.[24]

Scaramouch was one of Grimaldi's oldest and most frequently revived parts.

In her letter to Cassandra, Jane gives her usual precise details of the theatre visit, even down to the private box, 'directly on the stage'. Again, the Austens showed their support for the minor theatres, and Henry is arranging trips to the Lyceum. Perhaps he had an arrangement with his friend Mr Spencer to share each other's boxes at the minor theatres. Being seated in a box certainly meant that Jane could indulge in intimate discussion with Henry – as Elizabeth Bennet does with Mrs Gardiner in *Pride and Prejudice*.[25]

As planned, the very next night the party went to Covent Garden Theatre, where they had 'very good places in the Box next the stage box – front and second row; the three old ones behind of course'.[26] They sat in Covent Garden's new theatre boxes, presumably in full consciousness that, at the opening of the new theatre, riots had been occasioned by the extra number of private and dress boxes.[27] The parson and poet George Crabbe and his wife were in London and Jane Austen joked about seeing the versifying vicar at the playhouse, particularly as the 'boxes were fitted up with crimson velvet' (*Letters*, pp. 220–21). The remark skilfully combines an allusion to Crabbe's *Gentleman Farmer*, 'In full festoons the crimson curtains fell',[28] with detailed observation of the lavish fittings of the new Covent Garden Theatre, recently reopened after the fire of 1809.

Edward Brayley's account of the grand new playhouse also singled out the 'crimson-covered seats',[29] and described the grand staircase leading to the boxes, and the ante-room with its yellow-marble statue of Shakespeare.

The Austens saw *The Clandestine Marriage* by David Garrick and George Colman the Elder, and *Midas: an English Burletta* by Kane O'Hara, a parody of the Italian comic opera.[30] One of the attractions was to see Mr Terry, who had recently taken over the role of Lord Ogleby in *The Clandestine Marriage*.

> The new Mr Terry was Ld Ogleby, & Henry thinks he may do; but there was no acting more than moderate; & I was as much amused by the remembrances connected with Midas as with any part of it. The girls were very much delighted but still prefer Don Juan – & I must say I have seen nobody on the stage who has been a more interesting Character than that compound of Cruelty & Lust. (*Letters*, p. 221)

Daniel Terry (1780–1829) had made his debut at Covent Garden on 8 September, just a few days before Jane Austen saw him.[31] Sir Walter Scott was a great friend and admirer of Terry (who adapted several of the Waverley novels for the stage),[32] and claimed that he was an excellent actor who could act everything except lovers, fine gentlemen and operatic heroes. Scott observed that 'his old men in comedy particularly are the finest I ever saw'.[33] Henry Austen showed a little more tolerance than his sister in allowing Mr Terry teething troubles in the role of one of the most celebrated old men of eighteenth-century comedy.

Henry Austen's faith in Terry's capacity to grow into a beloved role reflects the performer-oriented tendency of the age. But Jane's powerful and striking description of *Don Juan* is a far less typical response. Here a more discerning and discriminating voice prevails. Rather than the performer being the main focus of interest, she is responding to the perverse appeal of the character beneath the actor. The famous blackguard was still obviously on her mind, belying her earlier insistence upon 'tranquil delight' and 'sober-mindedness'.

Jane Austen's reference to *Midas* confirms that she had seen this entertainment at an earlier date. Garrick and Colman's brilliant comedy *The Clandestine Marriage* had also been known to her for a long time. The title appears as a phrase in one of her early works, *Love and Freindship*, and, as will be seen, the play was a source for a key scene in *Mansfield Park*.

Austen was disappointed with her latest theatrical ventures, though had she stayed longer in London she might have been disposed to see Elliston in a new play, *First Impressions*, later that month.[34] When she wrote to her brother Frank, she complained of the falling standards of the theatres:

> Of our three evenings in Town one was spent at the Lyceum & another at Covent Garden; – the Clandestine Marriage was the most respectable of the performances, the rest were Sing-song & trumpery, but did very well for Lizzy & Marianne, who were indeed delighted; but *I* wanted better acting. – There was no Actor worth naming. – I beleive the Theatres are thought at a low ebb at present. (*Letters*, p. 230)

Austen's heart-felt wish for 'better acting', or, in Edmund Bertram's words, 'real hardened acting', was soon to be realised.

Drury Lane had indeed reached its lowest ebb for some years when it was rescued by the success of a new actor, Edmund Kean (1787–1833), who made his electrifying debut as Shylock in January 1814. The story of his stage debut has become one of the most enduring tales of the theatre. The reconstructed Drury Lane Theatre, rebuilt after it was destroyed by fire in 1809, was facing financial ruin, greatly exacerbated by the ruinous management of R. B. Sheridan, when a strolling player from the provinces, Edmund Kean, was asked to play Shylock.[35] Kean, in his innovative black wig, duly appeared before a meagre audience, mesmerising them by his stage entrance. At the end of the famous speech in the third act, the audience roared its applause. 'How the devil so few of them kicked up such a row', said Oxberry, 'was something marvelous.'[36] Kean's mesmerising appearance on the stage was given the seal of approval when Hazlitt, who after seeing him on the first night, raved: 'For voice, eye, action, and expression, no actor has come out for many years at all equal to him.'[37]

The news of Kean's conquest of the stage reached Jane Austen, and in early March 1814, while she was staying with Henry during the negotiations for the publication of *Mansfield Park*, she made plans to see the latest acting sensation:

> Places are secured at Drury Lane for Saturday, but so great is the rage for seeing Keen [*sic*] that only a third & fourth row could be got. As it is in a front box however, I hope we shall do pretty well. – Shylock. – A good play for Fanny. She cannot be much affected I think. (*Letters*, p. 256)

The relatively short part of Shylock is thus considered to be a suitably gentle introduction to Kean's powerful acting for the young girl. But Austen's own excitement is barely contained in her description of the theatre party: 'We hear that Mr Keen [*sic*] is more admired than ever. The two vacant places of our two rows, are likely to be filled by Mr Tilson & his brother Gen. Chownes.' Then, almost as if she has betrayed too much pleasure in the absence of her sister, she writes: 'There are no good places to be got in Drury Lane for the next fortnight, but Henry means to secure some for Saturday fortnight when You are reckoned upon' (*Letters*, p. 256).

Another visit to see Kean was intended, and Henry's acquaintance with the theatre world again emphasised. The party went to Drury Lane on the evening of 5 March, attending the eighth performance of *The Merchant of Venice*. Austen's initial response to the latest acting phenomenon was calm and rational: 'We were quite satisfied with Kean. I cannot imagine better acting, but the part was too short, & excepting him & Miss Smith, & *she* did not quite answer my expectations, the parts were ill filled & the Play heavy' (*Letters*, p. 257). Hazlitt, too, frequently complained that one of the problems of the star system was filling up the smaller parts. In his review of *The Merchant of Venice*, he was only grudgingly respectful of the minor roles.

Kean was still very much on Austen's mind, for in the same letter, in the midst of a sentence about Henry Crawford and *Mansfield Park*, she unexpectedly reverted to the subject of him with greater enthusiasm: 'I shall like to see Kean again excessively, & to see him with You too; – it appeared to me as if there was no fault in him anywhere; & in his scene with Tubal there was exquisite acting' (*Letters*, p. 258).

Jane Austen was conscious of the dramatic demands of Shylock's scene, which required the actor to scale, alternately, between grief and savage glee. Her singling out of this particular scene was no doubt influenced by the reports of the opening night, where the audience had been powerless to restrain their applause. Kean's biographer noted the subtle intricacies of the scene in the third act ending with the dialogue between Shylock and Tubal:

> Shylock's anguish at his daughter's flight, his wrath at the two Christians who had made sport of his suffering, his hatred of Christianity generally, and of Antonio in particular, and his alternations of rage, grief and ecstasy as Tubal enumerated the losses incurred in the search of Jessica – her extravagances, and then the ill-luck that had fallen on Antonio; in all this there was such originality, such terrible force, such assurance of a new and mighty master, that the house burst forth into a very whirlwind of approbation.[38]

For many critics, the greatest quality of Kean's as Shylock was his ability to change emotional gear at high speed, to scale the highest points and the lowest. Thus Hazlitt:

> In giving effect to the conflict of passions arising out of the contrasts of situation, in varied vehemence of declamation, in keenness of sarcasm, in the rapidity of his transitions from one tone and feeling to another, in propriety and novelty of action, presenting a succession of striking pictures, and giving perpetually fresh shocks of delight and surprise, it would be difficult to single out a competitor.[39]

Kean's acting style was hereafter characterised as impulsive, electric and fracturing. 'To see him act', Coleridge observed famously in his *Table Talk*, 'is like reading Shakespeare by flashes of lightning.'[40]

In contrast to her reaction to Kean, Jane Austen was disappointed with the performance of her old favourite Elliston. The programme that night included him in an oriental 'melodramatic spectacle' called *Illusion; or The Trances of Nourjahad*. The Austen party left before the end:

We were too much tired to stay for the whole of Illusion (Nourjahad) which has 3 acts; – there is a great deal of finery & dancing in it, but I think little merit. Elliston was Nourjahad, but it is a solemn sort of part, not at all calculated for his powers. There was nothing of the *best Elliston* about him. I might not have known him, but for his voice. (*Letters*, pp. 257–58)

Henry Crabb Robinson also saw Elliston as Nourjahad and wrote in his diary that 'his untragic face can express no strong emotions'. Robinson admired Elliston as a 'fine bustling comedian', but thought that he was a 'wretched Tragedian'.[41] Austen's observation that Elliston's brilliance lay especially in his comic powers was a view shared by his critics and admirers. Charles Lamb thought so too, but was afraid to say so when Elliston recounted how Drury Lane was abusing him. Lamb recorded: 'He complained of this: "Have you heard … how they treat me? they put me in *comedy*." Thought I – "where could they have put you better?" Then, after a pause – "Where I formerly played Romeo, I now play Mercutio."'[42]

Austen's 'best Elliston' was altered from his glory days at Bath and his early promise at Drury Lane as a result of physical deterioration brought on by hard drinking. His acting powers had steadily declined. From managing various minor and provincial theatres, he finally became the lessee and manager of Drury Lane from 1819 until 1826, when he retired, bankrupt through addiction to drinking and gambling.

Elliston's acting talent suffered when he threw his energies into his multifarious business ventures. The *London Magazine and Theatrical Inquisitor* observed that in later years he had fallen into 'a coarse buffoon-ery of manner' and Leigh Hunt oberved that he had 'degraded an unequivocal and powerful talent for comedy into coarseness and vulgar confidence'.[43]

Three days after seeing Kean and Elliston at Drury Lane, Jane Austen went to the rival house Covent Garden to see Charles Coffey's farce, *The Devil to Pay*. 'I expect to be very much amused', she wrote in anticipation (*Letters*, p. 260). Dora Jordan played Nell, one of her most famous comic roles. The party were to see Thomas Arne's opera *Artaxerxes* with Catherine Stephens (1794–1882), the celebrated British soprano who later became Countess of Essex. She was, however, less excited by the opera than the farce: 'Excepting Miss Stephens, I dare say Artaxerxes will be very tiresome' (*Letters*, p. 260). Catherine Stephens acted Mandane in *Artaxerxes*, a role in which Hazlitt thought she was superb, claiming that he could hear her sing 'forever': 'There was a new sound in the air, like the voice of Spring; it was as if Music had become young again, and was resolved to try the power of her softest, simplest, sweetest notes.'[44] Austen's response was just as she expected: 'I was very tired of Artaxerxes, highly amused with the Farce, & in an inferior way with the Pantomime that followed' (*Letters*, p. 260). However, she was unimpressed with Catherine Stephens and grumbled at the plan for a second excursion to see her the following night: 'I have had enough for the present' (*Letters*, p. 260).

Nevertheless, in spite of a cold, she joined the party to see Stephens as Mrs Cornflower in Charles Dibdin's *The Farmer's Wife*, a role created for her musical ability and her talent in low comedy:

> Well, we went to the Play again last night … The Farmer's Wife is a musical thing in 3 acts, & as Edward was steady in not staying for anything more, we were at home before 10 – Fanny and Mr J. P. are delighted with Miss S. & her merit in singing is I dare say very great; that she gave *me* no pleasure is no reflection upon her, nor I hope upon myself being what Nature made me on that article. All that I am sensible of in Miss S. is, a pleasing person & no skill in acting. We had Mathews, Liston and Emery: of course some amusement. (*Letters*, p. 261)

Though disappointed with Stephens, she enjoyed the performances of Mathews, Liston and Emery, who were three of the great comedians of the day. Tall and skinny, Charles Mathews was noted for his brilliance as 'officious valets and humorous old men'.[45] His long-time friend and fellow-actor, the inimitable John Liston, often appeared alongside him.[46]

Liston (1776–1846) was the highest paid comedian of his time.[47] Hazlitt described him as 'the greatest comic genius who has appeared in our time'.[48] He was noted for his bumpkin roles and humorous old men. Leigh Hunt observed that his 'happiest performances are ignorant rustics … he passes from the simplest rustic to the most conceited pretender with undiminished easiness of attainment'.[49] Liston's grave and serious face added to the effect of his comedy, Lamb wrote: 'There is one face of Farley, one of Knight, one (but what a one it is!) of Liston'.[50] For Hazlitt, Liston had 'more comic humour oozing out of his features and person than any other actor'.[51] He was a particularly fine Baron Wildenhaim in *Lovers' Vows*.

John Emery (1777–1822) also played in the same line of old gentlemen and rustics, and was compared to Liston: 'If our two stage-rustics, Emery and Liston, are compared, it will be found that the former is more skilled in the habits and cunning of rusticity, and the latter in its simplicity and ignorance.' But Hunt later claimed of Emery that, in playing the countrymen, the field was 'exclusively and entirely his'.[52] Hazlitt also observed that 'in his line of rustic characters he is a perfect actor'.[53]

The Farmer's Wife was a vehicle for the singing arts of Stephens and the comic talents of Mathews, Liston and Emery. It tells a rather tired tale of an innocent (Emma Cornflower) abducted by a debauched aristocrat (Sir Charles). Mathews plays a village apothecary, Dr Pother. Liston played a cunning London manservant to Sir Charles. This served as a comic contrast to Emery's ignorant but good-hearted Yorkshireman, servant to Farmer Cornflower.[54] The play's comic juxtapositions of high and low characters drew on a convention long associated with the stage: the contrast between town and country, a theme that Austen had been working on in *Mansfield Park*.

Jane Austen's blunt assertion that Stephens had 'no skill in acting' is refreshing and to the point, in an age distinguished by its over-elaborate encomiums of actors and their roles. Furthermore her remark reveals a strong and discerning voice, one that knows what 'good hardened acting' is, and isn't, and is confident in its own critical judgement without being unduly influenced by the current favourite of the stage. After revealing the details of the previous night's theatre to Cassandra, she wrote of plans for yet another excursion to Covent Garden to see Kean's rival, Charles Mayne Young (1777–1856), acting in *Richard III*: 'Prepare for a Play the very first evening. I rather think Covent Garden, to see Young in Richard' (*Letters*, p. 261).

Young had been the leading tragedian of the London stage before Kean challenged his supremacy in 1814. Young was in the Kemble school of acting, and was noted for his heroic, dignified acting style, though he was often compared unfavourably with his predecessor Kemble: 'His most striking fault, as a tragic actor, is a perpetual imitation of Mr Kemble.'[55] He was often criticised for his lack of passion: 'Mr Young never gives himself up to his feelings, but always relies upon his judgement – he never acts from the heart, but the head.'[56] Leigh Hunt was lukewarm about his abilities, describing him as an actor of 'elegant mediocrity', and Hazlitt was even more disparaging, especially of Young's Hamlet: 'he declaims it very well, and rants it very well; but where is the expression of the feeling?'[57] Since Cassandra was coming to London, and presumably accompanied her sister to see Young's Richard, there is no letter describing Jane's reaction to his rendering of the part. But the critical consensus was that the performance was not a success.

The opposition between the Kemble/Young and the Cooke/Kean school of acting was often couched as a conflict between reason and feeling, judgement and passion. It is striking that Austen, who is so often associated with 'sense' rather than 'sensibility', clearly admired Kean's acting but seems to have had little enthusiasm for the Kemble school. Though she names most of the major stars of the London stage in her surviving letters, there is not a single mention of John Philip Kemble himself.

Jane Austen did see Young again, this time with the new acting sensation, Eliza O'Neill, who had made her triumphant debut a month earlier as Juliet and was heralded as the only tragedian worthy to take over the mantle of Sarah Siddons. Just as Drury Lane had been saved from the brink of financial ruin by the advent of Kean, so Covent Garden was desperate to bring forward its own star in reply.[58] Byron refused to see O'Neill out of his loyalty to Kean and Drury Lane, and for fear that he would like her too much: 'No I'm resolved to be un-"Oneiled".'[59] As with Kean's debut earlier that year, audiences acclaimed O'Neill as a genius from the provinces; it was claimed that some spectators fainted under her spell.[60]

Jane Austen's last known visit to the professional theatre took place late in 1814. She was as keen to see Covent Garden's new star as she had been to see Kean, and on the night of 28 November Henry and Edward arranged for her to see *Isabella*, a tragedy adapted by Garrick from

Thomas Southerne's *The Fatal Marriage: or The Innocent Adultery*, in which O'Neill played the leading female role. Jane, writing to her niece Anna Lefroy, was disappointed with O'Neill's performance:

> We were all at the Play last night, to see Miss O'neal [*sic*] in Isabella. I do not think that she was quite equal to my expectation. I fancy I want something more than can be. Acting seldom satisfies me. I took two Pocket handkerchiefs, but had very little occasion for either. She is an elegant creature however & hugs Mr Younge [*sic*] delightfully. (*Letters*, p. 283)

She shows discernment in her rather cool response to O'Neill's performance. Even O'Neill's most ardent admirers admitted that she was less good in maternal parts, like *Isabella*, but was more suited to playing innocent young girls, such as the lovesick Juliet, and repentant fallen women, such as Jane Shore and Mrs Haller: 'She could not represent maternal affection; her love was all the love of fire, youth and passion.'[61]

Isabella, the tragedy of a devoted wife and mother who is persuaded to marry again only to find her beloved husband is alive, was considered to be one of Siddons's finest roles. She had established herself on the London stage with her performance in the part. O'Neill suffered from the inevitable comparisons drawn between the two women. Even Hazlitt, who admired O'Neill's Isabella, thought it lacked Siddons's grandeur and power: 'Nothing can be more natural or more affecting than her noble conception of the part. But there is not that terrible reaction of mental power on the scene, which forms the perfection of tragedy, whether in acting or writing.'[62] Oxberry's biography described her performance in *Isabella* as 'artificial' and suggested that it 'savoured strongly of adoption from the style of Kean'.[63]

Austen was clearly intimate enough with the theatre world to know about the nuances of O'Neill's acting style. Her joking reference to her two pocket handkerchiefs alludes to O'Neill's reputation as an actress of excessive sensibility whose magic was to 'raise the sigh' and who provoked tears rather than terror. O'Neill's biographer observed that her 'triumph, it has been justly said, is in tears'.[64] For Hazlitt, O'Neill's power lay in her extraordinary ability to draw sympathy from the audience. It was her 'reaction' to Romeo's death that characterised her unique acting style: 'In the silent expression of feeling, we have seldom witnessed anything finer.'[65]

The telling phrase '[she] hugs Mr Young delightfully' suggests that there was a kind of intimate theatrical code between Austen and her niece. As they were both aware, coupled with O'Neill's ability to elicit sympathy and tears was her reputation as a 'hugging actress'. This appellation appears to have been given by Thomas Amyot, according to the testimony of Crabb Robinson's diary: 'Saw Miss O'Neill in Isabella. She was as Aymot well said, "a hugging actress". Sensibility shown in grief and fondness was her forte, – her only talent.'[66]

The deleterious effects of excessive sensibility are a recurrent theme of Austen's fiction from her earliest jokes in *Love and Freindship* to *Sanditon*. Her joke about O'Neill's sensibility is shared not only with Anna but also with her other favoured niece Fanny Knight:

I just saw Mr Hayter at the Play, & think his face would please me on acquaintance. I was sorry he did not dine here. – It seemed rather odd to me to be in the Theatre, with nobody to *watch* for. I was quite composed myself, at leisure for all the agitation Isabella could raise. (*Letters*, p. 285)

Austen's ironic remark, 'It seemed rather odd to me to be in the Theatre, with nobody to *watch* for', comically portrays herself in the role of the chaperone of her young nieces, guarding their exposure to excessive sensibility or 'agitation'. Earlier, we saw her worrying about Fanny's agitation on seeing Kean. As indicated, both Kean and O'Neill were reputed to have the power of making their audience faint under their spell. Towards the close of this letter, Austen makes a striking reference to the two most famous tragediennes of the age, and uses the ardent acting style of O'Neill to express the contrasting natures of her young nieces:

That puss Cassy, did not shew more pleasure in seeing me than her Sisters, but I expected no better; – she does not shine in the tender feelings. She will never be a Miss O'neal; – more in the Mrs Siddons line. (*Letters*, p. 287)

This passage, perhaps more than any other single reference to the theatre, is revelatory of Jane Austen's intimacy with the late Georgian theatre. As she was clearly aware, one of the current debates in the theatre world was the contrasting acting styles of Mrs Siddons and Miss O'Neill. The latter's 'extreme natural sensibility' was played off against the former's classical nobility. For Hazlitt, Siddons was the embodiment of 'high tragedy', O'Neill of 'instinctive sympathy'.[67]

O'Neill's biographer, Charles Inigo Jones, complained of 'the rather too invidious comparisons constantly kept up betwixt her and Mrs Siddons', and yet proceeded to make his own comparisons, contrasting not only the acting styles of the two women but their physical attributes which, he believed, embodied their acting styles. Thus Siddons's 'grandeur and dignity are pictured in her appearance', and O'Neill's 'excess of sensibility is predominant ... and well pourtrayed in her countenance'.[68]

One of the best comparisons of the two tragedians is made in Oxberry's memoir of O'Neill:

> Miss O'Neill was a lovely ardent creature, with whose griefs we sympathized, and whose sorrows raised our pity. Mrs Siddons was a wonderful being, for whom we felt awe, veneration, and a more holy love ... Miss O'Neill twined most upon our affections, but Mrs Siddons made an impression on our minds, that time never eradicated.[69]

Austen's observations in the scanty correspondence that survives offer decisive, hitherto neglected, evidence of her deep familiarity with the theatre of Siddons and O'Neill. In addition, her manner of comparing social conduct to theatrical models such as her niece's Siddons-like dignified behaviour denoting a lack of sensibility ('the tender feelings') betrays a striking propensity to view life through the spectacles of theatre.

In January 1801, Cassandra Austen was compelled to abandon a trip to London, where she had intended to visit the Opera House to see the celebrated comic actress Dora Jordan (1761–1816). Jane wrote to her: 'You speak with such noble resignation of Mrs Jordan & the Opera House that it would be an insult to suppose consolation required' (*Letters*, p. 71).

The King's Theatre or Italian Opera House in the Haymarket had been built by Vanbrugh in 1705. The Opera House was destroyed by fire in 1789 and was rebuilt on a vast scale in 1791.[70] On the opening night, Michael Kelly sang in *The Haunted Tower* and Dora Jordan performed in Kemble's farce, *The Pannel*.[71] In 1799 the interior of the Opera House was partly remodelled by Marinari, the principal scene painter at Drury Lane.[72] Austen's sympathy for Cassandra's double disappointment was therefore equally distributed between seeing the new Opera House and seeing the great Mrs Jordan.

In 1801 Dora Jordan was at the height of her powers, and the star of Drury Lane. As Siddons was the Tragic Muse of the London stage, so Jordan was the Comic Muse.[73] Hoppner's portrait of Jordan as 'The Comic Muse' was a huge success at the Royal Academy in May 1786.[74] Not even Jordan's long-term liaison with the Duke of Clarence (to whom she bore ten children over a period of twenty years) could stem the tide of 'Jordan-Mania' that swept the country in the late eighteenth and early nineteenth centuries. Her image was everywhere: in the theatre, in theatrical engravings in print shop windows, and in the numerous caricatures by Gillray and Cruikshank. Sheet music of the songs that she sang at Drury Lane were sold on the streets.

Dora Jordan was unparalleled in comedy.[75] She appealed to both the critics and the theatre-going public who flocked to see her. Coleridge, Byron, Hazlitt and Lamb were among her admirers.[76] Hazlitt described her as 'the child of nature, whose voice was a cordial to the heart, because it came from it … whose laugh was to drink nectar … who "talked far above singing" and whose singing was like the twang of Cupid's bow'.[77] Leigh Hunt also singled out her memorable laugh and melodious voice: 'Mrs Jordan seems to speak with all her soul … her laughter is the happiest and most natural on the stage.'[78]

Jordan's extensive range was unusual in an era during which actors tended to be restricted to specific kinds of role. She played genteel ladies, such as Lady Teazle and Widow Belmour, and romantic leads such as Lydia Languish and Kate Hardcastle. She was also famous for her 'low' roles, playing chambermaids, romps and hoydens to much acclaim. Miss

Prue, Miss Hoyden, and Nell in *The Devil to Pay* were among her favourites. She was also famous for her 'breeches roles', playing the cross-dressed Hippolita, Harry Wildair, Rosalind, Viola, and Little Pickle in the farce *The Spoilt Child*. The theatre chronicler John Genest claimed that she 'sported the best leg ever seen on the stage'.[79]

Jordan's performance as the innocent country girl in Garrick's adaptation of William Wycherley's highly risqué Restoration comedy *The Country Wife* combined the role of a hoyden with a 'breeches part'. She played the Country Girl for fifteen seasons at Drury Lane from 1785 to 1800. In one of the most memorable scenes, Peggy takes a walk in St James's Park, disguised as a young boy, as her jealous guardian is determined to protect her from other men. In a letter of 1799, Austen uses the notion of the 'Country Girl' to express doubts about the behaviour of an acquaintance, Earle Harwood, who had married a woman of obscure birth:

> I cannot help thinking from your account of Mrs E. H. [Earle Harwood] that Earle's vanity has tempted him to invent the account of her former way of Life, that his triumph in securing her might be greater; – I dare say she was nothing but an innocent Country Girl in fact. (*Letters*, p. 48)

Austen's instinctive and imaginative way of using stage characters as a point of reference in her letters, coupled with her habit of weaving in quotations from favourite plays, offers yet another striking example of the range and extent of her familiarity with the drama. She is viewing the world around her through the spectacles of theatre, and, simultanously, showing her awareness of the intricacies and nuances of the kinds of social stratification reflected in the drama. The invention of 'Country Girl' innocents out of low-born characters in order to reflect favourable light upon the inventor is precisely the kind of dubious behaviour that Austen fictionalises so adroitly in *Emma*.

The life of the low-born and illegitimate Dora Jordan echoed the theatre's predilection for plays depicting social metamorphosis. From her humble, obscure origins, she had risen to be the mistress of a prince and a royal estate.[80] Epilogues were written for Jordan with pointed reference to her private circumstances. In 1791, when the Duke was stepping up his courtship of Jordan, she played for her benefit an adaptation of Fletcher's *The Humorous Lieutenant* called *The Greek Slave: or The School for Cowards*.[81] Jordan played the part of a slave girl who is in love with a prince, and is eventually discovered to be of noble birth. The epilogue drew attention to her assumption of genteel roles, both on and off stage:

> How Strange! methinks I hear a Critic say,
> What, *She* the serious Heroine of the Play!
> The Manager his want of Sense evinces
> To pitch on *Hoydens* for the love of Princes!
> To trick out *Chambermaids* in awkward pomp –
> Horrid! to make a Princess of a *Romp*.[82]

The epilogue also drew attention to the fact that, while she was acclaimed for her 'low' parts, her roles in polite comedy were often condemned. It seems that Jordan, even among her admirers, was considered to be a 'natural' at low parts. Even her adoring biographer Boaden described her low parts as 'natural … the genuine workings of nature within her'.[83] Leigh Hunt believed that Jordan was at her best in low comedy, and declared that she was 'all deficient in the *lady*' and unable to bring off genteel roles because of her lack of 'a certain graceful orderliness, an habitual subjection … of impulse of manner', claiming, however, that 'If Mrs Jordan were what she ought to be in the lady, we more than doubt whether she could be what she is in the boarding school-girl or the buxom woman'.[84]

Hunt's remarks betray a consciousness about the ease with which actresses could play the lady on stage and cross social boundaries off stage. Perhaps this was because so many former actresses married into aristocratic circles. Famously, one of Mrs Jordan's co-stars, Elizabeth Farren, quit the stage to marry the Earl of Derby.[85] Catherine Stephens married the Earl of Essex and Miss O'Neill retired early to become Lady Wrixon Beecher. Jordan's rise from illegitimate child-actor to royal mistress, crossing almost every social barrier, added an extra comic dimension to her role as Nell in Charles Coffey's farce *The Devil to Pay*.

In 1814 Jane Austen saw Jordan in this play, in what was perhaps her most famous role, that of a timid cobbler's wife who is magically transformed into an aristocratic society mistress.[86] Jordan played the part of the downtrodden wife who makes a better wife to Sir John, and a kinder mistress to her servants, than the irascible Lady Loverule. Lady Loverule's metamorphosis into the cobbler's wife eventually brings about her moral transformation. The rough treatment she experiences at the hands of the cobbler is partially responsible for the change in her attitude towards her exalted position:

> There's nought but the devil
> And this good strap
> Could ever tame a scold.[87]

The comedy had long amused the public, who enjoyed seeing Jordan's metamorphosis from rags into riches, just as she herself had been transformed, seemingly, by her liaison with the Duke of Clarence. Jordan was dubbed 'Nell of Clarence' by Horace Walpole, who intended a reference to her famous predecessor as royal theatrical mistress, Nell Gwynne.

By the time that Jane Austen saw *The Devil to Pay* in 1814, however, Jordan was separated from the duke and had returned to the stage.[88] Austen declared herself 'highly amused' with the farce. She was in good company – Hazlitt described Jordan's Nell as 'heavenly':

> Her Nell ... was right royal ... Miss Kelly is a dexterous knowing chambermaid: Mrs Jordan had nothing dexterous or knowing about her. She was Cleopatra turned into an oyster-wench, without knowing that she was Cleopatra, or caring that she was an oyster-wench. An oyster-wench, such as she was, would have been equal to a Cleopatra; and an Antony would not have deserted her for the empire of the world![89]

The Devil to Pay, the play that was so closely associated with Dora Jordan, exemplifies the drama's obsession with the concept of social mobility, and its endless play on rank and manners. The metamorphosis of a timid country girl and a termagant wife and society mistress highlighted the same sort of class tensions initiated by the unprecedented success of Richardson's *Pamela*. Goldsmith's *She Stoops to Conquer* was another

favourite eighteenth-century comedy that examined uneasy social strat-
ifications by a series of ironic reversals.

It is striking, but perhaps not surprising, that Austen favoured comedies where social roles were turned topsy-turvy, such as Coffey's *The
Devil to Pay*, Townley's *High Life Below Stairs* and Colman's *The Heir at
Law*.[90] Such comedies were popular with a wide and varied audience.
Theatre historians have shown how the need for public theatres to
appeal to a socially diverse audience of box, pit and gallery led to a
mixed programme of entertainment.[91] The opposition between 'high'
and 'low' became a perennial theme in eighteenth-century comedy,
depicting the dramatic situations and comic scenes that arise when a
person crosses the boundaries from low life to high, or vice-versa. The
device of bringing together contrasting types, whereby different styles
of action and language are attached to different classes and ironically
juxtaposed, allowed the writer to exploit the comic potential of 'high'
and 'low' life in Georgian England, and please the upper galleries as well
as the pit.

Pleasing the upper galleries and the boxes was, however, only part of
the intention. Writers for the theatre also knew that fashionable comedy
was genteel, and that its audience was predominantly middle class; therefore farces that criticised aristocratic manners and poked fun at 'low'
characters were particularly successful. The increasingly frequent
appearance of wealthy merchants, sympathetically treated in the plays of
the 1790s, has been ascribed to the development of 'middle-class'
attitudes.[92]

Ever since the success of Gay's *Beggar's Opera*, writers for the stage had
used low life as a means of satirising high. In Cowley's *Which is the Man?*
one of the 'low' characters duly exclaims: 'He must be a Lord by his want
of ceremony'. In *The Devil to Pay*, Nell's gentle manners and innate
dignity reflect badly on Lady Loverule. In *Pride and Prejudice*, Austen
was also to depict the moral defeat of a high-ranking aristocrat (another
Lady Loverule?) by a young woman 'of inferior birth … without family,
connections, or fortune' (*PP*, pp. 355–56). In *Mansfield Park* the rendi-
tion of Fanny's 'low' family in Portsmouth exploits the dramatic situations and comic scenes resulting from a woman's movement across the
boundaries between high life and low. Yet, in the end, it is the

lower-ranking Price children (William, Fanny and Susan) who turn out better than the high-bred Bertrams.[93]

It is evident throughout her work, distinguishable even from the early reference to Lewis and Quick, that Jane Austen was particularly attuned to the discrepancies between rank and manners within the tightly circumscribed social structure of her world. That understanding was shaped and informed by her interest in the drama. Her special interest in social metamorphosis, with its comic interplay between high and low types, was stimulated by the influence of eighteenth-century comedy.

The year 1814, in which *Mansfield Park* was published, saw the birth of a new age in the English theatre. Between the years of Kean's birth in the late 1780s and his death in 1833 the theatre underwent unprecedented change. The two patent houses had been closed by catastrophic fires in 1808–9 and had then been rebuilt on a more lavish and grander scale than had been seen before. Kemble's raised prices had incited sixty-seven nights of rioting in Covent Garden until he was forced to capitulate to the demands of the rioters. Edmund Kean and Eliza O'Neill had taken over the mantle of Kemble and Siddons, bringing to the stage a new style of intuitive acting characteristic of the 'Romantic' era. The rise of the illegitimate theatres and the impact of a 'theatrical revolution' in the advent of Kean (cemented by the praise of the cockney young literary radicals, Keats, Leigh Hunt and Hazlitt) marked a new age of vitality in the theatre.

This tumultuous period in the history of the theatre also happened to coincide with Jane Austen's own birth and death. She attended the first performances of Kean and O'Neill, witnessed the transformations taking place in the theatre, and remained in touch with its nuances and foibles. Austen's interest in the drama has been overlooked in the persistently mistaken notion that she was morally opposed to the theatre. Yet this assumption is in flagrant defiance of the evidence of the letters.

In the early part of 1814, in the middle of negotiations for the publication of *Mansfield Park*, and in the space of four days, Austen visited the professional theatre three times to see Kean, Jordan and Stephens. In the same short period she wrote of two more excursions to see Kean again and also his rival Young. It is a striking irony that the completion of

Mansfield Park, the novel that has been viewed almost universally as Austen's rejection of the theatre, coincided with a particularly busy theatre-going period for the author.[94]

Judging by Austen's earlier theatre-going periods, visits in such close proximity were not unusual. Her visit to Henry and Eliza in 1811 was planned with the Lyceum on Thursday, followed by two more visits to Covent Garden on Saturday and Monday. In 1813 she was found at the playhouse two nights in a row. This was by no means untypical and is an acute reminder of the frequency with which the Georgians visited the playhouse. On average, there were about 180 nights each season on which the patent houses offered the play-going public some kind of dramatic entertainment. The two winter patent houses alone could command a total of four hundred performances per season.[95] Whenever Jane made extended visits to town, she seems to have taken advantage of Henry's close connections with the theatre.

Theatre in the late Georgian period became an essential part of fash-ionable middle-class life.[96] One of the consequences of the system of stock companies was that the audience became familiar with the same actors, seeing them in a variety of different roles and plays of all types, coming to know not only their styles of acting, but the details of their private lives.[97] The proliferation of stage-related literature meant that readers were able to know the intimate details of actors' lives. In the words of one historian: 'The public's appetite for news, gossip and scan-dal about the stage was insatiable, its sense of intimate acquaintance with actors unique. A successful player could only have a public private life.'[98] To sate the audience appetite for theatre there were actors' diaries, jour-nals, memoirs, biographies of playwrights and managers, histories and annals of the theatre, periodicals, and magazines. Between 1800 and 1830 some one hundred and sixty different periodicals devoted exclu-sively to the theatre came into existence in Britain.[99]

William Hazlitt, in the preface to his *A View of the English Stage*, describes the allure of the theatre in late Georgian England: 'the disputes on the merits or defects of the last new piece, or a favourite performer, are as common, as frequently renewed, and carried on with as much eagerness and skill, as those on almost any other subject.'[100] With Hazlitt's words in mind, one of the most striking features of Austen's letters is her discussion of the theatre as a part of everyday conversation, to be written about as she writes about other quotidian matters like shopping and gossip.

Austen's letters are a neglected historical source for her interest in and love of the theatre. The fundamental place the theatre occupied in her life is revealed in the manner in which it can be joked about, admired, even be taken for granted. Her mock-insult to Siddons, 'I could swear at her for disappointing me', reflects the way in which the sisters often consoled one another for missing particular performers. Her tantalising observation that Mrs Edwin's performance 'is just what it used to be' speaks a language of intimate theatrical knowledge that we can only begin to guess at.

There is something paradoxically casual and yet essential about the way that Austen 'converses' about the theatre. At times her letters reveal a striking language of precision and economy in respect to the drama; details of the seating arrangements are often as important as descriptions of the plays, sometimes a cursory remark such as 'no skill in acting' is enough for the sisters and nieces, who are in tune with one another; no further elaboration is necessary, but it still needs to be said, because the interest is there between them. That interest lasted throughout Jane Austen's life and, as I will demonstrate, had a profound effect on her fiction.

PART TWO

The Theatre and the Novels

She partook largely in all the best gifts of the comic muse

Henry Austen, 'Biographical Notice' of his sister

4

Early Works

The impact of private theatricals and the vitality of the professional theatre in the late Georgian period gave Jane Austen a comprehensive and
longstanding interest in the drama. From her earliest attempts at
play-writing to the systematic incorporation of quasi-theatrical techniques into her mature novels, the influence of the drama rarely left her.
Throughout the canon there is an abundance of resonances and allusions
to eighteenth-century plays, many of which the author expected her
readers to recognise. It is, however, in Austen's juvenilia, written to amuse
her family, and not intended for public consumption, where the marks
of her early exposure to the drama can most clearly be seen.

Jane Austen's chief literary tool in her early works was the art of
burlesque.[1] In this she was influenced by her brothers' Oxford literary
journal, *The Loiterer*, which ran for sixty numbers between 1789 and
1790, and made a duty of burlesquing 'novel slang' and the absurdities of
popular fiction. Henry Austen's burlesque of the literary conventions of
courtship, entitled 'Peculiar Dangers of *Rusticus* from the Attacks of a
Female Cousin', is particularly striking.[2] In this parody of a sentimental
novel, the unlucky hero is besieged by the attentions of his cousin. The
hero of Henry's sentimental tale is lured into seducing his fair cousin:
'She begged me for the loan of an arm. My arm she accordingly took, and
in the course of all her frights and false steps, pinched it so hard and so
often, that it is still quite black and blue, through sheer tenderness.'
Following his cousin's admission of loving 'cropt Greys to distraction', he
is a lost man:

There was no standing this ... I thought she never looked so much like an angel. In short, I know not where my passion might have ended, had not the luckiest accident in the world at once roused me from this rapturous dream of fancied bliss, to all the phlegm of cool reflection and sober reality. A sudden puff of wind carried off two luxuriant tresses from her beautiful Chignon, and left her (unconscious to herself) in a situation truly ridiculous. The delicate thread of sentiment and affection was broken, never to be united.[3]

Henry Austen's burlesque technique of juxtaposing a serious and sentimental reflection with a quasi-farcical action is echoed throughout Jane Austen's *Volume the First*. Also typical is the taste for absurd detail and witty aphorism. Henry's tale ends with a description of the hero's unsuccessful attempts to be rid of his cousin; getting 'completely cut' and spilling lemonade over her dress prove fruitless: 'But she wouldn't be provoked, for when once a woman is determined to get a husband, I find trifling obstacles will not damp her hopes or sour her temper.'[4]

The Loiterer was not the only influence on Jane Austen. As has been shown, she was writing burlesque sketches at least two years before its publication, during the time of the Steventon private theatricals.[5] James and Henry's taste for satirical comedies ensured that she was exposed at a very early age to those masters of burlesque plays, Henry Fielding and Richard Brinsley Sheridan. Fielding's *Tom Thumb: or The Tragedy of Tragedies* (1730) and Sheridan's *The Critic* (1779) were two of the most successful examples of eighteenth-century theatrical burlesque. Jane Austen alludes to both plays in her juvenilia.

Fielding had been hailed as a master of political satire after the commercial success of his theatre burlesques, *The Author's Farce, Tom Thumb, Pasquin* and *The Historical Register*. His repeated attacks on the Whig government came to a head in *The Historical Register*, where he was more openly hostile to Sir Robert Walpole than he had been in his earlier burlesques. The success of this play finally provoked the government into passing the Theatre Licensing Act of 1737, whose long-term repercussions were to include the growth of closet drama and a transfer of creative energy from the theatre to the novel.[6] Fielding gave up writing and turned to the law, until the publication of Richardson's *Pamela*

(1740) provoked him into writing again. Once again he used burlesque to ridicule literary pretension and hypocrisy: *Shamela* and *Joseph Andrews* are different burlesques of the same book.

Fielding's theatre burlesques relied upon a subtle blending of theatrical and political satire. *Tom Thumb: or The Tragedy of Tragedies*, which the Austens acted at Steventon on 22 March 1788, was chiefly a parody of contemporary tragedy, although Walpole was implicitly satirised in the portrayal of Tom Thumb, 'the great man'. It was intended to be ludicrous and nonsensical. The original audience was delighted by the incongruity of a 'tragedy' designed to make them laugh. Fielding was satirising the way in which modern tragedy was unintentionally absurd.

Set in King Arthur's Court, Fielding's travesty ruthlessly caricatured conventional heroic tragedy. The play contains the full panoply of Neoclassical tragedy, but the superhuman giant-killing hero, Thumb – 'whose soul is as big as a mountain' – is a midget. The other 'noble' personages of the court are just as ridiculous. The royal couple are a quarrelsome pair. The noble King Arthur is bullied by his wife Dollalolla, a queen 'entirely faultless, saving that she is a little given to drink', and in love with the captive queen, Glumdalca, a giantess, who is in love with the dwarf, Thumb. The romantic sub-plot common in heroic tragedy is also parodied in the love triangle of the gluttonous Princess Huncamunca and her rivals, Lord Grizzle and Tom Thumb. The King's loyal courtiers, Noodle, Doodle and Foodle, are foolish and inept, and the play ends with a ludicrous massacre of all the characters.

Burlesque appealed to Austen, for her main concern in her early writings was to excite laughter. She approved of its uncomplicated aim to raise laughter by comic exaggeration and from the sheer absurdity of language and image. But, like Fielding, she was aware that parody acts as a form of criticism, a way of elucidating the absurdities and limitations of a particular art form.

Austen shared Fielding's irreverence for literary and artistic convention. Her characters are no more heroic than Fielding's, and often as physically odd or repulsive. In a deliberate echo of *Tom Thumb*, Austen set her stories in villages called Pammydiddle and Crankhumdunberry. Like Fielding, she took the clichéd situation and rendered it absurd. In 'Frederick and Elfrida' she parodied the novelistic convention of depicting two antithetical sisters, one beautiful and foolish, the other ugly and clever. In this topsy-turvy world it is the ugly Rebecca who charms the hero:

Lovely & too charming Fair one, notwithstanding your forbidding Squint, your greasy tresses & your swelling Back, which are more frightful than imagination can paint or pen describe, I cannot refrain from expressing my raptures, at the engaging Qualities of your Mind, which so amply atone for the Horror, with which your first appearance must ever inspire the unwary visitor. (*MW*, p. 6)

In *Tom Thumb*, Princess Huncamunca is confounded by the ugliness of Glumdalca: 'O Heaven, thou art as ugly as the devil.' Queen Dollalolla, meanwhile, is permanently drunk:

Oh, Dollalolla! do not blame my love;
I hoped the fumes of last night's punch had laid
Thy lovely eyelids fast.[7]

Just as Fielding's heroes are characterised by their unheroic qualities, such as physical ugliness, drunkeness and violence, Austen's earliest characters are also drunkards, murderers and adulterers. Jealous sisters poison each other, landowners beat their workers with a cudgel on a whim, and children bite off their mother's fingers. Austen's letters suggest that she long continued to find physical ugliness, illness and death amusing.[8]

Jane Austen does not raise a laugh merely through the employment of knockabout farce and violent imagery. Her grasp of verbal incongruities is equally impressive. Thus, in 'Frederic and Elfrida', the physically abhorrent Rebecca is finally sought in marriage by the aged Captain Rogers: 'Mrs Fitzroy did not approve of the match on account of the tender years of the young couple, Rebecca being but 36 & Captain Roger little more than 63. To remedy this objection, it was agreed that they should wait a little while till they were a good deal older' (*MW*, p. 7).

Absurdity of language is coupled with farcical action to achieve the maximum comic effect: 'From this period, the intimacy between the Families of Fitzroy, Drummond, and Falknor, daily increased till at length it grew to such a pitch, that they did not scruple to kick one another out of the window on the slightest provocation' (*MW*, p. 6). In this instance, Austen is parodying the formal rhetoric of the sentimental novel and elucidating its absurdities while simultaneously observing the quasi-farcical conventions of slapstick stage-comedy.

Similarly, in 'Jack and Alice', Austen moves swiftly from the educational motif of the 'improving' novel to a punch-line that is pure farce:

> Miss Dickens was an excellent Governess. She instructed me in the Paths of Virtue; under her tuition I daily became more amiable, & might perhaps by this time have nearly attained perfection, had not my worthy Preceptoress been torn from my arms, e'er I had attained my seventeeth year. I never shall forget her last words. 'My dear Kitty she said, Good night t'ye.' I never saw her afterwards', continued Lady Williams wiping her eyes, 'She eloped with the Butler the same night'. (*MW*, p. 17)

The technique of juxtaposing a mock-grandiose sentiment with a comic action is influenced by the burlesque methods of Henry and James Austen in *The Loiterer*. But, as this passage reveals, the rhythms and cadences of stage comedy also shape the narrative. The pompous diction of the second sentence culminates in the hackneyed sentimental expression 'torn from my arms', only to be comically deflated by the governess's brisk goodnight. The gesture of 'Lady Williams wiping her eyes' before continuing her story introduces a theatrical pause between the two clauses of the final sentence – and the governess eloping with the butler is a twist straight out of stage farce.[9]

The egocentricity of the heroine's blithe remark, 'I daily became more amiable, & might perhaps by this time have nearly gained perfection', is inserted almost incidentally into the narrative. Here the comic touch is more finely tuned. Jane Austen is already going beyond mere slapstick. Similarly, in the same story, the 'perfect' Charles Adams, a character based on Richardson's idealised hero Sir Charles Grandison, memorably remarks, 'I expect nothing more in my wife than my wife will find in me – Perfection' (*MW*, p. 26).

Austen's heroine in 'Jack and Alice' is an absurd figure whose only fault is, in the style of Fielding's Dollalolla, a propensity for liquor. Even

Lady Williams's benevolent nature is strained by her tippling companion: 'When you are more intimately acquainted with my Alice you will not be surprised, Lucy, to see the dear Creature drink a little too much; for such things happen every day. She has many rare & charming qualities, but Sobriety is not one of them. The whole Family are indeed a sad drunken set' (*MW*, p. 23).

As in the 'tragic' ending of *Tom Thumb*, 'Jack and Alice' becomes increasingly absurd and farcical. At the tender age of seventeen, Lucy is poisoned by the envious Sukey, who is promptly hauled off to the gallows for murder. The hero of the story (presumably 'Jack') is finally introduced only to be killed off instantly:

> It may now be proper to return to the Hero of this Novel, the brother of Alice, of whom I beleive I have scarcely ever had occasion to speak; which may perhaps be partly oweing to his unfortunate propensity to Liquor, which so compleatly deprived him of the use of those faculties Nature had endowed him with, that he never did anything worth mentioning. (*MW*, pp. 24–25)

The real hero and heroine of Austen's story are, of course, not the ludicrous drunkards Jack and Alice of Pammydiddle, but those more sinister figures, monsters of ego and self-interest, Lady Williams and Charles Adams, who are united in marriage having found their ideal of perfection in each other.

In *Volume the Second*, Austen continued to show her allegiance to burlesque. Where Henry Fielding had been an important influence in *Volume the First*, she now turned to Richard Brinsley Sheridan, his great successor in the art of literary parody. In *The History of England*, a burlesque of Oliver Goldsmith's 'partial, prejudiced and ignorant history', Austen mocks the way in which supposedly factual history is tempered by sensationalised fiction in order to popularise its appeal. To this end, she refers her readers to Sheridan's *The Critic*.

Sir Walter Raleigh flourished in this & the preceding reign, & is by many people held in great veneration & respect – But as he was an enemy of the noble Essex, I have nothing to say in praise of him, & must refer all those who may wish to be acquainted with the particulars of his life, to Mr Sheridan's play of the Critic, where they will find many interesting anecdotes as well of him as of his freind [*sic*] Sir Christopher Hatton. (*MW*, p. 147)

There are several further gestures towards *The Critic* in Austen's full-length burlesque of sentimentalism, *Love and Freindship*. This work was dedicated to Eliza de Feuillide, who had taken the part of Miss Titupp in the Steventon production of the Garrick's *Bon Ton*. As has been noted, the title of Jane's own burlesque had appeared as a phrase in Garrick's play: 'Love and Friendship are very fine names to be sure, but they are merely visiting acquaintance; we know their names indeed, talk of 'em sometimes, and let 'em knock at our doors, but we never let 'em in, you know.'[10]

Eighteenth-century 'sentimentalism' is a particularly slippery concept to define, not least because what was first an approbatory term increasingly became a pejorative label.[11] A quality of emotional excess – the indulgence or luxuriance in emotion for its own sake – was the particular target of Austen's satire in *Love and Freindship*.[12] This burlesque novella is a parody of the heroine-centred, epistolary novel of sensibility, exemplified by Charlotte's Smith's *Emmeline: or The Orphan of the Castle* and Fanny Burney's *Evelina*.[13] *Love and Freindship* duly contains all the clichés of romantic fiction: swooning heroines, unknown parentage and improbable chance meetings. But Austen's burlesque should not be viewed solely in the context of the sentimental novel. The deluded romantic heroine was also a theatrical type. So it was that *The Critic* gave Austen a precedent for her parody of the excesses of sentimentalism.

One of the traditions of sentimental drama was the 'discovery scene', in which some dramatic (and usually emotionally charged) revelation occurs. Sheridan parodied the device mercilessly. In the play-within-the-play, Puff's risible tragedy *The Spanish Armada*, there is the requisite improbable chance meeting with a stranger who is 'discovered' to be a long-lost relative:

JUSTICE:
What is thy name?

SON:
My name's Tom Jenkins – *alias*, have I none –
Tho' orphaned, and without a friend!

JUSTICE:
Thy parents?

SON:
My father dwelt in Rochester – and was,
As I have heard – a fishmonger – no more.

PUFF: What, Sir, do you leave out the account of your birth, parentage
    and education?
SON: They have settled it so, Sir, here.
PUFF: Oh! oh!

LADY:
How loudly nature whispers to my heart!
Had he no other name?

SON:
I've seen a bill
Of his, sign'd *Tomkins*, creditor.

JUSTICE:
This does indeed confirm each circumstance
The gypsey told! – Prepare!

SON:
I do.

JUSTICE:
No orphan, nor without a friend art thou –
I am thy father, *here's* thy mother, *there*
Thy uncle – this thy first cousin, and those
Are all your near relations!

MOTHER:
O ecstasy of bliss!

SON:
O most unlook'd for happiness!

JUSTICE:
O wonderful event!

[They faint alternately in each others' arms]

PUFF: There, you see relationship, like murder, will out.[14]

The specific object of Sheridan's parody is the famously sentimental discovery scene in John Home's immensely popular tragedy, *Douglas* (1756). In the second act, Lady Randolph 'discovers' a sheep-tender and is struck by the fact that, had her son lived,

He might have been like this young gallant stranger
And paired with him in features and in shape.

The stranger, who really is Lady Randolph's lost son, describes his life story in an eloquent, long-winded speech. In *The Critic*, the 'My name is Norval' speech is condensed into the two lines

My name's Tom Jenkins – *alias*, have I none –
Tho' orphaned, and without a friend!

In *Mansfield Park* Jane Austen alludes to the famous scene in *Douglas* when Tom Bertram recalls play-acting as a boy: 'How many times have we mourned over the dead body of Julius Caesar, and *to be'd* and *not to be'd*, in this very room for his amusement! And I am sure, *my name was Norval*, every evening of my life through one Christmas holidays' (*MP*, pp. 126–27). Long before this, in *Love and Freindship*, she had already parodied the obligatory discovery scene:

> Never did I see such an affecting Scene as was the meeting of Edward & Augustus.
>
> 'My life! my Soul!' (exclaimed the former) 'My adorable Angel!' (replied the latter) as they flew into each other's arms. It was too pathetic for the feelings of Sophia and myself – We fainted Alternately on a Sofa. (*MW*, p. 86)

The final line is a clear allusion to the parody of *Douglas* in *The Critic*, with its climactic stage direction, '*They faint alternately in each others' arms*'.

The allusion to Tom Jenkins's 'discovery scene' is sustained in the sentimental reunion of Austen's heroine, Laura. She also discovers, unexpectedly, the existence of a wealthy grandfather and benefactor: 'At his first Appearance my Sensibility was wonderfully affected & e'er I had gazed at him a 2*d*. time, an instinctive Sympathy whispered to my Heart, that he was my Grandfather' (*MW*, p. 91). Laura's friend and confidante, Sophia, discovers that the same venerable old man is a relative: '"Oh!" replied Sophia, "when I first beheld you the instinct of Nature whispered me that we were in some degree related – But whether Grandfathers, or Grandmothers, I could not pretend to determine"' (*MW*, p. 91).

Austen's heroines echo Sheridan's phrase, 'whispered to my heart'. This clichéd phrase indicates the trademark of sensibility: the heroine's grasp of the supremacy of instinctive intuition over the rational or intellectual. In *The Critic*, the implausible discovery scene is followed by a quick succession of equally implausible reunions:

I am thy father, *here's* thy mother, *there*
Thy uncle – this thy first cousin, and those
Are all your near relations!

Austen's own discovery scene is only completed when two more long-lost grandchildren, the strolling actors Philander and Augustus, enter the inn, much to the Grandfather's dismay:

'But tell me (continued he looking fearfully towards the Door) tell me, have I any other Grand-Children in the House'. 'None my Lord'. 'Then I will provide for you all without further delay – Here are 4 banknotes of 50£ each – Take them & remember I have done the Duty of a Grandfather –'. He instantly left the room & immediately afterwards the house ... You may imagine how greatly surprised we were by the sudden departure of Lord St Clair. 'Ignoble Grand-sire!' exclaimed Sophia. 'Unworthy Grandfather!' said I, & instantly fainted in each other's arms. (*MW*, p. 92)

The swooning scene once again borrows the stage direction in *The Critic* that calls for mutual fainting. The last-minute discovery of a benevolent guardian appears in most of the sentimental plays of the period. Celebrated examples include Stockwell in Cumberland's *The West Indian* and Sir Oliver Surface in Sheridan's own *The School for Scandal*.[15]

As well as the conventional discovery scene, Puff's tragedy incorporates fainting fits and madness, the symptoms of extreme sensibility in both drama and fiction. Hence the stage direction, '*Enter Tilburina and Confidante mad, according to custom*'.

TILBURINA:
The wind whistles – the moon rises – see
They have kill'd my squirrel in his cage!
Is this a grasshopper! – Ha! no, it is my
Whiskerandos – you shall not keep him –
I know you have him in your pocket –
An oyster may be cross'd in love! – Who says
A whale's a bird? – Ha! did you call, my love?

– He's here! He's there! – He's everywhere!
Ah me! He's no where![16]

In *Love and Freindship*, madness and swoons are the prerequisites for the distressed heroines, who witness the death of their husbands from an upturned carriage: 'Two Gentlemen most elegantly attired but weltering in their own blood was what first struck our Eyes … Yes dearest Marianne they were our Husbands. Sophia shrieked & fainted on the Ground – I screamed and instantly ran mad.' Laura descends into madness: 'My Eyes assumed a vacant Stare, My face became as pale as Death, and my Senses were considerably impaired' (*MW*, pp. 99–100). Laura's mad speech echoes the incongrous jumble of images in Tilburina's:

'Talk not to me of Phaetons' (said I, raving in a frantic, incoherent manner) – 'Give me a violin – I'll play to him & sooth him in his melancholy Hours – Beware ye gentle Nymphs of Cupid's Thunderbolts, avoid the piercing Shafts of Jupiter – Look at that Grove of Firs – I see a Leg of Mutton – They told me Edward was not Dead; but they deceived me – they took him for a Cucumber'. (*MW*, p. 100)

In *Love and Freindship*, Austen's allusions to *The Critic* are deliberate and blatant. Her mockery of the conventions of sentimentalism is shaped by Sheridan's burlesque techniques and she acknowledges the debt in her close and deliberate echoes of the play. But the Sheridan play that has most resonance with Austen's satire on sensibility is *The Rivals*. *Love and Freindship* has been seen as an early burlesque version of *Sense and Sensibility*, and in both works Austen is indebted to *The Rivals*.

One of the conventions of sentimentalism that both Sheridan and Austen exploit is the conflicting attitudes of the young and their more prudent elders, particularly when it comes to marriage.[17] What leads to a tragic outcome in *Clarissa*, the most influential example of parental tyranny in eighteenth-century fiction, is for Sheridan in *The Rivals* a subject for burlesque. *Love and Freindship* follows Sheridan's inversion of the convention, whereby the benign impulses of parents are wilfully misunderstood by their children. The absurd hero, Edward, opposes his father, even though the opposition is contrary to his own wishes:

'My father, seduced by the false glare of Fortune and the Deluding Pomp of Title, insisted on my giving my hand to Lady Dorothea. No never exclaimed I. Lady Dorothea is lovely and Engaging; I prefer no woman to her; but know Sir, that I scorn to marry her in compliance with your wishes. No! Never shall it be said that I obliged my Father.' (*MW*, p. 81)

The comic impact arises from the contrast between Edward's sentimental outburst and his father's level-headed response, which is to rebuke his quixotic son for using language that is inflated and melodramatic:

'Sir Edward was surprized; he had perhaps little expected to meet with so spirited an opposition to his will. "Where Edward in the name of wonder (said he) did you pick up this unmeaning Gibberish? You have been studying Novels I suspect." I scorned to answer: it would have been beneath my dignity.' (*MW*, p. 81)

The problem with Sir Edward's cretinous son is that he has read too many novels. In *The Loiterer*, Henry and James Austen had satirised women for reading trashy novels, but Austen retaliated in *Love and Freindship* by making a young *man* the target of her satire. Sir Edward accuses his son of gleaning absurdly romantic notions from the pages of sentimental fiction, just as Laura and Sophia make partial judgements based upon the sentimental novels they read:

We soon saw through his Character ... They said he was Sensible, well informed, and Agreeable; we did not pretend to Judge of such trifles, but as we were convinced he had no soul, that he had never read the Sorrows of Werter, & that his Hair bore not the slightest resemblance to Auburn, we were certain that Janetta could feel no affection for him, or at least that she ought to feel none. (*MW*, p. 93)

In the late eighteenth century, the epitome of the misguided reader of romantic novels was Lydia Languish in *The Rivals*. But Sheridan was not the first playwright to burlesque the giddy female novel reader. Lydia Languish follows on from a tradition of quixotic stage heroines such as

Richard Steele's Miss Biddy in *The Tender Husband* (1705) and George Colman the Elder's *Polly Honeycombe* (1760).

Sheridan, like Austen, had limited tolerance for financially imprudent marriages. Lydia embraces the idea of love in a cottage with Ensign Beverley – 'How charming will poverty be with him'. In *Love and Freindship*, Edward also prefers the romance of living in poverty, but the absurdity of his sentimental notions is made apparent by the cool scepticism of his clever sister, Augusta:

'Never, never Augusta will I so demean myself ... Support! What Support will Laura want which she can receive from him?'

'Only those very insignificant ones of Victuals and Drink' (answered she.)

'Victuals and Drink!' (replied my Husband in a most nobly contemptuous Manner) 'and dost thou then imagine that there is no other support for an exalted Mind (such as is my Laura's) than the mean and indelicate employment of Eating and Drinking?'

'None that I know of, so efficacious' (returned Augusta).

'And did you then never feel the pleasing Pangs of Love, Augusta?' (replied my Edward). 'Does it appear impossible to your vile and corrupted Palate, to exist on Love? Can you not conceive the Luxury of living in every Distress that Poverty can inflict, with the object of your tenderest Affection?'

'You are too ridiculous (said Augusta) to argue with.' (*MW*, pp. 83–84)

The device of contrasting a cool, level-headed character with a foolish one had also been deployed by Hugh Kelly in his play *False Delicacy* (1768), where Mrs Harley and Cecil provide a rational norm by which the excesses of absurd sensibility can be measured. The contrasts and conflicts arising from clashes between Romantic idealism and prudent conservatism provide the comic dynamic of both Austen's and Sheridan's satire, and – as will be shown later – Austen was to rework this comic device in *Sense and Sensibility*.

Even in her earliest works, the harmful effects of excessive emotion are satirised, although the chief emphasis in *Love and Freindship* is upon the hypocrisy of sentimentalism. The two anti-heroines, Laura and Sophia, justify selfish and malicious behaviour by their skewed vision of sentimental duty. In the name of sentimentalism, they persuade Janetta to elope with an unprincipled fortune hunter, and abandon the honourable man that she really loves:

> The very circumstance of his being her father's choice too, was so much in his disfavour, that had he been deserving her, in every other respect yet *that* of itself ought to have been a sufficient reason in the Eyes of Janetta for rejecting him … we had no difficulty to convince her that it was impossible she could love Graham, or that it was her duty to disobey her Father. (*MW*, pp. 93–94)

What is worse, their destructive interference in a young girl's happiness is twisted into the appearance of a noble and generous act. Beneath the veneer of sensibility lie egotism and selfishness. Laura and Sophia steal, lie and cheat – all in the name of sensibility. It was, after all, a code of conduct that unashamedly placed the individual first. Thus, when Sophia is caught *in flagrante delicto* stealing money from her host, in her own words 'majestically removing the 5th bank-note' from her cousin's private drawer, she responds in the injured tones of a virtuous heroine whose personal integrity has been violated, a parody on Clarissa Harlowe in Richardson's novel:

> Sophia … instantly put on a most forbidding look, & darting an angry frown on the undaunted culprit, demanded in a haughty tone of voice 'Wherefore her retirement was thus insolently broken in on?' The unblushing Macdonald, without even endeavouring to exculpate himself from the crime he was charged with, meanly endeavoured to reproach Sophia with ignobly defrauding him of his money … The Dignity of Sophia was wounded; 'Wretch' (exclaimed she, hastily replacing the Bank-note in the drawer) 'how darest thou to accuse me of an Act, of which the bare idea makes me blush.' (*MW*, p. 96)

Clarissa of course has every right to object to her violation, whereas Sophia does not, for she is stealing. Just as Laura and Sophia steal unashamedly from their guests, Edward and Augustus 'scorned to reflect a moment on their pecuniary distresses and would have blushed at the idea of paying their debts' (*MW*, p. 86). This 'gentlemanly' attribute derives from Charles Surface in *The School for Scandal*, who is encouraged by his friend Careless to put off paying his huge debts with the money that he has borrowed from Premium:

> CARELESS: Don't let that old Blockhead persuade you – to squander any of that money on old Musty debts, or any such Nonsense for tradesmen – Charles, are the most Exorbitant Fellows.
> CHARLES: Very true, and paying them is only Encouraging them.[18]

In *The Rivals* Sheridan had satirised absurd sentimentalism, but in *The School for Scandal* he made explicit the connection between sensibility and hypocrisy. Comedies by playwrights such as Steele, Colman and Kelly had satirised foolish sentimentalism, but the darker *School for Scandal* showed how the cult of sensibility was abused when it became a front for prudery and hypocrisy.[19]

In *Love and Freindship* Austen also shows how sensibility is abused by unscrupulous characters. In an allusion to Sheridan's smooth hypocrite Joseph Surface, Laura's 'refined' feelings are disturbed by the sound of 'loud and repeated snores' in a carriage journey, inciting a misplaced outburst of emotion:

> What an illiterate villain must that Man be! (thought I to myself) What a total Want of delicate refinement must he have who can thus shock our senses by such a brutal Noise! He must I am certain be capable of every bad Action! There is no crime too black for such a Character. (*MW*, p. 103)

This speech is an imitation of Joseph's hypocritical protestations when he persuades Sir Peter Teazle that his brother Charles is Lady Teazle's lover, rather than himself:

Oh, 'tis not to be credited – There may be a man capable of such Baseness to be sure – but for my Part 'till you can give me positive Proofs – I can not but doubt it. However if this should be proved on him He is no longer a Brother of mine! I disclaim kindred with him – for the Man who can break thro' the laws of Hospitality – and attempt the wife – of his Friend deserves to be branded as the Pest of Society.[20]

The 'artful, selfish and malicious' man who 'studies sentiment' and is a member of Lady Sneerwell's circle of malicious slanderers disguises his perfidy beneath a veneer of sensibility and tells the audience that, instead of the 'silver ore of pure Charity', he prefers to use 'the sentimental French plate'. Jane Austen's mockery of the hypocritical cant of sensibility owes much to Sheridan's example. Though her characters in *Love and Freindship* are rarely permitted to stray beyond the boundaries of burlesque, in *Sense and Sensibility* the genuine sensibility of the Dashwood sisters is used to reflect upon the false sensibility of other characters. Even in this later work, however, she doesn't altogether abandon burlesque methods.

Austen's roots were in literary parody: she loved burlesque and never altogether abandoned it. From her earliest full-length satire of the sentimental and Gothic novel, *Northanger Abbey*, to her final uncompleted novel, she continued to use elements of it in her work. *Sanditon* is extremely close in spirit to the juvenilia, a dying return to Austen's natural medium of satire and her love of the ridiculous.[21]

The Critic and *Tom Thumb* were probably the two most popular burlesques of the eighteenth century. Austen's development as a comic writer and her affinity with literary parody can be attributed, in part, to the example set by these plays. Furthermore, the distinctive element of both plays was the degree of authorial control maintained by the authors. Fielding's satirical author's notes to the text of *Tom Thumb*, and Sheridan's rehearsal play, with its author-within-the-play, permitted the writers an unusual degree of authorial control of a kind that greatly appealed to Jane Austen.

In the move from the drama to the novel, Fielding pioneered the way of successfully integrating quasi-theatrical techniques with third-person narration. Jane Austen also experimented with both dramatic and epistolary form – both of which lack a narrator's voice – before turning to third-person narration.

5

From Play to Novel

Jane Austen's chief models in the art of burlesque were Sheridan and Fielding in the dramatic tradition, and Charlotte Lennox's *The Female Quixote* in the novel tradition. In her mature fiction Austen honed her use of the technique without ever abandoning it fully. But before she began refining her first novels for publication in the early part of the nineteenth century, she put the finishing touches to two important transitional works: a play that burlesques Richardson's novel *Sir Charles Grandison* and an epistolary novel, *Lady Susan*.

An analysis of these works reveals a crucial development in the trajectory of Austen's writing career: her final experimentation with, and eventual rejection of, dramatic and epistolary forms, both of which lack a controlling narratorial voice, in favour of third-person narration. In this respect, the novels of Henry Fielding and Elizabeth Inchbald – both playwrights who became novelists – were an important influence on Austen's style. They assisted her in the search for a medium of writing that incorporated quasi-theatrical techniques with third-person narration.

Jane Austen's little five-act comedy 'Sir Charles Grandison' depends upon a close knowledge of Samuel Richardson's novel of the same name.[1] She sub-titled her play 'The Happy Man', in allusion to the way that Richardson irritatingly overused this phrase throughout his novel. Austen had previously made Richardson's 'perfect hero' the butt of many jokes in her juvenilia. He was the 'happy man' in 'Jack and Alice': 'an amiable, accomplished & bewitching young Man; of so dazzling a Beauty that none but Eagles could look him in the Face' (*MW*, p. 13).

The most obvious joke in Austen's 'Sir Charles Grandison' is its very brevity. It reduces Richardson's seven-volume, million-word novel into a stage lampoon of five short acts, without any marked alteration to the plot. The heroine, Harriet Byron, is stolen away at a masquerade ball by a notorious blackguard, Sir Hargrave Pollexfen, before being rescued and married to the hero Sir Charles Grandison. In the novel the reader, like the heroine, has to wait for five volumes before the hero is free to marry the woman he loves.

Samuel Johnson famously said that a man who read Richardson for the story might as well go hang himself. The telescoping of the notoriously long narrative into a short play is in the tradition of Fielding's reduction of *Pamela* into the sixty-page lampoon *Shamela*. The success of burlesque partly depends on its brevity, as Fielding realised, and Austen showed a similar awareness of this necessity in her juvenilia, where she rarely permitted the joke to be laboured. In 'Grandison' she compounded the comic impact by showing that Richardson's thin plot and million-word novel could be transposed into a short play.

It seems to have been written over a number of years.[2] Austen was probably working on it from the 1780s, when the family was engaged in private theatricals. For example, Act One is very similar in style to her playlets of this period, whereas the manuscript of Act Two is watermarked 1799. The final version was probably completed around 1805. The dating is important because it was the completion of 'Grandison' that heralded the way ahead for Austen's adoption of third-person narration.

By turning her favourite novel into a burlesque play, Austen showed her implicit awareness of Richardson's dramatic inheritance. Richardson was keen on the public theatre, and was friendly with such dramatists as Colley Cibber, Aaron Hill and Edward Young. He was deeply influenced by the drama and gleaned a diversity of techniques and materials from his knowledge of plays.[3] Indeed, he perceived himself as a dramatic novelist. In the postscript to *Clarissa*, he describes that work as a 'Dramatic Narrative', and at the front of *Clarissa* and *Sir Charles Grandison* he places the 'Names of *the* Principal Persons' as a *dramatis personae*. In all of his novels Richardson has parenthetical insertions like stage directions such as '*Enter Dorcas in haste*', '[*rising*]' and '[*Rising again*]' and even directions for the characters, '[Lips drawn closer: eye raised]'.[4]

One of the most striking theatrical borrowings in *Clarissa* is the scene before Hampstead, where Lovelace writes:

And here, supposing my narrative of the dramatic kind, ends Act the First. And now begins

ACT II. Scene, Hampstead Heath, continued

Enter my Rascal.[5]

Lovelace is a recognisable theatrical character (he is in many respects based on Nicholas Rowe's Lothario), and the fate of Clarissa may even have been based on the plot of a play called *Caelia* by Charles Johnson (1733), where a virtuous heroine is placed in a brothel.[6] Lovelace's relish for role-playing and for stage-managing the action of the novel reveal his open allegiance to the archetypal stage rake.[7]

A further development of Richardson's dramatic art in *Clarissa*, which he was to perfect in *Sir Charles Grandison*, was his implementation of dialogue in the style of a play-book. This can be seen in the comic description of Anna Howe's account of Uncle Anthony's courtship of Mrs Howe. The dialogue between mother and daughter is set out like a play:

I *think* you shall have the *dialogue* ...

MOTHER: I have a very serious matter to talk with you upon, Nancy, when you are disposed to attend to matters *within* ourselves, and not let matters *without* ourselves wholly engross you ...

DAUGHTER: I am *now* disposed to attend to everything my mamma is *disposed* to say to me.

MOTHER: Why then, child – why then, my dear – (and the good lady's face looked *so* plump! *so* smooth! and *so* shining!) – I see you are all attention, Nancy! – but don't be surprised! – don't be uneasy! – but I have – I have – where is it? – (And yet it lay next her heart, never another near it – so no difficulty to have found it) – I have a *letter*, my dear! – (and out from her bosom it came: but she still held it in her hand) – I have a *letter*, child – It is – it is – it is from – from a gentleman, I assure you! – lifting up her head, and smiling.[8]

Richardson knew that he was writing for a public used to reading play-books. Not for nothing had Pope quipped 'Our wives read Milton and our daughters plays'.[9] Though Richardson explicitly made use of play-book narration in *Clarissa*, he drew upon it even more extensively in *Sir Charles Grandison*. Though *Clarissa* (and *Pamela I*) were centred on a single plot situation that could be perceived as dramatic in origin, *Sir Charles Grandison* is more episodic. Richardson builds his script technique into the novel, recounting long dramatic conversations in the narrative with increasingly rare authorial intervention.

Paradoxically, *Sir Charles Grandison* has little dramatic action and is more concerned with everyday social behaviour, aside from the Clementina sub-plot. Yet Lady Bradshaigh, among others, saw the dramatic potential of the novel as genteel comedy when she remarked that a play worthy of David Garrick might be formed out of it.[10] The dramatic method of narrative is actually described in the novel itself, when Harriet explains her epistolary style to Lucy:

> By the way, Lucy, you are fond of plays; and it has come into my head, that to avoid all *says-I's* and *says-she's*, I will henceforth, in all dialogues, write names in the margin: so fansy, my dear, that you are reading in one of your favourite volumes.[11]

Richardson's pioneering method of narration was a significant influence on writers such as Fanny Burney and Jane Austen. Parts of Burney's early journals, for example, were written as conversations between different characters, following what she called 'the Grandison way of writing Dialogue'.[12] Later, she coined her own word to describe her method of writing: 'I think I shall occcasionally *Theatricalise* my Dialogues.'[13]

It is striking, but not surprising, that Jane Austen should have turned her very favourite novel into a burlesque, and in so doing have heightened many of its weaknesses. The very act of transcribing the novel into a play was a sly hit at Richardson's claim to be a dramatic novelist. Thus Austen parodies Richardson's use of elaborate stage-directions: '*The Library at Colnebrook, a few minutes later. Curtain draws up and discovers* Miss Grandison *reading*.'[14] Austen's stage directions mockingly recall the way in which Richardson describes action, gesture and facial expression in his dramatic dialogues:

> SIR CHARLES: I have a letter of his to answer. He is very urgent with me for my interest with you. I am to answer it. Will you tell me, my sister (giving her the letter) what I shall say?
>
> MISS GRANDISON: [*after perusing it*] Why, ay, poor man! he is very much in love.[15]

Though she admired *Grandison*'s comedy of manners, Austen was irreverent about the exaggerated parts that she found comically absurd and highly artificial. One example is the incident when Harriet Byron's stomach is squeezed in a door by the villainous seducer Sir Hargrave Pollexfen. Austen dramatises the action and mocks Richardson's melodramatic dialogue, 'So so, you have killed me, I hope – Well, now I hope, now I hope you are satisfied.'[16] Austen also parodies Richardson's stagecraft in act one scene two of her play, where there are twelve hurried entrances and exits centred upon Harriet's abduction. In Richardson's novel, Pollexfen behaves in the manner of a stage villain, and in the space of one paragraph makes numerous entrances and exits. Here it was easy to turn drama into farce.[17] The parts of *Sir Charles Grandison* that Jane Austen least enjoyed were the excessive sentimental and melodramatic elements, such as the abduction of Harriet and the madness of Clementina. Austen was aware that Richardson's debt to the dramatic tradition was best expressed in his conversations and the 'battle of the sexes' combats in the drawing room and the cedar parlour.

Richardson's comic types are drawn from Restoration and eighteenth-century comedy. In particular, Charlotte Grandison (later to become the married Lady G.) derives from the witty, teasing heroines of stage comedy – Harriet in Etherege's *The Man of Mode*, Harriot in Steele's *The Funeral* and Lady Betty Modish in Cibber's *The Careless Husband*.[18] Above all, Charlotte resembles Congreve's Millamant in *The Way of the World*. Though her wit and raillery provoke censure from her brother, he confesses that he loves her '*With all your faults, my dear*, and I had almost said, *for* some of them'.[19] Sir Charles is surely alluding to Mirabell's description of Millamant: 'I like her with all her Faults; nay, like her for her Faults. Her Follies are so natural, so artful, that they become her; and those Affectations which in another Woman wou'd be odious, serve but to make her more agreeable.'[20] Mirabell's remarks are also echoed in Knightley's feelings about Emma, when he describes her as 'faultless, in spite of all her faults' (E, p. 433) and claims that he has always doted on her 'faults and all' (E, p. 462).[21]

Austen's burlesque of Harriet, who loses all her spirit and interest as soon as she falls in love, is thrown into relief by her evident admiration of Charlotte Grandison. Throughout Richardson's *Sir Charles Grandison*, few characters get the better of Charlotte, and she is usually the winner in the various wit combats which pervade the narrative. Charlotte dislikes the subordination of women in marriage and delights in her own independence. Even as she is led up to the altar she is overheard to say, very much in the manner of Millamant, 'You don't know what you are about, man. I expect to have all my way: Remember that's one of my articles before marriage.'[22] Unusually for the fiction of the time, Charlotte remains an unreformed coquette even after her marriage to her bashful and doting husband.

Austen demonstrates her awareness of Charlotte Grandison's stature as the real heroine of the novel, and simultaneously burlesques one of Richardson's duller characters, Mr Reeves, by reversing his character, and enabling her own Charlotte to confess that Mr Reeves 'disputes charmingly. I thought he would have got the better of me.' Later Austen has Miss Jervois satirically observe of Lord G., Charlotte's betrothed: 'he will certainly get the better of you at last. He did it once, you know.'[23] Austen's dramatisation of *Sir Charles Grandison*, and in particular her use of the burlesque tradition to highlight its artificial elements, was a way of exorcising the parts of the novel she liked least, of escaping from the excessive sentimentality and melodramatic elements of Richardson's narrative method. It liberated her to produce her own ironised version of the sentimental novel. But she discovered that the dramatic form was unable to give her the authorial control she required, and she was now to reject it. It is surely no coincidence that she was also doing something similar with the epistolary tradition, that quasi-dramatic form of narration of which Richardson had been the pioneer.

*   *   *

Around the same time as she put the finishing touches to her burlesque play of *Sir Charles Grandison*, Jane Austen was completing *Lady Susan*. This short epistolary novel was probably first drafted around 1794–95, but Austen seems to have carefully copied it out around 1805, when she also added an author's conclusion in the third person.

Lady Susan is Jane Austen's most ambitious early work. It is her only extant epistolary novel of substance, and it is here that she really began to explore the possibilities of the letter as a narrative form. *Lady Susan* reveals how Austen recast inherited conventions by means of ongoing experiments with narrative voice. It also shows how she was still strongly influenced by Richardson.

Lady Susan playfully reworks the structure of Richardson's great tragic novel, *Clarissa*. It reproduces the first part of Richardson's plot, where a daughter is imprisoned for her refusal to marry the man of her parents' choice. As Lovelace is the traditional rake (of both stage and page), so Lady Susan is the temptress, manipulating men by employing her personal charms; she is charming and witty, and morally corrupt. Lady Susan justifies her attempt to ensnare the young hero on two accounts: partly to amuse herself with the challenge of subduing an 'insolent spirit', and also to avenge herself on the Vernon family, whom she despises, 'to humble the Pride of these self-important Courcies still lower' (*MW*, p. 254). These are exactly the two reasons why Lovelace literally ensnares Clarissa: 'Then what a triumph would it be to the *Harlowe pride*, were I now to marry this lady?'; 'Why will she not *if once subdued* be *always subdued*.'[24]

Lady Susan was Austen's first novel to contrast the town and the country. Events that occur at the country house of the Vernons are set against those which occur in London. This device, which the novel absorbed from stage comedy, was used to fine effect in Richardson; Jane Austen used it again in *Sense and Sensibility* and *Mansfield Park*. Unlike Richardson, who is brilliant in the London scenes, Austen is at her finest when she is depicting events in the country. She recast inherited stage conventions by having the Londoners entering the country and causing trouble, rather than the ingenues entering London society, as was conventional both in stage comedy and the novels of Fanny Burney and Maria Edgeworth.

Lady Susan was an important transitional work. Unlike *Love and Freindship*, which merely parodied the novel-of-letters, this work is a serious trial of the epistolary form. In *Clarissa*, Richardson mastered and perfected the epistolary form. The same characters and events are seen and judged from a variety of viewpoints; different characters reveal how all actions are open to many layers of interpretation and potential distortion.

The double yet separate correspondence of *Lady Susan* echoes that of Clarissa and Anne Howe, Lovelace and Belford. The psychological richness of Lovelace's character is rendered by Richardson's complex interweaving of letters between the four correspondents, and his careful manipulation of point of view. Just as Richardson's letters permit us to enter into the mind of the villainous Lovelace, Austen allows us into the mind of the equally unscrupulous Lady Susan. Through the juxtaposition of Lady Susan's first two letters, the novelist establishes her heroine's villainous potential. The tone and content of Lady Susan's deferential opening letter is contrasted and highlighted by the sheer force of her stylishly defiant second epistle, with its insolent self-justification of her villainous conduct. Despite the fact that Austen damns her heroine, Lady Susan's rebelliousness and her lively epistolary style, reminiscent of Lovelace's, make her an appealing villain. But, unlike Richardson, Austen does not sufficiently develop counter-balancing epistolary voices.

Lady Susan reproduces the first part of the *Clarissa* plot, but considers it from a different perspective. Like Clarissa, Lady Susan's daughter Frederica is imprisoned. Though Frederica is not imprisoned in a brothel, nor drugged, raped and left alone to die, her fate is nevertheless a devious form of confinement orchestrated by her mother. Clarissa is defined by her letters and her freedom to write; even after her 'literal death' her posthumous letters confirm and sustain her existence in the life of the novel. By contrast Frederica is forced to suffer a diametrically opposed, but equally significant, form of confinement. Frederica's punishment for trying to escape from her mother is the ban on her freedom to speak. Frederica has no voice. Nor does Austen give her a pen, save for one brief letter. The young heroine is silenced. This causes a potential problem for Austen; since we have Clarissa's letters, we can judge Lovelace's villainy. Without Frederica's letters, and without the counter-balancing voice of a strong male character, there is a danger that Lady Susan will completely dominate the novel.

Austen tries to get round this problem by contrasting her heroine with another strong female character, the sagacious and perceptive Mrs Vernon. Letter 24 is crucial in this regard. Here Austen demonstrates her own 'command of language' (*MW*, p. 251) in a scene that anticipates the vigour and sophistication of her later dialogues. This is a brilliant set-piece. Like so many of her later set-pieces, it is an arresting confrontation between two women in conflict over a young man. This motif reappears in the confrontation between Elinor Dashwood and Lucy Steele in *Sense and Sensibility*, and Elizabeth Bennet and Lady Catherine De Bourgh in *Pride and Prejudice*.

The dispute is induced by Frederica's plea for help, the substance of her first and only letter. Austen establishes the tone of this dramatic confrontation by Lady Susan's exultant acknowledgement of her manipulative powers: 'Did not I tell you, said she with a smile, that your Brother would not leave us after all?' (*MW*, p. 287). Lady Susan is barely able to contain her derision at her daughter's guilelessness: 'had Frederica possessed the penetration, the abilities, which I could have wished in my daughter, or had I even known her to possess so much as she does, I should not have been anxious for the match' (*MW*, p. 288). Mrs Vernon's defence of Frederica is equally spirited: 'It is odd that you alone should be ignorant of your Daughter's sense' (*MW*, p. 288).

The dialogue is continued in this vein, with Lady Susan's tears, vindications and excuses contrasted with Mrs Vernon's brusque, impatient rejoinders. Austen's delivery of Lady Susan's animated utterances, with its affected tone of injured virtue, is beautifully controlled. Before Letter 24 we have heard much of Lady Susan's linguistic arts, but in this letter we see them fully in action:

Can you possibly suppose that I was aware of her unhappiness? that it was my object to make my own child miserable, & that I had forbidden her speaking to you on the subject, from a fear of your interrupting the Diabolical scheme? Do you think me destitute of every honest, every natural feeling? Am I capable of consigning *her* to everlasting Misery, whose welfare it is my first Earthly Duty to promote? (*MW*, p. 289)

Through the dramatic force of this confrontation, Austen blurs the distinction between reported and immediate action. Following Richardson's model, Austen punctuates her speeches with added commentary, almost like stage directions: 'here she began to cry', 'with a smile', 'taking me by the hand'. Mrs Vernon's interjections are used to draw attention to Lady Susan's theatrical skills and they also reveal one of the strengths of the epistolary form. The letter simultaneously allows for the correspondent's retrospective viewpoint of the action, while providing immediate access to the character's writing 'of the moment'. Austen's device of switching between direct and reported speech also enables the flow of the heated exchange to gain full momentum. In response to Lady Susan's impassioned pleas and theatrical gestures, Mrs Vernon's reply is uncompromisingly brusque: 'The idea is horrible. What then was your intention when you insisted on her silence?' (*MW*, p. 289).

Mrs Vernon's resistance is, however, short-lived, and she is finally defeated by the sheer intellectual vigour of Lady Susan. That the day is the latter's is suggested in Lady Susan's closing barb: 'Excuse me, my dearest Sister, for thus trespassing on your time, but I owed it to my own Character; & after this explanation I trust I am in no danger of sinking in your opinion' (*MW*, p. 290).

Stunned by this final example of her opponent's effrontery, Mrs Vernon, like all Lady Susan's enemies (including her own daughter), is reduced to silence: 'It was the greatest stretch of Forbearance I could practise. I could not have stopped myself, had I begun' (*MW*, p. 291). Lady Susan's following letter rejoices over this major victory: 'I call on you my dear Alicia, for congratulations. I am again myself; gay and triumphant' (*MW*, p. 291).

Following the defeat of Mrs Vernon, the pace of the novel increases with a series of short letters, which serve to wind up the plot. Like Lovelace, Lady Susan wreaks revenge on all who have crossed her, and her favourite place to execute her plans is London. Richardson and Burney both made London the immoral centre of corrupt society. Lovelace's plot is chiefly dependent upon the lax morals of the prostitutes in the London brothel, and he insists that his intrigues can only work in a place that has the anonymity of the capital. Similarly, Lady Susan adores the bustle and intrigue of the town, 'for London will be always the fairest field of action' (*MW*, p. 294).

Austen devotes little space to the events in London, and swiftly moves to the denouement of plot, the exposition of Lady Susan's continuing affair with Manwaring, and its subsequent disclosure. The ensuing self-revelatory letters reveal the depths of Lady Susan's villainy. This is the weakest part of the novel; Austen seems impatient to wind up the plot. She abandons the letters and rounds off the ending with an author's summary, a cursory account of the fate of the main characters in a distinctive third-person narratorial voice that makes fun of the epistolary device that she has been used hitherto. Seemingly frustrated with a villain who has got out of hand, Jane Austen assumes a studied indifference to the fate of her essentially unsympathetic supporting cast. The novel ends rather predictably with the promise of Frederica's and Reginald's marriage, but by now the author doesn't really care: 'Frederica was therefore fixed in the family of her Uncle & Aunt, till such time as Reginald De Courcy could be talked, flattered & finessed into an affection for her ... Three months might have done it in general, but Reginald's feelings were no less lasting than lively' (*MW*, p. 313).

Austen's conclusion also represents a light-hearted attack on the epistolary style: 'This Correspondence ... could not, to the great detriment of the Post office Revenue, be continued longer' (*MW*, p. 311). The breakdown of the epistolary form is the price that Jane Austen has to pay for Lady Susan's domination of the narrative. In the absence of strong balancing forces, and with the silencing of Frederica and the defeat of Mrs Vernon in Letter 24, the epistolary form cannot provide Austen with a sufficiently powerful means of being both inside and outside her protagonist.

Far from guiding our moral responses, the brisk conclusion leaves readers to decide for themselves if the characters' fates are justified. Lady Susan marries the rich fop Sir James and we assume gets what she deserves: 'The world must judge from Probability. She had nothing against her, but her Husband, & her Conscience.' The author's own sympathy is devoted to one of her minor characters who loses her lover to Lady Susan: 'For myself, I confess that *I* can pity only Miss Manwaring, who coming to Town & putting herself to an expense in Cloathes, which impoverished her for two years, on purpose to secure him, was defrauded of her due by a Woman ten years older than herself' (*MW*, p. 313). And on that tantalising jibe, the novel ends, somewhat unsatisfactorily in its own terms, but leaving us eager to hear more of that ironically detached *I*.

Austen's rejection of Richardson, through her burlesque play 'Grandison' and through *Lady Susan*, was a casting aside of both epistolary and dramatic form. Neither of these were suitable mediums for her desire to be simultaneously inside and outside her characters, something which she eventually achieved by her use of irony and free indirect speech in third-person narration. Though *Lady Susan* was a serious experiment in epistolary narrative, Austen rejected it precisely because the epistolary technique is itself 'dramatic'; it formally banishes the authorial voice, though the 'author' or 'editor' is still implicit as the coordinator of juxtapositions, sequences, contrasting tones and parallelisms. Richardson's effacement of the authorial voice through the epistolary was clearly uncongenial to the mature Austen.

Austen also rejected the epistolary form's claim to be able to create the illusion of 'writing to the moment'. Lovelace's own phrase, 'I love to write to the moment',[25] suggests that the events are happening in the present tense, giving the reader a sense of the story's immediacy. The characters are always in the middle of their own experience, a feature which Fielding had been quick to satirise in *Shamela*: 'You see I write in the present Tense.'[26] Austen engaged in a similar parody in her juvenilia, notably in a story called 'Amelia Webster' (*MW*, pp. 47–49).

Anna Barbauld, in the introduction to her 1804 edition of Richardson's correspondence, described what she considered to be the differences between conventional methods of novelistic narration and the inherent drama of the epistolary method:

> This method unites, in good measure, the advantages of the other two; [the 'narrative' or 'epic' found for example in Cervantes and Fielding, and the 'memoir' found in Smollett and Goldsmith] it gives the feelings of the moment. It allows a pleasing variety of stile, if the author has sufficient command of the pen to assume it. It makes the whole work dramatic, since all the characters speak in their own persons.[27]

While writing *Sir Charles Grandison*, Richardson described to his friend, Lady Bradshaigh, the paradoxes of his narrative method in which the author's presence is banished and yet can simultaneously be identified with any one of the characters:

> Here I sit down to form characters. One I intend to be all goodness; All goodness he is. Another I intend to be all gravity; All gravity he is. Another *Lady G – ish*; All *Lady G – ish* she is. I am all the while absorbed in the character. It is not fair to say – I, identically I, am anywhere, while I keep within the character.[28]

This dramatic projection allows him to enter into the points of view of all of his characters; there is no single reliable authorial voice.

In her mature works Jane Austen used free indirect speech to achieve an even more sophisticated effect: she writes from both within and without her characters. Free indirect speech is the device whereby a novelist writes from the point of view of an individual character, but retains the distance provided by third-person narrative. Austen uses this technique most fully in *Emma*: 'The hair was curled, and the maid sent away, and Emma sat down to think and be miserable. – It was a wretched business, indeed! – Such an overthrow of every thing she had been wishing for … Such a blow for Harriet! – that was the worst of all' (*E*, p. 134). The first sentence appears to belong to the voice of the author, but as the passage continues, we seem to be given a verbalisation of the heroine's own thoughts.

It is for this reason that film and television adaptations – brilliantly as they may render the surface of Jane Austen's comic world – can never fully satisfy the serious reader of the novels themselves. Screenwriters find it almost impossible to render the ironic third-person authorial voice that is so important to Austen's narrative method.[29] Important as the drama was to the making of her fictional worlds, Austen was in the end a novelist.

Whereas dramatic dialogue and epistolary form render the *words* of the characters, free indirect discourse renders their *thoughts* – and, since it does so in the third person rather than the first, the author is able to be simultaneously inside and outside the consciousness of the character, to be both engaged and ironic. This technique is unique to the novel, but Austen only fully developed it after having experimented with dramatic and epistolary forms. In direct opposition to the Richardsonian imperative, she discovered that she favoured the authorial voice, the voice that we hear at the end of *Lady Susan*. By adding her author's conclusion to *Lady Susan*, Austen bid farewell to the epistolary form. It seems to have been after this that she reworked the epistolary 'Elinor and Marianne' into the third-person *Sense and Sensibility*.

Richardson remained, nevertheless, an important influence on Austen's narrative art. His pioneering use of dramatic-style dialogue was crucial to her development, and she assimilated both epistolary and quasi-theatrical techniques into her mature novels. Austen had parodied Richardson in her juvenilia and in 'Grandison', and in *Lady Susan* she had paid tribute to the epistolary tradition, before transcending her favourite writer. Paradoxically, the writer whose narrative style she now turned to was Richardson's great opponent, Henry Fielding, who pioneered the successful integration of quasi-theatrical techniques with third-person narration.

While she learned much from Richardson's mastery of revelation of character through dialogue, she also learned from Fielding. It is an irony that Richardson was singled out for his dramatic powers and imagination, while the playwright-turned-novelist Fielding was characterised by his obtrusive authorial presence, and his distrust of the epistolary form.

Fielding's metamorphosis into a novelist provided a powerful model for Austen. He began by burlesquing the epistolary tradition and highlighting its weaknesses and artificiality in *Shamela*, then developed a sophisticated third-person narratorial voice in *Joseph Andrews*. Austen not only shared his love of burlesque, but, like him, also successfully made the transition from burlesque to high comedy and from epistolary to third-person narration. Yet even as they rejected the drama, each of them retained a wealth of quasi-theatrical devices in their plotting, characterisation, dialogue, use of set-pieces and formal tableaux, coincidences, wit-combats and cross-purposes.[30] In direct opposition to Richardson's epistolary style, which they both parodied, Fielding and Austen favoured authorial mediation and a controlling intelligence. The stylisation wrought by theatrical techniques within the non-theatrical form of the novel highlighted the workings of that intelligence.

A comparable case is that of Elizabeth Inchbald, who, like Fielding, was a playwright turned novelist. Her highly acclaimed first novel, *A Simple Story*, was loosely based on Shakespeare's *Winter's Tale*. Austen knew Inchbald's adaptation of *Lovers' Vows*, which she used in *Mansfield Park*. She also perhaps alludes to Inchbald's controversial novel in *Emma*, where Mr Knightley describes the news of Harriet's engagement to Robert Martin as a 'simple story' (*E*, p. 471).

Inchbald's interpolation of dramatic detail into the novel, the product of her long experience as both a dramatist and an actress, was highly praised by her contemporaries. Like Fielding, she found new opportunities in her move from theatrical to narrative writing. An emphasis on direct speech and telling gesture was used to achieve dramatic revelation of character. The *Monthly Review* noted: 'The secret charm, that gives a grace to the whole is the art with which Mrs Inchbald has made her work dramatic. The business is, in a great degree, carried on in dialogue. In dialogue the characters unfold themselves. Their motions, their looks, their attitudes, discover the inward temper.'[31]

With the minimum of authorial intervention, Inchbald promised to let her heroine reveal herself: 'And now – leaving description – the reader must form a judgment of her by her actions; by all the round of great or trivial circumstances that shall be related.'[32] In her lively and irreverent dialogue, the heroine Miss Milner is indebted to the witty stage heroines of Restoration and eighteenth-century comedy. From her first exchange with the austere guardian/priest Dorriforth, she shows herself capable of forthright charm and candour: 'in some respects I am like you Roman Catholics; I don't believe from my own understanding, but from what other people tell me.'[33] In contrast, Dorriforth's repressed nature is conveyed in the stilted and wooden tones by which he endeavours to conceal his passion for his vivacious ward.

Inchbald's theatrical training is evident in the numerous reversals and parallels of incident and characterisation and the tightly-structured comedy of misunderstandings and misreadings between her intimate group of characters. Dorriforth ascribes Miss Milner's blushes to excessive modesty, but her embarrassment betrays something other than maidenly virtue:

> 'How can I doubt of a lady's virtue, when her countenance gives such evident proofs of them? Believe me, Miss Milner, that in the midst of your gayest follies; while you thus continue to blush, I shall reverence your internal sensations.'
>
> 'Oh! my lord, did you know some of them, I am afraid you would think them unpardonable.'[34]

The characters not only misunderstand each other, they also often dwell in ignorance of their own feelings. It is only Dorriforth's jealousy of a rival lover that forces him to acknowledge his illicit love for his ward.

Inchbald's art of dramatic presentation is further revealed in her deployment of comic parallels and contrasts to the main action. A comic device that she uses to great effect in *A Simple Story* is that of showing a series of reactions to the same incident. When Dorriforth's confessor, Sandford, tells the ladies that Dorriforth is to fight a duel over Miss Milner, they respond in a variety of ways:

> Mrs Horton exclaimed, 'If Mr Dorriforth dies, he dies a martyr.'
>
> Miss Woodley cried with fervour, 'Heaven forbid!'
>
> Miss Fenton cried, 'Dear me!'
>
> While Miss Milner, without uttering one word, sunk speechless on the floor.[35]

The dramatic detail that was absorbed into her novel elicited high praise from Maria Edgeworth: 'I am of the opinion that it is by leaving more than most other writers to the imagination, that you succeed so eminently in affecting it. By the force that is necessary to repress feeling, we judge of the intensity of the feeling; and you always contrive to give us by intelligible but simple signs the measure of this force.'[36] Edgeworth's remarks provide an important insight into Inchbald's technical innovation in narrative writing: the power of 'intelligible but simple signs'. Actions in *A Simple Story* often render dialogue or authorial elaboration unnecessary. The movement of a knife and fork in Miss Milner's hand, a mistake made while playing cards, or thrusting her head outside the window to cool her flushed face: all convey the strongest emotion beneath the exterior.[37]

Jane Austen's comparable interest in different reactions to the same incident, and the depiction of strong emotion beneath the surface of polite conduct, is evident in her first published novel, *Sense and Sensibility*. Signs or actions, as when a character rolls a paper or cuts with scissors, are used to suggest emotional turmoil within, very much in the manner of an actor's use of props and gestures on stage.

Fielding and Inchbald metamorphosed themselves from playwrights into novelists, and in so doing introduced theatrical effects into the novel. Austen correspondingly abandoned the dramatic and epistolary forms because they lacked a controlling narratorial voice. By adopting the best parts of Richardson's comedy of manners and the quasi-theatrical innovations of Fielding and Inchbald, she achieved a synthesis that enabled her to find her own unique novelistic voice.

6

Sense and Sensibility

Sense and Sensibility, Jane Austen's first published novel, is usually read in the context of the tradition of the sentimental novel, as *Northanger Abbey* is read in the context of the Gothic novel. But for Austen, the figure of the giddy female reader who falls into misadventures as a result of wishing to be like the sentimental heroines of fiction does not only derive from the novel form itself. There are other exemplars – and they offer further, hitherto neglected, evidence of the importance for her of the theatrical tradition.

In *Love and Freindship*, Austen had satirised sensibility and its harmful effect on the minds of young lovers who imbibe distorted romantic notions from the pages of sentimental novels. Like Henry Austen's burlesque heroine in *The Loiterer*, Austen's sentimental heroines, Laura and Sophia, are influenced by Goethe's *The Sorrows of Young Werther*. Literary parody associated with the harmful effects of reading on the young naive mind is to be found among the papers of the *Spectator* and in novels such as Charlotte Lennox's *The Female Quixote* (1752). Yet the key tradition in this respect was that of the theatre, where since 1705 there had been a comic paradigm of the giddy novel reader. Versions of this figure re-emerged in plays throughout the century. She was usually female, and she was often portrayed as mad or, at the very least, misguided and foolish.

In the late eighteenth century the epitome of the misguided reader of romantic novels was Lydia Languish in *The Rivals* (1775). Sheridan's brilliant portrayal of sentimental delusion made Lydia a household name, and helped to perpetuate the idea that novels were an inferior form of fiction, producing harmful effects on the minds of their undiscerning readers:

Here, my dear Lucy, hide these books. – Quick, quick. – Fling *Peregrine Pickle* under the toilet – throw *Roderick Random* into the closet – put *the Innocent Adultery* into *The Whole Duty of Man* – thrust *Lord Aimworth* under the sopha – cram *Ovid* behind the bolster – there – put *the Man of Feeling* into your pocket – so, so, now lay *Mrs Chapone* in sight, and leave *Fordyce's Sermons* open on the table.[1]

Sheridan's burlesque of the reader of the sentimental novel follows on from a tradition of quixotic stage heroines such as Richard Steele's Miss Biddy in *The Tender Husband* (1705) and George Colman the Elder's *Polly Honeycombe* (1760).[2]

Austen clearly knew *The Tender Husband*, as she alludes to Miss Biddy in *Love and Freindship*:

She was a Widow & had only one Daughter, who was then just Seventeen – One of the best of ages; but alas! she was very plain & her name was Bridget ... Nothing therefore could be expected from her – she could not be supposed to possess either exalted Ideas, Delicate Feelings or refined Sensibilities – She was nothing more than a mere good tempered, civil & obliging Young Woman; as such we could scarcely dislike her – she was only an Object of Contempt (*MW*, pp. 100–1).

Steele's Bridget objects to her own name: 'How often must I desire you, Madam, to lay aside that familiar name, Cousin *Biddy*? I never heard of it without Blushing – did you ever meet with an Heroine in those Idle romances as you call 'em, that was term'd *Biddy*?'[3]

The literary tradition of the female quixotic was popularised by Charlotte Lennox's novel, though her heroine Arabella was in fact based on Steele's Biddy Tipkin. When Polly Honeycombe condemns her loathed suitor she likens him to fictional characters from the novels she reads, 'you are as deceitful as Blifil, as rude as the Harlowes, and as ugly as Doctor Slop',[4] and is met with the same incredulous reaction as that of Lennox's lovely but absurd heroine, whose head has been turned by reading novels.[5] In *The Rivals*, Sir Anthony Absolute cries, 'the girl's mad! – her brain's turn'd by reading'.[6] If Lydia Languish and Polly Honeycombe should be viewed in the light of Lennox's heroine, attention should also be paid to Steele's earlier model from which it is more likely that they derive.

The final speech of Polly's exasperated father is a warning to fathers that 'a man might as well turn his Daughter loose in Covent garden, as trust the cultivation of her mind to a circulating library'. In *The Rivals*, Sir Anthony Absolute continues the tradition of fathers fulminating against the evils of the circulating library. Both Sir Anthony Absolute and Mr Honeycombe single out young girls as the targets for the circulating library, as did many other eighteenth-century critics.

Historically speaking, however, the flighty novel-reader was as likely to be male as female.[7] Certainly Jane Austen took this view from the beginning of her writing career to the end. In *Love and Freindship* it is Edward who is directly accused of gleaning absurd notions from reading novels, and in *Sanditon* Sir Edward Denham is a quixotic figure ludicrously enthralled by sensational novels and determined to be 'a dangerous man, quite in the line of the Lovelaces' (*MW*, p. 405). Willoughby loves 'all the same novels' as Marianne and has the same respectful, if detached, admiration for Pope, 'no more than what is proper'. Henry Tilney claims to have 'hundreds and hundreds' of novels and teasingly defends his rights as a male reader of novels, 'for they read nearly as many as women' (*NA*, p. 107).

Austen's fullest attempt at drawing her own giddy quixotic heroine, and avid reader of sensational fiction, Catherine Morland, paradoxically reveals a surprising doubleness, where the novel-reading heroine, contrary to expectation, *does* in fact learn about life from books.[8] Austen's defence of the novel in chapter 5 of *Northanger Abbey* is compounded by Catherine's epiphany at the end of the novel: 'Catherine, at any rate, heard enough to feel, that in suspecting General Tilney of either murdering or shutting up his wife, she had scarcely sinned against his character, or magnified his cruelty' (*NA*, p. 201).

Nor does Austen conform to the view that circulating libraries were the repositories of pap. She used circulating libraries and in 1798 commented on the opening of a subscription library which she intended to join: 'As an inducement to subscribe Mrs Martin tells us that her collection is not to consist only of Novels, but of every kind of Literature &c &c – She might have spared this pretension to *our* family, who are great Novel-readers & not ashamed of being so' (*Letters*, p. 26). One of Fanny Price's compensations for being exiled from Mansfield is the discovery of the joys of Portsmouth's circulating library.

The idea that giddy readers of fiction were not necessarily female is borne out by the practice of both the great comic dramatist and the great comic novelist of the period: as will be shown, both Richard Brinsley Sheridan and Jane Austen reveal that men as well as women are suscep- tible to absurd and self-destructive sentimentalism. Both writers burlesqued literary sentimentalism and its hackneyed features that arose in the genres of both fiction and drama, often interchangeably.[9] Austen and Sheridan's shared sense of literary parody has already been discussed. Here I want to suggest that the debate about the giddy female reader is but one aspect of a much more profound link between *The Rivals* and *Sense and Sensibility*. This connection is a paradigm for Austen's rework- ing of theatrical techniques from eighteenth-century dramatic models.

In *The Rivals*, Sheridan exploits the quasi-farcical device of mistaken identity in the character of Jack Absolute, who disguises himself as the penniless Ensign Beverley so that his lover can marry beneath her. *The Rivals* has two contrasting heroines: one sensible and level-headed (Julia Melville); the other excessively romantic and filled with quixotic notions (Lydia Languish). The amorous entanglement of Lydia and Jack is paral- leled by that of Julia and Faulkland.

By this principle of pairings Sheridan is able to provide contrasts and comparisons between his two female characters, as well as the male. The sensible Julia acts as a foil to the captious sentimentalist, Faulkland, as Lydia's sensibility is mocked by Absolute. But Julia also acts as a foil to Lydia's romantic attitudes, as Jack censures Faulkland's self-destructive impulses. The contrasts and conflicts arising from clashes between romantic idealism and prudent conservatism provide the comic dynamic of Sheridan's satire.

Lydia's quixotic notions threaten her own happiness. She invents a quarrel with Jack Absolute by writing a letter to herself, defaming his character, and is grievously disappointed to be denied a Gretna Green elopement. The association of the name Lydia with elopement is, of course, echoed in *Pride and Prejudice*, where the foolish Lydia writes to

Mrs Forster of her hopes of eloping to Gretna Green.[10] Both Lydia Bennet and Lydia Languish are denied the full romance of illicit love:

> LYDIA: There had I projected one of the most sentimental elopements!
> – so becoming a disguise! – so amiable a ladder of Ropes! –
> Conscious Moon – four horses – Scotch parson – with such
> surprize to Mrs Malaprop – and such paragraphs in the
> Newspapers! – O, I shall die with disappointment.
> JULIA: I don't wonder at it! …
> LYDIA: How mortifying, to remember the dear delicious shifts I used
> to be put to, to gain half a minute's conversation with this fellow! –
> How often have I stole forth, in the coldest night in January, and
> found him in the garden, stuck like a dripping statue! – There
> would he kneel to me in the snow, and sneeze and cough so
> pathetically! he shivering with cold, and I with apprehension! and
> while the freezing blast numb'd our joints, how warmly would he
> press me to pity his flame, and glow with mutual ardour! – Ah,
> Julia! that was something like being in love.
> JULIA: If I were in spirits, Lydia, I should chide you only by laughing
> heartily at you.[11]

Julia's level-headed response to her friend's misplaced misery throws into relief the comic absurdity of Sheridan's sentimental heroine. Furthermore, Julia is paralleled with Jack, for both characters needlessly suffer at the hands of their incorrigible lovers. The sympathy between them is suggested by Julia's heartfelt rebuke of Lydia's affectation: 'I entreat you, not to let a man, who loves you with sincerity, suffer that unhappiness from *caprice*, which I know too well caprice can inflict.' Lydia's response confirms the parallelism of character: 'What does Julia tax me with caprice? – I thought her lover Faulkland had enured her to it.'[12]

Absolute is frustrated by Lydia's 'dev'lish romantic, and very absurd' notions, and Julia is wearied by Faulkland's self-tormenting impulses. But as Julia criticises Lydia, Absolute censures Faulkland:

FAUKLAND: Now, Jack, as you are my friend, own honestly – don't you
 think there is something forward – something indelicate in this
 haste to forgive? …
ABSOLUTE: I have not patience to listen to you: – thou'rt incorrigible!
 … a captious sceptic in love, – a slave to fretfulness and whim –
 who has no difficulties but of *his own* creating – is a subject more fit
 for ridicule than compassion.[13]

The first critics of *The Rivals* do not seem to have shared Absolute's exasperation with his friend, but on the contrary took Faulkland as a model
of delicacy and refined sensibility.[14] Furthermore they felt that Lydia's
romantic notions would be best suited to Faulkland's neurotic musings,
although this would reduce the comedy arising from the contrasts
between the lovers and their counterparts.[15]

The Rivals employs a series of commonsense, sceptical figures who
provide an ironic contrast with the sentimental characters, and who
directly challenge their pretensions. Sheridan levels his critique at sentimentalism by contrasting sensible and rational figures with their opposites, who not only stand in direct contrast to their more foolish
counterparts but openly avow their disapproval of them. This principle
of pairings defines his comic effect. By doubling up the romantic leads,
Sheridan fully exploits the contrasts between the two female friends and
the two males, as well as those between the pairs of lovers.

The Rivals was an important influence on Jane Austen's exploration of
sensibility in her first published novel. Critics who have sought literary
antecedents in Austen's use of 'sense' and 'sensibility' characters as foils
to one another have neglected the influence of stage models.[16] *The Rivals*
was the most celebrated example of the 'sense' and 'sensibility' opposition in comic stage heroines, though other playwrights had explored the
comic potential of antithetical characters. This tradition of contrasting
foils is prevalent in the dramatic tradition. In *The Funeral: or Grief à-la-
Mode* (1701), Richard Steele dramatised two sisters of contrasting characters, Harriot and Sharlot. The coquettish and giddy Harriot is
contrasted with the graver Sharlot. In Cibber's *The Careless Husband*
(1704), the coquettish Lady Betty Modish is contrasted with her virtuous
friend Lady Easy. And in Hugh Kelly's *False Delicacy* (1768), another

play satirising excessive sensibility, the sentimental heroine Lady Betty is contrasted with the commonsensical Mrs Harley. When Lady Betty's personal happiness with Lord Winworth is compromised by her belief in the 'laws of delicacy' (one element being that 'a woman of real delicacy shou'd never admit a second impression on her heart'), she is roundly scolded by her friend Mrs Harley:

> What a work there is with you sentimental folks ... thank heaven my sentiments are not sufficiently refin'd to make me unhappy ... the devil take this delicacy; I don't know any thing it does besides making people miserable.[17]

Kelly's comedy, like *Sense and Sensibility*, shows that sustained mockery of sensibility may coexist with a strong sympathy for it.[18] Although there is no direct evidence that Austen knew the play, she certainly knew *The Rivals*, which, like Kelly's play, dramatises a giddy and a wise female duo.

Austen's principle of pairings is the structural base of *Sense and Sensibility*, and is developed in the contrasting and comparable characters of the two heroines. An antithetical position of representing one sister with sense, Elinor, and the other sister with sensibility, Marianne, is set up, only to be subsequently undermined. So much so that by the end of the novel it is the sensible sister who makes a romantic marriage, and the romantic sister who makes a sensible marriage. Like *False Delicacy*, Austen's satire of sensibility is less straightforward than it appears. The book is consciously structured around a series of ironic oppositions, which work to deflate fixed notions. Having two heroines allows the author's sympathy to be balanced between them as they are played off against one another.

The rationalism of Julia and Jack in *The Rivals*, which actively condemns sensibility, is reworked in *Sense and Sensibility*, where Elinor's dry responses to Marianne's impassioned outbursts often, though not always, prick the bubble of her excessive sensibility. In *The Rivals*, Julia Melville is amused and exasperated by her friend's distorted notions of romance, and provides a dramatic foil to Lydia's romantic notions. In *Sense and Sensibility*, Austen also uses contrasts and parallels between two seemingly different heroines to attack excessive sensibility. One of Marianne's most impassioned outbursts about falling autumnal leaves is dryly condemned by Elinor, 'It is not everyone who has your passion for dead leaves' (SS, p. 88). Julia Melville's genuine pain is keenly dramatised, whereas Lydia's pain is satirised because it is chiefly of her own making. Similarly, we feel limited sympathy for Faulkland's self-destructive impulses. In *Sense and Sensibility*, Elinor's internal suffering is keenly dramatised, while Marianne's is often satirised, largely because it is of her own creation: 'Marianne would have thought herself very inexcusable had she been able to sleep at all the first night after parting from Willoughby ... Her sensibility was potent enough' (SS, p. 83).

In *The Rivals*, Sheridan's principle of pairings allows him to exploit the comic possibilities that arise from the conflicts between reason and feeling, sense and sensibility. But we are meant to distinguish between Faulkland's problems of temperament and Lydia's quixotic errors. The quixotic figure is clearly to be considered differently to the melancholic figure, deriving from one of the most influential of all sentimental novels, Goethe's *The Sorrows of Young Werther*.

Though Faulkland's expectation of female decorum in courtship is derived from his distorted sentimental notions, the implication seems to be that they are imbibed not necessarily from romantic fiction, but from the effects of a melancholic, neurotic nature. After expecting that he is to be rejected by Julia, he is only more distressed to find that he has been forgiven; forgiveness does not accord with his preconceived notion that a lover must be made to suffer: 'Don't you think there is something forward – something indelicate in this haste to forgive? Women should never sue for reconciliation.'[19]

It is therefore striking that Faulkland puts Lydia's flaw down to 'the errors of an ill-directed imagination', while his own he describes as a problem of temperament and the effects of 'an unhappy temper'.[20] This perhaps makes Faulkland a closer model for Marianne Dashwood in *Sense and Sensibility*, and Benwick in *Persuasion*, whose melancholic temperaments are partly instrumental in their own misery. In *Northanger Abbey*, the quixotic Catherine Morland is famously reproached by Henry Tilney for the liberty of her imagination (*NA*, p. 199), but her danger to herself is not life-threatening.

Marianne Dashwood's romantic ideas, like those of Lydia Languish, are derived from the books that she reads. Jane Austen gains much comic mileage from her young heroine's faith in her own originality, although, ironically, her conduct places her as a rather conventional comic type. Both Lydia and Marianne are slavishly following the dictates of romantic novels where economic realities are disregarded. Lydia insists on marrying a penniless ensign and Marianne wonders 'What have wealth or grandeur to do with happiness?' (*SS*, p. 91). Her romantic sentiments are contrasted with her sister's more practical considerations, yet as Elinor paradoxically suggests, 'we may come to the same point. *Your* competence and *my* wealth are very much alike'. Ironically, Marianne's 'competence' of two thousand a year is greater than Elinor's 'wealth' of one thousand. This is an example of how the same thing or idea (wealth or competence) can be seen or be represented from two diametrically opposed and yet similar angles. This surprising doubleness becomes a main feature of the novel's dynamic.

In this conversation Austen is still drawing out the contrasts between her two heroines. Initially, she appears to be making broad antithetical judgements between the sisters. *Sense and Sensibility* is a deliberately undemanding title (each sister implicitly representing the antithetical position), suggesting a fairly primitive schematisation. But the novel subsequently proceeds to undermine this expectation. Both sisters have sense and sensibility, though in different proportions.

In the main plot a very similar situation of courtship is set up between the two sisters, and between the men that they are in love with, in order to invite parallels, contrasts and ironic reversals. Towards the end of volume one, Austen draws a structural parallel where both Willoughby and Edward have left Barton with no adequate explanation, nor any promise of return. In contrast to the conduct of her sister, Elinor 'does not adopt the method so judiciously employed by Marianne, on a similar occasion, to augment and fix her sorrow, by seeking silence, solitude and idleness' (*SS*, p. 104). Elinor's cheery selflessness spares her mother and sisters 'much solicitude on her account'. Nevertheless, she suffers quite considerably throughout much of the novel, especially as she is forced to endure Lucy Steele's spiteful taunting. Marianne's 'method' of coping with a broken heart is, of course, selfish and indulgent, and she sees nothing to be recommended in Elinor's self-control. For Marianne, bouts of hysterics, tears and melancholy are the legitimate response to thwarted love, and she equates Elinor's silent grief with an absence of 'strong affections'.

Jane Austen satirises the bullying egotism that is implicit in Marianne's excessive sensibility: 'She expected from other people the same opinions and feelings as her own, and she judged of their motives by the immediate effect of their actions on herself' (*SS*, p. 202). Didactic expectations are, however, confounded by the similarities between the sisters. Marianne's romantic notions are frequently punctured by Austen, who uses Elinor to expose her sister's contradictory views and lack of self-knowledge, just as Sheridan uses Julia Melville to counterbalance Lydia. But the irony is also pitted against Elinor, who is frequently mistaken and misguided in her notions. The irony is directed at both heroines and both types of conduct: 'Their means were as different as their objects, and equally suited to the advancement of each' (*SS*, p. 104).

At the end of volume two, in another structural parallel, both heroines prepare to leave London for home, having been jilted by their lovers, who are now engaged to other women. Marianne herself shows her awareness of the similarities of their positions when she shrewdly remarks that they are both behaving in a curiously similar and yet diametrically opposed way: 'We have neither of us anything to tell; you, because you communicate, and I, because I conceal nothing' (*SS*, p. 170).

Austen begins by satirising Marianne's sensibility but later moves to an imaginative imposition that is clearly on her side. Though Marianne is initially presented as a quixotic heroine, her genuine sensibility is never in doubt. Marianne is a far more vulnerable figure than Lydia Languish, whose conduct often borders on the absurd. Lydia's lack of intellectual curiosity is not to be compared with Marianne's inquiring mind. We cannot imagine Lydia reading Thomson's *The Seasons*, one of Marianne's favourites. Austen early on hints that Marianne's sensibility is a problem of temperament when Elinor perceptively comments that, though her sister is 'earnest' and 'very eager', she is 'not often really merry' (*SS*, p. 93).

Marianne's melancholy and intensity of feeling, like Faulkland's, add to her own misery. Even after her 'rupture' with Willoughby, Marianne blames herself, and seems bent on a similar course of excessive and obsessive self-destruction when she plans to spend her life in solitary study. Like Faulkland's, Marianne's sensibility can be seen as absurd and self-destructive, but its authenticity is not doubted. If there is any doubt of this, Austen contrasts Marianne's genuine sensibility with the false sensibility of the Steele sisters.

Austen's principle of pairings, as the structural base of *Sense and Sensibility*, allows her to mirror complex comparisons and contrasts between character and behaviour. Her principle of pairings makes the issue more complicated than one person being right and the other wrong. Not only does Austen draw upon comparisons and contrasts between the two Dashwood sisters, but by bringing in two other pairs of sisters who reflect upon our view of Marianne and Elinor, she further complicates the picture. Her principle of pairings is not confined to two heroines as in *The Rivals*, but is developed in two other pairs of sisters, the Jennings sisters (now Lady Middleton and Mrs Palmer) and the Steele sisters.

The discussion about the picturesque with Edward Ferrars allows Austen to draw further parallels between the sisters. Moreover, the arrival of Mr Palmer and the two Jennings sisters offers yet another perspective upon Edward and the Dashwood sisters. Austen juxtaposes the scenes one after another for comic effect, but also to suggest more serious alternative readings of Elinor and Marianne. Lady Middleton's elegance and coldness are contrasted unfavourably to her sister's 'prepossessing manners', her warmth and friendliness and lack of ceremony, which again encourage us to draw contrasts between Elinor and Marianne as sisters and as individuals. The controlled and coldly elegant Lady Middleton could be viewed as a more extreme version of Elinor, and Mrs Palmer, with her prettiness and warmth, as a crude version of Marianne. Mrs Palmer's claims to have almost married Brandon confirm this parallel.

Anne and Lucy Steele are introduced to provide yet another perspective on Elinor and Marianne. As with the Dashwoods, the Steeles are without financial means and are in need of the social patronage of the Middletons. The chief differences are initially summed up in the Dashwoods' refusal to ingratiate themselves into the Middletons' society;

it is always Sir John who presses the girls to accept his invitations. While the Dashwoods refuse to engage in sycophantic behaviour towards the Middletons, the Steeles have the 'good sense to make themselves agreeable' to the lady of the house through courting her odious, and very spoilt, children. This kind of 'sense' is shown in an unfavourable light by the Dashwood sisters, who refuse to pay any attention to the children. This is not lost on the shrewd Lucy Steele, who remarks on their indifference:

> 'I have a notion', said Lucy, 'you think the little Middletons rather too much indulged ... I love to see children full of life and spirits; I cannot bear them if they are tame and quiet'.
> 'I confess', replied Elinor, 'that while I am at Barton Park, I never think of tame and quiet children with any abhorrence.' (SS, pp. 122–23)

Elinor deflates yet another convention of sensibility: the idealisation of childhood innocence. One of the plays chosen by the Austen women for the family theatricals in 1805 was the popular farce *The Spoilt Child*, which dramatised the cunning and naughty conduct of a small child.[21]

Austen's principle of pairings is also developed in the contrasting characters of Brandon and Willoughby. They are even summed up like characters in a drama by the costumes they wear. Willoughby is first seen in his hunting clothes, which, to the smitten Marianne, is a mark of his manliness: 'of all manly dresses a shooting jacket was the most becoming' (SS, p. 26). In contrast, Brandon wears a flannel waistcoat which has drearily unromantic associations of 'aches, cramps, rheumatisms, and every species of ailment that can afflict the old and the feeble' (SS, p. 25). In the eighteenth-century farce *My Grandmother*, to which Austen directly alludes in *Mansfield Park*, one of the characters is ridiculed for wearing a flannel waistcoat. Austen's use of the flannel-waistcoat motif from a well-known farce is perhaps a deliberate gesture to suggest the crude contrasts of stage-heroes, whose costumes represent character.

Austen makes less crude comparisons and contrasts between Edward and Willoughby, though she uses a familiar stage device to reveal the differences between them. Both are dependent upon an older woman's authority, which means that they are unable to marry freely the women they love. But in Austen's hands, as in Sheridan's before her, the traditional comic motif of the antagonism between the old order and the new is reversed.

Parental tyranny exercised in the choice of spouse for a son, daughter or ward had long been traditional in comedy, and is paradoxically reworked in *The Rivals*.[22] Sheridan's inversion of this convention is to portray Mrs Malaprop and Sir Anthony Absolute, who, far from dividing the young lovers, only wish to encourage the union. That the marriage is delayed by Jack and Lydia's own perversity, rather than parental intervention, is the main comic thrust:

> ABSOLUTE: Sure, Sir, this is not very reasonable, to summon my
> affections for a lady I know nothing of!
> SIR ANTHONY: I am sure, Sir, 'tis more unreasonable in you to *object*
> to a lady you know nothing of.[23]

Sir Anthony's implacable demands of obedience from his son in matters matrimonial become a double-edged comic device in Sheridan's handling of the trope. As soon as Jack discovers that the girl intended for him *is* Lydia Languish, he is all too eager to submit to his father, in what becomes a brilliant inversion of a traditional motif of antagonism between the old and the young:

> ABSOLUTE: 'Tis just as Fag told me, indeed. – Whimsical enough,
> faith! My Father wants to *force* me to marry the very girl I am
> plotting to run away with! … However, I'll read my recantation
> instantly. – My conversion is something sudden, indeed – but I can
> assure him it is very *sincere* …
> SIR ANTHONY: Fellow, get out of my way.
> ABSOLUTE: Sir, you see a penitent before you.
> SIR ANTHONY: I see an impudent scoundrel before me.
> ABSOLUTE: A sincere penitent. – I am come, Sir, to acknowledge my
> error, and to submit entirely to your will … the result of my
> reflections is – a resolution to sacrifice every inclination of my own
> to your satisfaction.[24]

Austen's parody of secret engagements and parental interference makes use of a brilliant device clearly borrowed from *The Rivals*. The pivot of Sheridan's comic plot is his exploitation of the trope of filial disobedience. As discussed already, Austen had used this model in *Love and Freindship* in a reversal of the comic convention where an authority figure prevents the lovers' union. But in *Sense and Sensibility* Austen uses this motif in a far more complex and ambiguous way.

Both Elinor and Marianne wrongly attribute their lovers' inconsistent conduct to parental interference. Mrs Dashwood also falls into the sentimental trap set up by Austen, as she concocts a sentimentalised fantasy of Willoughby's conflict with his patron Mrs Smith: 'I am persuaded that Mrs Smith suspects his regard for Marianne, disapproves of it (perhaps because she has other views for him,) and on that account is eager to send him away' (*SS*, p. 78). Mrs Dashwood's account is highly ironic, as we later discover that Mrs Smith is no ogre, but wishes her nephew to act correctly by the woman he has seduced.

Similarly, Mrs Dashwood attributes Edward's low spirits to Mrs Ferrars's interference: 'attributing it to some want of liberality in his mother, [she] sat down to table indignant against all selfish parents' (*SS*, p. 90). The irony is intensified, as once more we have the same situation, and the same explanation as Mrs Dashwood had excused in the case of Willoughby. Elinor, as well as Marianne, is shown to be capable of error when she attributes Edward's inconsistent behaviour to his mother's influence. She mistakenly attributes Edward's 'want of spirits, of openness, and of consistency' to the interference of Mrs Ferrars, and Austen ironically notes, 'it was happy for her that he had a mother whose character was so imperfectly known to her, as to be the general excuse for every thing strange on the part of her son' (*SS*, p. 101).

The irony is clear: Elinor expresses doubt about Marianne's excuse of parental tyranny dividing her from Willoughby, yet Elinor is willing to use the same excuse when it comes to herself: 'she was very well disposed on the whole to regard his actions with all the candid allowances and generous qualifications, which had been rather more painfully exhorted from her, for Willoughby's service, by her mother' (*SS*, p. 101). Elinor is happy to blame Mrs Ferrars for her interference in her son's affairs: 'The old, well established grievance of duty against will, parent against child, was the cause of all' (*SS*, p. 102). Elinor could not be more wrong.

As in *The Rivals*, parental interference is a red herring. It is the lovers' own conduct and their own irresponsibility that causes them anguish. Although Mrs Ferrars conforms to the stereotype of parental power and authority, she is finally powerless to prevent both sons from marrying whom they want. Conversely, Mrs Smith is not the dictatorial authority figure of stage comedy, nor a Mrs Malaprop, hastening to marry her nephew off to a rich woman. To his horror Willoughby discovers that marrying the heiress Miss Grey has paradoxically alienated him from his benefactor. Miss Smith's desire that he should marry Eliza is a complex reversal of his expectations. So too is his discovery that 'had he behaved with honour towards Marianne, he might at once have been happy and rich' (*SS*, p. 379). It is Willoughby's own conduct that is responsible for his own fate: 'That his repentance of his misconduct, which thus brought its own punishment, was sincere, need not be doubted' (*SS*, p. 379).

Austen draws a final ironic parallel between Elinor and Marianne. On hearing the news of the public revelation of Lucy and Edward's secret engagement, Elinor is made even more painfully aware of this 'resemblance in their situations' (*SS*, p. 261). And Marianne confirms this by seeing Edward as a 'second Willoughby' (*SS*, p. 261).

Early on, when Elinor had been informed of the secret engagement between Edward and Lucy, she had considered the opposition of Mrs Ferrars to this match and perceived that 'melancholy was the state of the person, by whom the expectation of family opposition and unkindness, could be felt as a relief' (*SS*, p. 140). 'Relief' in this context seems to point towards Edward being relieved of his engagement to Lucy through parental opposition, but Elinor is confounded once again by Edward's defiance of his mother.

Edward's situation is now paralleled with Willoughby's – with one important difference, Edward's acceptance of his contract with Lucy Steele. Paradoxically, Edward's defiance of his mother, Mrs Ferrars, adds to his own misery, just as Willoughby's defiance of Mrs Smith brings its own punishment. This is yet another ironic reversal where defiance of parental authority works against the characters' best interests. Edward is made to conform to the picture of the romantic hero, who courageously defies parental authority for the sake of the woman he is engaged to. But this is satirically undermined by the fact that Edward is *not* in love with the young woman: 'Elinor's heart wrung for the feelings of Edward, while braving his mother's threats, for a woman who could not reward him' (*SS*, p. 268).

This is the sort of comic paradox that Sheridan explores to great effect in *The Rivals*. But Austen's ironic reversal of filial disobedience is more complex. Edward's 'honourable' refusal to extricate himself from a hastily formed and unwanted engagement is now compared favourably with Willoughby's refusal to honour either his implicit engagement with Marianne, or his more explicit contract with Eliza. While Mrs Jennings praises Edward's conduct in comparison with Willoughby's 'only Elinor and Marianne understood its true merit. *They* only knew how little he had had to tempt him to be disobedient' (*SS*, p. 270).

Edward's only respite is time: 'everything depended ... on his getting that preferment, of which, at present, there seemed not the smallest chance' (*SS*, p. 276). Not even Elinor predicts the final cruel twist, when Brandon, misunderstanding the true state of affairs between Edward and Elinor, provides the means for Edward to marry Lucy.

This is yet another reversal of a sentimental trope. One of the stalwarts of sentimental stage comedy is the last-minute benefactor who unites the young lovers against all odds. Perhaps the most famous eighteenth-century example was Stockwell in Cumberland's *The West Indian*. Brandon's benevolence is partly inspired by his (misplaced) admiration for Edward's chivalric conduct in opposing his mother for the sake of love: 'The cruelty ... of dividing, or attempting to divide, two young people long attached to each other, is terrible – Mrs Ferrars does not know what she may be doing – what she may drive her son to' (*SS*, p. 282). Brandon, of course, labours under a mistaken understanding of the situation, and the ironies increase as he makes Elinor his confidante. Brandon's generous interference unites the lovers (who are no longer in love), and seals Elinor's fate.

Austen's satirical inversion of this sentimental convention is in the spirit and manner of *The Rivals*, where the young lovers' union is threatened only by their own behaviour and not by parental interference. In *Sense and Sensibility*, the young men are financially dependent on older authority figures, but they are also free to make their own choices. Edward Ferrars's defiance of his mother for the sake of a woman he no longer loves is dangerously close to the absurd conduct of Edward Lindsay in *Love and Freindship*, who defies his father by his refusal to marry the woman he loves.

Austen's principle of pairings is the structural base of *Sense and Sensibility*. The pairing of Elinor and Lucy is developed through their parallel situation (both women are in love with the same man) in the final chapters leading up to the end of volume one and the closer paralleling of their behaviour in volume two. The revelation of Lucy's secret engagement at the end of volume one echoes the ambiguity surrounding the 'truth' of the secret engagement between Marianne and Willoughby and shows how contrasts, parallels and discordant similarities of action and exchange constantly resonate against each other. Austen thus ends the first volume with a theatrical flourish. And in volume two she deploys a further quasi-theatrical device, the 'set-piece' of a confrontation between two female rivals.

Jane Austen's set-piece between her 'two fair rivals' deliberately appeals to stage comic models. Scenes such as this, which contain pointed exchanges of dialogue and repartee, can be traced back to wit-comedies. The classic example of this kind of dramatic exchange, the 'polite quarrel' between two female characters, is the exchange between Célimène and Arsinoë in Molière's *Le misanthrope*. Henry Fielding used this model in his plays, and then more effectively in his novels.[25] But Austen's dramatic rendering of the polite quarrel in *Sense and Sensibility* achieves a realistic quality that transcends the burlesque absurdities of similar comically stylised exchanges in Fielding's plays and novels.

The scene is set in the Middletons' drawing room, and takes place in the stuffy, dimly-lit environment of the ladies' dining party. The controlling presence of the author is felt in the narrative preliminaries which sketch the unpleasant social atmosphere in which the dialogue takes place. On stage this would be achieved by the actors and the producer. The scene between Elinor and Lucy is introduced by Lady Middleton's proposal of a card game. Jane Austen invites the reader to consider the relationship between game-playing and social conduct.

The dialogue is preceded by a quasi-dramatic monologue in which Elinor's internal thoughts about Lucy's revelation are processed by a circuitous route of disbelief, indignation and, finally, acceptance. Austen thus sets the scene in the context of her heroine's disappointment and pain. Through this internalising of her heroine's thoughts, we discover the reason for Lucy's confidence in Elinor. Elinor discovers that, like Marianne, she has been jilted, but also that her rival is insistent on asserting her prior claim:

> What other reason for the disclosure of the affair could there be, but that Elinor might be informed by it of Lucy's superior claims on Edward, and be taught to avoid him in future? She had little difficulty in understanding thus much of her rival's intentions ... (SS, p. 142).

Elinor's desire to renew the topic with Lucy in order to ascertain further details is an ironic variant on the confidante role. Just as Austen satirises the stage-convention of filial defiance, she now parodies a favourite sentimental twist: a secret engagement due to the opposition of a cruel parent, and told to a best friend in confidence.

Elinor's decision to accept the role of Lucy's confidante threatens to compromise her integrity. The confidante or 'tame duenna', as Mary Crawford reminds us in *Mansfield Park*, is a conventional trope of stage comedy that had been successfully assimilated into the sentimental novel. In *The Rivals*, Julia acts as Lydia's confidante, although she expands the usual role by virtue of her criticism of her friend. Susanna Centlivre's comedy *The Wonder: A Woman Keeps a Secret* centres its plot on the role of the confidante. The title alone suggests that it is highly unusual for a woman to be trustworthy, even though Centlivre's heroine keeps her friend's secret at great personal cost. Austen's heroine also keeps a secret at great personal cost to her self-respect and dignity. Lucy and Elinor provide a cruel parody of the duenna trope, particularly as we know the reasons why Lucy is confiding in Elinor.

The theatrical tableau set up by Jane Austen is reminiscent of the opening of Congreve's *The Way of the World*. Two gamesters are at cards in a chocolate-house and, as the dialogue begins, the card-game dissolves to become a metaphor for the dramatic action. Mirabell and Fainall each seek to elicit information from the other without revealing his own hand. In Austen's tableau, Elinor and Lucy are working together on a filigree basket; this is extremely delicate ornamental work, which involves twisting, plaiting and weaving together the strands of the basket. While the 'remaining five draw their cards' (SS, p. 145), Lucy and Elinor engage in their more serious game: 'the two fair rivals were thus seated side by side at the same table, and with the utmost harmony in forwarding the same work' (SS, p. 145). Lucy's 'work' is to ensure that she is safe from the interference of Elinor, but she sadistically uses the opportunity to taunt her rival. Elinor's 'work' is to elicit information about the engagement.

The confrontation scene between Elinor and Lucy consists of a whole chapter written mainly in dialogue form. The dramatic element is reinforced by the relative absence of connectives ('he said', 'she said'). The scene is mostly unmediated in terms of authorial voice, although there appears to a conscious sense of a controlling presence from the opening line of the chapter:

> In a firm, though cautious tone, Elinor thus began.
> 'I should be undeserving of the confidence you have honoured me with, if I felt no desire for its continuance, or no farther curiosity on its subject. I will not apologize therefore for bringing it forward again.'
> 'Thank you,' cried Lucy warmly, 'for breaking the ice; you have set my heart at ease by it; for I was somehow or other afraid I had offended you by what I told you that Monday.'
> 'Offended me! How could you suppose so? …'
> 'And yet I do assure you,' replied Lucy, her little sharp eyes full of meaning, 'there seemed to me to be a coldness and displeasure in your manner, that made me quite uncomfortable.' (SS, p. 146)

The opening sentence seems to be the objective voice of the narrator, but a closer look reveals that this is Elinor's perspective shaping the narrative. The effect of Austen's free indirect speech in this instance is that Elinor's apprehension is conveyed in her desire to appear in control; the implication being that she is not.

Though the confrontation begins politely, the underlying tone of the exchange is established with added interjections, such as 'her little sharp eyes full of meaning'. Again, there is an ambiguity at play. The interjections are very much in the style of Richardson's 'conversations', but the point of view is deliberately muddied. If this is Elinor noting Lucy's aggressive body language, rather than an objective description by the author, the emotional content of the confrontation is intensified. Austen's free indirect speech gives her the means of being simultaneously inside and outside her character.

In the opening dialogue Austen creates a subtle instability of tone. The hints, evasions and insinuations convey the impression of much being withheld, and yet paradoxically revealed. The ritual of social nastiness and feminine swordsmanship truly gets underway with Elinor's sarcastic and uncharacteristic baiting: 'Could you have a motive for the trust, that was not honourable and flattering to me?' (SS, p. 146). Thus begins an intricate 'I know that you know that I know' dialogue in the tradition of the multi-layered exchanges to be found in Congreve.

In the opening dialogue of *The Way of the World*, the cause of tension between the two men is Mrs Marwood. Mrs Marwood has frustrated Mirabell's plan to gain Lady Wishfort's approval of his match with Millamant. Mirabell suspects Fainall of being Mrs Marwood's lover and privy to her design. In turn, Fainall suspects Mrs Marwood of being in love with Mirabell and seeks to establish whether Mirabell returns the sentiment or not. Furthermore, part of Mirabell's preoccupation is also to gauge Fainall's relationship with his wife, who happens to be Mirabell's lover. The exchange is thus fraught with innuendo, double meaning and insinuation, as the men play a complex double-game.

In *Sense and Sensibility*, Austen establishes a similar kind of narrative subtlety. Elinor wants to establish certain truths and details, and wishes to convince her rival of her indifference, while Lucy wants to taunt Elinor and keep her away from Edward. But, as the dialogue gets under way, the surface politeness and restraint become increasingly strained and the mutual dislike and jealousy of the two rivals are apparent:

[Lucy] 'If you knew what a consolation it was to me to relieve my heart by speaking to you of what I am always thinking of every moment of my life, your compassion would make you overlook everything else I am sure.'

135

[Elinor] 'Indeed I can easily believe that it was a very great relief to you, to acknowledge your situation to me, and be assured that you shall never have cause to repent it.' (*SS*, p. 146)

The point-scoring repartee reaches a natural climax in Elinor's (untruthful) plea of indifference:

'... the power of dividing two people so tenderly attached is too much for an indifferent person.'

''Tis because you are an indifferent person,' said Lucy, with some pique, and laying a particular stress on those words, 'that your judgement might justly have such weight with me. If you could be supposed to be biassed in any respect by your own feelings, your opinion would not be worth having.' (*SS*, p. 150)

Lucy implies that Edward has given himself away by talking too much of Elinor, and that she knows the full state of affairs between them, and with her malicious innuendo on 'indifference', incites Elinor's tactical withdrawal: 'Elinor thought it wisest to make no answer to this, lest they might provoke each other to an unsuitable increase of ease and unreserve' (*SS*, p. 150).

In a similar scene, earlier in the novel, Lucy reveals her secret engagement to Elinor. Austen punctuates the dialogue with dramatic interjections: 'eyeing Elinor attentively as she spoke'; 'amiably bashful, with only one side glance at her companion to observe its effect on her'; '"not to Mr Robert Ferrars – I never saw him in my life; but," fixing her eyes upon Elinor, "to his elder brother"' (*SS*, pp. 128–29). The dialogue is reinforced by Lucy's use of props, the reference to the ring and the 'taking a letter from her pocket', asides in the manner of stage directions.

As well as using quasi-theatrical interjections to suggest the emotional force of the confrontation, Jane Austen also shows how seemingly careless actions, such as the rolling of the papers, convey powerful emotional conflict beneath the calm surface. Towards the end of the novel, the unspoken but powerful emotion of Edward's revelation of his release from Lucy is given added force by his action of inadvertently cutting the sheath into pieces with the scissors. Mindless actions that suggest power-ful emotional conflict are in the tradition of the drama.

Jane Austen's set-pieces often have a semi-autonomous quality, making them resemble individual scenes in a play. But though they may be presented as self-contained and carefully patterned scenes, which rely mainly on character-revealing dialogue, they nevertheless establish a controlling, though often extremely delicate, authorial presence. In this instance, there is a disquieting sense that the moral order of the novel's world is threatening to collapse: the danger is that Elinor's aptitude for dissimulation and disingenuousness is alarmingly akin to Lucy's.

Elinor's complicity in the 'game' of confidences that is duplicitously set up by Lucy is undermined by the cruel truth that the Dashwood sisters do not confide in each other. Elinor now seems to be an extension of Lucy Steele:

> 'If the strength of your reciprocal attachment had failed, as between many people and under many circumstances it naturally would during a four years' engagement, your situation would have been pitiable indeed.'
>
> Lucy here looked up; but Elinor was careful in guarding her counte-nance from every expression that could give her words a suspicious tendency. (SS, p. 147)

The danger that is implied in the adoption and exploitation of Lucy's methods is swiftly curtailed. Elinor attempts this participation in what is really an unpleasant social game only once: 'From this time forth the subject was never revived by Elinor ... it was treated by the former with calmness and caution, and dismissed as soon as civility would allow; for she felt such conversations to be an indulgence which Lucy did not deserve, and which *were dangerous to herself*' (SS, p. 151, my italics).

A further aspect of Austen's principle of pairings between Elinor and Lucy is the implication for Marianne. If Elinor's extreme is Lucy at one end and Lady Middleton at the other, Marianne's extreme must be the garrulous, empty-headed Anne Steele, who at thirty is clearly beyond marriage prospects, and the rattling Mrs Palmer. Austen is perhaps invit-ing us to consider that Anne is a version of a character that Marianne might have become at the end of the novel, after having renounced sensibility, had she not been rescued by Colonel Brandon. As Lucy constantly smoothes over her sister's glaring *faux pas*, so Elinor 'screens' Marianne's deliberate rudeness. Anne Steele at one point is severely rebuked by Lucy for yet another social impropriety. The sharpness of Lucy's reprimand 'though it did not give much sweetness to the manners of one sister, was of advantage in governing those of the other' (*SS*, p. 219). This comment has significance for both pairs of sisters – although Elinor's gentler methods of 'governing' her sister's social conduct are more praiseworthy than Lucy's.

The paralleling of Anne and Marianne's social indiscretions also serves as a method of highlighting Marianne's virtues by contrasting them with an idiot version, much in the way that Mr Darcy is contrasted with Mr Collins. It is striking just how similar Collins's and Darcy's proposal speeches are. By the comparison between the two sets of sisters, Austen implies that Elinor's danger lies in becoming too adept at the social game, becoming dangerously close to Lucy. Through Austen's favourable comparison with Anne Steele, and the contrast between Marianne's genuine sensibility and the false sensibility of the Steeles, Austen is moving towards an imposition which is now on Marianne's side.

Austen's pairing of Lucy and Elinor enables her to make comparisons in ways that reflect favourably on Marianne. Thus when Elinor tries similar Lucy-like behaviour on her sister, Austen censures her duplicity and the authorial sympathy shifts to Marianne:

> Marianne looked at her steadily, and said, 'You know, Elinor, that this is a kind of talking which I cannot bear. If you only hope to have your assertion contradicted, as I must suppose to be the case, you ought to recollect that I am the last person in the world to do it. I cannot descend to be tricked out of assurances, that are not really wanted.' (*SS*, p. 244)

Marianne's outright refusal to participate in this form of social hypocrisy is revealed in an admirable light. The authorial sympathy, at this point, returns to Marianne. Nevertheless, aside from these temporary lapses, Elinor's social conduct perfectly illustrates her doctrine of the important disparity between independence of mind and outward behaviour. When Marianne takes her sister to task for her social conformity, she heartily disputes the accusation: 'No, Marianne, never. My doctrine has never aimed at the subjection of the understanding. All I have ever attempted to influence has been the behaviour. You must not confound my meaning' (*SS*, p. 94).

It was from the drama that Jane Austen received invaluable training for a novelist interested in scenes and dialogue. Scenes or set-pieces are units of action built around exits and entrances. How do you begin and end a scene except through entrances and exits? They are the markers of beginnings and endings, and of moments of surprise and suspense – of drama. But exits and entrances are not merely the units that mark beginnings and ends in a play; they can also come in the middle of a scene as an element of surprise. Throughout *Sense and Sensibility*, Austen provides us with a running motif of characters who are mistaken for others, as well as unexpectedly appearing and disappearing through doors, as in a farce.

This is particularly the case with her male characters. As one male character enters, the other exits. A morning walk in the country becomes an occasion of thwarted expectation for Marianne when she sees a man on horseback in the distance and immediately presumes that it is Willoughby, 'It is he; it is indeed; – I know it is!' (*SS*, p. 86), whereas the more sceptical Elinor is sure that it is not. Close up it in fact turns out to be Edward – Elinor is right. But later in the novel this scene is inverted when Elinor sees a gentleman on horseback and assumes it to be Colonel Brandon, only to discover that it is Edward (*SS*, p. 358). Austen's principle of pairings makes the issue more complex than one character being right and the other wrong. Both sisters misperceive. This exposes an important theme for the novel: the dangers of conjecture and subjective interpretation.

Austen's plot device of having people appear and disappear through doors is a means of exploring the discrepancy between illusion and reality. This is particularly the case with those male characters who disappear for unexplained reasons and reappear again unannounced. Edward absents himself indefinitely from Elinor, Brandon leaves for London unexpectedly, and Willoughby's abrupt departure from Barton cottage is equally mysterious and unexplained.

When the action of the novel shifts to London, a knock on the door is assumed by both sisters to herald Willoughby's long-awaited arrival in Berkeley Street:

> Elinor felt secure of its announcing Willoughby's approach, and Marianne starting up moved towards the door. Everything was silent; this could not be borne many seconds, she opened the door, advanced a few steps towards the stairs, and after listening half a minute, returned into the room in all the agitation which a conviction of having heard him would naturally produce; in the extasy of her feelings at the instant she could not help exclaiming, 'Oh! Elinor, it is Willoughby, indeed it is!' and seemed almost ready to throw herself into his arms, when Colonel Brandon appeared. (*SS*, p. 161)

The situation of a young girl throwing herself into the arms of the wrong lover is markedly theatrical. But Austen does not employ it here for comic effect. Marianne's disappointment is severe. Furthermore, this quasi-farcical moment points ahead to the union between Marianne and Brandon, in a way that not even Elinor anticipates. This is a scene of dramatic surprise, where the reader is kept in suspense as to who is behind the door.

The comic inversion of this incident is rendered in the great set-piece of Edward Ferrars's unpropitious arrival at Berkeley Street, only to find himself compromisingly positioned between the woman he wishes to marry and the woman he is engaged to marry:

> Elinor was prevented from making any reply to this civil triumph, by the door's being thrown open, the servant's announcing Mr Ferrars, and Edward's immediately walking in.
>
> It was a very awkward moment; and the countenance of each showed that it was so. They all looked exceedingly foolish; and Edward seemed to have as great an inclination to walk out of the room again, as to advance further into it.' (*SS*, pp. 240–41)

But this scene is one of dramatic irony. When Edward walks through the door to see Elinor, he has no idea that Lucy Steele is in the room. His innate social awkwardness is now ironically transformed to the acute embarrassment of being caught unaware, but being unable to explain himself to either of them. Caught thus between Lucy and Elinor, all he can do is look embarrassed: 'his embarrassment still exceeded that of the ladies in a proportion, which the case rendered reasonable, though his sex might make it rare; for his heart had not the indifference of Lucy's, nor could his conscience have quite the ease of Elinor's' (SS, p. 241).

If this is not sufficient discomfort for him, Austen compounds the comic impact with Marianne's arrival. Her customary directness is agonisingly misplaced as she heavily alludes to Edward's love for her sister in front of Lucy Steele: 'don't think of *my* health. Elinor is well, you see. That must be enough for us both' (SS, p. 242). The dramatic irony is intensified by Marianne's faith in Edward's honour, following her own disappointment in Willoughby, which leads her to magnify Edward's qualities. She is, of course, wildly off beam and misinterprets Edward's evident agitation 'to whatever cause best pleased herself'. Austen, meanwhile, invites us to enjoy his discomfort: 'Poor Edward muttered something, but what it was, nobody knew, not even himself' (SS, p. 243).

In *The Rivals* there are numerous examples of comic embarrassment built around untimely entrances and exits. In one memorable scene, Jack Absolute in the disguise of Ensign Beverley pretends to disguise himself as his own rival, Jack Absolute, in order to simultaneously deceive Mrs Malaprop and Lydia – who both know him as different characters. Just when he thinks that he has got away with deceiving the women, he is caught out by his father, who demands, along with them, that his son confess his true identity. Jack is placed in an impossible position when he is forced to admit his deception and confess his true identity to both Lydia and Mrs Malaprop; caught between offending one or the other and incurring the displeasure of both. In *Sense and Sensibility* we see how Jane Austen adopts similar theatrical devices to Sheridan. She builds her structure through 'scenes' woven around entrances and exits, and uses this as a device of comic embarrassment in the exact manner of eighteenth-century comedy.

If Edward's visit to Elinor is the comic apotheosis of unexpected entrances, Willoughby's equally unexpected arrival at Marianne's sickbed is surely the tragic. As with the mistaken identities of the men on horseback, Austen almost identically parallels Marianne's misconceptions with Elinor's. This time it is Elinor who almost rushes into the wrong man's arms. Upon hearing the sound of an approaching carriage, Elinor assumes that it heralds the imminent arrival of her mother and Brandon at Cleveland. Even though her common sense confounds the probability of this (she knows that it is far too early for their arrival), she vehemently wishes to believe in the truth of the 'almost impossibility of their being already come'.

Austen builds Elinor's anticipation of being reunited with her mother and Brandon in a way that echoes the earlier scene of Marianne's expectation of her imminent reunion with Willoughby: 'the night was cold and stormy ... the clock struck eight'. And, in a structural parallel typical of the novel's dynamic, Austen thwarts Elinor's expectations: 'Never in her life had Elinor found it so difficult to be calm, as at that moment ... The bustle in the vestibule, as she passed along an inner lobby, assured her that they were already in the house. She rushed forwards towards the drawing-room, – she entered it, – and saw only Willoughby' (SS, p. 316).

At various points in the novel Edward is mistaken for Willoughby, Edward is mistaken for Brandon, Brandon is mistaken for Willoughby, and Willoughby is mistaken for Brandon. In a novel that has pointedly alerted its characters to the discrepancies between illusion and reality, and the perplexities of interpretation and misconception, it is finally befitting that Willoughby should present his point of view. Indeed he refers explicitly to the dangers of subjective interpretation: "'Remember", cried Willoughby, "from whom you received the account. Could it be an impartial one?'" (SS, p. 322).

The confusion between the identities of the male characters, though quasi-farcical, poses a more sobering social reality for Austen's female characters. Behind such farcical or burlesque-like absurdities lies a cynical reminder that poverty is one of the best inducements for marriage, reminding us of Jane Austen's advice to her niece, Fanny, on the social and economic realities for dependent women: 'Single Women have a

Eliza O'Neill as Juliet: Jane Austen called her 'an elegant creature' who 'hugs Mr Younge [her co-star] delightfully' – but did not live up to the example of the great Mrs Siddons.

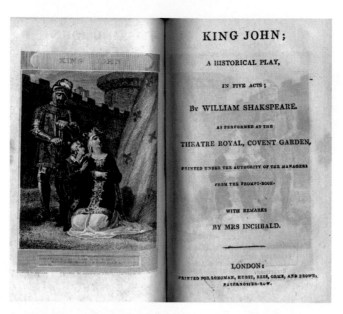

KING JOHN;

A HISTORICAL PLAY,

IN FIVE ACTS;

By WILLIAM SHAKSPEARE.

AS PERFORMED AT THE

THEATRE ROYAL, COVENT GARDEN.

PRINTED UNDER THE AUTHORITY OF THE MANAGERS

FROM THE PROMPT-BOOK.

WITH REMARKS

BY MRS INCHBALD.

LONDON:

PRINTED FOR LONGMAN, HURST, REES, ORME, AND BROWN,
PATERNOSTER-ROW.

Sarah Siddons as Constance in Shakespeare's *King John*: 'I should
particularly have liked seeing her in Constance, and could swear
at her for disappointing me,' wrote Austen in 1811.

Frontispiece to the published text of
Lovers' Vows, revealing its risqué content.

Mrs Inchbald's version of *Lovers' Vows* was
immensely popular. Staged at the Theatre
Royal, Bath, when Austen lived there, in
1799 it travelled as far as Philadelphia.

Emma Woodhouse, alias Alicia Silverstone as Cher, *Clueless* in Beverly Hills.

Fanny Price and Mary Crawford in Patricia Rozema's controversial *Mansfield Park*.

Mansfield Park made *Metropolitan* in upper-crust Manhattan.

Lady Susan: Whit Stillman's *Love & Friendship* takes Austen back to her comic origins.

dreadful propensity for being poor – which is one very strong argument in favour of matrimony' (*Letters*, p. 332).

The casualness of husband-hunting is suggested quite early in the novel when Charlotte Palmer claims that she might have married Brandon, 'if Mama had not objected to it', even though he had only seen her twice and had not owned an affection to her: 'he would have been very glad to have had me, if he could. Sir John and Lady Middleton wished it very much. But Mama did not think the match good enough for me, otherwise Sir John would have mentioned it to the Colonel, and we should have been married immediately' (*SS*, p. 117). Mrs Jennings's observation that she has 'the whip hand' of Mr Palmer because 'you have taken Charlotte off my hands, and cannot give her back again' (*SS*, p. 112) also emphasises how women were perceived as burdens on their family.

Austen had earlier observed that having married off her own daughters, Mrs Jennings had now 'nothing to do but to marry all the rest of the world' (*SS*, p. 36). Mrs Jennings shows no compunction in transferring her matchmaking plans from one lover to another. She has no trouble in switching Edward Ferrars's allegiance from Elinor to Lucy Steele, and again in transferring Brandon's from Marianne to Elinor. What is more, Elinor is also suspected by John Dashwood of making a conquest of Brandon: 'A very little trouble on your side secures him' (*SS*, p. 223).

It is not only stage routines, such as entrances and exits, that Austen uses to illustrate the harsh reality of the marriage market. Other artifices from the drama, such as comic misunderstandings and conversations heard at cross-purposes, are also employed to signal this theme. Austen taps into a long theatrical tradition of such overhearings that have either comic effects, as in *Much Ado About Nothing*, or tragic consequences, as in *Othello*. Mrs Jennings misconceives that she has 'overheard' a proposal of marriage between Brandon and Elinor when in fact Brandon has offered to save Edward and Lucy. Mrs Jennings's congratulations to Elinor are taken by Elinor to mean quite the opposite – the impending marriage of Edward and Lucy. The mistake persists, even though Mrs Jennings is amused and surprised by the coolness of the lovers: 'I have not heard of anything to please me so well since Charlotte was brought abed' (*SS*, p. 287). As Brandon apologises for the 'badness of his house', meaning the Delaford parsonage, Mrs Jennings takes it to mean his own estate: 'This set the matter beyond a doubt' (SS, p. 281). She is as eager to congratulate Elinor on her good luck, even though previously insistent that Brandon was in love with Marianne. Like John Dashwood, Mrs Jennings expresses indifference as to the identity of the future Mrs Brandon.

The misunderstanding is finally resolved by Mrs Jennings's direct reference to Elinor's marriage to Brandon: 'The deception could not continue after this; and an explanation immediately took place, by which both gained considerable amusement for the moment, without any material loss of happiness to either, for Mrs Jennings only exchanged one form of delight for another, and still without forfeiting her expectation of the first' (SS, p. 292). Comic misunderstandings persist to the very end with Mrs Jennings's letter to Elinor, which relates Edward's heartache at having been jilted by Lucy and reveals Brandon's delusions about Edward.

Austen's pointed use of artifices from the drama thus becomes a means of exposing her views on love and marriage. The confusion between the lovers and their arbitrary switching of partners, and the varying levels of deceit and mercenary considerations, provide a satirical exposé of the marriage market. As the various lovers pass in and out of doors, and are mistaken for each other right up to the very end, where Elinor believes that Edward is Brandon, we are encouraged to believe that the plot could go any way. Love becomes a chance encounter; whoever comes through the door could be the man you marry.

Therefore, contrary to critical consensus, no one should be surprised by Lucy's sudden marriage to Robert Ferrars (especially since he is now the new heir), nor by Marianne's union with Brandon, nor Elinor's with Edward. When John Dashwood informs Elinor that his family expect Robert to marry Miss Morton, his sister deftly sums up the situation: 'The lady, I suppose, has no choice in the affair … it must be the same to Miss Morton whether she marry Edward or Robert' (SS, p. 296). John Dashwood's brutal reply reflects the cynicism of the age when he answers, 'Certainly, there can be no difference' (SS, p. 297).

* * *

In *Sense and Sensibility*, Jane Austen exploits specific sentimental conventions from stage comedy, devices that had been assimilated into the sentimental novel: filial defiance, romantic heroes, giddy heroines, kindly benefactors. She satirises them in the way that Sheridan had done in *The Rivals*. Furthermore, Austen derives her principle of pairings from the example set by stage models in *The Rivals* and *False Delicacy*. In a kaleidoscopic fashion, her principle of pairings creates a diversion and shifting of sympathies, particularly between the two heroines. Like Sheridan and Hugh Kelly before her, Austen uses her principle of pairings to show that sustained mockery of sensibility may coexist with a strong sympathy for it.

Thus in the filigree basket scene between Elinor and Lucy, Elinor's 'sense' is shown to be as dangerous as Marianne's 'sensibility'. When Elinor feels in danger of entering into a form of social hypocrisy she quickly draws back, but not before the similarities between her and Lucy have been drawn. Austen's principle of pairings is the means to enable her to shift authorial sympathy from one heroine to the other, without a failure in the moral organisation of her fictional world.

In *The Rivals*, the doubling of the female leads enables the satire to be directed against the sentimental Lydia Languish, but Jane Austen's use of this device is far more elaborate than Sheridan's. In her hands, the pairing motif is further complicated. Individual sisters are compared not only with each other, but also with other pairs of sisters. As with Lucy and Anne, we are encouraged not only to draw comparisons between their conduct and that of Elinor and Marianne, but also to draw comparisons between Anne and Marianne, and Lucy and Elinor. Having extreme versions of the foils means that they are not just foils to each other. The Steele sisters and the Jennings sister provide almost caricature-like versions of the heroines, which encourages us to view Elinor and Marianne and 'sense' and 'sensibility' in different lights. Austen's use of the principle of pairings is far more complex and nuanced than Sheridan's for it enables her to ironise both heroines. Elinor's capacity to be as mistaken as Marianne allows for a shift in our perceptions and the displacement of our expectations, which is an important part of Austen's ironic method. Ironically, Elinor's and Marianne's similarities become more acute than their differences.

Towards the close of *Sense and Sensibility*, Austen upholds an ironic detachment from her characters. The authorial voice accords perfectly with the moral ambivalence achieved by the principle of pairings. Marianne, 'instead of falling a sacrifice to an irresistible passion', falls for a man 'she had considered too old to be married, – and who still sought the constitutional safeguard of a flannel waistcoat' (*SS*, p. 378). Elinor, after succumbing to a fit of sensibility in which she 'bursts into tears of joy', marries the disinherited Edward. The winner is the unscrupulous Lucy Steele:

> The whole of Lucy's behaviour in the affair, and the prosperity which crowned it, therefore, may be held forth as a most encouraging instance of what an earnest, an unceasing attention to self-interest, however its progress may be apparently obstructed, will do in securing every advantage of fortune. (*SS*, p. 376)

The authorial voice, at the end of *Sense and Sensibility*, is less ostentatious than the absurd Fieldingesque voice at the end of 'Jack and Alice',[26] and the satirical voice at the end of *Lady Susan*.[27]

Jane Austen's principle of pairings, derived from specific stage models, was the means of enabling her to achieve an ironic detachment from her characters which she was to perfect in her later novels by her increasing use of free indirect speech. The technique allows a shift in authorial sympathy and an ambiguity of moral tone. Her use of parallelism and contrast, which, for example, enables her to show a variety of different responses to the same situation, encourages us constantly to call into question the things we take for granted.

7

Pride and Prejudice

Of all Jane Austen's characters, with the possible (and intriguing) exception of Mary Crawford in *Mansfield Park*, Elizabeth Bennet most resembles the lively, witty, independent heroine of Shakespearean and Restoration comedy. And of all the novels, *Pride and Prejudice* most naturally lends itself to dramatic representation, mainly because of its reliance on dramatic speech. Perhaps Richard Brinsley Sheridan (always on the look-out for promising young writers) appreciated its quasi-dramatic qualities when he declared the novel 'one of the cleverest things he had ever read'.[1]

Austen's first critics, sensitive to the close affinity between stage and page in the late Georgian era, admired Elizabeth as a Shakespearean heroine. The *Critical Review* described her as the 'the Beatrice of the tale; [who] falls in love on much the same principles of contrariety'. The same reviewer also noted an allegiance to eighteenth-century, as well as Shakespearean, comedy: 'The character of Wickham is very well pourtrayed; we fancy, that our authoress had Joseph Surface before her eyes when she sketched it; as well as the lively Beatrice, when she drew the portrait of Elizabeth'.[2]

The so-called 'lively lady' and her more serious foil (Beatrice/Hero, Rosalind/Celia) were established character types in Restoration and eighteenth-century comedy. As has been shown, they were duly assimilated into the novel, but in the more sentimentalised comedy of the later eighteenth century there were changes and developments in the pairings. The secondary relationship between the duller and more serious couple was often given more emphasis and interest – consider the pairings of Julia and Faulkland in *The Rivals*, and Jane and Mr Bingley in *Pride and Prejudice*. The secondary love-plot was, furthermore, often interwoven with that of the witty courtship. Another important development was that the lively heroine was often given a sensible husband rather than a witty rake for a partner. The coquettish elements of the heroine were played down and, though clever and independent, she often proves to be mistaken in the matters of her own heart. In both *Pride and Prejudice* and *Emma*, Austen conforms to this new pattern of romantic comedy. She tempts the heroine with a witty rake (Wickham and Frank Churchill), but ultimately the heroine chooses a serious and steady lover, one who is characterised by his inability or refusal to speak florid protestations of love. When Elizabeth chides Darcy for his reluctance to demonstrate his love by talking to her at dinner, he replies, 'A man who felt less, might' (*PP*, p. 381). Mr Knightley similarly declares to Emma, 'If I loved you less, I might be able to talk about it more more' (*E*, p. 430).

Hannah Cowley's comedy *Which is the Man?* typifies the new kind of courtship model, where the lively heroine chooses a sensible lover (Beauchamp) rather than a reformed rake (Lord Sparkle). Lord Sparkle's cynicism and dissipation are revealed in his attempted seduction of an innocent country girl unaccustomed to 'the language of the day' which equates flattery with hard-nosed economics: 'Compliments are the ready coin of conversation. And 'tis every one's business to understand their value.'

In the contest for Lady Bell's heart, the superficially glamorous Lord Sparkle is rejected in favour of his less dazzling but more reliable rival: 'As caprice is absolutely necessary to the character of a fine lady, you will not be surpris'd if I give an instance of it now; and, spite of your elegance, your fashion, and your wit, present my hand to this poor soldier – who boasts only worth, spirit, honour, and love.'[3]

Lady Bell Bloomer is one of the most successful examples of the stock character of the witty, linguistically sophisticated and fearlessly outspoken lady, who arose from the drama and was developed by Richardson in the character of Lady G. in *Sir Charles Grandison*.[4] Lady Bell and Lady G. were two of Jane Austen's best-loved literary heroines. Strikingly, both hold a more powerful social position than, for example, Elizabeth Bennet. They are thus able to vent some of their intellectual frustration upon the men around them. Though Elizabeth is without 'family, connections and fortune', Austen ensured that her next spirited heroine Emma was not lacking in social status, wealth and power. Like Emma Woodhouse, the witty and popular Lady Bell only realises her love for Beauchamp when she mistakenly believes that he is in love with her friend and confidante, Julia. Lady Bell's jealousy of her friend inspires her moment of epiphany and the revelation that she does not know her own heart: 'the pangs of jealousy prov'd to me, in one moment, that *all* its sense is love'.[5]

Although Lady Bell promises to reform, she nevertheless continues to display her playful spirit with a quip that belies her intent. In response to Fitzherbert's vow to make Beauchamp his heir, Lady Bell protests against this measure to raise her husband's fortune from his modest pension as a soldier: 'Oh, I protest against that! – Our union would then appear a prudent, *sober* business, and I should lose the credit of having done a mad thing for the sake of the man my heart prefers.'[6]

Importantly, as with Elizabeth Bennet and Emma Woodhouse, the self-discovery of Lady Bell's folly and her ensuing marriage with a worthy man do not threaten to stifle her penchant for merriment. As Richardson's Lady G. protests her independence even as she walks up the aisle at her wedding ceremony, so Lady Bell's impending marriage promises not to suppress her spirit. In *Pride and Prejudice*, Darcy has to learn to be laughed at by his future wife, and, after they are married, she shocks his sister by continuing to talk to him 'in a lively, sportive manner' (*PP*, pp. 387–88). Critics have condemned Emma Woodhouse's failure to reform fully, or even to capitulate to her future spouse, but this is to misunderstand the workings of the lively heroine.[7]

Hannah Cowley's comedies also reveal the fascination in the drama of the period with conflict between social classes. In *Who's the Dupe?* (1779), the nimble-witted aristocrat Granger is shown making a fool of the *nouveau riche* merchant Doiley. Though his daughter Elizabeth is in love with Granger, Doiley is determined that she should marry the 'larned' scholar and pedant, Gradus. The witty and outspoken Elizabeth dislikes solemnity and gravity; she loves 'delightful nonsense'. She employs the help of her cousin and friend, Charlotte, to be rid of Gradus, leaving her free to marry Granger. Meanwhile, to Elizabeth's astonishment, Charlotte accepts a proposal of marriage from her rejected suitor.

In *Pride and Prejudice*, Austen echoes this plot-line, and even keeps the names of Elizabeth and Charlotte.

Austen's *Pride and Prejudice* may also have been alluding to another Cowley comedy, *The Belle's Stratagem* (1780), which begins with an account of five sisters from the country who come to town in the hope of finding rich husbands. This play was well known to Austen. She quoted a phrase in a letter to Cassandra in 1801: 'Mr Doricourt has travelled, he knows best.'[8] The vivacious heroine Letitia Hardy made this play Cowley's most popular and lasting comedy.

The plot of *The Belle's Stratagem* pivots upon the unpropitious first impressions of the fashionable Doricourt, when he meets Letitia for the first time. Determined to turn his indifference into love, she affects the manners of an ignorant country bumpkin to put him off, while enchanting him with her gaiety and wit (while in disguise) at a masked ball. When the lovers are finally united, Doricourt rejoices in her independence and liveliness, and confesses that he was deceived by his first impressions: 'You shall be nothing but yourself – nothing can be captivating that you are not. I will not wrong your penetration, by pretending that you won my heart at the first interview, but you have now my whole soul.'[9]

Unfavourable first impressions also provided the plot for *Pride and Prejudice*. Even if Austen was not consciously alluding to Cowley's play, she certainly used a similar comic motif of contrasting different social groups to express her views on morals and manners. The tension between town and country values had long been the staple of Restoration and eighteenth-century stage comedy, and in *Pride and Prejudice* Austen uses this motif for her thoroughgoing exploration of class and social prejudices.

Jane Austen's representation of social class requires an understanding of the indisputable fact – both celebrated and mocked in the drama of the period – of the fluidity and mobility of the middle classes in the late eighteenth and early nineteenth centuries.[10] The later novels, *Emma*, *Persuasion* and *Sanditon*, all register social and economic change, and enact social mobility.[11] But even in *Pride and Prejudice*, Austen celebrates her most upwardly mobile heroine in Elizabeth Bennet, and mocks the almost anachronistic social pride of the well-born Mr Darcy. She shows herself to be sympathetic to the claims of the rising middle classes, and gains much comic mileage from contrasts and comparisons between 'high' and 'low' characters. In this she was influenced by the dramatic tradition.

I have suggested in an earlier chapter that the drama's obsessive interest in the concept of social mobility, the rise of the middling classes, and the comic interplay between high life and low was fuelled by the widely divergent theatre-going public of the late eighteenth century. The usual convention in comic theatre for exploiting social difference was to depict the dramatic and comic situations that arise when a person crosses the boundary from low life to high. In the novel tradition, too, the social metamorphosis of a character such as Richardson's Pamela inspired other writers to explore the morals and manners of socially divergent groups. In *Evelina*, Fanny Burney provided satirical and sharply observed commentary on fashionable London society seen through the eyes of her intelligent ingénue.

The constant theme of Restoration and eighteenth-century comic drama is the contrast between genteel and mercantile values. In the novel tradition, Richardson's Sir Charles Grandison advocated the virtues of trade and commerce compared to mere gentility; Fanny Burney's novels and (unpublished and unproduced) stage comedies also suggest sympathy with the respectable merchant classes. Austen followed Burney in her unwillingness to ascribe bad behaviour to one particular class of society – most comedies satirised one social class at the expense of the other – and in her belief that morals and manners are inextricably linked.

The usual way to explore social difference in comedy was to bring the country girl to the town. In *Pride and Prejudice*, Austen brings the town to the country. This was a less conventional move, though Oliver Goldsmith in *She Stoops to Conquer* and Hannah Cowley in *The Runaway* had successfully used a country house setting for their comedies. In *She Stoops to Conquer*, Goldsmith opens his brilliantly conceived plot with two young men of fashion entering the country, one of whom (Marlow) arouses universal contempt for his haughty, supercilious manners, and subsequently falls in love with someone he believes to be a social inferior. The comedy, with its mix of genteel and low characters, is deeply concerned with the concept of social class. Kate Hardcastle, like Letitia Hardy in *The Belle's Stratagem*, deliberately reverses her social station to teach her lover a lesson and win his affections. However, her father's involuntary social metamorphosis – that is, Marlow's mistaken belief that he is an innkeeper – is dependent on the fact that Hardcastle cannot be recognised intrinsically as a gentleman. His lament, 'And yet he might have seen something in me above a common innkeeper',[12] reveals that rank and good breeding are not always concomitant.

In *Pride and Prejudice*, Elizabeth's most damning condemnation of Darcy is that he hasn't behaved as a gentleman.[13] Her stout refusal to equate high social status with intrinsic gentility sweeps away rigid class boundaries, and her marriage with Darcy heralds a more inclusive society. The final words of the novel reveal the realisation of Lady Catherine's fear that old money will mingle with new, that gentility will mingle with trade: 'she condescended to wait on them at Pemberley, in spite of that pollution which its woods had received, not merely from the presence of such a mistress, but the visits of her uncle and aunt from the city' (*PP*, p. 388).

The Gardiners are not the only family in the novel with trade connections. Mr Bingley's fortune has been acquired by trade, and the plot is initiated by his desire to purchase an estate. His sisters are 'fine ladies' who play down their associations with trade: 'They were of a respectable family in the north of England; a circumstance more deeply impressed on their memories than that their brother's fortune and their own had been acquired by trade' (*PP*, p. 15). Bingley's sisters are described as 'supercilious', unlike for example, Sir William Lucas, who has also acquired his fortune in trade, and has 'risen to the honour of knighthood', but 'though elated by his rank, it did not render him supercilious' (*PP*, p. 18).

The battle between town and country is invoked to play off different social groups. Darcy's first appearance at the Meryton Assembly, his slighting of Elizabeth, and his contempt for the 'collection of people in whom there was little beauty and no fashion' (*PP*, p. 16), perfectly express his indifference to the country. Even his swift change of heart towards Elizabeth asserts his town prejudice: 'in spite of his asserting that her manners were not those of the fashionable world, he was caught by their easy playfulness' (*PP*, p. 23). Caroline Bingley echoes this town prejudice with her disapproval of Elizabeth's 'country town indifference to decorum' (*PP*, p. 36). Her attempts to discredit Elizabeth in Darcy's eyes target her lowly origins, and her trade connections:

'I think I have heard you say, that their uncle is an attorney in Meryton.'

'Yes; and they have another, who lives somewhere near Cheapside.'

'That is capital,' added her sister, and they both laughed heartily.

'If they had uncles enough to fill *all* Cheapside,' cried Bingley, 'it would not make them one jot less agreeable.'

'But it must very materially lessen their chance of marrying men of any consideration in the world,' replied Darcy.

To this speech Bingley made no answer; but his sisters gave it their hearty assent, and indulged their mirth for some time at the expense of their dear friend's vulgar relations. (*PP*, p. 37)

Since the Restoration, dramatists and novelists had mocked the 'Cits', the new-moneyed, vulgar-mannered social class that lived in the City of London as opposed to the fashionable West End of London. Austen shows her awareness of London's strict social geography in a discussion between Mrs Gardiner and Elizabeth, where they debate the probability of an encounter between Jane and Bingley: 'Mr Darcy may perhaps have *heard* of such a place as Gracechurch Street, but he would hardly think a month's ablution enough to cleanse him from its impurities, were he once to enter it' (*PP*, p. 141). Elizabeth in particular comprehends the huge social distance between Gracechurch Street (home to the Gardiners) and Grosvenor Street (home to the Bingleys). The residence of the Gardiners in Gracechurch Street is dependent upon practical considerations rather than fashionable ones: 'The Netherfield ladies would have had difficulty in believing that a man who lived by trade, and within view of his own warehouses, could have been so well-bred and agreeable' (*PP*, p. 139).

As has been seen, one of the most important changes in the theatre of the late eighteenth century was the development of increasingly middle-class attitudes and values.[14] The frequent appearance of the newly-rich merchant classes in the drama of the period, sometimes treated sympathetically, sometimes not,[15] suggests the emergence of a new social group. In the novel tradition too, Fanny Burney's *Evelina* drew upon the eighteenth-century stage tradition of playing off different social classes. Burney's hilarious portrayal in *Evelina* of the Branghtons, an archetypal *nouveau riche* family, charmed everyone from Dr Johnson in London to Jane Austen in Steventon – she read the comic parts of the novel aloud to her nieces. Inspired by her success with the Branghtons, and encouraged by the playwright/manager Sheridan, Burney set about writing a comic play which would contrast different social classes. Burney's comedies never reached the stage, so Austen could not have known them when writing *Pride and Prejudice*, but one of her best plays, *A Busy Day*, is striking for the insights into the social structures and manners of the late eighteenth century that it shares with Austen's work.

Burney's *Evelina* and *A Busy Day* exploit the motif of embarrassing relations whose ignorance and selfishness threaten the heroine's happiness. In *A Busy Day*, the heroine Eliza Watts is led to believe that her well-born lover (Cleveland) is repelled by her vulgar relations and low connections. In particular, Cleveland's aristocratic Aunt (Lady Wilhemina) is determined to oppose the match, which she believes to be an injury to her station and rank. Unlike many of the comedies which exploit one social group at the expense of the other, Burney is keen to suggest that ignorance, ill-breeding and selfishness are not the province of one particular social class, but can be seen in all sections of society. Eliza's *nouveau riche* family are vulgar, selfish and money-grubbing, but Cleveland's aristocratic family (the Tylneys) are very much the same. Sir Marmaduke orders his nephew Cleveland to marry a rich heiress to pay off his mortgages, and Lady Wilhemina is the quintessential social snob who worships the aristocracy and despises the lower orders. Burney ends her play with the claim that 'Merit is limited to no spot, and confined to no Class'.

Like her admired Burney, Austen is keen to suggest that bad behaviour is not confined to caste but can be seen in all sections of society, and to emphasise that there are no class boundaries in moral obtuseness, selfishness, vulgarity and rudeness. Caroline Bingley's jealous taunting of Darcy targets his social pride through jibes at Elizabeth's 'vulgar relations': 'Do let the portraits of your uncle and aunt Philips be placed in the gallery at Pemberley. Put them next to your great uncle the judge. They are in the same profession, you know; only in different lines' (*PP*, pp. 52–53). Elizabeth's laughter is the usual corrective to such blatant snobbishness, but she is also made uneasy by the indisputable fact of her mother's vulgarity. The ambiguity of her position is caught in an early exchange between the two circles (town and country – Bingleys and Bennets), where Darcy is indulging a stereotypical notion of country-life:

'In a country neighbourhood you move in a very confined and unvary-ing society.'

'But people themselves alter so much, that there is something new to be observed in them for ever.'

'Yes, indeed,' cried Mrs Bennet, offended by his manner of mention-ing a country neighbourhood. 'I assure you there is quite as much of *that* going on in the country as in town'.

Everybody was surprised; and Darcy, after looking at her for a moment, turned silently away. (*PP*, pp. 42–43)

Elizabeth's blushes for her mother's social indiscretions reveal not simply a refined sensibility on the model of Burney's heroines but a deeper, more complex sense of the requirements of social conduct. Caroline Bingley's forced politeness fools Mrs Bennet, but not Elizabeth, who notes that 'she performed her part indeed without much graciousness' (*PP*, p. 45). However, Elizabeth also 'trembles … lest her mother should be exposing herself again'.

Ghastly relatives are a conventional trope in many of the comedies of the period. In Cowley's *Which is the Man?*, the low-born Sophy Pendragon, who is unexpectedly transported to London's high life, remarks, 'What dy'e think one has relations given one for? – To be asham'd of 'em'.[16] Comedies of the late eighteenth century, such as Burney's A *Busy Day* and Colman's *The Heir at Law*, also contain 'low' relations who specifically threaten the social pretensions and aspirations of the newly rich. The best scenes in these plays are the ones where the different sections of society meet in one room. Burney's final act of A *Busy Day* brings all the social classes together in order to play them off against each other. In *Pride and Prejudice*, the Netherfield Ball displays the Bennet family in the worst possible light, filtered through the eyes of the mortified heroine, and shows Austen drawing upon and yet departing from the comic conventions of the drama.

Social embarrassment is one of Austen's great themes in the novel, and at the Netherfield Ball she derives much of her comedy from this. Elizabeth's first mortification is her opening dance with Mr Collins; her 'shame and misery' due to the wrong-footedness and clumsiness of her partner set the tone for her exposure to the more severe embarrassments that are in store for her. Similarly, when asked to dance by Darcy, her unease is intensified by the knowledge that her every move is being closely observed. Strikingly, during the dance Elizabeth and Darcy both use the word 'performance' as a noun for drawing a person's character: 'I could wish, Miss Bennet, that you were not to sketch my character at the present moment, as there is reason to fear that the performance would reflect no credit on either' (*PP*, p. 94). Darcy is, of course, referring to Elizabeth's misreading of his own and Wickham's character, and though she claims that she 'must not decide on my own performance', she has already drawn Darcy's character. In this context, the word carries a resonance of the public perception of the case against Darcy: after all, a 'performance' requires an audience, and Elizabeth's prejudice has been enhanced by the opinions of others.

Ignoring Darcy's warning, Elizabeth blithely takes the bait when Caroline Bingley (rightly) defends Darcy against Wickham. Elizabeth's acute sense of social injustice is aroused by Caroline's attack on Wickham's socially dubious origins: 'he was the son of old Wickham, the late Mr Darcy's steward ... really considering his descent, one could not expect much better' (*PP*, pp. 94–95). Elizabeth's angry retort is typically sound: 'His guilt and his descent appear by your account to be the same ... for I have heard you accuse him of nothing worse than of being the son of Mr Darcy's steward' (*PP*, p. 95). However misguided she may be, her defence of Wickham's lowly origins reveals the heroine in a sympathetic light, in marked contrast to Mr Collins, who incurs contempt for ingratiating himself with those in a higher social position. Though Elizabeth speaks her mind freely when the occasion demands, she nevertheless has a highly developed sense of social protocol, which means that she is horrified when Mr Collins insists on paying his respects to Mr Darcy without a formal introduction. It is Elizabeth, not Mr Collins, who perceives Darcy's contempt, and her discomfort intensifies as her mother repeatedly breaches social etiquette by her indiscreet remarks about Jane and Bingley.

One of the supreme ironies of the novel is that Mrs Bennet is as bad as Darcy thinks she is, and, like Mrs Hardcastle in *She Stoops to Conquer*, has very little to redeem her. The scene is filtered mainly through the eyes of Elizabeth, whose discomfort is intensified by the fact that Darcy is also observing her mother's various improprieties: 'Elizabeth blushed and blushed again with shame and vexation' (*PP*, p. 100). Similarly, Mary's 'exhibition' is equally painful to her because she sees it through the contemptuous eyes of the Bingley sisters and Darcy:

> To Elizabeth it appeared, that had her family made an agreement to expose themselves as much as they could during the evening, it would have been impossible for them to play their parts with more spirit, or finer success ... she could not determine whether the silent contempt of the gentleman, or the insolent smiles of the ladies, were more intolerable. (*PP*, pp. 101–2)

The final mortification for Elizabeth is Mrs Bennet's deliberate ploy to delay their departure at the end of the evening, especially as the Bingley sisters fully understand the ruse. Both sisters are patently rude, and the delay provides ample opportunity for the Bennet family to humiliate themselves further. The only other person to be sensible of the awkwardness of the party is her father: 'Mr Bennet, in equal silence, was enjoying the scene' (*PP*, p. 103).

Unlike Mr Bennet, Elizabeth takes no pleasure from the spectacle. Austen's narrative technique ensures that she is not merely a witness to the scene of social embarrassment, but a mortified player. She is forced to endure not only the humiliation of her family's impropriety, but to witness the contempt of others observing her family's humiliation. Austen's doubling of perspectives, Elizabeth watching Darcy watching Mrs Bennet, is a means of intensifying and exacerbating the heroine's shame and embarrassment. This, of course, is more difficult to achieve in the drama. In *A Busy Day*, for example, Burney relies upon the less subtle devices of caricature and verbal exclamation to achieve a similar effect. In other words, the vulgar characters (both high and low) are exaggerated in order for Eliza to express both her distaste of and her distance from them. Furthermore, she often openly expresses her shame and embarrassment at the vulgarity of her family: 'O Cleveland! with elegance like yours, founded on birth, education and intellectual endowments, can I wonder if your mind should involuntarily recoil from an alliance in which shame must continually struggle against kindness, and Pride against Happiness.'[17]

Like Eliza Watts, Elizabeth is forced to endure the spectacle of her vulgar relations at their worst in front of the man she will eventually marry. As in Burney's play, however, Austen replays the motif later in the novel at Darcy's expense. Lady Catherine is Mrs Bennet's comic counterpart, and Austen pricks her pomposity with as much relish as she displays Mrs Bennet's vulgarity. Elizabeth's presentation at Rosings is a scene of high comedy, with its semi-parodic overtones of a presentation at court. Sir William Lucas (himself only recently risen to 'the honour of a knighthood') takes it upon himself to be the expert on the 'manners of the great': 'About the Court, such instances of elegant breeding are not uncommon' (*PP*, p. 160). His daughter Maria 'looked forward to her introduction at Rosings, with as much apprehension, as her father had done to his presentation at St James's' (*PP*, p. 161). Mr Collins's instruction to the ladies not to dress too finely, for Lady Catherine 'likes to have the distinction of rank preserved', makes Maria tremble further. Elizabeth alone remains composed: 'She had heard nothing of Lady Catherine that spoke her awful from any extraordinary talents or miraculous virtue, and the mere stateliness of money and rank, she thought she could witness without trepidation' (*PP*, p. 161).

The group is ceremoniously led into the entrance hall, and through an ante-chamber to where Lady Catherine awaits. Then Jane Austen's comic description of the different responses to the courtly presentation endorses her heroine's equanimity:

In spite of having been at St James's, Sir William was so completely awed, by the grandeur surrounding him, that he had but just courage enough to make a very low bow, and take his seat without saying a word; and his daughter, frightened almost out of her senses, sat on the edge of her chair, not knowing which way to look. Elizabeth found herself quite equal to the scene, and could observe the three ladies before her composedly. – Lady Catherine was a tall, large woman, with strongly-marked features, which might once have been handsome. Her air was not conciliating, nor was her manner of receiving them, such as to make her visitors forget their inferior rank. (*PP*, p. 162)

Lady Catherine is in the comic tradition of redoubtable aristocratic ladies, beloved by Fanny Burney (Lady Smatter, Mrs Delvile, Lady Wilhemina), monsters of egotism, selfishness and pride. She has the same contempt for the lower orders as these other fine ladies, and a misplaced love of her own dignity. Though she is obsessed with the minutiae of social decorum, she is also rude and unfeeling. The comic effect is enhanced by the pairing of the well-built, talkative and domineering mother with her thin, pale and silent daughter. But, on a more sinister note, Lady Catherine's social power is not confined to her own small circle, for, as Elizabeth discovers, she has an effective spy in Mr Collins:

She was a most active magistrate in her own parish, the minutest concerns of which were carried to her by Mr Collins; and whenever any of the cottagers were disposed to be quarrelsome, discontented or too poor, she sallied forth into the village to settle their differences, silence their complaints, and scold them into harmony and plenty. (*PP*, p. 169)

Elizabeth assesses her as self-important and opinionated, reflecting that 'nothing was beneath this great Lady's attention, which could furnish her with an occasion of dictating to others' (*PP*, p. 163). However, she resolutely refuses to be bullied:

'Upon my word', said her Ladyship, 'you give your opinion very decid-edly for so young a person. – Pray, what is your age?'

'With three younger sisters grown up', replied Elizabeth smiling, 'Your Ladyship can hardly expect me to own it'. Lady Catherine seemed quite astonished at not receiving a direct answer; and Elizabeth suspected herself to be the first creature who had ever dared to trifle with so much dignified impertinence. (*PP*, p. 166)

It is now Darcy's turn to blush for his relations, especially when his aunt offers Elizabeth the use of her pianoforte, in a part of the house that nobody uses: 'Mr Darcy looked a little ashamed of his aunt's ill breeding, and made no answer' (*PP*, p. 173).

Elizabeth is wrong in her estimation that Darcy is culpable of the 'worst kind of pride'. In her view, this is social pride, which distinguishes and elevates rank before any other considerations, what she describes as 'want of importance in his friend's connections, than from their want of sense' (*PP*, p. 187). Darcy's self-exculpatory letter, however, makes it abundantly clear that the real objection to Elizabeth's family is not their rank, but their behaviour: 'The situation of your mother's family, though objectionable, was nothing in comparison of that total want of propriety so frequently, so almost uniformly betrayed by herself, by your three younger sisters, and even occasionally by your father' (*PP*, p. 198). Most painful of all for Elizabeth is that 'Jane's disappointment had in fact been the work of her nearest relations' (*PP*, p. 209). She is made aware from this point on that breaches of social etiquette hold potentially damaging consequences.

Nevertheless, even though Elizabeth is finally brought to acknowledge the truth of Darcy's appraisal of her family, he too must learn to abandon the social pride that is manifested in his superciliousness towards trade. When Darcy asks Elizabeth to introduce him to the Gardiners, whom he mistakes for 'people of fashion', she obliges with the expectation of 'his decamping as fast as he could from such disgraceful companions' (*PP*, p. 255). His reformation forces a re-evaluation of his social prejudices: 'When she saw him thus seeking the acquaintance, and courting the good opinion of people, with whom any intercourse a few months ago would have been a disgrace; when she saw him thus civil, not only to herself, but to the very relations whom he had openly disdained ... the difference, the change was so great' (*PP*, p. 263). He later confesses that she alone has effected the change, 'By you I was properly humbled' (*PP*, p. 369).

Conversely, Lady Catherine's deeply rooted class prejudices show no such capacity for change. The set-piece of Lady Catherine's memorable encounter with Elizabeth relies upon traditional comic and quasi-theatrical techniques. One of the more classical conventions that Austen draws upon in this scene is the triumph of the new order over the old. Elizabeth's moral defeat of the older woman reveals the shallowness and ignorance of the social distinctions to which Lady Catherine is desperate to cling. Her speech about the importance of continuing the noble line by the union of Darcy and his cousin, and her insistence that Elizabeth – 'a young woman without family, connections, or fortune' – should not 'quit the sphere, in which [she] has been brought up' (*PP*, p. 356), wholly discredit the speaker. By now, it is impossible for the reader to imagine the possibility of a marriage between Darcy and the sickly Anne, especially given the extraordinary vigour of Elizabeth in this scene, and, as a result, Lady Catherine's anachronistic class distinctions lose all credibility and seem merely absurd. Her insistence that the union would 'ruin him in the opinion of all his friends and make him the contempt of the world' (a similar objection that Richardson's Mr B. makes to Pamela) is crushed by Elizabeth's fitting and final words: 'With regard to the resentment of his family, or the indignation of the world, if the former *were* excited by his marrying me, it would not give me one moment's concern – and the world in general would have too much sense to join in the scorn' (*PP*, p. 358).

During the confrontation, Lady Catherine accuses Elizabeth of being 'lost to every feeling of propriety and delicacy', a charge that she equates with her refusal to accept the distinctions of social class. But, as Elizabeth demonstrates, true propriety and delicacy are indicative of manners rather than rank. Furthermore, although Elizabeth refuses to be bullied by authority and exhibits courage and frankness in her private encounter with Lady Catherine, she also has a heightened awareness of the importance of observing social forms in public.

When Elizabeth taxes Darcy on his rudeness and incivility at their first public meeting, this opens up an important discourse on the art of social role-playing. Darcy professes that he lacks the necessary 'talent' for social intercourse, but Elizabeth reminds him that it is more a matter of practice and personal endeavour: 'My fingers do not move over this instrument in the masterly manner which I have seen so many women's do ... but then I have always supposed it to be my own fault – because I would not take the trouble of practising' (PP, p. 175). Elizabeth's remonstrance is gently phrased, and her analogy between practising the piano and practising social intercourse also resonates with Lady Catherine's earlier rudeness concerning the use of her piano. Darcy's response, 'we neither of us perform to strangers', is ambiguous; for although she is without affectation or false pretensions, Elizabeth is mindful of the necessity of social performance.

Jane Austen's heightened sense of the complexity of social performance means that even a matter such as a simple leave-taking presents potential conflicts. Elizabeth's farewell to Mr Collins, which 'tried to unite civility and truth in a few short sentences', epitomises the perennial problem of right social conduct. Even Elizabeth, despite her gift for social intercourse, struggles with this. She only succeeds by dint of her highly dexterous verbal skills which, for example, allow her to say with impunity to Mr Collins that 'she firmly believed and rejoiced in his domestic comforts' (PP, p. 216).

Elizabeth's social discretion is contrasted with Lydia's reckless want of delicacy. When the Bennet girls are waiting for their carriage at the roadside inn, Lydia is highly amused that Jane and Elizabeth send the waiter away before relating her gossip: 'Aye, that is just like your formality and discretion. You thought the waiter must not hear, as if he cared! I dare say he often hears worse things said than I am going to say. But he is an ugly fellow! I am glad he is gone. I never saw such a long chin in my life' (PP, p. 220).

As in Sense and Sensibility, Austen is comparing and contrasting different forms of social conduct. Lydia shows no compunction in expressing her feelings about Wickham and the heiress Mary King: 'I will answer for it he never cared three straws about her. Who could about such a nasty little freckled thing' (PP, p. 220). Elizabeth is shocked by her sister's candour, in part because she feels the same way: 'Elizabeth was shocked to think that, however incapable of such coarseness of *expression* herself, the coarseness of the *sentiment* was little other than her own breast had formerly harboured and fancied liberal!' (*PP*, p. 220). Once again, Austen illustrates the disparity between inward feeling and outward conduct that is so beautifully expressed by Elinor Dashwood in *Sense and Sensibility*: 'My doctrine has never aimed at the subjection of the understanding. All I have ever attempted to influence has been the behaviour' (*SS*, p. 94).

One of Elizabeth's rare lapses of decorum is brought on by the news of the match between Charlotte and Mr Collins. Her shock when she learns of the engagement is 'so great as to overcome at first the bounds of decorum ... "Engaged to Mr Collins! My dear Charlotte, – impossible!"' (*PP*, p. 124). It is Charlotte who is dismayed and confused by 'so direct a reproach' and Elizabeth ensures that her blunder is smoothed over and appropriate congratulations offered. In private, she laments the match and makes one of her most damning judgements when she refutes Jane's defence of Charlotte: 'You shall not, for the sake of one individual, change the meaning of principle and integrity, nor endeavour to persuade yourself or me, that selfishness is prudence, and insensibility of danger, security for happiness' (*PP*, pp. 135–36).

Elizabeth's own refusal of Mr Collins comically reveals the complexities of social conduct for young women on the subject of marriage. Mr Collins assumes her rejection of him is a ruse to increase his ardour, 'according to the usual practice of elegant females', but she insists 'I would rather be paid the compliment of being believed sincere ... Do not consider me now as an elegant female intending to plague you, but as a rational creature speaking the truth from her heart' (*PP*, pp. 108–9).

Elizabeth is mortified that her refusal is taken as the 'affectation and coquetry of an elegant female'. And although this is the sort of paradox in social conduct that Austen exploits for comic effect, there are moral implications too. Both Jane and Elizabeth discuss the impossibility of right female conduct within courtship. Jane defends Bingley's flirtation – 'Women fancy admiration means more than it does' – but her sister retaliates sharply: 'And men take care that they should.' Elizabeth, furthermore, assesses the moral implications of ambiguous social conduct, whereby harm can be done without design: 'but without scheming to do wrong, or to make others unhappy, there may be error, and there may be misery. Thoughtlessness, want of attention to other people's feelings, and want of resolution, will do the business' (*PP*, p. 136).

Elizabeth's belief in 'attention to other people's feelings' is reflected in her private conduct as well as public. She shows propriety and delicacy in her attitude towards Jane, in her refusal to speculate upon Mr Bingley's return to Netherfield, though 'no such delicacy restrained her mother' (*PP*, p. 129). Similarly, she shows her capacity to 'unite civility with truth' in her rapprochement with Wickham, and her tacit championing of Darcy: 'In essentials, I believe, he is very much what he was' (*PP*, p. 234). Her stout refusal to be once again drawn in by Wickham ensures that 'they parted at last with mutual civility, and possibly a mutual desire of never meeting again' (*PP*, p. 235).

It is striking that no such decorum is necessary for the union between Elizabeth and Darcy. Indeed, their relationship is defined by their mutual candour, and their unwillingness to dissemble, which is perhaps what Darcy implies in his remark that 'neither of us performs to strangers'. Their earliest exchanges convey a refreshing irreverence that belies their strong mutual attraction, as when Elizabeth's challenge, '*your* defect is a propensity to hate everybody', is countered with Darcy's swift return, 'And yours is wilfully to misunderstand them'. In a later erotically charged exchange, he shows that he is more than equal to her spirit of independence: 'I have had the pleasure of your acquaintance long enough to know, that you find great enjoyment in occasionally professing opinions which in fact are not your own' (*PP*, p. 174).

The quality of the wit-combats was what inspired Austen's first critics to see shades of Shakespeare's Beatrice in Elizabeth. They are independent-minded young women each of whom 'falls in love on the same principles of contrariety'. Certainly, as Darcy confesses, the effect of Lady Catherine's interference 'had been exactly contrariwise' and 'taught him to hope'. For, as Darcy well knows, 'had you been absolutely, irrevocably decided against me, you would have acknowledged it to Lady Catherine, frankly and openly'. Elizabeth's witty response accepts the veracity of his charge: 'Yes, you know enough of my *frankness* to believe me capable of *that*. After abusing you so abominably to your face, I could have no scruple in abusing you to all your relations' (*PP*, p. 367). Here, as so often, the development of the courtship proceeds through razor-sharp dialogue in the exact manner of that tradition of witty stage comedy which runs from *Much Ado About Nothing* through the Restoration to Hannah Cowley.

Elizabeth shows her grasp of the particular dynamic of their relationship when she assesses the qualities with which Darcy fell in love:

'My beauty you had early withstood, and as for my manners – my behaviour to *you* was at least always bordering on the uncivil ... Now be sincere; did you admire me for my impertinence?'

'For the liveliness of your mind, I did.'

'You may as well call it impertinence at once. It was very little less. The fact is, that you were sick of civility, of deference, of officious attention. You were disgusted with the women who were always speaking and looking, and thinking for *your* approbation alone. I roused, and interested you, because I was so unlike *them.*' (*PP*, p. 380)

It is precisely Elizabeth's irreverence and frankness that make possible a private language between them that transcends a society dependent upon conformity to social mores.

In her next two novels, *Mansfield Park* and *Emma*, Jane Austen returned to many of the themes of *Pride and Prejudice*. Her interest in the concept of social class and the quest to discover a language truthful to emotional experience were explored with even greater depth and insight. As this chapter has demonstrated, one of the great lessons that Austen took from the drama was the idea that social life always requires a strong element of role-playing. *Mansfield Park* and *Emma* are, respectively, her most complex and her wittiest explorations of this idea. In different ways, each novel owes much of its profundity to a highly fruitful engagement with the dramatic tradition.

8

Lovers' Vows

Mansfield Park is considered to be Jane Austen's problem novel, contrasting sharply with the comic brilliance of its predecessor, *Pride and Prejudice*.[1] Its depiction of an awkward, shy and socially displaced heroine – the diametric opposite of the lively, unrestrained Elizabeth Bennet – has aroused considerable hostility.[2] Yet Austen was an author who constantly experimented with narrative style and technique: it is characteristic that she should have transposed the role of the witty stage-heroine to the anti-heroine, Mary Crawford, and depicted the heroine, Fanny Price, as a reliable but dull understudy waiting in the wings.[3]

The theatrical metaphor is apt, as the novel ambitiously undertakes to depict the consciousness of not one, but a whole cast of characters. Jane Austen focuses her plot more broadly than usual, exploring the development of not one or two but four young women. With most of the action taking place in a large country house, the dynamics of the plot are rendered through the grouping and regrouping of her large cast of characters. As in the other novels, relationships are developed in the setting of the formal or semi-formal occasion: balls, outings, dinner parties, family visits.

Austen expressed dissatisfaction with the 'playfulness and epigrammatism' of *Pride and Prejudice*, and in *Mansfield Park* returns to the morally ambiguous and uncertain territory of *Sense and Sensibility*. In deliberate contrast to *Pride and Prejudice*, she sets a more sober tone from the outset. Nevertheless, comedy permeates the novel, especially in the events surrounding the amateur theatricals. Of all Austen's mature works, *Mansfield Park* is the one that most systematically engages with the drama. This is primarily because the novel's plot is interwoven with the plot of a controversial eighteenth-century play, *Lovers' Vows*.

* * *

The critical debate that continues to surround Jane Austen's use of *Lovers' Vows* is, in part, due to the ideological concerns raised by the play's authorship. The play rehearsed for the Mansfield theatricals is Elizabeth Inchbald's expurgated version of August Kotzebue's *Das Kind der Liebe*. Inchbald softens the original title, a literal translation of which would be *The Love-Child*. According to Mrs Inchbald's first biographer, James Boaden, a translation of Kotzebue's popular melodrama was brought to her in 1798 by the manager of Covent Garden, who 'desired her to fit it to the English stage'.[4] Under the title of *Lovers' Vows*, Mrs Inchbald's play was performed at Covent Garden in 1798. Its continuing popularity throughout the 1798–99 Covent Garden season (forty-two performances) was assured by favourable reviews and high receipts.[5] In the next few years the play was staged at Drury Lane, the Haymarket and the Theatre Royal, Bath. It was publicly performed in Bath at least seventeen times when the Austens lived there between 1801 and 1806.[6]

Much has been made in recent years of the political implications of the play-within-the-novel. For some critics, what is particularly attractive about Austen's choice of play is the opportunity it has given them to construe *Mansfield Park* as an attack upon the drama, and Kotzebue in particular.[7] One of the problems with this argument is that Austen enjoyed going to see Kotzebue plays. As has been shown, she saw various Kotzebue adaptations at the professional theatre, including *The Birth-Day*, *Of Age Tomorrow* and *The Bee-Hive*. She attended a performance of the last of these as late as 1813. Two of the most frequently performed roles of her admired Elliston were those of the heroes of immensely popular Kotzebue adaptations: *The Stranger* and *Pizarro*. She clearly also knew *Lovers' Vows* extremely well.

Jane Austen may even have attended an amateur version of *Lovers' Vows* in a private theatre. Three letters written to Cassandra in 1814 repeatedly refer to General Chowne, a family friend, as 'Frederick'.[8] In the same letters, there are comments about *Mansfield Park*. Austen remarks, 'I shall be ready to laugh at the sight of Frederick again' (*Letters*, p. 256), and finds Chowne much changed when she sits next to him at the theatre: 'he has not much remains of Frederick' (*Letters*, p. 258). Her final reference to Chowne connects him once again with 'Frederick': 'We met only Gen. Chowne today, who has not much to say for himself. – I was ready to laugh at the remembrance of Frederick, and such a different Frederick as we chose to fancy him to the real Christopher!' (*Letters*, p. 262). The most plausible explanation of this play on the name is that Chowne acted the part of Frederick in an amateur production of *Lovers' Vows*, and that this is what was being remembered with amusement by Jane and Cassandra.[9]

Speculative as this supposition may be, it cannot be disputed that Jane Austen attended rather than boycotted Kotzebue plays at the public theatre. She even took her impressionable young nieces along with her. As we have seen, she joked about her role as the young girls' chaperone. Equally, at the time she was reading the moralistic and anti-theatrical Thomas Gisborne, she was performing private theatricals with her nieces.

This is not to suggest that Austen was unaware of the controversial aspects of *Lovers' Vows*.[10] Indeed, she draws some of her most effective irony from her different characters' reaction to the chosen play. Edmund's sarcastic suggestion that the theatrical party put on a 'German play' shows him taking a rather conventional stance of high-minded prejudice against German drama. The Earl of Carlisle, writing his *Thoughts upon the Present Conditions of the Stage* in 1808, lamented a decline in standards due to 'those vicious productions of the German writers': 'This accounts for what appears to be a most vitiated taste of the public in the endurance of those childish pantomimes, Blue Beard, etc. on the very boards where Shakespeare and Otway once stormed the human heart'.[11]

When Edmund's ironic suggestion is turned against him and the group settles on *Lovers' Vows*, his shocked reaction to the female parts also conforms to a very stereotypical prejudice against the character of the fallen woman. Austen makes it clear that it is the fallen Agatha rather than the coquettish Amelia who is the cause for concern. When Edmund pointedly asks Maria 'what do you do for women?', she is unable even to speak the name of Agatha: 'I take the part which Lady Ravenshaw was to have done' (*MP*, p. 139).

The rendering of the plight of fallen women was not uncommon on the eighteenth-century stage. Nicholas Rowe's tragedy *Jane Shore*, which Austen satirised in her juvenilia, was a vehicle for stars like Siddons, and later O'Neill, to arouse pity and feeling for the abject figure of the fallen woman. Hastings's attempted rape of Jane Shore and the humiliating treatment she suffers at his hands are partly punishment for her lapse from virtue, but she is portrayed, ultimately, as a dignified and repentant figure. Though she attains her husband's forgiveness in her final moments, one of her most famous speeches is a reminder of the harsh, but inescapable, truth of the inequality of women:

> Why should I think that man will do for me
> What yet he never did for wretches like me?
> Mark by what partial justice we are judged:
> Such is the fate unhappy women find,
> And such the curse intail'd upon our kind,
> That man, the lawless libertine, may rove,
> Free and unquestion'd through the wilds of love;
> While woman, sense and nature's easy fool,
> If poor weak woman swerve from virtue's rule,
> If, strongly charm'd, she leave the thorny way,
> And in the softer paths of pleasure stray;
> Ruin ensues, reproach and endless shame,
> And one false step entirely damns her fame.
> In vain with tears the loss she may deplore,
> In vain look back to what she was before,
> She sets, like stars that fall, to rise no more.[12]

Charles Inigo Jones, in his memoir of Eliza O'Neill, was keen to stress her ability to impart purity to Kotzebue's fallen women. He isolated Jane Shore's speech as the linchpin of English morality: 'These sentiments of Rowe may be considered as the standard English opinion on the subject of female frailty, contrasted with the modern school of Kotzebue, as inferred by his portrait of Mrs Haller in *The Stranger*.'[13]

Kotzebue's fallen women, such as Elvira in *Pizarro* and Mrs Haller in *The Stranger*, are certainly more defiant figures than their English counterparts, and it was therefore vital that actors such as Siddons and O'Neill displayed the requisite purity and dignity: 'The sterling good sense of this country is not easily led astray by the sophistry of the new philosophy ... A Mrs Haller and a Mary Wolstancroft [*sic*] are the same; and if their morality is to be the guide and standard of female excellence, virtue will be but an empty name, and guilt lose all its turpitude.'[14]

William Dunlap in his memoir of G. F. Cooke took a rather more liberal view of Kotzebue's fallen women than the conventional one put by Austen into the mouth of Edmund Bertram: 'What torrents of abuse have been turned upon Kotzebue for uniting *Agatha Fribourg* in wedlock to her seducer, after twenty years of exemplary conduct and exemplary suffering.'[15] Dunlap complained that while George Colman the Younger's *Peregrine* was seen as a lesson in high morality – 'Its great object is to excite a just detestation of the character of a seducer, and to inculcate mercy and forgiveness to the seduced' – Kotzebue was damned for the same lesson: 'The reprehension of the crime, and the exhibition of the consequences are stronger in Kotzebue than in Colman. But German literature had become at one period too brilliant, too fashionable, and usurped too much attention – it became the interest of certain English writers to put it down.'[16]

Edmund thus adopts a conventional stance of trashing German drama and condemning the figure of Agatha Friburg, although his moral indignation does not prohibit him from taking part in *Lovers' Vows*. Dunlap's memoir of Cooke was first published in 1814, which suggest that the controversy about Kotzebue and Agatha Friburg was still topical when *Mansfield Park* was published (Dunlap had that same year also adapted *Lovers' Vows* in America).[17]

Kotzebue is only part of the story. Austen and her readers would also have been aware of the fact that *Lovers' Vows* was translated and adapted by Elizabeth Inchbald.[18] Inchbald's reputation as a writer was well-established and she was highly respected in literary London. She had at one time been in close association with Jacobin circles, yet in her preface to *Lovers' Vows* she indicates that she was no extremist.[19]

In her preface Inchbald also showed her sensitivity to the issue of female propriety. She accordingly altered Amelia's 'indelicately blunt' proposal of love to suit the sensibilities of her English audience by replacing 'coarse abruptness' with 'whimsical insinuations'.[20] Furthermore she removed sensitive political references such as Count Cassel's description of the attack on him in Paris at the start of the Revolution.[21] She also increased the comedy by building up the part of Verdun the butler.

Austen's deliberate omission of Kotzebue's name from the text of *Mansfield Park* only draws further attention to Mrs Inchbald.

The connection is particularly striking when viewed in the light of the fact that Inchbald had already invented a love affair between a priest and a coquette in her novel *A Simple Story*. *Lovers' Vows* ideally suited Austen's intentions of interweaving a dramatic counter-text with the plot of her novel. The particular rendering of a relationship between a coquette and a clergyman in this play, for example, has no other precedent in the drama. And the character of Agatha Friburg, perhaps one of the most notorious portrayals of a fallen woman, resonates with Austen's own depiction of a fallen woman.

Elizabeth Inchbald's play raises considerations about the right of women to choose their own husbands, about a father's responsibilities to his children, and, perhaps most radically, about the validity of innate merit rather than social position. In *Mansfield Park* Jane Austen is deeply engaged with all of these issues. In order for her to develop further her interest in the relationship between role-playing and social behaviour, she needed a play that could be interlinked with the characters in her novel. The sub-plot of *Lovers' Vows* parallels the main plot in *Mansfield Park* the prohibited love between a heroine and the clergyman/mentor who is responsible for forming her mind and her values. Additionally, the counter-text allows Austen to explore the 'dangerous intimacies' between the pairings of Edmund/Mary and Henry/Maria, with Fanny weaving between the two couples. There was simply no other play that could have done this as well as *Lovers' Vows*.

Austen describes the seemingly careless gesture of Tom Bertram flicking through the pages of the eclectic volumes of plays that line the table, only to chance upon the script of *Lovers' Vows* – but of course the choice has been carefully and consciously made, long before the heir of Mansfield Park triumphantly alights upon it. As Yates insists, 'After all our debatings and difficulties, we find there is nothing that will suit us altogether so well, nothing so unexceptionable, as Lovers' Vows' (*MP*, p. 131).

Jane Austen's intricate interweaving of novel and play depends upon an assurance of her readers' familiarity with *Lovers' Vows*. Notably, Fanny is the only principal character in the novel who has not read or seen the play. Tom Bertram defends the educational benefit of play-*reading*, and insists on its efficacy for improving public speaking. Tom's conviction of his father's tacit approval of the amateur theatricals is rather loosely based upon Sir Thomas's encouragement of youthful recitations – an essential part of male education. Even the relatively humble Robert Martin in *Emma* 'would read something aloud out of *Elegant Extracts*' (*E*, p. 29).

Tom, Edmund, Henry and Rushworth all refer to their visits to the public theatre, whereas among the female characters only Lady Bertram does so. This suggests that Maria and Julia have derived their prior knowledge of *Lovers' Vows* from reading rather than viewing. (The sale of the family's town house to settle Tom's debts could have made theatre-going more difficult for the young ladies.) When Edmund urges Maria to give the play up, he makes the assumption that she hasn't *read* it carefully enough, but Maria quickly confirms that she is 'perfectly acquainted' with *Lovers' Vows*. Play-reading is a prerequisite for a would-be heroine. Ironically, Maria, unlike Catherine Morland in *Northanger Abbey*, fails to learn the lessons from the printed text.[22]

Fanny Price has no qualms about 'reading' *Lovers' Vows*. Play-reading is her only source of dramatic entertainment until she is awakened, by Henry Crawford, to the pleasures of 'good hardened real acting' (*MP*, p. 124). In *Mansfield Park* Jane Austen not only directly shows her own heroine in the act of reading plays, she also indirectly encourages play-reading in her own readers by assuming prior knowledge of Mrs Inchbald's play – even today, readers who enjoy the novel are tempted to go on to the play. Much of the first volume of *Mansfield Park* is only partially intelligible without knowledge of *Lovers' Vows*. If Austen really did make the assumption that her readers had direct access to the play, this makes clear her reason for directly quoting only one speech from it. She simply believed that her readers, like herself, held the text in their memories or had it in their libraries. With this is mind I would like to argue for a closer reading of *Lovers' Vows* than has previously been attempted.[23]

* * *

In *Lovers' Vows*, Baron Wildenhaim has seduced and then abandoned a chambermaid, Agatha Friburg, in his youth. When the play opens Agatha is in a state of poverty, where she is found by her illegitimate son Frederick, now a soldier. When he learns the true story of his birth, he goes out to beg in order to help his mother. He happens to meet his father and tries to rob him. When he is arrested he reveals the identity of himself, the Baron and his mother. With the aid of the pastor, Anhalt, he persuades the Baron to marry Agatha. The Baron also consents to the marriage of his daughter, Amelia, to Anhalt, instead of forcing her to marry Count Cassel, a rich but brainless fop he had in mind for her.[24]

The casting eventually agreed at Mansfield is as follows:

MEN
Baron Wildenhaim – Mr Yates
Count Cassel – Mr Rushworth
Anhalt – Edmund Bertram
Frederick – Henry Crawford
Verdun the Butler – Tom Bertram
Landlord – Tom Bertram
Cottager – Tom Bertram

WOMEN
Agatha Friburg – Maria Bertram
Amelia Wildenhaim – Mary Crawford
Cottager's Wife – Fanny Price

Austen's introduction of *Lovers' Vows* into the action of *Mansfield Park* is a much more serious and far-reaching matter than the arbitrary choice of a play for an entertaining diversion during the absence of the father of the house. The choice of play signals Austen's engagement with the subject of prohibited relationships and with a long-standing debate about women's autonomy in courtship.

In *Northanger Abbey*, Austen had mocked Samuel Richardson's claim that no woman should fall in love with a man before he had made his proposal.[25] In her first published novel, *Sense and Sensibility* (1811), she had depicted two heroines who love without promise, and explored the implications of this condition for young, penniless women. In her later novels, *Mansfield Park* and *Persuasion*, she dramatises the effect of constrained love upon her displaced heroines. Throughout *Mansfield Park*, Fanny Price is portrayed in the uncompromising position of loving without invitation, and, much worse, loving without hope.

In *Mansfield Park* Austen explores female consciousness in four young women, and focuses upon the comparisons and contrasts of female conduct in the courtship process. The prototype for this type of narrative was her admired *Sir Charles Grandison*. Richardson's novel was among the first of its kind to describe female consciousness in detail, and its depiction of Harriet Byron's entrance into the world was a theme taken up most successfully by female authors such as Fanny Burney in *Evelina* (1771) and Maria Edgeworth in *Belinda* (1801).

The first three volumes of Richardson's lengthy novel depict his heroine's difficulty in deciding whether she should conceal or admit her love for Sir Charles before he has addressed her with a formal declaration. The character of Amelia Wildenhaim in *Lovers' Vows* is the stage prototype of a woman who unequivocally defends her right to love before her love is returned. From Richardson's portrayal of his heroine's dilemma in courtship to Inchbald's depiction of a brazen coquette initiating her own right to choose there is a huge leap in notions of female propriety. Inchbald, via Kotzebue, takes up the cause of a woman's right to court.

Lovers' Vows and *Mansfield Park* are both explorations of the *Grandison* theme: the difficulties of a prohibited relationship, from a woman's perspective.[26] The most obvious parallel between *Mansfield Park* and *Lovers' Vows* is that each work gives prominence to a relationship between a coquette and a clergyman. Inchbald was drawn to this kind of relationship partly for personal reasons – she was in love with John Kemble, who had abandoned his clerical vocation in order to become an actor – but the motif also arose from the eighteenth-century resurrection of the medieval love story of Eloise and Abelard.[27] Inchbald's first novel, *A Simple Story* (1791), depicts a prohibited love affair between a pious Catholic priest and his lively and outspoken ward, Miss Milner. Her interest in this kind of prohibited relationship perhaps contributed to her decision to adapt *Lovers' Vows*. In *Mansfield Park* Austen orchestrates parallels with and deviations from the coquette/clergyman theme brought to her by Inchbald.

Mansfield Park has its own triangle of lovers: a coquette, a prude and a clergyman. In seeking a model for Mary Crawford's attempt to divert Edmund from his calling, Austen would have had to look no further than Inchbald's *Lovers' Vows*. In seeking a model for Fanny Price's concealed passion, she would also find one in the play. It may even be that *Lovers' Vows* actually gave Austen the impulse to broach this set of relationships in her novel.

On a superficial level, when the amateur theatricals take place at Mansfield Park, the characters seem to be cast into roles that are appropriate for them. But on more detailed examination we see that this is not always the case. Jane Austen uses the play as a point of reference for the novel's principal relationship, that between Fanny and Edmund; but, rather than the heroine being characterised as a charming coquette, Fanny is divested of superficial sexual charisma and behaves as a model of modesty and prudence. In *Mansfield Park* the plot is complicated by the presence of a third force, and the character of the winning coquette is displaced onto the anti-heroine, Mary Crawford, whose role is that of the seductress who poses a threat to the heroine's happiness. Mary acts as a dramatic foil to the shy, prudish heroine, and Fanny's jealousy of her dazzling rival prompts much of the novel's dynamic.

In character and situation both Mary and Fanny present a variation on the *Lovers' Vows* theme. Amelia Wildenhaim, a beautiful coquette, is secretly in love with the clergyman who has been responsible for her education. In *Mansfield Park* Mary Crawford exhibits similar qualities of wit and vivacity that tempt the prudish Edmund to waver from his duty. But Fanny Price is also offered as a modification of the *Lovers' Vows* theme; she loves a man destined for the clergy who is prohibited to her, and refuses a more lucrative offer of marriage from an unworthy suitor.

As Fanny is willing to defy Sir Thomas in refusing a man she doesn't love, so Amelia disregards wealth and status in favour of love. Amelia's disregard of the binding rules of courtship decorum obscures neither her ability to recognise and value Anhalt's understated qualities, nor her readiness to put personal happiness before material considerations. Mary Crawford recognises Edmund's worth and is attracted by his steadiness and integrity, but cynically insists that there is no glamour in being 'honest and poor' – 'I have a much greater respect for those that are honest and rich' (*MP*, p. 213). Mary will not lower herself to marry a clergyman, in particular a clergyman with a serious vocation: 'It was plain that he could have no serious views, no true attachment, by fixing himself in a situation which he must know she would never stoop to' (*MP*, p. 228). Amelia, like Miss Hastings in Goldsmith's play, will 'stoop to conquer'. Mary will not.

Mary Crawford's faults are primarily attributed to a lack of the right sort of education: she has had an education in fashionable accomplishments rather than in good principles and morals. Her verbal indiscretions are the indelible marks of her educational deficiencies. They alert both Fanny and Edmund to her casual disregard of propriety. In the Sotherton chapel, Mary's indecorous quip about the 'former belles of the house of Rushworth' making eyes at the chaplain confirms the Abelard and Eloise theme of *Lovers' Vows* and *Mansfield Park*: 'The young Mrs Eleanors and Mrs Bridgets – starched up into seeming piety, but with heads full of something very different – especially if the poor chaplain were not worth looking at' (*MP*, p. 87).

Mary's irreverent remark also reveals an irony at her own expense, for it coincides with her discovery that Edmund is to be a clergyman. Mary's remark, pointedly made in a disused family chapel, is a covert hint at her contempt for Edmund's chosen profession, which she subsequently and quite openly attempts to undermine. Edmund Bertram is undoubtedly modelled upon the lover/clergyman hero of Pope and Rousseau, modified by Inchbald and Kotzebue, and brought to Austen's *Mansfield Park* directly and indirectly through Edmund's role as Anhalt in *Lovers' Vows*. Edmund closely resembles Anhalt in character and in situation. They have chosen the same profession: the church. They are both responsible for nurturing a young woman who responds by falling in love with them, and they are both captivated by a fashionably accomplished woman who happens to be attractive, witty and verbally imprudent. The incident in the chapel heralds the long conflict ahead for Mary and Edmund that ends with his discovery of her 'corrupted, vitiated mind' (*MP*, p. 456).

Mary's fondest memory of Edmund is recalling him in a position of sexual submission:

The scene we were rehearsing was so very remarkable! The subject of it
so very – very – what shall I say? He was to be describing and recommending matrimony to me. I think I see him now, trying to be as
demure and composed as Anhalt ought, through the two long speeches
… If I had the power of recalling any one week of my existence, it should
be that week, that acting week. Say what you will, Fanny, it should be
that; for I never knew such exquisite happiness in any other. His sturdy
spirit to bend as it did! Oh! it was sweet beyond expression. (*MP*, p. 358)

For Austen it is the friction ensuing from the clash between the sexually
confident coquette and the grave, prudish, religious figure that gives the
relationship its dynamic.[28] Mary Crawford's persistent attempts to
dissuade Edmund from his decision to be ordained not only reflect her
desire to continue in the lifestyle to which she has become accustomed:
they also increasingly become a struggle for the control of Edmund's
spirit, something she clearly finds thrilling. Although some critics have
puzzled over Mary's admiration of the rather stolid Edmund, this is to
misunderstand the workings of the coquette/clergyman relationship.
Mary's rival is the church. Mary's conflict with Edmund's religious vocation is no less than a fight for his soul, and this is why Fanny is so dead
set against Mary and why Edmund is portrayed as a character divided
against himself.

Mary's attempts to dissuade Edmund range from gentle persuasion
– 'You really are fit for something better. Come, do change your mind. It
is not too late. Go into the law' – to cruel attempts to emasculate him:
'Men love to distinguish themselves, and in either of the other lines,
distinction may be gained, but not in the church. A clergyman is nothing' (*MP*, pp. 92–93). Eventually, when she is no longer convinced of her
powers of persuasion, she pointedly insists that she 'never has danced
with a clergyman … and never *will*' (*MP*, p. 268). Later, she ridicules his
profession to his face (*MP*, p. 279). Having succeeded once in getting
him to change his mind over playing Anhalt, Mary is angered to discover,
during the card game Speculation, that she is deceived about her dreams
of Edmund as an unordained 'gentleman of independent fortune'.[29]

Austen makes the comparison between Edmund and Anhalt abundantly clear from the outset of the theatrical episode in her telling

description of Edmund caught 'between his theatrical and his real part' (*MP*, p. 163). Mary's comment about Edmund's performance of Anhalt's spiritual struggle, '*his* sturdy spirit to bend as it did', is thus deliberately ambiguous.

Edmund's long-drawn-out temptation is a source of provocation and anguish to his 'confessor', Fanny, who condemns him for his weakness and urges him to make up his mind: 'Finish it at once. Let there be an end of this suspense. Fix, commit, condemn yourself' (*MP*, p. 424). One of the cruelties of Fanny's position as confessor is that she is forced to listen to Edmund expressing both his admiration for, and his doubts about, Mary:

> 'I have been pained by her manner this morning, and cannot get the better of it. I know her disposition to be as sweet and faultless as your own, but the influence of her former companions makes her seem, gives to her conversation, to her professed opinions, sometimes a tinge of wrong. She does not *think* evil, but she speaks it – speaks it in playfulness – and though I know it to be playfulness, it grieves me to the soul'. 'The effect of education,' said Fanny gently. (*MP*, pp. 268–69)

Mary's verbal indiscretions frequently have a sexual content. Her remarks range from the mildly inappropriate – she jokes about the amorous servants lying in bed on a Sunday instead of going to chapel – to the more risqué joke about *Rears* and *Vices*. Her verbal improprieties, which reveal worldliness and knowingness, clearly hold a fascination for Edmund, which both attracts and repels. Yet although he is aware of her educational limitations, Austen reminds us that 'had he been able to talk another five minutes, there is no saying that he might not have talked away all Miss Crawford's faults and his own despondence' (*MP*, p. 270).

In *Lovers' Vows* Amelia promises to reimburse Anhalt's teaching by payment in kind. She will turn tutoress and so teach him how to love: 'none but a woman can teach the science of herself: and though I own I am very young, a young woman may be as agreeable for a tutoress as an old one'.[30] In contrast to the frivolously accomplished Bertram sisters and Mary Crawford, Fanny Price has had the 'proper' sort of education, nurtured by her cousin Edmund: she responds by loving him.

In both *Mansfield Park* and *Lovers' Vows* the young heroine falls in love with the man she holds responsible for her education. Paradoxically, then, it is Fanny, not Mary Crawford, who correlates with Amelia Wildenhaim in refusing a brilliant match with a rich but unworthy lover because her heart is pre-engaged to the man who has nurtured and educated her.

Alexander Pope in his poem *Eloise to Abelard* (1717) wrote of love:

Of all affliction taught a lover yet,
'Tis sure the hardest science to forget.[31]

The idea of love as a 'taught science' appears in all of the eighteenth-century resurrected versions of Eloise and Abelard. In *Lovers' Vows* the pious young clergyman, Anhalt, like Rousseau's St Preux in *La nouvelle Héloïse*, has been responsible for the tutoring of the Baron's family. Amelia unequivocally states, 'My father has more than once told me that he who forms my mind I should always consider as my greatest benefactor. And my heart tells me the same' (act 3, scene 2). Amelia inverts social convention when she candidly offers to teach Anhalt 'the science of herself', to repay him for the 'education' he has given her. This very closely parallels Rousseau, where Julie (the Eloise figure) explains to her father that her education is due to the exertions of her tutor: 'but all this could not be mine without a master: I told him mine, enumerating at the same time all the sciences he proposed to teach me, except one'.[32]

More radically, Amelia makes, in Fanny's words, 'very little short of a declaration of love' to her tutor: a shocking concept to Fanny, who is embarrassed by the similarity of her own situation to Amelia's. However, the idea of declaring that love, let alone making a proposal of marriage, is inconceivable to Fanny. Behind Fanny's discomfort of witnessing the 'dreaded scene' from *Lovers' Vows* is the cruel irony of her own similarity to Amelia. Edmund's searching out of Fanny to read Amelia's part against his Anhalt is potentially even more distressing than her being forced to watch Edmund and Mary rehearse the scene.

One of the ironies of Fanny's situation is that she is unable to express her true feelings directly to the one person who would listen, and a further cruel irony is that she is forced to accept the role of confidante to that same person. Fanny is aware of the cruelties of her position, yet is powerless to stem the force of her feelings:

> To think of him as Miss Crawford might be justified in thinking, would in her be insanity. To her, he could be nothing under any circumstances – nothing dearer than a friend. Why did such an idea occur to her even enough to be reprobated and forbidden? It ought not to have touched on the confines of her imagination. (*MP*, pp. 264–65)

Like Amelia in *Lovers' Vows*, Fanny is unmoved by the temptations of wealth, status and sexual conquest.[33] When she is given the rare opportunity to express her feelings, she does not hold back, as is shown in her gentle, but spirited, defence of her right to her 'negative':

> 'I *should* have thought ... that every woman must have felt the possibility of a man's not being approved, not being loved by some one of her sex, at least, let him be ever so generally agreeable. Let him have all the perfections in the world, I think it ought not to be set down as certain, that a man must be acceptable to every woman he may happen to like himself ... In my situation, it would have been the extreme of vanity to be forming expectation on Mr Crawford ... How then was I to be – to be in love with him the moment he said he was with me? How was I to have an attachment at his service, as soon as it was asked for?' (*MP*, p. 353)

This speech is remarkable for its encapsulation of the paradoxes of courtship conduct for women, particularly those of a low status.

Fanny's 'settled dislike' of Crawford is not enough for Sir Thomas, or indeed Edmund, because Crawford is perceived as a socially acceptable 'catch'; yet, paradoxically, it is precisely Fanny's lowly social status which precludes her from forming any expectations of Henry in the first place. Furthermore, when she is condescended to be noticed by a man of means, a man whom she has no right to consider in the first place, she is immediately expected to switch on her feelings, 'as soon as it was asked for'. The further layer of irony exposed by this double standard is Fanny's concealed love for Edmund, to whom she is making this speech. Fanny's own impropriety in imagining Edmund as a sexual partner has been reproved by her own conscience, for daring 'to have touched on the confines of her imagination'. But, paradoxically, the knowledge that Edmund 'could be nothing [to her] under any circumstances' does not stop the idea occurring to her 'even enough to be reprobated and forbidden' (*MP*, pp. 264–65). This is precisely because feelings cannot be switched off and on at random.

Fanny, of course, is not in Amelia's position of choosing her own husband, but she nevertheless exercises her right to refusal, as do most of Jane Austen's heroines. In *Sir Charles Grandison* Harriet Byron complains to her confidante about the unfairness of courtship decorum: 'What can a woman do who is addressed by a man of talents inferior to her own? She cannot pick and choose, as men can. She has only her negative.'[34] Austen has Henry Tilney advocating women's 'power of refusal' in *Northanger Abbey*,[35] but in *Pride and Prejudice* she conveys the limitations of a woman's 'no' in Mr Collins's and Darcy's refusal to accept Elizabeth's refusal.

In Henry Mackenzie's Rousseauistic novel *Julia de Roubigné* the heroine is frustrated by the Count's persistent pursuit of her hand, and complains of the injustice for women in courtship: 'Is this fair dealing … that his feelings are to be an apology for his suit, while mine are not allowed to be a reason for refusal.'[36] In *Mansfield Park*, Henry's reluctance to accept Fanny's refusal is proof of his gross selfishness. Even when she is softened by his conduct at Portsmouth, she still hopes to be released from his attentions: 'might not it be fairly supposed, that he would not much longer persevere in a suit so distressing to her?' (*MP*, p. 414).

Now it is Fanny who parallels Amelia in refusing an unwanted offer of marriage. While no one could claim that she shares Amelia's vivacity, she does share, to use Sir Thomas's term, an 'independence of spirit' (*MP*, p. 318). Neither Fanny nor Amelia will marry from a sense of duty. Amelia openly flirts with the reticent clergyman, but her intentions are deadly serious. She genuinely loves him and defiantly claims 'If you then love me as you say, I will marry; and will be happy – but only with you' (*LV*, act 3, scene 2). Paradoxically, it is Maria Bertram who, in refusing to be released from her engagement to Rushworth, does not exercise her right to refusal.

* * *

Many critics have noted the analogy between the two 'fallen woman', Agatha Friburg and Maria Bertram. The casting of Maria as Agatha is apt because, like her stage counterpart, she eventually becomes a social outcast through sexual misconduct. But Maria's character and situation are markedly different from those of her stage counterpart, just as Mary Crawford's and Amelia's situations are not as close as has usually been assumed. It is essential to the complex, ironic relationship between *Mansfield Park* and *Lovers' Vows* that not all the characters in the novel are, as superficially seems to be the case, cast in the parts that are appropriate for them – as we have seen from the greater resemblance of Amelia to Fanny Price than Mary Crawford.

Paradoxically, though Maria's situation as a fallen woman is different from Agatha's (she is the eldest daughter of a great family, not a seduced chambermaid), it does correspond with the role of the second female lead, Amelia. Both young women have an offer of marriage from men they despise, both are secretly in love with another man, both are under the jurisdiction of their fathers. Maria shares with her cousin, Fanny, the situation of being in love with an inaccessible man. Similarly, Sir Thomas's interviews with Maria and Fanny on the subject of the marriage transaction mirror each other.

One of the most striking parallels between *Lovers' Vows* and *Mansfield Park*, which is wholly lost on a reader unfamiliar with the play, is that between Sir Thomas Bertram and Baron Wildenhaim. As will be seen in the next chapter, Austen particularly relishes the great comic stage confrontation between Sir Thomas and Yates in the role of the Baron. In *Lovers' Vows* the loving and affectionate relationship between father and daughter is a striking reversal of the convention of the tyrannical Gothic father-figure so popular in late eighteenth-century fiction.

In *Mansfield Park* Wildenhaim's parental concern is echoed by that of Sir Thomas when he learns that his daughter's betrothed, James Rushworth, is empty and foolish. Rushworth's foppishness is likewise indicated by an 'unmanly' obsession with his 'finery'. His incessant references to his dressing-up clothes, in particular his pink satin costume, are a constant source of amusement to the other actors. That Rushworth is chosen to play the part of the despised suitor, Count Cassel, confirms the parallel between Sir Thomas and Wildenhaim.

Both Sir Thomas and the Baron hope for an improvement in their future sons-in-law: 'Mr Rushworth was young enough to improve; – Mr Rushworth must and would improve in good society' (*MP*, p. 201). Similarly Wildenhaim entreats the religious and spiritual guidance of Anhalt to improve Cassel, 'Take him under your care, while he is here, and make him something like yourself … Form the Count after your own manner' (*LV*, act 2, scene 2). Both fathers act responsibly in their attempts to gauge their daughters' happiness, both profess an unwillingness to 'sacrifice' that happiness to financial gain, and both wish to become better acquainted with their future sons-in-law before expressing their consent to marriage. Sir Thomas determines to spend more time with Rushworth in the hope of discovering the truth of Mrs Norris's promise that 'the more you know of him, the better you will like him' (*MP*, p. 190). Wildenhaim, likewise, is prepared to give his daughter time:

> No, I shall not be in a hurry: I love my daughter too well. We must be better acquainted before I give her to him. I shall not sacrifice my Amelia to the will of others, as I myself was sacrificed. The poor girl might, in thoughtlessness, say yes, and afterwards be miserable. (*LV*, act 2, scene 2)

The Baron's concern for his daughter's marital felicity places him as a considerate and responsible parent. Similarly Sir Thomas decides to 'observe' Maria and Rushworth to ascertain the strength of her feelings:

> He had expected a very different son-in-law; and beginning to feel grave on Maria's account, tried to understand *her* feelings. Little observation there was necessary to tell him that indifference was the most favourable state they could be in. Her behaviour to Mr Rushworth was careless and cold. She could not, did not like him … Advantageous as would be the alliance, and long standing and public as was the engagement, her happiness must not be sacrificed to it. (*MP*, p. 200)

Wildenhaim's soliloquy is strikingly echoed in Sir Thomas's internal monologue. Both fathers condemn the idea of 'sacrifice' by an unhappy liaison, regardless of material advantage. Both fathers use the same strategy to ascertain the truth by resolving to speak seriously to their daughters in a private interview. Both fathers seem to be a reversal of the Gothic patriarch of stage and page.

Austen takes from *Lovers' Vows* the scene of a confrontation between father and daughter on the subject of marriage, and extends and modifies it on two separate occasions. As in the play, the novel has a meeting between the Baron(et) and his daughter in which he (feebly) attempts to discover her true feelings for her suitor. Austen invites us to consider the similarities and differences between the two fathers.

In *Lovers' Vows* the interview between father and daughter is lighthearted and comic. Baron Wildenhaim begins his paternal speech by urging openness: 'Amelia, you know you have a father who loves you … tell me candidly how you like Count Cassel? … to see you happy is my wish' (*LV*, act 2, scene 2). The exchange is punctuated by Wildenhaim's insistence on candour: 'but be sure to answer me honestly – Speak truth,' and 'Nor ever *conceal* the truth from me' (*MP*, p. 495). The comic irony springs from the knowledge that Amelia is barely attempting to conceal her secret love for her tutor, but Wildenhaim is too blind to notice her hints:

> BARON: Psha! I want to know if you can love the Count. You saw him at the last ball when we were in France: when he capered around you; when he danced minuets; when he –. But I cannot say what his conversation was.
> AMELIA: Nor I either [*sic*] – I do not remember a syllable of it.
> BARON: No? Then I do not think you like him.
> AMELIA: I believe not.
> BARON: Do not you wish to take his part when his companions laugh at him?
> AMELIA: No: I love to laugh at him myself. (*LV*, act 2, scene 2)

The potential seriousness of the father/daughter scene is undercut by Amelia's casual indifference to the whole transaction. Her most serious stated reservation about marriage with Cassel is that he steps on her toes at balls. Although Cassel's status and wealth are vigorously stressed by the Baron, Amelia defends her view that 'birth and fortune are inconsiderable things, and cannot give happiness'. The convention that is being satirised in this scene is the confrontation with the tyrannical father. Far from being ill at ease and powerless, as is the expectation of a dependent daughter refusing a wealthy and approved suitor, Amelia upturns the convention by coolly and openly acknowledging her contempt for her betrothed, and it is Wildenhaim who is embarrassed and flustered by his own clumsy attempts to do his fatherly duty. In *Mansfield Park*, compared with the friendly banter between Amelia and the Baron, there is a chilling lack of feeling between Maria and her father, as he attempts to follow up the observations that have stared everyone else in the face since her hasty engagement.

The interview between father and daughter is deliberately brief. Austen sets out the position in reported speech: 'With solemn kindness Sir Thomas addressed her; told her his fears, inquired into her wishes, entreated her to be open and sincere, and assured her that every inconvenience should be braved, and the connection entirely given up, if she felt herself unhappy in the prospect of it. He would act for her and release her' (*MP*, p. 200). The lack of dramatic impetus in the rendering of Sir Thomas's 'paternal kindness' is a deliberate and conscious device of distancing. Maria's dismissal of his fears is dutiful and equally polite, but it strikes a false note, which conveys her proud intransigence in the face of her father's probings:

She thanked [Sir Thomas] for his great attention, his paternal kindness, but he was quite mistaken in supposing she had the smallest desire of breaking through her engagement, or was sensible of any change of opinion or inclination since her forming it. She had the highest esteem for Mr Rushworth's character and disposition, and could not have a doubt of her happiness with him. (*MP*, p. 200)

185

Any young woman on the verge of marriage might express fears or doubts if asked, but Maria's exaggerated claims of conviction produce little sympathy. Her stubborn bravado is expressed through her choice of words, and the rhythms of her speech: '*quite* mistaken', 'the *smallest* desire', 'the *highest esteem*', '*not a doubt of* her happiness with him'.

As in *Lovers' Vows*, there is dramatic irony at work in the daughter's concealment of knowledge from her father, in Maria's case that of her attachment to Henry Crawford and his rejection of her. In *Lovers' Vows* the irony is unambiguously directed against the father, who misinterprets his daughter's secrecy (the result of her love for Anhalt) as virgin modesty, while the audience enjoys her handling of the joke at his expense.[37] In *Mansfield Park*, on the other hand, the irony encompasses both Sir Thomas and Maria.

In the aftermath of the conference, both are left to reflect on their parts. His happiness in escaping 'the embarrassing evils of a rupture' assuages his doubts: 'Sir Thomas was satisfied; too glad to be satisfied perhaps to urge the matter quite so far as his judgement might have dictated to others' (*MP*, p. 201). Maria's response is to strengthen her resolve to 'behave more cautiously to Mr Rushworth in future, that her father might not be again suspecting her' (*MP*, p. 201). Austen reminds us that they have both got what they wanted: Maria has 'pledged herself anew to Sotherton' and prevented 'Crawford [from] destroying her prospects', and Sir Thomas has secured 'a marriage which would bring him such an addition of respectability and influence'. Austen spares neither father nor daughter: 'To her the conference closed as satisfactorily as to him.'

The Baron, like Sir Thomas, holds 'birth and fortune' high in the marital stakes, but Sir Thomas strikingly deviates from Wildenhaim in condoning a marriage without love, a reflection perhaps on his own mistake in marriage: 'A well-disposed young woman, who did not marry for love, was in general but the more attached to her own family' (*MP*, p. 201). A further irony is that Sir Thomas's timing is out: he is 'three or four days' too late, after Maria's wounded feelings have been tranquillised and replaced by 'pride and self-revenge' (*MP*, p. 202). Matrimony becomes her means of escape. She enters into marriage with a man she despises in order to get away from a father she resents:

Independence was more needful than ever; the want of it at Mansfield more sensibly felt. She was less and less able to endure the restraint which her father imposed. The liberty which his absence had given was now become absolutely necessary. She must escape from him and Mansfield as soon as possible, and find consolation in fortune and consequence, bustle and the world, for a wounded spirit. (*MP*, p. 202)

It is clear that Sir Thomas's intervention helps to push Maria over the edge. Ironically his 'solemn kindness', far from releasing her fears, precipitates her decision to marry Rushworth and leave Mansfield. In *Lovers' Vows*, Wildenhaim is more alert to the dangers of the kind of parental interference that is common in Gothic drama and fiction. He vows to remain impartial: 'I shall not command, neither persuade her to the marriage. I know too well the fatal influence of parents on such a subject' (*LV*, act 2, scene 2). Again the Gothic element is overturned in *Lovers' Vows*, but in *Mansfield Park* Sir Thomas's control and restraint are merely presented as a more subtle form of imprisonment.

So much for Maria and her father. Sir Thomas is pleased with the outcome of the conference. Once Maria and Julia have left for London, he is 'observing' once more, and this time it is an advantageous match for Fanny that interests him:

and though infinitely above scheming or contriving for any the most advantageous matrimonial establishment that could be among the apparent possibilities of any one most dear to him, and disdaining even as a littleness the being quick-sighted on such points, he could not avoid perceiving in a grand and careless way that Mr Crawford was somewhat distinguishing his niece – nor perhaps refrain (though unconsciously) from giving a more willing assent to invitations on that account. (*MP*, p. 238)

This passage is loaded with authorial irony. The mock-lofty tone of the first sentence deliberately undercuts the baronet's dignified intent; we already know that he has sanctioned an advantageous liaison for one 'most dear to him' in the full knowledge that it is marriage without affection or love, so we are clearly required to mistrust the authorial voice, and to accept this statement ironically. Nor are we meant to be fooled by Sir Thomas's casual admission of his observation of Henry's attention to Fanny, and his concession to the 'littleness' of such an observation. This is especially intriguing because the self-knowledge that is implied by such an admission is in fact more an assumption that Sir Thomas is making about himself, rather than a representation of his conscious thoughts. The inherent untrustworthiness of Sir Thomas's admission is subtly conveyed through free indirect speech, which simultaneously manages to excuse and condemn, to conceal yet reveal. The voice that seems to approve of the delicacy of Sir Thomas's motives is in fact exposing its distrust of his motives. Furthermore, the latter half of the sentence flatly contradicts the first. Sir Thomas's active encouragement of the Crawfords' company reveals that he is as scheming as Mrs Norris when it comes to contriving a lucrative marriage.

The irony, continuing in the same mocking vein, undermines Sir Thomas's screening of his own 'unconscious' scheming: 'for it was in the course of that very visit, that he first began to think, that any one in the habit of such idle observation *would have thought* that Mr Crawford was the admirer of Fanny Price' (*MP*, p. 238). Sir Thomas objectifies his observations to conceal his true motives from himself. This conscious concealment of his less honourable intentions is reinforced later in the novel, at the ball that he has so carefully stage-managed for the purpose of promoting Henry and Fanny's attachment. Austen deliberately employs an ambiguous language for Sir Thomas in which we can read his true motives beneath his words, even as he deludes himself in the process: 'He remained steadily inclined to gratify so amiable a feeling – to gratify *any body else* who might wish to see Fanny dance' (*MP*, p. 252, my italics). The 'any body else' is of course Henry Crawford, and this is confirmed by Sir Thomas's approval when Fanny is engaged for the first two dances by Henry, and his invitation to Henry at the end of the ball:

> and the readiness with which his invitation was accepted, convinced him that the suspicions whence, *he must confess to himself*, this very ball had in great measure sprung, were well founded, Mr Crawford was in love with Fanny. (*MP*, p. 280, my italics)

Most interesting in this passage is Sir Thomas's need to confess to himself fully. At last it is openly stated. Austen delivers her strongest indictment of Sir Thomas's control of Fanny: 'Sir Thomas was again interfering in her inclination by advising her to go immediately to bed. "Advise" was his word, but it was the advice of absolute power' (*MP*, p. 280). By the end of the ball, there is no ambiguity in Austen's presentation of Sir Thomas: 'In thus sending her away, Sir Thomas perhaps might not be thinking merely of her health. It might occur to him that Mr Crawford had been sitting by her long enough, or he might mean to recommend her as a wife by shewing her persuadableness' (*MP*, p. 281). This ironically anticipates Fanny's withstanding of Sir Thomas in her own conference scene, which forms a contrast to his scene with Maria. The complexity of Austen's use of narrative control to expose the workings of Sir Thomas's mind takes her far beyond *Lovers' Vows*.

The similarity of Fanny's position to that of her cousin Julia is made strikingly clear throughout the theatrical saga: neither of them wants to take part in the play because their rival is cast opposite the man they desire themselves. Less obviously, Fanny's correspondence with Maria is apparent from the similar situation in which they find themselves when in conference with Sir Thomas. Both girls are secretly in love, and unable to express that love to Sir Thomas, but are pressured into matrimony with a rich, unsuitable man. Fanny, in refusing Crawford, differs from her cousin, but shares the dilemma of being forced to conceal and dissemble.

Inchbald had parodied the theme of patriarchal power in *Lovers' Vows* by means of Amelia's control over her father. Austen has presented us early on in *Mansfield Park* with a kindly, if misguided father, who offers to release his daughter from her unhappy engagement. This time it is Fanny who is urged by a father-figure to accept a lucrative but unwanted marriage proposal, while she is forced to conceal the truth of a secret attachment. The contrast of this scene to Sir Thomas's early triumph with Maria is in its boldly theatricalised presentation of patriarchal power.

The scene with Sir Thomas in the East Room is preceded by Henry's passionate proposal to Fanny. This encounter between Fanny and Henry is almost comically presented, as her horror at his passionate words only increases his ardour. The comic irony springs from *her* disbelief of his intentions – 'it was like himself and entirely of a piece with what she had seen before' – and *his* misapprehension of her evident reluctance: 'to part with her at a moment when modesty alone seemed to his sanguine and pre-assured mind to stand in the way of the happiness he sought'. The quasi-farcical encounter is ended when Fanny 'bursts away from him' upon hearing Sir Thomas and 'rushed out at an opposite door from the one her uncle was approaching' (*MP*, p. 302).

The final volume of *Mansfield Park* opens with the heroine hiding in her room to avoid Henry. The sounds of her uncle's footsteps outside the door set her trembling like a Gothic heroine awaiting her terrible fate:

> Suddenly the sound of a step in regular approach was heard – a heavy step, an unusual step in that part of the house; it was her uncle's; she knew it as well as his voice; she had trembled at it as often, and began to tremble again, at the idea of his coming up to speak to her, whatever might be the subject. (*MP*, p. 312)

Sir Thomas comes his closest yet to making an apology to Fanny on his discovery that there is no fire in her room: 'you will feel that *they* were not least your friends who were educating and preparing you for that mediocrity of condition which *seemed* to be your lot' (*MP*, p. 313). Now that Henry's offer of marriage has raised the stakes, Sir Thomas entreats Fanny not to 'harbour resentment' over past grievances. His opening speech begins on the subject of 'birth and fortune'. In *Lovers' Vows* the Baron, when asked what can interest him in favour of a man 'whose head and heart are good for nothing', replies 'birth and fortune': as in *Mansfield Park*, the question of social status is raised as an important part of the marriage contract.

Just as in the interview with Maria, Sir Thomas is in control. He does not expect any problem at all from the shrinking girl he has fostered, and again the irony springs from the reversal of expectations. Sir Thomas expects problems from his daughter's 'disposition' but does not anticipate any struggle from Fanny's gentle nature. But it soon becomes clear that he is less concerned with romantic notions of marital felicity than with encouraging an advantageous alliance of means. He is stunned by Fanny's refusal to ally herself to a gentleman of such favourable prospects.

The scene is characterised by a fundamental clash of values. Sir Thomas's initial mistake is to assume that Fanny will behave as a dutiful daughter and accept the man of his choice. Given that Crawford is a man of sense, as well as fortune, he is even more confounded by Fanny's uncompromising refusal to accept him. Moreover, because she is without position and means, she has less reason to refuse him than the Bertram daughters would have:

> 'Am I to understand', said Sir Thomas, after a few moments' silence, 'that you mean to *refuse* Mr Crawford?'
> 'Yes, Sir'.
> 'Refuse him?'
> 'Yes, Sir'.
> 'Refuse Mr Crawford! Upon what plea? For what reason?'
> 'I – I cannot like him, Sir, well enough to marry him.' (*MP*, p. 315)

The fear that Fanny expresses to her uncle contrasts not only with Amelia's teasing but loving relationship with her father, but also with Maria's polite indifference to Sir Thomas. The tone of the interview shifts from friendly paternal consideration to outright emotional blackmail when Sir Thomas realises that she indeed means to defy him and refuse Crawford.

The scene gains suppleness from the quasi-theatrical device of dramatic irony whereby, like Maria and Amelia, Fanny is concealing vital information. Both Fanny and Sir Thomas are at cross-purposes. In *Lovers' Vows* the cross-purposes between father and daughter work effectively on a comic level. While it is obvious to the audience that Amelia is in love with Anhalt, when she drops hints to enlighten her father he blindly misinterprets her romantic allusions to the chaplain:

> BARON: Have you not dreamt at all tonight?
> AMELIA: Oh yes – I have dreamt of our chaplain, Mr Anhalt.
> BARON: Ah ha! As if he stood before you and the Count to ask for the ring.
> AMELIA: No: not that. (*LV*, act 2, scene 2)

Sir Thomas, too, is blind to the full state of affairs because Fanny with-holds information. But his lack of comprehension, and her dissembling, do not work for comic effect. Her motives can only be cleared by impli-cating those of her female cousins:

> her heart sunk under the appalling prospect of discussion, explanation and probably non-conviction. Her ill opinion of him was founded chiefly on observations, which, for her cousins' sake, she could scarcely dare mention to their father. Maria and Julia – and especially Maria, were so closely implicated in Mr Crawford's misconduct, that she could not give his character, such as she believed it, without betraying them. (*MP*, pp. 317–18)

Ironically the suitor is Henry Crawford, Maria's secret lover, and Fanny's secret lover is Edmund. The conference scene between Fanny and Sir Thomas is one of the most powerful in the novel. Fanny's motives are misunderstood and misrepresented by Sir Thomas, who is more and more bewildered by her refusal. His final admonishing speech is intended to hurt and humiliate. Sir Thomas accuses his niece of ingratitude, self-ishness and wilfulness. The kindly baronet has turned into a stage monster, rather as General Tilney, in *Northanger Abbey*, causes distress to the heroine which is more real to her than that inflicted by any Gothic tyrant she has read about.

The greatest blow to Fanny is her discovery that the uncle that she admires so much is inflexible in refusing to accept her rejection of Henry: 'She had hoped that to a man like her uncle, so discerning, so honoura-ble, so good, the simple acknowledgement of settled *dislike* on her side, would have been sufficient. To her infinite grief she found it was not' (*MP*, p. 318). In *Lovers' Vows*, we find a similar turn of phrase to express Wildenhaim's sense of the limit of parental pressure: 'Yet, if I thought my daughter absolutely disliked him.' For Amelia's father, 'settled dislike' *is* sufficient.

In *Mansfield Park*, the scene is not without comic irony. Sir Thomas's melodramatic accusation that Fanny is acting 'in a wild fit of folly' is utterly inappropriate for her gentle, hesitant repudiation of Henry: 'His attentions were always – what I did not like' (*MP*, p. 319). Similarly, Sir

Thomas's abrupt change of heart in keeping Fanny apart from Crawford is portrayed as a calculating move: 'When he looked at his niece, and saw the state of feature and complexion which her crying had brought her into, he thought there might be as much lost as gained by an immediate interview' (*MP*, p. 320). He still believes that he will win.

The most significant irony of this scene is Sir Thomas's refusal to perceive Fanny's true motives in refusing Crawford. In the scene with Maria, the thought that his daughter might have formed another attachment does not even enter his head. But with Fanny he permits the thought to enter his consciousness: 'Young as you are, and having scarcely seen anyone, it is hardly possible that your affections –' (*MP*, p. 316). At this juncture the close verbal parallels with *Lovers' Vows* resume significance. The Baron confides his fears for his daughter's impending marriage to the man that she is secretly in love with. The secret that Anhalt is the true recipient of Amelia's love is withheld from the unsuspecting father, just as Fanny's love for Edmund is concealed from Sir Thomas. The dramatic irony continues with Baron Wildenhaim's claim – addessed to Anhalt – that, although birth and fortune are important, love and affection must come first:

> Yet if I thought my daughter absolutely disliked him, or that she loved another, I would not thwart a first affection; no, for the world I would not. [*Sighing.*] But that her affections are already bestowed is not probable. (*LV*, act 2, scene 2)

The thought is allowed to flit across Wildenhaim's consciousness before he dismisses it as 'improbable', while the embarrassed chaplain squirms under his gaze. The same happens with Fanny, who, like Anhalt, is in love with her social superior. Sir Thomas momentarily permits the possibility of Fanny's affections being engaged, but, just as readily as he allows himself to be led out of his deep fears for Maria and Rushworth, he dismisses the idea of Fanny having a pre-engaged heart:

> He paused and eyed her fixedly. He saw her lips formed into a *no*, though the sound was inarticulate, but her face was like scarlet. That, however, in so modest a girl might be very compatible with innocence;

and chusing at least to appear satisfied, he quickly added, 'No, no, I know *that* is quite out of the question – quite impossible.' (*MP*, p. 316)

Amelia's lips would never have formed into a 'no' in this way. She is the least devious of the three young women. Her witty attempts to drop hints to her father are, at least, honest. Conversely, Fanny is forced to act a part: she would 'rather die than own the truth' (*MP*, p. 317).

In *Mansfield Park* Austen uses her two interview scenes to explore socially acceptable and unacceptable marriages. But the authorial voice probes critically at both Fanny and Sir Thomas, and Maria and Sir Thomas, in a way that is not possible in drama. On each occasion Sir Thomas chooses 'to appear satisfied' by his 'daughter's' attempts to deceive him. Yet on each occasion his conduct is reprehensible. He has no qualms at all about marrying the two young women to men they cordially loathe, as long as, in the eyes of the world, it looks like an advantageous match.

Sir Thomas and Baron Wildenhaim have different values. Both respect the dual claims of 'birth and fortune' in matrimony, but Sir Thomas is prepared to overlook the claims of love and affection. Austen ironises his propensity for righteous self-justification. Sir Thomas condones Maria's loveless marriage: 'without the prejudice, the blindness of love ... and if she could dispense with seeing her husband a leading, shining character, there would certainly be everything in her favour' (*MP*, p. 201). Conversely, he scorns Fanny for harbouring romantic notions: 'because you do not feel for Mr Crawford exactly what a young, heated fancy imagines to be necessary for happiness, you resolve to refuse him' (*MP*, p. 318).

In his defence, Sir Thomas is only partially aware of the truth. Fanny later comforts herself with this knowledge: 'and when she considered how much of the truth was unknown to him, she believed she had no right to wonder at the line of conduct he pursued' (*MP*, p. 331). But the irony begins again with a suggestion that, even if Sir Thomas had known 'the truth', it would not have made much difference. That he can describe Maria as 'nobly married' is proof enough of his insensibility (*MP*, p. 319). Fanny's harshest condemnation of her beloved uncle confirms this: 'He who had married a daughter to Mr Rushworth. Romantic delicacy was certainly not to be expected of him' (*MP*, p. 331).

Jane Austen reworks the interview scene from *Lovers' Vows* twice over, first with Maria, and then, more profoundly, with Fanny, to show the inadequacies of their relationship with Sir Thomas. She also shows that a woman who cannot admit her love has no choice but to conceal and deceive. Neither woman is in a position to reveal their secret passions, especially to a father-figure so insensitive to their feelings. Amelia and Baron Wildenhaim are revealed in a more favourable light by force of contrast.

As we have seen, the analogies between the play and novel are not solely to do with the casting parallels. The most important are the similarities and differences between Sir Thomas and Baron Wildenhaim in their relationship to their daughters, and the parallels and contrasts between Amelia and the three young women in *Mansfield Park*, Fanny, Mary and Maria. Both fathers urge candour and honesty, but both are patently blind to the fact that there may be a prior attachment. The fathers do not ask, and the daughters do not tell. But where Maria crucially deviates from Amelia is in lying about Rushworth. Maria's dissimulation is thus made clear.

The Baron's objections to the Count are not only his arrant stupidity: 'But when you find a man's head without brains, and his bosom without a heart, these are important articles to supply' (*LV*, act 2, scene 2). The man whose head is without brains is of course fitting for Rushworth, of whom even the tolerant Edmund cannot refrain from speaking ironically: 'If this man had not twelve thousand a year, he would be a very stupid fellow' (*MP*, p. 40). But the man whose 'bosom is without a heart' is, ironically, not the man Maria is engaged to, the Count Cassel figure, but the one who has secretly claimed her heart and who coolly endeavours to make a 'hole in Miss Price's heart': Henry Crawford.

Count Cassel in *Lovers' Vows* thus provides a character type for each of Maria's suitors. Cassel, although a rich fool, is a well-travelled, sophisticated man, 'an epitome of the world' (*LV*, act 2, scene 2). Part of his worldly education includes making and breaking lovers' vows: 'for me to keep my word to a woman would be deceit: 'tis not expected of me. It is in my character to break oaths in love.' Amelia's dislike of the Count is connected to his seduction techniques, which she describes as 'barbarous deeds', and his false promises of love: he has 'Made vows of love to so many women, that, on his marriage with me, a hundred female hearts will at least be broken' (*LV*, act 4, scene 2).

In *Mansfield Park*, Henry Crawford is the worldly, sophisticated seducer of women. When, like Cassel, he finally is conquered by one woman, Fanny Price, hundreds of woman are expected to be broken-hearted: 'Oh! the envyings and heart-burnings of dozens and dozens' (*MP*, p. 360). Mary Crawford entreats Fanny to bask in the conquest she has made over so many women, 'the glory of fixing one who has been shot at by so many'. But Fanny, like Amelia, 'cannot think well of a man who sports with any woman's feelings' (*MP*, p. 363).

Fanny and Amelia have no joy in such 'sportful' behaviour, unlike Mary Crawford and her friends. Amelia is unimpressed that marrying the Count means scoring off hundreds of heart-broken women, and instead she feels compassion for the waiting-girl who has been seduced. Fanny also shows female solidarity in both keeping Maria's secret from Sir Thomas and refusing to think well of a man who sports with any woman's feelings. I have already noted how Fanny is placed in an analogous situation with Amelia, in that both heroines are secretly in love with a clergyman/tutor. But their refusal to equate a good marriage with wealth and status, and their respect for other women, draws them even closer together. The surprising kinship between the superficially very different heroines of novel and play reveals the depth of Austen's engagement with *Lovers' Vows*.

A detailed analysis of the complex relationship between the two works suggests that, although Sir Thomas Bertram condemns the theatricals, Jane Austen does not. The opposite is more true, thanks to the contrast between the two fathers: it is the theatricals that condemn Sir Thomas.

9

Mansfield Park

I now want to set aside the play that is chosen at Mansfield Park and instead consider some other dimensions of the novel's interest in the drama, including the play that is not chosen. By doing so, I hope to demonstrate that, in both the range of its allusiveness and the variety of its quasi-dramatic techniques, *Mansfield Park* is much more deeply involved with the theatre than has hitherto been assumed.

We have already seen how thoroughly Jane Austen was indebted to the theatrical 'set-piece' or scene, how many of the most memorable moments in her works may be perceived in terms of their dramatic impact. Austen's novels are 'dramatic' in the sense that her scenes were often conceived and conducted in stage terms. The prevalence of character-revealing dialogue is the most far-reaching theatrical debt. It should be considered alongside the collecting of characters in appropriate groups, and the contriving of entrances and exits.

The first group activity in *Mansfield Park*, before the play sequence is introduced, is the outing to Sotherton Court, ostensibly for the purpose of advising its owner on the efficacy of landscape improvement. The family visit to Sotherton and the *Lovers' Vows* sequence are firmly linked in Fanny's consciousness as the two social events in which illicit misconduct goes unwarranted and unchecked.[1]

The outing to Sotherton is used primarily to explore the initial stages of the courtship between Mary and Edmund, and Maria and Henry. It also prefigures later important events: Edmund's ordination and Maria's marriage. Furthermore, the flirtations that get under way in the grounds of Sotherton between the two pairs of lovers (Mary and Edmund, Maria and Henry) are further developed in the rehearsals of *Lovers' Vows*.

There are parallels between the improving party and the theatrical party. Both schemes spring from the desire to alleviate boredom in the country, and both events incorporate the use of theatrical language to mask the unlicensed love-play that takes place between the characters. The events at Sotherton are the first steps in seduction, and, in the style of Restoration and eighteenth-century comedy, pairings of lovers are explored as the characters wander, aimlessly, around the grounds of Sotherton Court. The Sotherton episode could be described as a prelude to the mainpiece of *Lovers' Vows*.

It has been suggested that in the Sotherton episode Austen is alluding to Shakespeare's *As You Like It*. There is a pastoral setting and, more specifically, the mock marriage ceremony in the Jacobean family chapel (proposed by the jealous Julia) has shades of the mock marriage performed by Celia to unite Rosalind and Orlando.[2] *Mansfield Park* certainly shares with Shakespearean comedy an interest in role-play and overhearing. Fanny Price is accused by Mrs Norris of excessive 'lookings on': 'these are fine times for you, but you must not be always walking from one room to the other and doing the lookings on, at your ease, in this way' (*MP*, p. 166).[3]

The connection between the pastoral tradition and a kind of unlimited freedom of behaviour does derive from Shakespearean comedy, but the pastoral location is usually the wood or forest, as in the Italian tradition from which the genre derived. The use of the park or garden of a country estate is the Restoration variation of pastoral that was also the model for eighteenth-century comedy. Austen's use of the garden to dramatise freedom of conduct shows an allegiance less directly to Shakespeare than to recent and contemporaneous stage comedy. I believe that the Sotherton episode both alludes to and adapts one of the most popular comedies of the eighteenth-century stage.

From an early age, Jane Austen was familiar with George Colman and David Garrick's highly successful comedy, *The Clandestine Marriage*. She makes an explicit reference to the play in her early novel, *Love and Freindship*.[4] In 1813, she attended a production of the play at Covent Garden, commenting on the new Lord Ogleby, and complaining that the acting was only 'moderate'.[5] Colman and Garrick's comedy is the first of a number of contemporary plays that Austen deploys in *Mansfield Park*.

It has a heroine called Fanny and uses a garden setting to dramatise illicit love-play.

In *The Clandestine Marriage* the various love intrigues of the play are conducted in the extensive grounds of Sterling's country estate.[6] The conventional comic situation of love-play outdoors, assimilated from Restoration comedy, is given an eighteenth-century slant through an emphasis on the trend for landscape improvements. 'The chief pleasure of a country-house is to make improvements', remarks the master of the house, as he shows his guests around the grounds of his huge estate.[7] Sterling's 'improvements' naturally include the needless destruction of trees: 'We were surrounded with trees. I cut down above fifty to make the lawn before the house, and let in the wind and sun – Smack smooth – as you see.' Sterling's fashionably slavish desire for picturesque 'ruins' is mocked: 'It has just cost me a hundred and fifty pounds to put my ruins in thorough repair.'[8]

Austen provides her own parody of the picturesque in the portrayal of the foolish improver, Rushworth. He has already cut down 'two or three fine old trees ... that grew too near the house' and talks of cutting down the avenue at Sotherton, something that Fanny laments, quoting from Cowper's *The Task* in defence of the fate of the elm (*MP*, pp. 55–56).

The numerous puns on 'improvements' in *The Clandestine Marriage* are specifically given a lascivious *double entendre*. Sterling's fake church spire against a tree 'to terminate the prospect' is commented upon by the lecherous Lord Ogleby: 'Very ingenious, indeed! For my part, I desire no finer prospect than this I see before me. [*Leering at the Women*.] Simple, yet varied; bounded, yet extensive.' Ogleby continues to makes puns on this theme: 'We're in the garden of Eden, you know; in all the region of perpetual spring, youth and beauty [*Leering at the Women*].'[9]

The metaphor of the garden of Eden is extended by Ogleby's reference to a 'serpentine path':

STERLING: How d'ye like these close walks, my lord?
LORD OGLEBY: A most excellent serpentine! It forms a perfect maze, and winds like a true lover's knot.[10]

The lover's knot, which becomes increasingly entangled, is the secret love affair between Fanny and Lovewell. A comic love triangle is created when Fanny unburdens herself to Lord Ogleby, who mistakenly believes that he is the recipient of Fanny's secret affections. The 'lover's knot' is further complicated by the unexpected and genuine conversion of the rake, Sir John Melvil, who also falls in love with Fanny. It is out in the garden that Melvil makes the confession that, although engaged in a treaty of marriage with the elder sister, he is now in love with the younger. As in a Restoration comedy, the garden is the scene of seduction and intrigue. The physical landscape of the garden, its winding paths and sheltered walkways, screens the illicit behaviour of the characters.

Jane Austen adapts the theatrical device of love-play outdoors and uses a serpentine path symbolically to suggest her own 'lover's knot'. Edmund walks the path with Fanny and Mary on each arm. As in *The Clandestine Marriage*, a connection between sexual temptation and the Garden of Eden is suggested by the serpentine path. It is no coincidence that Mary first tries to tempt Edmund from his religious vocation on the serpentine path. Illicit misconduct and sexual temptation are suggested in Austen's language from the moment when the young people come to a door leading out to the garden, 'temptingly open on a flight of steps which led immediately to turf and shrubs, and all the sweets of pleasure-grounds, as by one impulse, one wish for air and liberty, all walked out' (*MP*, p. 90).

A second 'lover's knot' is explored in the secret flirtation between Henry Crawford and Maria Bertram, who is betrothed to John Rushworth. It is Mrs Grant who first makes a pun on the word 'improvements' with her insinuating remark that Maria will be Sotherton's finest 'improvement': 'Sotherton will have *every* improvement in time which his heart can desire', and this is spoken to Mrs Norris with 'a smile' (*MP*, p. 53). Henry Crawford picks up the metaphor when he is flirting with Maria before the iron gate: 'I do not think that *I* shall ever see Sotherton again with so much pleasure as I do now. Another summer will hardly improve it to me' (*MP*, p. 98).

Henry Crawford's surreptitious flirtation with Maria is conducted in quasi-theatrical terms. As Mary Crawford is the witty heroine of eighteenth-century comedy, so her brother is the charming rake of sentimental comedy, whose 'reformation' is at stake. Austen's implementation of a brother-sister duo who infiltrate a different society is a striking reversal of a popular eighteenth-century comic convention. Colman the Younger's *The Heir at Law* and Hannah Cowley's *Which is the Man?* rely upon a conventional comic plot device. Both plays introduce a pair of rustics, a brother and sister, whose entrance into London society gives rise to many incongruities and misunderstandings. In these plays, different styles of language and action are attached to different classes and ironically juxtaposed.

In *Mansfield Park* Austen reverses this convention. The brother-sister duo are sophisticated Londoners who leave town to enter the country. If the prosaic conversations of Fanny and Edmund seem dull by comparison, this is precisely the effect that Austen wants to create. As Edmund warns Mary, there is no fear of him saying 'a bon-mot, for there is not the least wit in my nature' (*MP*, p. 94). In contrast, the Crawfords' sparkling dialogue and witty repartee, with just a lacing of French phrases, reflect their cosmopolitan lifestyles: they are the kind of sophisticated Frenchified types parodied in Garrick's satire against fashionable gallantry, *Bon Ton: or High Life Above Stairs*.

In the chapel at Sotherton, Henry plays the part of the charming rake with characteristic aplomb. The striking tableau that is set up in the family chapel foreshadows and supplants the actual marriage ceremony between Maria and Rushworth, which later takes place 'off-stage'. Julia draws the group's attention to the 'performance': 'Do look at Mr Rushworth and Maria, standing side by side, exactly as if the ceremony were going to be performed' (*MP*, p. 88). As readers, we are encouraged to watch the group audience themselves watching the acting out of the future marriage ceremony between Maria and Rushworth that finally takes place unobserved by the reader. The emphasis on the visual tableau is undercut by Henry's whisper to the bride 'in a voice which she only could hear, "I do not like to see Miss Bertram so near the altar"' (*MP*, p. 88).

Maria's complicity is suggested in her acceptance of Henry's challenge and she continues the intimate banter by asking if he would 'give her away'. His response is equally provocative: '"I am afraid I should do it very awkwardly," was his reply with a look of meaning' (*MP*, p. 88).

Henry's flirtatious 'asides' to Maria set the tone for the repartee that is continued in the grounds in front of the iron gate. Austen contrasts the posed and confined indoor scene of the private chapel with the liberating outdoor scene. The indoor scene centres upon the legitimising of love-play by its public acknowledgement in marriage, while the outdoor scene embraces the idea of unlicensed, clandestine love-play. Thus, the cool chapel, where marital love is sanctioned, is contrasted with the flaming heat of the outdoors.[11]

The substantial stretch of direct speech between Maria and Henry, in front of the iron gate with Fanny as audience, is virtually a ready-made dramatic script, complete with directions for the actors (note the interjected instructions such as 'speaking rather lower' and 'smiling'):

[*Henry*] 'I find [Sotherton] better, grander, more complete in its style, though that style may not be the best. And to tell you the truth,' speaking rather lower, 'I do not think that *I* shall ever see Sotherton again with so much pleasure as I do now. Another summer will hardly improve it to me.'

After a moment's embarrassment the lady replied, 'You are too much of a man of the world not to see with the eyes of the world. If other people think Sotherton improved, I have no doubt that you will.'

'I am afraid that I am not quite so much the man of the world as might be good for me in some points. My feelings are not quite so evanescent, nor my memory of the past under such easy dominion as one finds to be the case with men of the world.'

This was followed by a short silence. Miss Bertram began again.

'You seemed to be enjoying your drive here very much this morning. I was glad to see you so well entertained. You and Julia were laughing the whole way.'

'Were we? Yes, I believe we were; but I have not the least recollection at what. Oh! I believe I was relating to her some ridiculous stories of an old Irish groom of my uncle's. Your sister loves to laugh.'

'You think her more light-hearted than I am.'

'More easily amused,' he replied, 'consequently you know,' smiling, 'better company. I could not have hoped to entertain *you* with Irish anecdotes during a ten miles' drive.'

'Naturally, I believe, I am as lively as Julia, but I have more to think of now.'

'You have undoubtedly – and there are situations in which very high spirits would denote insensibility. Your prospects, however, are too fair to justify want of spirits. You have a very smiling scene before you.'

'Do you mean literally or figuratively? Literally, I conclude. Yes, certainly the sun shines and the park looks very cheerful. But, unluckily that iron gate, that ha-ha, give me a feeling of restraint and hardship. I cannot get out, as the starling said.' As she spoke, and it was with expression, she walked to the gate; he followed her. 'Mr Rushworth is so long fetching this key.'

'And for the world you would not get out without the key and without Mr Rushworth's authority and protection, or I think you might with little difficulty pass round the edge of the gate, here, with my assistance; I think it might be done, if you really wished to be more at large, and could allow yourself to think it not prohibited.'

'Prohibited! nonsense! I certainly can get out that way, and I will. Mr Rushworth will be here in a moment you know – we shall not be out of sight.'

'Or if we are, Miss Price will be so good as to tell him, that he will find us near that knoll, the grove of oak on the knoll.'

Fanny, feeling all this to be wrong, could not help making an effort to prevent it. 'You will hurt yourself, Miss Bertram,' she cried, 'you will certainly hurt yourself against those spikes – you will tear your gown – you will be in danger of slipping into the ha-ha. You had better not go.' (*MP*, pp. 98–100)

This dialogue between Henry and Maria, the rake and the flirt, recalls the verbal fencing and lovers' wit-combat of Restoration and eighteenth-century stage comedy. Henry's challenging pun on 'improvement' is met with Maria's cool response: 'If other people think Sotherton improved, I have no doubt that you will.'

Many of Austen's dialogues consist of a rapid exchange of debating points, as in the confrontation between Lady Catherine and Elizabeth in *Pride and Prejudice*, and that between Elinor and Lucy in *Sense and Sensibility*. The set-piece between the clandestine lovers in *Mansfield*

Park is striking, however, for its use of silence to delineate the characters and attitudes of the speakers. Maria's jealousy and chagrin are expressed, finely, in the pause between her remarks regarding her impending marriage and her accusatory comments about Julia and Henry: 'You seemed to be enjoying your drive here very much this morning.'

The provision of 'stage directions' is a device that Austen uses to reinforce and sometimes contradict the spoken word. In Henry's case, the directions 'smiling' and 'speaking rather lower' reveal the hollowness of the verbal facade. The use of *double entendre* enhances the illicit tone of the banter; and, if we are in any doubt of the sub-text, Maria, with surprising clarity, focuses the reader with her question, 'Do you mean literally or figuratively?' With this breakthrough of consciousness, the authorial sympathy shifts to Maria momentarily with her poignant declaration 'I cannot get out, as the starling said'. Austen's allusion to Sterne's imprisoned starling in *A Sentimental Journey*, singing 'I can't get out, I can't get out', is highly significant. Shortly before he hears the bird's 'song for liberty', Yorick is contemplating confinement in the Bastille, which he describes as 'but another word for a house you can't get out of'. Maria Bertram describes Sotherton as 'dismal old prison' (*MP*, p. 53), and her words also resonate with those of another notorious Maria, Wollstonecraft's trapped heroine of *The Wrongs of Woman*, who declares that 'Marriage had bastilled me for life'.[12]

The remaining dialogue forecasts Maria's adultery, and the point of view moves to Fanny, who is suddenly reintroduced into the narrative with the warning cry: 'You will certainly hurt yourself against those spikes – you will tear your gown – you will be in danger of slipping into the ha-ha.'

This unexpected intrusion, with its overt prediction of sexual misconduct ('spikes', torn clothing, descent into ill-fame), has the effect of distancing Maria as it simultaneously draws the narrative focus back to Fanny. Just as Henry and Maria have forgotten about Fanny's presence, so too has the reader. The relative absence of authorial intervention in the long dialogue between Henry and Maria is emphasised by the sudden reappearance of the heroine, and the reader is jolted into remembering that Fanny has witnessed this highly-charged exchange. Only at this point does the authorial perspective return to Fanny's predictable conclusion: 'Fanny was again left to her solitude, and with no increase of pleasant feelings, for she was sorry for almost all that she had seen and heard, astonished at Miss Bertram and angry with Mr Crawford' (*MP*, p. 100).

The scene before the iron gate continues to be conducted in stage terms, not only in the use of dialogue but also in the contriving of exits and entrances. The single setting is retained throughout, with Fanny seated on the bench. The rest is as follows: initially Mary and Edmund exit from the bench as Rushworth, Maria and Henry enter. Rushworth exits for the key. Maria and Henry exit around the locked gate. Julia enters, and exits, around the locked door. Rushworth enters with the key and exits through the gate. Enter Edmund and Mary. Subordinate dialogues take place, leaving Fanny to contemplate the outcome of events from the central position of the bench. Confusingly, Fanny's ubiquitous presence, rather than focusing the ironies of the scene, offers a disarming lack of perspective. Throughout the quasi-farcical entrances and exits of the various characters, her thoughts are shaped, largely, by her jealous concern for Edmund. But though she seems to be little more than a conduit, it is significant that she should witness Henry in action. Her knowledge of his duplicitous conduct prepares her for her rejection of his advances in the third volume of the novel.

One of the most unexpected twists of *Mansfield Park* is the controversial reformation of the rake, Henry Crawford. The reformed rake had been a favourite stage type ever since the reformation of Loveless in the very first sentimental drama, Colley Cibber's *Love's Last Shift* (1696). In an important conversation that takes place shortly after Maria's marriage to Rushworth, Henry is reminded of Fanny's status as a silent witness to his conduct at Sotherton. Mary Crawford's commendation of her brother's behaviour at Sotherton makes her complicit in his misconduct: 'Only think what grand things were produced there by our all going with him one hot day in August to drive about the grounds and see his genius take fire. There we went, and there we came home again; and what was done there is not to be told!' (*MP*, p. 244). But it is Fanny's reaction to this comment that discomposes Henry:

Fanny's eyes were turned on Crawford for a moment with an expression more than grave, even reproachful; but on catching his were instantly withdrawn. With something of consciousness he shook his head at his sister, and laughingly replied, 'I cannot say there was much done at Sotherton; but it was a hot day, and we were all walking after each other and bewildered'. As soon as a general buz gave him shelter, he added, in a low voice directed solely at Fanny, 'I should be sorry to have my powers of *planning* judged of by the day at Sotherton. I see things very differently now. Do not think of me as I appeared then.' (*MP*, pp. 244–45)

For Henry, part of Fanny's charm is her indifference to him. What begins as a game to make 'a small hole in Fanny Price's heart' becomes a challenge when he discovers that she does, in fact, dislike him: 'Her looks say, "I will not like you, I am determined not to like you," and I say, she shall' (*MP*, p. 230). Henry's unexpectedly genuine conversion to love is of no greater surprise to anyone but himself: 'I am fairly caught. You know with what idle designs I began – but this is the end of them' (*MP*, p. 292).

The most influential example of a reformed rake in the novel tradition was Mr B. in Richardson's *Pamela*, who is tamed by the virtue and religious principles of a lowly maidservant.[13] But in the relationship between Fanny Price and Henry Crawford readers would have recognised allusions to *The Clandestine Marriage*, not least because its heroine Fanny Sterling – whose very name anticipates the solid worth and reliable qualities of Austen's heroine – rejects the proposals of a reformed rake. Sir Thomas comes to prize in Fanny 'the *sterling* good of principle' (*MP*, p. 471, my italics). Fanny Sterling is described as possessing 'delicacy' and a 'quick sensibility'. She is gentle and amiable, though is often misunderstood as being 'sly and deceitful': 'She wants nothing but a crook in her hand, and a lamb under her arm, to be a perfect picture of innocence and simplicity.'[14] Subjected to the jealousy of an elder sister, and in possession of a secret that renders her helpless to resist the unwanted attention of her sister's lover, Fanny is a target for ill-treatment – until the unexpected twist in the plot of *The Clandestine Marriage*, the conversion of the rake, Melvil.

I came into this family without any impressions on my mind – with an unimpassioned indifference, ready to receive one woman as soon as another. I looked upon love, serious, sober love as a chimera, and marriage as a thing of course, as you know most people do. But I, who was lately so great an infidel in love, am now one of its sincerest votaries. – In short, my defection from Miss Sterling [Fanny's elder sister] proceeds from the violence of my attachment to another ... who is she! who can she be, but Fanny – the tender, amiable engaging Fanny?[15]

The rake has become conscious of the superior attractions of the demure Fanny: 'was it possible for me to be indulged in a perpetual intercourse with two such objects as Fanny and her sister, and not find my heart led by insensible attraction towards her?'

Fanny's conduct is persistently misunderstood. Her repulsion of Melvil does not appease her sister, nor are her claims for female solidarity understood: 'If I forebore to exert a proper spirit nay, if I did not even express the quickest resentment at your behaviour, it was only in consideration of that respect I wish to pay you, in honour to my sister: and be assured, sir, that woman as I am, that my vanity could reap no pleasure from a triumph that must result from the blackest treachery to her.'[16]

Despite Fanny's protestations and anger at Melvil's persistence, his ardour is only increased by her resistance: 'And yet, opposition, instead of smothering, increases my inclination. I must have her.' Fanny's final declaration that she can never love Melvil likewise falls on stony ground: 'Hear me, sir, hear my final declaration. Were my father and sister, as insensible as you are pleased to represent them; were my heart forever to remain disengaged to any other, I could not listen to your proposals.' Unable and unwilling to return his affections, Fanny is 'packed off' to town to 'send her out of the way'.[17]

Like her predecessor, Fanny Price is in possession of a secret (her attachment to Edmund), and her attempts to conceal this secret cause her conduct to be consistently misunderstood. Fanny's gentle repulses only increase Henry's ardour, for he does not realise that she has a pre-engaged heart. Furthermore, she takes no pleasure in scoring against the opposite sex, or indeed her own sex, telling Mary that she cannot think highly of a man 'who sports with any woman's feelings' (*MP*, p.

363). Fanny Price's rejection of a reformed rake mirrors Fanny Sterling's rejection of Melvil, and, as a final remedy, she in turn is packed off to Portsmouth to be taught the 'value of a good income' (*MP*, p. 369). In *The Clandestine Marriage*, one of the most popular comedies of the period, there is a whole range of techniques that Austen assimilates into the Sotherton episode: the dramatic setting of the garden of a large country estate, the use of a serpentine path, flirtatious banter between quasi-theatrical types such as 'the flirt' and 'the rake', puns and innuendoes specifically linked to the idea of 'improvements', exits and entrances, and a keen sense of audience and looking on.

Furthermore, Austen borrows the name Fanny for her heroine (who has similar sterling qualities as Garrick and Colman's Fanny), and specifically uses the word 'clandestine' to describe Henry Crawford's conduct at Sotherton in a revealing passage that connects Sotherton with *Lovers' Vows*. Fanny firmly links the two episodes together when she too feels herself in danger of being seduced by Crawford: 'Mr Crawford was no longer the Mr Crawford who, as the clandestine, insidious, treacherous admirer of Maria Bertram, had been her abhorrence ... She might have disdained him in all the dignity of angry virtue, in the grounds of Sotherton, or the theatre at Mansfield Park; but he approached her now with rights that demanded different treatment' (*MP*, pp. 327–28).

The seed for Jane Austen's idea for the inclusion of private theatricals in a novel can be found in a short sketch written in about 1792. In 'The Three Sisters', the greedy, pleasure-seeking Mary Stanhope demands a private theatre as part of her marriage settlement: 'You must do nothing but give Balls & Masquerades. You must build a room on purpose & a Theatre to act Plays in. The first Play we have shall be *Which is the Man?*, and I will do Lady Bell Bloomer' (*MW*, p. 65).

Towards the end of *Love and Freindship*, Austen depicts the problems facing a small company of strolling actors in a manner that surely recalls her own family's difficulties in finding suitable plays for their amateur dramatics:

our Company was indeed rather small, as it consisted only of the Manager his wife & ourselves, but there were fewer to pay and the only inconvenience attending it was the Scarcity of Plays which for want of People to fill the Characters, we could perform –. We did not mind trifles however –. One of our most admired Performances was *Macbeth*, in which we were truly great. The Manager always played *Banquo* himself, his wife my *Lady Macbeth*. I did the *Three Witches* & Philander acted *all the rest*. (*MW*, p. 107–8)

The absurdity of Philander playing the parts of characters who appear on the stage at the same time, such as Macbeth and Macduff, and Gustavus playing all three witches, will especially amuse anyone who has had to work within the limitations of a small theatre company. The Austens sometimes solved their casting problems by inviting neighbouring families to take part in their performances. It is, of course, in order to avoid just such a measure that Edmund Bertram reluctantly agrees to join the theatrical ensemble in *Mansfield Park*.

The interest that was sparked by the Steventon theatricals and flickered through Jane Austen's juvenilia was rekindled in the writing of *Mansfield Park*. Significantly though, she focuses that interest on the pre-production, rehearsals and aftermath of *Lovers' Vows*, rather than the actual performance of the play, which is so memorably pre-empted by Sir Thomas's return. Her satirical treatment of the 'inconveniences' attached to 'scarcity of plays' in *Love and Freindship* is reworked in the Mansfield theatricals, where, ironically, the search for a suitable play is dramatised more fully than the play itself:

'Oh! no, *that* will never do. Let us have no ranting tragedies. Too many characters – Not a tolerable woman's part in the play – Anything but *that*, my dear Tom. It would be impossible to fill it up – One could not expect any body to take such a part – Nothing but buffoonery from beginning to end. *That* might do, perhaps, but for the low parts – If I *must* give my opinion, I have always thought it the most insipid play in the English language – *I* do not wish to make objections, I shall be happy to be of any use, but I think we could not choose worse.' (*MP*, p. 131)

Clearly Austen was no stranger to the exigencies of choosing a suitable play for home representation, and she delights in the sheer egomania of the would-be actors, who find it so hard to make a decision, chiefly because they all want the 'best characters'. Fanny Price, like her author, is 'not unamused' by this picture of 'disguised' selfishness. Fanny seems only too happy to observe the theatrical events: 'For her own gratification she could have wished that something might be acted, for she had never seen half a play, but everything of higher consequence was against it' (*MP*, p. 131).

Fanny forewarns Edmund that the group's theatrical preferences are markedly dissimilar: 'Your brother's taste, and your sisters', seem very different.' Edmund and Fanny even cherish hopes that the theatrical project will never get off the ground because there are too many people to be pleased. Austen ominously details the practical arrangements which begin to escalate in scale and expense – the carpenter has taken measurements and is already at work erecting a stage, the housemaids are making up the curtain – even before a choice of play has been fixed upon. The 'great irreconcileable difference' is over comedy or tragedy, and choosing a suitable play becomes an all-consuming task.

Shakespeare's tragedies, *Hamlet*, *Macbeth*, *Othello*, together with Moore's *The Gamester* and Home's *Douglas* (probably the two most popular 'sentimental' tragedies of the eighteenth century), are rejected as unsuitable. *The Rivals*, *The School for Scandal*, *The Wheel of Fortune* and *The Heir at Law* are eschewed by the tragedians 'with yet warmer objections' (*MP*, p. 131). While the majority view holds out for tragedy, Tom Bertram's preference is clearly for comedy; and, although he is tacitly seconded by Mary Crawford, 'his determinateness and his power, seemed to make allies unnecessary' (*MP*, p. 130). Tom insists upon a comedy, or at least a comic part for himself: 'I take any part you choose to give me, so as it be comic. Let it but be comic, I condition for nothing more' (*MP*, p. 131). Tom is 'exactly adapted to the novelty of acting' by dint of his 'lively talents' and 'comic taste'.

Tom Bertram is the character who is most deeply 'infected' by the vogue for amateur theatricals. Few have noticed how central he is to the theatricals.[18] Of all the characters, he appears to be the one with the most detailed and enthusiastic knowledge of the drama. Initially he doesn't want a sentimental play like *Lovers' Vows* – he wants to put on a comedy.

Tom's suggested plays, all well-established comedies of the London stage, represent a cross-section of some of the best works of a number of successful eighteenth-century playwrights, Sheridan, George Colman the Younger and Richard Cumberland. *The Rivals* and *The School for Scandal* were obvious choices for Austen, as both of these plays had been performed by her own family. Cumberland's sentimental comedy, *The Wheel of Fortune*, as the title suggests, presents a profligate, Woodville, who has squandered his fortune at the gaming table, enabling his arch enemy, Penruddock – a role made famous by John Philip Kemble – to exact revenge on him. It hardly hardly needs to be emphasised that Tom Bertram has already squandered part of his father's fortune on gambling losses, and cost Edmund his clerical living at Mansfield. *The Wheel of Fortune* dramatises a failed relationship between father and son. While the son has been off fighting for his country, his father has lost his home and wife through his addiction to gambling.

But it is *The Heir at Law* that Tom earnestly proposes five times. There are two parts that Tom considers for himself; one is the famed comic role of the great opportunist Dr Pangloss, the other is Lord Duberley – the comically displaced heir-at-law.[19] Tom's choice of play and role provide a significant insight into his character, which is wholly lost on a reader today.

George Colman the Younger, playwright and manager of the Haymarket Theatre, produced *The Heir at Law* on 15 July 1797.[20] The play enjoyed over a hundred years of success before disappearing from the boards; a performance was even noted as late as 1906.[21] Colman's play is another striking example of the era's devotion to comedies depicting social transformations. The device of bringing together contrasting 'types' allowed Colman to exploit fully the comic potential of the juxta-positions of 'high' and 'low' life in Georgian England, and to please the upper galleries as well as the pit.

The eponymous heir-at-law, Lord Duberley formerly Daniel Dowlas, is a common tradesman who in the absence of a natural heir has inher-ited a title and an estate belonging to a distant cousin. Uncomfortable with his role of nobleman, he secretly employs the services of Dr Pangloss for the purpose of 'fashioning his discourse' so that he can assume his 'rightful' place in genteel society. Meanwhile, the true heir, Henry Moreland, supposedly lost at sea, returns to England, only to find a common merchant in his father's place. The play is full of lively, displaced characters, uncomfortable with the roles that either society or fortune has apportioned them.

Colman's play shows that 'the fickle world is full of changes'. The plot revolves around inequalities of birth, where 'chance may remove one man so far from another, in the rank of life', and social mobility, where one's fortune can be made by improving a vulgar family's 'cacology', by becoming a rich man's mistress or by winning the lottery.[22] Colman's socially displaced characters are made miserable by their shifting roles and positions in society. At the play's denouement they are all restored to their original status, with the exception of the rustic, Zekiel Homespun, who confounds all social classifications by his win on the lottery. Daniel Dowlas is only too relieved to relinquish his burdensome rights and responsibilities to the real heir, Moreland, whose return from the 'watery grave' restores the authentic peer to his estate.

Plays depicting incongruous social reversals, such as *The Heir at Law* and Townley's *High Life Below Stairs*, were the particular favourites of the amateur theatricals of the public schools, military academies and spouting clubs. These exclusively male dilettante theatricals favoured comedies where social roles were turned topsy-turvy. Part of the attraction was the opportunity for enacting scenarios of social transformation. Navy theatricals, for instance, enabled officers to indulge themselves in coveted 'low-life' roles.[23] By the same account, Tom Bertram's interest in *The Heir at Law* and his desire to perform the role of Lord Duberley encourage us to reconsider his position of heir to the Mansfield Park estate.

His choice of the role of Lord Duberley is especially revealing, for the character is a fake aristocrat, a pretender. Thus the heir to the Mansfield estate wishes to play the part of the vulgar tradesman playing the part of the aristocratic lord. The desire to play the inauthentic peer instated by a 'freak of fortune' suggests Tom's uneasiness with the role of elder son – a role that he persistently rejects. Lord Duberley's character, decent and genial, but totally unfit for high office, accords well with Tom's cavalier attitude towards the responsibilities of his position and his light regard towards his duties as a future landowner. Mary Crawford quickly realises that the quickest way to Tom's heart is through horse-racing and gambling – his real love – and just as quickly perceives that his first priorities are to himself:

> his lengthened absence from Mansfield, without any thing but pleasure in view, and his own will to consult, made it perfectly clear that he did not care about her; and his indifference was so much more than equalled by her own, that were he now to step forth the owner of Mansfield park, the Sir Thomas complete, which he was to be in time, she did not believe that she could accept him. (*MP*, p. 114)

Mary's piqued reflections highlight the dangers which face the baronet in Antigua; at any moment Tom may be requested to 'step forth' into his father's shoes. The fear for Sir Thomas's safety is constantly emphasised, disproportionately by Mrs Norris who longs to be the bearer of the news of his untimely decease. One of Edmund's many reasons for opposing the theatricals is fear for his father's safety: 'It would show great want of feeling on my father's account, absent as he is, and in some degree of constant danger' (*MP*, p. 125). Although the danger is not specified, the threat is from not only the 'unfavourable circumstances' in Antigua, but more significantly the dangers of the voyage home. In the event of a disaster at sea, Sir Thomas's death would place Tom in the same position as Lord Duberley, who is heir at law by dint of the shipwrecked and supposedly drowned Henry Moreland.

Austen makes it clear that Tom is *in loco parentis* in the absence of his father: 'the inclination to act was awakened, and in no one more strongly than in him who was now master of the house' (*MP*, p. 123). Tom's wish to escape the role of 'the Sir Thomas complete' is undoubtedly reflected in his desire to play the part of Lord Duberley, the comically unsatisfactory heir to the estate. If he had had his way with the Colman play, his best scene as Lord Duberley, one of mistaken identity and misapprehension, would have suggested a particularly significant reading of his relationship to his father and the estate. In this scene, Stedfast, Moreland's friend, confuses Dowlas with the original Lord Duberley. The comic appeal is dependent upon the fragile equation of virtue with rank, which in this instance is shown to be falsifying:

> Ignorance may palliate meanness and buffoonery, and merely meet contempt, but want of feeling excites indignation. You have shocked me, and I leave you. From exalted rank like yours, my lord, men look for exalted virtue; and when these are coupled, they command respect, and grace each other: – but the coronet, which gives and receives splendour, when fixed on the brow of merit, glitters on the worthless head, like a mark of disgrace, to render vice, folly and inhumanity conspicuous.[24]

The joke is compounded by Stedfast's surprise at finding so little physiognomical evidence of the dignity and nobility that he has been encouraged to take for granted in a peer of the realm. Stedfast's high expectations stem from an earlier scene where the reputation of Lord Duberley has been warmly expounded by his son, who excuses his father's social reserve as a mark of his dignity:

> but I confess to those who are unacquainted with them, these qualities are concealed by a coldness in his manner ... a long habit too of haranguing in Parliament, gives a man a kind of dignity of deportment, and an elevation of style not to be met with every day you know. But Gentleman is written legibly upon his brow; erudition shines thro' every polished period of his language; and he is the best of men, and of fathers, believe me.[25]

In Colman's play appearances are deceptive. Dowlas neither looks nor speaks like a nobleman, and, although his good nature is undeniable, he is scorned for his natural vulgarity and 'lowness'. Conversely, Moreland's description of his father's noble physiognomy reminds us of another lofty baronet whose countenance is repeatedly described as being marked with solemn dignity, whose coldness is felt by his children, and whose conduct is not always presented as virtuous or gentlemanly: Sir Thomas Bertram. One of the most shocking moments for Fanny is when she realises that her uncle's motives and conduct towards her are far from disinterested and noble. To her own 'infinite grief', she discovers that she has been deceived by the baronet's outward appearance.

When Sir Thomas inadvertently makes his debut on the stage of his son's theatre, we are surely invited to consider the difference between the old Sir Thomas and the future 'Sir Thomas complete'. Tom Bertram is as uncomfortable with his future role as 'plain Daniel Dowlas of Gosport' is at playing the part of Lord Duberley. In Colman's comedy all comes right in the return of the true heir who restores everyone to their rightful social positions; the fake lord is ejected, and the social order is maintained. Of course, in the conventions of comic theatre, appearances that seem deceptive are revealed in their true light. It is only Daniel Dowlas who is surprised by the discovery that he has been merely *locum tenens* in the absence of Henry Moreland: a 'peer's warming pan'.[26]

In the more complex world of *Mansfield Park*, the social order is not so easily restored. Nor are appearances always a reliable guide to conduct, as Fanny discovers. Tom Bertram appears to be little more than a 'warming pan', as his self-inflicted illness almost threatens to grant Mary Crawford her desire to see the younger brother become 'Sir Edmund' Bertram. But the heir by birth, who is the fake heir by nature, finally does inherit Mansfield, and the heroine, the spiritual heir to the 'great' house, is displaced to the vicarage.

It is unsurprising that the other role to appeal to Tom's theatrical inclinations is that of Dr Pangloss. If he is not to play the part of Lord Duberley, he covets the great comic role of Colman's doctor-on-the-make. When he is denied his preferred choice of play by the opposition of the rest of the cast, he happily assents to *Lovers' Vows*, rejects the paternal role of Baron Wildenhaim and is content to appropriate a suitably humbler part to himself – the comic, rhyming Butler.[27] Even though he has not got his way over *The Heir at Law*, Tom is still able to make his descent down the social scale: the *de facto* master of the house adopts the stage role of a servant.

In the real life amateur theatricals of the period, Lord Barrymore played the roles of rustics and servants in his Wargrave playhouse. This kind of theatrical slumming was a striking reversal of the convention of the public theatre where a low-born actor could successfully portray the role of a gentleman. As we have seen, the actor William 'Gentleman'

Lewis was famous for his rendering of 'high society' roles. At Wargrave, the low-born professional actress Elizabeth Edwin often played the parts of aristocratic ladies to Lord Barrymore's rustics.[28]

When Elizabeth Farren, formerly a child actor in a company of strolling players in the provinces, became famous for her depiction of elegant and well-bred ladies at Drury Lane and Covent Garden, she was courted by the Earl of Derby.[29] Farren's meteoric rise from obscurity to the highest stratum of society, from 'a Barn to a Court', was complete when she became a countess and was presented at Court. She had become the very character that had sustained her in her numerous stage roles. Having grown to be highly respected – her behaviour won the approval of Queen Charlotte – she insisted that her former life should never be mentioned.

Austen's interest in social mobility is inextricably bound up with her knowledge of eighteenth-century theatre, both public and private, where reversals of rank and station were commonplace. Lord Barrymore's well-publicised theatricals were made even more notorious by the presence and 'princely patronage' of the Prince of Wales.[30] The Prince's connections with low-born actresses, most famously Mary 'Perdita' Robinson, no doubt added to the controversy. Austen's juvenilia shows her poking fun at the Prince's notorious relationships with low-born women.[31]

The first part of this book has demonstrated that Austen particularly relished cross-over farces such as *The Devil to Pay* and *High Life Below Stairs*, where reversals of rank and station were employed to reflect upon social conduct, and where low life was used to criticise high life. In *Mansfield Park*, her preoccupation with the blurring of the boundaries between the ranks is suggested from the opening pages where Sir Thomas and Mrs Norris are keen that Fanny should know her place and not be considered '*a Miss Bertram*' (*MP*, p. 10). Sir Thomas is keen to emphasise that the cousins are not 'equals': 'Their rank, fortune, rights, and expectations, will always be different' (*MP*, p. 11). However, by the end of the novel, he is compelled to reassess his thinking about the differences between the 'low' Price children and his own highly-bred children. Sir Thomas duly acknowledges, 'In [Susan's] usefulness, in Fanny's excellence, in William's continued good conduct, and rising fame, and in the general well-doing and success of the other members of the family, all assisting to advance each other ... the advantages of early hardship and discipline, and the consciousness of being born to struggle and endure' (*MP*, p. 473).

Jane Austen's unashamed delight in Elizabeth and Jane Bennet's social mobility in *Pride and Prejudice* is somewhat tempered in her depiction of the ascent of Fanny and Susan Price, where endurance and hard work are emphasised. With William Price – and Captain Wentworth in *Persuasion* – Austen uses the naval profession to emphasise the claims of innate merit and talent over social position and inherited wealth. In eighteenth-century comedies, such as *The Heir at Law* and *She Stoops to Conquer*, the stock character of the profligate son and heir to the estate who refuses to commit to his appropriate social role is used to reflect favourably upon lesser-ranking characters.

Tom's preoccupation with *The Heir at Law* suggests, even more forcibly, that Jane Austen was well attuned to the nuances of eighteenth-century social class and identity, as explored in the drama. Tom's uneasiness with his identity as heir to Mansfield Park is connected to his sense of the quasi-theatrical artifice of social behaviour. His amusing account of his social blunder over the mysteries of female protocol, of the Miss Anderson who was 'not out', and the Miss Sneyd who was 'out' (*MP*, p. 50), is in the style of eighteenth-century's comedy's playful confusion of rank and manners – to which, we must assume, he has been attuned by his theatre-going.

Miss Anderson's ambiguous social conduct is a source of embarrassment to Tom. Her behaviour when she is 'not out' is not so much excessive modesty as downright rudeness: 'I could hardly get a word or a look from the young lady – nothing like a civil answer – she screwed up her mouth, and turned from me with such an air!' (*MP*, p. 50). But when he meets her again when she is 'out', she displays a pushy, flirtatious manner in public: 'She came up to me, claimed me as an acquaintance, stared me out of countenance, and talked and laughed till I did not know which way to look. I felt that I must be the jest of the room at the time – and Miss Crawford, it is plain, has heard the story' (*MP*, p. 50). His sense of the absurd is tickled by the artificiality of the girl's social conduct, which verges from one extreme to another.

Likewise, Tom's 'dreadful scrape' at Ramsgate with the younger Miss Sneyd who is 'not out' is caused by misleading female dress codes that fail to denote behaviour. Mary Crawford's distinction between the protocol of the 'out' and the 'not out' girl is 'a close bonnet' (*MP*, p. 49), but Tom's blunder is occasioned by Miss Sneyd's failure to appear in an appropriately coded costume: 'The close bonnet and demure air ... tell one what is expected; but I got into a dreadful scrape last year from the want of them' (*MP*, p. 51).

In Goldsmith's *She Stoops to Conquer* (1771), a comedy premised on the ambiguities of social class and the discrepancies between rank and manners, the plot is based upon a similar social blunder by a young gentleman. Marlow mistakes a gentleman for an innkeeper partly because 'manners and appearance' are 'so totally different' (*MP*, p. 49). Furthermore, Kate Hardcastle's disguise as a barmaid is a voluntary undertaking of the reversal of the class roles in order to 'conquer' the socially awkward Marlow, who is reduced to inarticulacy by genteel women.[32] But it is Kate's father's insistence on her wearing a plain dress which first confuses Marlow, and the success of her plot is dependent upon the bonnet she wears in their first meeting which enables her to carry out her disguise.

Tom Bertram's impatience with the mores of civilised society is shown by his languid observations on dancing (an important and necessary part of the social environment), and his focusing of the scene into a fantasy of sexual intrigue:

> 'I only wonder how the good people can keep it up so long. – They had need be *all* in love, to find any amusement in such folly – and so they are, I fancy. If you look at them, you may see they are so many couple of lovers – all but Yates and Mrs Grant – and, between ourselves, she, poor woman! must want a lover as much as any one of them. A desperate dull life her's must be with the doctor.' (*MP*, pp. 118–19)

His observation on the Grants' ill-suited marriage comes straight out of stage comedy. Dr Grant's pretty wife is 'fifteen years his junior' and suffers at the hands of her gourmandising husband. Their type of union, the sexually deficient older man who risks being cuckolded by his beautiful young wife, had been a staple of comedy ever since its origins in ancient Greece. Eighteenth-century comedy is full of plot lines where young wives, like Sheridan's Lady Teazle, are tempted by rakes, repent of their flightiness, and are reconciled to their old spouses. Tom's speculation about Mrs Grant's sexually unfulfilled marriage suggests Yates as a candidate for the lover she needs to assuage her 'desperate dull life'.

Tom's aside reveals a comic propensity for viewing life through the spectacles of theatre, a propensity which should not be underestimated in a novel which uses theatricality and role-playing to comment upon social behaviour. It is in yet another of his seemingly careless asides that he first draws an explicit parallel between real life and theatricality. Yates's endless preoccupation with the termination of the private theatricals at Ecclesford, due to the death of a dowager grandmother, provokes another theatrical joke from Tom: 'An after-piece instead of a comedy … Lovers' Vows were at an end, and Lord and Lady Ravenshaw left to act My Grandmother by themselves' (*MP*, pp. 122–23).

Ostensibly, Tom's comment reveals how he has such a vast repertoire of eighteenth-century plays in his head that he can produce a theatrical witticism for any occasion. *My Grandmother*, a popular farce by Prince Hoare, was indeed performed as an 'afterpiece' to the main play, as were most eighteenth-century farces.[33] After the death of the dowager and the departure of the young people, Lord and Lady Ravenshaw are left to perform that ultimate after-piece, a funeral. But Tom's remark shows a more complex investment in theatricality than merely a knowledge of contemporary plays.

His pun is dependent upon us perceiving a literal interpretation of the plays' titles to convey the 'real' situation (the death of a grandmother, or love-play between young people), and it also confirms a literal understanding of the nature of the relationship between title and plot. This makes it startlingly clear that 'Lovers' Vows' is to be regarded as *double entendre* for young lovers engaging in love-play, making and breaking promises.[34] Tom is thus the first character to make the fertile connection between real life and theatricality, which is then further explored not only by the way in which the stage-lovers act out their real feelings by way of *Lovers' Vows*, but also by the broader correspondence between social conduct and artful play.

* * *

Once Edmund Bertram has finally been persuaded to participate in the theatricals, he soon begins to confuse 'his theatrical and his real part' (*MP*, p. 163). Although he initially expresses doubt about his closeness to the role of Anhalt – 'the man who chooses the profession itself, is, perhaps, one of the last who would wish to represent it on the stage' (*MP*, p. 145) – he is unable to resist the allure of Mary's bold request, 'What gentleman among you am I to have the pleasure of making love to?' (*MP*, p. 143). In 'making love' to Mary in their rehearsal scene, Edmund finds himself expressing his own real feelings as well as those of his character.

So too with Henry and Maria as Frederick and Agatha: acting gives the lovers freedom to express their real feelings. Fanny notes that 'Maria ... acted well – too well' (*MP*, p. 165). And Mary Crawford quips that 'those indefatigable rehearsers, Agatha and Frederick' should excel at their parts, for they are so often embracing: 'If *they* are not perfect, I *shall* be surprised' (*MP*, p. 169). Mary's reference to Henry and Maria by their stage names is a reminder of their emotional identification with the roles of Agatha and Frederick.

The stage directions of the first act of *Lovers' Vows* reveal the 'dangerous intimacy' of Tom's theatre (*MP*, p. 462): '[*Rising and Embracing him*]', '[*Leans her head against his breast*]', '[*He embraces her*]', '[*Agatha presses him to her breast*]', '[*Frederick with his eyes cast down, takes her hand, and puts it to his heart*].' This final direction is at the point where Henry and Maria are later interrupted by Sir Thomas's arrival. This shows how closely Austen followed Mrs Inchbald's stage directions. Ironically, Agatha's words preceding this direction are, 'His flattery made me vain, and his repeated vows –' (*LV*, act 1, scene 1). Henry's act of retaining Maria's hand after Julia's melodramatic announcement of Sir Thomas's arrival gives Maria the false impression that the gesture denotes an implicit lover's vow, and she fully expects that this will be followed by a formal declaration for her hand.[35] After days of anxious waiting, 'the agony of her mind was severe' when she discovers that no declaration is to be made: 'The hand which had so pressed her's to his heart! – The hand and the heart were alike motionless and passive now!' (*MP*, p. 193).

As well as watching Henry and Maria engaging in love-play, Fanny is compelled to be the 'judge and critic' of the rehearsal between Mary and

Edmund. She reflects afterwards on the unhappy experience: 'she was inclined to believe their performance would, indeed, have such nature and feeling in it, as must ensure their credit, and make it a very suffering exhibition to herself' (*MP*, p. 170). Fanny's observation is, of course, heavily ironic: she is referring, not to the acting abilities of Edmund and Mary, but to the display of their real feelings. The combination of the words 'nature and feeling' in the context of acting would, however, have had deep resonance for Austen's early readers, especially since at the time of the novel's publication Edmund Kean had recently made his electrifying debut on the London stage. Kean's 'natural' style fuelled a long-standing debate, going back to Charles Macklin and David Garrick, about traditional styles of acting in tragedy versus the new naturalism.

The declamatory, rhetorical approach, with its 'rants' and 'starts', represented by the Cibber school of acting was slowly reformed by a shift in emphasis from exaggeration to 'naturalism', from tradition to originality.[36] The formal, rhetorical tradition represented by James Quin was challenged by Macklin and Garrick, whose new 'naturalist' approach accepted the actor's right to freedom of interpretation. The birth of the new naturalist approach is memorialised in the story of Garrick's appearance at Goodman's Fields in *Richard III* and Quin's shocked exclamation, 'That if the young fellow was right, he, and the rest of the players, had been all wrong'.[37] Richard Cumberland, who saw Garrick and Quin acting the principal male leads in *The Fair Penitent*, was astonished by Garrick's performance: 'it seemed as if a whole century had been stepped over in the transition of a single scene'.[38] Even before Garrick, however, Macklin had challenged the rhetorical and formal tradition to acting. For example, his unconventional approach to Hamlet's first meeting with the ghost was played with an understated simplicity and respect rather than the expected exaggerated and bombastic 'starts' and 'rants'.[39]

The 'rant', which was the conventional mode of delivery for tragedy, became 'the most unvarying subject of attack by theatrical critics'.[40] Both Arthur Murphy and Thomas Davies in their biographies of Garrick describe him as having banished 'ranting'.[41] Jane Austen shows her own awareness of the practice of ranting in *Mansfield Park* when she depicts her dilettante actor John Yates as one who 'rants' and 'starts' in the style of the old school: 'Mr Yates was in general thought to rant dreadfully' (*MP*, p. 164). At Ecclesford, Yates had 'grudged every rant of Lord Ravenshaw's and been forced to re-rant it all in his own room' (*MP*, p. 132).

On the other hand, Henry Crawford is regarded by the theatrical party as an accomplished actor: 'he had more confidence than Edmund, more judgment than Tom, more talent and taste than Mr Yates' (*MP*, p. 165). It is little surprise that the only character, apart from Rushworth, to dislike Henry's acting style is Yates, who exclaims against 'his tameness and insipidity' (*MP*, p. 165). The histrionic, ranting Yates would, of course, find Henry's naturalism too tame. Fanny, on the other hand, finds Henry's style 'truly dramatic': 'His acting had first taught Fanny what pleasure a play might give' (*MP*, p. 337).

In Austen's era, actors such as Cooke and Siddons followed Garrick in their belief that it was not enough to copy nature. They believed that good acting also required emotional identification with the part. Leigh Hunt observes that Siddons 'has the air of never being the actress; she seems unconscious that there is a motley crowd called a pit waiting to applaud her, or that there are a dozen fiddlers waiting for her exit'.[42] But not every actor worked on the principle of emotional identification. Samuel Johnson enquired of Siddons's brother Kemble, 'Are you, sir, one of those enthusiasts who believe yourself transformed into the very character you represent?' Boswell records, 'Upon Mr Kemble's answering that he never felt so strong a persuasion himself; "to be sure not, Sir (said Johnson) the thing is impossible. And if Garrick really believed himself to be that monster, Richard III, he deserved to be hanged every time he performed it."'[43]

In *Tom Jones*, Henry Fielding's comic depiction of the debate is mediated through the less sophisticated viewpoint of Partridge. Tom Jones is eager for a criticism of Garrick 'unadulterated by art' and informed by 'the simple dictates of nature'. He therefore appeals to the foolish schoolmaster, only to discover to his amusement that Partridge dislikes Garrick's Hamlet because it is too true to life: 'why I could act as well as he myself. I am sure if I had seen a ghost, I should have looked in the very same manner, and done just what he did.'[44] Partridge prefers the exaggerated histrionic acting of the old-school player of Claudius because he 'speaks all his words distinctly, half as loud again as the other. – Any body may see he is an actor.'[45]

Fielding's fictionalising of Garrick's naturalistic performance seen through the eyes of the naive Partridge is a reminder of the way in which the actor's art became the subject of analysis and discussion in the Georgian era.[46] In *Mansfield Park*, Austen uses private theatricals rather than the public theatre to explore her own interest in the debate. Her allusions to the 'nature and feeling' of her four principals, and her comparison of the ranting Yates with the naturalism of Henry Crawford, would not have been lost on her first readers, especially as the novel was published soon after the debut of Edmund Kean, who was regarded as the first actor for a generation to raise stage feeling to the heights of Garrick.[47]

Although Kean made his debut shortly after Jane Austen finished *Mansfield Park*, it is nevertheless intriguing that she writes about him in the context of her novel. In the midst of her enthusiasm about her new novel, her train of thought slides from Henry Austen's reading of it to Henry Crawford to Kean:

> Henry has this moment said that he likes my M. P. better & better; – he is in the 3*d*. vol. – I beleive [*sic*] *now* he has changed his mind as to foreseeing the end; – he said yesterday at least, that he defied anybody to say whether H. C. would be reformed, or would forget Fanny in a fortnight. – I shall like to see Kean again excessively, & to see him with You too; – it appeared to me that there was no fault in him anywhere. (*Letters*, p. 258)

Critics have perceived a source for Henry Crawford in the theatre-loving, soldier-turned-banker-turned-clergyman Henry Austen. But what is striking about this letter is the enthusiasm for Kean and the theatre in the context of 'H. C.' It is highly appropriate that Henry Crawford wishes to 'undertake any character that ever was written, from Shylock or Richard III' (*MP*, p. 123), for those were the two parts with which Kean made his name.

Having just completed the novel that dealt most extensively with her interest in the relationship between art and life, Austen was disposed to be pleased with the style of acting heralded by Kean. Unlike Dr Johnson, she did not express any moral concern for the actor's emotional and intellectual identification with the role, but saw, on the contrary, that it created 'exquisite acting'. Even the sincere and demure Fanny takes pleasure in acting: she masters not only Rushworth's part, but every other role in the play in her unofficial capacity as prompter. So it is that she is eventually persuaded to play the role of Cottager's Wife.

Far from proposing that acting encourages a kind of insincere role-playing in life, Austen suggests in her depiction of polite society that an ability to perform socially is often a necessity.[48] Buoyed by her interest in the arts of the theatre, she explores how social mores require characters to adopt particular roles. In *Sense and Sensibility*, Mrs Dashwood anxiously demands if Willoughby has 'been acting a part' throughout his courtship of Marianne. In the morally ambiguous world of *Mansfield Park*, Austen consistently puns on the words 'act' and 'acting' to blur the distinctions between role-playing and social conduct. So, for instance, when Henry Crawford informs Fanny of his reformation from the role of absentee landlord to that of responsible master, Austen alerts us to the possibility of doubt: 'This was aimed, and well aimed, at Fanny. It was pleasing to hear him speak so properly; here, he had been acting as he ought to do' (*MP*, p. 404).

In contrast to the Crawfords, who have mastered the art of social role-playing, Tom Bertram is rendered uneasy by the rules of civilised society, for, as he has discovered with Miss Sneyd and Miss Anderson, they often breed deception and confusion. More than any other character in the novel, Tom is alert to the discrepancy between manners and appearance, and the theatricality of social conduct, and thus it is through his eyes that we witness the grand climax of the *Lovers' Vows* sequence: Sir Thomas Bertram's stage debut.

Austen distinguishes the fashionably elite theatricals of the aristocracy from those of the squirearchy in her portrayal of Tom's aristocratic 'friend', the Honourable Mr Yates, who brings the 'itch' for acting from the Ecclesford theatricals. The name Yates had a venerable theatrical pedigree. Richard Yates (1706–96) was the popular comedian who was the first Oliver Surface in Drury Lane's *The School for Scandal*. He was part of a famous acting couple, with his wife Mary Anne Yates (1728–87), one of Garrick's leading ladies, a famous tragedian often compared to Siddons.[49]

Mrs Yates was also often compared with another leading actress of the eighteenth-century stage, the tragedienne Mrs Ann Crawford (1734–1801).[50] Crawford was known as the 'lover of the stage'.[51] She was also part of a famous acting couple with the notoriously 'handsome, volatile, and noisy' Thomas (Billy) Crawford (1750–94).[52] Campbell wrote in his biography of Sarah Siddons: 'Next to Mrs Pritchard in point of time, our two greatest actresses were Mrs Yates and Mrs Crawford. They were contemporaries and great rivals; the former bearing the palm for dignity and sculpturesque beauty, while the latter, though less pleasing in looks, had more passion and versatility.'[53] The names Yates and Crawford were thus linked in the theatre world, not only because they were famous tragediennes in their own right, but because they were both married to famous actors.

Austen's use of the names Yates and Crawford in the context of her private theatre may well have been noted with amusement by readers familiar with the famous eighteenth-century theatrical dynasties. The romantic pairings of the real-life Yateses and Crawfords add an extra dimension to *Mansfield Park*. Ironically, the two characters who are excluded from the theatrical party, Fanny Price and Julia Bertram, come closer to the Georgian theatrical world when they (potentially, in Fanny's case) become Mrs Crawford and Mrs Yates.

The events at Ecclesford are curiously proleptic of the events at Mansfield Park. *Lovers' Vows* is provokingly interrupted on both occasions. The Ecclesford group are banished upon grounds of strict propriety: 'Lord Ravenshaw, who I suppose is one of the most correct men in England, would not hear of it' (*MP*, p. 122). Similarly, the impropriety of putting on a play when Sir Thomas is 'in some degree of constant danger' is one of Edmund's objections. Death has broken up the Ecclesford theatre. Even the public theatres closed for the day when a royal death occurred. The point is clear: that if news came back of Sir Thomas's death, the play would be interrupted in the same way as at Ecclesford, and *Lovers' Vows* would again be broken up, this time leaving Lady Bertram alone to act the after-piece of 'The Widow' or *The Distressed*

Mother. Lady Bertram certainly 'acts' the part of a grieving mother when she hears the news of Tom's decline: 'It was a sort of playing at being frightened' (*MP*, p. 427).

Lord Ravenshaw's theatrical party, which includes a scattering of the aristocracy (Lord and Lady Ravenshaw are joined by the Honourable John Yates, a Sir Henry, and even a Duke), is conducted on suitably lavish terms. Tom's desire to 'raise a little theatre at Mansfield' (*MP*, p. 123) evinces an ambition for something more extravagant than the makeshift theatres of the gentry. His longing for the 'Ecclesford theatre and scenery to try something with' is contrasted with Maria's entreaty to 'make the *performance*, not the *theatre*, our object' (*MP*, p. 124). Even Henry's suggestion that there is more to a theatre than the buildings and scenery fails to satisfy Tom: 'and for a theatre, what signifies a theatre? We shall only be amusing ourselves. Any room in this house might suffice.' Tom concedes to a makeshift theatre on the proviso that there are at least some theatrical accoutrements, a 'green curtain and a little carpenter's work' (*MP*, p. 127). Only then can he begin to envisage a prospective theatrical venue ensuing from the conversion of two rooms by 'merely moving the book-case in my father's room' (*MP*, p. 125).

Tom concentrates his theatrical energies behind the scenes. He is a committed manager, obsessed with the minutiae of stagecraft: he consults with the carpenters; he sets up a committee to pore over the text, to cut and lop where necessary; he suggests ideas for Fanny's costume and stage make-up; he is even prepared to ride across the country to find one more actor for his company (*MP*, p. 148). His efforts to professionalise the theatre are compounded by an adoption of theatrical language: he speaks of his 'company' and of Sir Thomas's study as the 'green room', while the billiard room is now '*the Theatre*'. Rather than respecting the 'privacy of the representation' he gives 'an invitation to every family who came in his way' (*MP*, p. 164). Having learned his part, 'all his parts', he is impatient to act.

Tom's attempts at *bon ton* theatricals are reminiscent of Lord Barrymore's theatrical excesses at Wargrave. Soon after his death, Barrymore was condemned for engaging in 'the most ridiculous, expensive, profuse and prodigal scheme, that ever signalized a predeliction for *private theatricals*'. Tickets were 'distributed to all the families of fashion and eminence in the surrounding neighbourhood', and 'sums exceeding all rational comprehension, all *common* credulity (to the amount of forty or fifty thousand) have been most degradingly lavished in every scene of riot, debauchery and extravagance'. Barrymore's 'infatuation' with his theatre was condemned: 'he became so severely infected with the deceptive *glee*, the affected *mirth*, the superficial *wit*, the interested *politesse*, the *political attachment*, the general *levity*, the characteristic *indigence*, and attracting tout ensemble of a green room'. Only after his death were the house and village rescued from 'the appearance of a *metropolis* in *miniature*' and restored to a 'truly remote and rusticated village'.[54]

Tom's desire to ape Lord Ravenshaw, not only by choosing *Lovers' Vows* but by longing for 'the Ecclesford theatre and the scenery', resonates with the fashionably elite theatricals of the aristocracy. His rendering of the 'low roles', the Butler and Cottager, also repeats Barrymore's performance of rustics and servants at Wargrave. Tom's responsibility for the theatricals is made clear: 'the inclination to act was awakened, and in no one more strongly than in him who was now master of the house' (*MP*, p. 123).

The disruptive consequences of Tom's theatricalising are most powerfully realised at the end of the first volume of *Mansfield Park* by the unexpected return of Sir Thomas. The first full dress rehearsal of *Lovers' Vows* has just begun when Sir Thomas makes his own melodramatic entrance from the West Indies. Sir Thomas interrupts a moment of high drama on stage, leading to a moment of high drama off stage.

The whole sequence of Sir Thomas's return and the termination of the *Lovers' Vows* is deliciously comic. The opening scene of the play is interrupted at the precise moment when Agatha is explaining the circumstances of her seduction and ruination to her son Frederick. At this point in Inchbald's play the stage directions reveal that Frederick 'takes the hand of Agatha and puts it to his heart'. Austen's specificity reveals her close knowledge of the play: 'Frederick was listening with looks of devotion to Agatha's narrative, and pressing her hand to her heart' (*MP*, p. 175). This moment occurs about ten minutes into the opening scene, at the end of Agatha's speech:[55]

he talked of love and promised me marriage … His flattery made me vain, and his repeated vows – Don't look at me, dear Frederick! – I can say no more. [*Frederick with his eyes cast down, takes her hand, and puts it to his heart.*] Oh! Oh! my son! I was intoxicated by the fervent caresses of a young, inexperienced, capricious man, and did not recover from the delirium till it was too late. (*LV*, act 1, scene 1)

The tableau on stage is framed, specifically, within the structure of the novel. In the chapel at Sotherton, Julia had directed the rest of the group to the visual tableau of the marriage between Rushworth and Maria. Now Austen repeats the motif, except that, even more spectacularly, she uses the moment to end the first volume of the novel. Furthermore, this time the tableau is itself a theatrical one – quite literally it forms the first scene of the first act of *Lovers' Vows*. Instead of Maria and Rushworth at the altar, a legitimate and formalised version of love, we now see Maria and Henry in a physical embrace. It is Julia who once again, as in the chapel, directs our gaze to the tableau, but this time there is a double focus: the reader watches a character in the novel watching a character on stage. Furthermore, the scene is not filtered through the eyes of Fanny, for she is also on the stage, about to take her part. It is Julia's re-entrance and horrified cry that ends the first volume: 'My father is come! He is in the hall at this moment' (*MP*, p. 172).

At the beginning of the second volume Austen raises the curtain to reveal the frozen tableau of the cast on stage, motionless and fearful in the 'terrible pause' which precedes 'the corroborating sounds of opening doors and footsteps' (*MP*, p. 175). Once again, silence is used to characterise the attitudes of the group. In *Mansfield Park*, Frederick's pointed gesture of retaining Agatha's hand close to his heart does not go unnoticed by Julia, who literally exits the stage in protest with a suitably frosty closing line, '*I* need not be afraid of appearing before him' (*MP*, p. 175). Austen's reference to Henry and Maria by their stage names signifies that we are watching the lovers on a stage, rehearsing their opening scene, the sentimental reunion of a mother and her son. But offstage we are also about to witness another reunion scene, that between Sir Thomas and his family.

The tone of the narrative lightens with the piqued exit of Julia breaking the on-stage tableau. The Bertram brothers also exit hastily, 'feeling the necessity of doing something'. While the Bertrams hurriedly leave the stage to face their father in the drawing room, Austen completes the scene with the rake, Henry, wickedly encouraging the fop, Rushworth, to 'pay his respects to Sir Thomas without delay' and sending him through the door after the others 'with delighted haste' (*MP*, p. 176). The Crawfords, naturally, make their own perfectly timed exit and Fanny exits hesitatingly, leaving Yates centre stage.

Sir Thomas's family reunion in the drawing room is one of intense dramatic irony, for we know, along with Fanny, that at any minute 'unsuspected vexation was probably ready to burst on him' (*MP*, p. 178). His entrance into the drawing room is comically marked by Mrs Norris's 'instinctive caution with which she had whisked away Mr Rushworth's pink satin cloak as her brother-in-law entered' (*MP*, pp. 179–80).

Jane Austen invites us to enjoy the discomfort of a pregnant and highly awkward social situation. Furthermore, rather than the Gothic father-figure that Fanny has come to expect, Austen delights in surprising her with a much-changed Sir Thomas. He has altered both physically and in character: 'His manner seemed changed; his voice was quick from the agitation of joy, and all that had been awful in his dignity seemed lost in tenderness' (*MP*, p. 178). Furthermore, 'the delights of his sensations in being again in his own house, in the centre of his family, after such a separation, made him communicative and chatty in a very unusual degree' (*MP*, p. 178).

But it is not only the master of the house who seems predisposed to chat. In the 'elation of her spirits Lady Bertram became talkative'. And it is her unusual garrulousness that so comically lets the cat out of the bag: 'How do you think the young people have been amusing themselves lately, Sir Thomas? They have been acting. We have been all alive with acting' (*MP*, p. 181). Austen adds, mischievously, 'and what were the sensations of her children upon hearing her'.

The culmination of the theatrical saga comes in the uproariously comic moment of Sir Thomas's own stage debut. Wishing to take a look at his 'own dear room' the master of the house enters his study to discover general confusion and upheaval, notably the removal of the bookcase from the adjoining door, which we know leads directly to 'the theatre'. Hearing a strange 'hallooing' in the next room Sir Thomas passes through the door and finds himself face to face with the ranting Yates 'who appeared likely to knock him down backwards' (*MP*, p. 182). This moment of quasi-farcical humour is compounded by the sardonic description of Yates 'giving perhaps the very best start he had ever given in the whole course of his rehearsals' as he almost knocks the august Sir Thomas off balance.

The moment of Sir Thomas's great comic entrance onto the stage at Mansfield crystallises Austen's interplay between life and theatre, novel and play. What is most striking about this scene is that it is witnessed by Tom Bertram from the back of what has become the auditorium. The ironies of the scene are focused through the eyes of Tom, who can barely contain himself with laughter at the sight of his father's embarrassment. Crucially, it is only Tom who witnesses this piece of real-life theatre.

Tom's amusement runs deeper than an impartial appreciation of the farcical potential of the scene: 'His father's looks of solemnity and amazement on this his first appearance on any stage, and the gradual metamorphosis of the impassioned Baron Wildenhaim into the well-bred and easy Mr Yates, making his bow and apology to Sir Thomas Bertram was such an exhibition, such *a piece of true acting*, as he would not have lost upon any account' (*MP*, p. 182, my italics). The fluidity of the sentence, itself metamorphosing through four personae from 'His father – to Baron Wildenhaim – to Mr Yates – to Sir Thomas Bertram', is richly suggestive of the blurring of distinctions between theatricality and reality. Yates and Sir Thomas are first startled, then recover themselves to perform their social roles, which create the exhibition of 'true acting'. 'His father', unintentionally, becomes an actor in a scene before reverting to his role as 'Sir Thomas Bertram'. Mr Yates is startled from his melodramatic posture as the ranting Baron Wildenhaim before he recovers to perform the social grace of a visitor presenting his formal compliments to his host.

The ability to adopt a social role is not to be confused with the polymorphic skills of Henry Crawford, but Yates's metamorphosis from the 'impassioned Baron Wildenhaim' into 'the well-bred and easy Mr Yates' is a complex reversal of the requirements of the acting process. In metamorphosing back into himself he is abandoning his usual histrionic style and is now acting naturalistically: what for Tom Bertram is 'true acting' is that absence of posturing which for Partridge, watching Garrick, was bad acting. But paradoxically, as Tom understands, Yates's bow and apology to 'Sir Thomas Bertram' is merely another form of social acting.

The ingenuity of describing this encounter through Tom's perspective is that, unlike Fanny, he understands the absurdities of social performance. Tom's desire to play the displaced Lord Duberley in Colman's *The Heir at Law* first identifies his understanding of the interchangeability of social roles, and the unstable relationship between status and conduct – perhaps first initiated by his confusion about Miss Anderson whose 'out' behaviour he found so perplexing. It is this understanding of the art of social role-playing that now shapes one of the most important scenes of the novel, the encounter between Yates and Sir Thomas, a slice of 'real-life' theatre: 'It would be the last – in all probability the last scene on that stage; but he was sure there could not be a finer. The house would close with the greatest eclat' (*MP*, pp. 182–83). Nowhere is Jane Austen's own *éclat* more evident than in this scene, with its dissolution of the distinction between acting on a stage and in social situations.

10

Emma

The *Lovers' Vows* debacle reveals that for Jane Austen acting is not so much an aberration as an inevitability. The great lesson she took from the drama, that social life requires a strong element of role-playing, is also one of the guiding principles of her next novel. In addition, *Emma* returns to the territory of *Pride and Prejudice*: the interplay of different social classes and the quest to discover a language truthful to emotional experience.

The depiction in *Pride and Prejudice* of a fine lady who is also an unregenerate snob is brilliantly reworked in *Emma*. This time, however, rather than the heroine being the victim of the cruelty and injustice of social snobbery, she is its perpetrator. Like Lady Catherine de Bourgh, Emma is concerned with preserving 'the distinctions of rank', and, in spite of the novel's deep engagement with the concept of social mobility, she is initially resistant to social change, unless upon her own terms.

The most traditional method of movement between the classes was through marriage and in *Emma* there are a number of intermarriages. The novel begins with the marriage between a former governess, Miss Taylor, and a highly respected, albeit self-made, gentleman, Mr Weston.[1] This union finds its correlation towards the close of the novel with the marriage between a woman on the brink of becoming a governess and a wealthy gentleman, who is the son of Mr Weston. Furthermore, the novel ends with the promise of future marriages (and matchmaking) between the daughter of the Westons and the offspring of the most genteel characters, the Knightleys.[2]

The assimilation of the social classes through marriage was one of the great themes of the drama, and alliances between 'blood' and 'money', or 'old' money and 'new', were the focuses of many successful comedies of the period.[3] In the novel tradition, Richardson's *Pamela* was the prime exemplar of an unlikely but successful union between a lowly servant girl and her master. In *Emma*, the theme of intermarriage comes full circle when Emma is faced with what she thinks is the probability, not merely the possibility, of a union between illegitimate Harriet and the well-born Mr Knightley: 'Mr Knightley and Harriet Smith! – Such an elevation on her side! Such a debasement on his! … Could it be? – No; it was impossible. And yet it was far, very far, from impossible' (*E*, p. 413). When Emma finally accepts that Harriet could well be 'the chosen, the first, the dearest, the friend, the wife to whom he looked for all the best blessings of existence', her wretchedness is increased by the reflection that 'it had been all her own work' (*E*, pp. 422–23).

While Harriet Smith is no Pamela or Evelina, resembling more the simple country girl of David Garrick's popular comedy, she does possess the capacity for improvement. Eventually, Mr Knightley is forced to reconsider his opinion of her character, and admit her to be Mr Elton's equal: 'An unpretending, single-minded, artless girl – infinitely to be preferred by any man of sense and taste to such a woman as Mrs Elton' (*E*, p. 331).

Austen's comedy of errors between Emma, Elton and Harriet in the first volume of the novel is, however, dependent on the finely nuanced renderings of rank and station so beloved of eighteenth-century comedy. The comic misunderstandings between the three characters are made possible by their tenuous grasp of social realities. Harriet believes (or is made to believe) that she is worthy of Mr Elton, while he, in turn, believes that he is worthy of Emma. Emma's concurrence in the misunderstandings is in no small part due to the fact that she is unable to conceive that Mr Elton could aspire to her own lofty level.

The misunderstandings within the Emma/Harriet/Elton love triangle are very much in the tradition of stage comedy. In Hannah Cowley's *The Runaway* a similar set of comic misunderstandings (known in the period as equivoques) occur between a father and son. The son (George Hargrave) mistakenly believes that the elderly Lady Dinah is intended for his father, and duly shows his happiness and approval of the match as he unwittingly courts the lady. The situation allows for many opportunities for comic misunderstandings until the son is suitably enlightened and horrified to learn that he, not his father, is the true object of desire. Likewise, Emma woos on behalf of Harriet until the comic epiphany of Mr Elton's proposal. Though aware of his drunken state, Emma foolishly believes that she can restrain his advances by talking of the weather, and is astonished to find her efforts repulsed: 'It really was so. Without scruple – without apology – without much apparent diffidence, Mr Elton, the lover of Harriet, was professing himself *her* lover' (*E*, p. 129).

In *Pride and Prejudice*, Austen had displayed the range of her comic skills in the great proposal scene between Elizabeth Bennet and Mr Collins, and in *Emma* she reworks the idea to depict the discrepancy between male and female behaviour in the courtship process. The high comedy of Elton's proposal is greatly enhanced by Emma's unknowing compliance in the mistake, yet the scene is also charged with the archetypal male arrogance which little expects anything but grateful acceptance from the female:

> 'I have thought only of you. I protest against having paid the smallest attention to any one else. Every thing that I have said or done, for many weeks past, has been with the sole view of marking my adoration of yourself. You cannot really, seriously, doubt it. No! – (in an accent meant to be insinuating) – I am sure you have seen and understood me.' (*E*, p. 131)

As with that other obtuse clergyman, Mr Collins, Elton interprets the lady's stunned silence as consent: 'allow me to interpret this interesting silence. It confesses that you have long understood me' (*E*, p. 131). Emma's incredulity at finding herself the object of Elton's desire is paralleled with his disdain at the discovery that the illegitimate Harriet is intended for himself: '*I* think seriously of Miss Smith! … no doubt, there are men who might not object to – Every body has their level' (*E*, pp. 131–32).

The narrative of *Emma* moves with great speed and skill between external events and the inner consciousness of the heroine. Dramatic dialogue is thus often followed by 'free indirect discourse' in which the third-person narratorial voice follows the unfolding of Emma's thoughts.[4] The carriage scene is mainly rendered in dialogue, but it is immediately followed by Emma's ruminations on Elton. She quickly realises that 'there had been no real affection either in his language or manners', though 'sighs and fine words had been given in abundance' (*E*, p. 135). Furthermore, she understands that he is a social climber who 'only wanted to aggrandize and enrich himself' (*E*, p. 135). The great comic paradox is that Emma is angry with Elton for looking down on Harriet, but is equally furious that he looks up to her level: 'that he should suppose himself her equal in connection or mind! – look down upon her friend, so well understanding the gradations of rank below him, and be so blind to what rose above' (*E*, p. 136). Having shown the worst effects of social snobbery in Elton's dismissal of Harriet, the authorial irony re-establishes its attack on Emma, whose snobbishness has yet to be purged: 'He must know that the Woodhouses had been settled for several generations at Hartfield, the younger branch of a very ancient family – and that the Eltons were nobody' (*E*, p. 136).

Eighteenth-century drama's obsession with the comic interplay of rank and manners depended upon discrepancies between outward appearance and inner reality. Plays such as *She Stoops to Conquer*, *The Heir at Law*, *The Belle's Stratagem* and *The Clandestine Marriage* all exploited the comic possibilities of mistaken identity and social displacement. Emma's lack of judgement is most apparent in her opinions of Mr Elton and Robert Martin. Her conviction that the handsome and gallant Mr Elton is a 'model' of good manners is as wrong-headed as her observation of Robert Martin's 'clownish' manners. Her comments are restricted to Martin's outward lack of polish, his 'unmodulated voice', and she duly condemns him as 'a completely gross, vulgar farmer – inattentive to appearances, and thinking of nothing but profit and loss' (*E*, p. 33). Emma's absurd remark that Robert Martin is 'not Harriet's equal' is angrily quashed by Mr Knightley: 'No, he is not her equal indeed, for he is as much her superior in sense as in situation' (*E*, p. 61).

The intricacies of social class are clearly understood by Robert Martin, who fears that Harriet is now 'considered (especially since *your* making so much of her) as in a line of society above him' (*E*, p. 59). Both Robert Martin and Mr Knightley know that Emma is to blame for her friend's recent social elevation. Yet again, there are distinctions made between different social levels. Emma thinks Robert Martin is unworthy of

Harriet, and Mr Knightley considers Harriet unworthy of Robert Martin: 'my only scruple in advising the match was on his account, as being beneath his deserts, and a bad connexion for him' (*E*, p. 61). Emma, sounding dangerously like Lady Catherine de Bourgh, stoutly refuses to concede: 'The sphere in which she moves is much above his. – It would be a degradation' (*E*, p. 62).

While Emma initially thinks of compatibility in terms of rank and station, Mr Knightley puts equal emphasis on compatibility of mind and disposition: 'A degradation to illegitimacy and ignorance, to be married to a respectable, intelligent gentleman-farmer'. Knightley approves of Robert Martin for being all that is 'open' and 'straightforward': 'Robert Martin's manners have sense, sincerity and good humour to recommend them; and his mind has more true gentility than Harriet Smith could understand' (*E*, p. 65). Mr Knightley perceives that Harriet's obscure origins are the insuperable social barrier to her making a good marriage (and Mr Elton's comments confirm this truth). Nevertheless, Emma is caught up in the romantic idea that the natural child is of noble birth: 'That she is a gentleman's daughter, is indubitable to me' (*E*, p. 62). Such is her faith in Harriet's true gentility that she fires a parting shot that will later rebound upon her: 'Were you, yourself, ever to marry, she is the very woman for you' (*E*, p. 64).

Social mobility achieved either through intermarriage between the classes or by means of trade and commerce provided stage comedy and fiction with the perfect vehicle for comparing and contrasting different social types. Austen's own fascination with social mobility, explored in *Pride and Prejudice*, is given fuller emphasis in *Emma*, where there is a greater depiction of the assimilation of the trading classes into gentility. While Miss Bates and Jane Fairfax are seen to be downwardly mobile, Mr Perry and the Coles are on the rise.[5] The Cole family, who are described as 'of low origin, in trade, and only moderately genteel', have risen to be 'in fortune and style of living, second only to the family at Hartfield', yet they still struggle to rise above the stigma of trade.

Emma initially sets herself against social mobility, for she has the common prejudice against trade and commerce, 'I have no doubt that he *will* thrive and be a very rich man in time – and his being illiterate and coarse need not disturb *us*' (*E*, p. 34). She dislikes visiting the Bateses at their humble home for fear of 'falling in with the second and third rate of Highbury, who were calling on them for ever'. Like Lady Catherine de Bourgh, Emma wishes to preserve the distinctions of rank, and is therefore rendered uncomfortable by events that dissolve social distinctions, such as the Coles's dinner party and the ball at the Crown Inn. Emma needs to be reassured that there will be no difficulty, 'in everybody's returning into their proper place the next morning' (*E*, p. 198).

But to her own astonishment, she discovers how much she enjoys the Coles's party (in contrast to the two more exclusive social gatherings at Donwell and Box Hill), finding the Coles to be 'worthy people', capable of giving 'real attention' (*E*, p. 208). This is in contrast to the vulgar Mrs Elton, who confirms Emma's worst prejudices about trade, with her airs and pretensions. Mrs Elton is a wonderful comic creation – in the mould of Fanny Burney's *nouveau riche* characters – with her incessant boasting of the Sucklings of Maple Grove and her horror of upstarts such as the Tupmans, 'encumbered with many low connections, but giving themselves immense airs' (*E*, p. 310). Her idiosyncratic speech captures her own particular brand of vulgarity: 'A cousin of Mr Suckling, Mrs Bragge, had such an infinity of applications; every body was anxious to be in her family, for she moves in the first circle. Wax-candles in the school-room! You may imagine how desirable!' (*E*, pp. 299–300). As with Burney's comic monsters, however, her moral inferiority is suggested in her treatment of her servants.[6] Whereas Emma and her father talk of James and Hannah with easy familiarity, Mrs Elton barely remembers the names of her servants: 'The man who fetches our letters every morning (one of our men, I forget his name)' (*E*, p. 295).[7]

Mrs Elton also uses her position of 'Lady Patroness' to bully Jane Fairfax and, together with her husband, to humiliate Harriet Smith: 'the enmity which they dared not shew in open disrespect to [Emma], found a broader vent in contemptuous treatment of Harriet' (*E*, p. 282). Mrs Elton takes up Jane Fairfax because timidity is prepossessing in those 'who are at all inferior' (*E*, p. 283). But, in an important speech, Mr Knightley conveys his understanding of the 'littleness' of her character:

Mrs Elton does not talk *to* Miss Fairfax as she speaks *of* her. We all know the difference between the pronouns he or she and thou, the plain-est-spoken amongst us; we all feel the influence of a something beyond common civility in our personal intercourse with each other – a some-thing more early implanted. We cannot give any body the disagreeable hints that we may have been very full of the hour before. We feel things differently. (*E*, p. 286)

This elusive 'something' that Knightley speaks of is crucial to an under-standing of the relationship between outward behaviour and inner feel-ing that permeates Austen's moral vision. The 'something beyond common civility' is of course precisely what Emma transgresses on Box Hill, but this must be understood as an uncharacteristic act, otherwise it would have no effect.

Jane Austen's interest in the disparity between what characters think and what they say and do is an essential part of her dramatic inheritance. We have seen how, from the juvenilia onwards, her works were in various ways shaped by the comic drama of the period. But more than this, her very vision of human beings in society is profoundly tied to her thinking about acting and role-playing. Throughout the novels, she resorts to a lexicon of theatre to explore the notion of the performed self. *Mansfield Park* explicitly revealed the theatricality of the self, above all in the great scene between Sir Thomas and Mr Yates; now in *Emma*, Austen explores this idea more implicitly, through social structure and the interplay of character more than in any particular incident.

Emma, though an 'imaginist', possesses a realistic grasp of the impor-tance of social performance. She duly enacts her disappointment on behalf of the Westons when Frank Churchill fails to appear at Randalls: 'She was the first to announce it to Mr Knightley; and exclaimed quite as much as was necessary (or, being acting a part, perhaps rather more) at the conduct of the Churchills, in keeping him away' (*E*, p. 145).

When Frank himself dissembles on the subject of his prolonged absence from Highbury, she accepts his duplicity with equilibrium: 'still if it were a falsehood, it was a pleasant one, and pleasantly handled' (*E*, p. 191). At the same time, she observes him closely to ascertain 'that he

had not been acting a part, or making a parade of insincere professions'
(*E*, p. 197). Emma comprehends that, while she must act a part, she must
also be on her guard to recognise acting in others. When sharing the
news of her engagement to Mr Knightley, she is happy that 'Mrs Weston
was acting no part, feigning no feelings in all that she said to him in
favour of the event' (*E*, p. 467).

While Emma accepts that 'acting a part', playing a social role, is
sometimes 'necessary', she draws the line at the sort of affectation and
disingenousness that disclaims the practice. On hearing Frank profess, 'I
am the wretchedest being at the world at a civil falsehood', Emma cannot
help but retort: 'I do not believe any such thing … I am persuaded that
you can be as insincere as your neighbours, when necessary' (*E*, p. 234).

The disparity between outward conduct and inner feeling is also a
source of endless amusement. Emma's impatience at having to observe
right social form is sometimes mocked, as, for example, when decorum
demands that she ask after Miss Fairfax, even though she doesn't want
to:

> 'Have you heard from Miss Fairfax so lately? I am extremely happy. I
> hope she is well?'
>
> 'Thank you. You are so kind!' replied the happily deceived aunt. (*E*,
> p. 157)

Miss Bates and even Jane Fairfax demand Emma's polite forbearance, but
most trying of all is Mrs Elton. Emma's solitary outbursts are all the more
comic, as they contrast so vividly with her repressed politeness:

> 'Knightley! – I could not have believed it. Knightley! – never seen him
> in her life before, and call him Knightley! – and discover that he is a
> gentleman! A little upstart, vulgar being, with her Mr E., and her *caro
> sposo*, and her resources, and all her airs of pert pretension and under-
> bred finery. Actually to discover that Mr Knightley is a gentleman! I
> doubt whether he will return the compliment, and discover her to be a
> lady.' (*E*, p. 279)

Though Emma heartily dislikes Mrs Elton, and finds that on occasion 'the forbearance of her outward submission' is put to the test, she (crucially) keeps her disgruntled feelings to herself.[8]

Austen's most discerning heroines, such as Elinor Dashwood and Elizabeth Bennet, possess the skill of appearing courteous in public without sacrificing their personal integrity. Emma also well understands the discrepancy between what Elinor describes as the 'behaviour' and the 'understanding'. Thus when Mr Weston claims that Mrs Elton 'is a good-natured woman after all', she finds the appropriate response: 'Emma denied none of it aloud, and agreed to none of it in private' (E, p. 353). Similarly, when Mr Elton's romantic attentions become annoyingly clear, Emma finds refuge in her ability to act a part but remain true to herself: 'she had the comfort of appearing very polite, while feeling very cross' (E, p. 119). Even when her forbearance is most sorely tested, by Harriet's disclosure of her love for Mr Knightley, Emma's response is magnanimous: 'She listened with much inward suffering, but with great outward patience' (E, p. 409). In each case, the phrasing is weighted by the opposites – denied/agreed, appearing/feeling, inward/outward – to express the conflict between social and private expression.

Even when dealing with extremely difficult family members, such as John Knightley and Mr Woodhouse, Emma shows her capacity for 'uniting civility with truth'. Thus, when John Knightley begins a typically antisocial rant concerning a dinner party at Randalls, Emma is unable to give him the 'pleased assent, which no doubt he was in the habit of receiving'. Rather, we are told, 'she could not be complying, she dreaded being quarrelsome; her heroism reached only to silence' (E, p. 114).

Throughout the novel, Austen explores the importance of silence, plain-speaking and non-verbal communication, offset against verbal ambiguities, equivocations, comic misunderstandings, riddles and word-games. In the first half of the novel, techniques such as riddles and verbal ambiguities are used with great effect to exploit the comic misunderstandings between Emma and Mr Elton. The novel's engagement with a more sophisticated exploration of language and communication coincides, however, with the arrival of Frank Churchill, who is the prime exemplar of verbal charm and social manipulation.

From the outset, the Knightley brothers are associated with a lack of gallantry and a love of plain-speaking. For instance, when the brothers meet, they welcome each other in the 'true English style', which though plain and unaffected is not lacking in feeling: "'How d'ye do, George?', and John, how are you?"… burying under a calmness that seemed all but indifference, the real attachment which would have led either of them, if requisite, to do every thing for the good of the other' (*E*, pp. 99–100). But whereas John Knightley's forthrightness often verges on rudeness, George's rarely does. Furthermore, he is attuned to the fact that the language of gallantry used by other men, such as Frank and Mr Elton, is merely a means to an end. He warns Emma that Mr Elton speaks a different language in 'unreserved moments, when there are only men present'. Mr Elton's more private language reveals that 'he does not mean to throw himself away' (*E*, p. 66).

George Knightley is similarly intolerant of Frank Churchill's dandyish manners. His own bluntness, which is contrasted with Frank's excessive gallantry, conceals his genuine concern for others. For example, Frank's insinuating praise and his importuning Jane Fairfax to continue singing, in spite of a hoarse voice, is contrasted with Mr Knightley's peremptory and blunt command: 'That will do … You have sung quite enough for one evening – now, be quiet … Miss Bates, are you mad, to let your niece sing herself hoarse in this manner? Go, and interfere' (*E*, p. 229). As Emma observes of Mr Knightley, 'He is not a gallant man, but he is a very humane one' (*E*, p. 223).

Frank Churchill's gallantry and charm, on the other hand, are manifested by his love and mastery of word-play. This is at its most skilful and scintillating when he is able to play Emma and Jane Fairfax off against each other, such as on the occasion when Emma discovers him mending Mrs Bates's spectacles, and at Box Hill. On both occasions, however, the verbal acrobatics and double-meanings are so brilliantly executed and multi-faceted that they become almost mentally wearying, especially when Emma invariably takes up Frank's challenge. Mr Knightley's habitual brevity of speech, which usually terminates the verbal games, is therefore welcomed. His barely concealed jealousy and disapproval of Frank Churchill, however, puts its own spin on the proceedings.

When Emma interrupts the lovers in the Bateses' sitting room to hear Jane Fairfax perform at her pianoforte, she mistakenly ascribes Jane's evident discomposure to nerves: 'she must reason herself into the power of performance'. However much Jane dislikes having to rouse herself to 'perform' a social lie, Frank relishes the opportunity to flex his verbal muscles by playing a flirtatious double game with the two women. He uses the opportunity to make love to Jane, while simultaneously continuing the Dixon pretence with Emma and using her as a blind. Thus he speaks of the pianoforte as a gift 'thoroughly from the heart. Nothing hastily done; nothing incomplete. True affection only could have prompted it' (*E*, p. 242). Emma, thinking he alludes to Dixon, is quick to reprimand Frank's indiscretion – 'you speak too plain' – but he replies with insouciance, 'I would have her understand me. I am not in the least ashamed of my meaning' (*E*, p. 243).

When Mr Knightley passes the window on horseback, he is drawn into conversation with Miss Bates. Not only does his bluntness amidst so much verbal ambiguity come as a most welcome relief, but the highly comical dialogue between him and the garrulous Miss Bates, which is audible to the small audience in the apartment, makes his feelings about Frank Churchill all too clear:

[Knightley] cut her short with,

'I am going to Kingston. Can I do anything for you?'

'Oh! dear, Kingston – are you? – Mrs Cole was saying the other day she wanted something from Kingston.'

'Mrs Cole has servants to send. Can I do anything for *you*?'

'No, I thank you. But do come in. Who do you think is here? – Miss Woodhouse and Miss Smith … Do put up your horse at the Crown, and come in.'

'Well,' said he in a deliberating manner, 'for five minutes, perhaps.'

'And here is Mrs Weston and Mr Frank Churchill too! – Quite delightful; so many friends!'

'No, not now, I thank you. I could not stay two minutes.' (*E*, p. 244)

It is unsurprising that Mr Knightley, the advocate of forthrightness, dislikes Frank Churchill, although jealousy distorts his judgement. When he and Emma discuss Frank's absence from Highbury, she shows herself to be highly sensitive to the social pressures upon a young man who is almost entirely dependent upon the will of a woman such as Mrs Churchill. As she sharply reminds Knightley, 'You are the worst judge in the world of the difficulties of dependence … You do not know what it is to have tempers to manage' (*E*, p. 146). No doubt she is alluding to the management of the more awkward members of her own family: 'Nobody, who has not been in the interior of a family, can say what the difficulties of any individual of that family may be' (*E*, p. 146).

Emma understands that forthrightness is a privilege of the powerful, not the disenfranchised. When Knightley suggests to her the simple and resolute speech that Frank should make to the Churchills in order to break free of their claims, she mocks his social naivety:

> Such language for a young man entirely dependent to use! – Nobody but you, Mr Knightley, would imagine it possible. But you have not an idea of what is requisite in situations directly opposite to your own. Mr Frank Churchill to be making such a speech as that to the uncle and aunt, who have brought him up, and are to provide for him! – Standing up in the middle of the room, I suppose, and speaking as loud as he could! How could you imagine such conduct practicable? (*E*, p. 147)

Paradoxically, although Austen is sensitive to the idea that it is not always 'practicable' to be forthright, especially where there is an imbalance of power, she also exploits the tragi-comic possibilities of social decorum that proscribes circumlocution. Emma's final and most painful misunderstanding occurs precisely because of social equivocations, which lead her to believe that Harriet is in love with Frank Churchill rather than Mr Knightley. Emma, resolving to herself that 'Plain dealing was always best' (*E*, p. 341), encourages Harriet to confess her new love, but adds an important codicil: 'Let no name ever pass our lips. We were very wrong before; we will be cautious now' (*E*, p. 342). The misunderstandings persist as the women, with due propriety, agree upon the superior merits of the 'gentleman' in question for rendering Harriet an elusive 'service':

'I am not at all surprised at you, Harriet. The service he rendered you was enough to warm your heart.'

'Service! oh! it was such an inexpressible obligation! – The very recollection of it, and all that I felt at the time – when I saw him coming – his noble look – and my wretchedness before. Such a change! … From perfect misery to perfect happiness.' (*E*, p. 342)

Emma, of course, refers to Frank's rescue of Harriet from the gypsies, whereas she remembers the far more painful social snub of being 'cut' by Mr Elton at the dance, and saved by Mr Knightley.

The confusion arises partly because social form dictates that the young women cannot be too explicit, that the man cannot be named. This is the sort of comic misunderstanding that is exploited in the drama. For example, in *The Clandestine Marriage* one of the best scenes involves a misunderstanding between the lovely young heroine and the lecherous Lord Ogleby. Fanny's equivocations on the delicate subject of her situation (she is secretly married and pregnant) mislead the debauched aristocrat to believe that she is in love with him. This is a classic example of the problems arising from the exigencies of female propriety. Of course, in *Emma*, the irony is intensified, as Emma is determined not to repeat her earlier misunderstanding with Harriet and Elton, and is therefore especially self-satisfied with her discretion and 'plain-dealing'. When the mistake finally comes to light, it is the catalyst for Emma's double epiphany: the revelation of her own love for Mr Knightley and the realisation of her own wrong-doing.

Jane Austen shows how language and propriety are vulnerable to evasions and misconstructions, but offsets this by demonstrating the unmistakable power of non-verbal communication. The most memorable moments in the novels are often those expressed by wordless actions. Few can forget the emotional impact of Captain Wentworth silently removing the small child from Anne's back in *Persuasion* or Mr Knightley almost kissing Emma's hand. Elinor Dashwood's tears of joy at the news that Edward is released from his engagement express her deep emotion, as do Emma's quiet, uncontrollable tears after Box Hill. Very often, strong feeling is rendered by the frequency with which characters look at each other. Darcy's love for Elizabeth is expressed by the manner in which he fixes his eyes upon her. Mr Knightley rumbles Frank Churchill and Jane Fairfax long before anyone else does because he has noticed the way they look at each other: 'I have lately imagined that I saw symptoms of attachment between them – certain expressive looks, which I did not believe meant to be public' (*E*, p. 350).

In *Emma* Jane Austen explores the impact of a particular kind of telepathy between couples. When Harriet is snubbed by Mr Elton at the Crown Inn ball, it is made clear that Mrs Elton is complicit: 'smiles of high glee passed between him and his wife' (*E*, p. 328). But when Harriet is saved by Mr Knightley, we witness the loving telepathy between him and Emma: 'She was all pleasure and gratitude … and longed to be thanking him; and though too distant for speech, her countenance said much, as soon as she could catch his eye again' (*E*, p. 328). Later, 'her eyes invited him irresistibly to come to her and be thanked' (*E*, p. 330). Similarly, Knightley expresses his own approbation and strength of feeling non-verbally when he discovers that Emma has visited Miss Bates following the Box Hill episode: 'It seemed as if there were an instantaneous impression in her favour, as if his eyes received the truth from her's, and all that had passed of good in her feelings were at once caught and honoured. – He looked at her with a glow of regard' (*E*, p. 385).

Their mutual respect and compatibility are also revealed by the frankness of expression in their conversation. They quarrel and spar in private, showing they are intellectual equals. Emma refuses to be intimidated by Knightley's brusqueness. She dares to contradict him, to accuse him of being manipulative and very fond of 'bending little minds' (*E*, p. 147), and of being full of 'prejudice' against Frank Churchill. She deliberately provokes him by taking views opposite to his. She confesses that even as a young girl she called him George, 'because I thought it would offend you' (*E*, p. 463). In public, their dialogue is distinguished by an economy of expression, which contrasts refreshingly with the tortuous, circuitous way in which, for example, Frank Churchill and Jane Fairfax are forced to communicate in public.[9]

In the dialogue between Emma and Mr Knightley there is an easiness and familiarity, even when they touch upon delicate subjects. When Emma attempts to ascertain his feelings towards Jane Fairfax, with the words 'The extent of your admiration may take you by surprise one day

or other', he blithely responds, 'Oh! are you there? – But you are misera-
bly behindhand. Mr Cole gave me a hint of it six weeks ago' (*E*, p. 287).
Strikingly, their romantic involvement is characterised by an absence of
sentimental language and false courtesy:

> 'Whom are you going to dance with?' asked Mr Knightley.
>
> She hesitated a moment, and then replied, 'With you, if you will ask
> me.'
>
> 'Will you?' said he, offering his hand.
>
> 'Indeed I will. You have shown that you can dance, and you know we
> are not really so much brother and sister as to make it at all improper.'
>
> 'Brother and sister! no, indeed.' (*E*, p. 331)

Even when the lovers discuss their impending marriage, there is a
distinct lack of sentiment: 'The subject followed; it was in plain, unaffected, gentleman-like English, such as Mr Knightley used even to the
woman he was in love with' (*E*, p. 448).

The association of a particular kind of brusqueness and forthrightness
with genuine feeling is used repeatedly in *Emma* to encapsulate the very
essence of Englishness. The true affection that belies the gruff exterior of
the language between the Knightley brothers, which Austen described as
'the true English manner', is now revealed in the union between Emma
and Mr Knightley. It is, furthermore, Frank Churchill's language,
expressed in a 'fine flourishing letter, full of professions and falsehoods',
which enables Mr Knightley to clarify the indefinable 'something' that
had previously eluded him in his early analysis of what constitutes right
moral conduct: 'No, Emma, your amiable young man can be amiable
only in French, not in English ... he can have no English delicacy towards
the feelings of other people' (*E*, p. 149). As in a long tradition within the
drama, English plainness is contrasted with French affectation.

As Austen makes clear, this 'English delicacy' is not confined to rank
or station. Even Emma recognises that Robert Martin and his sisters
possess 'genuine delicacy', and that their exemplary conduct following
Harriet's rejection is 'the result of real feeling' (*E*, p. 179). Yet this delicacy
eludes the Eltons, who in particular show 'injurious courtesy' towards
those who are socially inferior, and in need of protection, such as Jane

Fairfax and Harriet Smith. Momentarily, Emma makes a similar transgression to this when she humiliates Miss Bates at Box Hill.[10] Mr Knightley duly emphasises the matter of social inequality when he censures Emma's treatment of Miss Bates: 'Were she your equal in situation – but, Emma, consider how far this is from being the case' (*E*, p. 375). Emma swiftly make reparations with the consciousness of his words guiding her response: 'It should be the beginning, on her side, of a regular, equal, kindly intercourse' (*E*, p. 377).

Austen's happiest alliances are those between equals, not necessarily social equals, but those in whom there is compatibility of mind, and mutual respect and understanding. In the union between Emma and Knightley there is the promise of an equal discourse. Integral to Austen's resolutions is the way that her spirited heroines, in the best tradition of the lively ladies of comic tradition, never relinquish their penchant for merriment. Those critics who insist that Emma's reformation is not genuine cite the impudence of her remark to her future spouse: 'I always expect the best treatment, because I never put up with any other' (*E*, p. 474). To regard this as merely a continuation of Emma's egotism is to misunderstand the workings of the lively lady, such as Austen's favourites, Lady G. and Lady Bell Bloomer: comedy proposes that a woman may marry a worthy and upright man without fear that her high spirits will be stifled.

Mr Knightley declares to Emma after Box Hill: 'I will tell you truths while I can.' There is only one final agonising encounter when they fail to communicate fully, a last misunderstanding when each believes the other to be in love with someone else. But this is short-lived, for Emma, having first begged Mr Knightley not to speak of his love, will not ultimately sacrifice their friendship: 'I will hear whatever you like. I will tell you exactly what I think' (*E*, p. 429). When the misunderstanding is happily resolved, he shows his characteristic awkwardness with the language of sentiment: 'I cannot make speeches ... If I loved you less, I might be able to talk about it more. But you know what I am. You hear nothing but truth from me' (*E*, p. 430).

Paradoxically, however, Mr Knightley's pursuit of absolute truth is presented as touchingly idealistic: 'Mystery; Finesse – how they pervert the understanding! My Emma, does not every thing serve to prove more and more the beauty of truth and sincerity in all our dealings with each other?' (*E*, p. 446). His noble sentiment is ironically undercut by Emma's 'blush of sensibility on Harriet's account', for she is conscious that she is withholding the full truth of her friend's love for him, and her own part in it. It is only when Harriet is safely married to Robert Martin that 'the disguise, equivocation, mystery, so hateful to her to practise, might soon be over. She could now look forward to giving him that full and perfect confidence which her disposition was most ready to welcome as a duty' (*E*, p. 475). Whether or not Emma finally does reveal the whole truth to Knightley is left open. But this ambiguity should come as no surprise, for the authorial voice has already warned the reader: 'Seldom, very seldom, does complete truth belong to any human disclosure; seldom can it happen that something is not a little disguised, or a little mistaken' (*E*, p. 431). There is no escape from a little disguise, a little mistakenness: such is the lesson of the theatre.

The acknowledgement of the incompleteness of human disclosure strikes at the very heart of Jane Austen's creative vision. The novel, with its omniscient narrator, is in theory a genre that proposes the possibility of complete truth. Austen, however, is more akin to Shakespeare in her perception of the complexity and ambiguity of artistic truth. Her vision of how human beings behave in society is built on disguise and role-play, equivocation and mystery: arts inextricably associated with the dramatic tradition.

Jane Austen's insistence that all our disclosures are 'a little disguised' calls into question the argument of an influential line of critics who believe that she was suspicious of 'acting' because of the supposed insincerity of role-playing.[11] These critics maintain that the growth of the heroine towards authentic self-knowledge is the key to the moral world of the novels. Such critics are themselves more Knightleys than Austens: they are susceptible to an ideal of truth that is surely unattainable. Rather, from Jane Austen's earliest beginnings in the amateur theatricals at Steventon and her experiments with dramatic form in the juvenilia to her systematic engagement with the drama in the mature novels, we find an implicit belief that the social self is always *performed*. The ultimate model for this way of seeing is the theatre.

11

Why She Is a Hit in Hollywood

Hollywood fell in love with Jane Austen in the mid-1990s, when six film and television adaptations of her novels exploded onto the small and big screen, all of them critical and box-office successes. In 1995, the British actors Emma Thompson and Kate Winslet appeared as Elinor and Marianne Dashwood, alongside Hugh Grant and Alan Rickman, in a lushly romantic film of *Sense and Sensibility*, directed by the Taiwanese-born Ang Lee, who had established his reputation with a sequence of films about family conflicts in the context of traditional Chinese values. In *Eat Drink Man Woman*, a master chef in Taipei struggles with his three daughters' distinctly western views of love and marriage. This interest in the tension between the 'modern' notion of romantic passion as the route to marriage and the traditional idea of marrying for the sake of respectability and property inheritance, in accordance with parental wishes, meant that Lee appeared an ideal candidate to direct *Sense and Sensibility*. Manners matter in Chinese culture, as they did in the world of Jane Austen, and in this respect the marriage between director and material proved a good match. The film duly won critical plaudits and seven Academy Award nominations, with Emma Thompson taking the Oscar for Best Adapted Screenplay.

Persuasion was the debut movie of South African-born Roger Michell, who went on to direct *Notting Hill*, one of late twentieth-century British cinema's most commercially successfully romantic comedies. Michell had cut his directorial teeth in the British stage tradition, with work at the Royal Court and the Royal Shakespeare Company. He knew how to get exceptionally nuanced performances out of a host of established classical actors such as Corin Redgrave, Fiona Shaw, Phoebe Nicholls and Simon Russell Beale. Reviewers especially praised *Persuasion*'s gritty realism and Amanda Root's moving and understated performance of Anne Elliot. The film originally aired on 16 April 1995, when it was broadcast on BBC Two television. It won the BAFTA for the year's best single television drama. Sony Pictures Classics released the film in American cinemas on 27 September 1995. Critics hailed its 'unhurried delicacy' and its authenticity to the novel.[1] The *Los Angeles Times* described it as the most faithful to the spirit of Austen of the several Hollywood adaptations.[2]

On the small screen, also in 1995, the BBC's *Pride and Prejudice*, memorably starring Colin Firth as Mr Darcy in a wet shirt, garnered over eleven million viewers in Britain alone.[3] In America, 3.7 million Americans watched the first broadcast on the A&E Network. The series was spread out over six episodes, and adapted by Andrew Davies, a seasoned converter of classic novels for television. He wanted to produce 'a fresh, lively story about real people', and wanted to emphasise the themes of sex and money that underpin the novel.[4] Davies added extra scenes, including the infamous lake scene, and portrayed Austen's men in sporting activities such as billiards and fencing. He also used voice-overs and flashbacks, and revealed character via letters that the actors were seen reading to themselves and to one another. The series was critically acclaimed and award-winning, and it is still perceived by many as the definitive adaptation. The appearance of three such contrasting but equally well-achieved screen dramatisations meant that 'Austen Mania' was truly underway.

The following year Gwyneth Paltrow starred in a lavish, highly decorative, period drama of *Emma*, directed by Douglas McGrath, with Jeremy Northam as Mr Knightley. Despite its outstanding supporting cast (Juliet Stevenson stole the film with her pitch-perfect rendering of the odious snob Mrs Elton), there was a shallow sheen to the adaptation that belied the complexity of the novel. Beautiful to look at, the movie failed to capture the interior life of the more complex characters. Of all Austen's novels, *Emma* is the most technically proficient in the layering of narrative arc and psychological insight. Adapter and director Douglas McGrath could not find any equivalent for the authorial voice upon which the book is so dependent. The main failure of the movie was Paltrow. Austen's intention was to create an unsympathetic heroine: 'I am going to take a heroine whom no one but myself will much like.' But she was too shrewd a novelist not to be aware that her readers still needed to feel sympathy or admiration for the main character. In the novel, Austen gets around this problem of Emma's 'unlikeability' by two means. First, there is her complex use of irony directed against the heroine, multi-layered and beautifully orchestrated from the opening lines. This is facilitated by Austen's increasing command of the key technique of free indirect speech, in which the reader finds herself both inside and outside the heroine as the narrative is written from her point of view but in the third-person, allowing for the ironic exposure of her prejudices. Secondly, there is the censure of Mr Knightley: 'Better be without sense, than misapply it as you do.'[5]

Here is the opening sentence of the novel: 'Emma Woodhouse, handsome, clever, and rich, with a comfortable home and happy disposition, seemed to unite some of the best blessings of existence; and had lived nearly twenty-one years in the world with very little to distress or vex her.' The word 'seemed' is a vital clue to what will unfold in the course of the narrative. By the time we get to Emma's (faulty) judgement of both Harriet Smith and Jane Fairfax, Austen's use of free indirect speech to ironise her heroine, and to deflate her ego, is in full force:

> She was not struck by any thing remarkably clever in Miss Smith's conversation, but she found her altogether very engaging – not inconveniently shy, not unwilling to talk – and yet so far from pushing, shewing so proper and becoming a deference, seeming so pleasantly grateful for being admitted to Hartfield, and so artlessly impressed by the appearance of every thing in so superior a style to what she had been used to, that she must have good sense and deserve encouragement.[6]

And here is Emma on her rival, Jane Fairfax:

> She could never get acquainted with her: she did not know how it was, but there was such coldness and reserve – such apparent indifference whether she pleased or not – and then, her aunt was such an eternal talker! – and she was made such a fuss with by every body! – and it had been always imagined that they were to be so intimate – because their

ages were the same, every body had supposed they must be so fond of each other. These were her reasons – she had no better.[7]

In both these passages, the reader is being directed by Austen to distrust Emma's judgement. We know that we are present in the company of a flawed heroine, who has great, misguided, faith in the powers of her own intelligence. McGrath's essential problem was that he was too in love with Paltrow's beauty. The camera lingered lovingly on her face; she was lit in the most transcendent light, which made her appear angelic. Without the corrective of Austen's lethal irony and with no cinematic equivalent of her free indirect speech, Emma is a two-dimensional, shallow mannequin. Later, I will suggest how Amy Heckerling circumvents the technical problem of ironising the heroine within the genre of film.

Since 1996, there have been over thirty Jane Austen adaptations and spin-offs, including a dog cartoon series based on *Pride and Prejudice* and *Northanger Abbey* called *Wishbone*; Angel Gracia's *From Prada to Nada*, a Latina spin on *Sense and Sensibility* set in East Los Angeles; and *Scents and Sensibility*, where Elinor is a cleaner in a spa and Marianne makes scented products. The novel *Bridget Jones's Diary* reworked the plot of *Pride and Prejudice*. Colin Firth, who played the role of Darcy in the BBC adaptation, played the role of Helen Fielding's modern-day Darcy in the film of the book. Then there was *Lost in Austen*, a fantasy reworking of *Pride and Prejudice* set in modern times, and *The Lizzie Bennet Diaries*, an American web series conveyed in the form of vlogs. We have had a dramatisation of Austen's own purported love life in *Becoming Jane*; Austen goes to Bollywood in *Bride and Prejudice*; Austen meets murder mystery in P. D. James's *Death Comes to Pemberley*; and Austen meets the horror genre in Seth Grahame-Smith's *Pride and Prejudice and Zombies*, which was first a book and then a movie. The list is endless. One wonders whether there will soon be a TV channel entirely devoted to Jane Austen.

Many explanations have been offered for the resurgence of interest in Jane Austen during the two decades between the mid-1990s and the 2016 celebrations of her endurance two hundred years after her death. Typically, the success of the adaptations has been ascribed to a nostalgic desire to escape from the uncertainties of modern life and return to an age of politeness and social order. As we will see, Jane Austen has been popular in times of war. A key aspect of this explanation is what might be described as 'Big House Syndrome'. The televised *Brideshead Revisited* of 1981 filmed at Castle Howard, the 1995 *Pride and Prejudice* using the National Trust property Lyme Park, and, more recently, *Downton Abbey*, which sent thousands of tourists to Highclere, were all of a piece. They idealised the world of 'upstairs, downstairs'. One of the characteristics of the 'heritage' dramatisations of Austen novels was that the houses were all too big. There was an undifferentiated view of the great families and estates of the past: the productions' designers and location scouts failed to see that Austen tends to speak for the values of the lesser gentry and to scorn such idle, vain aristocrats as Lady Catherine de Bourgh (the embodiment of both pride and prejudice) and the Dowager Viscountess Dalrymple (in *Persuasion*).

The power of escapism and romantic fantasy cannot be gainsaid, but the key to the difference between the merely escapist and romantic screen renditions of Jane Austen and those that truly succeed as works of art in their own right is the adaptation's truth not to the letter of her text – and certainly not to correctness of period detail – but to the spirit of her comedy. The spirit, that is, which she herself learned from the comic theatre.

Austen's career in Hollywood began in 1938. *Pride and Prejudice* was a box-office hit in the MGM movie starring Laurence Olivier and Greer Garson. The idea for a movie version came from Harpo Marx, who saw a theatre adaptation of *Pride and Prejudice* in 1935 and thought it would make a good film, and a perfect vehicle for the actress Norma Shearer. However, there is an even more fascinating, though little known, back-story to the history of *Pride and Prejudice* dramatisation.

One of England's most successful playwrights in the 1920s was a man called Alan Milne, who specialised in comedies with a satirical edge. His work was often compared with that of Noël Coward. By 1922, his plays were being performed simultaneously in London, America and Liverpool. He had also turned his hand to screenwriting, though he considered himself first and foremost a playwright. It was only in the late 1920s that he published the stories for his son Christopher Robin that have totally eclipsed his theatrical achievements: *Winnie-the-Pooh* and *The House at Pooh Corner*.

In 1936, shortly after German troops re-entered the demilitarised zone of the Rhineland, A. A. Milne wrote a letter to his friend Charles Turley Smith, deploring the international situation: 'The world is foul. I hate the insular egotism of France, I loathe the German government, I detest Musso, I abominate Communism.' He was taking comfort in an enterprise that he had been working on for some months; to turn his 'favourite book' into a stage play: 'It was nearly a year's job – six months reading and thinking, six months writing.' It was a labour of love: an adaptation of Jane Austen's *Pride and Prejudice*. For him, his 'liaison with Miss Jane Austen' was one of the most 'difficult' and the 'most delightful' things he had ever done.[8]

His 'liaison' went back a long way and had served him well in difficult times.[9] During the First World War, Milne enlisted as an officer in the Warwickshire Regiment. He was sent out to France in July 1916. After serious action on the Somme, his battalion was resting out of the line before going up again. He had travelled to France with a quiet young boy, whose elder brother had been killed a few months earlier. One evening as the soldier was just settling down to take his tea he was hit by a shell and blown to pieces in front of Milne.

In August 1916, the regiment took part in a new attack. In his dug-out, Milne offered to run out a telephone line on the front line, and asked his sergeant to pick two men to accompany him. Losses had been severe, and the colonel told Milne that he could not afford to lose three signalling officers in a month. Milne knew few of the men, but he had bonded with a young man, Lance Corporal Grainger, over a shared passion for Jane Austen. Like the men in Rudyard Kipling's great story 'The Janeites', they would talk about the novels in the trenches. Alan had loved Austen since he had been a boy at Westminster, as had his schoolmate Lytton Strachey. *Pride and Prejudice* was his favourite novel, along with *The Wind in the Willows*.

Milne's sergeant volunteered himself with a cheery 'I'll come for one, sir'. Grainger was nowhere to be seen. And off they went over the top and into the front line. One of the signal stations had been blown to smithereens and was a pancake of earth. Bodies all around him, Milne expertly joined up the telephone. Pressing the buzzer, he made contact with the colonel, glad to be alive. Milne recounted the story in his autobiography:

> Then with a sigh of utter content and thankfulness and the joy of living, I turned away from the telephone. And there behind me was Lance Corporal Grainger.
> 'What on earth are *you* doing here?' I said.
> He grinned sheepishly ...
> 'I thought I'd just like to come along, sir.'
> 'But *why*?' ...
> 'Well, sir, I thought I'd just like to be sure *you* were all right.'
> Which is the greatest tribute to Jane Austen that I have ever heard.[10]

Soon after this episode of Jane Austen in the trenches, Milne was invalided out of the Army. As the war came to an end, he began his career as one of the most successful playwrights of the age.

Milne's first intention for the honouring of his passion on stage was to write a play about the life of Jane Austen. But as he began work on the play, he began to see that he was in fact writing about Elizabeth Bennet. In his preface to the published play, Milne wrote about his change of heart:

> I began by telling myself proudly that I was the one dramatist in England who had not written a play about the Brontës; who, moreover, had no slightest wish to write a play about the Brontës; who, indeed, if ever he wrote that sort of play at all, could only want to write about the divine and incomparable Austen. Having allowed that thought a moment's lodgings in my mind, I was immediately at its mercy. The characters began to assemble on the stage: Mr and Mrs Austen, Cassandra, the cheery brothers, Uncle Leigh; and at her table in a modest corner, busy, over the chatter, at what the family would call 'Jane's writing', Miss Austen herself. Soon she will have to say something. What sort of a young woman is she? What will she have to say? And as soon as she had said it, I knew that it was just Miss Elizabeth Bennet speaking. So the play, then, must be about Elizabeth Bennet. It must in fact be a

dramatisation of *Pride and Prejudice*. Quite impossible, I decided at last, but considerable fun to try.[11]

Milne's play is a *tour de force*, as one might expect from the author of one of the funniest children's books ever written adapting the funniest of female authors. In his preface to the published text, Milne drew attention to the golden rules of dramatisation of novels. The dramatist should be guided by 'truth to the characters' (especially in the case of a beloved classic), but always remember that he is writing a play. Though Austen excelled in dramatic dialogue, Milne insists that the dramatist must 'please himself as to how much or how little of the original dialogue he uses'. 'The play must be written throughout as the dramatist would naturally write it, not as Miss Austen would have written it. That is to say, he must never ask himself: "would Jane Austen have made So and So say this?" But "would So and So have said it?"' This is the absolute key to the distinction between adaptations that succeed and those that fail: the test of every line of fresh dialogue is truth to the character, not truth to the original text. And this, of course, is something that Austen herself had learned from reading and seeing plays, whether by Shakespeare, Sheridan or the now forgotten female playwrights of the eighteenth century: be it in the dialogue of a novel, on stage or on screen, the characters must always maintain *consistency of voice*.

Milne added extra scenes where he felt it necessary. He was puzzled, for example, as to why Austen does not permit the reader to witness a conversation between Jane Bennet and Mr Bingley. Their romance takes place 'off stage':

It is strange that Miss Austen does not give us a single scene between Jane and Bingley. The dramatist cannot afford a similar reticence; for it is Bingley's attraction to Jane which sets the story moving. Bingley was 'lively' – we have Jane's word for it. At a dance, in the company of the girl he loved, a happy carefree Bingley might almost become a 'rattle'. I maintain that I am historically accurate in saying that he did become a rattle. At least there is no evidence to the contrary.

Thus, Milne reveals what Austen denies the reader: a scene between Jane and Mr Bingley, which fleshes out their characters and develops their burgeoning romance:

BINGLEY: I am the biggest fool at compliments. I think of them just too late.

JANE: But why should you wish to pay me compliments?

BINGLEY: I don't. I wish to talk very seriously to you about Tithes, my Lord Chatham and the Rotation of Crops. I want you to think to yourself: 'This is the most intelligent man I have ever spoken to in my life, he knows all about the rotation of tithes at Chatham, and one day he will stand for Parliament, and people will cry "Vote for Bingley!"' And all the time I want to talk to you like this I find myself thinking 'Her eyes, her hair, her expression, her smile' – and I am dumb. Miss Jane, as a prospective member of Parliament, can I rely upon you to vote for Bingley when the moment comes?

JANE: [*smiling*] I cannot quite see you in Parliament, sir.

BINGLEY: Nor I. And yet there must be bigger fools there, or else they wouldn't be there at all.

Another clever modification was to include the five daughters in the opening scene, which means that he can establish the different characters of the sisters efficiently:

MR BENNET: Kitty has no discretion in her coughs. She times them ill.

JANE: Do tell us, ma'am.

MARY: Pray tell us, mamma.

MRS BENNET: Well you must know Lady Lucas tells me that Netherfield is really taken at last by a handsome young man of large fortune from the north of England. He came down …

LYDIA: Did she see him? Is he *very* handsome?

MR BENNET: *All* young men with large fortunes are handsome, Lydia.

MRS BENNET: He came down in a chaise and four –

MR BENNET: In a chaise and four they are particularly handsome.

Milne elaborated upon the character of Mr Bennet, and emphasised the strong bond between father and daughter. It is striking that the final scene of the play is a touching one between father and daughter, not a romantic union between Elizabeth and Darcy. Darcy's character is more open than in the novel. After Elizabeth rejects his marriage proposal, he does not write her a letter explaining his actions, as in the novel, but speaks to her directly. Elizabeth, shocked to hear of Wickham's infamy, expresses her disbelief: 'I do not believe it! It is your jealousy which makes you say so … it is your story against his … horrible, horrible! I will *not* believe it.'[12]

Another of Milne's ground rules for adaptation was not to try to improve on Austen's dialogue, but to move seamlessly between the dramatist's voice and Austen's own: 'The two styles should be equal to each other, simply because they are equal to the same thing: namely, the way these actual people would have talked in those days, and in those situations.'[13] His command of the dialogue is so astonishing that there are moments when it's difficult to distinguish Austen from Milne. Here is Lizzy refusing to dance with Mr Darcy, in a speech that anticipates, brilliantly, her later refusal of his marriage proposal: 'No, Mr Darcy, you may not beg it. Let the refusal seem to come from yourself rather than from me, and your pride will be saved.'

Miss Elizabeth Bennet is faithful to the original, but witty and captivating in its own right. Milne's only egregious mistake was the inclusion of Mrs Norris, who is mentioned as an aunt to the sisters. When a friend spotted the error, Milne was mortified: 'Yes, Norris must have come from *Mansfield Park*. God knows how, I have been going hot and cold ever since. I knew I should make some fantastic mistake somewhere, and this is it.'[14]

On the very day that the play was finished, Milne was dismayed to read that a dramatised version of *Pride and Prejudice* was about to be produced on the New York stage:

Apparently it was Jane Austen who was now fashionable. However, there was still England. Should one hurry to get the play on with any cast that was available, or should one wait for the ideal Elizabeth, now unavailable? In the end the risk was taken; arrangements were made for the early autumn; the Elizabeth I had always wanted began to let her hair grow; the management, the theatre, the producer, all were there ... and at that moment the American version landed in London.[15]

An Australian writer called Helen Jerome had got there first: 28 October 1935 was the night that Harpo Marx attended a Philadelphia preview of Jerome's Broadway-bound dramatisation of *Pride and Prejudice*, which was subtitled 'a sentimental comedy in three acts'. The very next day, Harpo sent the following telegram to film producer Irving Thalberg in Hollywood: 'Just saw Pride and Prejudice. Stop. Swell show. Stop. Would be wonderful for Norma. Stop.'[16]

Production was about to begin in October, with Norma Shearer in the role of Elizabeth and Clark Gable in the role of Darcy, when the boy genius Thalberg suddenly died, and the film stalled. Meanwhile, Milne opened his *Miss Elizabeth Bennet* in Liverpool on 3 September 1936. He went to the opening night and made a speech 'in the absence of Miss Austen'.[17] Eighteen months later, the play opened in London but only for a short run at the People's Palace.

In Hollywood, MGM now decided that the role of Mr Darcy should be given to Laurence Olivier, rather than Gable. Olivier had achieved box-office success with *Wuthering Heights* and *Rebecca*. His dark, brooding looks and proud manner, they reasoned, would be perfect for Austen's Darcy. Olivier wanted to appear alongside his lover, Vivien Leigh, in the role of Elizabeth, but the studio, anxious to avoid a scandal, as Olivier was a married man, eventually decided on Greer Garson.[18]

The studio approached the renowned novelist Aldous Huxley, who was living in Hollywood, to co-write the screenplay with writer Jane Murfin. When war broke out, Huxley was reportedly anxious about being paid so handsomely while his 'family and friends were being starved and bombed in England'. He overcame his scruples and the film was a huge success during the early years of war. The advertising campaign announced: 'Bachelors Beware! Five Gorgeous Beauties are on a Madcap Manhunt'. The movie drew the largest weekly August audience in Radio City Music Hall's history.

The 1940 *Pride and Prejudice* set the mould for most of the Hollywood adaptations of the 1990s. The novel's romantic plot between Elizabeth and Darcy was given emphasis, costumes were elaborate (famously 'Hollywoodised' into Victorian frills rather than streamlined Regency clothes), and settings were sumptuous. It won an Academy Award for Art Direction.

The film was a sentimental and idealised vision of nineteenth-century England: it begins 'It happened in Old England ... in the village of Meryton.' Sequences were added, such as the archery scene with Elizabeth and Darcy, and some of the encounters were radically altered, such as the encounter between Lady Catherine and Elizabeth towards the end of the film. Rather than Lady Catherine doing her utmost to separate the lovers, she is seen to actively encourage the union. However, in contrast with A. A. Milne's seamlessly integrated added dialogue, the extra speeches sometimes have a wholly incongruous tone:

> LADY CATHERINE: She's right for you, Darcy. You were a spoiled child, and we don't want to go on spoiling you. What you need is a woman who can stand up to you. I think you've found her.
>
> ELIZABETH: You're very puzzling, Mr Darcy. At this moment, it's difficult to believe that you're so ... *proud*.
>
> DARCY: At this moment, it's difficult to believe that you're so ... *prejudiced*. Shall we not call it quits and start again?

The *New York Times* film critic praised the film as 'the most deliciously pert comedy of old manners, the most crisp and crackling satire in costume that we in this corner can remember ever having seen on the screen'. He also praised the two leads: 'Greer Garson as Elizabeth – "dear, beautiful Lizzie" – stepped right out of the book, or rather out of one's fondest imagination: poised, graceful, self-contained, witty, spasmodically stubborn and as lovely as a woman can be. Laurence Olivier is Darcy, that's all there is to it – the arrogant, sardonic Darcy whose pride went before a most felicitous fall.'[19]

For Huxley, it was a hack job. There is none of the astringency of his own novels of social satire such as *Crome Yellow* and *Antic Hay*. Helen Jerome had bequeathed Hollywood a version of Jane Austen as 'sentimental comedy in three acts'. Had the Milne adaptation been used instead, there might have been a better understanding of Austen as social satirist, verbal ironist and daughter of the muse of comedy as opposed to sentiment.

Back in England, Milne lamented his ill-luck, but the publication of his *Miss Elizabeth Bennet* was well received. And, when war broke out, it found a new life as a radio play. In November 1940, the play was broadcast on the Home Service with Celia Johnson in the role of Elizabeth Bennet. Then in March 1944, it was broadcast again as a special play on Forces radio, with Margaret Rutherford in the role of Mrs Bennet.[20]

Jane Austen's novels were clearly perceived as a morale booster, and an escape from the horrors of war. In the light of his experience on the Somme, Milne was duly gratified. A further example of Jane Austen's capacity to boost spirits during wartime was discovered by the American film critic Kenneth Turan, who was granted access to director Robert Z. Leonard's scrapbooks in the Motion Picture Academy library. Turan noticed a letter tucked away in a scrapbook from a fan in England, telling him that the Olivier/Garson *Pride and Prejudice* movie had produced much-needed comic relief and respite from the desperate realities of bombed-out Southampton:

> My husband is a Naval Officer and a few days ago he had one of his rare afternoons in port and a chance to visit the cinema. We went to see your film made from the book we know and love so well and to our delight were carried away for two whole hours of perfect enjoyment. Only once was I reminded of our war – when in a candle-lit room there was an uncurtained window and my husband whispered humorously, 'Look – they're not blacked out.'
>
> You may perhaps know that this city has suffered badly from air raids but we still have some cinemas left, and to see a packed audience enjoying *Pride and Prejudice* so much was most heartening. I do thank you very much as well as all the actors and actresses for your share in what has given so much pleasure to us.[21]

Milne's *Miss Elizabeth Bennet* succeeded as a play both on the stage and on the radio because, as an experienced dramatist, he instinctively understood that he should not be intimidated by the original version.

The best adaptations of Austen are those that, in Milne's words, reveal 'truth to character', without a slavish devotion to the purity of the text. Indeed, it was vital that he ensured his adaptation was intelligible to anyone who had not heard of *Pride and Prejudice*: 'To assume no special knowledge in an audience is the golden rule of play-writing.'[22]

The Austen film adaptations that work best are those that succeed as films in their own right. Patricia Rozema's audacious *Mansfield Park* (1999) eschews the heritage-style whimsy of the conventional period drama. Its deployment of feminist, gender and post-colonial themes nods to academic literary criticism of Austen, and provides a fascinating shadow story to this most complex of novels. Amy Heckerling's *Clueless* (1995) and Whit Stillman's *Love & Friendship* (2016) are two of the most creative and innovative adaptations: again, they eschew whimsy and sentimentalism. They work as films in their own right, they take risks, and yet they remain true to the spirit of the novels and the essence of the characters. They assume no special knowledge. In both films, the writer/director captures the comic brilliance of the original, the skilfulness of Austen's plotting and characterisation, her verbal dexterity, and the lack of sentimentality that imbues her novels.

Amy Heckerling made her directorial debut in 1982 with *Fast Times at Ridgemont High*, one of the best coming-of-age teen comedies of the modern era, with a script by Cameron Crowe and outstanding performances from a group of young, not yet famous actors including Sean Penn, Nicolas Cage, Jennifer Jason Leigh, Phoebe Cates, Eric Stoltz and Forest Whitaker. Dissatisfied with the quality of the scripts she was subsequently sent, Heckerling began writing her own. Her first 'written and directed by' credit came in 1989 with *Look Who's Talking*, featuring John Travolta, Kirstie Alley and a baby voiced by Bruce Willis. The voice-over from the baby's point of view revealed to Heckerling that it was possible to achieve a narrative equivalent of the novelist's ironising device of free indirect speech. Her next move was to put together this voiceover technique and the material of *Fast Times* – female friendship, coming-of-age, inter-generational conflict (youthful transgressions, uptight teachers), rock soundtrack. The result was *Clueless*. Released in July 1995, it was an immediate box-office hit, the 'sleeper' success of the year, and soon a cult movie spawning a spin-off television series and innumerable imitations. What the credits did not mention and the first wave of appreciative movie critics did not notice was that Heckerling's script was a close adaptation of *Emma* – transposed to the *Fast Times* setting of a Californian high school.

The plot and most of the characters are faithfully preserved, but Highbury is reinvented as modern-day Beverly Hills, home to the fabulously rich and famous. It retains the air of an English village riven with petty jealousies, competitive consumer consumption, superiority complexes and gossipy cliques. Heckerling reveals the intricate workings of the contemporary American class system (based on beauty, wealth and celebrity) with all the finesse of Austen's take on the gentry of early nineteenth-century England.

The heroine Cher (Alicia Silverstone, nineteen years old and in only her second film) is good-looking, clever and rich. She is at the top of the pecking order in her rarefied, though confined, world. As suggested earlier, the key to *Emma* is Austen's use of free indirect speech, so that she can ironise her flawed heroine, which is difficult to achieve in the genre of film. *Clueless* circumvents this by the use of a first-person voice-over, with which Heckerling had experimented in *Look Who's Talking*. It is clear from the opening that Cher/Emma is being ironised. Her lack of self-knowledge and her skewed perspective are made evident from the first two minutes of the film.

It begins with a montage of glamorous, gorgeous young people, shopping at Tiffany's, swimming in luxurious outdoor pools and driving expensive cars. Cher's voiceover says: 'OK, so you're probably going, "Is this like a Noxzema commercial or what?" But seriously, I actually have a way normal life for a teenage girl. I get up, brush my teeth and I pick out my school clothes.' Noxzema is a cleansing cream, intended to make the skin look young and fresh, a point reinforced by the Supergrass song that soon follows on the soundtrack, with its refrain 'We are young! We run green! Keep our teeth nice and clean!'

Cher then programs her sartorial choices into a computer, which matches up the perfect outfit from a selection of exquisite designer clothes. We thus know instantly that she has a skewed sense of reality; she assumes that everyone has the same lifestyle and privileges. She does not have 'a way normal life'.

Nevertheless, her perfect Hollywood life is not all it seems: 'seemed', that key word in our introduction to Emma Woodhouse. Bored and frustrated, Cher is consumed by matchmaking and 'makeovers'. She sees her opportunity for the ideal makeover when Tai, a Latina girl from a deprived background, allows herself to be transformed by stylish clothes, cosmetics and hairstyle into a Beverly Hills high school girl, a clone of Cher herself.

Cher's catchphrase for her makeovers is 'project'. It's a word that seems contemporary, but it's actually used by Austen in *Emma* on several occasions: 'Emma's *project* of forgetting Mr Elton for a while'; 'It was the discovery of what she was doing; of this very *project* of hers'; 'Your views for Harriet are best known to yourself; but as you make no secret of your love of matchmaking, it is fair to suppose that views, and plans, and *projects*'. In the novel, matchmaking and projects (in Cher's parlance 'makeovers') are inextricably linked, but in *Clueless*, Heckerling breathes new life into the word and reveals her close reading of the original text.

Heckerling is astute in her understanding that Cher must be a sympathetic, indeed lovable, character. Despite her flaws, she is a devoted daughter; she is kind, witty and has a good heart. Above all, *Clueless* shines because of Heckerling's mastery of rapier-quick comic dialogue. She has learned from Austen the art that Austen learned from the comic theatre:

TAI: Cher, you're a virgin?
CHER: You say that like it's a bad thing.
DIONE: Besides, the PC term is 'hymenally challenged.'
CHER: You see how picky I am about my shoes and they only go on
 my feet.

There is the joke that also makes a point about Tai/Harriet's lack of education:

TAI: Do you think she's pretty?
CHER: No, she's a full-on Monet.
TAI: What's a monet?

CHER: It's like a painting, see? From far away, it's OK, but up close, it's a big old mess.

There is the art of repartee:

AMBER: Ms Stoeger, my plastic surgeon, doesn't want me doing any activity where balls fly at my nose.
DIONE: Well, there goes your social life.

And the affectionate put-down of Cher/Emma by the Knightley character:

CHER: I want to do something for humanity.
JOSH: How about sterilisation?

Heckerling's inventive use of teen jargon ('buggin'', 'Baldwin', 'Betty', 'cake boy' 'Boinkfest', 'As if!') is combined with satirical pseudo-intellectual academic jargon: when Cher's best friend Dione chastises her teenage boyfriend for addressing her as 'woman', he replies: 'Street slang is an increasingly valid form of expression. Most of the feminine pronouns do have mocking but not necessarily misogynistic undertones.'

Clueless is as much a satire on teen movies as it is an homage to *Emma*. Few people, at the time of the release, realised that the film was indeed an adaptation of a Jane Austen novel. The only clue is that the Mr Elton figure is called Elton. It works brilliantly (as A. A. Milne would say) in its own right. But it perfectly captures Austen's interest in class, hierarchy, social status, social mobility, manners, and, at its heart, the film has a moral imperative. Cher learns that before she can help others (or inter-fere with their lives, and meddle with their happiness) she needs to trans-form herself: 'I decided I needed a complete makeover, except this time, I'd *makeover my soul.*'

It is her willingness to accept that she is wrong and to make amends that redeems her. Milnean 'truth to character' is upheld throughout. Here is Cher on American isolationism, showing her essential goodness of heart:

So like, right now for example. The Haitians need to come to America. But some people are all, 'What about the strain on our resources?' Well it's like when I had this garden party for my father's birthday, right? I put R.S.V.P. 'cause it was a sit-down dinner. But some people came that like did not R.S.V.P. I was like totally buggin'. I had to haul ass to the kitchen, redistribute the food, and squish in extra place settings. But by the end of the day it was, like, the more the merrier. And so if the government could just get to the kitchen, rearrange some things, we could certainly party with the Haitians. And in conclusion may I please remind you it does not say R.S.V.P. on the Statue of Liberty.

If ever an Austen adaptation film set out to shock its viewers from their complacency and vapid sentimentality, then Patricia Rozema's 1999 *Mansfield Park* was the one. In perhaps the cleverest of all overt Austen adaptations, Rozema set out her goal firmly from the beginning, saying that *Mansfield Park*, which she wrote and directed, was not a Jane Austen film: 'It's a Patricia Rozema film. My job as an artist is to provide a fresh view.'[23] Which was primarily that this is a novel about the corrupt spoils of slavery, though Rozema throws in some incest and lesbianism for good measure. Harold Pinter – an inspired piece of casting – portrays Sir Thomas Bertram as a sadistic patriarch who takes an unhealthy interest in his female slaves.

The novel is the least loved of the Austen canon due to the dullness of its heroine, Fanny Price, who has always divided readers and critics. That was true even among Austen's own family. Her pious Christian brother, Frank, thought Fanny a 'delightful character', but her niece Anna 'could not bear Fanny'. Her mother 'thought Fanny insipid' and her nephew George 'disliked Fanny (interested by nobody but Mary Crawford)'.[24]

Perhaps the long-held reluctance to film *Mansfield Park* was precisely bound up with the essential problem of depicting a dull heroine set against a sexy, witty anti-heroine. In an interview about her adaptation, Rozema described Fanny Price as 'annoying', 'not fully drawn' and 'too slight and retiring and internal'.[25] Rozema's modification was to conflate the character of Fanny Price with the author herself, drawing upon Jane Austen's juvenilia and letters to add colour and spirit to the unpopular heroine.

Given that the young Fanny Price's respite from loneliness, bullying at the hands of Mrs Norris and homesickness for her Portsmouth family is the conduit of writing letters home, then this seems to be a legitimate modification. Furthermore, Austen's mature Fanny Price becomes an avid reader. Her love of books proves to be the most durable and sustainable of all her relationships. A turning point in Fanny's character is when she introduces her sister Susan to the pleasures of a good book and the delights of a circulating library: a lifesaver for both of them.

Rozema's Fanny Price is no shrinking violet trembling at the sound of her uncle's footsteps in the passage, as she is in Austen's novel. It remains to be seen whether it is possible for there to be a faithful dramatisation of *Mansfield Park*, which dares to portray a diffident, anxious heroine who nevertheless displays an iron will. In this regard, Fanny Price is the most interesting of Austen's heroines and the one whom the conventions of modern cinema and television are least well qualified to serve. It was striking that when ITV jumped on the Austen bandwagon with a series of adaptations in 2007, the *Northanger Abbey* with Felicity Jones perfectly caught the naivety of Catherine Morland (not least by playing her off against Carey Mulligan's glorious selfish Isabella Thorpe), whereas the *Mansfield Park* failed because even as fine an actor as Billie Piper failed to capture the simultaneous strength and weakness of Fanny Price.

The problem with Rozema's depiction of Fanny as a young woman who is as spirited and sexy as Mary Crawford was that it lost something vital that Austen was trying to explore: the quiet, watchful, moral, bookish girl who becomes indispensable. Austen is interested in characters who fall in love slowly, stealthily. She is always suspicious of the conventional, sentimental idea of love at first sight. That is why the truest adaptations of her novels are those that cut against the grain of Hollywood convention. Rozema certainly does that, especially in the Sapphic dimension, which owes more to her own earlier films than to any warrant in the novel – though it does nod to a notorious essay of that key Austen year of 1995, in which the lesbian literary theorist Terry Castle proposed in a review of a new edition of Austen's letters that, in the light of her deep affection for her sister Cassandra, the novelist's closest emotional attachments were female, an interpretation that some shocked commentators translated into 'Jane Austen may have been gay'.[26] But the refiguring of Fanny comes at the expense of Austen's very deliberate intention to create a heroine who was the opposite of Miss Elizabeth Bennet.

Mansfield Park is not a coming-of-age novel in any conventional sense. It is an ensemble piece of a group of young people on the brink of adulthood. Edmund Bertram loves Mary Crawford, who makes a play first for Tom Bertram before transferring her attentions to Edmund, who is beloved by Fanny Price, who is loved by Henry Crawford. Sisters Julia and Maria Bertram both love Henry Crawford but Maria is engaged to Rushworth (whom she doesn't love). Henry and Maria have an adulterous affair, and Fanny and Edmund are finally united. In many respects this is a novel about ennui and boredom. Stuck in the country with nothing much to do except fall in and out of love, the group try various schemes to alleviate the hopelessness that seems to envelope them all. Despite it being written at the beginning of a new century, there is a *fin-de-siècle* nihilism that suffuses the novel. Rozema's interpretation captures some of this darkness.

The critic David Monaghan argues that viewers should approach Rozema's *Mansfield Park* as 'an independent work of art rather than an adaptation of Austen's novel'.[27] However, Monaghan takes issue with Rozema's depiction of Fanny's 'enlightened attitudes towards issues of gender, class and race'. He sees this as anachronistic (viewing the past through 'modern values') and as trendy liberal humanism that seeks to make this awkward heroine more acceptable to a modern audience. This seems puzzling as both Jane Austen and her heroine Fanny Price do indeed share enlightened attitudes towards gender, class and race. *Mansfield Park* celebrates meritocracy above the inherited values and privileges of the landed gentry. It is the hard-working, ill-educated lower-class Price children who are the victors in this story. Fanny Price exercises her right of refusal in the marriage market (limited power it may be, but it's effective) and she will not be coerced into marrying Henry Crawford, no matter how good a match.

Nevertheless, as Monaghan explains, 'In the England depicted by Rozema (and indeed by Austen), a woman was made extremely vulnerable by her sexuality'. Those such as Maria Bertram who choose to act on libidinous impulses are ostracised. That Rozema's Fanny Price catches

Maria and Henry *in flagrante delicto* is a stark reminder of her own vulnerability: 'The sight of Maria, naked and exposed to shame and ridicule, is all the evidence Fanny needs of what could well have been her own fate had she let herself fall prey to Henry's undoubted charms.'[28]

Monaghan points out the repeated presence of caged birds in the background of interior shots involving female characters. One of the most memorable scenes in the adaptation comes with Henry's arrangement of a choreographed flock of doves as part of his seduction of Fanny in Portsmouth.[29] Then at the film's close, a flock of wild starlings swoop upwards above the house into the sky. This cinematic device is a perceptive and brilliant reference to female enslavement and oppression. In the novel, Maria Bertram enters into a lucrative but loveless engagement with the foolish Rushworth. In the extensive grounds of his estate, Sotherton Court, she looks out at an iron gate and quotes a passage from Laurence Sterne's *A Sentimental Journey*: 'I cannot get out, as the Starling said.' This is one of the rare instances when the authorial sympathy shifts to Maria. She wants to get married to escape her home and her oppressive father, but is merely exchanging one form of slavery for another. She feels trapped and oppressed, just like the starling in the cage, longing to get out (Sterne makes a reference to the Bastille prison in the same passage). Maria is enslaved by her choices, and her desire for status and power, but also by a culture that, in the first place, views her as a commodity.

For Rozema, another kind of enslavement underpins her adaptation. She wanted to use the film to expose the brutal horrors of the slave trade that bankrolls the lifestyle of the Bertrams. Fanny herself is not exempt from this. A pivotal scene (again, with no source in the novel) is that in which Fanny finds Tom's portfolio of sketches of his time in Antigua on his father's slave plantation. There are drawings of white men raping black women, slaves being tortured and Sir Thomas whipping a slave. Another sketch depicts Sir Thomas forcing a female slave to perform a sexual act. It's a shocking and disquieting scene, all the more powerful when we know that this was a common occurrence among slave owners.[30]

If the backdrop to the novel of *Mansfield Park* is the dark story of the slave trade, then Rozema's film is a *tour de force*. We are never permitted to escape its all-pervading influence. The character of Sir Thomas, played to extremely sinister effect by Harold Pinter, is given extra lines, making clear his views on the female slaves: 'The mulattos are in general well-shaped and the women especially well-featured. I have one – so easy and graceful in her movements and intelligent as well. But strangely, you know, two mulattos will never have children. They are of the mule-kind in that respect.'

Unlike so many of the more conventional adaptations, such as Ang Lee's *Sense and Sensibility*, Rozema eschews the sentimental. This is not the world of heritage Jane Austen. This Georgian country house is not a haven of beauty and elegance. It is no Pemberley in the guise of Chatsworth, as used for the BBC's *Pride and Prejudice*. It's barren and bare, crumbling under the weight of its uneasy past. It's a house built on the blood of slaves. At the end of the film, Fanny and Edmund depart to the parsonage and not to the house with all its corrupt associations. This is not a film for the Austen purists, but it's a powerful and unsettling depiction of this most dark and complex of novels.

For Rozema, the central problem of adapting *Mansfield Park* for a modern audience was the passivity of its heroine. How does one make Fanny Price interesting when all eyes, like those of Austen's nephew George, are on Mary Crawford? Is it possible for a modern audience to like Fanny Price? Whit Stillman, who may lay claim to have been the first writer and director of what has been called the post-heritage genre of Austen adaptation,[31] explores this idea in his superb coming-of-age drama, *Metropolitan* (1990).

The film, a contemporary refashioning of *Mansfield Park*, set in Manhattan's Upper East Side and the Hamptons, has at its centre a shy, moral heroine (Audrey Rouget), who is obsessed by Jane Austen. As in *Mansfield Park*, the group of intelligent, well-bred and educated young people on the verge of adulthood are mainly left to their own devices, without the guiding influence of their parents. The parents (and step-parents) are perceived as feckless and selfish, giving no moral or ethical guidance. It's a brilliant depiction of the manners and mores of upper-class WASP society.

In *Metropolitan*, the young people, who are all first-year college students, are on winter break during the Manhattan debutante season.

The boys form a group calling themselves the Urban Haute Bourgeoisie (UHBs), while the girls form the Sally Fowler Rat Pack. Sally's is the apartment where the highly articulate young people converge after the dinners and dances to discuss issues such as the uncertainties of the future, and questions of class and morality.

The narrative is developed through the eyes of Tom, a cynical, poor but clever outsider accepted into the elite group. Audrey is the moral compass and she falls in love with Tom, while he is still smitten with Serena Slocum, the beautiful, witty and amoral girl, modelled on Mary Crawford. At one point in the film, Audrey and Tom have a debate about Fanny Price as a virtuous heroine, quoting from Lionel Trilling's influential essay on the novel:

> I think he's very strange. He says that 'nobody' could like the heroine of *Mansfield Park*. I like her. Then he goes on and on about how 'we' modern people, today, with 'our' modern attitudes 'bitterly resent' *Mansfield Park* because its heroine is virtuous. What's wrong with a novel having a virtuous heroine? Finally, it turns out he really likes *Mansfield Park*, so what's the point?[32]

Tom agrees with Lionel Trilling about the absurdity of the notion that there is something morally wrong about the young people putting on a play. When Audrey presses him on the issue, he admits that he hasn't in fact read the novel, only the criticism: 'I don't read novels. I prefer good literary criticism – that way you get both the novelists' ideas and the critics' thinking.'

The young people, bored and restless, decide to play a game of 'Truth or Dare'. Audrey refuses to play and as a result is isolated from the group, the equivalent of the *Lovers' Vows* episode in the novel. Unpleasant truths are revealed and the group is irrevocably fractured. Audrey leaves Manhattan for the Hamptons in the company of rich, handsome womaniser Rick von Sloneker, the Henry Crawford figure. While she is there, Tom realises that Audrey is the girl he really loves and sets out to rescue her. The film ends with them hitchhiking back to New York.

Stillman's debut film received an Oscar nomination for Best Original Screenplay. He claimed that *Metropolitan* sparked Hollywood's interest in Jane Austen, and he was asked to direct Emma Thompson's *Sense and Sensibility*, but declined after he read the script.[33] But he wasn't finished with Austen. In 2016, he wrote and directed *Love & Friendship*, a period drama based on Austen's novella *Lady Susan*. But this being Whit Stillman, it is not a conventional Austen period drama. There is no probing of the human heart in this adaptation. It's all about the money. It's an audacious, witty, fast-paced paean to Austen's great comic powers, which restores her to her burlesque and satirical roots. Viewers wanting the Austen of romance and sentiment will not find her in this film. This is not the safe, cosy Regency spinster restoring us to a comforting world of gentility and manners. This is the 'sick and wicked' Austen of the letters: the 'mad beast' who 'cannot help it'. Austen's juvenilia is full of arch manipulators such as Lady Susan, though few have her 'diabolical genius' and charm.

'Love & Friendship' is not of course the title of *Lady Susan*, which Austen herself left untitled – only when it was published after her death was the manuscript named for its anti-heroine. Stillman has borrowed his title from another of Austen's early comic works, in order, very cleverly, to echo *Pride and Prejudice* and *Sense and Sensibility*.

The story revolves around the machinations of Lady Susan, a *femme fatale* in the Mary Crawford model, except that, unlike Mary Crawford, she is allowed both to play the game and win the game. The game is the marriage market, and Lady Susan (Kate Beckinsale) seeks a rich husband for both herself and her (dull) daughter, Frederica (Morfydd Clark). Stillman's relish for Lady Susan, Austen's most naughty, clever and sexy heroine, is evident. She is better than all the men around her, because she is more intelligent and resourceful. She is self-aware, selfish and not self-deluded. She wreaks havoc on those around her, and is gloriously unrepentant. Her beauty, style and grace serve her as currency in the Georgian marriage market, but if she's a commodity then she will play the game her own way, breaking the rules from the inside, along the way. She is a magnificent monster, who imposes her will on her world, but also a liberated woman in an era and culture where women are usually restricted. She's like the bad girls in Austen's juvenilia who refuse to be good daughters, good sisters, good wives. She defies social convention not only by her pursuit of men, but by her refusal to accept the norms of motherhood. She delights in being a bad mother: and is all the more refreshing for it. She is indeed the heroine and not the victim of her own life. *Love & Friendship* feels like a film that celebrates women.

Kate Beckinsale (who twenty years earlier played Emma Woodhouse in Andrew Davies's rather flat 1996 television dramatisation for the BBC) is perfect casting for the role, combining beauty and wit with a calculating, predatory cynicism. She does, of course, have all the best lines. Of her best friend's companion she quips: 'What a mistake you made in marrying that man! Too old to be governable, too young to die.' And, 'Facts are horrid things,' she sighs after deflecting an assault on her reputation. When a young rake solicits her on a street, she threatens him with a whipping.

Part of the problem with Austen's incomplete novella is that Lady Susan dominates the narrative. There are few counterbalancing figures of the sort that create such vital foils in her finished novels. Stillman gets around this problem by fleshing out some of the other characters. He builds up the role of Lady Susan's companion, Alicia Johnson, who in his film is American, an opportunity for some colonial jokes from Lady Susan. She describes her friend as an American 'who has none of the uncouthness but all of the candour' of that young country. The colonists who have recently won their independence are 'American ingrates'. Lady Susan confesses her schemes to Alicia, to put the audience in the picture.

The film is visually stunning, juxtaposing town and country brilliantly. In tribute to the epistolary form of *Lady Susan*, Stillman creates intertitles that introduce his characters, in the manner of a silent movie. The contents of letters are also flashed up on the screen. Like A. A. Milne in *Miss Elizabeth Bennet*, Stillman seamlessly interweaves his own masterful comic dialogue with Jane Austen's. After shooting the film, he penned his own tie-in version of *Lady Susan*, rewriting it from the point of view of a minor character whom we never meet. The narrative voice is that of Rufus Martin-Colonna de Cesari-Rocca, nephew to Sir James Martin, who hopes that his book will rehabilitate the reputation of Lady Susan. Austen is the unkind and unfair 'spinster Authoress' who has impugned Lady Susan. Stillman explained in an interview that the idea for Rufus came from the real life character of Austen's stuffy and rather dim nephew, Edward Austen-Leigh, who wrote the first life of Austen and saw *Lady Susan* into print in 1871.[34] This is a witty and Austen-like joke.

Stillman uses many of Austen's wonderful phrases: for example, 'the Vernon milkiness' to describe the sappiness of the Vernon family, whom Lady Susan is out to destroy. But he adds plenty of his own: 'Partial truth is Falsehood's fiercest bodyguard.' There is a wonderful exchange between Lady Susan and her young toy-boy lover, where she is trying to persuade him that her meek and dutiful daughter is a selfish rebel: 'I would never represent my daughter as worse than her actions show her to be.' That is a sentence truly worthy of Jane Austen's barbed verbal economy.

Stillman's deft literary interpolations and command of voice and irony actually improve on the original. It's the advice that A. A. Milne gave in his preface to *Miss Elizabeth Bennet*: don't try to improve on a Jane Austen sentence, and if you are adding extra lines, write what you think the character might say, not what you think Jane Austen would say.

Critics described Stillman's film as being like an undiscovered Oscar Wilde, revealing a different aspect to Jane Austen, far more risqué, more dangerous than anything in the line of costume dramas and sentimental romances descended from the old Hollywood *Pride and Prejudice*. Stillman's vision is far more true to Austen's comic powers than many of the other period dramas. There's a comic exuberance and joy that restores Austen to herself.

If Jane Austen were alive today, she'd probably be appalled by the movie adaptations of her books. She would be baffled by the fact that the majority of films emphasise the romantic aspect of her novels, when her intention was to subvert and undermine the romantic. Perhaps she would be vexed that her comic genius, and precise social satire, have been subsumed by Regency frocks, beautiful houses and impeccably landscaped gardens. Though the performances in Ang Lee's *Sense and Sensibility* were outstanding, the film's insistence on a highly idealistic presentation of romantic love ultimately promulgates and vindicates precisely the values that the novel satirises.

The adaptations and spin-offs that succeed best – *Miss Elizabeth Bennet*, *Clueless*, *Metropolitan* and *Love & Friendship* – do so because they stand up as works of art in their own right, without requiring the spectator to have any prior knowledge of the original work. Staying true to the spirit of Austen, A. A. Milne, Amy Heckerling and Whit Stillman show how uproariously comic she is, and draw attention to her careful manipulation of character and plot. They do this almost instinctively because they are themselves such brilliant writers of comic dialogue and exponents of the great tradition of comedy of manners. Their union with Jane Austen is a marriage not of convenience but of perfection.

Exits and entrances, great comic types, the move from high to low, supreme skill in comic dialogue that allows characters to reveal themselves through the words they speak, narrative structure in the form of scenes with climactic theatrical 'set-pieces': all these Austen devices, which this book has explored, were derived from her immersion in the great tradition of English drama from Shakespeare to Sheridan to Hannah Cowley and Elizabeth Inchbald. That is why the novels are natural candidates for 'revisioning' in the modern dramatic medium of film. The television sitcom and Hollywood romantic comedies are our equivalents of the theatrical comedies to which Jane Austen and her original readers flocked in London and Bath. The Comic Muse passed from those glorious playhouses to Austen's playful pen, and from her it has been passed onto the screen by way of such modern classics as *Clueless*.

As for the more conventional adaptations, they are above all excellent gateways to the novels. They can enhance our appreciation of Austen's comic genius, but we should not forget that she chose the genre of the novel, becoming one of its chief apologists and transforming the art of English fiction into something entirely original. Ultimately, the value of the direct dramatisations such as Emma Thompson's *Sense and Sensibility* screenplay and Andrew Davies's *Pride and Prejudice* television script was that they introduced new readers to the novels, and sent those who had already read Austen back to the pleasures and rewards of re-reading her.

Notes

Introduction
1. [Richard Whately], 'Modern Novels: *Northanger Abbey and Persuasion*', *Quarterly Review*, 24 (1821), p. 362.
2. In reviews of 1847 and 1851, George Henry Lewes cited an 1843 essay by Thomas Macaulay for the phrase. Macaulay does not use the precise wording, but does describe Austen as second only to Shakespeare. See *Jane Austen: The Critical Heritage*, ed. B. C. Southam, 2 vols (London: Routledge and Kegan Paul, 1968–87), i, pp. 122–25 and 130.
3. George Lewes, 'The Novels of Jane Austen', *Blackwood's Magazine*, 86 (1859), p. 105.
4. [Thomas Lister], *Edinburgh Review*, 53 (1830), p. 449.
5. Henry Austen, 'Biographical Notice', *NA*, p. 7.
6. Caroline Austen, *My Aunt Jane Austen: A Memoir* (Winchester: Sarsen Press, 1991), p. 10.
7. Lewes, 'Novels of Austen', p. 105.
8. In an especially influential essay, Lionel Trilling made the *Lovers' Vows* debacle the starting-point for an argument that hostility to role-playing was crucial to Austen's vision of the integrity of the individual. Trilling, 'Mansfield Park', in *The Opposing Self* (London: Secker and Warburg, 1955), pp. 206–30. In particular, Trilling singles out 'the fear that the impersonation of a bad or inferior character will have a harmful effect upon the impersonator, that, indeed, the impersonation of any other self will diminish the integrity of the self' (p. 218). In a later study, Trilling also compares Plato's moral objection to acting with Rousseau's, suggesting that it encourages a falsifying of the self and a weakening of the fabric of society. See Lionel Trilling, *Sincerity and Authenticity* (London: Oxford University Press, 1972), pp. 64–79.
9. Its dramatic elements are, however, ably discussed by Claude Rawson in his introduction to the World's Classics edition of the novel (Oxford: Oxford University Press, 1990).
10. The most influential reading along these 'conservative' lines is Marilyn Butler, *Jane Austen and the War of Ideas* (Oxford: Clarendon Press, 1975).
11. See Henry James, *The Art of the Novel*, ed. R. P. Blackmur (New York and London: Scribners, 1947), p. 110.

1: Private Theatricals

1. See Sybil Rosenfeld, *Temples of Thespis: Some Private Theatres and Theatricals in England and Wales, 1700–1820* (London: The Society for Theatre Research, 1978), p. 11.

2. Barrymore had employed Cox, the carpenter to Covent Garden, to erect his theatre, which was described by the *London Chronicle* as a model of Vanbrugh's King's Theatre in the Haymarket. Its seating capacity was more likely 400. See Anthony Pasquin, *The Life of the Late Earl of Barrymore: Including a History of the Wargrave Theatricals* (London, 1793), pp. 15–16; *Temples of Thespis*, pp. 16–33. See also Evelyn Howe, 'Amateur Theatre in Georgian England', *History Today*, 20 (1970), pp. 695–703; and George Holbert Tucker, *Jane Austen: The Woman* (New York: St Martin's Press, 1994), pp. 87–88.

3. See Gillian Russell, *The Theatres of War: Performance, Politics, and Society, 1793–1815* (Oxford: Clarendon Press, 1995), pp. 122–30. Amanda Vickery, *The Gentleman's Daughter: Women's Lives in Georgian England* (New Haven and London: Yale University Press, 1998), pp. 235–36.

4. See *Theatres of War*, pp. 122–28.

5. See Sybil Rosenfeld, 'Jane Austen and Private Theatricals', *Essays and Studies*, 15 (1962), pp. 40–51.

6. In 1770 Fanny Burney had objected to performing in the 'shocking' farce *Miss in her Teens*, but in 1771 she was happy to perform scenes from Colley Cibber's *The Careless Husband* in front of a small audience. See Fanny Burney, *The Early Journals and Letters of Fanny Burney*, ed. Lars E. Troide, 3 vols (Oxford: Clarendon Press, 1988), i, pp. 116, 161–63, 171; ii, pp. 238–48.

7. Family tradition records that the plays were presented either in the dining room or the outside barn. See *Jane Austen: A Family Record*, by William Austen-Leigh and Richard Arthur Austen-Leigh, revised and enlarged by Deirdre Le Faye (London: The British Library, 1989; repr. 1993), p. 43. See also George Holbert Tucker, 'Amateur Theatricals at Steventon', in *The Jane Austen Handbook: With a Dictionary of Jane Austen's Life and Works*, ed. J. David Grey (London: Athlone, 1986), pp. 1–5.

8. The collected verses of James Austen, including his prologues and epilogues, were copied out by James Edward Austen-Leigh, c. 1834–40. Two copies exist, with some slight differences in content and wording, in the Austen-Leigh archive at the Hampshire Record Office and at Chawton House.

9. Hampshire Record Office, Austen-Leigh Archive, James Austen's verses, copied by James Edward Austen-Leigh, 23 M93/60/3/2.

10. Strikingly, the phrase 'Love and Friendship' (the title of one of Austen's early burlesques) appears in one of Siward's speeches:

    Alas! it rives my soul
    To see the tender bonds of amity
    Thus torn asunder by the very means
    I fondly thought for ever would unite them;

And the fair structure, which my hopes had raised,
Of love and friendship, in a moment shrunk
From its weak base, and buried all in ruin.

See Elizabeth Inchbald, *The Modern Theatre*, 10 vols (London, 1811), vi, p. 43.

11. Hampshire Record Office, James Austen's verses, 23M93/60/3/2.
12. The prologue begins with James's imploring indulgence from his friends and ends with a similar plea to the 'blooming fair' members of the audience.
13. *A Family Record*, p. 46.
14. Claire Tomalin, *Jane Austen: A Life* (London: Viking, 1997), p. 40.
15. Hampshire Record Office, 23M93/60/3/2.
16. Hampshire Record Office, Austen-Leigh Archive, Eliza de Feuillide's Letters, 1790s to 1830s, 23M93/M1, letter 21, from Eliza de Feuillide to Philadelphia Walter, 17 January 1786, on microfiche. Letters are sequentially numbered and subsequent references will be numbered and dated.
17. *A Family Record*, pp. 63–64.
18. R. A. Austen-Leigh, *Austen Papers, 1704–1856* (London: Spottiswoode, 1942), p. 126.
19. *A Family Record*, p. 57.
20. Ibid., p. 58.
21. Ibid.
22. Hampshire Record Office, letter 26, 16 November 1787.
23. Ibid.
24. Hampshire Record Office, letter 27, 28 November 1787.
25. Ibid.
26. Ibid.
27. Claire Tomalin observes: 'It seems that Eliza finally got her chance to play Miss Titupp, and to say the lines which reflected well on her own unsatisfactory marriage: "We must marry, you know, because other people of fashion marry; but I should think very meanly of myself, if, after I was married, I should feel the least concern about my husband". *Jane Austen: A Life*, p. 56. See also *Bon Ton: or High Life Above Stairs*, in *The Plays of David Garrick*, ed. Gerald M. Berkowitz, 4 vols (New York and London: Garland, 1981), ii, p. 2.
28. *The Wonder: A Woman Keeps a Secret*, in *The Plays of Susanna Centlivre*, ed. Richard C. Frushell, 3 vols (New York and London: Garland, 1982), iii, p. 8.
29. Marilyn Butler describes *The Wonder* as 'the only unequivocally feminist work we know Austen knew', arguing that this was the play that Austen covertly used in *Mansfield Park*, because her choice of *Lovers' Vows* with its plot feature 'the woman's proposal of marriage' mirrored that of *The Wonder*. However, Butler's contention that Austen disapproved of this 'outright challenge to the masculine prerogative' flies in the face of everything that she was exposed to at Steventon. See Jane Austen, *Mansfield Park*, ed. James Kinsley, with a new introduction by Marilyn Butler (Oxford: Oxford University Press, 1990), pp. xxi–xxv.

30. Hampshire Record Office, 23M93/60/3/2.
31. See *The British Theatre: or A Collection of Plays ... with Biographical and Critical Remarks by Mrs Inchbald* (London, 1808), vol. vi.
32. See Q. D. Leavis, 'A Critical Theory of Jane Austen's Writing', *Scrutiny*, 10 (1941–42), pp. 114–42.
33. James Edward Austen-Leigh, *A Memoir of Jane Austen*, ed. R. W. Chapman (Oxford: Clarendon Press, 1926), p. 49.
34. See Butler's introduction to the Oxford edition, p. xxiii.
35. Hampshire Record Office, 23M93/60/3/2.
36. See *A Family Record*, p. 63.
37. *The Sultan: or A Peep into the Seraglio*, in *The Plays of Isaac Bickerstaffe*, ed. Peter A. Tasch, 3 vols (New York and London: Garland, 1981), iii, p. 13.
38. Hampshire Record Office, 23M93/60/3/2.
39. The private theatricals staged by the Burneys were *Tom Thumb* and *The Way to Keep Him*. Burney's niece took the part of Tom Thumb: 'The meaning & energy with which this sweet Child spoke, was really wonderful; we had all done our best in giving her instructions, & she had profitted with a facility & good sense that, at her age, I do believe to be unequalled.' See *The Early Journals and Letters of Fanny Burney*, ii, p. 246. In the public theatres the part of Tom Thumb was often played by child actors, 'sometimes girls and sometimes as young as five, who would have spoken the heroic bombast with high-pitched voices': see Peter Lewis, *Fielding's Burlesque Drama: Its Place in the Tradition* (Edinburgh: Edinburgh University Press, 1987), p. 119. Jane Austen would have been thirteen when it was performed at Steventon.
40. In a letter to her nephew, James Edward, Austen asks him to thank his father for a present of pickled cucumbers and quotes Lady Bell Bloomer's phrase, 'tell him what you will'. See *Letters*, p. 323.
41. Hampshire Record Office, 23M93/M1, letter 30, 11 February 1789.
42. There is a discrepancy in the dating of James's epilogue for *The Sultan*, which he dates January 1790, though the evidence points to 1789. The Cooper cousins came to Steventon for the Christmas of 1788–89, and in February 1789 Eliza wrote to Philadelphia Walter with news of the performances of *The Sultan* and *High Life Below Stairs*.
43. See Margaret Anne Doody, 'Jane Austen's Reading', in *The Jane Austen Handbook*, p. 351.
44. In writing about the life of Henry IV, Austen parodies Goldsmith's bowdlerising style: 'his son the Prince of Wales came and took away the crown; whereupon the King made a long speech, for which I must refer the Reader to Shakespear's Plays, & the Prince made a still longer' (*MW*, p. 139).
45. See Chapman's index of allusions in his edition of *NA & P*, pp. 317–29.
46. See David Gilson, *A Bibliography of Jane Austen* (Oxford: Clarendon Press, 1982), pp. 438–39.
47. William Hayley, *Poems and Plays*, 6 vols (London, 1785).
48. Ibid., vi, p. 256.
49. Ibid., vi, p. 254.
50. James Austen, *The Loiterer*, 2 vols (Oxford, 1789–90), no. ix, pp. 4–7.

51. Ibid., pp. 6–7.
52. *The Children's Friend: Translated from the French of Mr Berquin by Lucas Williams*, 6 vols (London, 1793), preface in vol. 1 (subsequent quotations also from this preface).
53. Ibid., v, p. 18.
54. Ibid., v, p. 32.
55. Ibid., v, p. 36.
56. Austen's juvenile stories and plays were written for family amusement, and were handed down to family members as treasured heirlooms. Brian Southam suggests that the transcription of the juvenilia into the three-volume notebooks was probably for the purpose of reading aloud to the rest of the family. See B. C. Southam, *Jane Austen's Literary Manuscripts: A Study of the Novelist's Development through the Surviving Papers* (London: Oxford University Press, 1964), p. 14.
57. Southam dates *The Mystery* and *The Visit* around 1787–90 (*Literary Manuscripts*, p. 16). As mentioned earlier, Deirdre Le Faye has suggested that they were probably performed as comic after-pieces to the main play at the Steventon theatricals.
58. Claire Tomalin has also noted Austen's subversion of Berquin: 'Where he sought to teach and elevate, she plunged into farce, burlesque and self-mockery, and created a world of moral anarchy, bursting with the life and energy Berquin's good intentions managed to squeeze out'. (*Jane Austen: A Life*, p. 45).
59. Austen's biographer David Nokes views 'The Visit' as a comic counterpart to Townley's topsy-turvy world where servants feed on 'claret, burgundy and champagne' and eat French delicacies: 'In her own short play, *The Visit*, Jane imagined the exact opposite, a dinner-party of elegant aristocrats consuming the meanest labourer's food: cowheel, tripe and suet pudding, washed down with home-made elderberry and gooseberry wines. Something about the anarchy of such incongruous social reversals appealed to her sense of fictional adventure.' Nokes, *Jane Austen: A Life* (London: Fourth Estate, 1997), p. 113.
60. *A Family Record*, p. 63.
61. See Southam's notes to *MW*, p. 458.
62. There are no 'whispering scenes' in *The Critic*, although there are ludicrously ambiguous 'asides' spoken to great comic effect by two of the characters.
63. George Villiers, Duke of Buckingham, *The Rehearsal*, ed. Montague Summers (Stratford: Shakespeare Head, 1914), p. 16.
64. The ballad-opera, such as Gay's *The Beggar's Opera* (1728), was popular in the first part of the eighteenth century, but after 1750 the comic opera, the operatic farce, the burletta and the musical interlude took over. For the subtle differences between these miscellaneous forms, see Allardyce Nicoll, *A History of English Drama, 1660–1900*, 6 vols (Cambridge: Cambridge University Press, 1955–59), iii, pp. 191–208.
65. *New Brooms*, in *The Plays of George Colman the Elder*, ed. Kalman A. Burnim, 6 vols (New York and London: Garland, 1983), iv, p. 21.

66. The most successful comic opera of the time was perhaps Sheridan's *The Duenna* (1775); unusually for comic opera, it was particularly commended for the richness of its plot. *The Duenna* ran for seventy-five performances, see Nicoll, *History of English Drama*, iii, p. 205. Reviews in the *Morning Post* and the *London Chronicle* praised its richness of plot, as did Hazlitt in his *Lectures on the English Comic Writers*.

67. Oliver Goldsmith's comedy *She Stoops to Conquer* is set in a house that is mistaken for an inn, and contains comical scenes with Tony Lumpkin in a roadside tavern called 'The Three Pigeons'.

68. The 'Chorus of Ploughboys' is probably a parody of the choruses in Frances Brooke's ballad-opera *Rosina* (1782), which contains a semi-pastoral element, although there is also a chorus of rustic harvesters in Dryden and Purcell's *King Arthur* (1691).

69. See below for the influence of the drama on Austen's early works of fiction.

70. Kent County Archives, Centre for Kentish Studies, Knatchbull Manuscript, Fanny Knight's Journals, U951 F24, vols 1–10, on microfilm.

71. Although there is a play called *Irish Hospitality: or Virtue Rewarded* by Charles Dibdin, the characters listed by Fanny Knight suggest that this play was specifically written for the children. *Virtue Rewarded* was the sub-title of Richardson's *Pamela* (1740).

72. Claire Tomalin claims that Anne Sharp wrote this play for the children to perform to amuse the servants. See *Jane Austen: A Life*, p. 136.

73. Kent County Archives, U951 F24/1.

74. Thomas Gisborne, *An Enquiry into the Duties of the Female Sex* (London, 1797), p. 175.

75. The influential critic Marilyn Butler has led the way unchallenged in her conviction that Austen's supposed disapproval of private theatricals echoed Gisborne's. Butler's contention that the theatrical saga in *Mansfield Park* implicitly embraces Gisborne's moral conservatism sits oddly with Austen's evident disregard for Gisborne's strident criticism of private theatricals. Butler's insistence that Austen read Gisborne with approval in 1805 does not square with the Kent private theatricals. See *Jane Austen and the War of Ideas* (Oxford: Clarendon Press, 1975; repr. 1987), pp. 231–32.

76. Gisborne, excerpted in Jane Austen, *Mansfield Park*, ed. Claudia L. Johnson (New York and London: Norton, 1998), p. 401.

77. Although for many years the play's authorship was attributed to the seven-year-old Anna, B. C. Southam has set the record straight, arguing that the extent of Anna's collaboration was to make a few suggestions and alterations (there are pencil scribblings in a childish hand): *Jane Austen's 'Sir Charles Grandison'*, ed. Brian Southam (Oxford: Clarendon Press, 1980), p. 11. Southam argues for composition at an earlier date, but the evidence of Anna's hand suggests completion or revision at this time.

78. See Deirdre Le Faye, 'The Business of Mothering: Two Austenian Dialogues', *Book Collector* (1983), pp. 296–314.

79. Ibid., p. 302.

80. Ibid., p. 308.

81. See Ellen Jordan, 'Mansfield Park', *Times Literary Supplement*, 23 June 1972, p. 719.

2: The Professional Theatre

1. See William Dunlap, *The Life and Time of George Frederick Cooke*, 2 vols (London, 1815), i, p. 183.
2. *Dramatic Essays by Leigh Hunt*, ed. William Archer and Robert W. Lowe (London, 1894), p. 41.
3. *The Complete Works of William Hazlitt*, ed. P. P. Howe, 21 vols (London: Dent, 1930–34), xviii, p. 274.
4. The testimony of Thomas Bellamy, in his *Miscellanies*, 2 vols (London, 1794), i, p. 23.
5. See *A Biographical Dictionary of Actors, Actresses, Musicians, Dancers, Managers and Other Stage Personnel in London, 1660–1800*, ed. Philip H. Highfill, J. R. Kalman, A. Burnim and Edward A. Langhans, 16 vols (Carbondale: Southern Illinois University Press, 1984), xii, p. 222.
6. *Works of Hazlitt*, xviii, p. 274.
7. See *Biographical Dictionary of Actors*, ix, pp. 219–22.
8. See Thomas Frost, *Circus Life and Circus Celebrities* (London, 1875), p. 22, and Isaac J. Greenwood, *The Circus: Its Origin and Growth Prior to 1835* (New York: Dunlap, 1898), p. 19.
9. See Watson Nicholson, *The Struggle for a Free Stage in London* (London: Constable, 1906), p. 283; and Ernest Watson, *Sheridan to Robertson: A Study of the Nineteenth-Century London Stage* (Cambridge, Massachusetts: Harvard University Press, 1926), p. 71.
10. See Edward Wedlake Brayley, *Historical and Descriptive Accounts of the Theatres of London* (London, 1826), p. 62. In 1798, it was styled Astley's Royal Amphitheatre. In 1808, it was known as Astley's Amphitheatre, specialising in 'equestrian melodrama and spectacle'. See Allardyce Nicoll, *A History of Early Nineteenth-Century Drama, 1800–1850*, 2 vols (London, Cambridge University Press, 1930), i, pp. 224–25.
11. See Frost, *Circus Life*, pp. 45–46.
12. The term 'burletta' was used as an umbrella term for performances at the minor theatres that, for legal purposes, included five or six songs per act. For a full account of the circumvention of the law by the illegitimate theatres, see the following: Nicholson, *The Struggle for a Free Stage in London*; Ernest Watson, *Sheridan to Robertson: A Study of the Nineteenth-Century London Stage*, pp. 20–57; Joseph Donohue, 'Burletta and the Early Nineteenth-Century English Theatre', *Nineteenth-Century Theatre Research*, 1 (1973), pp. 29–51; and Dewey Ganzel, 'Patent Wrongs and Patent Theatres: Drama and the Law in the Early Nineteenth Century', *PMLA*, 76 (1961), pp. 384–96.
13. *Restoration and Georgian England, 1660–1778*, ed. David Thomas, *Theatre in Europe: A Documentary History* (Cambridge: Cambridge University Press, 1989), p. 208. See also Joseph Donohue, *Theatre in the Age of Kean* (Oxford: Blackwell, 1975), pp. 2–3; and John Brewer, *The Pleasures of the*

Imagination: English Culture in the Eighteenth Century (London: HarperCollins, 1997), pp. 385–89.

14. See Thomas and Hare, *Theatre in Europe*, pp. 220–23. See also Allardyce Nicoll, *The Garrick Stage: Theatres and Audience in the Eighteenth Century*, ed. Sybil Rosenfeld (Manchester: Manchester University Press, 1980), pp. 4–5.
15. Donohue, *Theatre in the Age of Kean*, p. 38.
16. Brayley's account includes the Adelphi Theatre, Astley's Royal Ampitheatre, the East London Theatre, the English Opera House, the King's Theatre, the Olympic Theatre, the Pantheon, the Regency, the Royal Coburg and Sadler's Wells. Tomlins lists the Adelphi, Astley's Amphitheatre, the English Opera House, the Garrick, the Haymarket, the Little Theatre in the Strand, the Olympic, the Pavilion, the Queen's Theatre, Sadler's Wells and the St James's. See F. G. Tomlins, *A Brief View of the English Stage* (London, 1832), p. 60. More recently, Raymond Mander and Joe Mitchenson have accounted for twenty-eight 'lost theatres' of nineteenth-century London.
17. See *Emma*, chapters 28 and 29.
18. The amphitheatre was closed from Michaelmas to Passion week, see Greenwood, *The Circus*, p. 30.
19. See Raymond Mander and Joe Mitchenson, *The Lost Theatres of London* (New York: Taplinger, 1968), p. 253.
20. See Frost, *Circus Life*, p. 48.
21. Greenwood, *The Circus*, p. 30.
22. See *The Life and Enterprises of Robert William Elliston* (London, 1857), p. 210. See also Mander and Mitchenson, *The Lost Theatres of London*, pp. 255–56, and Christopher Murray, *Robert William Elliston: Manager* (London: Society for Theatre Research, 1975), p. 48.
23. This conflicts with Brayley's observation, in 1826, that the theatre, when full, housed 1300 people. See Greenwood, *The Circus*, pp. 30–31; and Brayley, *Theatres of London*, p. 88.
24. Tomlins, *Brief View*, pp. 60–61.
25. See Brayley, *Theatres of London*, p. 66.
26. See *Emma*, p. 472.
27. The amphitheatre contained one full tier of thirteen boxes, three private boxes to the side and two boxes above the stage doors. See Brayley, *Theatres of London*, p. 65.
28. Elliston also had to pay an annuity to Astley for twenty pounds, see *Life and Enterprises*, p. 211.
29. Frost, *Circus Life*, p. 27. Jane Moody has argued that, although the minor theatres were 'neither unequivocally genteel nor unequivocally plebeian places', they were considered as 'artisan domains' by reviewers, and therefore discriminated against. Not only were they housed in insalubrious locations, they were unrespectable and vulgar, even linked with immorality and disorder. Moody invokes the hostility of genteel reviewers towards populist adaptations of Shakespeare in the minor theatres to make a broader argument about patrician anxiety for the preservation of social and cultural hierarchies: 'The presence of mixed social groups watching these

performances no doubt seemed all the more incomprehensible in view of the increasing segregation of domestic and cultural spaces by class taking place outside the theatre', Jane Moody, 'Writing for the Metropolis: Illegitimate Performances of Shakespeare in Early Nineteenth-Century London', *Shakespeare Survey*, 47 (1994), pp. 61–69. See further, Moody, *Illegitimate Theatre in London, 1770–1840* (Cambridge: Cambridge University Press, 2000).

30. Prices for admission in Astley's were 4s. for boxes, 2s. for pit and 1s. for gallery; whereas in the patents, they were 7s. for boxes, 3s. 6d. for pit, 2s. for middle gallery and 1s. for upper gallery. See Brayley, *Theatres of London*, p. 88.

31. Kent County Archives, Centre for Kentish Studies, Fanny Knight's Journals, 1 October 1807, U951 F24/4.

32. Towards the end of the novel Charles Musgrove secures a box at the theatre for the party, see *PP*, pp. 223–24.

33. Joshua Reynolds painted her formal portrait as Miss Prue; it was much copied and engraved. See *Biographical Dictionary of Actors*, i, p. 19.

34. See *Biographical Dictionary of Actors*, iv, p. 386. See also George Holbert Tucker, *Jane Austen the Woman* (New York: St Martin's Press, 1994). Tucker cites the review from the *Bath Herald and Reporter* for 29 June 1799, p. 96.

35. See James Boaden, *Life of Mrs Jordan*, 2 vols (London, 1832), ii, p. 14.

36. Chris Viveash, 'Jane Austen and Kotzebue', *Jane Austen Society Report* (1994), pp. 29–31.

37. Thomas Dibdin, *The Birth-Day*, in *A Collection of Farces and Other Afterpieces, Selected by Mrs Inchbald*, 7 vols (London, 1809), ii, p. 8.

38. Captain Bertram discovers Mrs Moral's treachery when Jack Junk persuades him to hide in the closet so as to overhear them plotting. The Bertram brothers are united and the cousins marry one another.

39. Margaret Kirkham has proposed that *Emma* is a conscious adaptation of Kotzebue's play, sharing a similar heroine and major plot-line. See *Jane Austen: Feminism and Fiction* (London: Athlone, 1997), pp. 121–29.

40. Though there are four surviving letters written during May 1801, there is a gap in Austen's correspondence until one isolated letter of 14 September 1804 (*A Family Record*, p. 119).

41. The theatre flourished in these years. The receipts for benefits averaged nearly £150 a night, compared to the usual fifty and sixty pounds. In 1799 Dimond, the manager, realised £161 (Mrs Siddons was playing) and Elliston £146. In 1800 Dimond's benefit brought him £137, Elliston's £150 and Mrs Edwin's £150. See Belville S. Penley, *The Bath Stage* (London, 1892), p. 81.

42. By 1800 royal patents had been granted to Aberdeen, Bath, Bristol, Cheltenham, Chester, Cork, Dublin, Edinburgh, Hull, Liverpool, Manchester, Margate, Newcastle-upon-Tyne, Norwich, Richmond, Weymouth, Windsor, Yarmouth and York. See Donohue, *Age of Kean*, p. 28, and Brewer, *Pleasures of Imagination*, p. 388.

43. The first patent was given to Edinburgh. Within months, the first provincial English city was petitioning for the same protection. An Enabling Act was

passed for the licensing of a playhouse in Bath and was given the royal
assent on 29 January 1768. See Thomas, *Restoration and Georgian England*,
pp. 222–25. See also Penley, *The Bath Stage*, p. 35.

44. See Allardyce Nicoll, *A History of English Drama, 1660–1900*, 6 vols
(Cambridge: Cambridge University Press, 1955), iv, p. 234.

45. Penley, *The Bath Stage*, pp. 50, 82.

46. Siddons returned to Bath in 1799 and again in April and August 1801. See
*Theatre Royal Bath: A Calendar of Performances at the Orchard Street
Theatre, 1750–1805*, ed. Arnold Hare (Bath: Kingsmead Press, 1977), pp.
178–79, 190–93. See also Penley, *The Bath Stage*, p. 88.

47. Elliston contemplated at different times entering the church. His
biographer records that in 1799 he undertook a series of lectures at Bath
and Bristol on morals and general criticism, 'in which the moralist and the
critic, pleasantly impregnated with the popular actor, drew together very
profitable assemblies at both cities' (*Life and Enterprises*, p. 48). He had
even considered buying Albemarle chapel, 'having serious thoughts of
taking Holy Orders and preaching therein himself' (*Life and Enterprises*,
p. 158).

48. See George Raymond, *Memoirs of Robert William Elliston*, 2 vols (London,
1844).

49. See Genest, *Some Account of the English Stage from 1660–1830*, 10 vols
(Bath, 1832), vii, p. 638.

50. See ibid., vii, p. 640.

51. William Reitzel has noted six performances of *Lovers' Vows* during the time
of the Austens' residence in Bath: 7 November 1801, 22 April 1802, 28
January 1803, 2 June 1803, 17 November 1803 and 17 January 1805. See
William Reitzel, '*Mansfield Park* and *Lovers' Vows*', *RES*, 9 (1933), p. 454.
However, Arnold Hare's calendar of Orchard Street performances,
compiled from newspapers and playbills, records a further eleven
performances, as follows: 25 May 1801, 21 September 1801, 13 February
1802, 13 November 1802, 13 June 1803, 21 October 1803, 19 November
1803 (not 17 November, as Reitzel suggests), 22 June 1804, 23 June 1804, 12
November 1804, 17 January 1805 and 10 July 1805. See Hare, *Theatre Royal
Bath*, pp. 191–218.

52. See Joseph Donohue, *Dramatic Character in the English Romantic Age*
(Princeton: Princeton University Press, 1970), p. 147. For the numerous
performances of Kotzebue adaptations between 1801 and 1805, see Hare,
Theatre Royal Bath, pp. 187–218.

53. See Genest, *Some Account of the English Stage*, vii, p. 562.

54. R. A. Austen-Leigh, *Austen Papers, 1704–1856* (London: Spottiswoode,
1942), p. 238.

55. According to Dunlap, Kean moved Cooke's remains from the Stranger's
Vault of St Paul's church to a more prominent location in the centre of the
churchyard: 'it may hereafter be found that his surgeon possesses his scull,
and his sucessor, Kean, the bones of the forefinger of his right-hand – that
dictatorial finger'. See William Dunlap, *A History of the American Theatre*
(New York, 1832), p. 393. This gave birth to one of the strangest legends in

theatre history. One version of the fate of the finger claims that Kean's wife had it thrown away, upon which point Kean left the stage. The skull had supposedly been used in productions of Hamlet after Cooke's death, and was located in Jefferson Medical College in 1967. See Don B. Milmeth, 'The Posthumous Career of George Frederick Cooke', *Theatre Notebook*, 24 (1969–70), pp. 68–74.

56. Dunlap, *Life of Cooke*, i, p. 50.
57. Cooke acted with Siddons in the provinces before she became a London star. See *Life of Cooke*, i, p. 43.
58. Dunlap, *Life of Cooke*, i. p. 206.
59. Penley, *The Bath Stage*, p. 81.
60. See *DNB*, vii, p. 302, and *Memoirs of Elliston*, i, pp. 215–23.
61. See Hunt, *Dramatic Essays*, pp. 85, 90.
62. See *DNB*, vii, p. 302.
63. 'R. W. Elliston, Esq', *Gentleman's Magazine*, 101, part 2 (1831), p. 184.
64. *Oxberry's Dramatic Biography and Histrionic Anecdotes: or The Green-Room Spy*, 6 vols (London, 1825–27), iii, p. 88.
65. See Charles Lamb, *The Last Essays of Elia*, ed. Edmund Blunden (London: Oxford University Press, 1929), p. 23.
66. See Deirdre Le Faye, 'Journey, Waterparties and Plays', *Jane Austen Society Report* (1986), pp. 29–35.
67. See A. Temple Patterson, *A History of Southampton, 1700–1914*, 11 vols (Southampton: Southampton University Press, 1966), i, pp. 115–16.
68. See R. A. Austen-Leigh, *Jane Austen and Southampton* (London: Spottiswoode, 1949). pp. 30–31.
69. See John Adolphus, *Memoirs of John Bannister*, 2 vols (London, 1839), and *Biographical Dictionary of Actors*, p. 270.
70. Fanny Knight's Journals, U951 F24/1.
71. Arthur Murphy, *The Way to Keep Him*, in *Bell's British Theatre*, 34 vols (London, 1797), xvii, p. 52.
72. Hunt, *Dramatic Essays*, p. 31. Samuel de Wilde painted Bannister as 'Ben the sailor'. See *Biographical Dictionary of Actors*, p. 273.
73. Hunt, *Dramatic Essays*, p. 32.
74. See Thomas Dibdin, *Reminiscences*, 4 vols (London, 1827), ii, p. 239.
75. Michael Kelly, *Reminiscences*, 2 vols (London, 1826), ii, pp. 150–52.
76. Ibid., ii, p. 152.
77. Charles Dibdin, *Of Age Tomorrow* (London, n. d.), p. 18.
78. Kelly, *Reminiscences*, ii, p. 151.
79. Bannister's other cross-dressed role was as Jenny Diver in *The Beggar's Opera Metamorphosed*, which he played alongside his father's Polly Peachum in his first season at the Haymarket. Bannister was also painted in the role of Polly Peachum, so he probably took over this role from his father. See *Biographical Dictionary of Actors*, pp. 268, 273.
80. Charles Dibdin (1745–1814), not to be confused with his illegitimate older son Charles Dibdin the younger (1768–1833), and his illegitimate younger son Thomas Dibdin (1771–1841).
81. Patterson, *History of Southampton*, p. 104.

82. See Paul Ranger, *The Georgian Playhouses of Hampshire, 1730–1830*, Hampshire Papers, 10 (Winchester: Hampshire County Council, 1996), pp. 17–18.
83. Patterson, *History of Southampton*, p. 114.
84. Austen-Leigh, *Jane Austen and Southampton*, p. 46.

3: Plays and Actors

1. Pope's career on the London stage spanned fifty-two years and, from playing sprightly comic roles, she became in Hazlitt's words, 'the very picture of a duenna, a maiden lady or antiquated dowager'. See *Biographical Dictionary of Actors*, xii, pp. 77–84.
2. See David Nokes, *Jane Austen: A Life* (London: Fourth Estate, 1997), p. 323.
3. See Claire Tomalin, *Jane Austen: A Life* (London: Viking, 1997), p. 204.
4. See Raymond Mander and Joe Mitchenson, *The Lost Theatres of London* (New York: Taplinger, 1968), pp. 322–34.
5. Frances Burney, *Evelina*, ed. Edward A. Bloom (London: Oxford University Press, 1970), p. 104.
6. See Thomas Campbell, *Life of Mrs Siddons* (New York, 1834), p. 87.
7. Ibid., p. 89.
8. The 'rant', representing the formal and highly rhetorical approach to tragedy, was decried by the critics. See further discussion in Chapter 9 below.
9. See Leigh Hunt, *Dramatic Criticism*, ed. L. H. and C. W. Houtchens (New York: Columbia University Press, 1949), p. 39.
10. Campbell, *Life of Siddons*, pp. 86–87.
11. For her final season at Covent Garden she also acted Queen Katherine six times, Mrs Beverley five times, Elvira four times, Isabella twice and Lady Randolph once. See Genest, *Some Account of the English Stage*, viii, p. 239.
12. The Drury Lane Company remained at the Lyceum until 1812.
13. Dowton was a notorious figure for reviving the burlesque play *The Tailors* at the Haymarket in 1805, inciting a riot by aggrieved London tailors. See *Oxberry's Dramatic Biography*, iv, pp. 256–57.
14. Hunt, *Dramatic Criticism*, p. 97.
15. Hunt, *Dramatic Essays*, p. 32.
16. Mathews describes his unprepossessing figure in his memoirs, where he relates that from a child he was 'a long, thin skewer of a child' with distorted comical features. Mathews's son, who resembled his father, became known as 'Twig'. See *The Life and Correspondence of Charles Mathews*, ed. Edmund Yates (London, 1860), pp. 5–6, 130. For his account of Wilkinson, see ibid., p. 72.
17. *Life and Correspondence of Mathews*, pp. 148–49.
18. Bickerstaffe's musical version of the play was adapted from Cibber. The witty heroine of Restoration comedy had been replaced in Georgian drama by a new character assimilated from Richardsonian models, in particular the freely spoken, independent Lady G. (née Charlotte Grandison). See below, Chapter 5.
19. The Edwins were at Bath, Bristol and Southampton from 1797–98 to 1803–4. Edwin acted in the provinces throughout the acting career. See

Biographical Dictionary of Actors, p. 34, and Hare's *Orchard Street Calendar*, pp. 170–212.

20. C. Baron Wilson, *Our Actresses*, 2 vols (London, 1844), i, p. 105.
21. Ibid., p. 119.
22. *Oxberry's Dramatic Biography*, iv, p. 209.
23. See James J. Lynch, *Box, Pit and Gallery: Stage and Society in Johnson's London* (Berkeley: University of California Press, 1953), pp. 5–6.
24. *Lord Byron: The Complete Poetical Works*, ed. Jerome J. McGann, 7 vols (Oxford: Clarendon Press, 1986), v, p. 9. Byron became friends with Grimaldi. He first saw him in 1808, and always took a box ticket for his benefit. See *Memoirs of Joseph Grimaldi*, ed. Boz (London, 1869), p. 196. See also *The Theatre of Don Juan: A Collection of Plays and Views, 1630–1963*, ed. Oscar Mandel (Lincoln: University of Nebraska Press, 1963).
25. See *PP*, pp. 152–54.
26. There were three boxes on each side of the proscenium, three tiers or circles of boxes in the auditory (each containing twenty-six) and above them spacious slip boxes (on a level with the gallery). Brayley, *Theatres of London*, p. 19.
27. See Marc Baer, *Theatre and Disorder in Late Georgian England* (Oxford: Oxford University Press, 1992), pp. 135–65, and Gillian Russell, 'Playing at Revolution: The Politics of the O.P. Riots of 1809', *Theatre Notebook*, 44 (1990), pp. 16–26.
28. See *Letters*, p. 419.
29. See Brayley, *Theatres of London*, p. 19.
30. See Donohue, *Theatre in the Age of Kean*, p. 47.
31. He made his debut as Leon in *Rule a Wife and Have a Wife*. See Genest, *English Stage*, viii.
32. See J. G. Lockhart, *Life of Walter Scott* (New York: Cromwell, 1848), p. 271.
33. See *The Letters of Sir Walter Scott*, ed. H. J. C. Grierson, 12 vols (London: Constable, 1932), iii, p. 32.
34. See Genest, *English Stage*, viii, pp. 400–1.
35. By the close of the first fortnight of the 1813–14 season the receipts were worryingly low, averaging £250 a night, compared to £500 in the 1807–8 season. See Harold Newcombe Hillebrand, *Edmund Kean* (New York: Columbia University Press, 1933), pp. 106–13.
36. See F. W. Hawkins, *The Life of Edmund Kean*, 2 vols (London, 1869), i, p. 131.
37. *Works of Hazlitt*, v, p. 179.
38. Hawkins, *Life of Kean*, i, p. 130.
39. *Works of Hazlitt*, v, p. 179.
40. *The Romantics on Shakespeare*, ed. Jonathan Bate (London: Penguin, 1992), p. 160. Coleridge's patron Sir George Beaumont also observed of Kean that 'there was a fire in his acting that was electric'. See Hillebrand, *Edmund Kean*, pp. 119, 365.
41. *The London Theatre, 1811–1866: Selections from the Diary of Henry Crabb Robinson*, ed. Eluned Brown (London: Society for Theatre Research, 1966), pp. 36, 56.

42. Lamb, 'Ellistonia', p. 25.
43. See *DNB*, vii, p. 302, and Hunt's *Dramatic Criticism*, p. 96.
44. *Works of Hazlitt*, xviii, pp. 219, 343.
45. See Hunt, *Dramatic Essays*, p. 67.
46. The success of *Killing no Murder* was attributed to the ability of Mathews and Liston to play into each other's hands.
47. When he first joined Drury Lane he was paid £40 a week, though he was rumoured to have earned £100 a week when he joined the Olympic.
48. *Works of Hazlitt*, v, p. 252.
49. Hunt, *Dramatic Essays*, p. 49.
50. *The Works of Charles and Mary Lamb*, ed. E. V. Lucas, 2 vols (London: Methuen, 1903), ii, p. 148.
51. *Works of Hazlitt*, xviii, p. 402.
52. Hunt, *Dramatic Essays*, p. 60; *Dramatic Criticism*, p. 100.
53. *Works of Hazlitt*, xviii, p. 279.
54. See Genest, *English Stage*, viii, p. 422.
55. See *Oxberry's Dramatic Biography*, iv, p. 8. Hazlitt also complained that Young's Hamlet was a poor imitation of Kemble's.
56. *Oxberry's Dramatic Biography*, iv, p. 10.
57. Hunt, *Dramatic Criticism*, p. 25; *Works of Hazlitt*, xviii, p. 244.
58. See *Oxberry's Dramatic Biography*, i, p. 95.
59. See *Byron's Life, Letters and Journals*, ed. Thomas Moore (London, 1854), p. 252.
60. See Joseph Donohue, *Dramatic Character in the English Romantic Age*, p. 167.
61. *Oxberry's Dramatic Biography*, i, p. 97.
62. *Works of Hazlitt*, xviii, p. 196.
63. *Oxberry's Dramatic Biography*, i, p. 97.
64. See Charles Inigo Jones, *Memoirs of Miss O'Neill* (London, 1816), pp. 8, 47.
65. *Works of Hazlitt*, v, p. 199.
66. Crabb Robinson, *Selections from the Diary*, p. 299.
67. *Works of Hazlitt*, v, pp. 198–99.
68. Jones, *Memoirs of O'Neill*, pp. 50, 90–91.
69. *Oxberry's Dramatic Biography*, i, p. 98.
70. See Brayley, *Theatres of London*, p. 29.
71. Kelly observed that the new Opera House 'was by far the best for sound I ever sang at', and that Mrs Jordan received a great share of the applause. See Kelly's *Reminiscences*, pp. 186–87.
72. See Brayley, *Theatres of London*, p. 29.
73. Her fellow actor William Macready observed, 'If Mrs Siddons appeared a personification of the tragic muse, certainly all the attributes of Thalia were most joyously combined in Mrs Jordan'. See *Macready's Reminiscences*, ed. Sir Frederick Pollock (New York, 1875), p. 46. See also Boaden, *Life of Mrs Jordan*, 2 vols (London, 1831), i, p. 2.
74. The full title of the painting was *The Comic Muse Supported by Euphrosyne, who Represses the Advances of a Satyr*. See Claire Tomalin, *Mrs Jordan's Profession* (New York: Knopf, 1994), pp. 69–71.

75. Genest claimed that she never had a superior in her line and that she was 'second to none', *English Stage*, viii, p. 429. Sir Joshua Reynolds declared that she 'vastly exceeded every thing that he had ever seen, and really *was* what others only affected to be', Boaden, *Life of Jordan*, p. 220.

76. Coleridge sent her a copy of *Lyrical Ballads*, and praised her verse-speaking to Byron as the best he had ever heard. He also claimed that Jordan intended to sing stanzas of 'The Mad Mother' in *Pizarro*. See Tomalin, *Mrs Jordan's Profession*, pp. 179, 181, 270.

77. See *Works of Hazlitt*, xviii, p. 277.

78. See Leigh Hunt, *Dramatic Essays*, pp. 80–81. See also his 'The Comic Actress', in *Dramatic Criticism*, pp. 87–91.

79. Genest, *English Stage*, viii, p. 431.

80. In 1796, the King had presented William with Bushy, a part of the Hampton Court Palace estates. See Tomalin, *Mrs Jordan's Profession*, pp. 156–57.

81. See Genest, *English Stage*, vii, p. 18, and *The London Stage, 1660–1800*, ed. Emmett L. Avery, Charles Beecher Hogan, Arthur H. Scouten, George Winchester Stone Jr and William Van Lennep, 11 vols (Carbondale: Southern Illinois University Press, 1960–68), v, p. 1332.

82. *The Greek Slave*, Huntington Library, MS Larpent 894.

83. *Life of Mrs Jordan*, i, p. 142.

84. Hunt, *Dramatic Criticism*, pp. 87–88.

85. See 'Petronius Arbiter', *Memoirs of the Present Countess of Derby* (London, 1797).

86. Genest notes that Dora Jordan played Nell on 7 March, *English Stage*, viii, p. 423.

87. Elizabeth Inchbald, *A Collection of Farces and Other Afterpieces: Selected by Mrs Inchbald*, 7 vols (London, 1809), vii, p. 119.

88. Jordan had quit the stage in 1811 on the terms of her separation with the Duke of Clarence, which stated that if she returned to the stage she would lose custody of her daughters. She did return to the stage in 1812 in order to pay the debts of her son-in-law and secured an engagement at Covent Garden, making her debut in February 1813.

89. *Works of Hazlitt*, xviii, pp. 277, 234.

90. The three mentioned here, which Austen knew, represent merely a fraction of farces and comedies with a similar theme, dating from Gay's *The Beggar's Opera*, which first combined genres from 'high' and 'low' culture.

91. Garrick's famous epilogue to Murphy's *All in the Wrong* is often seen as representative of the social and architectural stratification of theatre audiences. After the main play, people were admitted into the theatre for half price. Although the assumption is that the upper and middle classes left after the main play and the lower classes gained a low ticket price for entrance to the farce, this wasn't always the case. Austen often seemed to prefer the after-piece to the main play. Nor can we make the assumption that the social stratification of the box, pit and gallery was as circumscribed as is sometimes assumed. Joseph Donohue has shown that the architectural and social division of the auditorium 'by no means created mutually exclusive seating areas', *Theatre in the Age of Kean*, p. 15.

92. See Donohue, *Theatre in the Age of Kean*, p. 17, and Lynch, *Box, Pit and Gallery*, p. 2. The rise of sentimental drama has been ascribed, in part, to the idealising of the aspiring middling classes, and the depiction of the heroic merchant figure, as in *The London Merchant* and *The West Indian*. See Arthur Sherbo, *English Sentimental Drama* (Ann Arbor: Michigan State University Press, 1957), and Ernest Bernbaum, *The Drama of Sensibility: A Sketch of the History of English Sentimental Comedy and Domestic Tragedy, 1696–1780* (Gloucester, Massachusetts: Peter Smith, 1958).

93. D. G. Greene proposes that the unifying theme of Austen's novels is the clash of the rising middle class with the established aristocracy: 'In *Pride and Prejudice* it is the middle-class Bennets and Gardiners who compel the noble Fitzwilliams and Darcys to take them seriously; in *Persuasion*, it is Wentworths against Elliots; in *Northanger Abbey*, Morlands against Tilneys; in *Sense and Sensibility*, Dashwoods against Ferrarses … her middle-class protaganists are as good a class as those who treat them superciliously.' See D. G. Greene, 'Jane Austen and the Peerage', *PMLA*, 68 (1953), pp. 1017–31, at p. 1028.

94. Naturally, her letters during this time contain various references to *Mansfield Park*, in particular Henry's comments and criticisms. Though Jane Austen wrote that she hoped to see it published 'before the end of April' (*Letters*, p. 262), it was announced by Egerton the publisher in the *Morning Chronicle* of 23 and 27 May and was no doubt published soon afterwards. See introductory note to Chapman's edition of *MP*.

95. During the first few weeks of the winter season, the two patent houses scheduled performances on three nights of the week, moving to six performances per week as the season progressed. See James J. Lynch, *Box, Pit and Gallery*, pp. 12–13.

96. Theatre historians have shown that interest in the theatre was by no means limited to certain social classes or economic groups. See Lynch, *Box, Pit and Gallery*, p. 199.

97. See Lynch, *Box, Pit and Gallery*, p. 143.

98. John Brewer, *The Pleasures of Imagination: English Culture in the Eighteenth Century* (London: HarperCollins, 1997), p. 340.

99. Donohue, *Theatre in the Age of Kean*, p. 144.

100. *Works of Hazlitt*, v, p. 173.

4: Early Works

1. Samuel Johnson's definition of the adjective is: 'Jocular; tending to raise laughter by unnatural or unsuitable language and images', and he defines the noun as 'ludicrous language or ideas; ridicule'. Samuel Johnson, *A Dictionary of the English Language*, 4 vols (London, 1756; repr. 1805). John Loftis in *Sheridan and the Drama of Georgian England* (Oxford: Blackwell, 1976), p. 144, cites the first definition of the noun by the *Oxford English Dictionary*. 'That species of literary composition, or of dramatic representation, which aims at exciting laughter by caricature of the manner or spirit of serious works, or by ludicrous treatment of their subject'. The

key point is that the comic effect is achieved by exaggeration of the original in order to elucidate its absurdities and limitations.

2. Park Honan argues that this article was written with Eliza de Feuillide in mind. She had visited the Austen brothers at Oxford in 1788. Honan, *Jane Austen: Her Life* (1987; revised edn, London: Phoenix, 1997), p. 56. This argument is supported by the fact that one of the sisters in Henry's burlesque is called Eliza. That Eliza was keen on burlesque is perhaps comfirmed by Jane Austen's dedication of *Love and Freindship* to her cousin.

3. James Austen, *The Loiterer*, 2 vols (Oxford: C. S. Rann, 1789–90), no. 32, pp. 13–14.

4. Ibid., p. 14.

5. See above, Chapter 1, for the playlets 'The Visit' and 'The Mystery'. Many of the non-dramatic sketches in *Volume the First*, written around 1787–90 when Jane Austen was between the ages of twelve and fifteen, incorporate farcical action. *Volume the Second* contains the two most sustained burlesques, 'Love and Freindship' and 'The History of England', dated 'June 13 1790' and 'November 26 1791' respectively (*MW*, p. 109 and p. 149). *Volume the Third* (1792–93) begins to show Austen intermingling burlesque with her first experiments in realistic social comedy.

6. John Loftis argues unequivocally that 'the most profound literary consequence of the Act has been the impulse that it gave to the development of the novel'. See John Loftis, *The Politics of Drama in Augustan England* (Oxford: Clarendon Press, 1963), pp. 128–53.

7. *The Tragedy of Tragedies: or Tom Thumb the Great*, in *The Beggar's Opera and Other Eighteenth-Century Plays*, ed. John Hampden (London: Dent, 1974), pp. 192, 201.

8. The most notorious example being the cruel jibe she makes about miscarriage: 'Mrs Hall of Sherbourn was brought to bed yesterday of a dead child, some weeks before she expected, oweing to a fright. – I suppose she happened unawares to look at her husband' (*Letters*, p. 17).

9. Garrick's farce *Bon Ton: or High Life above Stairs* and Townley's *High Life below Stairs* spring to mind.

10. David Garrick, *Bon Ton: or High Life Above Stairs*, in *The Plays of David Garrick*, ed. Gerald M. Berkowitz, 4 vols (New York and London: Garland, 1981), ii, p. 257. 'Love and Friendship' is a familiar phrase in eighteenth-century literature. Austen would have known it from Richardson's *Sir Charles Grandison* (1754), v, pp. 74–75, and from Henry Austen's article in *The Loiterer*. 'Let every girl who seeks for happiness conquer both her feelings and her passions. Let her avoid love and freindship' (no. 29). There is also a novel of the same name listed in the preface to Colman's after-piece *Polly Honeycombe*, which lists novels from a typical eighteenth-century circulating library.

11. The problem of accurately defining sentimentalism is explored by Arthur Sherbo in *English Sentimental Drama* (Ann Arbor: Michigan State University Press, 1957). See also Ernest Bernbaum's *The Drama of Sensibility: A Sketch of the History of English Sentimental Comedy and Domestic Tragedy*,

1696–1780 (Gloucester, Massachusetts: Peter Smith, 1958) for the standard work on English sentimental drama. John Loftis shows the 'two faces' of Sheridan's sentimentalism in *Sheridan and the Drama of Georgian England* (Oxford: Blackwell, 1976). See also Richard Bevis, *The Laughing Tradition* (Athens: University of Georgia Press, 1980), pp. 45–47, and John Mullan, *Sentiment and Sociability: The Language of Feeling in the Eighteenth Century* (Oxford: Clarendon Press, 1988; repr. 1997).

12. At the end of *Volume the First*, Austen had written a fragment called *A Beautiful Description of the Different Effects of Sensibility on Different Minds*. The excessive swooning fits of the dying heroine excite compassion from the author, indifference from her insensible sister, sighs from her melancholy husband and bad puns from the doctor who visits her on her death bed (*MW*, pp. 72–73).

13. Both texts are burlesqued in *Northanger Abbey*. For further examples of the sentimental novel see J. M. S. Tompkins, *The Popular Novel in England, 1770–1800* (Lincoln: University of Nebraska Press, 1932; repr. 1961).

14. *The Dramatic Works of Richard Brinsley Sheridan*, ed. Cecil Price, 2 vols (Oxford: Clarendon Press, 1973), ii, pp. 539–41. Centred text indicates lines from the play-within-the-play.

15. In *The West Indian*, Belcour is reunited with his father:

> STOCKWELL: I am your father.
> BELCOUR: My father! Do I live? … It is too much.

Richard Cumberland, *The West Indian: A Comedy* (London, 1771), repr. in *The Beggar's Opera and other Eighteenth Century Plays*, p. 405. Austen's scene is also a burlesque of Burney's *Evelina*, where Sir John Belmont discovers numerous unknown relatives: 'I have already a daughter … and it is not three days since, that I had the pleasure of discovering a son; how many more sons and daughters may be brought to me, I am yet to learn, but I am already, perfectly satisfied with the size of my family' (*Evelina*, p. 371).

16. *Dramatic Works of Sheridan*, ii, p. 548. Tilburina's speech is most obviously a parody of Ophelia. *Hamlet* was the mainpiece performed on the opening night of *The Critic*.

17. Loftis thus argues: 'His burlesque of the tyranny of the older generation in the persons of Sir Anthony Absolute and Mrs Malaprop should not conceal the force of the social reality which lay behind that tyranny – the custom among affluent families of arranging marriages with close attention to property settlements. Sheridan wrote in the interval between Richardson's *Clarissa*, and Jane Austen's *Pride and Prejudice*'. Loftis, *Sheridan and the Drama of Georgian England*, p. 46.

18. *Dramatic Works of Sheridan*, i, p. 408.

19. See Fintan O'Toole, *A Traitor's Kiss: The Life of Richard Brinsley Sheridan* (London: Granta, 1998), p. 125.

20. *Dramatic Works of Sheridan*, i, p. 415.

21. *Sanditon* also contains some of Austen's funniest satire on sensibility. The absurd Sir Edward Denham's taste for sentimental fiction is satirised, and

his penchant for modelling himself on Richardson's Lovelace suggests the corrupting effects of the 'exceptionable parts' of Richardson's novels (*MW*, p. 358).

5: From Play to Novel

1. Austen's play is quoted from *Jane Austen's 'Sir Charles Grandison'*, ed. Brian Southam (Oxford: Clarendon Press, 1980). For ease of reference, it is cited as 'Grandison', Richardson's novel as *Sir Charles Grandison*.
2. 'Grandison', ed. Southam, pp. 1–34.
3. See Mark Kinkead-Weekes, *Samuel Richardson: Dramatic Novelist* (London: Methuen, 1973); Margaret Anne Doody, *A Natural Passion: A Study of the Novels of Samuel Richardson* (London: Oxford University Press, 1974); Ira Konigsberg, *Samuel Richardson and the Dramatic Novel* (Lexington: University of Kentucky Press, 1968).
4. See George Sherburn, 'Samuel Richardson's Novels and the Theatre: A Theory Sketched', *Philological Quarterly*, 41 (1962), p. 328.
5. Samuel Richardson, *Clarissa*, ed. Angus Ross (London: Penguin, 1985), p. 764. This example is cited by Sherburn, 'Richardson's Novels', p. 328.
6. Sherburn, 'Samuel Richardson's Novels', p. 327.
7. See Konigsberg, *Dramatic Novel*, pp. 33–47.
8. Richardson, *Clarissa*, p. 626.
9. 'The First Epistle of the Second Book of Horace Imitated', line 172, *The Poems of Alexander Pope*, ed. John Butt (London: Methuen, 1963), p. 641.
10. 'What a delightful play might be form'd out of this piece. I am sure Mr Garrick will have it upon the stage': quoted, Doody, *A Natural Passion*, p. 280.
11. Samuel Richardson, *The History of Sir Charles Grandison*, ed. Jocelyn Harris, 3 vols (London: Oxford University Press, 1972), i, p. 273.
12. See *The Early Journals and Letters of Fanny Burney*, ed. Lars E. Troide and Stewart J. Cooke, 3 vols to date (Oxford: Clarendon Press, 1988–94), i, p. 202.
13. Kate Chisholm has noted this as one of many instances where Burney coined words that are now cited in the *OED*. See *Fanny Burney: Her Life* (London: Chatto and Windus, 1998), p. 83.
14. 'Grandison', p. 46. Austen had previously used the same joke in 'The Visit', where two characters are 'discovered': a theatrical term used in stage-directions to indicate that the characters are already on the stage when the curtain rises.
15. Richardson, *Sir Charles Grandison*, ii, p. 408.
16. 'Grandison', p. 44.
17. It is also noteworthy that there were a number of school-room abridgements of *Sir Charles Grandison*. Austen's burlesque play was a mockery not only of the original novel, but also of these popular bowdlerisations. 'The schoolroom versions were notably reticent in retailing the events at Paddington, where the threat of rape hangs heavy in the air. Jane Austen makes this the high point of her comic melodrama.

Far from closing her eyes to the strain of erotic titillation in Richardson, Jane Austen laughs it off the stage.' Southam, introduction to 'Grandison', p. 22.

18. In *The Funeral*, Steele dramatises two sisters of contrasting characters, Harriot and Sharlot. The coquettish and giddy Harriot is contrasted with the graver Sharlot. Doody suggests that Richardson has given his heroines the same names but reversed the roles, Doody, *A Natural Passion*, p. 287.

19. *Sir Charles Grandison*, ii, p. 99.

20. William Congreve, *The Way of the World*, ed. Brian Gibbons (2nd edn, London: A & C Black, 1994), act 1, scene 3, pp. 140–45.

21. See Frank W. Bradbrook, *Jane Austen and her Predecessors* (Cambridge: Cambridge University Press, 1966), p. 74.

22. *Sir Charles Grandison*, ii, p. 340.

23. 'Grandison', pp. 45, 51.

24. *Clarissa*, pp. 426, 430.

25. Ibid., p. 721.

26. Henry Fielding, *The History of the Adventures of Joseph Andrews and of his Friend Mr Abraham Adams and An Apology for the Life of Mrs Shamela Andrews*, ed. Douglas Brook-Davies (Oxford: Oxford University Press, 1980), p. 330.

27. *The Correspondence of Samuel Richardson*, ed. A. L. Barbauld, 6 vols (London, 1804), i, pp. xxviii.

28. *Selected Letters of Samuel Richardson*, ed. John Carroll (Oxford: Oxford University Press, 1964), p. 286.

29. The devices that come closest to doing so are voiceover and ironic editing. It was these techniques that made *Clueless* the most successful of the 1990s adaptations, despite its being the one that was least faithful to the surface of its original. The film took the plot of *Emma* and translated it to Beverly Hills, jettisoning the dialogue and yet retaining the spirit of a young girl's growth to self-knowledge. At the same time, the heroine was ironised by means of an art of directorial control strikingly akin to Austen's own authorial control. On this, see Nora Nachumi's excellent essay, "'As If!'": Translating Austen's Ironic Narrator to Film', in *Jane Austen in Hollywood*, ed. Linda Troost and Sayre Greenfield (Lexington: University of Kentucky Press, 1998), pp. 130–37, and my final chapter.

30. This point is very well made by Claude Rawson, *Satire and Sentiment, 1660–1830* (Cambridge: Cambridge University Press, 1994), p. 281.

31. See Elizabeth Inchbald, *A Simple Story*, ed. Pamela Clemit (Harmondsworth: Penguin, 1996), p. viii.

32. See Elizabeth Inchbald, *A Simple Story* (1791) ed. J. M. S. Tompkins with a new introduction by Jane Spencer (Oxford: Oxford University Press, 1988), p. 15.

33. Ibid., p. 16.

34. Ibid., p. 110.

35. Ibid., p. 67.

36. James Boaden, *Memoirs of Mrs Inchbald*, 2 vols (London, 1833), ii, pp. 152–53.

37. Gary Kelly has suggested that the use of gestures supplanting that which words often fail to express came from Inchbald's experience as an actress on the London stage. See Gary Kelly, *The English Jacobin Novel, 1780–1805* (Oxford: Clarendon Press, 1976), p. 88.

6: Sense and Sensibility

1. *The Dramatic Works of Richard Brinsley Sheridan*, ed. Cecil Price, 2 vols (Oxford: Clarendon Press, 1973), i, p. 84.
2. Colman's hostility towards his female quixotic is suggested by the fact that she loses her lover by the end of the play without being cured of her romantically absurd notions. Furthermore, in the first edition of *Polly Honeycombe* (1760), Colman provides a preface warning of the dangers of novel-reading for young women.
3. *The Plays of Richard Steele*, ed. Shirley Strum Kenny (Oxford: Clarendon Press, 1971), p. 233.
4. See *Polly Honeycombe*, in *The Plays of George Colman the Elder*, ed. Kalman A. Burnim, 6 vols (New York and London: Garland, 1983), p. 41.
5. The lovely Arabella is considered to be out of her senses, and Colman picks up the motif: 'She's downright raving – mad as a March hare – I'll put her into Bedlam'. *Plays of Colman*, p. 41.
6. *Dramatic Works of Sheridan*, i, p. 123.
7. See John Brewer, *The Pleasures of the Imagination: English Culture in the Eighteenth Century* (London: HarperCollins, 1997), pp. 169–97.
8. Paradoxically, what Austen's foolish, deluded, novel-reading heroine ultimately discovers is that reading books can prepare you for life, and teach you to distrust paternal authority. See Claudia L. Johnson, *Jane Austen: Women, Politics and the Novel* (Chicago: University of Chicago Press, 1988), pp. 39–43.
9. Colman's exemplification of the traffic between drama and the novel is apparent not only in *Polly Honeycombe*, but also in *The Jealous Wife*, which openly acknowledges a debt to Fielding's *Tom Jones*. See John Loftis, *Sheridan and the Drama of Georgian England* (Oxford: Blackwell, 1976), p. 28.
10. See *PP*, p. 274. Both girls are attracted to 'a bit of red cloth' and show disrespect for Fordyce's sermons. Lydia Languish tears out pages of Fordyce's sermons for curl papers. See also E. E. Phare, 'Lydia Languish, Lydia Bennet, and Dr Fordyce's Sermons', *Notes and Queries*, 209 (1964), pp. 231–32.
11. *Dramatic Works of Sheridan*, i, p. 135.
12. Ibid., i, pp. 135, 82.
13. Ibid., i, pp. 130–31.
14. Ironically, Faulkland was first admired by the public as a true picture of a sentimental hero. As John Loftis argues, 'Faulkland serves as a reminder that the "age of sensibility" had not passed, and Sheridan shares an affectionate regard for sensibility even while burlesquing it'. See Loftis, *Sheridan and the Drama of Georgian England*, p. 51. Eighteenth-century

audiences had more sympathy for him than we have, judging by the reviews. The *Morning Chronicle* wrote, 'he is a beautiful exotic, and tho' not found in every garden, we cannot deny it may be in some; the exquisite refinement in his disposition, opposed to the noble simplicity, tenderness, and candor of Julia's, gives rise to some of the most affecting sentimental scenes I ever remember to have met with'. See *Dramatic Works of Sheridan*, i, p. 47. However John Bernard, in *Retrospections of the Stage* (1830), acidly commented that 'Faulkland and Julia (which Sheridan had obviously introduced to conciliate the sentimentalists, but which in the present day are considered heavy incumbrances) were the characters most favourably received' (ibid., i, p. 55). Sheridan's critique of sentimentalism is perhaps clouded by his ambiguous attitude towards Faulkland, and the fact that he pragmatically increased some of his sentimental speeches after the first unsuccessful performance of the play.

15. See Loftis, *Sheridan and the Drama*, p. 52.
16. See Kenneth Molar, *Jane Austen's Art of Allusion* (Lincoln: University of Nebraska Press, 1977), and J. M. S. Tomkins, '"Elinor and Marianne": A Note on Jane Austen', *Review of English Studies*, 16 (1940), pp. 33–43.
17. *False Delicacy* in *The Plays of Hugh Kelly*, ed. Larry Carver and Mary J. H. Gross (New York and London: Garland, 1980), pp. 19–20.
18. See Claude Rawson's 'Some Remarks on Eighteenth-Century "Delicacy", with a Note on Hugh Kelly's *False Delicacy* (1768)', *JEGP*, 61 (1962), pp. 1–13, at p. 12. Rawson also provides notes on 'Delicacy' in *Order from Confusion Sprung: Studies in Eighteenth-Century Literature from Swift to Cowper* (London: Allen and Unwin, 1985), pp. 341–54.
19. *Dramatic Works of Sheridan*, i, p. 130.
20. Ibid., i, p. 144.
21. This was one of the plays performed in the Kent private theatricals in 1805, with Fanny Knight.
22. Polly Honeycombe's closing lines to her lover, Scribble, are: 'You may depend upon my constancy and affection. I never read of any lady's giving up her lover, to submit to the absurd election of her parents', *Polly Honeycombe*, p. 41. Lydia Languish is distressed to find that her romantic fantasies are dashed when she discovers that she has her guardian's consent to marriage: 'So, while *I* fondly imagined we were deceiving my relations … my hopes are to be crush'd at once, by my Aunt's consent and approbation!' *Dramatic Works of Sheridan*, ii, p. 26.
23. *Dramatic Works of Sheridan*, i, p. 97.
24. Ibid., i, p. 103.
25. See Rawson, *Order From Confusion Sprung*, pp. 271–84, a study of dialogue and authorial presence in Fielding's novels and plays that also has striking implications for Jane Austen's implementation of theatrical devices.
26. 'It may be proper to return to the hero of this Novel, the brother of Alice, of whom I beleive I have scarcely ever had the occasion to speak' (*MW*, pp. 24–25).

27. 'For myself, I confess that *I* can only pity Miss Manwaring, who coming to Town & putting herself to an expense in Cloathes, which impoverished her for two years, on purpose to secure him, was defrauded of her due by a Woman ten years older than herself' (*MW*, p. 313).

7: Pride and Prejudice

1. See W. and R. A. Austen-Leigh, *Jane Austen: A Family Record*, rev. and enlarged by Deirdre Le Faye (London: British Library, 1989), p. 175. Sheridan, as manager of Drury Lane, was quick to persuade the young Fanny Burney to write a stage comedy after the success of *Evelina*. He was impressed with Burney's handling of different social classes, and felt that her comic juxtapositions of vulgar and aristocratic characters would translate well to the stage. The quasi-dramatic qualities of *Evelina* also appealed to Austen, who read the comic parts aloud to her family, her niece Caroline describing the experience as being like a play.

2. *Jane Austen: The Critical Heritage*, ed. Brian Southam, 2 vols (London: Routledge and Kegan Paul, 1968–87), i, pp. 45–46.

3. *Which is the Man?*, in *The Plays of Hannah Cowley*, ed. Frederick M. Link, 2 vols (New York and London: Garland, 1979), i, pp. 51, 53.

4. Cowley's comedy frequently alludes to *Sir Charles Grandison* – Richardson's endless debates between the sexes were often refashioned in the plays of the period.

5. *Which is the Man?*, p. 47.

6. Ibid., p. 54.

7. See, for example, Marvin Mudrick, *Jane Austen: Irony as Defense and Discovery* (Princeton: Princeton University Press, 1952), p. 205.

8. *Letters*, p. 74, quoting act 5, scene 5 of *The Belle's Stratagem*. See *Plays of Hannah Cowley*, i, p. 79.

9. *Plays of Hannah Cowley*, i, p. 81.

10. As one sensitive critic of *Emma* suggests: 'The social world of the novel is peopled with upwardly and downwardly mobile individuals. It is viewed not from the perspective of frozen class division but from a perspective of living change. It is not France in the 1780s but England at the beginning of the nineteenth century.' Julia Prewitt Brown, *Jane Austen's Novels: Social Change and Literary Form*, chapter on *Emma* reprinted in *Jane Austen's 'Emma', Modern Critical Interpretations*, ed. Harold Bloom (New York: Chelsea House, 1987), p. 57.

11. See Marilyn Butler, 'History, Politics, and Religion', in *The Jane Austen Handbook*, ed. J. David Grey (London: Athlone, 1986), p. 202.

12. Act 5, scene 1, in Oliver Goldsmith, *She Stoops to Conquer*, ed. Tom Davis (London: Ernest Benn, 1979), p. 79.

13. Darcy admits how her words stung him: 'Your reproof, so well applied, I shall never forget: "had you behaved in a more gentleman-like manner." Those were your words. You know not, you can scarcely conceive, how they have tortured me' (*PP*, p. 367).

14. See discussion above in Chapter 2. Also Joseph Donohue, *Theatre in the Age of Kean* (Oxford: Blackwell, 1975), p. 17.

15. Plays such as John Burgoyne's *Heiress* (1786), George Colman the Elder's *Man of Business* (1774), Arthur Murphy's *The Citizen* (1761), Hannah Cowley's *Who's the Dupe?* and George Colman the Younger's *The Heir at Law* (1797) crudely satirised the merchant classes as ignorant, ill-educated and money-grubbing.
16. *Plays of Hannah Cowley*, i, p. 16.
17. *A Busy Day*, act 3, scene 3, in *The Complete Plays of Frances Burney*, ed. Peter Sabor, 2 vols (Montreal: McGill-Queen's University Press, 1995), i, p. 350.

8: Lover's Vows

1. See Marvin Mudrick's influential *Jane Austen: Irony as Defense and Discovery* (Princeton: Princeton University Press, 1952). '*Mansfield Park* has always been more respected than loved', observes Marilyn Butler: Jane Austen, *Mansfield Park*, ed. James Kinsley with a new introduction by Marilyn Butler (Oxford: Oxford University Press, 1990), p. vii.
2. Notably from Kingsley Amis in his 'What Became of Jane Austen?' *Spectator*, 4 October 1957, p. 339. Tony Tanner has observed that 'nobody has ever fallen in love with Fanny Price'. See Tony Tanner, *Jane Austen* (London: Macmillan, 1986), p. 143. Jane Austen's mother thought her 'insipid' and Reginald Farrer declared that Henry Crawford had a 'near miss', since 'fiction holds no heroine more repulsive in her cast-iron self righteousness and steely rigidity of prejudice' than Fanny. See Reginald Farrer, 'Jane Austen's *Gran Refiuto*', in *Sense and Sensibility, Pride and Prejudice and Mansfield Park: A Casebook*, ed. B. C. Southam (London: Macmillan, 1976), pp. 210–11.
3. Pam Perkins has argued that Mary Crawford and Fanny Price represent (respectively) 'laughing' and 'sentimental' comedy. See 'A Subdued Gaiety: The Comedy of *Mansfield Park*', *Nineteenth-Century Literature*, 48 (1993), pp. 1–25.
4. See James Boaden, *Memoirs of Mrs Inchbald*, 2 vols (London: 1833), ii, p. 20.
5. See *The London Stage, 1660–1800*, ed. Emmett L. Avery et al., 5 parts in 11 vols (Carbondale, Illinois: Southern Illinois University Press, 1960–68), part 5, 1776–800, ed. Charles Beecher Hogan, p. 2116, for receipts and *Times* review (13 October 1798): '*Lovers' Vows* continues to exercise a resistless controul over the feelings of the audience. The fifth act is, without exception, worked up with more art and nature, and is more impressive in its termination, than any denouement which the English stage has hithero furnished.'
6. See above, Chapter 2.
7. Marilyn Butler, for instance, has argued that Kotzebue's name alone would have alerted readers to the moral and political dangers of *Lovers' Vows* because his works were synonymous with the German drama so despised by anti-Jacobins: 'There could be no doubt in the minds of Jane Austen and most of her readers that the name of Kotzebue was synonymous with everything most sinister in German Literature of the period.' Kotzebue is

said to be synonymous with political subversion and dangerous Jacobin messages about 'freedom in sexual matters and defiance of traditional restraints'. Marilyn Butler, *Jane Austen and the War of Ideas* (Oxford: Clarendon Press, 1975), pp. 233–34. This sort of political reading has condemned Austen to the status of a conservative propagandist. Even though Butler has softened her position since the publication of her influential *Jane Austen and the War of Ideas*, she still insists upon 'Austen's evident detestation of Kotzebue's play' (introduction to 1990 Oxford World's Classics edition of *Mansfield Park*). Butler supports her anti-Kotzebue argument with the false supposition that Austen was influenced by the Evangelical movement in her suspicion of theatre. For a demonstration that Austen was not Evangelical, see Michael Williams, *Jane Austen: Six Novels and their Methods* (London: Macmillan, 1986), pp. 92–97; see also David Monaghan, '*Mansfield Park* and Evangelicalism: A Reassessment', *Nineteenth-Century Fiction*, 33 (1978), pp. 215–30.

Butler's influential reading of *Lovers' Vows*, along with the older but still frequently cited work of Lionel Trilling on the novelist's rejection of 'the histrionic art', has put the seal on the critical orthodoxy that asserts Austen's condemnation of private theatricals. Even though the evidence of Austen's life conflicts strongly with the arguments advocated by Butler and Trilling, and even though a plethora of critical ambiguity surrounds the play-acting sequence in *Mansfield Park*, few have challenged the assumption that Austen was hostile to the drama.

8. Margaret Kirkham, 'The Theatricals in *Mansfield Park* and "Frederick" in *Lovers' Vows*', *Notes and Queries*, 220 (1975), pp. 389–99.

9. *Mansfield Park* has often been misread as a result of the misinterpretation of another Austen letter, in which she asks a question about 'ordination' – she does *not* say, as was once supposed, that ordination would be the 'subject' of her new novel. Margaret Kirkham neatly suggests that we would do better to begin *Mansfield Park* with knowledge of the 'Frederick' letter, rather than the 'ordination' one: 'Almost everyone who reads *Mansfield Park* now reads some kind of brief introduction first, so he is more likely than not to believe before he starts that Jane Austen said its subject was ordination and that in this period of her life she had become sympathetic to the Evangelical outlook. If the reader started instead with the knowledge that Jane Austen had once seen a very funny performance of *Lovers' Vows* and that a good many years later, just after *Mansfield Park* was finished, she was ready to laugh at the remembrance of the chief male character in it, he might perhaps begin reading what he would expect to be a comedy. The benefits that this might eventually bring, even if improperly derived, would be very considerable', Kirkham, 'Theatricals', p. 390. Kirkham raises a most telling point when she observes that the misunderstanding of the notorious ordination letter and the misleading application of remarks about the Evangelicals, made in very select circumstances to Fanny Knight, are interpretations that have influenced critical writings on *Mansfield Park*. It is an irony, she argues, that the laughter associated with *Lovers' Vows* has been twisted into moral disapprobation and censure.

10. William Reitzel cites a theatre review from the *Porcupine* in 1801 condemning the play for its dangerous political sentiments as well as its dramatic inferiority: 'Independent of the morality of this piece, the first act is the heaviest bundle of dramatic lumber ever tolerated on the boards of an English theatre.' William Reitzel, '*Mansfield Park* and *Lovers' Vows*', *Review of English Studies*, 9 (1933), p. 453.

11. Frederick Howard, Earl of Carlisle, *Thoughts upon the Present Conditions of the Stage* (London, 1808), pp. 5, 22.

12. Nicholas Rowe, *Jane Shore: A Tragedy as Performed at the Theatre-Royal in Drury Lane, Regulated from the Prompt-Book, by Permission of the Managers, by Mr Hopkins, Prompter* (London, 1776), p. 18.

13. See Charles Inigo Jones, *Memoirs of Miss O'Neill* (London, 1816), p. 61.

14. Ibid., p. 49.

15. See William Dunlap, *The Life and Time of George Frederick Cooke*, 2 vols (2nd edn, London, 1815), p. 295.

16. Ibid., p. 295.

17. William Dunlap, *A History of the American Theatre* (New York, 1832), p. 95.

18. Gary Kelly considers the authorship of Mrs Inchbald's *Lovers' Vows* in *Mansfield Park* as controversial 'because of the impropriety of its social *mores* rather than the Jacobinism of its political views'. See *The English Jacobin Novel, 1780–1805* (Oxford: Clarendon Press, 1976), p. 65.

19. The question of Inchbald's politics remains ambiguous. Although *Lovers' Vows* was rendered less controversial than Kotzebue's original play, Inchbald's liberal sympathies with radical and bohemian circles had been noted in the reaction to many of her works. Her play *Every One Has His Fault* was particularly controversial, inciting a riot in the Portsmouth Theatre in 1795. But according to evidence from her biographer James Boaden, her royalist sympathies and strict sense of female decorum defy stringent readings of her supposed radicalism.

20. Inchbald's phrase for her revision of Amelia's style of language might fittingly be applied to Mary Crawford, the mistress of 'whimsical insinuations'. See *MP*, p. 478.

21. Sheridan's adaptation of Kotzebue's *Pizarro* was also highly successful. Like Inchbald, he showed prudence and business acumen in excising the controversial aspects of Kotzebue's play. In particular the part of Elvira, played by Sarah Siddons, was heightened from a soldier's whore to a dignified fallen woman.

22. In *Northanger Abbey* Austen plays a double game in her literary satire. Far from discovering that books do not equip one for dealing with the harsh realities of social snobbery, Catherine's reading of Gothic fiction *does* prepare and influence her distrust of General Tilney's character, so that by the end of the novel her initial suspicions are confirmed: 'in suspecting General Tilney of either murdering or shutting up his wife, she had scarcely sinned against his character, or magnified his cruelty' (*NA*, p. 247).

23. The most stimulating of previous comparisons of *Lovers' Vows* and *Mansfield Park* is by Dvora Zelicovici, who interprets the allusive relationship as one of calculated counter-effectiveness: 'Far from exalting

sexual liberty, *Lovers' Vows* exposes the viciousness of immoral conduct and its miserable consequences. It does not condone and reward licence, but requires repentance and restitution (not retribution).' The point is that the characters in *Mansfield Park* fail to learn the moral messages of the play. Zelicovici, 'The Inefficacy of *Lovers' Vows*', *English Literary History*, 50 (1983), pp. 531–40.

24. Tony Tanner, *Jane Austen* (London: Macmillan, 1986), p. 164; plot summary based on *The Oxford Companion to English Literature*.

25. In 1751 Samuel Richardson had written in Johnson's *Rambler* (no. 97) 'That a young lady should be in love, and the love of the young gentleman undeclared, is an heterodoxy which prudence, and even policy, must not allow.' Samuel Johnson, *The Rambler* (London: Dent, 1953), p. 168. Austen wittily responded in *Northanger Abbey*: 'for if it be true, as a celebrated writer has maintained, that no young lady can be justified in falling in love before the gentleman's love is declared, it must be very improper that a young lady should dream of a gentleman before the gentleman is first known to have dreamt of her' (*NA*, pp. 29–30).

26. There are different kinds of prohibition dividing the hero from the heroine, ranging from religion in *Grandison* to social status in *Lovers' Vows*.

27. The notorious lovers re-emerged in Pope's *Eloise to Abelard* (1717), in Rousseau's *La nouvelle Héloïse* (1761) and Mackenzie's *Julia de Roubigné* (1777). On this tradition, see my article 'A Simple Story: From Inchbald to Austen', *Romanticism*, 5 (1999), pp. 161–72.

28. Professed indifference to her charms is precisely what animates Lady Susan's interest in De Courcy: 'There is an exquisite pleasure in subduing an insolent spirit, in making a person predetermined to dislike, acknowledge one's superiority' (MW, p. 254).

29. Throughout Speculation, both Edmund and Mary are found surreptitiously continuing the underground debate that has been running between them ever since the visit to Sotherton. Under cover of the card game, they make their intentions known to each other in coded comments ostensibly spoken to others. Edmund's guarded remark to Henry that the humble Thornton Lacey 'must suffice me; and I hope all who care about me' is answered by Mary, as is intended, by her equivocal comment to William Price that 'she will stake her last like a woman of spirit'. Both Mary and Edmund continue this surreptitious debate until Sir Thomas's 'sermon' unceremoniously puts an end to it, and 'all the agreeable of *her* speculation was over for that hour' (*MP*, p. 248).

30. Act 3, scene 2 (*MP*, p. 506). *Lovers' Vows* is quoted from the text in Chapman's Oxford edition of *MP*, but so that references may be traced in other editions, references are given in the form of act and scene number. The most readily accessible text is that in the World's Classics, *Five Romantic Plays*, ed. Paul Baines and Edward Burns (Oxford: Oxford University Press, 2000).

31. *Alexander Pope: Selected Poetry* (London: Penguin, 1985), p. 71.

32. Jean-Jacques Rousseau, *Eloisa: or A Series of Original Letters*, 2 vols (1803; repr. Oxford: Woodstock Books, 1989), i, p. 114.

33. Fanny and Amelia show little respect for libertines who trifle with women. Fanny tells Mary: 'I cannot think well of a man who sports with any woman's feelings' (*MP*, p. 363), and Amelia censures Count Cassel for his ill treatment of young women: 'For our Butler told my waiting-maid of a poor young creature who has been deceived, undone; and she, and her whole family, involved in shame and sorrow by his perfidy' (*MP*, p. 516).

34. Richardson, *Sir Charles Grandison*, ed. Jocelyn Harris, 3 vols (London: Oxford University Press, 1972), ii, p. 230.

35. In *Northanger Abbey*, Henry Tilney compares women's choice in marriage to their limited powers in choosing a dancing partner – an effective image of courtship ritual: 'I consider a country dance as an emblem of marriage … in both, man has the advantage of choice, woman only the power of refusal' (*NA*, pp. 76–77). Women are not initiators of choice in courtship, but they can resist an offer, as Elizabeth Bennet proves by her refusal of Collins and Darcy.

36. Henry Mackenzie, *The Man of Feeling: and Julia de Roubigné* (London, 1832), p. 162.

37. Wildenhaim's misapprehension gives rise to a number of puns and *double entendres*:

> BARON: However, I will send Mr Anhalt to you –
> AMELIA: [*much pleased*] Do, papa.
> BARON: He shall explain to you my sentiments. [*Rings.*] A clergyman can do this better than – [*Enter servant.*] Go directly to Mr Anhalt, tell him that I shall be glad to see him for a quarter of an hour if he is not engaged. [*Exit servant.*]
> AMELIA: [*calls after him*] Wish him a good morning from me. (*LV*, act 2, scene 2; in *MP*, p. 496)

9: Mansfield Park

1. Fanny's low opinion of Henry Crawford is compelled to undergo a change when he shows himself capable of 'ardent, disinterested love', though she connects his previous ill-conduct with Sotherton and the private theatricals (see *MP*, p. 328).

2. See Isobel Armstrong, *Jane Austen: Mansfield Park*, Penguin Critical Studies (Harmondsworth: Penguin, 1988), pp. 62–65.

3. Fanny's presence in the rehearsals of *Lovers' Vows* is essential, of course, as she alone must be privy to Henry Crawford's conduct.

4. 'After having so nobly disentagled themselves from the shackles of parental authority, by a Clandestine Marriage …' (*MW*, p. 87).

5. Austen saw *The Clandestine Marriage* on 15 September 1813, at Covent Garden. Her lukewarm reaction to the new Lord Ogleby suggests that she had seen the play before. See above, Chapter 3. *Mansfield Park* was begun about February 1811 and finished 'soon after June 1813' (see Chapman's introductory note to *MP*, p. xi).

6. The plot of Garrick's and Colman's comedy turns upon a secret – the clandestine marriage between Fanny Sterling and Lovewell – which gives

rise to various incongruous and comic misunderstandings. Fanny is bound by a promise to her husband to keep her marriage to Lovewell a secret, until an appropriate time, but in the meantime is harassed by other would-be suitors, one of whom has switched his affections from her elder sister. Lovewell wishes to delay the news, fearing that Fanny's avaricious father and interfering aunt will disinherit them. The lecherous Lord Ogleby mistakenly believes that Fanny's secret love is for him, when she unburdens herself to tell him that she is devoted to another man, and places herself under his protection in a comic scene of misunderstandings and cross-purposes.

7. Elizabeth Inchbald, *The Clandestine Marriage, in The British Theatre: or A Collection of Plays, with Biographical and Critical Remarks by Mrs Inchbald*, 25 vols (London, 1808), xvi, p. 36.

8. *The Clandestine Marriage*, pp. 36, 38.

9. Ibid., pp. 38–39.

10. Ibid., p. 37.

11. Both the corpulent Rushworth and the delicate Fanny are rendered breathless by the heat and emotion of the day. The hot weather contributes to the mishaps and confusions.

12. Mary Wollstonecraft, *Mary and The Wrongs of Woman*, ed. James Kinsley and Gary Kelly (Oxford: Oxford University Press, 1980), p. 155. See also Margaret Kirkham, *Jane Austen: Feminism and Fiction* (London; Athlone, 1997), p. 37.

13. In *Clarissa*, the rake Lovelace doesn't repent, unlike the reformed rake Loveless in *Love's Last Shift*. Richardson's deliberate and ironic allusion to Loveless/Lovelace is yet another telling example of the traffic between the drama and the novel. Richardson's assumption is that the reader will know the dramatic repertoire, so the irony of expectation is intensified when Lovelace does not reform.

14. *The Clandestine Marriage*, p. 56.

15. Ibid., pp. 39–40.

16. Ibid., p. 43.

17. Ibid., pp. 44, 63, 64.

18. Tom's importance for the novel more generally is recognised by Roger Sales in *Jane Austen and Representations of Regency England* (London and New York: Routledge, 1994), pp. 93–106.

19. Duberley is spelt thus by Austen and I will use her spelling, although 'Duberly' is printed in the text of *The Heir at Law*.

20. *The Heir at Law*, in *The Plays of George Colman the Younger*, ed. Peter Tasch, 2 vols (New York and London: Garland, 1981).

21. See introduction to Colman's *Plays*, i, p. xli. The play was performed twenty-eight times during the summer of 1797. Austen stayed in Bath during the latter part of 1797, and may well have attended a performance of the play on 19 November.

22. *Heir at Law*, p. 41. 'Cacology' means 'Bad choice of words; bad pronunciation'. Dowlas mispronounces it as 'cakelology'.

23. See Gillian Russell, *The Theatres of War: Performance, Politics, and Society, 1793–1815* (Oxford: Clarendon Press, 1995), p. 132.

24. *The Heir at Law*, p. 38.
25. Ibid., p. 31.
26. Ibid., p. 64.
27. As A. Walton Litz points out, Tom takes on a triple role in *Lovers' Vows*, playing Butler, Landlord and Cottager. A. Walton Litz, *Jane Austen: A Study of her Artistic Development* (London: Chatto and Windus, 1965), p. 123. Tom later regrets this and wishes that the play could be changed.
28. C. Baron Wilson, *Our Actresses*, 2 vols (London, 1844), i, p. 105.
29. See 'Petronius Arbiter', *Memoirs of the Present Countess of Derby* (London, 1797).
30. See *Truth Opposed to Fiction: or An Impartial Review of the Late Earl of Barrymore by a Personal Observer* (London, 1793).
31. See *MW*, p. 29.
32. In Goldsmith's comedy, it is not only Marlow who is uncomfortable with genteel women and happy in the company of 'females of another class'. Tony Lumpkin and Mr Hardcastle are more relaxed in the company of their servants than of their genteel guests. At the arrival of Marlow and Hastings, Lumpkin asks his yokel friends to leave with the words, 'Gentlemen … they mayn't be good enough company for you'. See Oliver Goldsmith, *She Stoops to Conquer*, ed. Tom Davies (London: A&C Black, 1979), p. 18.
33. *My Grandmother* was first performed 16 December 1793 at the Haymarket Theatre, but soon became so popular that it was performed as a mainpiece.
34. The significance of the play's deeply ironic title is made doubly clear later on in Mrs Norris's description of the play to Lady Bertram, 'It is about Lovers' Vows' (*MP*, p. 167). I cannot concur with Chapman's proposal (*MP*, p. 544) that Austen is suggesting Mrs Norris's theatrical ignorance in this comment. I would suggest quite the reverse: that, although she earlier claims that she doesn't know the play, she knows enough about it to screen her sister from watching the rehearsal. As Mrs Norris bluntly confirms, the play *is* 'about Lovers' Vows'. On the other hand, Rushworth's comment in the first edition *is* highly suggestive of theatrical ignorance. In the first edition he says 'it is to be called Lovers' Vows', but this was changed in the second edition to 'it is to be Lovers' Vows' (*MP*, p. 138). Chapman writes that Austen 'may have repented of the hit at poor Mr Rushworth (perhaps in consideration of his having seen the play in London)', *MP*, p. 544. This seems a good explanation, although we must lament this loss of Rushworth's blunder, which would have played off nicely against Tom's theatrical sophistication and wit.
35. See *MP*, pp. 176 and 191–94.
36. See Alan S. Downer, 'Nature to Advantage Dressed: Eighteenth-Century Acting', *PMLA*, 58 (1943), pp. 1002–37; Lily B. Campbell, 'The Rise of a Theory of Stage Presentation in England during the Eighteenth Century', *PMLA*, 32 (1917), pp. 163–200.
37. See Thomas Davies, *Memoirs of Garrick*, 2 vols (Boston, 1818), i, p. 46.
38. *Memoirs of Richard Cumberland*, ed. Henry Flanders (1856; repr. New York: Benjamin Blom, 1969), p. 47.

39. Davies records: 'After the short ejaculation of "Angels and ministers of grace, defend us!" he endeavoured to conquer that fear and terror into which he was naturally thrown by the first sight of the vision, and uttered the remainder of the address calmly, but respectfully, and with a firm tone of voice, as from one who had subdued his timidity and apprehension.' Thomas Davies, *Dramatic Miscellanies*, 3 vols (London, 1785), iii, p. 30.

40. See Downer, 'Nature to Advantage Dressed', p. 1021.

41. Murphy describes Garrick's rescue of the drama 'from its lowest ebb: in tragedy, declamation roared in a most unnatural strain; rant was passion; whining was grief; vociferation was terror, and drawling accents were the voice of love'. See Murphy's *Life of David Garrick*, 2 vols (London, 1801), i, p. 17. Davies records: 'Mr Garrick shone forth like a theatrical Newton; he threw new light on elocution and action; he banished ranting, bombast and grimace; and restored nature, ease, simplicity, and genuine humour' (ibid., i, p. 45).

42. See Hunt's *Dramatic Essays*, ed. William Archer and Robert W. Lowe (London, 1894), p. 13.

43. See Boswell's *Life of Johnson*, ed. George Birkbeck Hill, 6 vols (Oxford, 1937), iv, pp. 243–44.

44. Henry Fielding, *The History of Tom Jones*, ed. Fredson Bowers, 2 vols (Oxford: Oxford University Press, 1975), ii, pp. 852–57.

45. Ibid., ii, p. 857.

46. A number of acting handbooks were published during the latter part of the eighteenth century. Macklin even established a training school to advocate his naturalistic approach. See *Restoration and Georgian England*, ed. David Thomas, and Arnold Hare, *Theatre in Europe: A Documentary History* (Cambridge: Cambridge University Press, 1989), pp. 342–48.

47. The words 'nature' and 'feeling' were often applied to Kean. Sir George Beaumont raved that 'no actor since Garrick exhibited so much genuine *feeling of nature*', praising Kean as 'wholly free from the measured and artificial practise of the Kemble school'. See Harold Newcombe Hillebrand, *Edmund Kean* (New York: Columbia University Press, 1933), p. 119. Byron was mesmerised by Kean and recorded his impression in his journal: 'Just returned from seeing Kean in Richard. By Jove, he is a soul! Life – nature – truth – without exaggeration or diminution … Richard is a man; and Kean is Richard.' See *Byron's Life, Letters and Journals*, ed. Thomas Moore (London, 1854), p. 222.

48. Austen is keenly aware of the necessity of certain kinds of social conduct, which may conflict with the beliefs of the individual. In *Sense and Sensibility*, Elinor's prudent social conduct is contrasted with Marianne's often ill-judged insistence upon being true to herself. See above, Chapter 6.

49. See *Biographical Dictionary of Actors*, xvi, pp. 314–19.

50. See William Hawkins, *Miscellanies in Verse and Prose and Theatrical Biography* (London, 1792), p. 63.

51. See John Bernard, *Retrospections of the Stage*, 2 vols (London, 1830), i, pp. 278–80.

52. This was Hannah More's description of Crawford in a letter to Garrick. See *Biographical Dictionary of Actors*, iv, p. 34. When Crawford married Ann, in 1778, she was the leading tragedienne at Covent Garden and was able to get an engagement for her husband. They then went to Drury Lane, but left after a season. She soon left him and tried to recover her previous glory. See Thomas Gilliland, *Dramatic Mirror*, 2 vols (London, 1808).
53. Thomas Campbell, *Life of Mrs Siddons* (New York, 1834), p. 87.
54. *Truth Opposed to Fiction*, pp. 34–45.
55. The play opens with a short scene between Landlord/Tom and Agatha/Maria, then with Frederick/Henry, Agatha/Maria and Landlord/Tom, and then the Landlord exits, leaving Agatha and Frederick centre stage.

10: Emma

1. Mr Weston comes from a 'respectable family, which for the last two or three generations had been rising into gentility and property' (*E*, p. 15). His fortune, acquired by trade, has enabled him to purchase a small estate. See Juliet McMaster, 'Class', in *The Cambridge Companion to Jane Austen*, ed. Edward Copeland and Juliet McMaster (Cambridge: Cambridge University Press, 1997), pp. 115–30.
2. Emma is delighted when Mrs Weston gives birth to a daughter: 'She would not acknowledge that it was with any view of making a match for her, hereafter, with either of Isabella's sons' (*E*, p. 461).
3. *The Clandestine Marriage* and *A New Way to Pay Old Debts* held the stage with notable success throughout Austen's lifetime.
4. This technique has been much discussed by critics. See especially A. Walton Litz, *Jane Austen: A Study of her Artistic Development* (London: Chatto and Windus, 1965), pp. 146–47.
5. Julia Prewitt-Brown has noted that Miss Bates's small apartment joins the older gentry (Woodhouses and Knightleys), the new rich (Coles), and the lower-middle to lower-class townspeople and clerks: 'She represents Highbury's fluidity and mobility'. See Prewitt-Brown, 'Civilizations and the Contentment of *Emma*', in *Modern Critical Interpretations: Jane Austen's Emma*, ed. Harold Bloom (New York and Philadelphia: Bloom's Literary Criticism, 1987), p. 55.
6. In Burney's play *A Busy Day* the heroine is devoted to her servant, Mungo, whereas her newly rich family treat him with contempt.
7. Critics have noted the similarities between Emma and Mrs Elton, but, as Claudia Johnson suggests, Austen contrasts them to distinguish between the proper and improper use of social position. Mrs Elton's leadership, for example, depends upon the insistent publicity of herself as Lady Patroness, and the humiliation of those who are socially inferior to her. See Claudia L. Johnson, *Jane Austen: Women, Politics and the Novel* (Chicago: University of Chicago Press, 1988), pp. 129–30.
8. One exception is when she enters a private discussion with her trusted friends, Mrs Weston and Mr Knightley, concerning Mrs Elton's injurious treatment of Jane Fairfax (*E*, pp. 286–89).

9. They conduct a polite row on Box Hill, unbeknown to the rest of the party: 'How many a man has committed himself on a short acquaintance, and rued it all the rest of his life' (*E*, p. 372). Jane replies: 'I would be understood to mean, that it can be only weak, irresolute characters (whose happiness must be always at the mercy of chance), who will suffer an unfortunate acquaintance to be an inconvenience, an oppression for ever' (*E*, p. 373).

10. 'There is a pattern in the novel of vulnerable single woman, whom it is the social duty of the strong and the rich to protect': Marilyn Butler, *Jane Austen and the War of Ideas* (Oxford: Clarendon Press, 1975; repr; 1987), p. 257.

11. Lionel Trilling remains especially influential in this regard. See, in particular, his *Sincerity and Authenticity* (London: Oxford University Press, 1972), pp. 75–78. My own reading of Austen is closer to that of Joseph Litvak in his *Caught in the Act: Theatricality in the Nineteenth-Century Novel* (Berkeley: University of California Press, 1993). Jane Austen's characters act all the time, so even Fanny Price cannot help but play a part: 'All along in eschewing acting, Fanny has in fact been playing a role, albeit "sincerely"... From Henry's performance she learns not the necessity of acting, but the impossibility of *not* acting.' Litvak, *Caught in the Act*, p. 21.

11: Why She Is a Hit in Hollywood

1. Desson Howe, '"Persuasion": Worth Waiting For', *Washington Post*, 20 October 1995.

2. Kenneth Turan, 'Movie Review: An Austen-tatious Year', *Los Angeles Times*, 13 December 1995.

3. Linda Troost and Sayre Greenfield (eds), *Jane Austen in Hollywood* (Lexington: University of Kentucky Press, 1998), p. 130.

4. Sue Birtwistle and Susie Conklin, *The Making of Pride and Prejudice* (Harmondsworth: Penguin, 1995).

5. *E*, chapter 8, p. 64.

6. Ibid., pp. 23–4.

7. Ibid., pp. 166–7.

8. A. A. Milne, *Miss Elizabeth Bennet, A Play from 'Pride and Prejudice'* (Chatto and Windus, 1936), p. viii.

9. The following paragraphs are based on the account in Ann Thwaite, *A. A. Milne: The Man behind Winnie-the-Pooh* (London: Random House, 1990), pp. 175–7.

10. A. A. Milne, *It's Too Late Now: The Autobiography of a Writer* (London: Methuen, 1939), p. 42.

11. Milne, *Miss Elizabeth Bennet*, p. vii.

12. Ibid., pp. 85–6.

13. Ibid., p. x.

14. Thwaite, *A. A. Milne*, p. 413.

15. Milne, *It's Too Late Now*, p. viii.

16. Kenneth Turan, '*Pride and Prejudice*: An Informal History of the Garson-Olivier Motion Picture', *Persuasions*, 11 (1989), 140–43.

17. Thwaite, *A. A. Milne*, p. 413.
18. Turan, '*Pride and Prejudice*', p. 140.
19. See Bosley Crowther, '"*Pride and Prejudice*", a Delightful Comedy of Manners', *New York Times*, 9 August 1940.
20. *Miss Elizabeth Bennet* was broadcast again in 1960 with Dorothy Tutin as Elizabeth and Arthur Lowe as Mr Bennet, and in 1967 with Derek Jacobi as Mr Darcy.
21. Turan, '*Pride and Prejudice*', p. 143.
22. Milne, *Miss Elizabeth Bennet*, p. x.
23. Barbara Kantorowitz, 'Making an Austen Heroine More Like Austen', *New York Times*, 31 October 1999, pp. 17, 26. Quoted in Kathi Groenendyk, 'Modernizing *Mansfield Park*: Patricia Rozema's Spin on Jane Austen', http://www.jasna.org/persuasions/on-line/vol25no1/toc.html.
24. Jane Austen, 'Opinions of Mansfield Park', *MW*, pp. 431–5.
25. David Monaghan, 'In Defence of Patricia Rozema's *Mansfield Park*', http://www.jasna.org/persuasions/printed/number28/monaghan.pdf.
26. Terry Castle, 'Sister-Sister', *London Review of Books*, 3 August 1995, and her follow-up letter of 24 August 1995: http://www.lrb.co.uk/v17/n15/terry-castle/sister-sister.
27. Monaghan, 'In Defence', p. 60.
28. Ibid., p. 62.
29. Ibid.
30. See Paula Byrne, *Belle: The True Story of Dido Belle* (London: William Collins, 2014).
31. See Suzanne R. Pucci and James Thompson (eds), *Jane Austen and Co* (Albany, State University of New York, 2003). Spin-offs such as *Bridget Jones's Diary* and *Ruby in Paradise* are other examples of this genre.
32. Quoted R. V. Young, 'From Mansfield to Manhattan: The Abandoned Generation of Whit Stillman's *Metropolitan*', *Intercollegiate Review*, Spring 2000, pp. 20–27.
33. http://observer.com/2016/05/whit-stillman-talks-love-friendship-austen-adaptations-and-the-rules-of-comedy/.
34. See Ryan Gilbey, http://www.newstatesman.com/culture/film/2016/06/whit-stillman-love-friendship-his-postmodern-love-letter-jane-austen.

Bibliography

JANE AUSTEN

Austen, Jane, *The Novels*, ed. R. W. Chapman, 5 vols (Oxford: Oxford University Press, 1923, 3rd edition, 1932–34).

—, *Minor Works*, ed. R. W. Chapman, revised by B. C. Southam (Oxford: Oxford University Press, 1975).

—, *Sir Charles Grandison*, transcribed and edited by Brian Southam (Oxford: Clarendon Press, 1980).

—, *Lady Susan: A Facsimile of the Manuscript in the Pierpont Morgan Library and the 1925 Printed Edition*, ed. A Walton Litz (New York: Garland, 1989).

—, *Jane Austen's Letters*, ed. Deirdre Le Faye (3rd edn, Oxford: Oxford University Press, 1995).

Austen, Caroline, *My Aunt Jane Austen: A Memoir* (Winchester: Sarsen Press, 1991).

Austen, Henry, 'Biographical Notice', in *Northanger Abbey and Persuasion* (London: John Murray, 1818).

Austen-Leigh, James Edward, *A Memoir of Jane Austen*, ed. R. W. Chapman (Oxford: Clarendon Press, 1951).

Austen-Leigh, R. A., *Austen Papers, 1704–1865* (London: Spottiswoode, Ballantyre, 1942).

Austen-Leigh, William and Richard Arthur, *Jane Austen: A Family Record*, rev. and enlarged by Deirdre Le Faye (London: The British Library, 1989).

Gilson, David, *A Bibliography of Jane Austen* (Oxford: Clarendon Press, 1982).

MANUSCRIPTS AND ARCHIVAL MATERIAL

Bath Public Library
Theatre Royal Playbills, 1771–1805 and 1806–20.

Hampshire Record Office, Winchester
23M93/60/3/2, James Austen's Verses, copied by James Edward Austen-Leigh.
23M93/M1, Eliza de Feuillide's Letters, 1790–1830, on microfiche.

Huntington Library, San Marino, California, USA
HM 31201, Anna Larpent's Methodised Journal, 1773–87.
Larpent Collection of Plays.

Kent Archives Office, Centre for Kentish Studies, Maidstone
U951f24/1–69, Fanny Knight's Journals, 1804–72.

OTHER PRIMARY MATERIAL

Adolphus, John, *Memoirs of John Bannister*, 2 vols (London, 1839).
Arbiter, Petronius [pseudonym], *Memoirs of the Present Countess of Derby* (London, 1797).
Austen, James, *The Loiterer*, 2 vols (Oxford, 1789–90).
Bell's British Theatre, 34 vols (London, 1797).
Bellamy, Thomas, *Miscellanies*, 2 vols (London, 1794).
Bernard, John, *Retrospections of the Stage*, 2 vols (London, 1830).
Berquin, Arnaud, *L'ami des enfans*, 12 vols (London, 1782–83).
—, *The Children's Friend, Translated from the French of Mr Berquin*, by Lucas Williams, 6 vols (London, 1793).
Bickerstaffe, Isaac, *The Plays*, ed. Peter A. Tasch, 3 vols (New York and London: Garland, 1981).
Biographia Dramatica, ed. Stephen Jones, 3 vols (London, 1812).
Boaden, James, *Life of Mrs Jordan*, 2 vols (London, 1831).
—, *Memoirs of Mrs Inchbald*, 2 vols (London, 1833).
Boswell, James, *Life of Johnson*, ed. Birkbeck Hill, 6 vols (Oxford, 1937).
Brayley, Edward Wedlake, *Historical and Descriptive Accounts of the Theatres of London* (London, 1826).
Burney, Fanny, *A Busy Day*, ed. Tara Ghoshal Wallace (1801; New Brunswick, New Jersey: Rutgers University Press, 1984).
—, *Camilla: or A Picture of Youth*, ed. Edward and Lillian Bloom (1796; Oxford: Oxford University Press, 1983).
—, *Cecilia: or Memoirs of an Heiress*, ed. Anne Raine Ellis, 2 vols (London: George Bell and Sons, 1882).
—, *Cecilia: or Memoirs of an Heiress*, ed. Margaret Anne Doody and Peter Sabor (1782; Oxford: Oxford University Press, 1992).
—, *Evelina*, ed. Margaret Anne Doody (1778; Harmondsworth: Penguin Classics, 1994).
—, *The Early Journals and Letters of Fanny Burney*, ed. Lars E. Troide and Stewart J. Cooke, 3 vols to date (Oxford: Clarendon Press, 1988–94).
—, *The Journals and Letters of Fanny Burney (Madame D'Arblay)*, ed. Joyce Hemlow et al., 12 vols (Oxford: Clarendon Press, 1972–84).
—, *The Wanderer*, ed. Margaret Anne Doody and Peter Sabor (1814; Oxford: Oxford University Press, 1991).
—, *The Witlings* (1781), *in The Meridian Anthology of Restoration and Eighteenth-Century Plays by Women*, ed. Katharine M. Rogers (New York: Meridian, 1994).

Byron, Lord, *The Complete Poetical Works*, ed. Jerome J. McGann, 7 vols (Oxford: Clarendon Press, 1980–93).

Campbell, Thomas, *Life of Mrs Siddons* (New York, 1834).

Centlivre, Susanna, *The Plays*, ed. Richard C. Frushell, 3 vols (New York and London: Garland, 1982).

Coleridge, Samuel Taylor, *Specimens of the Table Talk of the Late Samuel Taylor Coleridge*, ed. H. N. Coleridge, 2 vols (London, 1835).

Colman the Elder, George, *The Plays*, ed. Kalman A. Burnim, 6 vols (New York and London: Garland, 1983).

Colman the Younger, George, *The Plays*, ed. Peter Tasch, 2 vols (New York and London: Garland, 1981).

Congreve, William, *The Way of the World*, ed. Brian Gibbons (2nd edn, London: A&C Black, 1994).

Cowley, Hannah, *The Plays of Hannah Cowley*, ed. Frederick H. Link, 2 vols (New York and London: Garland, 1979).

Davies, Thomas, *Dramatic Miscellanies*, 3 vols (London, 1785).

—, *Memoirs of Garrick*, 2 vols (Boston, 1818).

[Dickens, Charles], *Memoirs of Joseph Grimaldi*, ed. Boz (London, 1869).

Dibdin, Charles, *Of Age Tomorrow* (London, n. d.).

Dibdin, Thomas, *Reminiscences*, 4 vols (London, 1827).

Dunlap, William, *A History of the American Theatre* (New York, 1832).

—, *The Life and Time of George Frederick Cooke*, 2 vols (London, 1815).

Edgeworth, Maria, *Belinda* (1801; repr. London: Pandora, 1986).

—, *Patronage* (1814; repr. London: Pandora, 1986).

Fielding, Henry, *The History of the Adventures of Joseph Andrews and of his Friend Mr Abraham Adams and An Apology for the Life of Mrs Shamela Andrews*, ed. Douglas Brooks-Davies (Oxford: Oxford University Press, 1980).

—, *The History of Tom Jones*, ed. Fredson Bowers, 2 vols (Oxford: Oxford University Press, 1975).

Frost, Thomas, *Circus Life and Circus Celebrities* (London, 1875).

Garrick, David, *The Plays*, ed. Gerald M. Berkowitz, 4 vols (New York and London: Garland, 1981).

Genest, John, *Some Account of the English Stage from 1660–1830*, 10 vols (Bath, 1832).

Gilliland, Thomas, *Dramatic Mirror*, 2 vols (London, 1808).

Gisborne, Thomas, *An Enquiry into the Duties of the Female Sex* (London, 1797).

Goldsmith, Oliver, *She Stoops to Conquer*, ed. Tom Davis (London: A&C Black, 1979).

Greenwood, Isaac J., *The Circus: Its Origin and Growth Prior to 1835* (New York: Dunlap, 1898).

Hawkins, F. W., *The Life of Edmund Kean*, 2 vols (London, 1869).

Hawkins, William, *Miscellanies in Verse and Prose* and *Theatrical Biography* (London, 1792).

Hayley, William, *Plays for a Private Theatre* (London, 1784).

—, *Poems and Plays*, 6 vols (London, 1785).

Hazlitt, William, *The Complete Works*, ed. P. P. Howe, 21 vols (London: Dent, 1930–34).

Home, John, *The Plays*, ed. James S. Malek (New York and London: Garland, 1980).

Howard, Frederick, Earl of Carlisle, *Thought upon the Present Conditions of the Stage* (London, 1808).

Hunt, Leigh, *Dramatic Criticism*, ed. L. H. and C. W. Houtchens (New York, 1949).

—, *Dramatic Essays*, ed. William Archer and Robert W. Lowe (London, 1894).

Inchbald, Elizabeth, *A Collection of Farces and Other Afterpieces: Selected by Mrs Inchbald*, 7 vols (London, 1809).

—, *A Simple Story*, ed. J. M. S. Tompkins (1791; Oxford: Oxford University Press, 1988).

—, *A Simple Story* (1791; repr. Harmondsworth: Penguin, 1996).

—, *Lovers' Vows: A Play in Five Acts, Performing at the Theatre Royal, Covent Garden. From the German of Kotzebue* (London: G. G. Robinson, 1798). For ease of reference all quotations are taken from the text of the fifth edition in Chapman's edition of *Mansfield Park*. Also reprinted in *Five Romantic Plays*, ed. Paul Baines and Edward Burns (Oxford: Oxford University Press, 2000).

—, *The British Theatre; or A Collection of Plays ... with Biographical and Critical Remarks by Mrs Inchbald* (London, 1808), vi.

—, *The Modern British Drama*, 5 vols (London, 1811).

—, *The Modern Theatre: A Collection of Successful Modern Plays, as Acted at The Theatre Royal, London*, 10 vols (London, 1811).

Jones, Charles Inigo, *Memoirs of Miss O'Neill* (London, 1816).

Kelly, Hugh, *The Plays*, eds. Larry Carver and Mary J. H. Gross (New York and London: Garland, 1980).

Kelly, Michael, *Reminiscences*, 2 vols (London, 1826).

Lamb, Charles, *The Last Essays of Elia*, ed. Edmund Blunden (London: Oxford University Press, 1929).

—, *The Works of Charles and Mary Lamb*, ed. E. V. Lucas, 2 vols (London: Methuen, 1903).

Lewes, George, 'The Novels of Jane Austen', *Blackwood's Magazine*, 86 (1859), pp. 99–113.

[Lister, Thomas], 'Women as They Are', *Edinburgh Review*, 53 (1830), pp. 444–63.

Lockhart, J. G., *Life of Walter Scott*, 6 vols (New York, 1848).

Macready's Reminiscences, ed. Sir Frederick Pollock (New York, 1875).

Murphy, Arthur, *Life of David Garrick*, 2 vols (London, 1801).

Oxberry's Dramatic Biography and Histrionic Anecdotes: or The Green-Room Spy, 6 vols (London, 1825–27).

Pasquin, Anthony [pseudonym], *The Life of the Late Earl of Barrymore Including a History of the Wargrave Theatricals* (London, 1793).

Peake, Richard Brinsley, *Memoirs of the Colman Family* (London, 1841).

Penley, Belville S., *The Bath Stage* (London, 1892).

Pope, Alexander, *The Poems*, ed. John Butt (London: Methuen, 1963).

Raymond, George, *Memoirs of Robert William Elliston Comedian*, 2 vols (London, 1844).
—, *The Life and Enterprises of Robert William Elliston* (London, 1857).
Richardson, Samuel, *Clarissa: or The History of a Young Lady*, ed. Angus Ross (1747–48; repr. Harmondsworth: Penguin, 1985).
—, *Selected Letters of Samuel Richardson*, ed. John Carroll (Oxford: Oxford University Press, 1964).
—, *The Correspondence of Samuel Richardson*, ed. A. L. Barbauld, 6 vols (London, 1804).
—, *The History of Sir Charles Grandison*, ed. Jocelyn Harris, 3 vols (1753–54; repr. London: Oxford University Press, 1972).
Robinson, Henry Crabb, *The London Theatre, 1811–1866: Selections from the Diary of Henry Crabb Robinson*, ed. Eluned Brown (London: Society for Theatre Research, 1966).
Rowe, Nicholas, *Jane Shore: A Tragedy as Performed at the Theatre-Royal in Drury Lane, Regulated from the Prompt-Book, by Permission of the Managers, by Mr Hopkins, Prompter* (London, 1776).
Scott, Sir Walter, *The Letters of Sir Walter Scott*, ed. H. J. C. Grierson, 12 vols (London: Constable, 1932).
Sheridan, Richard Brinsley, *The Dramatic Works*, ed. Cecil Price, 2 vols (London: Oxford University Press, 1973).
Steele, Sir Richard, *The Plays*, ed. Shirley Strum Kenny (Oxford: Clarendon Press, 1971).
Tomlins, F. G., *A Brief View of the English Stage* (London, 1832).
Wilson, C. Baron, *Our Actresses*, 2 vols (London, 1844).
[Whately, Richard] 'Modern Novels: *Northanger Abbey and Persuasion, Quarterly Review*, 24 (1821), pp. 352–76.
Yates, Edmund, ed., *The Life and Correspondence of Charles Mathews* (London, i860).

SECONDARY MATERIAL

Amis, Kingsley, 'What Became of Jane Austen?', *Spectator*, 4 October 1957, p. 339.
Armstrong, Isobel, *Jane Austen: Mansfield Park*, Penguin Critical Studies (Harmondsworth: Penguin, 1988).
Austen-Leigh, R. A., *Jane Austen and Southampton* (London: Spottiswoode, 1949).
Avery, Emmett L. et al., eds, *The London Stage, 1660–1800*, 5 parts in 11 vols (Carbondale: Southern Illinois University Press, 1960–68).
Babb, Howard, *Jane Austen's Novels: The Fabric of Dialogue* (Columbus: Ohio University Press, 1962).
Baer, Marc, *Theatre and Disorder in Late Georgian England* (Oxford: Clarendon Press, 1992).
Barish, Jonas, *The Anti-Theatrical Prejudice* (Berkeley: University of California Press, 1981).
Bate, Jonathan, ed., *The Romantics on Shakespeare* (Harmondsworth: Penguin, 1992).

Bateson, F. W., *English Comic Drama, 1700–1750* (Oxford: Clarendon Press, 1929).

Bernbaum, Ernest, *The Drama of Sensibility: A Sketch of the History of English Sentimental Comedy and Domestic Tragedy, 1696–1780* (Gloucester, Massachusetts: Peter Smith, 1958).

Bevis, Richard, *The Laughing Tradition* (Athens: University of Georgia Press, 1980).

Bradbrook, Frank W., *Jane Austen and her Predecessors* (Cambridge: Cambridge University Press, 1966).

—, 'Style and Judgement in Jane Austen's Novels', *Cambridge Quarterly*, 4 (1951), pp. 515–37.

Brewer, John, *The Pleasures of the Imagination: English Culture in the Eighteenth Century* (London: HarperCollins, 1997).

Butler, E. M., '*Mansfield Park* and Kotzebue's *Lovers' Vows*', *MLR*, 38 (1933), pp. 326–37.

Butler, Marilyn, Introduction to *Mansfield Park*, ed. James Kinsley (Oxford: Oxford University Press, 1990).

—, *Jane Austen and the War of Ideas* (Oxford: Clarendon Press, 1975).

Campbell, Lily, B., 'The Rise of a Theory of Stage Presentation in England during the Eighteenth Century', *PMLA*, 32 (1917), pp. 163–200.

Castle, Terry, Introduction to *Northanger Abbey, Lady Susan, The Watsons, and Sanditon*, ed. John Davie (Oxford: Oxford University Press, 1990).

Chapman, R. W., *Jane Austen: Facts and Problems* (Oxford: Clarendon Press, 1948).

—, 'Jane Austen's Library', *Book-Collector's Quarterly*, 11 (1933), pp. 28–32.

Chisholm, Kate, *Fanny Burney: Her Life* (London: Chatto and Windus, 1998).

Conger, Sydney McMillen, 'Reading *Lovers' Vows*: Jane Austen's Reflections on English Sense and German Sensibility', *Studies in Philology*, 85 (1988), pp. 92–113.

Cope, Zachary, 'Who Was Sophia Sentiment? Was She Jane Austen?', *Book Collector*, 15 (1966), pp. 143–51.

Donkin, Ellen, *Getting into the Act: Women Playwrights in London, 1776–1829* (London and New York: Routledge, 1995).

Donohue, Joseph W., 'Burletta and the Early Nineteenth-Century English Theatre', *Nineteenth-Century Theatre Research*, 1 (1973), pp. 29–51.

—, *Dramatic Character in the English Romantic Age* (Princeton: Princeton University Press, 1970).

—, *Theatre in the Age of Kean* (Oxford: Blackwell, 1975).

Doody, Margaret Anne, *A Natural Passion: A Study of the Novels of Samuel Richardson* (London: Oxford University Press, 1974).

—, *Frances Burney: The Life in the Works* (New Brunswick, New Jersey: Rutgers University Press, 1988).

Downer, Alan, S., 'Nature to Advantage Dressed: Eighteenth-Century Acting', *PMLA*, 58 (1943). pp. 1002–37.

Duckworth, Alistair M., *The Improvement of the Estate: A Study of Jane Austen's Novels* (Baltimore: Johns Hopkins University Press, 1971).

Flanders, Henry, ed., *Memoirs of Richard Cumberland* (1856; repr. New York: Benjamin Blom, 1969).

Fleishman, Avrom, *A Reading of 'Mansfield Park'* (Minneapolis: University of Minnesota Press, 1967).

Ganzel, Dewey, 'Patent Wrongs and Patent Theatres: Drama and the Law in the Early Nineteenth Century', *PMLA*, 76 (1961), pp. 384–96.

Garside, Peter, and Elizabeth McDonald, 'Evangelicalism and *Mansfield Park*', *Trivium*, 10 (1975), pp. 34–49.

Gray, Charles Harold, *Theatrical Criticism in London to 1795* (New York: Columbia University Press, 1931).

Greene, D. G., 'Jane Austen and the Peerage', *PMLA*, 68 (1953), pp. 1017–31.

Grey, J. David, ed., *The Jane Austen Handbook* (London: Athlone Press, 1986).

Hahn, Emily, *A Degree of Prudery: A Biography of Fanny Burney* (New York: Doubleday, 1950).

Hare, Arnold, ed., *Theatre Royal Bath: A Calendar of Performances at the Orchard Street Theatre, 1750–1805* (Bath: Kingsmead Press, 1977).

Harris, Jocelyn, *Jane Austen's Art of Memory* (Cambridge: Cambridge University Press, 1989).

Hemlow, Joyce, *The History of Fanny Burney* (Oxford: Clarendon Press, 1958).

Highfill, Philip H., Jr, Kalman A. Burnim and Edward A. Langhans, eds, *A Biographical Dictionary of Actors, Actresses, Musicians, Dancers, Managers and Other Stage Personnel in London, 1660–1800*, 16 vols (Carbondale: Southern Illinois University Press, 1984).

Hillebrand, Harold Newcombe, *Edmund Kean* (New York: Columbia University Press, 1933).

Holland, Peter, 'The Age of Garrick', in *Shakespeare: An Illustrated Stage History*, ed. Jonathan Bate and Russell Jackson (Oxford: Oxford University Press, 1996), pp. 69–91.

—, *The Ornament of Action: Text and Performance in Restoration Comedy* (Cambridge: Cambridge University Press, 1979).

Honan, Park, *Jane Austen: Her Life* (London: Weidenfeld and Nicolson, 1987).

Howe, Elizabeth, *The First English Actresses: Women and Drama, 1660–1700* (Cambridge: Cambridge University Press, 1992).

Howe, Evelyn, 'Amateur Theatre in Georgian England', *History Today*, 20 (1970), pp. 695–703.

Hubback, J. H., 'Pen Portraits in Jane Austen's Novels', *Cornhill Magazine* (July 1928), pp. 24–33.

Hufstader, Alice Anderson, *Sisters of the Quill* (New York: Mead, 1978).

Husbands, Winifred H., '*Mansfield Park* and *Lovers' Vows*: A Reply', *MLR*, 29 (1934), pp. 176–79.

James, Henry, *The Art of the Novel*, ed. R. P. Blackmur (New York and London: Charles Scribner's Sons, 1947).

Johnson, Claudia L., *Equivocal Beings: Politics, Gender and Sentimentality in the 1790s* (Chicago: University of Chicago Press, 1995).

—, *Jane Austen: Women, Politics and the Novel* (Chicago: University of Chicago Press, 1988).

Jordan, Elaine, 'Pulpit, Stage and Novel: *Mansfield Park* and *Lovers' Vows*', *Novel: A Forum on Fiction*, 20 (1987), pp. 138–48.

Kelly, Gary, 'Reading Aloud in *Mansfield Park*', *Nineteenth-Century Fiction*, 37 (1982), pp. 29–42.

—, *The English Jacobin Novel, 1780–1805* (Oxford: Clarendon Press, 1976).

Kenny, Shirley Strum, *British Theatre and the Other Arts, 1660–1800* (Washington: Associated University Presses, 1984).

Kinkead-Weekes, Mark, *Samuel Richardson: Dramatic Novelist* (London: Methuen, 1973).

Kirkham, Margaret, *Jane Austen: Feminism and Fiction* (London; Athlone Press, 1997).

—, 'The Theatricals in *Mansfield Park* and "Frederick" in *Lovers' Vows*', *Notes and Queries*, 220 (1975), pp. 389–90.

Konigsberg, Ira, *Samuel Richardson and the Dramatic Novel* (Lexington: University of Kentucky Press, 1968).

Lascelles, Mary, *Jane Austen and Her Art* (Oxford: Clarendon Press, 1939).

Leavis, Q. D., 'A Critical Theory of Jane Austen's Writing', *Scrutiny*, 10 (1941), pp. 61–90, 114–42.

Le Faye, Deirdre, 'Jane Austen and William Hayley', *Notes and Queries*, 232 (1987), pp. 25–26.

—, 'Journey, Waterparties and Plays', *Jane Austen Society Report* (1986), pp. 29–35.

—, 'The Business of Mothering: Two Austenian Dialogues', *Book Collector* (1983), pp. 296–314.

Lewis, Peter, *Fielding's Burlesque Drama: Its Place in the Tradition* (Edinburgh: Edinburgh University Press, 1987).

Linklater Thomson, C., *Jane Austen: A Survey* (London: Horace Marshall, 1929).

Littlewood, S. R., *Elizabeth Inchbald and her Circle* (London: Daniel O'Connor, 1921).

Litvak, Joseph, *Caught in the Act: Theatricality in the Nineteenth-Century Novel* (Berkeley: University of California Press, 1993).

Litz, A. Walton, *Jane Austen: A Study of Her Artistic Development* (London: Chatto and Windus, 1965).

Loftis, John, *Sheridan and the Drama of Georgian England* (Oxford: Blackwell, 1976).

—, *The Politics of Drama in Augustan England* (Oxford: Clarendon Press, 1963).

Lynch, James, J., *Box, Pit and Gallery: Stage and Society in Johnson's London* (Berkeley: University of California Press, 1953).

McMillin, Scott, ed., *Restoration and Eighteenth-Century Comedy* (New York and London: Norton, 1973).

Mandel, Oscar, *The Theatre of Don Juan: A Collection of Plays and Views, 1630–1963* (Lincoln: University of Nebraska Press, 1963).

Mander, Raymond, and Joe Mitchenson, *The Lost Theatres of London* (New York: Taplinger, 1968).

Manvell, Roger, *Elizabeth Inchbald: A Biographical Study* (Lanham: University Press of America, 1987).

Milmeth, Don. B., 'The Posthumous Career of George Frederick Cooke', *Theatre Notebook*, 24 (1969–70), pp. 68–74.

Molar, Kenneth, *Jane Austen's Art of Allusion* (Lincoln: University of Nebraska Press, 1977).

Monaghan, David, '*Mansfield Park* and Evangelicalism: A Reassessment', *Nineteenth-Century Fiction*, 33 (1978), pp. 215–30.

Moody, Jane, *Illegitimate Theatre in London, 1770–1840* (Cambridge: Cambridge University Press, 2000).

—, 'Writing for the Metropolis: Illegitimate Performances of Shakespeare in Early Nineteenth-Century London', *Shakespeare Survey*, 47 (1994). pp. 61–69.

Mudrick, Marvin, *Jane Austen: Irony as Defense and Discovery* (Princeton: Princeton University Press, 1952).

Mullan, John, *Sentiment and Sociability: The Language of Feeling in the Eighteenth Century* (Oxford: Clarendon Press, 1997).

Murray, Christopher, *Robert William Elliston: Manager* (London: Society for Theatre Research, 1975).

Nicoll, Allardyce, *A History of Early Nineteenth-Century Drama, 1800–1850*, 2 vols (London: Cambridge University Press, 1930).

—, *A History of English Drama, 1660–1900*, 6 vols (Cambridge: Cambridge University Press, 1955–59).

—, *The Garrick Stage: Theatres and Audience in the Eighteenth Century*, ed. Sybil Rosenfeld (Manchester: Manchester University Press, 1980).

Nicholson, Watson, *The Struggle for a Free Stage in London* (London: Constable, 1906).

Nokes, David, *Jane Austen: A Life* (London: Fourth Estate, 1997).

Page, Norman, *The Language of Jane Austen* (Oxford: Oxford University Press, 1972.).

Patterson, A. Temple, *A History of Southampton, 1700–1914*, 11 vols (Southampton: Southampton University Press, 1966).

Ranger, Paul, *The Georgian Playhouses of Hampshire, 1730–1830*, Hampshire Papers 10 (Winchester: Hampshire County Council, 1996).

Rawson, Claude, Introduction to *Persuasion*, ed. John Davie (Oxford: Oxford University Press, 1990).

—, *Order from Confusion Sprung: Studies in Eighteenth-Century Literature from Swift to Cowper* (London: Allen and Unwin, 1985).

—, *Satire and Sentiment, 1660–1830* (Cambridge: Cambridge University Press, 1994).

—, 'Some Remarks on Eighteenth-Century "Delicacy", with a Note on Hugh Kelly's *False Delicacy* (1768)', *JEGP*, 61 (1962), pp. 1–13.

Reitzel, William, '*Mansfield Park* and *Lovers' Vows*', *Review of English Studies*, 9 (1933), pp. 451–56.

Rosenfeld, Sybil, 'Jane Austen and Private Theatricals', *Essays and Studies*, 15 (1962), pp. 40–51.

—, *Temples of Thespis: Some Private Theatres and Theatricals in England and Wales, 1700–1820* (London: The Society for Theatre Research, 1978).

Russell, Gillian, 'Playing at Revolution: The Politics of the O. P. Riots of 1809', *Theatre Notebook*, 44 (1990), pp. 16–26.

—, *The Theatres of War: Performance, Politics, and Society, 1793–1815* (Oxford, Clarendon Press, 1995).

Sales, Roger, *Jane Austen and Representations of Regency England* (London: Routledge, 1996).

Selwyn, David, *Jane Austen and Leisure* (London: Hambledon Press, 1999).

Sherbo, Arthur, *English Sentimental Drama* (Michigan: Michigan State University Press, 1957).

Sherburn, George, 'Samuel Richardson's Novels and the Theatre: A Theory Sketched', *Philological Quarterly*, 41 (1962), pp. 325–29.

Southam, B. C., *Critical Essays on Jane Austen* (London: Routledge and Kegan Paul, 1968).

—, *Jane Austen: The Critical Heritage*, 2 vols (London: Routledge and Kegan Paul, 1968–87)

—, *Jane Austen's Literary Manuscripts* (London: Oxford University Press, 1964).

—, *Sense and Sensibility, Pride and Prejudice, and Mansfield Park: A Casebook* (London: Macmillan, 1976).

Spring, David, 'Aristocracy, Social Structure, and Religion in the Early Victorian Period', *Victorian Studies*, 6 (1963), pp. 263–80.

Staves, Susan, 'Evelina: or Female Difficulties', *Modern Philology*, 73 (1976), pp. 368–81.

Tanner, Tony, *Jane Austen* (London: Macmillan, 1986).

Tasch, Peter A, *The Dramatic Cobbler: The Life and Works of Isaac Bickerstaff* (Lewisburg: Bucknell University Press, 1971).

Thaler, Alwin, *Shakespeare to Sheridan* (Cambridge: Cambridge University Press, 1922).

Thomas, David and Arnold Hare, eds, *Restoration and Georgian England, Theatre in Europe: A Documentary History* (Cambridge: Cambridge University Press, 1989).

Tinker, Chauncey Brewster, *Dr Johnson and Fanny Burney* (New York: Moffat, Yard, 1911).

Tomalin, Claire, *Jane Austen: A Life* (London: Viking, 1997).

—, *Mrs Jordan's Profession* (New York: Knopf, 1994).

Tompkins, J. M. S., '"Elinor and Marianne": A Note on Jane Austen', *Review of English Studies*, 16 (1940), pp. 33–43.

—, *The Popular Novel in England, 1770–1800* (Lincoln: University of Nebraska Press, 1932; repr. 1961).

Trilling, Lionel, *Sincerity and Authenticity* (London: Oxford University Press, 1972).

—, *The Opposing Self* (London: Secker and Warburg, 1955).

Troost, Linda, and Sayre Greenfield, eds, *Jane Austen in Hollywood* (Lexington: University of Kentucky Press, 1998).

Trusler, Simon, ed., *Burlesque Plays of the Eighteenth Century* (London: Oxford University Press, 1969).

Tucker, George Holbert, *A Goodly Heritage: A History of Jane Austen's Family* (Manchester: Carcanet Press, 1983).

—, *Jane Austen: The Woman* (New York: St Martin's Press, 1994).

Vickery, Amanda, *The Gentleman's Daughter: Women's Lives in Georgian England* (New Haven and London: Yale University Press, 1998).

Viveash, Chris, 'Jane Austen and Kotzebue', *Jane Austen Society Report* (1994), pp. 29–31.

Watson, Ernest, *Sheridan to Robertson: A Study of the Nineteenth-Century London Stage* (Cambridge, Massachusetts: Harvard University Press, 1926).

Watt, Ian, ed., *Jane Austen: A Collection of Critical Essays* (Englewood Cliffs, New Jersey: Prentice-Hall, 1963).

Williams, Michael, *Jane Austen: Six Novels and their Methods* (London: Macmillan, 1986).

Zelicovici, Dvora, 'The Inefficacy of *Lovers' Vows*', *English Literary History*, 50 (1983), pp. 531–40.

Index